TExES™
TEXAS EXAMINATIONS OF EDUCATOR STANDARDS™

CORE SUBJECTS EC-6 (391)

T0291071

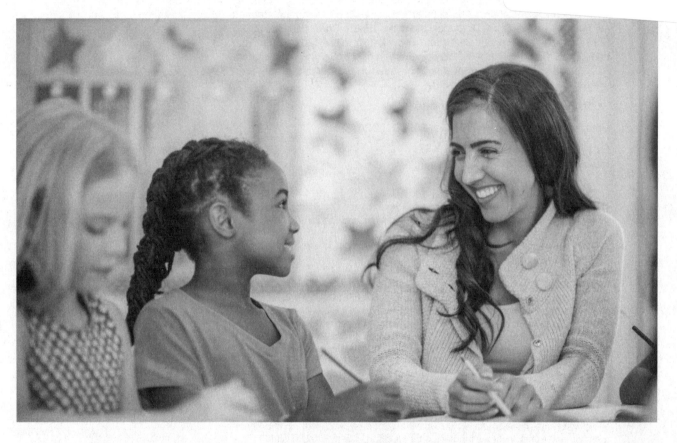

By Luis A. Rosado, Ed.D.

Contributing Authors

Ann Cavallo, Ph.D.
Mary Curtis, Ph.D.
Dean Ferguson, Ph.D.

Diane M. Lange, Ph.D.
Larry P. Nelson, Ph.D.

Kathleen C. Tice, Ph.D.
Jason Wardlaw, Ph.D.

Research & Education Association

www.rea.com

Research & Education Association
1325 Franklin Avenue, Suite 250
Garden City, NY 11530
Email: info@rea.com

TExES™ Core Subjects EC–6 (391) with Online Practice Tests, First Edition

Published 2024

Printed in the United States of America

Library of Congress Control Number 2022911720

ISBN-13: 978-0-7386-1277-5
ISBN-10: 0-7386-1277-4

The competencies presented in this book were created and implemented by the Texas Education Agency and Pearson Education, Inc., or its affiliates. Texas Examinations of Educator Standards and TExES are trademarks of the Texas Education Agency. All other trademarks cited in this publication are the property of their respective owners.

Cover image: © iStockphoto.com/FatCamera

REA® is a registered trademark of Research & Education Association.

Contents

TEXES CORE SUBJECTS EC–6

CONTENTS

TExES Core Subjects Practice Test Battery 1
Also available online at: www.rea.com/studycenter

TExES Core Subjects Practice Test Battery 2
Available online at: www.rea.com/studycenter

Practice Subject Test 2: English Language Arts and Reading

Practice Subject Test 2: Mathematics

Practice Subject Test 2: Social Studies

Practice Subject Test 2: Science

Practice Subject Test 2: Fine Arts, Health, and Physical Education

About the Author

Dr. Luis A. Rosado is a Professor of Bilingual Education and the Founding Director of the Center for Bilingual and ESL Education in the College of Education and Health Professions at the University of Texas at Arlington. He holds degrees from the University of Puerto Rico, Boston State College, and Texas A&I University, now Texas A&M–Kingsville. Prior to coming to UT Arlington, Dr. Rosado held academic appointments at Pontifical Catholic University of Puerto Rico, Texas Southern University, and Texas Woman's University. Dr. Rosado has more than three decades of teaching experience at the elementary, high school, and college levels. He has taught in Puerto Rico, Massachusetts, and Texas.

In 2011, Dr. Rosado was the co-recipient of a $1.9 million grant from the U.S. Department of Education's Office of English Language Acquisition to improve preparation for teachers serving English learners. In total, Dr. Rosado has received more than $5.6 million in state and federal funding to prepare bilingual and ESL teachers as well as school administrators, and to provide services to support high school students.

Dr. Rosado has written extensively in the areas of pedagogy and professional responsibilities, parental involvement, cross-cultural communication, preparation for teacher certification exams, and Spanish for bilingual teachers. Among his publications are a series of books to prepare preservice teachers for certification tests, including REA's best-selling *TExES Bilingual Generalist EC–6 (192)*, and *Desarrollo del Español para Maestros en Programas de Educación Bilingüe* (Spanish Development for Teachers in Bilingual Education Programs), for which, with co-author Lidia Morris, he earned first place in the 2014 International Latino Book Awards in the category of Best Reference Book—Spanish or Bilingual. The book, which is intended, Dr. Rosado says, "to polish Spanish, not to teach Spanish," has been used by several universities and a number of Texas school districts.

Author's Dedication

This book is dedicated to Kelly, Koko, and Alex because through their natural behavior and development, they guided me to see the connection between theory and practice.

About the Contributing Authors

English Language Arts and Reading

Dr. Kathleen Copeland Tice is the Program Coordinator for Literacy Studies in the Department of Curriculum & Instruction at the University of Texas at Arlington. She also teaches courses in literacy studies at both the undergraduate and graduate level. Her research has focused upon teacher knowledge development and service-learning in teacher preparation. She has served as the annual conference Program Chair for the Service-Learning & Experiential Education–Special Interest Group of the American Educational Research Association. She is a co-editor of the *International Journal of Research on Service-Learning in Teacher Education.* Dr. Tice won a 2015 Literacy Grant from the Honor Society of Phi Kappa Phi, the nation's oldest and most prestigious collegiate honor society for all academic disciplines. Her teaching awards include the University of Texas System Regents' Outstanding Teacher Award. She received her master's degree in reading education from the University of Houston, and earned her Ph.D. in reading and in English/language arts education from the University of Texas at Austin.

Health and Physical Education

Dr. Larry P. Nelson is an Associate Professor in the Department of Kinesiology at the University of Texas at Arlington. He holds a Ph.D. in Sport & Exercise Science from the University of Northern Colorado; an M.S. in Physical Education Pedagogy from Colorado State University; and a B.S. in Exercise and Sport Science from Colorado State University. His research interests include physical education program assessment and evaluation, developing service-learning models that improve preservice teachers' efficacy, and testing active-learning strategies for critical thinking development. Dr. Nelson is a co-founder of Dancing Classrooms North Texas 501(c)(3) and is the Research Coordinator for Dancing Classrooms (National Network). He was awarded the *Fort Worth Star-Telegram*'s Community Service-Learning Award in 2008, the inaugural UT Regents' Outstanding Teaching Award in 2009, and was named Citizen of the Year by the YMCA of Arlington in 2011. Dr. Nelson enjoys coaching soccer in the Arlington community.

Mathematics

Dr. Jason Wardlaw is an analog integrated circuit design engineer. He received a B.S. and a Ph.D. in Electrical Engineering from Texas A&M University. Dr. Wardlaw was a Teaching Assistant and Assistant Lecturer for the Department of Electrical and Computer Engineering at Texas A&M University from 2005 to 2008. From June 2008 to December 2010, he was involved in a National Science Foundation GK–12 program for enhancing STEM awareness in rural middle school classrooms.

Music

Dr. Diane Lange is Professor and Area Coordinator of Music Education at the University of Texas at Arlington, where she oversees the music education area and teaches undergraduate and graduate courses in Early Childhood and Elementary Music Education. She also teaches early childhood music at her private studio, The Musical Treehouse. Dr. Lange has taught elementary music for ten years in both Michigan and Nevada. She received her Orff Levels and Master Class at Memphis State University and GIML Level I and II at Michigan State University. She is a certified faculty member where she teaches GIML Level I around the country. Dr. Lange received both her Bachelor of Music in Education and Master of Music degrees from Central Michigan University, and earned her Ph.D. from Michigan State University. She has presented clinics and workshops at multiple state, national, and international conferences. Dr. Lange has published three books, numerous book chapters and articles, and is a coauthor of *Jump Right In: The Elementary Music Curriculum, Grades Kindergarten and 5*. Dr. Lange has received the Outstanding Educator Award from the Crawford AuSable School District and was inducted into the Academy of Distinguished Teachers at the University of Texas at Arlington in 2019.

Science

Dr. Ann Cavallo is Assistant Vice Provost and Director of the Center for Research on Teaching and Learning Excellence, Co-director of UTeach Arlington, and Distinguished University Professor of Science Education at the University of Texas at Arlington. Dr. Cavallo earned her B.S. from Niagara University, and her M.S. in Science Education/Biology, M.S. in Natural Science, and Ph.D. in Science Education from Syracuse University. She holds secondary teacher certification in Biology, Chemistry, Earth Science, and General Science, and taught middle and high school science prior to earning her graduate degrees. She has held faculty appointments at the University of Oklahoma, the University of California–Davis, and Wayne State University. She joined the faculty at the University of Texas at Arlington in 2006 as Associate Professor and earned the rank of Professor in 2009 in her field of Science Education. Dr. Cavallo received the 2015 Distinguished Record of Research or Creative Activity Award from UT Arlington. She is Principal Investigator of three National Science Foundation (NSF) grants totaling over $3 million. Dr. Cavallo's research has investigated high school and college students' learning approaches and strategies, scientific reasoning, self-efficacy, and their acquisition of conceptual understandings of science. Dr. Cavallo has been published in more than 40 internationally and nationally refereed journals and proceedings, as well as having authored several books and book chapters (including REA's top-selling *TExES Core Subjects 4–8 Book + Online* prep pack). In total, she has secured more than $12 million in grants and gifts from various funding agencies to support her work. She serves on the STEM Teacher Preparation Advisory Board for NSF and the American Association for the Advancement of Science. She has made over 70 presentations at professional conferences, and has held significant leadership positions in professional education organizations.

Social Studies

Dr. Mary D. Curtis is Assistant Professor of Curriculum and Instruction in the College of Education at the University of Houston–Clear Lake. Dr. Curtis earned her B.A. in Political Science from Texas A&M University, M.S. in Instructional Technology from the University of Houston–Clear Lake, and Ph.D. in Geography Education from Texas State University. She worked 10 years as a Social Studies teacher in the Clear Creek Independent School District, League City, Texas. In 2007 Dr. Curtis received the K–12 Distinguished Teaching Award from the National Council for Geography Education. In 2008 and again 2010, she was named a Gilbert M. Grosvenor Scholar, the only candidate to earn this distinction twice. Grosvenor Scholars manage political outreach to build geography awareness and conduct research in conjunction with the National Geographic Education Foundation and Education Program division of the National Geographic Society. Dr. Curtis was also named the 2017 Professor of the Year by the Arlington Sunrise Rotary.

Contributing to the history section was **Dr. Dean Ferguson**, Professor of History at Texas A&M University–Kingsville, where he has been based since 1998. He earned his master's degree in History from Central Michigan University and his Ph.D. in European History from Purdue.

Dr. Ferguson is an old hand at Texas's TExES exams. He served as a content reviewer and developed a program at Texas A&M–Kingsville to prepare teacher candidates for success on the social studies and history certification exams.

About REA

Founded in 1959, Research & Education Association (REA) is dedicated to publishing the finest and most effective educational materials—including study guides and test preps—for students of all ages. Today, REA's wide-ranging catalog is a leading resource for students, teachers, and other professionals. Visit *www.rea.com* to see our complete catalog.

Publisher's Acknowledgments

Publisher: Pam Weston

Editorial Director: Larry B. Kling

Digital Content Prep: Heidi Gagnon

Copyediting: Fiona Hallowell, John Kupetz, Miriam Perkoff, Sandra Rush, and Stu Schwartz

Indexing: Terry Casey, Casey Indexing and Information Service

Composition Services: Caragraphics

File Prep: Jennifer Calhoun

Getting Started

Congratulations! By taking the TExES Core Subjects EC–6 (391) test, you're on your way to a rewarding career as a teacher of young students in Texas. Our book, and the online tools that come with it, give you everything you need to succeed on this important exam, bringing you one step closer to being certified to teach in Texas.

This TExES Core Subjects test prep package includes:

- A **complete overview** of the TExES Core Subjects EC–6 (391) test

- A **comprehensive review** for all five subject tests in the TExES Core Subjects test battery

- An **online diagnostic test** to pinpoint your strengths and weaknesses and focus your study

- **Two full-length practice tests:** one in the book and an additional test online that comes with powerful diagnostic tools to help you personalize your prep

HOW TO USE THIS BOOK + ONLINE PREP

About Our Review

The review chapters in this book are designed to help you sharpen your command of all the skills you'll need to pass the Core Subjects EC–6 test. The test is composed of five domains and 44 competencies. Each of the skills required for all five domains is discussed at length to optimize your understanding of what the test covers.

Keep in mind that your schooling has taught you most of what you need to know to answer the questions on the test. Our content review is designed to reinforce what you have learned and show you how to relate the information you have acquired to the specific competencies on the test.

Studying your class notes and textbooks together with our review will give you an excellent foundation for passing the test.

About the REA Study Center

We know your time is valuable and you want an efficient study experience. At the REA Study Center (*www.rea.com/studycenter*), you will get feedback right from the start on what you know and what you don't to help make the most of your study time.

Here is what you will find at the REA Study Center:

- **Diagnostic Test**—Before you review with the book, take our online diagnostic test. Your score report will pinpoint topics for which you need the most review, to help focus your study.

- **2 Full-Length Practice Tests**—These practice tests give you the most complete picture of your strengths and weaknesses. After you've studied with the book, test what you've learned by taking the first of two online practice exams. Review your score reports, then go back and study any topics you missed. Take the second practice test to ensure you've mastered the material.

Our online exams simulate the computer-based format of the actual TExES test and come with these features:

- **Automatic scoring**—Find out how you did on your test, instantly.

- **Diagnostic score reports**—Get a specific score tied to each competency, so you can focus on the areas that challenge you the most.

- **On-screen detailed answer explanations**—See why the correct response option is right, and learn why the other answer choices are incorrect.

- **Timed testing**—Learn to manage your time as you practice, so you'll feel confident on test day.

AN OVERVIEW OF THE TEST

What is assessed on the Core Subjects EC–6 test?

The TExES Core Subjects EC–6 test is a criterion-referenced examination constructed to measure the knowledge and skills that an entry-level educator in Texas public schools must have. The test is a requirement for candidates seeking a Core Subjects EC–6 certificate. Because it's a computer-administered test, the Core Subjects EC–6 exam is available throughout the year at numerous locations across the state and at select locations nationally. To find the test center near you, visit *www.tx.nesinc.com*.

Candidates are limited to five attempts to take any of Texas's teacher certification tests, but in the event you don't pass the Core Subjects EC–6 test, you need to retake only the individual subtest(s) where your score falls short.

Below are the five domains that correspond with the Core Subjects exam's five subject tests. The table covers the percentage and number of questions in each domain, as well as the time allocated for each section of the test. These domains and the competencies rooted in them represent the knowledge that teams of teachers, subject area specialists, and district-level educators have determined to be important for beginning teachers.

A Snapshot of the TExES Core Subjects EC–6 Test (391)

Subject Exam	Competencies	Percentage	Total Items and Item Type	Time
Exam I: English Language Arts and Reading (901)	10	21.5%	45 selected-response	1 hour and 10 minutes (70 minutes)
Exam II: Mathematics (902)	6	19%	40 selected-response	1 hour and 10 minutes (70 minutes)
Exam III: Social Studies (903)	5	19%	40 selected-response	50 minutes
Exam IV: Science (904)	18	21.5%	45 selected-response	55 minutes
Exam V: Fine Arts, Health and Physical Education (905)	5	19%	45 selected-response	35 minutes
Total	44	100%	210	4 hours and 40 minutes

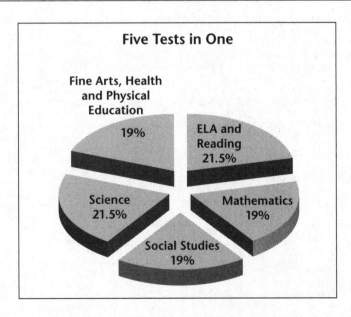

Five Tests in One

Fine Arts, Health and Physical Education 19%
ELA and Reading 21.5%
Science 21.5%
Mathematics 19%
Social Studies 19%

What is the format of the TExES Core Subjects EC–6 test?

The test includes a total of 210 selected-response questions. Each selected-response question that you answer correctly earns you one raw score point. The total raw score is the number of scored questions answered correctly on the entire exam. Scores for the entire TExES series are reported on a scale of 100 to 300. A score of 240 is the minimum you need to pass.

Multiple-Choice Questions

Though all the questions on the test are multiple-choice, they may not all be the type of multiple-choice question with which you're familiar. The majority of questions on the Core Subjects test are standard multiple-choice items. The questions are not intended merely to test your command of facts but also your critical-thinking skills. For example, you may be asked to analyze information and compare it with knowledge you have, or make a judgment about it. To acquaint yourself with all the standards and competencies covered on the test, be sure to download Pearson's test framework at *www.tx.nesinc.com*.

Some multiple-choice questions are self-contained while others are clustered, branching off a common stimulus. Each question will generally have four choices: A, B, C, and D. (Some questions may have five options.) In most cases, the correct answer will require you to identify the single best response. Some questions, however, will require you to select *all* the responses that answer the question correctly. In such instances, you will click check boxes instead of ovals. Also be aware that this test occasionally presents non-traditional formats for multiple-choice items, both to present the information and to allow you to select the best answer. A rundown of these new formats follows.

Unfamiliar Question Types

There are several unfamiliar question types that may show up on the Core Subjects test. First, let's look at the kind of question that asks test-takers to identify more than one correct response option to a question.

Example

1. Which of the following led to the American Revolution? Select *all* that apply.

    A. the French and Indian War

    B. the Intolerable Acts

    C. the French Revolution

    D. the Articles of Confederation

Answer and Explanation

Options (A) and (B) are correct. The French and Indian War (A), fought from 1754 to 1763, served as a powerful vehicle by which the British Empire extended its reach in North America. The British sought to impose taxation on the colonists to finance the defense of the newly acquired territory, which aggravated growing discontent with British governance. The Intolerable Acts (B) embraced measures enacted by the British Parliament in 1774 to strike back at the colonists' defiance (e.g., the Boston Tea Party in 1773) of British rule. The move backfired, spawning the First Continental Congress later that year. Simple chronology helps you root out the French Revolution (C) as an incorrect option. The French Revolution, fought from 1787 to 1799, is an anachronistic response that could not have led to the American Revolution, which ended in 1783. Finally, the Articles of Confederation instead of leading to the American Revolution actually *resulted from* it. The Articles were drafted in 1776–77 and adopted by Congress on Nov. 15, 1777, as the first U.S. constitution.

According to Pearson, the Core Subjects EC–6 test may use interactive questions that may include audio or video clips instead of, say, a static map or reading passage.

Item formats may ask you to select the correct answer(s) by any of these means:

1. Click on a sentence or sentences, or on parts of a graphic representation, such as a map, chart, or figure – sometimes termed a "hot spot."

2. Drag and drop answer options into "target" areas in a table, piece of text, or graphic.

3. Use a drop-down menu.

More than anything, these innovative item types require that you read the instructions carefully to be sure you are fully responsive to the question.

The TExES Core Subjects test is scored based on the number of questions you answer correctly. With no penalty for guessing, you won't want to leave any item unanswered.

When should the test be taken?

Traditionally, teacher preparation programs determine when their candidates take the required tests for teacher certification. These programs will also clear you to take the examinations and make final recommendations for certification to the Texas State Board for Educator Certification (SBEC).

A candidate seeking EC–6 certification may take the appropriate Core Subjects test at such time as his or her Educator Preparation Program (EPP) determines the candidate's readiness to take the test, or upon successful completion of the EPP, whichever comes first. The EPP will determine readiness through benchmarks and structured assessments of the candidates' progress throughout the preparation program.

For those seeking certification right out of college, the TExES Core Subjects EC–6 (391) is generally taken just before graduation. Earning your Core Subjects EC–6 certificate in Texas also means that you have to pass the standalone TExES Science of Teaching Reading (293) test to meet your content pedagogy requirements.

How do I register for the test?

To register for the TExES 391 test, you must create an account in the Pearson online registration system. Registration will then be available to you online, 24/7, during the regular, late, and emergency registration periods. Visit Pearson's TExES website at *www.tx.nesinc.com* and follow the instructions.

The site also offers a rundown of test dates and locations, as well as information on testing accommodations for those with special needs. The registration bulletin is available at *www.tx.nesinc.com*.

Registration bulletins are also available at the education departments of Texas colleges and universities. To address issues that cannot be solved at the teacher preparation program level, you can contact the offices of SBEC at (888) 863-5880 or (512) 469-8400.

You must pay a registration fee to take the TExES tests, and you will also incur additional late fees if registering after the scheduled date.

What's the passing score?

There are 210 selected-response questions on the TExES 391 test. Your score on each of the TExES 391's subtests (test codes 901 to 905) will be reported on a 100–300 scale. A scaled score of 240 is set as the minimum passing score. To put this in context, you want to be confident you can answer between 70% and 80% of the questions correctly. To achieve the 70% level, you must get 147 questions correct; to reach the 80% level, you need to get 168 questions correct. As you work your way through our practice tests, scores in this range will suggest that you are sufficiently absorbing the test content. There is no holistic score for the full Core Subjects EC–6 battery; your combined results are reported as "passed" or "not passed" because, as Pearson puts it, "there is no total scaled score for the overall exam."

If you do not get a passing score on our online diagnostic test or the practice tests, review your online score report and study the detailed explanations for the questions you answered incorrectly. Note which types of questions you answered wrong, and re-examine the corresponding review content. After further review, you may want to retake the practice tests online.

When will I receive my score report?

As part of the registration process to take TExES examinations, test candidates set up an account with Pearson in which they are assigned a username and password. Use this account to access your score report information on Pearson's TExES website. Score reports will be posted by 5 p.m. CT on the score reporting date and will be available for 90 days.

What if I don't pass each subject area subtest?

You must pass all parts of the Core Subjects EC–6 (391) test—as well as the Science of Teaching Reading (293) test—in order to meet the content pedagogy examination requirement for Texas's Core Subjects EC–6 certificate. If, after taking the whole Core Subjects test battery, you do not pass one or more of the subject tests, you are eligible to retake (a) any single subject test if you passed all of the other subject tests, or (b) the entire Core Subjects battery if you do not pass two or more subject exams. You may retake any portion of the Core Subjects exams up to four times. After the first attempt, each testing session counts as another try, regardless of whether the session includes the entire exam or one of the subject area subtests. You must wait 30 days between attempts.

How should I prepare for the test?

It is never too early to start studying for the TExES. The earlier you begin, the more time you will have to sharpen your skills. Do not procrastinate. Cramming is not an effective way to study, since it does not allow you the time needed to learn the test material. It is important for you to choose the time and place for studying that works best for you. Be consistent and use your time wisely. Work out a study routine and stick to it.

When you take REA's diagnostic test and practice tests, simulate the conditions of the actual test as closely as possible. Turn your television and radio off, and go to a quiet place free from distraction. Read each question carefully, consider all answer choices, and pace yourself.

As you complete each test, review your score reports, study the diagnostic feedback, and thoroughly review the explanations to the questions you answered incorrectly. But don't overdo it. Take one problem area at a time; review it until you are confident that you have mastered the material. Give extra attention to the areas giving you the most difficulty, as this will help build your score.

Because the TExES 391 test covers EC–6 content areas, you should review the state curricula for these grades. Convenient access to the curricula, known as the Texas Essential Knowledge and Skills, is offered by the Texas Education Agency at *https://tea.texas.gov/*.

It is also important to familiarize yourself with the released examinations that students in Grades 3 to 6 take to demonstrate mastery of the state curriculum. These tests are released after each administration.

TEXES CORE SUBJECTS EC–6 (391) STUDY SCHEDULE

Week	Activity
1	Take the online Diagnostic Test at the REA Study Center. Your detailed score report will identify the topics where you need the most review.
2–3	Study the review chapters. Use your score report from the Diagnostic Test to focus your study. Useful study techniques include highlighting key terms and information and taking notes as you read the review. Learn all the competencies by making flashcards and targeting questions you missed on the diagnostic test.
4	Take Practice Test Battery 1 either in the book or online at the REA Study Center. Review your score report and identify topics where you need more review.
5	Reread all your notes, refresh your understanding of the test's competencies and skills, and review your college textbooks. This is also the time to consider any other supplementary materials that your advisor or the Texas Education Agency suggests. Review the agency's website at *https://tea.texas.gov/*.
6	Take Practice Test Battery 2 online at the REA Study Center. Review your score report and restudy the appropriate review section(s) until you are confident you understand the material.

Are there any breaks during the test?

Although there is no designated break during the Core Subjects test, you do have a little time to use for the restroom or snacking or stretching outside the testing room. As you can see from our earlier recap, the total time allotted for all the subtests is 4 hours and 40 minutes. But the grand total for the entire appointment time is 5 hours. That leaves you 20 minutes to make your own break.

Bear in mind the following:

- You need to get permission to leave the testing room.

- You cannot take a break during any of the subtests – only between tests.

- The overall test clock never stops.

- The timer for individual subtests starts only when you begin a test.

- Consult your test admission materials for further details, including updates from Pearson.

What else do I need to know about test day?

The day before your test, check for any updates in your Pearson testing account. This is where you'll learn of any changes to your reporting schedule or if there's a change in the test site.

On the day of the test, you should wake up early after a good night's rest. Have a good breakfast and dress in layers that can be removed or added as the conditions in the test center require.

Arrive at the test center early. This will allow you to relax and collect your thoughts before the test, and will also spare you the anguish that comes with being late. As an added incentive to make sure that you arrive early, keep in mind that no one will be admitted into the test center after the test has begun.

Before you leave for the testing site, carefully review your registration materials. Make sure you bring your admission ticket and two unexpired forms of identification. Primary forms of ID include:

- Passport

- Government-issued driver's license

- State or Province ID card

- National ID card

- Military ID card

You may need to produce a supplemental ID document if any questions arise with your primary ID or if your primary ID is otherwise valid but lacks your full name, photo, and signature. Without proper identification, you will not be admitted to the test center.

Strict rules limit what you can bring into the test center to just your ID; we recommend that you consult the Texas Education Agency's "Texas Educator Certification Registration Bulletin" for a complete rundown. You may not bring watches of any kind, cellphones, smartphones, or any other electronic communication devices or weapons of any kind. Scrap paper, written notes, books, and any printed material is prohibited.

No smoking, eating, or drinking is allowed in the testing room. Consider bringing a small snack and a bottle of water to partake of beforehand to keep you sharp during the test.

Good luck on the TExES Core Subjects EC–6 (391) test!

Proven Test-Taking Strategies for TExES Core Subjects

1. Guess Away

One of the most frequently asked questions about the TExES Core Subjects test is: Can I guess? The answer: absolutely! There is no penalty for guessing on the test. That means if you refrain from guessing, you may lose points. To guess smartly, use the process of elimination (see Strategy No. 2). Your score is based strictly on the number of correct answers. So answer all questions and take your best guess when you don't know the answer.

2. Process of Elimination

Process of elimination is one of the most important test-taking strategies at your disposal. Process of elimination means looking at the choices and eliminating the ones you know are wrong, including answers that are partially wrong. Your odds of getting the right answer increase from the moment you're able to get rid of a wrong choice.

3. All in

Review all the response options. Just because you believe you've found the correct answer—or, in some cases, answers—look at each choice so you don't mistakenly jump to any conclusions. If you are asked to choose the *best* answer, be sure your first answer is really the best one.

4. Choice of the Day

What if you are truly stumped and can't use the process of elimination? It's time to pick a fallback answer. On the day of the test, choose the position of the answer (e.g., the third of the four choices) that you will pick for any question you cannot smartly guess. According to the laws of probability, you have a higher chance of getting an answer right if you stick to one chosen position for the answer choice when you have to guess an answer instead of randomly picking one.

5. Use Choices to Confirm Your Answer

The great thing about multiple-choice questions is that the answer has to be staring back at you. Have an answer in mind and use the choices to *confirm* it. For the Math test, in the cases in which you're given a problem to solve, try to find the match among the choices. Or try the opposite: *backsolving*—that is, working backwards—from the choices given.

6. Watch the Clock

Among the most vital point-saving skills is active time management. The breakdown and time limits of each section are provided as you begin each test. Keep an eye on the timer on your computer screen. Make sure you stay on top of how much time you have left for each section and never spend too much time on any one question. Remember: Most multiple-choice questions are worth one raw point. Treat each one as if it's the one that will put you over the top. You never know, it just might. The last thing you want on test day is to lose easy points because you ran out of time and focused too much on difficult questions.

7. Read, Read, Read

It's important to read through all the multiple-choice options. Even if you believe answer choice A is correct, you can misread a question or response option if you're rushing to get through the test. While it is important not to linger on a question, it is also crucial to avoid giving a question short shrift. Slow down, calm down, read all the choices. Verify that your choice is the best one, and click on it.

8. Take Notes

Use the scratch paper provided to you to make notes to work toward the answer(s). If you use all the scratch paper you're initially given, you can get more.

9. Isolate Limiters

Pay attention to any limiters in a multiple-choice question stem. These are words such as *initial, best, most* (as in *most appropriate* or *most likely*), *not, least, except, required,* or *necessary.* Especially watch for negative words, such as "Choose the answer that is *not* true." When you select your answer, double-check yourself by asking how the response fits the limitations established by the stem. Think of the stem as a puzzle piece that perfectly fits only the response option(s) that contain the correct answer. Let it guide you.

10. It's Not a Race

Ignore other test-takers. Don't compare yourself to anyone else in the room. Focus on the items in front of you and the time you have left. If someone finishes the test 30 minutes early, it does not necessarily mean that person answered more questions correctly than you did. Stay calm and focus on *your* test. It's the only one that matters.

11. Confirm Your Click

In the digital age, many of us are used to rapid-clicking, be it in the course of emailing or gaming. Look at the screen to be sure to see that your mouse-click is acknowledged. If your answer doesn't register, you won't get credit. However, if you want to mark it for review so you can return later, that's your call. Before you click "SUBMIT," use the test's review screen to see whether you inadvertently skipped any questions.

12. Creature of Habit? No Worries.

We are all creatures of habit. It's therefore best to follow a familiar pattern of study. Do what's comfortable for you. Set a time and place each day to study for this test. Whether it is 30 minutes at the library or an hour in a secluded corner of your local coffee shop, commit yourself as best you can to this schedule every day. Find quiet places where it is less crowded, as constant background noise can distract you. Don't study one subject for too long, either. Take an occasional breather and treat yourself to a healthy snack or some quick exercise. After your short break—5 or 10 minutes can do the trick—return to what you were studying or start a new section.

13. Knowledge is Power

Purchasing this book gave you an edge on passing the TExES Core Subjects test. Make the most of this edge. Review the sections on how the test is structured, what the directions look like, what types of questions will be asked, and so on. Take our practice tests to familiarize yourself with what the test looks and feels like. Most test anxiety occurs because people feel unprepared when they are taking the test, and they psych themselves out. You can whittle away at anxiety by learning the format of the test and by knowing what to expect. Fully simulating the test even once will boost your chances of getting the score you need. Meanwhile, the knowledge you've gained will also save you the valuable time that would have been eaten up puzzling through what the directions are asking. As an added benefit, previewing the test will free up your brain's resources so you can focus on racking up as many points as you can.

14. B-r-e-a-t-h-e

Anxiety is neither unusual nor necessarily unwelcome on a test. Just don't let it stifle you. Take a moment to breathe. This won't merely make you feel good. The brain uses roughly three times as much oxygen as muscles in the body do: Give it what it needs.

Now consider this: What's the worst that can happen when you take a test? You may have an off day, and despite your best efforts, you may not pass. Well, the good news is that this test can be retaken. Fortunately, the TExES Core Subjects test is something you can study and prepare for, and in some ways to a greater extent than other tests you've taken throughout your academic career. In fact, study after study has validated the value of test preparation. Yes, there will be questions you won't know, but neither your teacher education program nor state licensing board (which sets its own cut scores) expects you to know everything. When unfamiliar vocabulary appears or difficult math problems loom, don't despair: Use context clues, process of elimination, or your response option of the day (i.e., choose either A, B, C, or D routinely when you need to resort to a guess) to make your choice, and then press ahead. If you have time left, you can always come back to the question later. If not, relax. It is only one question on a test filled with many.

Take a deep breath and then exhale. You know this information. Now you're going to show it.

Subject Test I: English Language Arts and Reading (901)

COMPETENCY 001: ORAL LANGUAGE

The teacher understands the importance of oral language, knows the developmental processes of oral language, and provides the students with varied opportunities to develop listening and speaking skills.

Oral Language Acquisition and Development

Long before children begin their schooling, they have made strides in their language development. By the time children are 5 years old, most of them are able to speak and listen in at least one language. Because oral language acquisition occurs so regularly, educators can overlook its significance. However, between birth and the start of their schooling, children engage in the complex, abstract thinking that is needed for them to acquire a language.

What factors help determine how language is acquired? A child's environment plays a role. Parents, caretakers, and others surround a child with authentic speech, and children will acquire the language in a subconscious manner. However, children have an innate ability to acquire language, and they actively construct their knowledge of language. People do not formally teach a child with a sequence of lessons. Instead, children discern the underlying principles of language on their own.

Research shows that children apply these underlying language principles, based on real reasons to communicate. Adults surely know how to create messages in the language, and they know how to reply to messages from others, but they do not know consciously how letters and words are combined to create language. Adults know how sounds can be combined when they pronounce words and how words can be combined when they talk and listen, but they cannot specify the principles.

In the process of acquiring language, children do not just imitate the language of people around them. Studies of children's language acquisition have shown that children use forms of language they have not heard, such as when they overgeneralize a rule they are learning. For example, a child may say *went* but at a later point say *goed* as part of learning about adding -*ed* to form the past tense. Or a child may say *feets* in the course of learning to form plurals. Eventually the child then uses the conventional forms, figuring out the linguistic rules.

Understanding the factors that contribute to children's successful language acquisition can provide guidance for teachers to foster language development once children are in school. Developing students' oral language should continue throughout schooling, and oral language development can work in tandem with reading and writing development.

Components of Oral Language

In the process of acquiring oral language, children gain mastery of the sounds of the language—the **phonemes**—and how sounds can be combined. They also develop knowledge of **semantics**, or the ways meaning is generated in a language, which includes not only the meanings of words but also the way words, phrases, and sentences combine to convey meaning. The semantic component entails morphemes, the smallest units of meaning that can be combined. Some morphemes are **free morphemes** because they can occur alone in a word such as *car*. Other morphemes are **bound morphemes** because they cannot occur alone as a word, such as the -*s* used to form a plural. For example, the word *cats* consists of two morphemes, *cat* and -*s*. Additionally, children learn how words/morphemes can be combined—the **syntax** of the language— to create meaning. Children combine two words, such as in the phrase "more juice," to convey meaning, but later create complex statements and types of questions.

Language development also includes **pragmatics**, or knowing how to use language appropriately depending upon the context. Pragmatics is part of communicative competence, or knowing how to adjust speaking to fit the situation. A person can talk about the same event in different ways, depending on whom they are talking with and whether it is an informal or formal situation.

Social Dimensions of Language Use

When children acquire language, they do so as part of communicating with others for authentic purposes. Examples include connecting with others and making sense of their experience. These social dimensions of language growth cannot be disentangled from the cognitive growth that takes place. Teachers can provide opportunities for students to continue to grow in oral language when they let students use language for real reasons in the classroom and value opportunities for letting students talk in a variety of situations for different purposes. Talking also can continue to be a tool for thinking and learning.

Stages of Oral Language Acquisition

By the time children are around 12 to 18 months old, they typically produce one word at a time. When they enter the **telegraphic stage**, they use two or more words together to create sentence-like utterances, such as "more juice" to communicate "I want more juice" to the parent. At age 4 to 4½ years old, the child's language becomes more complex in the types of statements, questions, as well as the vocabulary (or lexicon) that is acquired. At 5 years old, children are able to talk fluidly with others who speak the same language or dialect.

Children vary in exactly when they begin to talk and when they make gains. Some children begin to talk before they reach 12 months old, while others take longer. Some may use more complex sentences at 3½ years old as compared to other children who do so at 4½ years old.

Theories of Language Acquisition

Behaviorist theory explains that language acquisition entails children gradually acquiring language by moving from the simple to the more complex utterances. Children begin with babbling and then say one- and two-word utterances until they are able to produce longer messages. They can be positively reinforced, such as when a mother smiles or brings a glass of juice when the child says "juice."

Although children do move through this progression in a predictable format, and people do respond to children's talk, cognitive theorists have argued that the behaviorists do not account for many other aspects of language acquisition. For example, adults are able to produce and understand language they have never heard before, so it is clear that language acquisition goes beyond mere imitation of the speech of parents and caregivers.

According to linguist Noam Chomsky, children are born with an innate mechanism that allows them to understand an infinite number of possibilities in the formation of sentences and utterances. Chomsky called this innate mechanism a Language Acquisition Device (LAD).

Chomsky theorized that children are born with Universal Grammar, which contains all the information children need to acquire the grammar of the language(s) they experience. However, psycholinguists did not totally accept Chomsky's notion and they proposed that children might use more general cognitive principles. According to this line of thinking, children are born with the ability to acquire language, and the development is gradual. Children hearing a sufficient number of types of linguistic constructions will discern the patterns and eventually use them in their own communication. Bruner set forth another theory of language acquisition, interactionist theory. According to Bruner, children are born with the capacity to acquire language, but language acquisition requires meaningful interactions with speakers of a language.

Important Factors of Oral Language Development in Schooling

Educators can assume that by the time students reach the middle grades, they know enough about speaking and listening, and even younger children know enough. In addition, oral language development can be misinterpreted by educators as a low priority because much remains to be accomplished in reading and writing. However, theory and research have shown that students' oral language development has an impact on their development in reading and writing. Additionally, students need the opportunities to grow in the use of the content-based and academic language that schooling provides and that are not as likely to be a part of everyday uses of oral language. Moreover, knowing how to communicate through speaking and listening is important throughout students' lives beyond schooling.

Students who are proficient in reading and writing have had certain types of oral language experiences that prepare them for successful reading and writing development. Even when students can engage in everyday speaking and listening, their vocabulary may not be strong enough to develop the skills of reading and writing in school. Nonetheless, a good vocabulary by itself is an insufficient foundation for successful reading and writing. Students need to know how to create meaning by bringing together individual words, sentences, or thoughts to develop a mental representation of the message.

When students engage in everyday listening, they are not called upon to understand longer texts. Similarly, in everyday speaking, students do not have to compose longer texts when talking with people, which typically takes place in spurts. When students gain opportunities to listen to longer texts, such as in hearing books read aloud, they gain in the listening comprehension abilities they need for reading. Composing longer, more complex thoughts in speech helps students acquire the proficiency needed for writing.

Oral language development also is valuable in its own right. The language development opportunities that schooling provides can be built upon and expand the oral language at home. As students continue their schooling, their opportunities for growth in speaking and listening should continue. Schooling provides all students experiences to grow by providing opportunities to use everyday language as well as the academic language learned in subject areas. Schooling can contribute in special ways stemming from speaking and listening opportunities that expand students' experience horizons in terms of types of audience, function (or purpose), and situation (or register).

Planning for oral language development does not require teachers to add another area to be taught. Rather, speaking and listening can be readily integrated as part of students' experiences. Teachers should ensure that students engage in a range of types of speaking and listening situations that concomitantly enhance the learning in reading, writing, and subject-matter learning.

Audience

In planning, teachers should incorporate opportunities for students to engage in a range of situations that vary according to audience. The size of the audience for oral language situations can of course range widely. The demands of using language differ depending on whether students are talking to another individual, in a small group, or in a whole-class or other large group. Audience also varies in terms of familiarity; how a speaker knows a person or a group calls upon differentiated treatment across oral language situations. The age of the participants also plays a role. Thus, speakers may need to adjust their comments depending upon the age and familiarity of the person listening.

Functions of Language

Halliday (1973) has provided a description of various functions of language, and teachers can use them to ensure that students engage in using language for various **purposes**.

Students can gain proficiency if they receive scaffolding and support by engaging in these functions:

- **Instrumental**—to obtain something

- **Regulatory**—to request or control

- **Interactional**—to make contact with others

- **Personal**—to express self

- **Heuristic**—to gain information or explore

- **Imaginative**—to create

- **Representational**—to inform

Providing ways for students to engage in these functions does not require additional lessons. In fact, educational objectives can be enhanced as students interact with their peers for various purposes. For example, rather than completing an assignment on their own, students can work with partners or small groups in math or science. As the students learn in the subject area, they also engage in heuristic, representational, and regulatory functions.

Language Register

In both oral and written language development, growth includes knowing how to situationally adjust the level and style of language. For example, a formal register is appropriate for some situations, whereas an informal register is most appropriate when communicating with family and friends. By giving students multiple opportunities to use language that range from informal to formal registers, students expand their ability to communicate.

Fostering Oral Language Development

Speaking and listening development is required in curriculum, but it is reading and writing development that tends to command attention in the school setting. This is because educators often assume that students who are native speakers already know what they need to know about speaking and listening. Students often are expected to work on their own. Yet in our communities and the workplace, successfully interacting with others (and even obtaining a job) often hinges on proficiency in speaking and listening. Research tells us that proficiency in oral language depends upon people using language for a range of purposes, in different situations, with various sizes of audiences.

The guidelines that follow highlight how to foster students' abilities in speaking and listening.

- **Integrate listening and speaking skills in subject-matter learning.** Teachers may think that they lack time to add speaking and listening to their schedules. In addition, they know that formal assessments focus on reading and writing. However, many written language experiences can be tweaked to include talking and listening. Learning experiences where each student writes in isolation can be reworked so that students talk about the information. In fact, the demonstrations and collaboration provided by speaking and listening can actually enhance learning. Ultimately, though students need to be able to work independently, their achievement will be enhanced when oral and written language are intertwined in a mutually supportive way.

- **Provide students an array of opportunities to engage in authentic speaking and listening.** Being able to talk easily with family and friends does not necessarily mean that a person can easily chat up a person she or he has recently met. Think, for example, of the dynamic of a job interview. Different types of language situations make different demands on speakers and listeners. Devise ways to let students use language for **different purposes** and in **various types of situations** that range from informal to formal situations, such as talking with another classmate about a book and/or having a panel discussion. Consider also how to deal with **various types of audiences**, for instance people who are familiar or less familiar, those who are the same age, and those who are younger or older. Audiences also can vary in terms of speaking with another individual, in a small group, or in a large group.

- **Provide modeling.** Students can gain linguistic and content-area knowledge when teachers engage in discussions with an individual or a group of students. The adult modeling the teacher provides expands the models provided in the home and the community. Moreover, teachers should be sensitive to the fact that school usage may have no parallel at home.

- **Provide helpful growth in using conventional language rather than focusing upon errors.** Students need to learn about conventional ways of speaking. However, rather than criticizing the student for saying something that is "wrong" or incorrect, the teacher can respond by modeling the conventional form of expression and focusing on the intended meaning. For example, if the child says, "He goed with me yesterday," in the course of sharing an event, the teacher could reply, "Oh, it is great that he went with you." With such a response, the students hear the conventional form while also feeling safe in talking with the teacher. Keep in mind that the expressions students use could be a reflection of how their parents and other loved ones speak. Over time, students also can acquire more fully conventional uses of language when opportunities to participate in conversations center on conventional usage.

- **Let students engage in talking and listening daily as part of a routine.** Research on language development tells us that we grow in language by using it daily, for authentic reasons. Talking and listening are ways we form connections, and the social dimensions of learning cannot be disentangled from cognitive processes.

- **Rather than focusing on what students cannot do, adults should focus on what students *can* do.** The majority of students have been quite successful in acquiring at least one language by the time they are 5 years old. A student may mispronounce a word or not use a word exactly in a conventional way. Nevertheless, most students will eventually use the more conventional forms through engaging in talking and listening. Some students are more reticent, and some are more talkative, and perhaps more so in certain situations. As certain situations become more familiar, many students who are initially reticent begin to talk more. If teachers make it possible for students to engage in a range of types of authentic talking situations, students will grow in their use of language.

- **Seek advice when needed.** If a student has difficulty hearing or seems to be far behind peers in communicating, the teacher should seek advice; the child may need the help of other professionals who specialize in speech and hearing.

- **Keep in mind that students rely upon knowing a language through speaking and listening to be able to read and write in that language.** Students do not need to wait until they are proficient in speaking to begin reading and writing instruction, but they draw upon knowing vocabulary and how to combine sounds and words when they read and write. Short-changing oral language development hampers growth in reading and writing.

Conditions for Learning Oral and Written Language

We have established that in learning to speak and listen, children do more than imitate what they hear. Rather, they learn the underlying principles for how words can be combined, which makes it possible for language learners to understand sentences they have never heard before and to produce sentences they have never spoken before.

However, parents, caretakers, and others play an invaluable role in children's language acquisition. Children hear language being used, or are provided modeling. Also, others respond to the child's utterances. Moreover, through interactions with others, children are given real reasons to communicate. Jerome Bruner (1985) has suggested that this kind of support is needed for successful language development.

Brian Cambourne (1995) identified eight conditions that facilitate the development of oral and written language in children. When these conditions are present in their environment, students acquire language more readily.

Table 3-1. Cambourne's Eight Conditions of Literacy Development

Condition of Learning	Explanation
1. Immersion	Students should be immersed in oral and written language in ways that are authentic throughout the curriculum, such as reading aloud to students, letting them work in small groups, and giving them daily opportunities to write.
2. Demonstration	Students need demonstrations of the use of oral and written language. Model for, and involve children in, writing notes, letters, stories, recipes, and lists. Teachers should make it a point to stress the various ways in which language is used in books.
3. Engagement	Regardless of their proficiency levels, help students actively engage and see that they can read and write when they are placed in a supportive environment where they can freely experiment with language.
4. Expectation	Set high but realistic expectations for each student, knowing they will make gains in language development over time.
5. Responsibility	With meaningful support, students can make choices about what they read and write and take responsibility for their learning.
6. Approximation	Students gradually attain proficiency in oral and written language use when their best efforts are valued and when they are guided toward accuracy and self-correction.
7. Use	Students need multiple opportunities to use oral and written language in a variety of ways for meaningful reasons.
8. Response	Students gain most when teachers and others listen to them, read their writing, invite their questions, and provide helpful feedback and praise for progress.

Source: Dr. Brian Cambourne, Centre for Studies in Literacy, Wollongong University, New South Wales, Australia: http://www.cambournesconditionsoflearning.com.au. Cambourne, B. (1988). The whole story: Natural learning and the acquisition of literacy in the classroom. New York: Ashton.

Ways Oral and Written Language Development Can Work in Tandem

Speaking and listening can contribute to students' growth in reading and writing. By incorporating effective instructional practices on a daily basis, teachers can capitalize on speaking and listening opportunities to help their students grow as readers and writers. These practices make an impact, over time, when they become part of classroom routines. Some gains can be seen immediately, but even greater gains come once students gain familiarity with procedures and experiences.

These instructional practices also make it possible for teachers to provide oral language experiences that enable students to participate in different types of language situations that vary according to (1) **types of audiences**, (2) **informal to more formal registers**, and (3) **purposes or functions**.

Reading Aloud

Being a successful reader entails more than just identifying words correctly. Even when students can say words correctly, many still cannot comprehend what they are reading. Reading can become all the more difficult as students enter the reading-to-learn phase in the third and fourth grades, when the amount of reading expands and fewer pictures provide support. A major reason that students may find reading more challenging at this juncture is because they have not developed the abilities needed for reading longer texts. Developing students' listening comprehension can allow them to navigate longer texts when they read based on the very types of thinking that tie back to gains in listening comprehension.

When students talk with others outside of school, they encounter brief snatches of language. In speaking with friends and family, the exchanges are typically short, with one person saying something and the other person replying in bursts of conversation. Through these oral language experiences, students gain much, but they do not gain the listening comprehension that will foster success when reading. Students who have experienced mostly shorter language exchanges are at a disadvantage when facing longer segments of language. This stems from their inability to sustain attention or bring together ideas to create understanding.

We also know that students' oral language experiences alone do not rival the wide range of vocabulary they encounter in reading. However, students' listening comprehension and vocabulary can be developed in a relatively short time by reading quality literature aloud. Quality literature for youth engages students, which in turn leads to vocabulary and comprehension development. Literature at this level lengthens students' attention spans and creates a foundation for understanding as they gradually encounter longer passages cutting across different types of books. Though students should read independently every day, they also can gain from daily read aloud experiences, which will gradually increase their listening comprehension over time if done daily. In fact, it needs to be done daily. Reading aloud is the *single most important predictor* of success in reading. Reading aloud also is critical for showing students the value of books. As many teachers have seen, assigning reading may or may not work with reluctant readers. Yet it's also true that when teachers read aloud quality literature that students enjoy, even reluctant readers may be motivated to read—and choose to read independently.

Writing Conferences

Writing conferences with students help them talk about a topic, which in turn provides scaffolding for writing. Similarly, individual and whole-class writing conferences with students support writing development as fellow class members tell the student what they liked or learned and then pose genuine questions that reveal where the work can benefit from greater clarity or elaboration.

Buddy Reading or Partner Work

Reading with partners creates opportunities to participate in productive reading as well as to foster the development of oral language. Rather than completing an activity on their own, students can learn content more efficiently when they and the teacher collaborate or when students are shown how to work in small groups.

Grand Conversations

Traditionally, reading assignments to measure understanding have entailed writing answers to questions or completing packets. The same learning objectives can be met by engaging in grand conversations with students on a daily basis. Rather than simply being question-and-answer recitations, the teacher and students can instead share their thoughts about big ideas that emerge from the reading selection. This student-led, whole-class discussion works especially well when the teacher models sharing and participates in the conversation. In the real world, readers talk about books; students, too, enjoy this as well when given the opportunity. In addition, students' comments show that they can think at high levels about what they have read as they make inferences, evaluate, share connections to their lives and other reading experiences. Such discussions also can provide the basis for subsequent discussion of literary elements featured in a work. The talking that takes place regularly also can provide support for students as they learn how to write about what they have read. The students' oral composing development in turn makes it easier for them to compose when writing because they have gained valuable practice in telling a story, that is, narrative development.

Retelling

After students have read a section or part of a selection independently, the teacher can ask the group to retell what was read. This should be a casual conversation so students feel safe to express themselves. If students leave out a part, the teacher can add the missing piece to provide modeling for accurate plot sequencing (e.g., "Yes, that happened, but just before that..."). If students stop midway, the teacher can provide a brief prompt, such as "What happened next?" to encourage them. If students are reluctant to begin, the teacher can start to model and invite them to share.

Retelling is a way to encourage students to pay attention to the text as they read. Using this strategy each time a story is read independently or in the course of reading expository texts, students can gain in proficiency in remembering and retelling.

Retelling also can be used to assess whether students have understood what they read. A student's retelling may not reveal higher levels of comprehension, but higher levels of comprehension can be developed through conversations about the book. Moreover, recalling what was read through retelling provides a basis for making inferences, evaluations, synthesis, and applications.

Technology and Audio-Assisted Reading

Students can receive additional experiences in hearing texts read through audiobooks. Quality literature can be shared beyond the reading aloud experiences provided. These experiences contribute to gains in vocabulary and listening comprehension.

Cooperative Learning

Students can make greater strides in vocabulary and overall oral language development by participating in small-group work on some assignments and by working in pairs. These learning experiences also can be used to provide scaffolding for students who need more assistance before being able to complete a task independently. English learners as well as other students can gain from cooperative learning.

"Turn and Talk"

Traditionally, teachers ask an entire group of students a question or set of questions as part of broader learning experiences. But some children are reluctant to share because they lack confidence in talking in a whole-group setting in school. Giving them the opportunity to talk and listen with another classmate first can instill the confidence they need to get in front of a group.

"Turn and Talk" can be used when the teacher would like students to think more about a topic or experience. Instead of an individual child answering the teacher's question, children turn and talk to a partner to help crystallize their thinking and develop their oral language abilities. After talking with a partner, the children then share what they have talked about with the whole group. For instance, suppose a group of children learn about the function of the bark of a tree one day in science class. The teacher could ask the children to turn and talk about one thing they learned about the tree bark. Then the children could share and talk as a whole group. The teacher also could make a list of ideas that could be reviewed in later lessons of the unit on trees.

"Turn and Talk" works best when the teacher makes sure all students have partners who can help them grow in speaking and listening. For example, it may be best to place a reticent child with a child who is confident but also supportive. Teachers also should help students learn about how to be polite listeners.

Demonstrating how to "turn and talk" also provides invaluable help for students. Many teachers use this strategy in situations where the children can address the topic at hand in 30 to 60 seconds, or through a brief talking situation. Letting students talk with a partner or work together could also be a part of classroom learning for longer periods of time.

Assessing Listening and Speaking

Performance-based activities are another way to create opportunities to use language. Such activities also can provide a context for assessing a student's proficiency in listening and speaking.

These listening and speaking activities work best when they are an enduring part of learning in the class. Students' speaking abilities also can be assessed in the classroom with a structured checklist identifying specific features that teachers want to observe. The checklist can be organized to feature social as well as academic situations and/or proficiency levels. See the observation checklist below.

Table 3-2. Observation Checklist for Speaking and Listening Skills

Speaking and Listening Skills	Students' Names								
Student as audience									
Listens to others during whole-class conversations									
Listens to others during small-group conversations									
Asks questions related to topic									
Student as speaker									
Contributes to whole-class conversations									
Contributes to small-group conversations									
Talks with individual students									
Speaks clearly									
Uses appropriate social registers									
Uses courteous language									
Stays on topic									

Language Assessment of English Learners (ELs[1])

The Texas Education Agency (TEA) designed the Texas English Language Proficiency Assessment System (TELPAS) to assess the progress that English learners (ELs) make in learning the English language. English language proficiency assessments in Grades K–12 are required by the federal government to evaluate the progress of ELs. The TELPAS assesses proficiency in listening, speaking, reading, and writing. For students in Grades K–1, the TELPAS includes ratings based on classroom observations. Students in Grades 2–12 receive a score on the multiple-choice questions of the TELPAS reading test. Speaking and listening proficiency ratings are based on classroom observations, and writing scores are based on a portfolio of each student's writing. Students receive a rating based upon four levels of English proficiency, presented in the table that follows.

Table 3-3. ELPS-TELPAS Proficiency Level Descriptors

Proficiencies	Descriptors
Beginning	English learners at this level have a small vocabulary of common words and little ability to use English in academic settings. These students often communicate by using basic English words and phrases they have memorized.
Intermediate	English learners at this level are able to communicate about familiar topics, are able to understand some conversations, but may miss some details. These students use basic English, and they need language support to understand.
Advanced	English learners at this level understand most of what they hear in social situations, but they have difficulty with unfamiliar academic vocabulary and grammar. These students understand and use grade-appropriate academic English with support.
Advanced High	English learners at this level are able to communicate in most situations. They use grade-appropriate academic English with little support even when encountering new information.

English Proficiency Standards (ELPS)

ELs can learn English and the new subject matter within various disciplines. English Proficiency Standards (ELPS) delineate what ELs must know and do to become proficient in academic English. The ELPS are used across the curriculum for learning in disciplines, and the Texas Essen-

---

[1] The term *English Learner (ELs)* is rooted in the federal Every Student Succeeds Act, the main education law for public schools in the United States, which was signed into law in 2015. The coinage describes students participating in special language programs. The term represents an attempt to eliminate the deficit model represented in terms like *Limited English Speaking Ability (LESA)* and *Limited English Proficient (LEP)* previously used in the federal and state legislation.

tial Knowledge and Skills (TEKS) requires teachers to integrate these student expectations as they teach subjects to ELs.

The ELPS address expectations for student mastery of (1) learning strategies, (2) listening, (3) speaking, (4) reading, and (5) writing. In other words, ELs need to be able to learn within a discipline and make gains in speaking, listening, reading, and writing. Supporting ELs requires making sure they have numerous targeted opportunities to use English across the curriculum.

Using pictures and gestures can help children who are new to English. Providing scaffolding and support for leaning in disciplines is necessary for all students, but especially ELs.

Fully supporting all learners hinges on these factors:

1. Students use language daily

2. Language use builds upon what is known in English and about a topic

3. Students experience interesting learning opportunities

4. Students are able to participate by way of appropriately calibrated pacing and levels of difficulty

These four approaches are effective for all students, so ELs and native speakers alike can participate in the same types of learning experiences. However, more scaffolding is needed for ELs, implemented according to their language proficiency.

COMPETENCY 002: WORD ANALYSIS AND IDENTIFICATION SKILLS

The teacher understands the importance of word analysis and identification skills for reading comprehension and provides many opportunities for students to practice and improve these skills.

Foundations of Literacy Development

Instruction in word identification gives students the ability to analyze unknown words or recognize words encountered when reading. Word identification is necessary for reading, but students also need to be able to comprehend what they read. Early literacy instruction must help students decode print, but from the outset, students need to see word identification as a means to understanding what they read.

Proficiency and Rationale for Instruction

By the time students have reached fourth grade, many are proficient in correctly pronouncing the words they encounter in reading materials at their grade level. Along with knowing words, these students can figure out or decode words they have not seen before. At the same time, many students are not able to recognize words when reading materials at their grade level. In fact, students in a sixth-grade classroom could be reading on the first- or second-grade level.

Being able to identify words immediately is critical in reading. When students have to focus attention on figuring out a word, a type of "bottleneck" occurs with short-term memory, causing them to lose track of meaning or comprehension. However, it's also possible for students to correctly read every word in a passage and yet not comprehend what they have read.

Third grade has been thought to mark a pivotal point in literacy development. Some in literacy education contend that up to third grade, students' literacy development focuses more on learning how to read, while after third grade, their focus centers on reading to learn. Moreover, the effort needed to build proficiency becomes ever more daunting for those unable to function at least at grade level. But the reality is that not all students read on grade level. For a variety of reasons, some students read below—or even far below—grade level. Researchers know even these students can make progress, but this often requires that they have a teacher with the expertise to help them learn how to identify words after third grade.

How Readers Identify Words

Readers use four major ways to identify/recognize words: (1) sight words, (2) phonics, (3) structural analysis, and (4) context clues—using surrounding words in a sentence and/or pictures to figure out an unknown word or glean specific information from the text. Capable readers are able to use all four ways to identify words, so instruction should include assessment of what students know and then teaching in view of students' needs.

Sight Words: Assessment and Instruction

Sight words are common enough that they should be instantly recognized without sounding them out. The first sight words that students need to know are the high-frequency words they will encounter when they read and which they will use when they write. To achieve fluency, children need to know how to read and write 20 to 30 sight words before they can engage in guided reading lessons. Children who are not ready for guided reading can read the text with the teacher, pointing to the words to make a voice–print match, which is termed **choral reading**.

One noted sight word list is the Dolch list, named for Dr. Edward W. Dolch, who developed the list by studying the most common words students encounter when reading. The list includes approximately 300 words. The words are organized in groups of 100 or by grade levels, ranging from Pre-K through Grade 3.

The Fry list, developed by Dr. Edward Fry, is an expanded version of the Dolch list. Known as Fry's Instant Words, or Fry Words, the list contains 1,000 words and it, too, is based on the most common words that readers need to be able to recognize. The Fry Words on average represent approximately 90% of the words in a typical book, website, or news article. The Fry Words are listed in order of the frequency with which they occur and are often broken down into groups of 100. Thus, the first 100 words are the most frequently occurring words in the English language.

Sight-word lists are presented by levels. Thus, students can be assessed by reading a list of words. Once a student is able to read the words fluently at a given level, the teacher assesses the student at the next level.

Students also should be able to spell high-frequency words because of the extent they will use these when they write. A student may be able to read a word but not be able to spell it even if the student is reading on grade level. Spelling tests can be given to determine the words students are struggling with. Isolating these words gives students the opportunity to learn how to spell them.

Phonics: Assessment and Instruction

Phonics pertains to the relationship of sounds and letters. Many words in English have irregular spellings, defying readers' efforts to sound them out. Still, knowing the major phonics generalizations allows students to rely on patterns as they read and spell. The phonics generalizations presented next are that ones that occur often enough to be helpful for teachers to help students discern the generalizations.

One effective way to assess students' understanding of phonics is to ask them to write/spell one-syllable words that feature the generalization. In this way, students will begin to see the pattern, as, for instance, in learning short vowel sounds in words such as *cap*, *had*, *bat*. From words that students learn to read/spell, they can also learn word families. Once they know how to read/spell *bat*, for example, they can learn, by way of the analogic approach, words such as *cat*, *fat*, *hat*, *mat*, *sat*. With this approach, students learn how to detect patterns. In a synthetic approach, students blend individual sounds. Effective instruction can include both approaches, and provides for sufficient practice in reading and spelling words so that students master phonics generalizations.

Major Phonics Generalizations

Effective phonics instruction ensures that students can apply phonics generalizations as part of word identification. However, effective instruction does not ask students to memorize rules. Rather, it entails providing enough practice in reading words that exemplify a generalization so that students can internalize the pattern.

Consonants

In English, the alphabet is composed of vowels and consonants. The vowels are *a*, *e*, *i*, *o*, *u*— and sometimes *y* (e.g., pl**ay**) and *w* (e.g., sn**ow**), when they team up with the vowel next to them to create a single vowel sound. Consonants are the other letters of the alphabet.

Here's a summary of various consonant sounds found in English:

- **Initial consonant sounds:** The single consonant at the beginning of a word is the initial consonant. For example, in the words *yellow* and *with*, the *y* and *w* are the consonants in the first position.

- **Final consonant sounds:** Once students know final consonant sounds, they typically do not have difficulty identifying sounds of the letters in the final position, but, as we saw earlier, *y* and *w* can take the role of vowels when combined with a vowel, together creating a vowel sound, such as in *play*, *cow*, and *snow*.

- **Consonant blends:** Consonant blends are when two or three consonant sounds, unseparated by vowels, blend together. Adults may not see these combinations as different from single initial consonant sounds because they know how to read, but children can perceive differences, such as making the distinction between the initial sound of *brown* and that of *boat*. Common consonant blends include the following:

  l-blends (such as **bl, cl, fl, pl**)

  r-blends (such as **br, cr, dr, fr, pr, tr**)

  s-blends (such as **st, sp, str, spr**)

Consonant sounds that do not blend are called **consonant digraphs**. In such instances, two consonants together create a single sound, such as these: **ch (church), ch (choral), ng (ring), ph (phone), sh (shout), th (then), th (thing), wh (when)**.

Vowels

Vowel sounds are not as consistent as those of consonants. The sound of a vowel depends upon orthographic patterns, or the letters that surround the vowel. Students do not need to be able to say whether the vowel is "long" or "short" to read words with vowels. Instead, they need to be able to discern the pattern by seeing many examples of it. For example, children discern the pattern of short *a* by seeing instances of short *a* words in a spelling list when first learning these words (rather than having short *a* words combined with other short vowel words). Later on, they can be shown how the sounds change depending upon what surrounds the *a* (such as *can* vs. *car* or *can* vs. *cane*).

Here's a summary of various vowel sounds found in English:

1. **Short vowels:** The Consonant-Vowel-Consonant (CVC) pattern—a vowel connecting two consonants—always signals short vowels, as shown in these examples:

CVC Short A	CVC Short E
cap	jet
man	set
had	ten

CVC Short I	CVC Short O
sit	dog
fish	hot
ship	mop

CVC Short U
cut
rug
must

2. **Long vowels:** The vowel "says" its name, and this takes place in three major patterns:

   • **Two vowels together:** In the first pattern, the first vowel says its name, and the second one is silent.

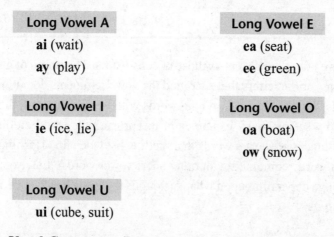

Long Vowel A	Long Vowel E
ai (wait)	**ea** (seat)
ay (play)	**ee** (green)

Long Vowel I	Long Vowel O
ie (ice, lie)	**oa** (boat)
	ow (snow)

Long Vowel U
ui (cube, suit)

   • **VCe-Vowel-Consonant-silent e pattern.** In this pattern, the first vowel is long and the second is silent.

Long Vowels—CVe
a name
e Pete
i kite
u flute

- **Single vowel after a consonant:** These words are learned as sight words (such as *me* or *so*), so they usually are taught that way.

3. **R-controlled vowels:** The vowel appears as a CVC pattern, but it is not a short vowel found because the *r* changes the sound of the vowel.

R-Controlled Vowels
car
fern
stir
corn
turn

4. **Vowel digraphs:** Two vowels come together to create a new sound that is neither long, short, nor **r**-controlled.

Vowel Digraphs
au, **aw**—haul, saw
oo—look, book; soon, pool

5. **Dipthongs:** Diphthongs entail the slurring of two-letter vowel combinations and are a special case of digraphs.

Dipthongs—oy, oi	Dipthongs—ou, ow
boy	house
boil	cow

Structural Analysis or Word Parts Instruction: Assessment and Instruction

Readers use structural analysis to identify meaning in words by examining parts of a word. Students begin to develop this ability in the early grades once they know sight words. As students progress, they use structural analysis as they encounter words that have more than one syllable and when they examine word roots and affixes (pre and post) to identify the meaning of words.

Here is a snapshot of how students are introduced to structural analysis in the early grades.

Forming plurals

In general, the plural of a noun is formed by adding *-s* to the noun.

Singular	Plural
cat	cats
rake	rakes

However, if the word ends in a **consonant** + **y**, drop the -*y* and add -*ies*.

Singular	Plural
puppy	puppies
baby	babies

If the word ends in a **vowel** + **y**, just add -*s*.

Singular	Plural
day	days
toy	toys

If the word ends in –*x*, -*s*, -*sh*, or -*ch*, add -*es*.

Singular	Plural
box	boxes
bus	buses
dish	dishes
church	churches

Then there are the special cases of plurals…

Singular	Plural
wolf	wolves
foot	feet
deer	deer
sheep	sheep
potato	potatoes
child	children

Inflectional Endings

For **inflectional endings**, a word part added to the end of a base word changes the number or tense of a base word. English has eight inflectional morphemes or inflectional endings— -*s* (plural), -*es* (long plural), -*s* (third person singular), *'s* (the possessive), -*ed* (past tense), -*en* (past participle), -*er* (the comparative), -*est* (superlative), and -*ing* (present progressive). Note: Short and long plurals count for one of the eight inflectional morphemes.

Compound Words

Compound words are composed of two or more words that, when combined, make a new word with its own unique meaning. The components of the word can help in the identification of the meaning, such as in *birdhouse*, *windshield*, *cupcake*, *snowball*, and *mailbox*. However, other compound words do not provide clues to meaning, such as *nightmare*, *hotdog*, and *butterfly*.

Contractions

Contractions are formed by using the apostrophe to show where one or more letters or syllables have been omitted to create a shorter form of a word or set of words. When students are shown this, it is easier to learn to spell contractions because they can then see the logic of where the apostrophe is placed. Some common examples of English contractions are: *it's* for *it is*, *can't* for *cannot*, *I've* for *I have*, *didn't* for *did not*, and *I'll* for *I will*.

Prefixes

A **prefix** is an affix at the beginning of a word. It contains meaning in itself and can change the meaning of the word. Some common prefixes are listed in the table that follows:

Table 3-4. Common English Prefixes

Prefix	Meaning	Example
un-	not or opposite of	unhappy, unaware
dis-	not, opposite of	disappear, discover
trans-	across	transportation, transmit
sub-	underneath, lower	submarine, subway

Suffixes

A **suffix** is an affix at the end of a word. As with prefixes, suffixes also convey meaning and can change the meaning of the word.

Table 3-5. Common English Suffixes

Suffix	Meaning	Example
-ful	full of	helpful, playful
-less	without	home, homeless
-ly	manner of	sad, sadly
-able, -ible	can be done, capable of being	preventable, audible

A **syllable** is a unit containing one vowel sound or a vowel with one or more consonants, which may form a complete word or become part of a word.

Knowing syllable patterns can help students as they spell and read. Common types of syllables are as follows:

- **Open syllable** occurs with one vowel at the end of the combination of letters, such as *me* or *so*, which are one-syllable words, or in multisyllabic words, such as <u>ho</u>-*tel* or <u>me</u>-*te-or*. The vowel makes a long sound in an open syllable.

- **Closed syllable** occurs when a vowel is "closed" by a consonant, such as *bag* or *bag-gage*. The vowel makes a short sound in a closed syllable.

- **Vowel-Consonant-Silent e (VCe) syllable** has a long vowel sound spelled with a vowel/consonant/silent *e*, such as in *bike* or *com-plete*.

- **Vowel Teams syllable** occurs when two vowels are together and make one sound. The sound can be the long vowel sound, such as in *play*, *wait*, *keep*, *seat*, *boat*, *snow*, *fruit*, *pie* or *snow-ing*, *playing*. **Vowel digraphs** can be considered vowel teams, such as in *paw* and *aw-ful* or *book* and *book-ing*. Vowel teams also can include **dipthongs**, such as in *joy*, *joy-ful*, *cow*, *pow-er*.

- **Vowel-r (or r-controlled) syllable** contains *ar*, *er*, *ir* or *or*, *ur*, such as in *turn*, *pur-chase*, *bark*, *bark-ing*.

- **Schwa syllable** contains the schwa vowel sound, which is common but does not have one standard sound. The schwa sound is close to the short *u* sound and is an unaccented syllable, such as in *dam-**age***, ***oc***-*cur*, *em-**pha**-size*.

The knowledge students gain in learning phonics and sight words helps them as they learn syllable patterns. Through systematically learning to spell words that highlight different types of syllables, students gain understanding of how to read and write multisyllabic words.

Morphemic Analysis

Morphemic analysis is related to **structural analysis**; this takes place when students use prefixes, suffixes, and roots or base words to determine or remember the meanings of words. Research shows morphemic analysis fosters stronger vocabulary development.

A morpheme is a unit of meaning in a language which has these traits:

- It is a word or part of a word that has meaning.

- It is not necessarily a word.

- A **bound morpheme** is not a word on its own, so it cannot stand on its own. A bound morpheme appears with a root. Bound morphemes include affixes (prefixes or suffixes), such as *dis-* in *disappear*, or *-s* in *dogs*.

- A **free morpheme** can stand on its own, as we see in *appear*.

- A **compound word** (e.g., *football*) is composed of **two free morphemes**.

Through structural or morphemic analysis, students analyze parts of words to identify and understand them. Structural analysis begins early on as students learn to apply plurals, such as *cat → cats*, or adding an inflectional ending such as *-s, -ed, -ing* to a verb, as in *walks → walked → walking*.

Structural and morphemic analysis becomes more complicated as students learn to read and spell plurals such as *puppies* for *puppy*. It also becomes more complicated as students learn to identify multisyllabic words and break them into syllables.

Learning Latin and Greek roots and derivations can help students increase their vocabulary and understand new words they encounter more readily, especially as they become able to apply context clues to the text. Teaching derivational morphemes on a daily basis can increase the ability of students to decode and interpret new words. The use of derivational morphemes can change the syntactic classification of the word. For example, the noun *caution* becomes an adjective or an adverb when we add derivational morphemes—*cautious* (adjective) and *cautiously* (adverb). The following table presents examples of derivational morphemes, together with examples of English words they help create.

Table 3-6. Common Greek and Latin Roots and Derivation

Root	Origin	Meaning	English Example
auto-	Greek	self	autobiography
bio-	Greek	life	biography
homo-	Greek	same	homogenous, homophone
hydr-	Greek	water	hydration, dehydrated
-logy	Greek	study of	biology, geology
cord-, cor-, cardi-	Latin	heart	cordial, discord, cardiogram
duc-, duct-	Latin	to lead	conduct, reduction
fract-, frag-	Latin	break	fraction, fragment
loc-	Latin	place	location, relocate
port-	Latin	to carry	export, transportation

The Greek and Latin languages have enriched the lexicon of a large number of European languages, including English and Spanish. As a result, these two languages have numerous cognates. **Cognates** are words in two or more languages that share a similar meaning, spelling, and pronunciation. English learners can benefit from using these types of words. However, most cognates are content-based academic words; thus, most likely these words are not part of the daily vocabulary of ELs. However, teachers can present these academic words in the native language of the child, so students can connect them with their English equivalent.

The following table shows examples of English–Spanish cognates derived from Greek and Latin.

Table 3-7. Greek and Latin Roots

Root	Origin	English Example	Spanish Example
astron- ("star")	Greek	astrology, astronaut	astrología, astronauta
bio- ("life")	Greek	biology, geology	biología, geología
phon- ("sound")	Greek	microphone, phoneme	micrófono, fonéma
aud- ("to hear")	Latin	auditorium, audience	auditorio, audiencia
dict- ("to tell, speak")	Latin	dictate, dictator	dictar, dictador
hospit- (host)	Latin	hospital, hospitality	hospital, hospitalidad

Context Clues

Using **context clues** is a decoding strategy to derive meaning from unknown words. When implementing context clues, readers study the words surrounding an unknown word to identify the unknown word. Context clues also can be illustrations that picture what the text or the setting is about.

Knowing how words can be put together requires knowledge of syntax, or language structure. In using context, students use their knowledge of language structure because they know what types of words can be placed together. For example, in the sentence below, the blank for the unknown word would be a thing, not a verb or preposition.

I like to eat _____.

Children who know English also intuitively know this even though they do not know the grammatical term *noun*, nor do they need to know the parts of speech to figure out the unknown word. Even young children intuitively will know this because they discern principles of language as they acquire language.

Because we, as adults, know English and know about what people can eat, we know that the unknown word (the blank) will be a kind of food (e.g., *tacos, shrimp, carrots, cake*)—rather than *car*, for example.

Children, especially beginning readers, should be guided to use context and picture cues to determine unknown or unfamiliar words they encounter in text selections. Suppose, for example, that a student turns to a page in a book with an illustration showing a child eating a piece of cake. The student can look at the illustration on the page to infer that the unknown word in the following sentence is *cake*:

I like to eat _____.

To use context clues, students need to know sight words because they need to be to be able to read some of the words in the sentence.

Now let's take it a step further by providing the student with an additional clue to a missing word. Readers often use context clues and phonics and/or structural analysis as they figure out the word that should go in the blank, as shown immediately below. In the following sentence, the reader is given the initial consonant sound of the unknown word (which is phonics) to be used in tandem with context clue.

I will ride to school on the b_____.

Initial consonant sounds and context clues are especially helpful for readers to identify unknown words. In the following example, the student cannot immediately decode the word *instead* but may break it into syllables, a process that deploys structural analysis and context clues to decide what would make sense:

I want to eat this dessert _____ (*instead*).

When children know how to speak English, they can use context more readily. How to speak is undergirded by knowledge of semantics (meaning) and syntax (language structure).

Using context clues is the most efficient way for students to figure out words. In fact, students can use this even before they know all of the phonics and structural analysis generalizations. Therefore, oral language development is critical in teaching students how to recognize words in English.

In the cloze procedure, students are asked to read a passage and supply missing words, which requires students to use context clues. The cloze procedure is used to assess comprehension, but it also can be used to encourage students to use context clues.

Effective Word Analysis Development

Spelling

One of the best ways for students to learn word analysis or identification skills is through spelling. Spelling helps students focus on each letter of a word, and as students learn to spell words, they learn to read words. Through a systematic spelling program, students gain mastery of various ways readers identify words that feature phonics generalizations, sight words, and structural/morphemic analysis. By focusing on a designated list of sight words and either phonics or structural analysis generalizations, teachers can ensure that students are learning what they need to know. Once students have mastered basic word analysis, teachers can focus on systematic study of Latin and Greek derivational morphemes to help students see patterns in roots.

Word Games

To strengthen students' learning of words, teachers can provide small-group learning or learning stations where students play word games such as bingo. Once students have been shown how to work together in playing the game, they will be able to do so while the teacher works with other students. And as students learn new words, the teacher adds them to the game.

Demonstrations Using Context and Cloze Procedure

Teachers also can show students how to use context clues by demonstrating how to use surrounding words in a sentence to figure out an unknown word. This can take place by listening to students read aloud individually or as part of group instruction, including guided reading groups. Using sentences from the reading section, the teacher can model how to reveal an unknown word by reading up to and after the word in the sentence to decide what would make sense. Cloze passages leave blanks at designated points to see whether students can read and understand the texts even with the missing words. Students are asked to supply the missing words, which hinges on their ability to use context clues. Students need to be able to read the surrounding words to be able to supply the missing word, or alternatively, teachers need to read the sentences for the student. Cloze activities also can help students review words they are learning by asking them to complete sentences by making selections from a word bank.

Independent Reading

Students will become more proficient in word identification by daily reading. Gains in reading are associated with the amount of time students spend reading texts. Specific instruction in spelling and skills is needed, but it is critical that students refine and orchestrate their skills by engaging in sustained reading. Daily instruction should provide opportunities for students to independently read books they select. Even if books are easy to read, students still advance because reading easy books makes it possible to make gains in fluency. Students whose teachers read aloud daily will be more apt to want to read because they see what books offer, and they often will select a book or author of a book the teacher has read aloud.

Guided Reading

Guided reading is small-group reading instruction that makes it possible for the teacher to help the student make gains in reading by providing texts at the students' instructional level. Instructional-level texts are slightly more difficult than the independent-level texts that students can read on their own. Independent-level texts are ones the students can read once the teacher provides support before reading by introducing new words and activating/building background for reading. The teacher also supports growth by fostering comprehension. Through multiple readings of a text, students are able to strengthen word recognition, which in turn supports fluent reading.

Shared Reading

In shared reading, the teacher reads first to model, and students follow along. In subsequent readings, the students read with the teacher until they can read on their own. Shared reading can take place daily when the teacher and students read a text together, making it possible for students to learn words and then be able to read on their own that day or after subsequent readings with the teacher. Poems that students find enjoyable are ideal for this purpose. Shared reading can also take place when students need to read a text in content areas. This approach can help keep students from being overwhelmed by unknown words in new nonfiction. After all, children encounter unfamiliar words all the time. So this shared-reading approach can help turn a reluctant reader into one who relishes books.

Students also can read with a partner or read along with an audiobook during small-group work while the teacher works with a group for guided reading. These learning experiences work especially well for many students who are not able to engage in sustained silent reading for longer periods of time.

COMPETENCY 003: READING FLUENCY

The teacher understands the importance of fluency for reading comprehension and provides many opportunities for students to improve their reading fluency.

Fluency

Fluency in reading is essential for comprehension. When students read fluently, it means they can focus more on constructing the meaning of the text because of the automaticity of their decoding skills. Additionally, fluency is important because if students do not read easily and with understanding, they are less apt to enjoy it. Students who do not enjoy reading tend to read less and do not make the gains in reading development that come from reading for its own sake. Although fluency metrics include timed readings, fluency should not be confused with speed reading. Fluency entails **accuracy**, **rate**, and **prosody**.

Accuracy and rate gains stem from strong word identification skills. This means that students not only can identify a word but also identify words automatically. Thus, creating meaning is not disrupted by a slow rate or word-by-word reading, enabling readers to make connections between ideas presented in the text and their background knowledge. The student who reads fluently frees up the attention needed to figure out unfamiliar words. Readers who deploy sight words, phonics, structural/morphemic analysis, and context clues draw upon a wide repertoire of knowledge and skills to identify words they read.

- Phonics helps students see patterns in words rather than needing to memorize every word.

- Knowledge of sight words/high-frequency words helps students automatically deal with many of the words they will encounter, including those with irregular spellings that do not adhere to phonics patterns, such as *said* and *come*.

- Structural/morphemic analysis provides expertise in identifying multisyllabic words, including base words with prefixes or suffixes.

- Students familiar with context clues can use their knowledge of language structure (or syntax) along with meaning (or semantics) as they decode, which helps them monitor their word identification of visually similar words as they decide whether what they're reading makes sense or sounds like the way something is said, such as in this example:

We ride to school <u>in</u> our car (not <u>on</u> our car).

Prosody (or expression) includes appropriate phrasing, which requires that attention be paid to punctuation. Students who read with expression, using appropriate intonation and phrasing, are more apt to derive what's being conveyed in the text. Likewise, paying attention to punctuation includes being able, for example, to treat a sentence that ends with a question mark differently than one that ends with a period – which enhances the student's command of the text's rhythm and intonation.

Still, students may be able to read words accurately and automatically, yet not comprehend the text. Prosody marks the distinction as to whether students are constructing meaning (comprehending) as they read rather than merely word calling.

Fluency Assessment

Here are keys to assessing reading fluency:

- Screening, diagnosing, and progress monitoring make it possible to support students' growth in fluency.

- By listening to students read, teachers can make sure they are reading fluently.

- Assessment for fluency needs to address accuracy, rate (automaticity), and prosody (expression).

- If only rate is observed, comprehension and expression may suffer for the lack of attention to prosody. Furthermore, when only rate is stressed, students and teachers may confuse fluency with speed reading.

- If only accuracy is observed, students may be only "word calling" and thus reading so slowly that they cannot devote attention to constructing meaning as they read.

Procedures for Assessing Fluency

Here is an overview of critical procedures for assessing reading fluency:

- Use a passage from a grade-level text to know how well a student performs at grade level. The passage can be 100 to 245 words.

- Students should individually read the text aloud for 1 minute.

- Count the number of words the student read correctly to obtain words read correctly per minute (WCPM).

- Because the one-minute testing time is short, multiple passages can be read, and the median (or middle) score used.

- Research studies have established norms for **reading rates**, or how many words a student reads per minute. These rates are established for the beginning of the school year as well as later in the year to determine whether students are making progress.

- Teachers can compare a student's reading rates to average rates. Hasbrouck and Tindal (1992) have provided guidance for Grades 1–8, and the rates are provided for three assessments during a school year, as shown in the following chart:

Table 3-8. Oral Reading Fluency (ORF) Target Rate Norms

Grade	Fall WCPM	Winter WCPM	Spring WCPM
1		10–30	30–60
2	30–60	50–80	70–100
3	50–90	70–100	80–110
4	70–110	80–120	100–140
5	80–120	100–140	110–150
6	100–140	110–150	120–160
7	110–150	120–160	130–170
8	120–160	130–170	140–180

Source: Hasbrouck, J.E., & Tindal, G. (1992). Curriculum-based oral reading fluency norms for students in Grades 2 through 5. *Teaching Exceptional Children*, 24, 41–44.

- To find the **accuracy rate**, count the number of errors the student did not self-correct to obtain a percentage of words read accurately. For example, if a student makes 10 errors after reading 100 words, the accuracy is 90%.

- The **accuracy rate** can help determine whether the grade-level text is at the independent, instructional, or frustration level.

  - To find the **accuracy rate**, count the number of errors the student did not correct to obtain a percentage of words read accurately. For example, if a student makes 10 errors in the course of reading 100 words, the accuracy rate is 90%.

  - The accuracy rate can help determine whether the grade-level text is at the independent, instructional, or frustration level.

  95%–100%   Independent Level (easy)

  90%–94%   Instructional Level (can be read with support/instruction)

  Below 90%   Frustration Level (too difficult)

- **Prosody** can be assessed by noting the extent to which the student reads with expression. This includes whether the student consistently reads in a natural way, notes punctuation, and speaks at an appropriate conversational volume. Prosody assessment can include noting whether students read mostly word by word, in two- to three-word phrases, or by using longer, smooth phrasing.

Instructional Support for Fluency

Using Assessment to Inform Teaching

How should assessment inform teaching to improve reading fluency? Here's a brief rundown:

- If a student does not read a text accurately, he or she may need more instruction in a particular area of word identification.

- If the student has difficulty in word identification, the teacher needs to determine what type of word identification is needed. Additional support may be needed in phonemic awareness, letter identification, sight vocabulary, phonics, structural analysis, or in the student's grasp of context clues within the framework of oral language development.

- Students who lack expression may need practice in reading the text more smoothly, with expression, and/or paying attention to punctuation.

- Even students who can identify words may still need the teacher to model how to read fluently, such as by paying attention to punctuation and reading with expression.

- If the text used for fluency assessment is too difficult for the reader, a text at a lower reading level should be tried. Students who cannot identify at least 90% of the words in a text are reading at their frustration level, making the text too difficult.

- Using an easier text may help the student to read more fluently and understand the text.

Students make gains in fluency when they can read at least 95% of the words, which means they won't be diverting attention to word analysis. It is best when the student can read 98%–100% of the words of a text.

Reading Materials

Give careful thought to the reading materials available in your classroom. Providing opportunities for students to read independently daily helps develop fluency. Students should be able to self-select what they read so they experience reading the way readers do in the real world, and they should have ample materials to choose from that are at their independent reading level and thus easy for them to read.

Even grade-level books can be too hard for some students to read independently. When students have to struggle to identify words, they are unable to gain in fluency. Grade-level texts used for assessment provide a way to see how a student performs versus grade-level proficiency, but easy texts are where students make gains in fluency.

Rereading

Reading texts again for instruction can make it possible for students to reach the independent reading level for the texts. Thus, having students reread a text on a subsequent day after a guided reading lesson can be a valuable instructional activity.

Multiple readings are feasible when students can read shorter texts a second time. Poetry, generally a short form, is ideal for this. Many teachers provide shared reading of a poem daily, which is optimal. Quality poetry for youth allows for an enjoyable reading experience.

Choral Reading and Shared Reading

Choral reading takes place when the teacher and students read a text or part of a text together. Choral reading can take place through a projected text a group of students can see at once, online (when necessary or appropriate), or it can take place when the teacher and students read printed copies of the same text in unison.

In shared reading, the teacher reads first to model, and students follow along. In subsequent readings, the students read with the teacher until they can do so on their own. Choral reading and shared reading begin with the teacher reading the selection aloud so that (1) the teacher models fluent reading, and (2) students can then enjoy the story or poem and think about its meaning.

As we've said, many teachers present a poem for daily shared reading. Once students master reading the poem, a new one is introduced, either during the same or the following week. Shared reading provides differentiated instruction because students will gain what they need, whether it is new words or reading with expression.

The multiple readings of poetry can include pointing out to students how to abide by punctuation and provide the proper expression that the punctuation signals. Students can be shown to not pause (even when they reach the end of a line) until they see a comma, period, or question mark in the poem. Students also can be shown how to consider the "voice" of the poem so that they'll read it with the proper expression.

Showing Fluent Reading

Teachers can model how to read fluently. This can take place during daily read-alouds. Teachers also can model at the end of a guided reading lesson or when working with students individually. The teacher can read a short segment to model, and then let the students read with her or him. The students then read alone.

Audio-Assisted Reading

In audio-assisted reading, students read along with the voice on an audio recording of a text. If the reading materials is easy for the student, the student can focus on reading smoothly and with expression. Audio-assisted reading can take the shape of a learning station or independent activity. Students participate while the teacher works with a small group for guided reading or small-group work. Students will enjoy the reading if the teacher selects quality poetry, picture books, or short stories that meet the needs of youth.

Readers' Theater

Readers' theater is a type of drama where the presentation takes place through reading a script. Readers' theater does not involve memorizing lines of a script as in a formal play. The presentation does not involve movement, as would story dramatization. Instead, reading comes alive through the readers' voices.

Readers' theater can be a rewarding way for students to revisit a story or content in textbooks. The subsequent reading can help foster comprehension and vocabulary development as students review content. The rereading also helps with word recognition as students strive to read fluently as they practice the script in advance of presenting it. Fluency also is enhanced as students aspire to become the character and say something the way the character would by observing punctuation rules and using the correct intonation.

Readers' theater does not involve costumes and memorizing, so it is an easy drama activity to incorporate while also fostering fluency, vocabulary, and comprehension and oral language development. Oral language development takes place as the presenters talk and their classmates listen.

Readers' theater is an ideal way to develop oral and written language because students are using language for real reasons, not dummy runs. Various forms of literature can provide the basis of the script, but it needs to be at students' independent reading level for fluency development. By reading the script with the teacher or with classmates, students can practice at their instructional level (90%–94% word identification). With practice, students can reach 100% of the words they read in the script.

Partner Reading

Students can be shown how to read in pairs by practicing reading a poem they have read during shared reading. With the teacher's help, students make gains in fluency. Students also can reread the story they had read during their guided reading instruction with the teacher. When students are shown how to read together in productive ways, partner reading can take the form of a beneficial literacy station or independent activity while the teacher meets with small groups for guided reading or other instruction.

COMPETENCY 004: READING COMPREHENSION AND APPLICATIONS

The teacher understands the importance of reading for understanding, knows the components and processes of reading comprehension, and teaches students strategies for improving their comprehension, including using a variety of texts and contexts.

Reading Comprehension and Applications

Successful reading entails being able to comprehend what is being read. By the time students reach the middle grades of elementary school, many can correctly pronounce the words they read, yet they may struggle in understanding what they're reading. Accurate word identification is necessary for comprehension, but reading words accurately does not guarantee that students understand what they are reading.

Levels and Types of Comprehension

To be able to comprehend, students need to be engaged in learning experiences in which they are able to understand at varying levels of comprehension and across various types of texts.

- **Literal comprehension** entails being able to recall what is explicitly stated in a text. This can be the main idea along with important details. Literal comprehension is the least difficult. However, knowing what is explicitly written is important for interpreting and evaluating stories and expository texts in subject-matter learning, as well as persuasive texts or arguments.

- **Inferential comprehension** requires that readers discern or arrive at understandings when information is not explicitly stated in the text. Competent readers are able to use what is stated in the text to make inferences. Students need to make inferences as they connect ideas to comprehend what takes place in a story (or animates the plot), to make predictions, and to uncover themes that emerge. Students also need to know how to make inferences as they work their way through informational text and persuasive texts or arguments by drawing conclusions based on what is presented in the text. Many students assume that comprehension entails only understanding what is explicitly stated, but authors assume readers will make inferences.

- **Evaluative comprehension** also requires readers to think at higher levels as they analyze, evaluate, and decide on their own position or stance. Students need to be able to understand what is presented in the text as they engage in evaluating, and they need to be able to explain and support evaluations by using evidence in the text to support or prove their case.

Learning to Read versus Reading to Learn

Students in Grades EC–3 are learning how to decode or identify words. In other words, **learning to read** is a large part of literacy development in those grades. By the time students reach Grade 4, students who are on grade level will know how to recognize words and decode the unfamiliar ones. Word study for students in Grades 4–6 focuses upon morphemic analysis and understanding words, or increasing vocabulary.

Comprehension can start to become difficult for students in Grades 4–6, as the texts they read become longer and more complex. Students must rely increasingly on the print to construct meaning rather than relying on illustrations. Along with reading longer fictional stories, students read longer nonfiction texts in their subject-matter learning. Therefore, a shift takes place where reading to learn becomes a large focus in Grades 4–6. Nevertheless, comprehension development needs to begin as students progress along the trajectory of learning to read up to **reading to learn** in the upper grades. This critical development puts students in a position to understand longer stories and navigate informational or expository texts, which demand that the reader understand, synthesize, and remember new information.

Dyslexia and Comprehension Assessment

Students also can have high levels of listening comprehension and adequate levels of intelligence indicating they can comprehend texts well, but these same students may struggle when processing text as readers, so their comprehension is hindered.

Students' inability to read words accurately may be the result of the lack of effective instruction, but it also could signal the need for assessment to determine whether the student has dyslexia or some other learning disability. Dyslexia creates difficulty with single-word recognition, reading fluency, and spelling. Consequently, it also gets in the way of comprehension and written expression. Teachers are required to seek assessment for students who display potential signs of dyslexia or other disabilities so that appropriate instruction is not delayed.

Dimensions of Comprehension

Questioning students about a text can be a way to assess comprehension if the questions are well developed. However, comprehension instruction should not be limited to providing passages and how to answer particular types of questions.

Attention should also be given to instruction in comprehension to help students deal with aspects of comprehending texts that can be challenging. Reading is an active, constructive process that is a transaction between the reader and the text. Readers need to create a text model in their mind, using the information in the text. In constructing meaning, readers use their knowledge of (1) **language**, (2) **the world**, and (3) **navigating print**. The meaning created also can depend upon the **reader's purpose for reading**; different texts and **text structures** make different types of demands on readers.

Young readers' unique experiences and abilities may give them a strong basis for comprehension, but teachers are in a unique position to improve students' proficiency. Here are specific opportunities for instruction:

- Because readers use knowledge of language to comprehend texts, teachers can help students grow by imparting their own knowledge of language.

- Teachers can activate and build background knowledge students need as they read a selection of fiction, poetry, and nonfiction.

- Teachers can help students learn to navigate various types of texts and adjust how they read to match their purposes.

- Teachers can help students learn to monitor their reading to heighten awareness of whether they are comprehending as they read so they can revise their approach along the way.

Knowledge of Language and Comprehension

As we've said, teachers can help students increase their knowledge of language by providing oral language experiences where students are able to use language in a variety of ways on a daily basis. This leaves the challenge of meeting the demands of written language. Even though students may be able to communicate proficiently in informal/daily talking and listening, this may not translate into proficiency in written language. Specific challenges and opportunities for instruction include the following:

- In using their knowledge of language, students must be able to understand words they encounter in the text, which may include some that are rarely or never used in their oral language experiences.

- To read and comprehend, students must learn to know how to understand syntax – that is, the ways sentences are developed in language. In oral language situations, the communication takes place in ways (e.g., face-to-face, video links) where people can rely on gestures or ask questions as they construct meaning. In reading, readers must rely solely on the text in constructing meaning.

- Daily teacher-led read alouds and in-school independent reading let students begin to see how written language works, just as they did when acquiring oral language.

- Students who write daily also can learn more about how text is used to convey meaning.

- Reading experiences inform the students' writing, but students also grow as readers as they make choices akin to those that other writers make in developing a message.

Knowledge of the World and Comprehension

Before students read a selection, teachers can **build or activate background knowledge** needed to comprehend the text well. Capable readers draw upon their background knowledge without being aware that they are doing so, and thus teachers may assume all students will do likewise. But students can benefit from having teachers activate their background knowledge. Teachers may want to activate background knowledge when students are reading a text that is similar to one that was previously read. For example, if students are reading a variant of a folktale, the teacher may remind students of the version of the tale that students read previously. Or if students are reading another book in a series, the teacher may want to briefly discuss connections between the two texts.

Activating background knowledge by reviewing concepts read previously can help enhance students' understanding of the next section in a textbook. If students do not have the background knowledge they need for a given text, teachers should fill in the gaps. For example, if students are reading a work of historical fiction that takes place during the Great Depression, teachers may want to explain the national mood and setting at the time, as well as what led to the economic downturn.

Preparing students to read a text can include helping students build their vocabulary. Vocabulary development includes understanding concepts as well as how to pronounce unfamiliar words. Asking students to look up the definition of words in a glossary is not an effective way to learn unfamiliar concepts. Rather, teachers need to explain a concept and provide examples, as needed. The amount of instruction needed can vary depending upon the demands of the text, the students' lived experiences, and the difficulty of the concept itself. For example, for a story that takes place at a circus, the teacher may briefly explain terms, such as *trapeze* or *big top*. Or the teacher may need to briefly explain what *mill* means when students read *The Little Red Hen*. Some concepts and vocabulary require more discussion so that students can absorb the new information they are encountering in informational (or expository) texts or to understand the plot of a story.

Navigating Print: Knowledge of Text Structure, Purposes for Reading, Monitoring

Along with being able to identify and understand words, students need to be prepared for dealing with various types of **text structure**. For example, **narrative texts** encountered when reading stories make different demands on readers as compared to informational or expository texts. Even young children can remember and retell stories they hear because they have a schema, or cognitive framework, for stories, or for organizing and interpreting stories. Similarly, older students may be able to readily comprehend fiction, but may struggle when reading informational texts.

If students can read the words and pay attention to the content as they read a story, they can read and then retell the story with accuracy, especially as they gain practice with what a retelling is. **Arguments or argumentative essays** are where an author takes a position or presents a thesis. The author then provides evidence to support the position. In comprehending an argument, students need to be shown how to decide the strength of an argument by evaluating the evidence that supports it.

Expository or informational text is structured differently than fictional stories. This places different demands on readers. Whereas readers have a schema for stories, they need to invest time and effort to figure out the text structure of informational texts, which focus on presenting the essential facts of a topic.

Even capable readers can struggle when reading informational texts and their textbooks because they may assume they can read these tests like they read a story. Thus, more than one straight-through reading may be necessary. The text structures of informational texts can vary, depending upon how the information is organized in the discipline or is needed for relating the information. For example, when presenting a chapter on rocks, the authors may use headings that signal how the information is organized, such as *igneous*, *sedimentary*, and *metamorphic*. Within each section, each type of rock is described. If students use these headings to guide their reading, they have a way of organizing the individual facts or units of information. Students also can use headings to understand how concepts relate to one another, such as the role of *magma* when thinking about igneous rocks or what *sediments* are.

As students reach the middle grades, they increasingly are required to read longer informational texts, which make greater demands upon their memory. Teachers can help students understand and remember information by demonstrating how it's organized. Students struggle if they try to remember a list of facts presented in a section of a textbook chapter. However, they are more apt to remember important ideas when they can relate ideas to each other and to the overall topic.

Following are **major types of text structures** that writers use when producing informational texts:

- **Description**—The writer describes the topic by presenting a list of characteristics.

- **Sequence**—The writer presents a series of steps in a process or sequence of events.

- **Compare/contrast**—The writer compares or contrasts concepts and events by showing how they are alike or different.

- **Problem/solution**—The writer presents a problem followed by a solution.

- **Cause/effect**—The writer presents information that explains a relationship of one or more causes and their effect(s).

While different types of text structures can exist and be described individually, students should be shown how more than one type of text structure can exist within a text. For example, a chapter in a history textbook may use sequencing to present the chronology of the American Revolution while also demonstrating cause and effect and describing the events that led up to and stemmed from it.

Of prime importance is students' ability to apply knowledge of text structure as they read actual texts rather than just defining text structures per se. Familiarity with text structures is crucial to reading to learn successfully. As students apply knowledge of text structures as they read in various disciplines, they will gain in flexibility and expertise. Still, frustration can set in when students are asked to use text structure without having enough scaffolding from the teacher.

Self-Monitoring

Comprehension requires forming connections among ideas while reading. Proficient readers monitor their understanding of texts as they read. They know how to adjust their rate of reading according to the purpose for reading and the difficulty of the text. A proficient reader will read a section again or pause to think more about ideas that are difficult to understand.

One way teachers can encourage students to monitor their reading is through effective prompts that address students' miscues, asking whether what they said makes sense when a miscue (or oral reading error) shows that the student is not paying attention to meaning. Many students in the upper grades identify words without making many errors or miscues, but, even so, not all students are on grade level. Teachers also assist students in self-monitoring by discussing short segments of text rather than waiting until the end. These discussions encourage students to heed meaning and see that texts are not necessarily just read but require greater consideration of the ideas embedded in the text material.

Role of Quality Literature in Meeting Students' Needs

Students whose teachers point them to a variety of types of literature are more apt to make more extensive gains. Besides reading fiction and poetry aloud, teachers should do the same with nonfiction books. Nonfiction is actually a favorite type of literature for many students, as well as for adults. Nonfiction also particularly enhances subject-matter learning in science and social studies. Numerous books have been published for youth, but they vary widely in quality and in how well they meet students' needs.

Genres of Literature & Multicultural Literature

Literature can be divided into two major categories: **fiction** and **nonfiction**. **Poetry** is also a type of literature. In planning a read aloud and independent reading program, teachers should incorporate a wide range of literature that meets the interests of students. Teachers should work to help students understand the perspectives of others. Likewise, teachers should expose students to quality literature that features the students' own cultural background. Offering authentic reading experiences, through the many quality books that are available, allows students to discover a wide range of rewarding literature.

Nonfiction

Nonfiction is literature that shares factual information. It includes biography, autobiography, memoir, and informational books.

- Biography is a factual account of a person's life.
- Autobiography is actual account of the author's own life.
- Memoir is autobiographical but focuses upon selected parts of the person's life.
- Informational books provide factual information about a topic or event.

Fiction

Fiction can be realistic and believable, but the story conveyed is not entirely factual. Even though the author may be inspired by an actual event or person, all the characters, episodes, and/or settings are products of the imagination.

- Realistic fiction offers stories that could have happened in the real world.
- Historical fiction offers stories of history that could have happened and are based upon facts although the actual characters and episodes are fictional.
- Traditional literature includes folktales, fairy tales, legends, and myths, which are narratives that take place in an alternate reality.

- Fantasy and science fiction offer stories that are much like traditional literature in terms of exploring an alternate reality, but these stories flow from the author's pen rather than being oral tales that share a culture's beliefs, values, and morals.

- Science fiction relies upon scientific concepts or technologies.

Poetry

Poetry does not readily fit into a category under either fiction or nonfiction. Poetry is often recognized by its form or the way its words are arranged on a page. Poetry often, but not always, rhymes but is typically characterized by rhythm. Carefully chosen and arranged words evoke ideas and emotions to convey a message that is often presented through metaphor.

Literary Elements

Students need to know about literary elements to understand how literature works. Knowing literary elements can provide understandings that can guide students in their writing stories, poetry, and nonfiction. Still, to be most successful in analyzing literature, students need to see that their thoughts about literature are legitimate. Teachers can support students' gains by providing instruction that recognizes the role of personal responses in reading. Students need to first read and share their personal responses to a work before they analyze it. Through their responses, students read and reflect upon a work of literature by making their own personal connections. As they formulate their thoughts in speaking, they consider what they like or did not like in regard to what happened, and derive the big ideas that emerge from the work—which in turn allows them to make their connections.

Through discussions/grand conversations, students can hear the views of others, including the teacher. These exchanges expand student experiences with a literary work. Competent readers' responses are consistent with what the text presents, so students also should be encouraged, as they form a response, to look more closely at the text to see whether they have overlooked anything.

The text lookback strategy teaches students that reinspecting a text allows for greater focus on literary elements such as the following:

- **Plot** is what happens in the story, and the plot should proceed in ways that are logical, even in imaginative works. Even in historical fiction, what takes place needs to be accurate, that is, something that *could have taken place.*

- **Setting** is the time and place of a story. Setting is especially important in historical fiction to determine what can take place based on realistic touchstones. This goes to credibility and believability. Even a fantasy universe should be consistent and cohere to support detailed, vivid description.

- **Theme** relates to messages, big ideas, or larger meanings that emerge from a story.

- **Characterization** is how the authors reveal characters. Readers learn about characters through what a character says, does, and/or thinks. Readers also become familiar with a character through what other characters say about him or her. Characters can grow and change, but their existence and what they do should be plausible even when the work is not based upon real events.

- **Style** is the way a writer tells a story. The style of the author determines the types of words used, the way words are arranged, and the tone of the narrative. The style emerges from the unique **voice** of the author.

- **Point of View** is who is telling the story—the narrator—and the way the narrator reveals the story. The third person omniscient point of view lets readers know what each character is thinking, saying, and doing, and the author can speak directly to the readers, just as a storyteller would. Limited third person point of view involves the narrator knowing only what one character feels, thinks, says, and understands; in other words, the story is told from that character's viewpoint. Other characters are revealed through what they say and do. First person narrative is when a character tells the story.

Guided Reading Groups and Small-Group Instruction

Guided reading is small-group instruction, which has the teacher work with students reading at approximately the same reading level. Although students can profit from heterogeneous groups for independent work, guided reading groups work best with homogeneous grouping where students are reading a text at the instructional level for all.

Students can be overwhelmed and stymied from making gains when reading texts that are not too hard because too many words are unknown. The texts for guided reading are ones the student can read with some support from the teacher, making student gains possible. With small-group instruction, the teacher can also provide more individualized attention.

Guided reading/small-group reading can take place during language arts blocks, but it also can take place during science and social studies when students learn from textbooks that are more difficult to read. If students cannot read the textbook, teachers can use shared reading, where students follow along as the teacher reads. Over time, students make gains in their sight vocabulary so that they can read a text.

The three parts of a guided reading lesson work together to help the students learn how to be more proficient readers: before reading, during reading, and after reading. A story the students read with a teacher during one week could be one the students are able to subsequently read independently. Through support in learning how to read textbooks or other types of informational texts, students will be better equipped to read as they advance in their schooling.

Before Reading

Before reading, the teacher builds or activates background knowledge helpful for understanding the text. The teacher also helps students be prepared for reading sections of the text that they are not familiar with, such as unknown words and concepts.

These unknown components can be words that the students cannot decode, or words and concepts that the students do not understand. To close these gaps, the teacher can help students preview the text to examine speech bubbles, charts, bold print, and headings by pointing out how these features of the text play a role in reading the text successfully.

During Reading

During reading, the students read the story or designated segment silently (or in a soft voice if they are young children/beginning readers). Some students might finish reading before others have, so they read the selection again, which helps with fluency. The teacher listens to individual students read aloud to assess each student's ability to recognize words and to provide prompts to help figure out unknown words. The teacher typically cannot listen to all read in one day, but can listen to some students read one day and the rest the next day.

During reading is a critical time because the teacher can determine what needs to be addressed during word study, such as which words students do not know, whether students read fluently, and whether students know how to use multiple cues for word analysis. Lower-ability readers often will exhibit an overreliance on context clues such as illustrations or what makes sense because they lack strong word identification abilities. Teachers create brief anecdotal notes so they can address the needs of students during word-study instruction.

Teachers also can teach during reading as they respond to a student's miscues or oral reading errors. Through prompts, teachers can help students learn to use a variety of sources of information or cueing systems: to look at the text (visual cues), to think about what sounds right (language structure cues), and to decide what makes sense (meaning cues).

During reading is prime time to devote additional time to develop comprehension. When students are not dealing with complex text as they read, they can do so without support from the teacher. However, for students having difficulty with comprehension of stories, during reading can be a time to guide the students by reading short segments with them and helping them visualize what they have read. Informational texts present cognitive demands that stories do not, so even capable readers can profit from the teacher showing them strategies for comprehension. The amount of support necessary from the teacher depends upon the students' ability, the purpose for reading, and how complex the informational text is for students. If students are reading expository texts as part of subject-matter learning, all can profit from the teacher showing a strategy for not only comprehending but also learning information. Students may be able to understand what they read as they encounter ideas, but that does not ensure they are able to connect and remember relationships among ideas.

After Reading

After reading, the teacher and students discuss the story. Teachers can begin by asking students to recall what took place in the story while also helping them remember and compose their thoughts. After retelling, students can discuss the story to engage in higher levels of comprehension by making inferences, forming connections between and among texts (text-to-text connections) or connections to their lives (text-to-self connections). In addition, students can discuss themes or lessons that emerge from the text. Through authentic discussions, students can learn through the contributions or modeling of the teacher how important ideas can be raised without a question-answer recitation. Moreover, students can learn from each other.

Reading informational texts requires reading short segments and then discussing ideas covered in the text to help students understand and remember. Working with students can take place during reading or afterward as they apply a strategy to read a text more carefully and process the information. Students can discuss ideas, and how to take notes with headings to remember details about a topic. The after-reading stage also is devoted to word study, during which the teacher can teach students how to spell a few words and address meanings if that is needed to provide vocabulary instruction. Teachers also can share reading strategies that students may not yet know well, such as how to use context, how to read with expression, or how to read charts.

Providing Scaffolding for Students' Silent Reading

Round-robin reading takes place when students take turns reading a segment of a passage aloud. Even though round-robin reading is prevalent, reading experts agree that it is not effective and can actually hamper students' progress in word identification. Students read at different rates, and a student who reads at a slower rate will have trouble following the reading of the student who reads faster. Faster readers are asked to slow down to follow along with the slower readers, which works against fluency. Letting students read silently or in a soft voice avoids embarrassing less capable students, who, if put on the spot, can come to dread reading. Teachers should be on the lookout for students who may not actually read much because they rely on following along when others read and thus read only when it is their turn. Many teachers use the round-robin approach because they are familiar with it. They justify using it because they are not sure whether students will, or can, read the text on their own.

What's a good alternative to round-robin reading? Show students how to read softly or silently with guided reading/small-group instruction. Teach students in small groups while the rest of the class engages in independent reading activities. If students cannot identify the words in a text, use shared reading, with the teacher leading and students following along. If students can read individual words but are unable to stay engaged, ask them to read and then discuss short segments; this helps students monitor their reading while also building stamina.

Formal Comprehension Assessments

Schools use formal assessments to obtain data on students' progress in literacy. As students reach the middle grades, they are expected to read longer, more complex texts, which requires connecting the ideas of longer texts. Formal assessment, such as the following, helps readers stay on track and document progress in reading.

- **Criterion-Referenced Tests** are developed to assess a specific set of skills or concepts or criteria at a designated level of difficulty. These exams can be used to determine how much a student knows before and after instruction. Each skill or concept is measured to obtain an adequate sample of students' knowledge. This type of test is standards-based, and presents individual performance using percentages.

- **Norm-Referenced Tests** are standardized tests that compare a student's test performance with a sample of similar students (e.g., of the same grade level) who took the test at the same time of the school year. The administration and scoring of the test is standardized by using the same procedures for giving the exam and scoring it. Norms are obtained from the standardization sample. The scores provide information about how the student's achievement compares to other students at national levels. A percentile score can range from 1–99. A score at the 60th percentile means that 60% of the norm group performed at the same level or below the student's score. This would mean that 59% of the norm group scored below the student's score.

Strategies and Instruction for Comprehension Development

Retelling

After reading a story or segment of a story, students retell what they have read. **Retelling** can be used to assess students' understanding, but it also can help students learn to monitor their reading. Retelling helps students recall what they just read as they tell what happened in their own words.

Before students are asked to retell, the teacher should model and join in students' retellings when students leave out important information. A basic retelling would include the setting, characters, and the plot. In retelling what takes place, students should include the major events of the story as well as the problem and its resolution. Retelling can help ensure students have understood the plot. As students' retellings become more advanced, they include inferences gleaned from the plot, as well as evaluations.

Grand Conversations

A critical way to help develop students' comprehension is to provide time for them to share their personal responses as part of reading aloud, and guided and independent reading. Rather than assessing comprehension by asking questions, the teacher contributes by sharing thoughts about what took place and big ideas that emerge from the literature. Rather than dominating the conversations, the teacher strives to be a participant, facilitating and scaffolding the student-led discussion. The teacher shares ideas to model how a competent reader thinks about literature by sharing thoughts about the plot or big ideas that emerge from the literature. Rather than asking a question to draw attention to something important, the teacher raises the idea as a contributor, setting the stage for a shared exchange with the students.

Visualizing

If students visualize or create images of what they read, they are engaged. Visualizing is especially helpful for comprehension when reading fiction. When students can identify the words well when reading a story, but they cannot retell what they have read, they may profit from visualizing as they read. The teacher can model visualizing to show students. The teacher reads a segment of text aloud and the students follow along. The teacher stops at a certain point and thinks aloud to share the mental picture that can include the characters, the setting, and the action. As the teacher shares, students are invited to do the same, and the teacher can point out that different people may hold varying but equally accurate pictures in their minds even though they don't visualize exactly the same thing.

Story Maps

Story maps can be used to help students learn elements of fiction. Through a visual representation, students discuss setting, characters, plot, problem resolution, and theme(s). As part of implementing story maps, teachers should model and work with students to complete the map. After the initial reading and discussion of a story, teachers can use story maps to help students learn about elements of fiction. Teachers should keep in mind that story maps are a means to help students understand how literature works; they should avoid placing undue emphasis on the mechanics of how to create a story map. When students are shown how literature works, they become more proficient readers and writers.

Previewing and Text Features

Previewing can help students anticipate what they are going to read. When students read expository text, they may overlook features of text that are important for comprehending and learning. Proficient reading necessitates recognizing these features and using them as tools to understand the text as a whole.

Features include illustrations, images, diagrams, labels, captions, graphs, charts, timetable, bold and italic text, headings and subheadings, glossary, table of contents, and index. Students will learn best about the roles of text features when they are shown how to use a text feature that is relevant to the text they are reading.

Students have a schema for stories or the narrative structure of fiction. Topics in the expository text of social studies, science, and other subjects have their own structure, which is largely determined by how a subject is inherently organized. The author of an informational or expository text uses the organization in presenting ideas and in connecting ideas. Successful reading and learning requires understanding the major ideas, important supporting details, and how these ideas relate to one another to create a larger understanding of the broader topic.

Students cannot be expected to readily remember new information, but teachers can help them learn how to read and study when reading informational or expository texts. Students need to be shown that proficient readers should be adept at changing their approach when reading to learn. Through modeling and guidance, teachers can help students understand the major ideas (and associated headings), supporting details and how these major ideas relate to each other in presenting information about a topic. Authors may not always use headings, so students should be equipped to infer what the major ideas are by reading the section.

In teaching strategies to improve understanding and retention, it is critical that students be given sufficient modeling on how to use a given strategy. Guided practice also is essential. The idea is to gradually release responsibility by following this sequence:

1. The teacher demonstrates while the students watch.

2. The teacher and students do the task together.

3. The students work together while the teacher provides monitoring to make sure they know what to do.

4. The students are able to work on their own.

Students will vary in regard to when they are able to apply a strategy on their own. However, guided practice is instruction, and it is valuable because students can learn in their current subjects and be primed for future schooling. Teachers who fail to provide enough modeling and guidance may find that their students do not gain much from strategy instruction.

Another way to help students learn is to show them how to read a few short chunks at a time. Students can be asked to read shorter segments before discussing. The length of an appropriate chunk depends upon the difficulty of the materials and the student's abilities.

Levels of Thinking

Critical-thinking skills include analysis, synthesis, and evaluation. Benjamin Bloom (1956) created a taxonomy for categorizing levels of thinking. The taxonomy presents a structure to categorize the levels of thinking required to ask and answer questions. These questions have been used to guide children from the **recalling of information (knowledge)** and **understanding information (comprehension)** to using such **higher-order thinking skills as analysis, synthesis, and evaluation.**

Recalling and understanding are important parts of reading comprehension, but teachers must help children move from literal comprehension and explicit ideas to figurative comprehension and implicit ideas. Teachers must guide children to analyze the ideas presented in text and then make inferences (analysis), to assess their inferences (evaluation), to draw conclusions about the ideas (synthesis), and perhaps to apply the ideas to new situations (application). Children who can go beyond the literal and explicit information in text develop a deeper understand of the content areas and manipulate the content at higher levels of thinking.

Question-Answer Relationships (QAR)

QAR is a strategy used after reading to help students deal with the variable nature of questions presented about a passage. Often, students assume that they need to search the passage to find an answer, unaware that questions may ask them to use their background/prior knowledge to connect information in the text. In this strategy, the types of questions are categorized on the basis of the question–answer relationship:

"Right There" Questions—Answers to these questions are found "right there" in the text. These are literal questions that often have the same words as the text.

"Think and Search" Questions—Answers to these questions can be found in the text, too. However, it requires searching various parts of the text to put the required information together.

"Author and You" Questions—These questions require the student to connect their prior/ background knowledge with information in the text.

"On Your Own" Questions—These questions require students to use just their prior/background knowledge to answer the questions. The answers are found by drawing only on the reader's experiences. Such questions are inspired by, but not in, the text.

Directed Reading Thinking Activity (DRTA)

DRTA (Stauffer, 1969) is a comprehension strategy that encourages students to activate their prior knowledge, make predictions, and monitor their understanding. Teachers need to provide modeling and other support as students engage so that the experiences in applying the strategy are effective. The procedures entailed in DRTA are as follows:

- **Direct**—The teacher calls attention to the title, chapter heading(s), illustrations, and captions, and any other related text features. Teachers ask a general question based on the title and heading of material to be read during the lesson (e.g., "Based on the title, what do you think we will learn?" "Look at this heading. What do you think we will learn?"). As with any strategy, teachers need to think aloud when introducing the strategy. Teachers also need to be prepared to help by providing prompts or adding to what students say to provide differentiated instruction for students who are English learners, less capable readers, or have a learning disability.

- **Read**—In advance, the teacher decides what is a good stopping point for students as they read, keeping in mind that students often need to read smaller chunks rather than an entire section. The amount to be read is based upon the difficulty of the material and the reading ability of the students. After students read, the teacher asks students what they found out and how this relates to their predictions. Then the students continue in this way until they have read the section of the passage or textbook.

- **Think**—When students have finished reading a section, the teacher guides the students in thinking about their predictions and what they have read. Students can think about what they have found out, and whether they need to modify their predictions. Teachers may write down students' predictions— and what they have learned—to provide a record for their thinking which they can later review with respect to the passage or chapter at hand. This modeling by the teacher provides instruction on note-taking, which focuses not only on how to read but also how to study to learn and retain information.

Reciprocal Teaching

Reciprocal teaching (Palinscar and Brown, 1984) is instruction that encourages students to be active readers by monitoring their reading. Reciprocal teaching entails four strategies to attack text:

Summarizing—Students read a chunk of the information in a section of the text. As a summarizer, students tell what the key ideas are so far.

Question Generating—After the summarizer shares, the questioner asks questions about any unclear parts and/or asks about how ideas connect to other ideas or concepts presented so far.

Clarifying—The clarifier answers the questions presented by the questioner.

Predicting—The predictor anticipates what the author will present next in the text.

To implement reciprocal teaching, teachers model and ensure students have had ample practice to learn each strategy of reciprocal teaching. Once teachers are sure students know what to do, the teacher places them in groups of four, and assigns each student a role written on an index card.

- Students read up to the stopping point determined by the teacher so the students read appropriate, small chunks of the section.

- Students assume their roles in leading the dialogue and teaching each other.

- Students change roles, passing the card to the right, and repeat the process.

- The teacher guides and monitors to ensure students are successful. The teacher's participation can decrease as students become more proficient.

The time teachers devote to making sure students can apply reciprocal teaching strategies is worthwhile because (1) students are learning the content through the teacher's guidance, and (2) the payoff is large as students can work successfully on their own once the teachers equip the students to use the strategies on their own.

Think-Pair-Share (TPS)

Think-Pair-Share (TPS) is a strategy that encourages students to think on their own in response to a question the teacher provides and then share their thoughts with another student. TPS provides scaffolding for students as they share with a classmate, helping students learn concepts and develop oral language abilities. The procedures are the following:

- The teacher determines both when to ask a question as well as the question to ask. The question can be general, such as, "What did you learn from what you just read?" or "What did the author tell us?"

- The teacher provides demonstrations for using each part of TPS by working with a small or whole group to let students learn what to do. The teacher models and then uses a gradual release of responsibility to let students participate with the teacher's guidance and make sure students know what to do before students apply TPS:

Think—After reading or viewing, students individually think about the question the teacher has presented.

Pair—Students have a partner or small group to share what they have been thinking.

Share—Students share what they have been thinking. They then also can share with a whole group, which the teacher can then use as the basis of a whole-group discussion.

Concept Maps

A concept map is a visual display that serves as an organizer that enhances students' understanding and retention. Through the visual organizer, students are able to tangibly see the main ideas and how concepts relate to each other. The organizer, for example, may present a concept with lines connecting to provide elaboration and show connections. The visual organizer could be a web, timeline, or Venn diagram.

Concept maps also can be used to show a process along with terms associated with the process, such as photosynthesis. The visual organizer includes photos or illustrations, such as a plant with the parts of the plant explained. Concept mapping also can be used as semantic maps for vocabulary development and for representing concepts. At the center of a web, the word is placed.

Each concept will have at least three associations that can be important for students to know: associations of class, property, and example. *Class* is the type of things the concept is part of, such as *hurricanes* being in the class of "types of storms." *Property* refers to attributes or properties of the concept, such as defining characteristics.

Concept and semantic maps can be used before, during, and after reading or unit of study:

- **Before**—Students can tell what they know or what comes to mind when they think of the topic/concept/word. The teacher adds students' thoughts to the map. Activating students' prior knowledge can help them form a basis for relating new information.

- **During**—As students read, they can discuss what they are learning and add that to the map.

- **After**—Once developed, the map can be reviewed after various points in the unit of study to assist with review and recall.

SQ4R

SQ4R is a comprehension and study strategy that has been used for years to help students navigate expository text. This method adds one step to the original strategy, SQ3R, by including a step for students to create notes. The steps of the strategy are as follows:

- **Survey**—To survey, the students skim the chapter title, headings, illustrations, and bold text to get an overall idea of the topic and how the information is being framed by the author.

- **Question**—When starting to read a section, students turn a heading into the question(s) they anticipate will be answered later on in the text.

- **Read**—Students read to gain answers, and a stopping point can be determined based on the material's difficulty level.

- **Recite**—After reading a section, students should discuss what they have found out in their own words.

- **Record**—Once students confirm their understanding of a section of the material and can paraphrase it, they record that understanding by making notes. Teachers can support students by modeling how to proceed from talking about what they have just read (via the "recite" step) to summarizing the ideas in their notes.

- **Review**—The review can take place at the end of a section, and it also can take place after reading all of the sections and by reviewing the notes the students have developed.

K-W-L

K-W-L (Ogle, 1986) is a strategy where students discuss and complete three columns of a chart as part of reading text (an example of which follows): What I Know, What I Want to Learn, and What I Learned.

K-W-L Chart		
Topic: _____		
What I Know	What I Want to Learn	What I Learned

The K-W-L strategy helps students think about their prior knowledge, set purposes for reading, and monitor their comprehension.

Before reading, students discuss what they know about the topic and the teacher or students list those ideas, which activates their background knowledge. Next, students discuss and list specific questions they think will be answered in the text, which helps them be purposeful and think about what they are reading.

After reading the text or text segment, the students discuss and write about what they learned in the column for that. Any answers to questions can be written next to the question. Putting what they've learned into their own words makes students better able to process information. Doing so makes students better able to see for themselves which ideas they pick up from the reading and which ideas merit further attention. This strategy is effective when teachers model for students and guide the development of the K-W-L chart.

Questioning the Author

By questioning the author, students read a segment of the text and then collaborate with the teacher to understand the text as well as learn how to deal with comprehension problems as they read. Setting active reading in motion gives students the perspective that the text is created by someone. Questioning the author takes place as students read a text, not after.

When planning, the teacher first decides on what are the major understandings students should construct as they read the text as well as what could create difficulty. Next, the teacher decides on the best way to segment the texts, that is, where to insert stopping points. In addition, the teacher develops questions or queries that help students promote understanding.

The questions are designed to be *queries* rather than comprehension questions. Queries are designed to foster discussion of the information and to encourage students to use their own words as they construct meaning from the text.

Initial queries about the text help students discuss what the text is saying and prepares them for the next segment as they construct meaning: What is the author saying here? Am I understanding the author?

Follow-up prompts can help students look at what a text means, not just what is said: How does this connect with what the author said before? Does the author explain this sufficiently so that it makes sense?

The teacher and students collaborate. The teacher strives to help students develop and share their observations with each other, fostering an effective discussion.

COMPETENCY 005: VOCABULARY DEVELOPMENT

The teacher knows the importance of vocabulary development and applies that knowledge to teach reading, listening, speaking, and writing.

What's in a Word?

Being a proficient reader depends on the ability to immediately recognize and understand individual words. Once this milestone is achieved, readers are able to devote attention to creating meaning, which underpins comprehension. Students also rely upon understanding the meanings of words to be successful in instructional experiences that rely upon listening and speaking.

Before children enter school, they are able to improve their speaking and listening vocabularies through meaningful interactions with others. Even without being taught directly, children gradually acquire and refine their knowledge of words. Schooling provides opportunities for students to expand their speaking and listening vocabularies while also expanding their reading and writing vocabularies.

Although students continue to make gains in vocabulary development through less formal interactions with others instruction at school plays a decisive role in helping students make the gains they need to succeed as fully functional adults and citizens. Acquiring vocabulary entails being able to (1) understand a word when it is used, (2) define a word in one's own words, (3) decode and spell a word, and (4) know multiple meanings and how they apply.

Effective Vocabulary Development

Children's vocabulary and concept development are closely intertwined. And the former drives improvement of the latter. The number of words that children hear during interactions with adults (e.g., conversations, book reading, play) is predictive of vocabulary growth. With a more developed vocabulary comes the ability to grasp and describe more sophisticated, complex concepts such as time, space, and size and categories of things. Though children should be encouraged to learn how to use a dictionary, gains in vocabulary development do not take place when students look up words and memorize definitions. Knowing how to use a word requires more in-depth understanding.

The child needs to be able to connect concepts with words, relating new concepts to existing labels or words they know, such as the *bark* of a dog versus the *bark* of a tree. In school, children should learn both a concept and a label. How this is taught depends. A brief example may be sufficient when students understand a concept and are learning a new word for it. On the other hand, English learners will need more experiences if they know a concept but are learning a word for it in a language other than their native tongue. Especially challenging can be grasping a concept while also learning new words.

Many of the concepts students encounter in content areas (such as science and social studies) are abstract, so instruction must be devoted to building an understanding of the concept. In the case of the term *photosynthesis*, for example, it is effective to teach the word alongside the process it represents for how plants convert sunlight into energy. At the same time, instruction must help students acquire the vocabulary that is needed to discuss and learn the concept. When students understand a concept at a deeper level, they understand how concepts relate to other related concepts. Students gain in conceptual development by encountering a concept firsthand, viewing media, and in written language. Teachers play a critical role in providing the learning experiences that foster students' vocabulary development.

Instructional Approaches for Vocabulary Development

Reading Aloud and Independent Reading

Students encounter words in reading materials that are not likely to be a part of their oral language experiences. Students understand and learn new words by using **contextual analysis**, which involves teasing out meaning by evaluating surrounding words and illustrations. Thus, even when teachers are not teaching vocabulary directly, students will still make substantial gains through their engagement with reading. Words that become a part of their reading vocabularies then migrate to their speaking, listening, and writing vocabularies. The more teachers make sure students encounter a variety of types of literature, the more apt students will be to make more extensive gains. Along with reading fiction and poetry aloud, teachers need to do the same with nonfiction to show children how to find and evaluate information.

Systematic Vocabulary Instruction

Vocabulary development also needs to include systematic instruction that gives students strategies for gaining vocabulary. Ways to help students gain in vocabulary development include the following:

1. Describe the concept.

2. Give examples and analogies.

3. Discuss how the concept fits in a category.

4. Use actions or gestures to show verbs. Provide illustrations, charts, graphs, and media to clarify concepts.

5. Provide additional reading aloud experiences on the topic.

6. Make a deliberate attempt to use new words on subsequent days (following instruction).

Teachers should provide instruction before, during, and after reading. Deciding when to teach or review vocabulary should take account of the tasks students need to engage in and their overall oral and written language development.

Vocabulary development can take place **before reading** to help students encounter new concepts and words so that they can comprehend the text. Teachers need to consider students' background knowledge and the ways they can relate new concepts to previous learning or background knowledge. Rather than simply asking students to look up a word in the dictionary or the book's glossary, teachers should provide examples, gestures, features, pictures, or visual diagrams to clarify new words and concepts. Teachers also need to show students how to use illustrations or diagrams available in the text to help understand vocabulary and associated concepts.

Students can use context clues or surrounding words and illustrations to understand unknown words. When teachers interact with students **during reading**, they help students learn to use the context of the sentence, text, or surrounding illustrations to figure out what a word means. This instruction should aim to have students read independently, for the instances when they will not have someone immediately at their side to deal with unfamiliar words.

Vocabulary instruction that takes place **after reading** can help students review concepts. Instruction afterward also can help students understand how concepts relate to each other. Instruction can include semantic maps or diagrams as well as talking about concepts. Writing experiences also can be helpful, but students are not likely to learn by simply copying definitions.

Morphemic Analysis

Systematic instruction includes using word structure to understand and remember new words. Morphemes are the smallest units of meaning in language; they can be free morphemes, that is, words that have meaning (e.g., *happy*). Morphemes can be bound morphemes, or word parts that cannot stand alone with meaning but rather change or expand the meaning of words when they are added. Bound morphemes include prefixes (e.g., *un-*) and suffixes (e.g., *-ment*). Helping students see connections between spelling and meaning can be beneficial. Words can be related in meaning even when their sounds change, such as the sound shift between *nation* and *national*. Learning Latin and Greek roots and derivations also helps students understand and remember new words. Look, for example, at the common Latin root of *cordial*, *accord*, and *discord*.

Using the Dictionary

It's one thing to tell students to use the dictionary, and quite another to ensure they know *how*. Students need to be shown how to locate the word, which may not be apparent if, for instance, it has an inflectional ending (e.g., *repairs*, *repairing*). So they may need instruction on deciphering the base word. In addition, care must be taken to find the definition that fits the sentence they are reading, taking into account the entire context.

Word Tiers

Teachers need to decide which words to teach of the many words students will encounter as they read. Unfamiliar words and concepts will require more deliberate instruction. Beck, McKeown, and Kucan (2008) have described three levels, or tiers, of words that indicate the difficulty students can have in understanding words, and these are described next.

Tier 1 Words

The most basic words, such as *puppy* or *house*, usually will not require instruction for native speakers. These are Tier 1 words. Students are likely to encounter and use these words in their daily oral language experiences, so explicit instruction is not typically needed. Teachers, however, should not assume that English learners know these words because they may not have encountered them. However, English learners *will* typically know the concepts (e.g., *family*, *butterfly*) in their native language, making such words easier to teach. Tier 1 instruction includes some expressions or idioms (e.g., "give it a shot" or "piece of cake") that may be especially confusing for ELs.

Tier 2 Words

Tier 2 words are more apt to require instruction because students are not likely to encounter these words (such as *inhibit*, *adjacent*, and *guarantee*) in their daily talking and listening situations. Tier 2 words are those that students are most likely to encounter in print. Tier 2 words also can include words that are commonly confused, such as the homophones *fowl* and *foul*. Tier 2 words are used across various disciplines, and may appear in technical and literary texts.

Tier 3 Words

Tier 3 words (such as *condensation*, *diameter*, *senator*) are associated with a specific field or content area. These words are a critical part of understanding and learning concepts presented in texts. Instruction is often needed for students to read and understand the text. Often, instruction is needed after students read so that students can remember or learn concepts and how the concepts are connected. Teachers should be prepared to offer more in-depth instruction typically needed to introduce new concepts. Research has shown that merely supplying definitions does not help students understand and learn new concepts. Examples or illustrations can be used to bolster instruction. Students can then be asked to explain the concept in their own words or create a picture or symbolic representation. To help students retain the new vocabulary, they can keep vocabulary notebooks, adding new terms as they arise. All this can be fun. In fact, students can play games that use the vocabulary or talk with a partner about the vocabulary they have accumulated in their notebooks.

Teaching Vocabulary for Understanding and Learning in Subject Areas

Teaching all the new words in a reading selection often is not necessary, and it may not even be effective. Teachers need to set a hierarchy, deciding which words are critical to understand the selection. Teachers also decide whether students can gain enough understanding by the way the word is used in the selection; whether this is so will vary among students depending upon their stage of language development. For example, a word that is decoded instantaneously by a native speaker may not be amenable to being understood—even with context clues—by an English learner. Teachers also need to decide how much instruction is needed without disrupting the enjoyment and process of the reading experience. Often, vocabulary in informational materials requires direct instruction because the concepts are new to students.

COMPETENCY 006: READING, INQUIRY, AND RESEARCH

The teacher understands the importance of inquiry and research skills to students' academic success and provides instruction that promotes students' acquisition and effective use of these skills in the content areas.

Transition from "Learning to Read" to "Reading to Learn"

Children from Pre-K to second grade must learn to decode and make sense of written language. Traditionally, illustrated short stories with a specific structure and predictable story line are used to guide the child in "learning to read." However, in the upper elementary grades, students read longer texts of fiction and also face larger demands as they read informational texts or engage in what's known as "reading to learn."

In reading to learn, students encounter unfamiliar vocabulary and unfamiliar concepts. Additionally, students must not only comprehend a text but also know how to remember or learn content. Students need to be reading and hearing informational texts from the outset of their schooling to help them make the transition to reading to learn. At the same time, teachers can help students navigate expository and informational texts.

Structure of Text

Students must examine the structure of the text to comprehend it. Students have a schema for stories, so they can remember the plot and retell stories if the text is not too difficult for them to read and if they realize that they should pay attention to meaning and not just identify words.

To work toward this goal, teachers should guide students through a picture, table, and graphic walk-through of the text while pointing out useful text features to the students. However, when reading expository/informational texts, students must figure out how important ideas are organized so they can retain the details and discern how those details relate to create a larger picture or improve the reader's understanding. Many informational texts have titles and headings which help in showing how ideas are organized. Some texts do not have headings, but students can be shown how to discern the focus of the section as they discuss a section they have read. Figuring out the structure of a text helps students to read more efficiently. Once they understand textual structure, children can anticipate what information a selection will reveal.

Understanding the pattern of the text helps students organize ideas and recognize the author's textual organization or organizational patterns. However, students should not be asked to determine the text structure as the goal of teaching. Rather, discerning the text structure should be part of reading and learning content. A chapter in a textbook or any text may use more than one type of text structure, and being able to identify the text structure will not help students learn the ideas. However, by guiding students in reading informational text and using appropriate strategies, they can discern the text structure as they notice how individual important details relate to a sub-topic and overall topic. Following are common organizational patterns used in expository text:

- Chronological order relates events in a temporal sequence from beginning to the end

- Cause-and-effect relationships between events, with the causes identified or implied

- Problem description, followed by solutions

- Comparisons and/or contrasts to describe ideas

- Sequential materials, presented as directions to be followed in a prescribed order

Reciprocal Teaching

Reciprocal teaching is a strategy that also pertains to Competency 004 (Reading Comprehension and Applications). The strategy is discussed under that competency.

SQ4R

SQ4R (Survey, Question, Read, Recite, Record, and Review) is a strategy that also pertains to Competency 004 (Reading Comprehension and Applications). The strategy is discussed under that competency.

K-W-L

K-W-L (Know, Want to Learn, Learned) is a strategy that also pertains to Competency 004 (Reading Comprehension and Applications). The strategy is discussed under that competency.

Directed Reading Thinking Activity (DRTA)

DRTA (Directed Reading Thinking Activity) is a strategy that also pertains to Competency 004 (Reading Comprehension and Applications). The strategy is discussed under that competency.

Graphic Organizers, Concept Maps, and Semantic Maps

Graphic organizers are a visual way to help students put ideas in categories as a way of understanding the ideas. We can use them to refer to ideas. The ability to organize information and ideas is fundamental to effective thinking and learning. Choosing the right type of graphic organizer depends on what is being taught and how best to show the relationships between and among concepts. For example, a chart with headings across might work best to list the branches of the federal or state government, with key information added as students learn. Or teachers might want to use a flow chart to show a process or sequence. Illustrations can work best in some instances, such as learning the functions of the parts of a plant or what takes place in photosynthesis. A Venn diagram can be used when comparing and contrasting to see how two topics are alike or overlap in some ways and yet different in other ways.

A concept map is a visual display that serves as an organizer that enhances students' understanding and retention. Using a visual organizer, students are able to see the main ideas and how concepts relate. The organizer, for example, may present a concept with lines to provide elaboration and show connections.

Concept maps can be used to help students develop an in-depth understanding of a concept. Each concept will have at least three associations revolving around class, property, and example. *Class* is the what the concept is part of, such as trains being in the class of transportation. *Property* refers to attributes or traits of the concept, such as defining characteristics.

Concept and semantic maps can be used before, during, and after reading a unit of study:

- **Before**—Students can tell what they know or what comes to mind when they think of the topic/concept/word. The teacher adds students' thoughts to the map. Activating students' prior knowledge can help them have a basis for relating new information.

- **During**—As students read, they can discuss what they are learning to add to the map.

- **After**—The map developed can be reviewed after various points in the unit of study to review and remember.

Note-Taking

Note-taking is a skill that is rarely taught explicitly in school. Teachers may assume incorrectly that taking notes is a skill that students will learn naturally. Learning this skill can have multiple cognitive advantages for students. Taking notes help students identify and summarize relevant information. In the process of note-taking, students receive and process information, and write it in their own words. Moreover, taking legible and relevant notes will guide students to develop a better understanding of the content. Additionally, students use note-taking when gathering information as part of writing reports and developing arguments.

A key challenge in note-taking is to decide what is most relevant. One way to help students is to take notes together to model the process and provide support as students gain proficiency. If note-taking is a regular part of reading in content areas, students will develop the expertise. One way to provide note-taking is when reading expository texts. For example, as students are reading about types of rocks, the teacher can ask students to tell what they just learned. As we discussed earlier in Chapter 3, the teacher can create headings, such as SEDIMENTARY ROCKS, and then write what the students say. In this way, students are learning together how to read and put what was said in your own words without copying word for word. By not having to actually write the notes, the students focus on the process of reading and extracting. The notes the teacher records can be typed and used for reviewing each day and for studying for a test. On their own, many students would not take notes effectively, but when the teacher models and guides the development of the notes, students gain in expertise over time. Additionally, the note-taking actually enhances learning subject matter.

Similarly, the teacher can help students master note-taking as they conduct research for class reports. Rather than telling students what to do, the teacher and students can take notes together as they read from a book, view a video, or observe something pertinent (e.g., plant growth) in the course of gathering information. The notes gathered can be placed on note cards or sticky notes under headings created to organize the information.

Once students have worked with the teacher, they can split into small groups to gather information on a topic, where students can support each other towards learning how to take notes on their own.

Think-Aloud

Think-alouds let the teacher and students problem-solve together. The teacher poses a question. Then, the teacher, group of students, or entire class responds. This strategy can increase reading comprehension in the content areas. In modeling a think-aloud, the following steps are used (Wilhelm, 2001).

1. The teacher explains *what* the strategy is and describes the strategy and its purpose.

2. The teacher explains *why* the strategy is important for improving reading comprehension.

3. The teacher explains *when* to use the strategy.

4. The teacher models *how* to use the strategy with an **authentic text**.

5. The teacher guides student practice using authentic text.

6. The teacher gradually releases responsibility for doing the think-aloud to students.

7. Students practice the strategy in pairs or independently.

8. The teacher asks that students do a think-aloud in which they explain and articulate their thinking for using the strategy.

Skimming and Scanning

Students with strong comprehension skills and decoding ability are ready to become more efficient readers by practicing the techniques of **scanning** and **skimming** to extract content information. To help students with scanning, the teacher shows them how to look for specific information by using the headings, indices, boldface and italics to guide them to specific words or content. In skimming, students are shown how to read major headings, table of contents, bold letters, graphic materials, and summary paragraphs to get the main idea of the content.

To improve content comprehension, teachers can acquaint students with several study plans to help them read content materials. As students use strategies, they will discuss ideas that can then be recorded for further study.

Study Skills and Study Plans

Some students often assume they know information if they understood the information when reading or if they can provide a definition of major terms. Other students assume they must memorize every sentence they read in a chapter to study. If students know how to study effectively, they are more apt to be successful in reading to learn. Along with supporting students as they use strategies and note-taking, teachers need to demonstrate how to use notes and other materials to study. Rather than "telling" students to study, teachers should provide modeling and devote time for students to practice studying as part of subject-matter learning.

Linguistic Accommodation Testing for ELs and Special Education Students

Texas provides for linguistic accommodation for ELs and special education children taking the content portion of the State of Texas Assessment of Academic Readiness (STAAR) examination in Grades 3–8 and 10 to ensure that reading comprehension and other aspects of language development do not interfere with assessing content mastery. Based on specific recommendations from the Admission, Review, and Dismissal (ARD) and/or the Language Proficiency Assessment Committee (LPAC), districts can allow linguistic accommodations for special education and ELs when taking the STAAR basic skills test. Following is a list of allowed linguistic accommodations (TEA, 2020–2021):

1. Presenting the information in two languages side by side.

2. Allowing the test administrator to read the questions or translate words, phrases, and sentences.

3. Using dictionaries to find translations.

4. Allowing the use of bilingual or English-language glossaries.

5. Allowing the test administrator to present the information using simple language.

6. Using visual and nonverbal communication to make content clear.

7. For a detailed analysis of accommodations for students in special program, see TEA, 2020–2021.

CHAPTER 3

COMPETENCY 007: WRITING CONVENTIONS

The teacher understands the conventions of writing in English and provides instruction that helps students develop proficiency in applying writing conventions.

Role and Importance of Writing Conventions

Think of writing conventions as a way to be "polite" to the reader by making the text as accessible as possible. These are the widely accepted practices—the "rules of the road"– that enable readers to understand and navigate text. While establishing content may be the most challenging part of writing, teachers need to devote time to writing conventions, including handwriting, capitalization, punctuation, usage, and spelling. Instruction needs to regularly include time for skill development and for students to apply writing conventions as they write. Mastering writing conventions lets students focus more on higher-order facets of writing such as syntax and ideation.

Handwriting instruction focuses on manuscript (printing) and cursive writing. Why does this merit attention in a world where students spend so much time on keyboards attached to computers and mobile devices? Many legal documents require a signature, and some documents require printing as well as a signature. Even in a world where e-signatures have become common, students still benefit by being able to tangibly root themselves in the value of a signature. Additionally, some people prefer to write manuscript and then type the final draft, and people use writing in their lives in other ways, such as signing a greeting card. Handwriting instruction should help students write in legible, efficient ways. Letter formation guides have been developed for teachers to show students how to form letters; these guides show students how to write more efficiently. Handwriting instruction also anchors students in writing and reading from left to right.

Among the other mechanics in the writing convention toolbox is systematic spelling instruction. Once students can identify and write letters, they can learn to spell words. Start with high-frequency words, which appear often not only when students read but also when they write. Once students have a corpus of sight words, they have a basis for learning. Students in the early grades should be able to spell words that feature phonics generalizations. But they also need to learn to spell words that feature different aspects of morphemic/structural analysis, including multisyllabic words. As students progress in spelling, they can learn commonly confused words and commonly misspelled words.

When it comes to lessons on capitalization, punctuation, and usage, English handbooks provide guidance to help teachers provide the right instruction at the right time. By developing checklists and using anecdotal records, teachers can ensure that students master the skills they need. Skill instruction of any type is best provided for no more than 10 to 20 minutes at a time, focusing on one type of skill, or, when spelling is taught, taking just a few words at once. Spending more time can lead to diminishing returns and detract from other important facets of instruction. What is taught one day can be reviewed and built upon so that over time students retain what they learn.

Role of Proofreading and Publishing Conferences

Along with systematic skills instruction, students need to be able to apply skills for real-world reasons. During the publishing conference, the teacher meets with a small group of students to guide them as they proofread their draft to create a final draft that they can publish. Students understand that just as professional writers rely on proofreading, they, too, should develop a polished product. Students may write a final draft to be displayed on the bulletin board, or they can develop a book to be added (or "gifted") to the class library. Or students could be adding finished writing products to a classroom document. Writing for a broader audience beyond just the teacher motivates students to invest time in proofreading.

To prepare for the conference, the teacher reads each student's draft, choosing two skills to teach during the conference with the student. During the conference, the teacher demonstrates how to use an editing checklist to check for spelling, capitalization, and punctuation. The children use a color of ink different from what the teacher will use later to mark the checklist. Proofreading checklists become more sophisticated as students learn more about writing conventions (i.e., spelling, capitalization, punctuation, and usage).

The teacher gives short lessons on one or two aspects of writing conventions with each student while the others listen. The teacher should always start by noting what the student did well, and then move to what needs to be changed for the one or two aspects. The teacher focuses on just a few things to avoid having the student become overwhelmed with too much input. Nonetheless, the final draft will not contain errors because the teacher now uses a different color of ink to make needed changes for typing a final draft.

Stages of Spelling Development

Researchers who study the writing of children have described five stages of spelling development. Progression from one stage to the next is typically gradual, and a speller may display aspects of more than one stage at any given point. The age levels are approximate, and children can vary depending upon their experiences with print and their spelling instruction. In fact, some literacy experts recommend not treating development in terms of grade levels, but instead considering each student individually and providing the requisite instruction.

Table 3-9. The Five Stages of Spelling Development

STAGE 1— PRECOMMUNICATIVE		
Description	**Hallmarks of spelling**	**Examples**
In the precommunicative stage (typically 3 to 5 years old), the child uses letters, but there is no correspondence between letters and words when the child reads the writing. The child exhibits knowledge that letters are used in writing.	Writing looks like a random array of letters with no apparent meaning even though the child has a meaning in mind.	**M E M M S** (I am with my dog.)

STAGE 2— SEMIPHONETIC		
Description	**Hallmarks of spelling**	**Examples**
In the semiphonetic stage (typically 4 to 6 years old), the child uses letters, but there is no correspondence between letters and words when the child reads what she or he has written. The child may not know that writing in English moves left to right on the page.	The child knows that letters are used in writing. The child has a message in mind, but a reader would not be able to understand it.	R (are) U (you) B (be)

STAGE 3— PHONETIC		
Description	**Hallmarks of spelling**	**Examples**
In the phonetic stage (typically 5 to 6 years old), the child represents all of the major speech sounds she or he can hear in a word.	Although words may not be spelled correctly or conventionally, the spellings are systematic and can be understood.	**TAK** (take); **CHRAN** (train); **CHRUK** (truck)

STAGE 4— TRANSITIONAL		
Description	**Hallmarks of spelling**	**Examples**
In the transitional stage (typically 6 to 11 years old), the child starts to rely less on spelling by representing sounds. The child starts to also use visual and morphological information.	Many common words are known, and the child may use common letter strings, such as *igh*. Using visual information may result in the reversal of letters within words.	**siad** (said); **yousual** (usual)

(continued)

STAGE 5— CORRECT		
Description	**Hallmarks of spelling**	**Examples**
Once the correct stage (typically 10 to 11 years old) is reached, the speller knows nearly all the sound-symbol principles. The speller has learned generalizations as well as irregular spellings of words. The speller can use prefixes, suffixes, and silent consonants. Commonly misspelled words and instances of individual words may create difficulty.	The speller can use prefixes, suffixes, and silent consonants, consonant clusters, and digraphs. Commonly misspelled words (e.g., homophones) and instances involving exceptions to prevailing rules may create difficulty.	said unhappy against

COMPETENCY 008: WRITTEN COMMUNICATION

The teacher understands that writing to communicate is a developmental process and provides instruction that promotes students' competence in written communication.

Process and Product in Writing

Writing instruction should help students learn the strategies and techniques successful writers use, and the conditions for writing should be ones that foster growth in writing proficiency. Much of traditional writing instruction focuses solely or mostly on the end product. Students get a writing assignment and work on their own to complete it. The teacher then grades the finished assignment. The grade may depend on how well the writing establishes content or presents ideas. The grade also could be based upon how well the student applied correct spelling, punctuation, capitalization, and usage. This focus on the final product fails to keep in mind the process of writing—what occurs when people write. Focusing on a finished product provides feedback only at the end and offers no support during the writing process.

Current theory and research emphasize that effective writing instruction should support students during the process to help them learn and develop a better product and become proficient writers. During the process, attention first focuses on establishing content, but instruction should not dismiss the application of writing conventions when writing is going to be "published" or shared with others. Students thus should be shown how to proofread their writing for others to read.

By writing drafts, students learn to establish content and share their writing so that others can understand it. By paying attention to the final product, students then further learn to apply conventions of spelling, punctuation, capitalization, and usage.

Current theory and research also points out that writing is a recursive process that can include more than just writing itself. In fact, it is part of a broader process that includes pre-writing or thinking about what to write, composing or actually writing, revising or changing content, and editing or proofreading. Additionally, writers do not write in a lock-step manner, where, for example, they brainstorm on Day 1 and write a rough draft on Day 2. Instead, good writing follows a spiraling process that begins with a rough draft and undergoes refinement as the process progresses.

Writing instruction should recognize that students can vary where they are in the process even when they all are writing daily. Some students may finish a piece on the second day, while others may work on a piece for several days. Students should be instructed that when they finish one piece, they should begin another. After, say, a few weeks, the students select their best piece for "publishing," sharing its final draft. They then do further proofreading so that what they share adheres to conventions of spelling, punctuation, capitalization, and usage.

Daily Writing Instruction and Structure of Writing Workshop

By using a writing workshop approach, teachers can provide conditions for learning that are akin to how writers write in the real world. In a writing workshop, students write daily to gain fluency through practice, as they do when engaging in reading and other learning. Students cannot progress with occasional writing or writing only for assessments. Students need to build momentum and gain confidence, which daily writing can afford alongside sound instruction from teachers.

A writing workshop is structured to help students gain proficiency. Each part plays a role, and the combined parts support students' development by helping them learn strategies and techniques as well as providing authentic writing experiences and conditions for learning. The simple, predictable structure of a workshop helps students because they know what to expect each day. Students who know they will write each day also think about topics even when they are outside of school. A predictable structure also helps teachers because they know what they will do rather than choreographing something each day or week. Structure should not be confused with regimentation.

Through **mini-lessons**, teachers help students based on their abilities and the writing they need to learn. At the start of the writing workshop each day, students can meet as a group. Through mini-lessons, teachers show what students need to learn. Mini-lessons are usually brief, but they have the same focus more than one day, depending on students' needs. The teacher first must devote attention to procedures of the writing workshop; these include how to get such materials as each student's writing folder as well as paper and pencils. Procedures also include writing names and dates on drafts and starting another writing when a draft is finished. Mini-lessons focus mostly on the craft of writing, including the strategies and techniques that writers use. Instead of lecturing, teachers should think aloud and *show* students the writing process. For example, the teacher can model how to select a topic by brainstorming and listing what the teacher knows and cares about. Likewise, the teacher might illustrate the revision process by sharing a draft the teacher is working on and then add needed details to it. Literature previously read aloud also can be reviewed as a **mentor text** to show students how a professional writer uses a strategy or technique.

Small-group work can build upon mini-lessons. For additional scaffolding, teachers can provide small-group instruction while other students write. Each student should meet the teacher according to a daily schedule created for each group.

During **writing conferences**, the teacher and students write. After about 10 minutes, the teacher should move about the room for **rough-draft conferences** with students. These conferences should run about one to three minutes and focus solely on establishing content, with later proofreading reserved for addressing conventions. As most writers do, the student or the teacher reads the piece aloud. The teacher then "receives" the work by telling the student what the teacher heard or learned, using the student's exact words. Next, the teacher asks genuine questions about anything that needs clarifying. This structure lets students know what is working and what needs to be clearer. The conference also can let the teacher help a student with a problem, such as selecting a topic. Teachers should not assign a topic, allowing students to maintain ownership, but teachers can talk to students and help them pick a topic they know and care about.

Whole-class sharing can occur daily to let students share their writing beyond the teacher. A few students can share each day, and students can sign up to do so. All who want to share should have that opportunity, but sharing should not be required of students reluctant to do so. Students learn from each other in whole-group conferences, which should be structured like the rough-draft conferences with the teacher. The student reads the piece aloud. The other students then "receive" the work by telling the student what they heard or learned. Then, the students ask genuine questions that can show where the piece needs clarification.

The structure of a writing workshop can remain the same with any writing. The content to be learned changes according to what students need and what needs to be taught. The structure provides opportunities for growth while managing the class. The structure also provides differentiated instruction because students participate according to their abilities while getting support from the teacher as well as their classmates.

Publishing Conferences

Publishing conferences can occur while students write. Kindergartners and early first grade students do not proofread, and their invented spelling should be recognized as positive, not as errors. Invented spelling contributes to phonemic awareness, an important ability in learning to read and write, and should not be discouraged. When students master conventional spelling, however, teachers should have publishing conferences. After two or three weeks, students should select one piece to be published from their folders. Students can move at their own pace in writing, but they should write daily. During those two or three weeks, students should put a piece for "publishing" in an editing tray. When enough students do this, the teacher conducts a publishing conference at the table. For rough-draft conferences, the teacher moves among students, but publishing conferences take place in small groups at a table.

The teacher prepares for publishing conferences by reading each draft to determine what the student can do and where the student needs help. The teacher records this on an anecdotal record sheet kept for each student to document skill development. When focusing on writing to capture their thoughts, students devote attention to establish content. First drafts thus may have errors in such writing conventions as spelling, punctuation, capitalization, and usage (the way, according to convention, that a word or phrase is correctly used) even when they can otherwise spell a word or use another convention correctly. As students gain proficiency, they will apply greater skill more often when writing drafts.

During the publishing conference with a small group, the teacher shows how to use an editing checklist for spelling, capitalization, punctuation, and usage. Students' checklists become more sophisticated as they learn about the conventions.

The teacher conducts short lessons on one or two writing conventions with each student while the others listen. The teacher starts by telling the student what works and then suggests what should be revised based on the lessons. By limiting the focus of the revision, the teacher avoids overwhelming the student, but the goal is a final draft without errors.

The teacher corrects errors in a different ink color from the student's to distinguish the teacher's corrections from the student's. This is done before a final draft is typed or written and not during the conference. If the students can do it well, the teacher lets them type the final draft, but reluctant and less capable writers may rely on the teacher to type a final draft without errors.

Records of Students' Work

The children have a writing folder for rough drafts, and the teacher develops a system for passing out folders for the writing workshop. A cumulative folder is kept for each child and includes a copy of rough and final drafts dated to show progress. Through the process approach, students write daily, select topics, write rough drafts, revise their work, and share writing with others.

Strategies and Techniques of Effective Writing

The most difficult part of writing is establishing content that will be understood by the reader as the author intended it. Since the reader has only the writing from which to get the intended meaning, the writer must: (1) form the thoughts while writing to express what the writer intends, and (2) determine how to write it so that the audience understands the intended meaning, which requires the writer to have audience awareness. To develop the best possible piece, writers must develop more than one draft, even if the initial drafts are solely thought about and not committed to writing. Like most adults, students must write more than one draft to establish content.

In trying to help students meet the demands of writing a draft, teachers can show students strategies and techniques that writers use, much as a coach does. Rather than just "telling" someone what to do, a coach also "shows" what to do and provides support while the person tries to follow the strategy or technique.

Depending on the students' needs and the type of writing being taught, the teacher shows strategies and techniques that writers use, showing how to engage in the following:

- Select a topic

- Write rough drafts that focus on establishing content rather than disrupting the process by devoting attention to writing conventions

- Add or delete a word, sentence or set of sentences

- Spell a word the best you can rather than using a less effective word that is easy to spell

- Elaborate by adding details

- Select a title

- Add dialogue

- Create a picture with words to convey what happened

- Use strong verbs rather than adverbs + verbs (**NO:** "She held on tightly to the baseball bat." **YES:** "She gripped the baseball bat.")

- Locate and organize information for writing reports

- Use resources for reports without plagiarizing

Voice and Types of Writing

The teacher first helps students write stories about themselves because personal narratives are meaningful. In a personal story, the student is already in command of a scenario, making it easier to use details and dialogue to create a picture with words. Likewise, students may select topics they know and care about (e.g., soccer, game apps, pets) for informal reports that, again, let them share information they already have. When students select the topic, they are more likely to be invested in the writing versus a topic the teacher would choose. Professional writers often write what they know and care about, and it is reasonable to assume that beginning writers will progress more when they share their own experiences and ideas.

State exams and school reports assign topics, but when students get experience at forming their thoughts when writing, they develop abilities that will help them respond to assigned topics. By writing about what they know and care about, students learn they have something to say when they write. Exams and assigned reports also often provide a choice of topics or prompts.

As the school year progresses, students can learn about writing reports, essays, fiction and poetry. The structure of the writing workshop stays the same, with teachers adapting mini-lessons and group work to the particular form of writing to be learned.

Teachers consider the strategies and techniques required to develop the writing and plan mini-lessons to show them to students and let them practice the strategies and techniques. For example, in teaching students how to take notes for a report, the students and teacher can read the information together. The students then write notes that put the ideas into their own words.

Publishing Conferences of the Writing Workshop

After a specified time, students select a piece to publish from their rough-draft folders. The teacher reads the pieces before having a publishing conference with a small group. Other students continue writing at their desks or tables. During a publishing conference, the teacher calls a group of students together to use a proofreading list. The teacher shows students how to use the proofreading list, which becomes more sophisticated as students learn more about punctuation and usage.

The teacher provides guidance and selects one or two skills to teach each child. Students are not expected to find all the errors in spelling, punctuation, and usage. As in similar cases we've discussed, the teacher will later use a different color of ink to correct remaining errors. The teacher or the students type a final draft for publication. Outlets for publication can be books published for classroom libraries or gifts, framed displays, and bulletin boards. The children have a writing folder for rough drafts, and the teacher develops a system for passing out folders for the writing workshop.

A cumulative folder is kept for each child and includes a copy of rough and final drafts dated to show progress. Through the process approach, students write daily, select topics, write rough drafts, revise their work, and share writing with others.

Traits of Writing

The 6+1 Trait Writing, developed by the Northwest Regional Educational Laboratory (NREL), is a system that emphasizes seven elements of writing (2021). Knowing traits of writing can guide teachers as they make sure they foster students' writing development:

1. **Organization**—the internal structure of the sample.

2. **Ideas**—how ideas are presented in the sample.

3. **Voice**—the uniqueness of the author and how ideas are presented.

4. **Word Choice**—the vocabulary used to convey meaning.

5. **Sentence Fluency**—the flow of ideas and the use of connectors.

6. **Conventions**—the use of capitalization, punctuation, and spelling.

7. **Presentation**—how the final product looks in print.

Similarly, the Texas Education Agency has set forth traits of writing as follows:

1. **Focus and Coherence**—how the main idea is introduced and supported in the composition.

2. **Organization**—the organization of ideas, including connectors.

3. **Development of Ideas**—how the ideas are presented and supported.

4. **Voice**—the uniqueness of the author and how ideas are projected.

5. **Conventions**—the use of capitalization, punctuation, and spelling.

Both the 6+1 Trait Writing and the TEA writing programs guide children to show knowledge of writing traits. To assess students' performance, both programs develop a four-point rubric for each writing trait.

Identifying the Characteristics of Modes of Writing

Writing serves different functions. The main functions are to narrate, describe, explain, and persuade. These four categories are neither exhaustive nor mutually exclusive, but they can guide instruction. A sound writing program can provide students the opportunities to write for different functions, especially when writing is incorporated in subject learning, such as science and social studies.

The narrative is a story or an account. It may recount an incident or a series of incidents. The account may be autobiographical to make a point. It may be fiction or nonfiction. Descriptive writing provides information about a person, place, or thing. Descriptive writing can be fiction or nonfiction. Description is a powerful tool in advertising. Advertisements describe items using factual information, but the information is presented to persuade prospective buyers.

Expository writing explains and clarifies ideas. Students are probably most familiar with this type of writing. The expository essay may have a narrative, but the storytelling or recounting is minor and serves the explanation. Expository writing is found in textbooks. For instance, a textbook on the history of Texas would likely be expository.

Persuasive writing tries to convince the reader of something. Persuasive writing fills online and print magazines and newspapers and permeates the internet. The writer may be trying to push a political candidate, convince neighbors to vote for a zoning ordinance, or promote a diet plan. Effective persuasive writing presents a viewpoint and provides factual and/or anecdotal evidence to support it. The structure should address counterarguments that readers might have in mind. Topics for persuasive writing for students could include, for instance, whether homework is necessary or whether pets should be allowed to come to school. Whatever the topic, the writer works to win the reader over. An argument presents a viewpoint to persuade, but in developing the argument, writers rely upon research to support their view. Topics for writing an argument could, for example, include whether genetically modified crops should be permitted to be developed, or whether menthol cigarettes should be banned.

Authors choose their form of writing not only to tell a story but also to present ideas. Whether choosing the narrative, descriptive, expository, or persuasive format, writers have something on their minds that they want to convey to readers.

Writing for Audiences, Occasions, and Purposes

Teachers should encourage children to write for meaningful purposes. Meaningful writing can be incorporated into daily classroom activities and enhance not only writing skills but also content area mastery. Over the school year, students can use writing for a range of purposes and use different formats to share their thoughts. Students also need to be provided the option of writing for various audiences, not solely the teacher.

Some writing can be a rough draft, more like talk written on paper, such as a dialogue journal where the student writes to the teacher to talk about a book the student has read and the teacher writes back on a weekly basis. Similarly, students can be shown how to create notes as well as learning logs in various subject areas.

During the writing workshop, students also can be shown how to develop personal narratives, reports, fiction, and poetry. This writing can include writing rough drafts and learning to revise content towards a product that is written for others to read.

COMPETENCY 009: VIEWING AND REPRESENTING

The teacher understands skills for interpreting, analyzing, evaluating, and producing visual images and messages in various types of media, including electronic media, and provides students with opportunities to develop skills in this area.

According to the Texas K–12 curriculum standards, TEKS (rev. 2019–2020), students in EC–6 grades must develop the skills needed to create and understand images and messages presented in different media. The skills increase in complexity as students move from lower to upper elementary grades. For instance, students in Grades 1–3 must produce visual representations of what they learn as well as of the tasks they do (e.g., create an image summarizing a story they have read). Students also must know how to discuss the visual representations they have created. In Grades 4–6, students must understand, interpret, analyze, critique, and produce these visual representations as well as discuss their meaning or significance through the multiple media, including newsletters, charts, and electronic presentations.

Students also should understand an author's purpose and choice of elements used to get his or her message across via multiple media. The characteristics and functions of the different media are explained next.

Types and Characteristics of Media

A medium is considered to be any means used to convey information to others. At least three main media are available: **print**, **visual**, and **electronic**. Print media disseminate information mainly via newspapers, magazines, and direct mail. Print media are static; that is, once the information is published, it cannot be changed. Visual media incorporate visual imagery to complement or supplement the message. Visual media can also stand alone. For example, photographs and paintings can convey meaning without text. Moreover, visual media are also an integral part of print media to illustrate messages. As such, visual media can take many forms, including photography, film, and even cartoons. Visual media can be static (e.g., still photographs) or dynamic, as with movies or videos.

Besides incorporating print and visual imagery, electronic media require such external devices as a television, computer, or mobile device to display the information and images. Electronic media are used in different fields, including journalism, fine arts, commerce, education, and communications. A primary electronic medium that encompasses different electronic tools is the internet, which contains photographs, videos, blogs, email, and multiple articles. In addition, e-books also are available on the internet.

When using these electronic media, teachers must remember that technology changes fast.

Many tools for presenting information are improved and refined almost daily. For instance, photography has evolved from being created on photographic plates and then film to now being created digitally. Teachers should realize a vast array of possibilities to create and display information is available via existing media. As the need for using and sharing massive amounts of information with others becomes necessary, some media will take precedence over others. For example, the use of online information has become so pervasive that static media, like print media, are now being channeled electronically (e.g., newspapers and books). The use of online resources and websites has become a staple. Students expect those around them to know how to use these tools. Students seek opportunities to use and produce different products through different media.

Representing Messages and Meanings Through Media

Charts, tables, graphs, pictures, and print, and non-print media are examples of materials used to present or summarize information and/or to complement messages. For instance, a chart can summarize much information without written explanations. Students should understand that visual representations are important and that their purpose is to present information and facilitate communicating the message. Visual images should also be used to make information more understandable.

A graphic can expand or illustrate a concept, support points, summarize data, organize facts, add a dimension to the content (such as a cartoon adding humor), compare information, show change over time, or furnish additional information. Through graphics, the reader can interpret, predict, and apply information with careful observation. Questioning students as they create visual images (e.g., asking what they are trying to convey or how they think someone will interpret their image) as well as providing ongoing feedback may help students to focus and clarify the information they are presenting with graphics.

Understanding How Students May Interpret and Evaluate Visual Images

Teachers should realize that even a graphic that looks uncomplicated may challenge a reader's interpretive skills. Many inferences may be necessary for even the simplest visual aid or graphic. Students may first skip the graphics or skim them without interpreting them. Students also may just focus on the graphics without paying attention to the written explanations. Even students with training in the use of graphic information may fail to transfer that knowledge to other content areas or have trouble going from print to graphic and then back to print. In either case, students may not have been taught how to use multiple representations of information. Teachers can help students use multiple representations of information via open-book and guided reading. A teacher can also show how to use a chart or graph via electronic tools, including overhead projectors and interactive whiteboards. Examples of effective presentations and how to create them can be shared with the students. Resources and software to improve their writing (mentor texts) (Dorfman & Cappelli, 2007) can give students examples of how to select images to use with text (e.g., consideration of how the image parallels or complements the text).

Visual design can be viewed as containing its own grammar (Kress & van Leeuwen, 2001). Teachers can help students to understand and apply such visual grammar by teaching its component parts (Wysocki, et al., 2004) Johnson-Eilola, Selfe, & Sirc, 2004). Some of these key components are:

- **Visual impact:** how the overall visual design appeals to the reader (e.g., through detail, layout, and color).

- **Visual coherence:** how the design creates unity and wholeness (e.g., via shapes, line, imagery).

- **Visual salience:** using design features to generate a desired effect (e.g., through varying size, colors, clip art, etc.)

- **Organization:** how the layout of the page creates a unique pattern understandable to the reader (e.g., through consideration of how items in the layout might be arranged on the page).

These features of visual literacy overlap and can guide students toward an awareness of visual literacy.

Teachers should model how to read, complement, and interpret visual images whenever students are required to create them. Pictures and other graphics can arouse interest and stimulate thinking. Graphics also can add clarity, prevent misunderstanding, show step-by-step development, and exhibit the status of things, events, and processes, as well as demonstrate comparisons and contrasts (Vacca and Vacca 1989).

Integrating Technology for Producing Communications

Teachers should provide students with opportunities to use state-of-the-art technology and tools. Doing so will motivate children to read and write as well as monitor their writing and enable them to communicate with different media. For instance, one could assume that the goal of word-processing software is simply to record written information. With technological advances, such software now offers writers help with editing their documents. Other uses of this software include creating semantic maps, tables, charts, and graphs. Such writing-related elements as spellcheck, definitions of terms, a thesaurus, and even suggestions for sentence constructions are commonly available in programs like Microsoft Word. A spell checker (even with its inherent limitations) not only helps identify misspelled words but also frees students from the pressure of spelling things right, at least at the drafting stage. Students should be encouraged to put their ideas in writing without stopping to check spelling. When they finish writing, they address other important concerns like spelling. Students should be reminded that the spell checker won't always work. Therefore, children should be guided to pay attention to corrections and learn from them.

Teachers should show children how to take advantage of programs available for communicating and creating electronic products. The products they can create include a classroom newsletter, a multimedia presentation, and a video response to a group project. Students should keep their audience and purpose in mind when they create their pieces. Doing so will also help them make sure the language they use is appropriate and understandable for their audience.

COMPETENCY 010: ASSESSMENT OF DEVELOPING LITERACY

The teacher understands the basic principles of literacy assessment and uses a variety of assessments to guide literacy instruction.

Knowledge and Use of Literacy Assessment

The two main types of assessment are formal and informal. Each has a place in the classroom, especially in the literacy classroom. Teachers understand the importance of ongoing assessment as an instructional tool and use both informal and formal assessment measures to assess students' learning in their classroom. However, teachers should not group children permanently because of one assessment, either formal or informal. Any grouping should come about after considering several assessments, and the grouping should be flexible to recognize differences among the students in each group.

Informal Assessments

Teachers can learn valuable information about their students by observing them at work. Through systematic observation and documentation, teachers can assess their students in ways that are more comprehensive than tests alone. Teachers can use informal assessments from literacy education books, and they also can develop their own informal reading assessments based on indicators of students' progress. Informal assessments are beneficial because they provide specific feedback about a student on a daily basis during instruction and not solely when a test is given so that teachers can provide additional support. The assessments also can help teachers revise instruction, monitor progress, and share comprehensive measures of progress with parents.

Running Records

Running records are an assessment tool in which teachers listen to students read aloud to know how to meet their needs. The teacher records what students say via shorthand. The notations represent what the students did or said for each word they read, whether the student: (1) correctly read a word, (2) made an oral reading error or miscue, (3) repeated a word or series of words, (4) self-corrected, or (5) was unable to try to read a word.

At the beginning of the school year, running records can be used to assign students to a guided reading or small instructional group. A group must be homogeneous so that its members have similar needs. Similarly, running records can be used to find the best level of book for students. When students read a text that is too hard, they cannot use the sources of information and will not understand what they are reading. Teachers can use benchmark books or selections at varying levels of difficulty that correspond to different reading levels.

Teachers can use running records throughout the year to make sure students are progressing in the books they have read once or twice during their guided reading instruction. Teachers can gauge progress when they listen to students read individually while other students read silently during guided reading, or they can assess at other times.

Teachers also can analyze running records to determine which type of instruction a student needs to progress in reading. Running records are a valuable tool to document a student's progress over time.

Running records provide insights about students' oral reading. A student's comprehension of a text can be determined by asking the student to retell what was read or by asking questions about the text. If students are proficient in word identification, teachers will rely more on assessing students' comprehension to determine the level of text and how to meet students' needs.

Taking a Running Record

Here are the steps necessary for taking a running record:

- Select the text to use for assessment. When forming reading groups, different levels may be needed. If the assessment is for reading instruction in guided reading groups, the text will be a current one or one that was recently finished.

- Students need not read an entire story or book. Students should read enough for the teacher to obtain an understanding of the reading ability of the student.

- Use a blank sheet of notebook paper or Running Record form. Make notes on the paper, not on copies of the reading.

- Write the student's name, the title of the selection, and the date of the assessment on the sheet.

- Sit next to the student to see each word as the student reads.

- On the sheet of paper or Running Record form, use the notation system and mark the sheet for each word in the text to show what the student did.

- Arrange the marks as the words on the page are arranged. Move from left, starting a new line when the text does. Show page numbers so that you will know what the student said.

- Use a horizontal line to show new page numbers.

- Use a check mark to show each word read correctly. The following example shows the words in the text, what the student read, and what the running record would be.

Text:	After school, we are going to my friend's house.
Student:	After school, we are going to my friend's house.
Running Record:	✓ ✓ ✓ ✓ ✓ ✓ ✓ ✓

- Use other marks to show errors. What the student says goes above a line, and what the text says or the teacher says goes below the line. Do not include punctuation.

Text:	After school, we are going to my friend's house.
Student:	After stool, we are going to my friend's house.
Running Record:	✓ <u>stool</u> ✓ ✓ ✓ ✓ ✓ ✓ ✓
	school

Students' Reading, Notation, and Error Count

- **Accurate Reading**—The student reads the word correctly.

✓

Types of Miscues Counted as an Error:

- **Substitution**—The student says a word different from the word in the text. The teacher's substitution is counted as an error unless the student self-corrects. Names are counted wrong just once even when they appear multiple times in the text.

  Student   <u>depended</u>

  Text   decided

- **Omission**—The student leaves out the word in the text.

  Student   <u>—</u>

  Text   a

- **Insertion**—The student adds or inserts a word not in the text.

  Student   <u>the</u>

  Text   —

Not Counted as an Error:

- **Repetition**—A repetition takes place when a student repeats a word or section of words. A repetition is not counted as an error because the student knows the words, but this behavior is noted because the student may be unable to recognize a word automatically. A line is drawn over the word or words repeated.

  ↓————————— R

  ✓ ✓ ✓ ✓ ✓ ✓ ✓

- **Self-Correction**—The student substitutes a word but then corrects the error. This is not counted as an error, but it is noted.

  Student   <u>depended|</u> SC

  Text   decided

Intervention—One Error:

- **Appeal/Told**—Each word told is counted as an error. During assessment, the teacher strives to tell a student a word or give prompts for word identification to obtain an accurate assessment of what the student can do. Teachers provide prompts during instruction because the goal is teaching with assessment when listening to students read aloud individually during guided reading or small-group work. However, when a student does not make an attempt, the teacher tells the word after waiting 5–10 seconds for the student to figure out the word.

Student   _____ A
Text   decided T

Scoring a Running Record

Scoring a running record is based upon the total of correctly read words. The running words (RW) are the number of words the student read. Errors (E) is the number of miscues counted as an error.

The **accuracy rate** is found by determining the percentage of words read correctly of the number of words read:

$$RW - E/RW \times 100$$

Example:

RW = 100

Errors = 2

$$100 - 2/100 \times 100 = 98\%$$

The accuracy rate can help determine whether a text is at the independent, instructional, or frustration level.

95%—100%   Independent Level (easy)

90%—94%   Instructional Level (can be read with support/instruction)

Below 90%   Frustration Level (too difficult)

Analyzing Miscues

By analyzing the miscues of a running record, the teacher can determine the sources of information a student is using. If a student is using **visual cues**, she or he is using the print to identify words.

Students use their knowledge of (language) **structure cues** when they use what they know about how words combine in the language to figure out an unknown word, such as in the following: I like to eat _____.

Although the student may not know terms, the student would know the kinds of words that could fit for the unknown word (i.e., the blank), such as knowing intuitively that a verb would not be the unknown word. Knowing how words can combine is using **knowledge of syntax**, or language structure.

Students use their knowledge of **meaning** when they consider what would make sense, such as in the following: Mary likes to ride a _____. Because the student knows what people can ride, the student knows that the unknown word (i.e., the blank) will be a mode of transportation. Using meaning entails **knowledge of semantics**.

If a student fails to use **visual cues** (the way a word is written/spelled), the student may have a problem in word identification. Instruction in phonics, structural analysis (or morphemic analysis), and sight words helps students gain in using **visual cues**.

Students who fail to use **structure cues** may need help in using context clues or may need more oral language development to gain expertise in English syntax. Similarly, students who fail to use **meaning cues** may need help in using context clues or may need more oral language development to increase their grasp of English syntax. They may also may need to monitor comprehension.

Example 1: Miscue Analysis Using Running Records

> Student: I have a bag dog.
> Text: I have a big dog.
>
> ✓ ✓ ✓ <u>bag</u> ✓
> big

A. meaning cues: No, the miscue does not make sense or does not show using knowledge of semantics.

B. structure cues: No, the miscue does not show knowledge relevant to syntax.

C. visual cues: Yes, the miscue indicates the reader has used visual cues because of using initial and final consonant letters.

D. needed instruction: The student used short *a* and did not know or recognize the word. Therefore, short *i* must be taught.

Example 2: Miscue Analysis Using Running Records

> Student: This vase is under because it is broken.
> Text: This vase is unacceptable because it is broken.
>
> ✓ ✓ ✓   <u>under</u>   ✓   ✓ ✓   ✓
> unacceptable

A. meaning cues: No, the miscue does not make sense or show using knowledge of semantics.

B. structure cues: No, the miscue does not show using knowledge of syntax.

C. visual cues: Yes, the reader used *un-* when trying to identify the word.

D. needed instruction: The student must be taught how to identify multisyllabic words by examining the prefix and base word. The student also may not know the base word, *acceptable*.

Other forms of assessment include:

Sight Words—Students are asked to read leveled lists of high-frequency sight words. Students also can be assessed to determine whether they can spell the words. The teacher keeps a record sheet for each student.

Phonics Generalization Word Lists—Students are asked to read and spell lists of words that feature phonics generalizations. For example, if students can read and spell the word, *tape*, they show they can read long *a* words with the vowel, consonant, silent *e* pattern. Reading *chop* shows understanding the sound of the digraph *ch*. Students also can be assessed to determine whether they can spell the words. The teacher keeps a record sheet for each student.

Reading Logs—Students write the title, author, and illustrator of each book they read during independent reading. This assessment documents independent reading and the literature the student is reading.

Anecdotal Notes—Teachers jot comments or write longer entries to remember what a student did and said, such as when asking a student to read individually during guided reading or to document what happened during a writing conference.

Writing Samples and Written Checklists—Teachers maintain a cumulative folder for students with checklists that correspond to the students' ability to (1) compose and (2) to deal with spelling, punctuation, and usage. Students' writing samples are dated, and they can include rough drafts stapled to the final draft.

Story Retelling

Asking a child to retell a story is another informal assessment. The ability to retell a story can show whether a child remembers what took place in the story (the plot). Informal assessment also can take place through observations, journals, conversations, and written drafts.

Structured Informal Observations

The teacher may also observe individual or group work. Usually, the teacher makes a checklist of competencies, skills, or requirements and then uses the list to check those for student or group displays. A teacher wishing to emphasize interviewing skills could devise a checklist that includes personal appearance, mannerisms, and confidence as well as addressing the questions asked. A teacher who wants to emphasize careful listening might observe a discussion with a checklist that includes paying attention, summarizing others' ideas, asking questions, and not interrupting. Checklists let teachers capture behaviors that cannot be measured with a paper-and-pencil test, such as following the correct sequence of steps in a science experiment or including all important elements in a speech in class. The structure of a checklist can be both an advantage and a disadvantage. The structure provides consistency but lacks flexibility. An open-ended comment section at the end of a checklist can help overcome this deficit.

Anecdotal Records

Anecdotal records sometimes help. For example, they can capture how a group of students solves a problem. The anecdotal records can be useful when giving feedback to the group. Students can also be taught to write explanations of the procedures they use for their projects or science experiments. An anecdotal record can include all relevant information, but it also takes a good deal of time. Assigning a grade for it also can be difficult, but if the anecdotal record is used solely for feedback, no grade is necessary.

Portfolio and Cumulative Folder Assessment

Portfolios provide a collection of students' work to represent their progress. Like a portfolio created by an artist, model, or performer, a student portfolio provides a succinct picture of the child's achievements over time. Portfolios may contain essays or articles written on paper, videotapes, multimedia presentations on computer disks, or a combination of these. Language arts teachers often use portfolios to collect the best samples of student writing during the school year and could include various types of writing.

Cumulative folders provide a way for teachers to collect a copy of all final drafts of students' writing, with a copy of rough drafts attached to the final draft. Teachers can show students how to view their work in portfolios or cumulative folders to self-assess. Teachers also can discuss students' entries (in a portfolio or cumulative folder) with parents to help them see their child's progress.

Formal Assessments

Formal measures may include teacher-made tests, district exams, and standardized tests. Formative and summative evaluations are part of effective instruction. Formative evaluation occurs when the teacher or the students monitor progress during the period when instruction can still be modified. Summative evaluation occurs at the end of a specific time or course of study. Usually, a summative evaluation applies a single grade or score to represent a student's performance.

Teachers should use a variety of formal assessments. Teacher-made instruments should be developed as part of planning goals and outcomes rather than after the completion of the lessons. Carefully planned objectives and assessment instruments guide lesson development for the teacher. Paper-and-pencil tests are the most common method for evaluating progress.

Criterion-Referenced Tests

In criterion-referenced tests (CRTs), the teacher tries to measure each student against uniform objectives or criteria (standards). CRTs allow the possibility that all students can score 100% on the test because they understand the concepts being tested. Teacher-made tests are criterion-referenced because the teacher develops them to measure the achievement of predetermined course outcomes. If teachers have properly prepared lessons based on the outcomes and if students have mastered the outcomes, scores on CRTs should be high. Students are not competing with each other for a high score because this test does not limit the number of students who can score well. Some commercially developed tests are criterion-referenced, but most are norm-referenced.

The State of Texas Assessments of Academic Readiness (STAAR) is a criterion-referenced basic skills test for children in Grades 3 to 12. This criterion-referenced test assesses the implementation and the mastery of the Texas Essential Knowledge and Skills (TEKS), the Texas state curriculum.

Norm-Referenced Tests

A norm-referenced test (NRT) is designed to compare the performance of groups of students. This test is competitive because a limited number of students can score well. A plot of NRT scores resembles a bell-shaped curve, with most scores clustering around the center and a few scores at each end. The midpoint is the average of test data, and half will score above average and half below. The bell-shaped curve is a mathematical description of the results of tossing coins. It represents the chance, or normal, distribution of skills, knowledge, or events across the general population. A survey of the height of sixth-grade boys will result in an average height, with half the boys above average height and half below. A small number will have heights far above average, and a small number will have heights far below. However, most heights will cluster around the average. A percentile score (not to be confused with a percentage) is a way of reporting a student's NRT score. The percentile score indicates the percentage of the population whose scores fall at or below the student's score. For example, if a group of students score at the 80th percentile, it means that the group scored as well as or better than 79% of the students who took the test. A student with a score at the 50th percentile has an average score. Percentile scores rank students from highest to lowest. By themselves, percentile scores do not indicate how well the student has mastered the content objectives. Raw scores indicate how many questions the student answered correctly and are thus useful in computing a percentage score.

The Texas Education Agency (TEA) has a comprehensive list of approved norm-referenced tests from which districts can choose to assess students' achievement in the state. This list includes the California Achievement Test (CAT), Stanford Achievement Test, and the Iowa Test of Basic Skills (ITBS).

Performance-Based Assessment

Some states and districts are moving toward performance-based tests, which assess students on how well they perform certain tasks. Students must use higher-level thinking skills to apply, analyze, synthesize, and evaluate ideas and data. For example, assessing content using a performance-based test might require students to read a problem, design and carry out a lab experiment, and then write summaries of their findings. The performance-based assessment would evaluate both the process students used and the output they produced. An English performance-based test might ask students to read a selection of literature and then write a critical analysis. A mathematics performance-based test might state a problem, require students to invent one or more methods for solving the problem, use one of the methods to arrive at a solution, and then write the solution and an explanation of the processes they used.

Performance-based assessments let students create solutions to problems or questions and require them to use higher-level skills. This approach has weaknesses, however. It can be time-consuming, and it often requires multiple resources, which can be expensive. Teachers also must get training in how to apply the test. However, many schools consider performance-based testing to be a more authentic measure of achievement than traditional tests.

Constructing Classroom-Based Tests

Teachers must consider professional and technical factors when designing tests. They first must recognize that test construction is as creative, challenging, and important as the rest of their teaching. The planning and background that contribute to teaching are incomplete unless evaluation of student performance provides accurate feedback to the teacher.

Good tests stem from careful planning, creative thinking, and hard work as well as technical knowledge about the methods of measuring student knowledge and performance. Classroom tests that accomplish their purpose result from the development of a pool of items and the constant revision of those items based on feedback. This process improves the validity and reliability of the instrument. Tests provide a valuable instructional aid because they help determine student progress and provide feedback to teachers about their own effectiveness. The tests reveal misunderstanding and problems that can help the teacher recognize areas that need instructional development. This information also provides the basis for the remediation of students and the revision of teaching procedures. The construction, administration, and proper scoring of classroom tests are thus among the most important activities in teaching.

Essay Tests

There are advantages and disadvantages to essay tests. Advantages include the possibility for students to be creative in their answers, the opportunity for students to explain their responses, and the potential to test for higher-level thinking skills. Disadvantages of essay questions include the time students need to formulate meaningful responses and the time teachers need to evaluate the essays consistently. In addition, language difficulties can make essay tests extremely difficult for some students, including ELs. Consistency in evaluating essays can also be a problem for some teachers, but an outline of the acceptable answers—a scoring rubric—can help the issue. Teachers who write specific questions and know what they are looking for are more likely to be consistent in grading. Also, if there are several essay questions, the effective teacher grades all student responses to the first question, then moves on to all responses to the second, and so on.

Using Rubrics for Assessment

A rubric is a checklist with assigned point values. To create a rubric, a teacher uses the lesson objectives. Students should get an explanation of the rubric when they get their writing assignment so that they can use it as a guide while they work. The teacher then uses the rubric to evaluate the completed assignment. Rubrics help teachers provide clear, well-planned instructions and guidelines for activities and can decrease student frustration. When teachers model what they expect and state clear objectives or goals for each assignment, students perform better.

Scoring Compositions

Holistic scoring is used to evaluate the writing of students in Texas. The scoring of the whole writing sample is based on pre-established criteria contained in a rubric. The writing rubric used to score the performance on STAAR is based on four performance-level descriptors—masters grade level (4), meets grade level (3), approaches grade level (2), and does not meet grade level (1) (TEA, 2007–2020). Students need to score at level three or four to pass the test.

Assessing English Learners

The Texas English Language Proficiency Assessment System (TELPAS) is the Texas assessment instrument for English learners (ELs) (TEA, 2007–2020). This instrument was designed to comply with the accountability requirements of the federal Elementary and Secondary Education Act, now renamed the Every Student Succeeds Act (ESSA) of 2015 (USDE, n.d.).

This instrument assesses the progress of ELs in Grades K–12 in the four language domains: listening, speaking, reading, and writing. The federal legislation requires that all ELs be assessed yearly in all four language areas to document progress toward English language mastery. This includes students in special language programs (Bilingual/ESL), as well as those whose parents have declined bilingual and ESL services (TEA, 2021–2022). This test is also required for ELs with intellectual and adaptive behavior challenges served through the Special Education Program. A TELPAS Alternate examination is used for students in the special education program. Students begin taking TELPAS in Kindergarten and stop only when they are reclassified as fluent English speakers (TEA, 2021–2022).

For students in Grades K–1, TELPAS uses a holistic approach and classroom observations to assess the four language domains. In Grades 2–12, TELPAS uses a multiple-choice format to assess reading comprehension and uses holistically rated instruments based on classroom observations to assess listening, speaking, and writing.

The TEKS and the English Language Proficiency Standards

TELPAS is aligned with the K–12 Texas state curriculum and the English Language Proficiency Standards (ELPS) mandated by state and federal legislation (TAC Chapter 74.4). When instruction to ELs is delivered in English, the ELPS are implemented as part of an ongoing content area support for ELs. To implement this support, teachers delivering content instruction in English are required by state and federal law to add language proficiency objectives to their daily lesson plans (TAC Chapter 74.4). The implementation of the ELPS objectives requires content-area teachers to select the appropriate ELPS objective for the lesson so that ELs can develop the academic proficiency to benefit from instruction and master the state curriculum.

Diversity in the Classroom

Teachers need to understand and appreciate diversity in the school and the community. An instructor recognizes the prime importance of creating a classroom that accepts and celebrates the uniqueness of individuals. In such an environment, the teacher and the students view the race, ethnicity, religion, national origin, preferred learning modality, and gender of learners and the teacher as strengths that foster learning with and from each other. When teachers involve parents and resources from beyond the schoolhouse doors, there blossoms a greater sense of a learning environment where inclusion, diversity, acceptance, and a sense of belonging are valued and appreciated.

Sources

Adams, M.J. (1994). *Beginning to read: thinking and learning about print*. Boston: MIT Press.

Anderson, R.C.; Hiebert, E.H, Scott, J.A.; Wilkinson, I.A.G. (1985) *Becoming a Nation of Readers: The Report of the Commission on Reading*. Washington, DC. National Academy of Education.

Anderson, R.C., & Pearson, P.D. (1984). A schema-theoretic view of basic processes in reading. In P.D. Pearson, R. Barr, M.L. Kamil, & P. Mosenthal (Eds.), Handbook of reading research. White Plains, NY: Longman.

Atwell, N, (2015). *In the middle: A lifetime of learning about reading, writing, and adolescents.* Portsmouth, NH: Heinemann Educational Books

Beck, I., McKeown, M. & Kucan, L (2013). *Bringing words to life: Robust vocabulary instruction.* New York: The Gilford Press.

Bruner, J. (1985). The Role of Interaction Formats in Language Acquisition Language and Social Situations. https://link.springer.com/chapter/10.1007/978-1-4612-5074-6_2

Calkins, L. (1994). *The Art of Teaching Writing,* 2nd ed. Portsmouth, NH: Heinemann.

Cambourne, Brian (1995). Toward an educationally relevant theory of literacy learning: Twenty years of inquiry. *The Reading Teacher,* Vol. 49, No. 3.

Cullinan, B. (2000). Independent reading and school achievement. *School Library Media Research,* 3, 1–24.

Chard, D.J., & Osborn, J. (1998). *Suggestions for examining phonics and decoding instruction in supplementary reading programs.* Austin, TX: Texas Education Agency.

Durkin, D. (1978–79). What classroom observations reveal about reading comprehension instruction. Reading Research Quarterly, 14, 481–533.

Ehri, L.C., Dreyer, L.G., Flugman, B., & Gross, A. (2007). Reading Rescue: An effective tutoring intervention model for language minority students who are struggling readers in first grade. *American Educational Research Journal,* 44(2), 414–448.

Fisher, D., & Frey, N. (2013). *Better learning through structured teaching: A framework for the gradual release of responsibility.* ASCD.

Fountas, I.C., & Pinnell, G.S. (1996). *Guided reading: Good first teaching for all children.* Portsmouth, NH: Heinemann.

Freeman, D. & Freeman, Y. (2008). *Academic language for struggling readers and English language learners.* Portsmouth, NH: Heinemann.

Graves, D.H. (1983). *Writing: Teachers and children at work.* Portsmouth, NH: Heinemann Educational Books.

Graves, D. (1994). *A Fresh Look at Writing.* Portsmouth, NH: Heinemann.

Halliday, M.A.K. (1973). *Explorations in the Functions of Language.* Amersterdam, Netherlands: Elsevier Science Publisher.

Hasbrouck, J. & Tindal, G. (2017). *An update to compiled ORF norms* (Technical Report No. 1702). Eugene, OR: Behavioral Research and Teaching, University of Oregon.

Hiebert, E.H. & Reutzel, D.R.(Eds.) (2010). *Revisiting silent reading: New directions for teachers and researchers.* Newark, DE: International Reading Association.

Kelley, M.J., & Clausen-Grace, N. (2008). From picture walk to text feature walk: Guiding students to strategically preview informational text. *Journal of Content Area Reading*, 7(1), 9–31.

Kibby, M.W. (1995). The organization and teaching of things and the words that signify them. *Journal of Adolescent & Adult Literacy*, 39(3), 208–233.

Krashen, S.D. (1989). We acquire vocabulary and spelling by reading: Additional evidence for the Input Hypothesis. *Modern Language Journal 73*, 440–64.

LaBerge, D., & Samuels, S.J. (1974). Toward a theory of automatic information processing in reading. *Cognitive Psychology*, 6, 293–323.

Lesaux, N.K. & Geva, E. (2006). Synthesis: Development of literacy in language minority learners. In D.L. August & T. Shanahan (Eds.) *Developing Literacy in a second language: Report of the National Literacy Panel*. (pp. 53–74). Mahwah, NJ: Lawrence Erlbaum Associates, (2006).

Lindfors, J.W. (1987). *Children's Language and Learning. Englewood Cliffs*, NJ: Prentice-Hall.

Meyer, B.J.F., Middlemiss, W., Theodorou, E., S., Brezinski, K.L., McDougall, J., & Bartlett, B.J. (2002). Older adults tutoring fifth-grade children in the structure strategy via the internet. *Journal of Educational Psychology*, 94 (3), 486–519.

Moats, L. (2020). *Teaching Reading is Rocket Science: What Expert Teachers of Reading Should Know*. Washington, DC: American Federation of Teachers.

Moss, B. & Young, T.A. (2010). *Creating lifelong readers through independent reading*. International Reading Association.

Nagy, W.E., & Scott, J.A. (2004). Vocabulary processes. In R.B. Ruddell & N.J. Unrau (Eds.), *Theoretical models and processes of reading* (5th ed., pp. 574–593). Newark, DE: International Reading Association.

National Center for Education Statistics (2019). *The Nation's Report Card: NAEP Reading Assessments*. Institute of Education Sciences, U.S. Department of Education, Washington, DC.

National Reading Panel. (2000, April). *Report of the National Reading Panel: Teaching children to read*. Washington, DC: National Institute of Child Health and Human Development, National Institutes of Health, U.S. Department of Health and Human Services.

National Reading Panel. (April, 2000). *Report of the National Reading Panel. Teaching Children to Read: An Evidence-Based Assessment of the Scientific Research Literature on Reading and Its Implications for Reading Instruction. National Institute of Child Health and Human Development*.

Palincsar, A.S., & Brown, A.L. (1984). Reciprocal teaching of comprehension-fostering and monitoring activities. *Cognition and Instruction*, 1, 117–175.

Pearson, P.D., & Dole, J.A. (1987). Explicit comprehension instruction: A review of research and a new conceptualization of instruction. *Elementary School Journal*, 88, 151–165.

Pearson, P.D., & Fielding, L. (1991). Comprehension instruction. In R. Barr, M.L. Kamil, P.B. Mosenthal, & P.D. Pearson (Eds.), *Handbook of reading research: Volume II* (pp. 815–860). White Plains, NY: Longman.

Peregoy, S.F., O.F. Boyle, & Cadiero-Kapplan, K. (2008). *Reading, writing and learning in ESL: A Resource Book for K–12 Teachers* (5th ed.). New York: Pearson.

Pikulski, J.J., & Chard, D.J. (2005). Fluency: Bridge Between Decoding and Reading Comprehension. *The Reading Teacher*, 58, 510–5.

Pressley, M. (2000). What should comprehension instruction be the instruction of? In M.L. Kamil, P.B. Mosenthal, P.D. Pearson, & R. Barr (Eds.), *Handbook of reading research: Volume III* (pp. 545–561). Mahwah NJ: Erlbaum.

Rasinkski, T., & Padak, N. (1996). *Holistic reading strategies: Teaching children who find reading difficult*. Englewood Cliffs, NJ: Merrill/Prentice Hall.

Rosenblatt, L.M. (1978). The reader, the text, the poem: The transactional theory of the literary work. Carbondale, IL: Southern Illinois University Press.

Roskos Kathleen, Neuman Susan B. (2014). Best Practices in Reading: A 21st Century Skill Update. *The Reading Teacher*, 67(7), 507–511.

Rupley, W.H., Logan, J.W., & Nichols, W.D. (1998). Vocabulary instruction in a balanced reading program. *The Reading Teacher*, 52(4), 336–346.

Snow, C.E., Burns, M.S., & Griffin, P. (1998). *Preventing reading difficulties in young children*. Washington, DC: National Academy Press.

Stahl, K.A.D. (2004). Proof, practice, and promise: Comprehension strategy instruction in the primary grades. *The Reading Teacher*, 57(7), 598–609.

Stauffer, R.G. (1969). Directing reading maturity as a cognitive process. New York: Harper & Row.

Wysocki, A.F., Johnson-Eilola, J., Selfe, L., & Sirc, G. (2004). Writing new media: Theory and applications for expanding the teaching of composition. Logan, UT: Utah State University Press.

Subject Test II: Mathematics (902)

COMPETENCY 001: MATHEMATICS INSTRUCTION

The teacher understands how students learn mathematical skills and uses that knowledge to plan, organize, and implement instruction and assess learning.

In 2000, the National Council of Teachers of Mathematics (NCTM) published the *Principles and Standards for School Mathematics*. The national organization's goals include the development and improvement of mathematics education. In the NCTM publication, the association identified six principles and ten standards that children in Kindergarten through Grade 12 should be able to master. The document guides states and district curricula development and specifies the mathematics content knowledge students should develop.

Principles of Mathematics

The NCTM (2000) identified six principles that should guide mathematics instruction. These include equity, curriculum, teaching, learning, assessment, and technology.

- **Equity**—Excellence in mathematics education requires equity: high expectations and strong support for all students.

- **Curriculum**—A curriculum must be coherent, focused on important and well-articulated mathematics concepts across the grades.

- **Teaching**—Effective mathematics teaching requires understanding what students know and need to learn while challenging and supporting students to learn it well.

- **Learning**—Students must learn mathematics with understanding, actively building new knowledge from experience and previous knowledge.

☞ To focus your study, go online to take the diagnostic test for this subject at *www.rea.com/studycenter*.

- **Assessment**—Assessment should support the learning of important mathematics concepts, and furnish useful information to both teachers and students.

- **Technology**—Technology is essential in teaching and learning mathematics; it influences the teaching of mathematics while enhancing and facilitating students' learning.

Mathematics and English Learners

Contrary to popular belief, mathematics is not a universal language. It is a language with special nomenclature and unique concepts. Even the way that people perform mathematical processes is often different across cultures. For example, the processes used for division in Mexico and the Dominican Republic differ from the process used in the United States. In Mexico, the problem is set up in a similar fashion but most of the steps are done mentally, as opposed to the American way in which students write every step as part of the process. As an example, for the problem "11 divided by 2," children in Mexico are taught to multiply 2 by 5 to obtain 10, but they do not write the 10 under the 11—they do it mentally and write the remainder below the 11. In the Dominican Republic, children do not use the division bracket traditionally used in the United States and Mexico; instead, they use a bracket similar to an elongated **L**, and they place the **divisor** inside the bracket and the **dividend** outside. Thus, children from Mexico and the Dominican Republic might experience confusion when asked to perform division "the American way."

Table 4-1 illustrates three different processes used to perform division.

Table 4-1. Division in Three Cultures

American	Mexican	Dominican Republic
$\begin{array}{r} 5 \\ 2\overline{)11} \\ -10 \\ \hline 1R \end{array}$	$\begin{array}{r} 5 \\ 2\overline{)11} \\ 1R \end{array}$	$\begin{array}{l} 11\ \underline{\lvert 5} \\ -10\ \ 2 \\ 1R\ \ \ 0 \end{array}$

The use of Arabic numbers does not present problems for English learners (ELs). The real challenge is to comprehend the **explanation** of the process in a language that ELs have not yet mastered. Providing examples of the mathematical process and modeling while describing the process can definitely improve comprehension. Students who enjoy **inductive teaching**—learning through examples—will definitely benefit from this approach. However, students who enjoy the **deductive approach**—learning step by step—might experience comprehension problems.

The Nomenclature of Mathematics

In addition to the obvious English communication problems, ELs face a number of challenges with the technical vocabulary or the nomenclature of mathematics for at least three reasons. First, the mathematics classroom tends to abound in assumptions concerning students' prior knowledge of specialized terms, such as **denominator**, **subtraction**, **minuend**, **divisor**, and **subtrahend**, among others. Second, the terms having one meaning in one subject domain can take on an entirely different meaning in the vocabulary of mathematics; these terms include **quarter**, **column**, **product**, **rational**, **even**, and **table**. Third, the vocabulary tends to encompass a variety of homophones (words pronounced the same way but having different meanings), which can be troublesome for English learners who are unaccustomed to the new language. **Table 4-2** lists various mathematics terms, and **Table 4-3** presents unfamiliar structures that may be confusing for all students.

Table 4-2. Terminology of Mathematics

Terminology	Generic Meaning	Mathematical Meaning
Even	Equal amount, same level	Numbers divisible by 2 yielding no remainder
Face	Front of human head	Surface of a geometric solid
Plane	Flat surface, aircraft, or without adornment (plain)	A two-dimensional surface
Mean	Not nice, or to express a particular message	Arithmetic average of a set of values
Right	Correct, proper, or a direction	Forming a 90° angle
Some/Sum	A small amount (some)	Answer to addition problem
Volume	Loudness of sounds	Quantity of liquid

Table 4-3. Unfamiliar Structures

Technical terms (e.g., equation, exponents, inequalities, quotient)
Varied degrees of focus on problem solving versus computation and notation
Use of passive voice for most problem-solving questions and statements
Use of various mathematical symbols unfamiliar to ELs (e.g., π, \$, $<$, $=$, $\pm$, and $\neq$)
Multiple words or phrases indicating the same operations (e.g., fractional parts, divide, separate, equivalent parts, etc.)
Unclear "if . . . then . . ." problem statements
Specific examples in word problems drawn from culturally unfamiliar situations
Focus on problem solving using cultural bias strategies or context unfamiliar to ELs
Multiple words with similar meanings (e.g., sum, total)
New information that does not fit with prior knowledge of subject matter (e.g., time, temperature, money, measurement, use of manipulatives in the classroom)

Developmentally Appropriate Instruction

Children develop a basic understanding of numbers at two years of age or even younger. Infants and toddlers understand the concepts of "one" or "more," usually within the context of food. Rote counting, or the verbal repetition of numbers, begins around the age of two to three years. This rote memorization can be used as a foundation for building an understanding of the number concepts of combining, separating, and naming amounts using concrete objects as soon as language develops. In their effort to develop the idea of amount, children must first know the language of number words (Fuson & Hall, 1983). Sometimes children appear to be counting when, in fact, they are naming the objects. For example, when a child has eight red blocks and begins to count out loud, "One, two, three, four, five, six, seven, eight," pointing to each block as he/she goes, and then says, "Eight," we need to ask questions. "How do you know?" or "Can you show me eight?" will tell us whether the child recognizes that the entire set makes up "eight" or that the last block is named "Eight." They need to understand that the idea of amount is inclusive of all the previously counted blocks, not just the name of the last block.

Children should be encouraged to think about numbers and the quantity of objects in meaningful situations. For example, children may be asked to hold up five crayons or hand out five crayons to each student. Kamii (2000) states that, to deepen quantification knowledge, students should compare sets in real-life situations rather than just counting out objects. It is important for children to use movable objects, moving to larger quantities, in order to create their own internal mental relationships while interacting with various types of objects (Pepper & Hunting, 1998).

In making the move from quantification to computation, it is helpful to pose an addition question by using concrete objects. Using a context for the objects helps children make their own sense and helps them to develop their own autonomy about the operation of addition. For example, a simple addition problem can be introduced by putting beads on a string and asking children to add or subtract the various colors to create a necklace or bracelet. Many times children will prefer to "use paper and pencil" instead of objects, so they can externalize their own ideas and use drawings instead. This is probably why children do not choose to use counters to solve word problems (Kamii, 2000).

Several materials or concrete objects can be used to help children demonstrate the mathematics of the problems. It is important to distinguish between **discrete models** (e.g., counters) and **continuous models** (e.g., number lines that children might choose for solving problems). Personal algorithms can grow directly from meaningful experiences acting out problems, whether through direct modeling or counting until the mathematics concepts make sense to the child.

Cognitive Development and Mathematics

The cognitive development of children in Pre-kindergarten (Pre-K) through Grade 6 represents a special challenge when attempting to learn the symbolic and abstract representation used in mathematics. Children are expected to learn an entire organized discipline, usually represented in symbolic form. They may learn to deal with symbols well enough to perform arithmetic operations. However, having learned arithmetic procedures is not sufficient for real understanding of the concepts that symbolic manipulations represent. There is no guarantee that children will be able to use those concepts to solve problems.

Learning mathematics requires children to create and recreate mathematics relationships in their own minds. Children need direct and concrete interaction with mathematical ideas; these ideas are not accessible from abstractions and symbols. Continuous interaction between a child's mind and concrete experiences in the real world are necessary to learn concepts in math.

As a developmental biologist, **Jean Piaget** (1896–1980) observed and recorded the intellectual abilities of infants, children, and adolescents. His stages of intellectual development were related to brain growth and led him to conclude that the thinking and reasoning of children were dominated by preoperational thought—a pattern of thinking that is egocentric, centered, irreversible, and nontransformational (Piaget & Inhelder, 1969). His theory concerned the growth of intelligence, the emergence and acquisition of schemata, or schemes of a child using "developmental stages," to explain how children acquire new information. Piaget divided the schemes children use into four main stages:

- Sensorimotor stage (birth–2 years)

- Preoperational stage (years 2–7)

- Concrete Operational stage (years 7–11)

- Formal Operational stage (years 11–adult)

The importance of these stages of development as conceptualized by Piaget is the recognition of the child's ability to integrate symbolic referents (objects or experiences) and to interpret the mathematical concept. Children around six years old (first graders in the Preoperational stage) tend to fix their attention on a single aspect of a relationship. For example, if two rows of the same number of coins are lined up, one-to-one, equally spaced, and children are asked whether the number of coins in the two rows are the same, they are likely to judge the two to be equal. When the appearance of one of the rows is changed, either by spreading the coins out farther or stacking them, children are more likely to judge them as being unequal. Their response is not based on logical reasoning but on their own perception.

According to Piaget, the **Preoperational stage** of development includes the processes of symbolic functioning, centration, intuitive thought, egocentrism, and inability to conserve. Children in the **Concrete Operational stage** exhibit the developmental processes of decentering, reversibility, conservation, serialization, classification, and elimination of egocentrism. The **Formal Operational stage** of cognitive development begins around eleven years of age (puberty) and continues into adulthood. The characteristics of this stage focus on the ability to use symbols and think abstractly.

Sperry Smith (2008) reports that children in the Preoperational stage experience problems with at least two perceptual concepts—centration and conservation.

- **Centration**—Focusing on only one aspect of a situation or problem. For example, let's say we take two 5″ × 8″ cards and roll each into a tube, rolling one the short way and the other the long way. We then tape them to make cylindrical containers, and fill each tube with beans to compare how much each holds. When presented with the two cylinders, a preschool child might judge the quantity of beans in the tall cylinder to be more than the shorter, based on his or her perception of tall and short as opposed to the actual volume of the container.

- **Conservation**—Understanding that quantity, length, or number of items is unrelated to the arrangement or appearance of the object or items. This limitation can affect children's ability to measure volume and to understand the value of money. For example, children may think a nickel is worth more than a dime because the coin is larger, or that five nickels are more than a quarter.

During the Concrete Operational stage of cognitive development (Grades 2 to 7) children experience rapid growth in cognitive development. This stage is characterized by the ability to think logically about concrete objects or relationships. Some of the characteristics of children at this stage are as follows:

- **Decentering**—The child can take into account multiple aspects of a problem to solve it; the child can form a conclusion based on reason rather than perception.

- **Reversibility**—The child understands that the objects can be changed and then returned to their original state; the child can determine that $4 + 4 = 8$ and $8 - 4 = 4$, the original quantity.

- **Conservation**—The child understands that quantity, length, or number of items is unrelated to the arrangement or appearance of the object; the child can discern that if water is transferred from a filled cup to a pitcher, it will conserve the quantity and be equal to the original filled cup.

- **Serialization**—The child is able to arrange objects in an order according to size, shape, or any other attribute; the child can arrange geometric forms by shape, size, color, and thickness of the form.

- **Classification**—The child can name and identify sets of objects according to appearance, size, or other characteristics; the child can arrange objects based on characteristics.

- **Elimination of Egocentrism**—The child is able to view things from another's perspective; the child can retell a story from another child's perspective.

Since Piaget completed his work, contemporary researchers (often referred to as neo-Piagetian and post-Piagetian researchers) found that Piaget had underestimated the abilities of children in the preschool and early elementary years. Even before the second or early third grade, some students develop more sophisticated thinking and reasoning skills, especially if they have had adequate instruction and opportunities to interact with adults and competent peers (Vygotsky, 1986). Children's intellectual development appears to proceed continuously, and their cognitive development is influenced by their culture and by instruction (Santrock, 2003). This relates to cognitively guided instruction (CGI) (Carpenter, Fennema, Franke, Levi & Empson, 1999; Flavell, 1985; Kamii, 2000). The CGI model depends heavily on a well-developed structure of how children learn a given topic and on the ability of the teacher to assess the knowledge of each child and provide appropriate experiences. Kamii's work and CGI's researchers connect their respective research to understanding how children learn mathematics concepts and how to recognize different strategies young children use when they execute operations.

Mathematics in Real-Life Situations

Mathematical concepts are an integral part of our daily life. Children should be encouraged to pay attention to daily activities and identify the mathematical principles used to perform the activity or the task. A simple visit to the local supermarket requires some level of mathematical development to communicate effectively. For instance, reading product labels requires an understanding of weights and measurements. It also requires knowledge of the standard and metric systems and the value of money. Without this kind of knowledge, it would be practically impossible to make product comparisons.

Consider the following situation:

A consumer is trying to decide between two products—a kilogram of coffee for $3.99 or 2 pounds of the same coffee for $3.99. What item represents the best value?

In order to make this decision, the consumer must have an understanding of the **standard** and **metric** systems of measurement. Most consumers in the United States will probably go with 2 pounds because they are familiar with the **standard** system of measurement. However, this option is not the best value for the money because 1 kilogram is equivalent to 2.2 pounds. Parents can present this kind of problem to children and ask them to help in the decision-making process. When mathematics is used in real-life situations, it becomes more meaningful and easier to internalize.

As seen in this example, it is important for children to learn to use mathematical principles to assist with their day-to-day lives. As children reach adulthood, they should already understand some basic real-life situations and meanings, such as the purpose of banks, different taxes and to what they apply, and how to use credit responsibly. One method of teaching the students these topics is to allow them to balance a budget for a family. They would understand the cost of groceries, bills for a home, and how much money it takes to raise children.

Manipulatives in Mathematics

Children can benefit from group instruction and the use of concrete objects and manipulatives. Manipulatives can be used to provide "hands-on-learning" for Kindergarten to high school students. Manipulatives enhance student understanding, enable students to have conversations that are grounded in a common model, and help students to recognize and correct any misconceptions they may have.

Manipulatives also are an excellent way for students to develop self-verbalizing learning strategies. As they use the senses of sight, touch, and hearing, students should be encouraged to talk their way through each problem, either with peers or to themselves. Physical materials can model the situation and illuminate some of the aspects of the processes of various operations, such as multiplication and division. It is important that the concept is understood by the student and that the manipulative is appropriate for the concept so the materials can be used in ways that make sense. It is important that students first develop relationships that are mental abstractions about the mathematics being represented by the physical materials and then develop a corresponding symbolic representation. Teachers have to ask appropriate questions and listen to students explain their thinking to know whether they have abstracted the idea from the physical models.

In addition to the manipulatives used in mathematics, the typical classroom contains a variety of instructional materials to support children in the learning process (see **Table 4-4**). Teachers should be encouraged to use these aids to make mathematics more engaging and meaningful to children.

Games are highly motivational for children in Pre-K through Grade 6. A simple game using dice can be used to teach counting, place value, probability, and fractions. Color tiles, unifix cubes, two-color counters, and pattern blocks can be used to teach sequencing, patterns, odd and even numbers, probability, and statistics. Children learn best when they can manipulate materials to check their understanding and link what they are learning to real-life situations. In fact, they learn about fractions initially outside the school. For example, children often hear adults use fractions in various conversations : "You can have half of my cookie." "My gas tank is half full." "The recipe calls for two-thirds of a cup of cereal."

**Table 4-4. Types of Manipulatives and Instructional Materials
Used in the Mathematics Classroom**

Grades K–1	Grade 2	Grade 3	Grade 4	Grade 5	Grade 6
Beads, string, sewing cards	Blocks	Base-ten blocks	Geometric Solids	Cuisenaire rods	Cuisenaire rods
Snap cubes, straws	Cubes	Tangrams	Geoboards	Virtual manipulatives	Virtual manipulatives
Color tiles	Chips	Pattern blocks	Calculators	Calculators	Calculators
Two-color counters	Measuring cups	Playing cards	Protractors	Graduated cylinders	Attribute logic blocks
Macaroni, beans, cereal, candy, raisins, crackers	Attribute shapes	Scales: customary and metric	Tangrams	Timers	Algebra tiles
	Money models	Magnetic numbers, chalk boards	Pentominoes	Metric beaker set for volume	Video games
Buttons, sticks, stones, shells	Number lines	Spinners, dice	Graphing paper	Metric trundle wheel	Math software games
	Dominoes		Fraction kit		iPods
Paper clips	Unifix cubes	Calendar	Platform scale	Fraction tower cubes	Balance metric weight set
Toothpicks	Clock faces	Fractional shapes	Customary weight set	Connecting cubes	Computer/ internet
Legos	Ruler, yard stick, metric stick	Games	Metric weight set	Board games	Smart boards
Egg cartons	Balance scales	Measuring tape	Graphing boards	Fraction tiles	Digital cameras, camcorders
Teddy bear counters	Linear graphs	0–99 charts	Scatter plot graphs	Geoboards	Computer templates
Board games		Bar graphs		Pie charts and graphs	
Pictographs					

Numbers and fractions represent a challenge to elementary students. A number of ideas about fractions take shape informally in children's minds from their experiences. They may have heard of one-half, one-fourth, and one-third of a unit—but not two-thirds or three-fourths. Therefore, their understanding may be incomplete and confused. Children think of "half" as any part of a whole, rather than one of two equal parts, and refer to one-half being larger than another. For example, they may say, "Your half is bigger than mine." Additionally, they may not understand relationships, such as three-fourths of an inch is one-fourth less than one inch. Classroom instruction should build on children's previous experiences and focus within the context of real life before moving to the symbolic representations. Fractions may be taught using fraction kits, where students cut and label the pieces to relate the fractional notation to the concrete pieces and compare the sizes of the fractional parts. They are able to see that $\frac{1}{4}$, for example, is larger than $\frac{1}{8}$, and they can measure to prove that two of the $\frac{1}{8}$ pieces are equivalent to $\frac{1}{4}$. **Table 4-5** presents an analysis of fractions.

Table 4-5. Equivalent Fractions

One Whole = $\frac{1}{1}$							
One-half = $\frac{1}{2}$				One-half = $\frac{1}{2}$			
One-fourth = $\frac{1}{4}$		One-fourth = $\frac{1}{4}$		One-fourth = $\frac{1}{4}$		One-fourth = $\frac{1}{4}$	
$\frac{1}{8}$	$\frac{1}{8}$	$\frac{1}{8}$	$\frac{1}{8}$	$\frac{1}{8}$	$\frac{1}{8}$	$\frac{1}{8}$	$\frac{1}{8}$
$\frac{1}{16}$ $\frac{1}{16}$	$\frac{1}{16}$ $\frac{1}{16}$	$\frac{1}{16}$ $\frac{1}{16}$	$\frac{1}{16}$ $\frac{1}{16}$	$\frac{1}{16}$ $\frac{1}{16}$	$\frac{1}{16}$ $\frac{1}{16}$	$\frac{1}{16}$ $\frac{1}{16}$	$\frac{1}{16}$ $\frac{1}{16}$

Use of Technology

As rapidly as technology is changing and improving, educators are challenged to keep up with those advances and learn how to use technology to improve instruction. Clearly, changes need to be made in how schools acquire access to these new advances. These changes must be equitably implemented so that students who live in poverty have the same access to technology and challenging mathematics as their affluent peers. The newest advancements in hand-held computers present educators with both opportunities and responsibilities. The primary opportunity is that of allowing access to challenging mathematics for every student, regardless of the student's past mastery of arithmetic or rote skills.

Digital videos provide opportunities for students to evaluate their own explanations of problem solutions. Students may present their videos and discuss similarities and differences in approaches to solving problems. These may be uploaded onto a website to allow for online discussions using discussion board tools, blogs, and various communication tools with other students. Students can develop effective presentations, online resources, wikis, and other projects for sharing with learners around the world. Additional digital presentation tools may help students to develop effective presentations that communicate mathematical ideas. Programs such as PowerPoint and HyperStudio allow students to integrate graphics, digital images and video, and text into their presentations.

Learning Environment

The *Professional Standards for Teaching Mathematics* (NCTM, 2007) presents standards for the teaching of mathematics, organized under four categories: tasks, discourse, environment, and analysis. These four strands are integrated and interdependent, and are crucial in shaping what goes on in mathematics classrooms.

- Tasks—the projects, questions, problems, constructions, applications, and exercises in which students engage

- Discourse—the manner of representing, thinking, talking, agreeing, and disagreeing that teachers and students use to engage in these tasks

- Environment—the setting for learning

- Analysis—the systematic reflection in which teachers engage

The mathematics teacher should create a learning environment that fosters the development of each student's mathematical ability by doing the following:

- Providing and structuring the time necessary to explore sound mathematics and grapple with significant ideas and problems

- Using the physical space and materials in ways that facilitate learning mathematics

- Providing a context that encourages the development of mathematical skill and proficiency

- Respecting and valuing students' ideas, ways of thinking, and mathematical dispositions

Included in the *Professional Standards for Teaching Mathematics* are five major shifts in the environment of mathematics classrooms from current practice to teaching for the empowerment of students. These major shift areas include:

- Treating classrooms as mathematical communities rather than simply a collection of individuals

- Students using logic and mathematical evidence as verification rather than students relying solely on the teacher for correct answers

- Students employing mathematical reasoning rather than merely memorizing procedures

- Emphasizing problem solving rather than an emphasis on mechanistic answer-finding

- Students connecting mathematics, its ideas, and its applications rather than viewing mathematics as a body of isolated concepts and procedures

The Texas Essential Knowledge and Skills

The Texas Essential Knowledge and Skills (TEKS) is the state's required curriculum. The implementation of TEKS for mathematics requires a well-balanced curriculum beginning in Kindergarten and continuing through Grade 12. (See: 19 TAC Chapter 111. Texas Essential Knowledge and Skills for Mathematics.)

Pre-kindergarten content has been aligned with the TEKS and may be found in the Texas Education Agency's Pre-kindergarten Curriculum Guidelines (2015) at *http://tea.texas.gov*.

Both the TEKS and the Pre-K Curriculum Guidelines incorporate the NCTM principles and standards, which provide early experiences and exploration of number concepts using concrete objects to learn about one-to-one correspondence. In the first and second grades, students continue exploring number concepts and begin learning basic computation skills. In the third through fifth grades, they continue developing number concepts to include multiplication, division, fraction and decimal representations, geometric principles, and algebraic reasoning. **Table 4-6** presents the focal points from Pre-K through Grade 6.

Table 4-6. Mathematics Curriculum: Number Concepts Strand for Pre-K through Grade 6

Grade Level	Numbers and Operations
Pre-K	1. Explores concrete models and materials; begins to arrange sets of concrete objects in one-to-one correspondence; counts to 10 or higher by ones, by fives or higher; combines, separates, and names "how many" concrete objects. 2. Begins to recognize and can describe the concept of zero (meaning there are none); identifying first and last in a series; compares numbers of concrete objects by using language (e.g., "same" or "equal," "one more," "more than," or "less than").
Kindergarten	1. Uses whole number concepts to describe how many objects are in a set (through 20) by using verbal and symbolic descriptions; uses sets of concrete objects to represent quantities given in verbal or written form (through 20); uses one-to-one correspondence and language such as "more than," "same number as," or "two less than" to describe relative sizes of sets of concrete objects; names the ordinal positions in a sequence, such as first, second, third, etc. 2. Begins to demonstrate the concepts of "part of" and "whole" with real objects. 3. Sorts to explore numbers; uses patterns; and is able to model and create addition and subtraction problems in real situations with concrete objects.

Grade Level	Numbers and Operations
First Grade	1. Has the ability to create sets of tens and ones using concrete objects to describe, compare, and order whole numbers; reads and writes numbers to 99 to describe sets of concrete objects; compares and orders whole numbers up to 99 (e.g., "less than," "greater than," or "equal to") by using sets of concrete objects and pictorial models. 2. Separates a whole into two, three, or four equal parts and uses appropriate language to describe the parts, such as "three out of four equal parts." 3. Models and creates addition and subtraction problem situations with concrete objects and writes corresponding number sentences. 4. Identifies individual coins by name and value and describes relationships among them.
Second Grade	1. Uses concrete models of hundreds, tens, and ones to represent a given whole number (up to 999) in various ways; begins to use place value to read, write, and describe the value of whole numbers to 999; uses models to compare and order whole numbers to 999; records comparisons using numbers and symbols ($<$, $=$, $>$). 2. Uses concrete models to represent and name fractional parts of a whole object (with denominators of 12 or less). 3. Models addition and subtraction of two-digit numbers with objects, pictures, words, and numbers; solves problems with and without regrouping; is able to recall and apply basic addition and subtraction facts (to 18). 4. Determines the value of a collection of coins up to one dollar; describes how the cent symbol, dollar symbol, and decimal point are used to name the value of a collection of coins.
Third Grade	1. Uses place value to read, write (in symbols and words), and describe the value of whole numbers; compares and orders whole numbers through 9,999. 2. Uses fraction names and symbols to describe fractional parts of whole objects or sets of objects; compares fractional parts of whole objects or sets of objects in a problem situation using concrete models 3. Selects and uses addition or subtraction to solve problems involving whole numbers through 999; uses problem-solving strategies; is able to use rounding and compatible numbers to estimate solutions to addition and subtraction problems. 4. Applies multiplication facts through 12 by using concrete models and objects (up to two digits times one digit); uses models to solve division problems; uses number sentences to record solutions; identifies patterns in related multiplication and division sentences (fact families).

(continued)

Grade Level	Numbers and Operations
Fourth Grade	1. Uses place value to read, write, compare, and order whole numbers through 999,999,999 and decimals involving tenths and hundredths, including money, using concrete objects and pictorial models. 2. Uses concrete objects and pictorial models to generate equivalent fractions. 3. Uses multiplication to solve problems (no more than two digits times two digits); uses division to solve problems (no more than one-digit divisors and three-digit dividends). 4. Uses strategies, including rounding and compatible numbers, to estimate solutions to addition, subtraction, multiplication, and division problems.
Fifth Grade	1. Uses place value to read, write, compare, and order whole numbers through 999,999,999,999 and decimals through the thousandths place. 2. Identifies common factors of a set of whole numbers; uses multiplication to solve problems involving whole numbers (no more than three digits times two digits); uses division to solve problems involving whole numbers (no more than two-digit divisors and three-digit dividends), including solutions with a remainder.
Sixth Grade	1. Compares and orders nonnegative rational numbers; generates equivalent forms of rational numbers, including whole numbers, fractions, and decimals; uses integers to represent real-life situations. 2. Is able to write prime factorizations using exponents; identifies factors of a positive integer, common factors, and the greatest common factor of a set of positive integers.

Analysis of Teaching and Learning

The teacher of mathematics should engage in ongoing analysis of teaching and learning by doing the following:

- observing, listening to, and gathering other information about students to assess what they are learning

- examining the effects of the task, discourse, and learning environment on students' mathematical knowledge, skills, and dispositions in order to ensure that every student is learning sound and significant mathematics and is developing a positive disposition toward mathematics

- challenging and extending students' ideas

- adapting or changing activities while teaching

- making both short- and long-range plans

- describing and commenting on each student's learning to parents and administrators as well as to the students themselves

Making Connections with the Real World

The U.S. Department of Labor (2012) developed a list of the top professions that require a strong knowledge of mathematics. Some of the most prominent jobs are as accountants and auditors, computer programmers, computer scientists, computer engineers and system analysts, economists and marketing research analysts, managers, mathematicians, operations research analysts, statisticians, and financial planners.

The preceding list of professions is useful for emphasizing the importance of mathematics in our lives; however, most children in early childhood might not be aware of, and cannot relate to, these kinds of jobs. The best way to link mathematics to real jobs or activities is to guide students to develop a list of jobs available in their community. For example, a unit about community helpers will yield a large list of occupations, such as nurses, physicians, sanitary workers, home builders, landscapers, plumbers, carpenters, and tile installers. Teachers can assign readings about these professions and invite community sources to describe and demonstrate how they use mathematics in their profession. The interactive and concrete approach can easily present the need for mathematics in our daily lives.

One of the key challenges in promoting interest in mathematics is to convince children that mathematics plays an important role in their lives. Based on this assumption, teachers need to introduce mathematics concepts in a problem-solving format using real-life situations. Some examples for Pre-K through Grade 6 are the following:

- Purchase inexpensive items at the dollar store and set up a "classroom store" where the students can purchase items using play money. Children can earn play money as part of the classroom management program, which can reward students with play money for good behavior.

- Organize cooking activities at home or in school using recipes requiring specific units of measurement; this activity can also be linked to science, particularly to chemistry.

- Guide students to identify the most appropriate measuring system to compute the size of objects and the area of spaces in the classroom or school.

- Plan a field trip for which students have to estimate the cost of the trip. Children have to use computation skills to determine the cost of the activity.

- Plan a road trip app like Mapquest to calculate distances between places and then use distance to calculate travel time and gas expenses based on mileage.

- Create tables or graphs of the expenses versus travel time to estimate costs associated with taking shorter or longer trips based on the average daily costs from the previous examples.

Thematic Instruction

Thematic instruction is the organization of curriculum content based on themes or topics. Thematic instruction integrates basic disciplines (e.g., reading, math, music, art, and science) with the exploration of broad subjects, such as *American Indians*, *Six Flags over Texas*, *state symbols*, *river systems in Texas*, *the rain forest*, *recycling resources*, and so on. The selection of the theme can be done school-wide, by grade, or by individual teacher.

Thematic planning provides opportunities for the students to hear similar information in various instructional segments and from a variety of sources. Additionally, it allows opportunities for students to apply cognitive processes and creativity through content-area instruction based on real-life situations.

Planning and Organizing Thematic Units

Teachers must consider several important elements when planning and organizing thematic units. The basic steps are selecting the theme, designing the integrated curriculum, gathering materials for the unit, and arranging thematic activities (Fredericks, Blake-Kline, and Kristo, 1997).

Selecting the Theme

Identify a theme, taking into account its interest to children, the relevance of the topic, and the connection to the state curriculum. The theme should be broad enough to allow the integration of content areas. For example, a topic such as "our solar system" is broad enough to cover every content area in the curriculum. However, the topic of "goldfish" might be too limited in scope to allow the easy integration of subjects.

Designing the Integrated Curriculum

The state curriculum (TEKS) should be the guiding force in the organization of the integrated curriculum. Once this connection is established, teachers must identify the main principles or generalizations about the theme. Using these generalizations, teachers need to identify the key objectives to involve each content area and the materials needed to implement instruction.

Thematic instruction minimizes the artificial boundaries created through traditional course scheduling. The fixed course scheduling for the content areas can now be combined into larger segments where multiple content areas are delivered in an integrated manner. When designing instruction for children in the early grades, teachers must take into account the developmental characteristics of the children to keep them focused and engaged.

Gathering Materials for the Unit

Gathering materials for the unit can be challenging for first-year teachers. They should request input from veteran teachers and from the school librarian. Some of the key considerations when selecting materials are as follows:

- The materials should focus on the same set of generalizations and principles in each of the content areas.

- Materials should include narratives, expositions, drama, poems, and a variety of materials and resource books, magazines, newspapers, movies, internet materials, videotapes, and audiotapes.

- Materials should also represent a range of thinking abilities and literacy development, including materials written in a language other than English.

- Materials should represent the home as well as the school culture and language of the students.

Arranging Thematic Activities

Traditionally, thematic units are organized into three main segments—introduction to the unit, presentation of the content, and a closing activity. The opening activity is designed to motivate children and to get them interested in the theme. Children are exposed to the goals and the steps in the presentation of the theme. The presentation of the content is done through various coordinated lessons and activities. The closing activity is designed to review and pull together the concepts learned and to celebrate the mastery of the content.

Types of Questioning Strategies

Clearly, all teachers should use open questions that do not have simple yes/no answers. Questions should focus students' thinking, require them to think critically, and help them to "clarify or justify their ideas orally and in writing." Good questions "elicit language and challenge each student's thinking" (NCTM, 2000, p. 35). Teachers need to model these questioning strategies. The NCTM Professional Standards propose five categories of questions that teachers should ask to elicit justification and reasoning, as shown in **Table 4-7**, along with sample questions.

Table 4-7. Questioning Strategies for Mathematics Discourse

Category 1—Questions that help students learn how to make learning math meaningful.

"Do you agree (disagree) with the correct answer?"

"Does anyone use a different strategy to get the correct answer? Explain it."

Category 2—Questions that help students to become self-reliant and determine whether something is mathematically correct.

"Does that make sense?"

"Tell me what makes this a reasonable solution to the task?"

Category 3—Questions that help students learn to reason mathematically. "What have you tried that has worked or not worked?"

"How could you explain this in your own words?"

Category 4—Questions that help students learn to solve problems. "What would happen if...?"

"What would happen if not . . . ?"

"What pattern do you see, and how would you explain your answer?"

Category 5—Questions that relate to helping students connect mathematics, its ideas, and its applications.

"Have we solved a problem that is similar to this one?"

"Can you write another problem like this one?"

Source: Adapted from Charles A. Dana Center, Mathematics TEKS Toolkit. UT-Austin. Available online at: http://www.utdanacenter.org/mathtoolkit/support/questioning.php

Using Formal and Informal Assessment

The State of Texas Assessments of Academic Readiness (STAAR) is the state assessment for reading, math, writing, science, and social studies. The STAAR test evaluates student learning based on the state-required curriculum, the Texas Essential Knowledge and Skills. STAAR is a "high-stakes" testing system that provides accountability for districts, schools, administrators, teachers, and students. By law, Texas students must pass the STAAR test to be promoted at certain grade levels and to graduate from high school.

COMPETENCY 002: NUMBER CONCEPTS AND OPERATIONS

The teacher understands concepts related to numbers, operations and algorithms, and the properties of numbers.

Number Concepts

One of the key challenges in mathematics education is the teaching of technical vocabulary and concepts. Teachers as well as students need to have an understanding of the key terms used in mathematics to communicate effectively in the classroom. A summary of key mathematical terms and concepts follows.

Integers

An **integer** is a whole number that includes all positive and negative numbers, including zero. This may be represented on a number line that extends in both directions from 1. You might have −45, −450,000, 0, 234, or 78,306. Integers do not include decimals or fractions. The members of the set {..., −6, −5, −4, −3, −2, −1, 0, 1, 2, 3, 4, 5, 6...} are all integers.

Many real-life situations are represented with integers.

Natural Numbers

A **natural number** is a positive integer or a nonnegative integer. There is a small difference because nonnegative integers also include "0." A list of positive integers would include whole numbers but not zero. Natural numbers include 1, 2, 3, 4, 5 ... ∞, where ∞ is the symbol for infinity. Natural numbers are all whole numbers. They do not include negative numbers, fractions, or decimals.

Rational Numbers

A number that can be expressed as a ratio or quotient of two nonzero integers is known as a **rational number**. Rational numbers can be expressed as common fractions or decimals, such as $\frac{3}{5}$ or 0.6. Finite decimals, repeating decimals, mixed numbers, and whole numbers are all rational numbers. Nonrepeating decimals cannot be expressed in this way, and are said to be irrational.

Irrational Numbers

An irrational number is a number that cannot be represented as an exact ratio of two integers. The decimal form of the number never terminates and never repeats. Examples include the square root of 2 ($\sqrt{2}$) and pi (π).

Real Numbers

A **real number** describes any number that is positive, negative, or zero and can be used to measure continuous quantities. A real number also includes numbers that have decimal representations, even those with infinite decimal sequences, such as π.

Place Value

Place values are the basic foundation for understanding mathematic computation. The simple number 1984 can be explained based on the positions of the numbers in the value scale. See the example in **Table 4-8**.

Table 4-8. Place Values

Thousand	Hundred	Ten	One
1000	900	80	4
1	9	8	4

Basic Operations and Their Algorithms

This section discusses some of the basic operations covered in the EC–6 curricula, as well as the algorithms for these operations. An **algorithm** is an established and well-defined step-by-step problem-solving method used to achieve a desired mathematical result.

Addition

Addition is the mathematical operation of combining two or more quantities into a sum. The quantity is often a number with one or more digits. The term **digit** in mathematics is a number symbol (e.g., 1, 2, or 3) used in numerals to represent numbers (these are real numbers or integers) in positional numeral systems. In addition of whole numbers, the key element is to align the numbers based on place value—ones, tens, hundreds, thousands, and so forth. Following the alignment, proceed to add beginning with the ones—in a right to left progression.

$$\begin{array}{r} 25 \\ + 32 \\ \hline 57 \end{array}$$

Step 1: Add the numbers in the ones place (5 + 2 = 7)

Step 2: Add the numbers in the tens place (2 + 3 = 5)

Subtraction

Subtraction is the process/operation of removing objects from a larger group, or finding parts of a whole. It is the opposite of addition. Subtraction is indicated by the minus sign (–). When a number (formally called a *subtrahend*) is subtracted from another number (formally called a *minu-*

end), the resulting number (the *difference*) is smaller than the minuend. As an example, see the following operation:

    25   minuend
    –20   subtrahend
    ───
    05   remainder or difference

Step 1: Beginning with the ones, subtract the bottom number from the top number.

Step 2: Subtract the tens by using the same process to get the result.

A typical subtraction problem would be: "From a group of 25 cars, 20 were sold. How many are left?" The child might know the operation but may not understand that the word "left" in the problem calls for subtraction. Teachers need to develop a list of key words linked to each of the four basic operations.

Like addition, subtraction is a process in which children must see their learning task as one of making sense of whatever they are studying. It is not appropriate to teach children how to do a procedure without teaching them how to reason. Students should not be expected to do things by rote or be made to say things they do not honestly understand.

Additionally, the complexity of the language can create problems for all children, especially for ELs. For example, some common phrases used in forming subtraction word problems include: (1) How many are left (or left over)? (2) How many more are needed? (3) How many less (or fewer)? (4) How many more than . . .? (5) How many would you have if half were subtracted? Words and phrases used for explaining subtraction include: *minus, take away, decrease, reduce, deduct, remove, less than,* and *how many do you need to take away to get* a certain number.

Children need to make sense of the procedure. The most obvious message to a child is that addition and subtraction require that you follow the "rules." Teaching "what to do" in mathematics is a widespread practice in the classroom. However, it is important to understand that just teaching procedures and teaching procedures in relation to their meaning are two very different approaches to teaching mathematics. When students do not have the broader understanding, they may lack the cognitive flexibility to deal with situations that may differ (even slightly) regarding the format of the problem or question from the particular situation learned. Have children describe their thinking processes and explain why their answers make sense. When children know the "why" of what they are doing, their understanding and skills can be applied more easily to new tasks.

Multiplication

Multiplication is a mathematical operation of combining groups of equal amounts. Multiplication may be described as repeated addition or the inverse of division (discussed next). Traditionally, multiplication requires students to learn the multiplication facts and develop computation facility. After learning all the "times tables," children learn to multiply with paper and pencil, first practicing with one-digit multipliers ($24 \times 5 =$) and progressing to two-digit and three-digit multipliers, and so on. Word problems provide a way for children to apply the concepts of multiplication in various situations. An example of the steps in the process is shown below.

$$
\begin{array}{r}
\overset{3}{9}5 \quad \text{factor} \\
\times 7 \quad \text{factor} \\
\hline
665 \quad \text{product}
\end{array}
$$

Step 1: Multiply $7 \times 5 = 35$.

Step 2: Since the number has more than one digit (i.e., 3 tens and 5 ones), place the 3 at the top of the tens column and the 5 in the ones column of the product.

Step 3: Multiply the digit in the tens place (9) by the factor (7) to get $7 \times 9 = 63$.

Step 4: Add the 63 to the 3 placed in the tens place; this equals 66.

Step 5: Place the 66 to the left of the ones column to obtain the final result of 665.

Teachers should link multiplication to real-world contexts. Having children explore with groups of objects helps them link the idea of multiplication as repeated addition. Children need to interact with the concept of multiplication pictorially by drawing sets of objects, symbolically by writing the multiplication sentences ($4 \times 6 = 24$), and verbally by reading the sentences (4 sets of 6 equals 24; 4 groups of 6 equals 24; 4 times 6 equals 24). Children need opportunities to see mathematics in their daily lives, not as existing in the classrooms or on the pages of their textbooks.

Division

Division is a mathematical operation involving two numbers that tells how many groups there are or how many are in each group. It may be thought of as the inverse of multiplication. The symbol for division is $\div$ or /. For example, $58 \div 8$ or $\dfrac{58}{8}$, which both can be set up in long division as

$$
\begin{array}{r}
7 \text{ R2} \\
8\overline{)58} \\
-56 \\
\hline
2
\end{array}
$$

Step 1: Place the **divisor** (number doing the dividing) outside the division bracket on the left-hand side and the **dividend** (number being divided) inside it.

Step 2: Examine the first digit of the dividend. If this is smaller than the divisor, then use the first two digits of the dividend.

Step 3: Identify how many times the divisor (8) can fit into the dividend (58).

Step 4: Place the result (7) on top of the 8 in 58.

Step 5: Multiply the quotient (7) by the divisor (8), which equals 56.

Step 6: Subtract the 56 from 58 to identify a possible remainder.

Step 7: Place the remainder (i.e., R2) in the **quotient** (answer).

Fractions

A **fraction** is a number that represents part of a whole, part of a set, or a quotient in the form $\frac{a}{b}$, which can be read as "a divided by b." The number above the fraction bar is called the numerator, and the number below the fraction bar is called the denominator.

Finding Equivalent Fractions, or Simplification of Fractions

To identify an equivalent fraction, follow these steps, using the example $\frac{2}{4}$.

   Step 1:   Find a number that can be divided evenly into the numerator and the denominator. For example, in the fraction $\frac{2}{4}$, the number 2 can be divided evenly into 2 and 4.

   Step 2:   Divide the numerator and denominator by 2 and get the result:. $\frac{2}{4} = \frac{1}{2}$.

Adding and Subtracting Homogeneous Fractions

When adding or subtracting fractions with the same denominator (**homogeneous** fractions), add or subtract the numerators and keep the denominator the same. For example,

$$\frac{2}{5} + \frac{1}{5} = \frac{3}{5} \qquad \frac{7}{9} - \frac{5}{9} = \frac{2}{9}$$

Changing Improper Fractions to Mixed Numbers

To change an improper fraction, such as $\frac{5}{2}$, to a mixed number (a number with a whole number part and a fractional part), divide the numerator by the denominator and represent the remainder as a fraction. For example:

$$\frac{5}{2} = \frac{4+1}{2} = \frac{2 \times 2 + 1}{2} = \frac{4}{2} + \frac{1}{2} = 2\frac{1}{2}$$

Adding and Subtracting Mixed Numbers

To add and subtract mixed numbers, follow the algorithm provided in the example below.

$$2\frac{5}{10} \qquad\qquad 7\frac{9}{12}$$
$$+1\frac{4}{10} \qquad\qquad -5\frac{4}{12}$$

$$3\frac{9}{10} \qquad 2\frac{5}{12}$$

Add or subtract the fractions, then add or subtract the whole numbers.

If necessary to complete the operation, change the top mixed number by "borrowing" from the whole number part. Reduce the whole number part by 1 and increase the fraction part by adding a fraction that is equivalent to 1. For example,

$$5\frac{2}{7} = 4\frac{2}{7} + \frac{7}{7} = 4\frac{9}{7}$$

Reduce = 5 to 4, add $\frac{7}{7}$ to $\frac{2}{7}$, then proceed as usual.

$$-3\frac{4}{7} = -3\frac{4}{7} = -3\frac{4}{7}$$

$$1\frac{5}{7}$$

Changing Mixed Numbers to Improper Fractions

To change a mixed number to an improper fraction (a fraction with the numerator greater than the denominator), multiply the denominator by the whole number; then add the result to the numerator to obtain the new numerator. For example,

$$2\frac{3}{4} = \frac{2 \times 4 + 3}{4} = \frac{8 + 3}{4} = \frac{11}{4}$$

Adding Fractions with Different Denominators

To work with fractions with different denominators, it is necessary to rewrite the fractions using a **common denominator**, or a number that is a multiple of the original denominators. For example, to rename the fractions $\frac{1}{2}$ and $\frac{2}{3}$, it is necessary to find a common denominator for both of them. In this case the lowest common denominator is 6 because 6 is a multiple of both of the original denominators. Another way to say this is that both original denominators are factors of 6. So, by multiplying each original fraction by $\frac{6}{6}$ (which equals 1 and thus doesn't change the value of the original fraction), $\frac{1}{2} \times \frac{6}{6} = \frac{6}{12} = \frac{3}{6}$ and $\frac{2}{3} \times \frac{6}{6} = \frac{12}{18} = \frac{4}{6}$. The fractions now have the same denominator. Thus,

$$\frac{1}{2} + \frac{2}{3} = \frac{3}{6} + \frac{4}{6} = \frac{7}{6}.$$

Multiplying Fractions

Multiplying fractions involves multiplying the numerators together and the denominators together (horizontally), then simplifying the product (note that the term used is **simplify**, not *reduce*; the value of the fraction remains unchanged). For example,

$$\frac{2}{3} \times \frac{3}{4} = \frac{2 \times 3}{3 \times 4} = \frac{6}{12} = \frac{1}{2}$$

If the numbers to be multiplied are mixed fractions, first rewrite them as improper fractions, such as $\frac{6}{2}$, and then proceed to multiply as described earlier.

Dividing Fractions

To perform this operation, take the reciprocal of the second fraction (the one doing the dividing) and multiply the numbers as just described for multiplying fractions. A **reciprocal** is a fraction with the numerator and denominator switched.

For example, to perform $\frac{1}{5}$ divided by $\frac{3}{8}$, follow these steps. Obtain the reciprocal of the second fraction, so $\frac{3}{8}$ is changed to $\frac{8}{3}$. Then proceed to multiply:

$$\frac{1}{5} \div \frac{3}{8} = \frac{1}{5} \times \frac{8}{3} = \frac{8}{15}$$

Decimal Numbers

Decimal numbers are fractional numbers that are written using base ten. A mixed decimal number has a whole number part as well; for example, 0.28 is a decimal number and 3.9 is a mixed decimal number.

Decimal numbers are fractions whose denominators are powers of 10 (i.e., 10, 100, 1000, and so forth). For example, 0.098 is equivalent to $\frac{98}{1000}$.

Adding and Subtracting Decimals

To add or subtract decimal numbers, arrange them vertically, align the decimal points, inserting zeros if necessary for the alignment, then add or subtract the same as done for whole numbers. The decimal point remains in the same location. For example, for 23.5 + 237.04,

```
   23.50
+237.04
 260.54
```

Multiplying Decimals

Multiplication of decimals does not require aligning decimal points; the numbers can be arranged vertically, with right sides aligned. The numbers can then be multiplied as if they were whole numbers. The numbers of digits to the right of the decimal point in the product should be equal to the sum of the number of digits to the right of the decimal point in the two factors. For example,

$$1.25 \quad \text{Two numbers to the right of the decimal point}$$
$$\times 0.6 \quad \text{One number to the right of the decimal point}$$
$$\overline{0.750} \quad \text{Therefore, three numbers to the right of the decimal point.}$$

Dividing Decimals

Division of decimals is done like traditional whole number division. The number of digits to the right of the decimal point in the divisor (number doing the dividing) is how far the decimal point in the dividend (number being divided) should be moved to the right. Then the decimal point in the quotient (answer) will appear above this point. For example, when dividing 1.44 by 0.3, since the divisor (0.3) has one digit after the decimal point, the decimal point in the dividend (1.44) is moved one digit to the right, and the decimal point in the quotient (4.8) is aligned above it.

$$0.3\overline{)1.44} = 03.\overline{)14.4}^{\,4.8}$$

Percents

Percent is another way of expressing a fractional number. Percent always expresses a fractional number in terms of $\frac{1}{100}$, or 0.01. Percents use the "%" symbol. For example, 40 parts out of 100 is 40%.

A percent is easily converted to a common fraction or decimal representation. To convert a percent to a common fraction, place the percent in the numerator and use 100 as the denominator (simplify as necessary). To convert a percent to a decimal fraction, divide the percent by 100, or move the decimal point two places to the left. Thus,

$$100\% = \frac{100}{100} = 1.0 \quad 25\% = \frac{25}{100} = 0.25 \quad 150\% = \frac{150}{100} = 1.5$$

The fraction equivalents of a percent often can be simplified by dividing by a common factor. Thus, $25\% = \frac{25}{100} = \frac{\frac{25}{25}}{\frac{100}{25}} = \frac{1}{4}$.

To convert a common fraction to a percent, follow this procedure: Carry out the division of the numerator by the denominator of the fraction to get the decimal equivalent. Then, to convert the decimal to a percentage, move the decimal point two places to the right (adding 0's as placeholders, if needed) and round as necessary. For example,

$$\frac{1}{4} = 1 \div 4 = .25 = \frac{25}{100} = 25\%$$

$$\frac{2}{7} = 2 \div 7 = .286 = \frac{286}{1000} = 28.6\%, \text{ which can be rounded to } 29\%$$

To find the **percentage** of a known quantity, change the percent to a common fraction or a decimal fraction, and multiply the fraction times the quantity. The percentage is expressed in the same units as the known quantity. For example, to find 25% of 360 books, change 25% to 0.25 and multiply times 360, or $0.25 \times 360 = 90$. The result is 90 books.

Mathematical Terms and Operations

Exponential Notation

Exponential notation is a symbolic way of showing how many times a number or variable is used as a factor. In the notation 5^3, the exponent 3 shows that 5 is a factor used three times, calculated in the following way: $5^3 = 5 \times 5 \times 5 = 125$.

A negative exponent indicates a reciprocal. Therefore, $5^{-3} = \frac{1}{5^3} = \frac{1}{5 \times 5 \times 5} = \frac{1}{125}$.

Absolute Value

Absolute value is the distance of a number from zero on the number line. This action ignores the + or − sign of a number. The notation for absolute value is two vertical lines, so $|x|$ is the graphic used to describe the action of absolute value. For example, $|-5| = 5$ or $|5| = 5$.

Expanded Form

The expanded form of numbers shows the place value of each digit. For example: $263 = 200 + 60 + 3$, which is equal to 2 hundreds, 6 tens, and 3 ones.

Expanded Notation

Expanded notation, just as expanded form, shows place value by multiplying each digit in a number by the appropriate power of 10. For example,

$$523 = 5 \times 10^2 + 2 \times 10 + 3 \times 1 \; \textit{or} \; 5 \times 10^2 + 2 \times 10^1 + 3 \times 10^0$$

Scientific Notation

Scientific notation is a form of writing a number as the product of a power of 10 and a decimal number greater than or equal to 1 and less than 10. For example,

$$2{,}400{,}000 = 2.4 \times 10^6; \quad 240.2 = 2.402 \times 10^2; \quad 0.0024 = 2.4 \times 10^{-3}$$

Estimation and Rounding

Estimation is used to make an approximation that is still close enough to be useful. When using estimation, use the leading or the left-most digit to make an estimate.

Rounding may be used to estimate a sum, difference, or product and to make mental approximations. Look at the digit to be rounded and use the following rules for rounding.

- If the digit is 0, 1, 2, 3, or 4, leave the digit as is.

- If the digit is 5, 6, 7, 8, or 9, round up (e.g., 5 is changed to a 6).

- All of the digits after the rounded digit become zeros.

For example, an estimation can be obtained by rounding up or down:

$$532 + 385 + 57 = 500 + 400 + 60 = 960.$$

The result certainly is less precise than doing the actual addition, but it is easier to perform mentally in most cases. This example is sometimes referred to as **front-end estimation** because it uses the leading, or left-most digit to make an estimate quickly and easily.

Rounding may also be used to reduce the number of digits in a number. Rounding is especially useful to have fewer digits in the answer when dividing numbers with remainders. For example, to divide a 20-cm-long wire into 3 equal pieces and to find the length of each piece, divide 20 by 3 to get the length of each piece.

$$\frac{20}{3} = 6.66666666666666\ldots$$

The 6 repeats an infinite number of times. This is known as a **repeating decimal**. Typically, the answer is based on the required number of decimal places. Decimal places here refers to the number of digits to the right of the decimal point. Usually rounding to the tenths or hundredths place is sufficient. To round the answer (6.666 . . .) to the nearest hundredths place, the next digit in the thousandths place is 6, so the 6 in the hundredths place is rounded up, giving 6.67 as the desired answer.

A decimal in which one or more digits repeat infinitely is indicated by a bar over the repeating digits; for example: 0.3333 . . . or $0.\overline{3}$ and 5.272727 . . . or $5.\overline{27}$.

Number Theory

Teacher candidates have to have a solid command of basic number theory. This section discusses some of the elements required for the EC–6 curricula.

Prime Factorization

Prime factorization involves knowledge of two sets of numbers:

- **Prime numbers** are natural numbers greater than 1 that are divisible only by themselves and 1. The first eight prime numbers are {2, 3, 5, 7, 11, 13, 17, 19}.

- **Composite numbers** are natural numbers greater than zero that are divisible by at least one other number besides 1 and themselves. Composite numbers have at least three factors; for example, 9 is a composite number because it has three factors: 1, 3, and 9.

Every composite number can be written as a product of prime numbers. This is called the **prime factorization** of the number. To perform prime factorization, start by factoring a known prime number into the given number. Then repeat this procedure on all factors until no more factorization can take place. When a factor is repeated in a prime factorization, express the repeated factor by using an exponent.

A factor tree can also help in finding the prime factorization of a composite number. It does not matter which factor pair is used first, as long as factoring continues until there are only prime numbers.

The prime factorization of 48 follows. Note the use of an exponent for repeat factors.

$48 = 3 \times 16$	Start by factoring 48 by a known prime, 3.
$48 = 3 \times 2 \times 8$	Factor 16 by 2, the lowest divisible prime of 16.
$48 = 3 \times 2 \times 2 \times 4$	Factor 8 similarly.
$48 = 3 \times 2 \times 2 \times 2 \times 2$	Factor 4 similarly.
$48 = 3 \times 2^4$	Express $2 \times 2 \times 2 \times 2$ as 2^4.

The exponent 4 shows how many times the base number 2 is used as a factor. The factor 3 is used only once. It has an exponent of 1. Exponents of 1 do not need to be written because they are implied. Prime factorizations are usually written in order from least to greatest base number. The prime factorization of 48 is usually written as $2^4 \times 3$.

Greatest Common Divisor

The **greatest common divisor** (GCD) of two or more nonzero integers is the largest positive integer that divides into the numbers without producing a remainder. Sometimes the term used is "divides evenly into." This is useful for simplifying fractions into their lowest terms. For example, to simplify $\frac{42}{56}$, find the GCD of 42 and 56, which is 14, and factor it out of the numerator and denominator: $\frac{42}{56} = \frac{3 \times 14}{4 \times 14} = \frac{3}{4}$.

Note that although 42 and 56 are each divisible by larger numbers (21 and 28, respectively), the largest number that is a factor of *both* 42 and 56, is 14.

Common Multiple

A common multiple is a whole number that is a multiple of two or more given numbers. For example, the common multiples of 2, 3, and 4 are 12, 24, 36, 48 . . .

Numbers and their Properties

Numbers have basic properties that can help simplify mathematics problem solving and reasoning skills. Some of these are:

Commutative Property

The order of the **addends** (terms being added) or **factors** (in multiplication) do not change the result.

$a + b = b + a$ and $a \times b = b \times a$

Addition: 6 + 8 = 14 is the same as 8 + 6 = 14

Multiplication: 5 × 8 = 40 is the same as 8 × 5 = 40

Associative Property of Multiplication and Addition

The order of the addends or factors will not change the sum or the product.

$(a + b) + c = a + (b + c)$ and $(a \times b) \times c = a \times (b \times c)$

Addition: (2 + 3) + 5 = 10, 2 + (3 + 5) = 10

Multiplication: (2 × 3) × 5 = 30, 2 × (3 × 5) = 30

Property of Zero

The sum of a number and zero is the number itself, and the product of a number and zero is zero.

Addition: 8 + 0 = 8

Multiplication: 8 × 0 = 0

Distributive Property

The distributive property says that everything within the parentheses needs to be multiplied by the number on the outside.

You can add and then multiply or multiply and then add.

$a(b + c) = a \times (b + c)$ or $a(b + c) = (a \times b) + (a \times c)$

$8(5 + 2) = 8 \times 7 = 56$ or $8(5 + 2) = (8 \times 5) + (8 \times 2) = 56$

The distributive property also works with subtraction, so that $4(8 - 5) = 4(8) - 4(5) = 32 - 20 = 12$, Again, if the quantity in the parentheses is evaluated first, $4(8 - 5) = 4(3) = 12$.

Students may first learn the distributive property when they are learning order of operations, which is discussed next.

Order of Operations

The solutions of many problems in mathematics involve a series of calculations, or steps. Consider the equation $3 + 2 \times 6 = n$. Should this be calculated "left to right" by doing the + first and get 30? Or should the multiplication be calculated first and get 15? To avoid confusion and to obtain the correct answer, mathematicians decided long ago that all calculations should be done in the same order.

An arithmetic expression is evaluated by following these ordered steps, called the **order of operations:**

1. Simplify within grouping symbols, such as parentheses or brackets, starting with the innermost.

2. Apply exponents—powers and roots.

3. Perform all multiplications and divisions in order from left to right.

4. Perform all additions and subtractions in order from left to right.

You may have learned this order of operations as being

Please Excuse My Dear Aunt Sally!

The words in this sentence stand for *Parentheses, Exponentiation, Multiplication, Division, Addition*, and *Subtraction*, or generally, using the first letter of the order, as **PEMDAS**. So what is the correct answer for our problem? The order of operations would say that in the absence of parentheses, multiply 2×6 first, and then add 3, so the answer should be 15. If you were to add $3 + 2 = 5$, then multiply 5×6 that would be 30, a very different (and wrong) answer! If the $3 + 2$ were supposed to be added first, the problem should be written $(3 + 2) \times 6$ because then PEMDAS says to do the operations in the parentheses first.

COMPETENCY 003: PATTERNS AND ALGEBRA

The teacher understands concepts related to patterns, relations, functions, and algebraic reasoning.

Problem-Solving Situations

The role of operations in problem solving involves developing critical thinking and rational powers. The uses of operations in problem solving include applications, study of patterns and relationships, translation of word problems with a variety of structures and situations into symbolic representations using equations, and the selection of problem-solving strategies, all of which are topics covered in this competency.

Linear and Nonlinear Functional Relationships

Many functions can be represented by pairs of numbers. A real-valued function assigns to each real number x in a specified set of numbers, called the domain of f, a single real number designated as $f(x)$. The variable x is called the independent variable. If $y = f(x)$, we call y the dependent variable. Then, $f(0)$ is the value of the function when $x = 0$.

A function can be specified in the following ways: (1) numerically by means of a table, (2) algebraically by means of a formula, or (3) graphically by means of a graph. A **numerically specified function** is shown in **Table 4-9**, which shows the values: $f(0) = 3.01$ and $f(1) = -1.03$.

Table 4-9. Numerically Specified Function

x	0	1	2	3
$f(x)$	3.01	−1.03	2.22	0.01

Suppose an algebraically specified function f is specified by

$f(x) = 3x^2 - 4x + 1$.

Then by substituting 2 for x,

$f(x) = 3x^2 - 4x + 1$

$f(2) = 3(2)^2 - 4(2) + 1$

$f(2) = 12 - 8 + 1 = 5$

Likewise, $f(-1) = 3(-1)^2 - 4(-1) + 1 = 3 + 4 + 1 = 8$.

The graph of a **linear function** is a straight line (that is why it is called "linear"). A linear function is one of the most fundamental and important relationship concepts used as a foundation for advanced mathematics. A linear function is one that always satisfies the following: $f(x + y) = f(x) + f(y)$ and $f(\alpha x) = \alpha f(x)$. In this definition, x and y are input variables and α is a constant.

For example, consider the function $f(x) = 2x$. For any two input values a and b, suppose $x = a + b$. The function now becomes $f(x) = f(a + b) = 2(a + b) = 2a + 2b$. We see that if we substitute, $x = a$ and then $x = b$, we obtain $f(a) = 2a$ and $f(b) = 2b$ and $f(a + b) = f(a) + f(b)$, which satisfies the first rule. Checking the second constraint, $f(\alpha x) = 2\alpha x$, which is equivalent to $\alpha f(x) = \alpha 2x$ due to the associative/commutative properties of multiplication.

A **nonlinear function** does not satisfy the constraints of a linear function. For example, the function $f(x) = x^2$ is nonlinear because $f(a + b) = (a + b)^2 = a^2 + 2ab + b^2$ is not equal to $f(a) + f(b) = a^2 + b^2$.

We will revisit the concept of linear and nonlinear functions later.

Function

Functions can be used to understand how one quantity varies in relation to (or is a function of) changes in the second quantity. For example, there is a functional relationship between the price per pound of a particular type of meat and the total amount paid for ten pounds of that type of meat. You can see that the values of one variable determine the values of another.

Patterns

A **pattern** can be a design (geometric) or sequence (numeric or algebraic) that is predictable because some aspect of it repeats and/or can be represented by an equation. For example, a numeric pattern that adds increments of 3 looks like this: 4, 7, 10, 13. . . . An algebraic pattern that adds one to the multiple: x, $2x$, $3x$ . . . ; or when students are asked to identify patterns using fact families. A fact family is a set of numbers that are related using different mathematical operations. For example, 1, 2, and 3 are a fact family because of the following fact family relationships: $1 + 2 = 3$, $2 + 1 = 3$, $3 - 2 = 1$, and $3 - 1 = 2$. A fact family will always have at least four math facts relating the family. This can also be seen in the following example from the STAAR Objective 2, item (3.6) – Patterns, relationships, and algebraic thinking:

(C) Identify patterns in related multiplication and division sentences (fact families) such as $2 \times 3 = 6$, $3 \times 2 = 6$, $6 \div 2 = 3$, $6 \div 3 = 2$.

In the above example there is only a single fact family listed. However, there are many other fact family relationships that can be found that will allow students to identify patterns in addition, subtraction, multiplication, and division sentences.

Algebraic Pattern

An **algebraic pattern** is a set of numbers and/or variables in a specific order. An example would be a chart showing the distance in feet Max travels on his bicycle versus the time in seconds, as shown in the chart below. What is one way to find the number of feet Max travels on his bicycle in 1 second?

No. of seconds	6	8	9
No. of feet	90	120	135

First, students need to be able to understand the algebraic pattern presented in the chart and how the numbers are listed. Students should divide the number of feet by the number of seconds to find the correct answer. However, in this problem the answer 15 does not answer the test question, which asks which operation was used to derive the answer to the question.

Algebraic Expression

An **algebraic expression** is a mathematical phrase that is written by using one or more variables and constants, but does not contain a relation symbol (e.g., $5y + 8$).

A **variable** or an unknown is a letter that stands for a number in an algebraic expression.

A **coefficient** is the number that precedes the variable to give the quantity of the variable in the expression. Algebraic expressions are comprised of terms, or groupings of variables and numbers. An algebraic expression with one term is called a **monomial**; with two terms, a **binomial**; with three terms, a **trinomial**; with more than one term, a **polynomial**. When writing algebraic expressions, coefficients are always written before variables. For example, $2a$ is correct, whereas $a2$ is not.

For example, $2ab - cd$ is a binomial (two-term) algebraic expression with variables a, b, c, and d, and terms $2ab$ and $(-cd)$. The coefficient of ab is 2, and the coefficient of cd is -1. As another example, $x^2 + 3y - 1$ is a trinomial algebraic expression using the variables x and y, and terms x^2, $3y$, and (-1); likewise, $z(x - 1) + uv - wy - 2$ is a polynomial with variables z, x, u, v, w, and y, and terms $z(x - 1)$, uv, $(-wy)$, and (-2).

Operations with algebraic expressions are governed by various rules and conventions.

- For **addition and subtraction**, *only like algebraic terms (same variable bases with the same exponents) can be added or subtracted* to produce simpler expressions. For example, $2x^3$ and $3x^3$ can be added together to get $5x^3$ because the terms are *like* terms; they both are x^3 terms. In contrast, $7m^3$ and $6m^2$ cannot be added together because they have *unlike* exponents. (*Note*: To *evaluate* an algebraic expression means to simplify it by using conventional rules.)

- When **multiplying exponential terms** together, the constant terms are multiplied, but the *exponents of the terms with the same variable bases are added together*, which is somewhat counterintuitive. For example, $4w^2$ multiplied by $8w^3$ gives $32w^5$ (not $32w^6$, as one might guess).

- When like algebraic terms are **divided**, exponents are subtracted. For example, $\dfrac{2x^7}{5x^3}$ becomes $\dfrac{\frac{2x}{7-3}}{\frac{5x}{3-3}} = \dfrac{2x^4}{5}$.

Multiplication of Binomials

In algebra, it is frequently necessary to multiply two binomials. The FOIL method is one way to multiply binomials. FOIL stands for "first, outer, inner, last" or "first, outside, inside, last." Multiply the first terms in the parentheses, then the outermost terms, then the innermost terms, then the last terms, and then add the products together and simplify the expression by combining like terms. For example, to multiply $(x + 3)$ and $(2x - 5)$, multiply x by $2x$ (the first terms), x by -5 (outer terms), 3 by $2x$ (inner terms), and 3 by -5 (last terms). The four products ($2x^2$, $-5x$, $6x$, and -15) add up to $2x^2 + x - 15$. If the polynomials to be multiplied have more than two terms (trinomials, for instance), make sure that *each* term of the first polynomial is multiplied by *each* term of the second.

The opposite of polynomial multiplication is factoring. **Factoring** a polynomial means rewriting it as the product of factors (often two binomials). The trinomial $x^2 - 11x + 28$, for instance, can be factored into $(x - 4)(x - 7)$. (You can check this by "FOILing" the binomials.) When attempting to factor polynomials, it is sometimes helpful to first factor out any factor that might be common to all terms. The two terms in $5x^2 - 10$, for example, both contain the factor 5. This means that the expression can be factored as $5(x^2 - 2)$.

Algebraic Relationship

It is important to express the relationship between two or more numbers by using an algebraic expression. The algebraic relationship that represents 2, 4, 6, 8, . . . is $2n$ (where $n = 1, 2, 3, . . .$) and the algebraic relationship that represents 4, 7, 10, 13, . . . is $3n + 1$ (where $n = 1, 2, 3, . . .$).

Algebraic Solution

An **algebraic solution** is the process of solving a mathematical problem by using the principles of algebra.

Performing Operations with Negative and Positive Numbers

When performing operations on negative and positive numbers, the key component is to pay attention to the sign. Rules for multiplication and division are the same—two positives or two negatives make a positive, and mixing negative with positive makes a negative. See the following examples.

- negative × negative = positive (−6 × −5 = 30)

- positive × positive = positive (6 × 5 = 30)

- positive × negative = negative (6 × −5 = −30)

Graphs and Symbolic Representations

A graph is an image or chart representation used to show a numerical relationship. On the TExES, teacher candidates are required to study graphs, charts, and tables, and answer questions based on the information presented. A **table** is a systematic or orderly list of values, usually in rows and columns. Tables often are organized from a function or relationship. Four kinds of **graphs** are generally used in Grades Pre-K to 6—pictorial, bar, line, and pie.

Pictorial graphs are the most concrete representations of information. They represent a transition from the real object graphs to symbolic graphs (Sperry Smith, 2008). These graphs usually are used to introduce children to graphing in Pre-K through Grade 1. For example, the teacher can use pictures of pizzas and hot dogs to represent the number of children that prefer one food over the other.

Bar graphs are used to represent two elements of a *single* subject. For example, the bar graph that follows presents the number of books read by a group of students. This graph presents in a concrete fashion that student E was the top reader, with 5 books, and student A read the lowest number of books.

Line graphs present information in a fashion similar to bar graphs, but they use points and lines. This type of representation is more abstract for children and is therefore more challenging for them. A line graph tracks one or more subjects. One element is usually a time period over which the other element increases, decreases, or remains static. The following line graph depicts U.S. immigration statistics from 1820 to 2013.

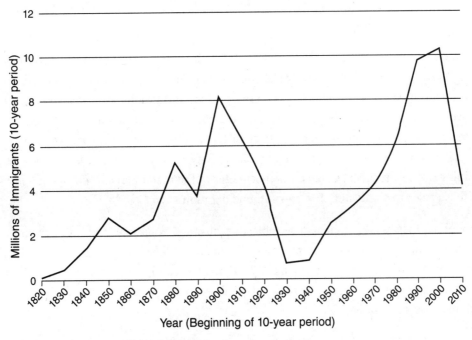

Volume of U.S. Immigration by Decade, 1820–2013

Data Source: U.S. Department of Homeland Security

Pie charts are used to help visualize relationships based on percentages of a possible 100%. This graph appears to be easy to read, which is deceptive. It requires an understanding of percentages, which makes it inappropriate for children in the early grades. A pie graph representing food preferences follows.

Food Preferences

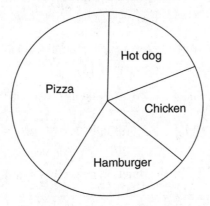

Identifying Patterns Using Concrete Models

Kindergarten students begin to use concrete models to construct, describe, extend, and determine what comes next in repeating patterns. To identify and construct repeating patterns, students must be able to identify the attributes of the objects in the pattern. Therefore, students sort objects by their attributes before they begin constructing their own patterns. Students construct patterns with two (AB, AAB, ABB) or three (ABC, ACB, BAC, BCA, CAB, CBA) elements. As students become more familiar with the structure of patterns they are able to begin to think about how two patterns are similar and different.

By Grade 5, students continue their work from Grades 3 and 4 by examining, representing, and describing situations in which the rate of change is constant. Students move from using concrete models to using figures and numbers. They create tables and graphs to represent the relationship between two variables in a variety of contexts and are able to describe the rules for each situation. For example, consider the perimeters of a set of rectangles made from rows of tiles with three tiles in each row. If the value of one variable (the number of rows of three tiles) is known, the corresponding value of the other variable (the perimeter of the rectangle) can be calculated. Students express these rules in words and then in symbolic notation.

Throughout their work, students use tables, graphs, and equations and relations among those representations and the situation they represent. Their work with symbolic notation is closely related to the context in which they are working. By moving back and forth between contexts, their own ways of describing general rules in words, and symbolic notation, students learn how notation can carry mathematical meaning.

Linear and Nonlinear Functions

As stated previously, a **linear function** is one whose graph is a straight line. The equation for a linear function, which is a first-degree polynomial function of one variable, can be written in the form of $y = mx + b$, called the **slope-intercept form** of the equation. The constant m is called the **slope** or **gradient**, and b is the **y-intercept**, or the point of intersection between the graph of the function and the y-axis. Changing m makes the line steeper or more gradual; changing b moves the line up or down.

The form of the equation in function form and equation form are given below. Note that x is the independent variable and y is the dependent variable.

$f(x) = mx + b$ (function form)   Example: $f(x) = 3x - 1$ ($m = 3$, $b = -1$).

$y = mx + b$ (equation form)   Example: $y = 3x - 1$

A partial table of values of the linear function $f(x) = 3x - 1$ follows.

x	−4	−3	−2	−1	0	1	2	3
y	−13	−10	−7	−4	−1	2	5	8

This linear equation has $m = 3$ (slope), $b = -1$ (y-intercept). Notice that $x = 0$ gives $y = -1$, the value of b. Numerically, b is the value of y when $x = 0$. On the graph, the corresponding point $(0,-1)$ is the point where the graph crosses the y-axis. The role of m in the equation $y = 3x - 1$ means that the value of y increases by 3 for every increase of 1 in x.

The graph of this function is a straight line rising by 3 for every 1 we go to the right. We say that we have a *rise* of 3 units for each *run* of 1 unit. Similarly, we have a rise of 6 for a run of 2, a rise of 9 for a run of 3, and so on. Thus we see that $m = 3$ is a measure of the steepness of the line. Geometrically, the graph of a linear function $f(x) = mx + b$ rises by m units for every 1 unit move to the right.

Examples of functions whose graph is a line include the following:

- $f_1(x) = 2x + 1$

- $f_2(x) = \dfrac{x}{2} + 1$

- $f_3(x) = \dfrac{x}{2} - 1$

The graphs of these equations are shown below:

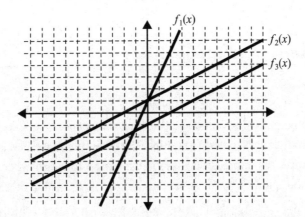

A **nonlinear** function, as the name implies, is not linear. An example is the quadratic $x^2 + x - 1 = 0$. Although nonlinear, this simple example may be solved exactly by using a formula (called the quadratic formula, a topic for higher grades) and is very well understood. To determine whether a function is linear or nonlinear, see the following examples.

$y = 4x$	$y = x^2 + x - 2$	$y = \dfrac{7}{x}$
Linear. $y = 4x$ can be written as $y = mx + b$	Nonlinear. $y = x^2 + x - 2$ cannot be written as $y = mx + b$ because it has an x^2 term	Nonlinear. $y = \dfrac{7}{x}$ cannot be written as $y = mx + b$ because x is in the denominator

Proportional Reasoning

Proportional reasoning is important in preparing students for algebra. Students in 5th grade begin to use a ratio chart to solve proportion problems. Proportions may present a challenge for students. Often they involve two unlike values that are related in a certain way. Students can be influenced by the context, so it is important to expose students to various examples, as in the following types of problems:

1. The office copier uses 5 reams of paper every 2 weeks. At the end of 6 weeks, how many reams of paper will the office copier have used?

2. Each table in the restaurant has a vase with three long-stem roses. The restaurant has 15 tables. How many flowers are there altogether?

3. The soccer coach orders new soccer balls for the team. She orders 3 out of 4 soccer balls in the school colors. If she orders 36 soccer balls, how many of these will be painted in the school colors?

Variables, Equations, and Inequalities

Equations

An equation is a mathematical sentence stating that two expressions are equal. Many mathematical expressions include letters called **variables**. Variables are classified as either independent (free) or dependent (bound). An expression may be evaluated for a given combination of values for the independent variables, although for some combinations, the value of the expression may be undefined. For example, the expression $\frac{x}{y}$ evaluated for $x = 10$, $y = 5$, will give 2; but it is undefined for $y = 0$. Thus an expression represents a function whose inputs are the values assigned to the independent variables and whose output is the resulting value of the expression.

The evaluation of an expression is dependent on the definition of the mathematical operators and on the system of values applied in the context of the expression. See Formal Semantics and Interpretation (logic) for the study of this question in logic.

Two expressions are said to be equivalent if, for each combination of values for the free variables, they have the same output, i.e., they represent the same function.

In equations, the '+' and '–' (addition and subtraction) symbols have their usual meanings. Division can be expressed as either $x/2$ or $\frac{x}{2}$ (like a fraction); both are perfectly valid. Multiplication can use the symbols $\times$, $\cdot$ (a multiplication dot), parentheses, or the sign can simply be omitted when multiplication is implicit. So $2 \cdot x$, or $2 \times x$, or $2(x)$, or $2x$ are all acceptable. Notice how the "times" symbol resembles an "x" and also how the " $\cdot$ " symbol resembles a decimal point, so to avoid confusion it may be best to use one of the latter two forms (depending on the problem).

An algebraic expression must be well formed. That is, the operators must have the correct number of inputs, in the correct places. As examples, the expression $2 + 3$ is well formed, but the expression $*2 +$ is not—at least, not in the usual notation of arithmetic.

Algebraic Inequality

An **algebraic inequality** is an algebraic statement about the relative size of one or more variables and/or constants. Inequalities are used to determine the relationship between these values. For example, taking x as a variable and saying, "x is less than 5," may be written as $x < 5$. An algebraic inequality also may use one or more variables and constants that shows a greater than or less than relationship, such as $2x - 8 > x + 24$.

Solving an algebraic inequality means finding all of its solutions. A "solution" of an inequality is a number or group of numbers that, when substituted for the variable (for example, x) make the inequality a true statement. As was the case for solving equations, certain manipulations of the inequality do not change the solution. Consider the list of manipulations shown below for the algebraic inequality $2x + 8 > 24$.

1. Adding or subtracting the same number on both sides: $2x + 8 > 24$ has the same solution as the inequality $2x > 16$. (The second inequality was obtained from the first one by subtracting 8 from both sides.)

2. Switching sides and changing the orientation of the inequality sign: $2x + 8 > 24$ has the same solution as $24 < 2x + 8$. (Merely switch the sides of the inequality and turn the ">" into a "<")

3a. Multiplying or dividing by the same *positive* number on both sides.

Last, the operation that is the source of all the trouble with inequalities:

3b. Multiplying or dividing by the same *negative* number on both sides *and* changing the orientation of the inequality sign.

This does not seem too difficult. The inequality $2x > 6$ has the same solution as the inequality $x > 3$ (dividing by +2 on both sides). The inequality $-2x \geq 4$ has the same solutions as the inequality $x \leq -2$ (dividing by (–2) on both sides and switching "$\geq$" to "$\leq$").

The inequality $x^2 > x$, however, does not have the same solutions as the inequality $x > 1$. Dividing both sides by x is not possible, because x can be either positive or negative. In fact, it is easy to check that $x = -2$ solves the first inequality but does not solve the second inequality.

COMPETENCY 004: GEOMETRY AND MEASUREMENT

The teacher understands concepts and principles of geometry and measurement.

Geometry and measurement are significant strands of mathematics. In the elementary classroom, children's experience in geometry should provide for the development of the concepts of direction, shape, size, symmetry, congruence, and similarity in using two-dimensional and three-dimensional shapes. Experiences for children should begin with exploring, playing, and building with shapes using familiar objects and a wide variety of concrete materials. Children must use these experiences to develop appropriate vocabulary and build on their understanding. Middle school students use formal generalizations to understand geometric relationships.

Concepts and skills in the measurement strand of mathematics deal with making comparisons between what is being measured and the standard for measurement. Children need first-hand experiences with measuring activities that require them to practice the skill. Additionally, children should be aware that measurement is never exact, but instead is actually an estimation. However, it is important that children learn to practice making estimates. Measuring gives children practical applications to apply their computation skills. It also provides a way to link geometric concepts to number concepts.

The Van Hiele Theory

Although the Van Hiele theory (Van Hiele, 1986) has been recognized for its role in describing the levels of thinking associated with the learning of geometry, it also has been developed as a general theory of mathematics education. In 1988, Fuys, Gedds, and Tischler interpreted much of that work. The Van Hiele theory is a stage theory, set out in levels. The theory does not stop at the description of "levels of thinking," but provides a foundation for understanding the movement between these levels, and the role of the teacher in assisting with this progression. The theory goes beyond the concerns of Piaget, who did not address the question of how students may be encouraged to progress from level to level. The Van Hiele theory, in addition to describing levels of thinking, offers an important addition. This is the notion of *stages of learning* as a means by which the learner may be assisted to use higher-level thinking skills. Five such stages (levels 0–4) are specified in **Table 4-10** (Van Hiele, 1986).

Table 4-10. Van Hiele's Levels of Geometric Thinking

What the teacher needs to know	What the learner can do
Van Hiele's Levels **0—Visualization** Learners develop a mental picture of each shape; therefore, teachers need to provide a multitude of good physical examples and nonexamples for exploration.	**Learner is able to:** • Select a specific shape from a set of shapes • Sort and match shapes • Identify shapes in the environment • Point out shapes (e.g., a baseball diamond, etc.)
1—Analysis Learners begin to talk and notice the properties of the shapes. Teachers can focus on the various components of the geometric shape.	**Learner is able to:** • Predict a shape's final form after seeing only a part of it • List several attributes of each shape • Subdivide a shape into parts, describe the various pieces, and create a shape from parts
2—Informal Deduction Students stop relying on visualization, and now use relationships to make a conclusion. Focus is on the first two levels for students in K–8.	**Learner is able to:** • Recognize that squares belong in both the rectangle and rhombus category • Use "if" statements describing the shape • Divide a rectangle into two congruent triangles • Identify parallelograms based on the criteria regarding opposite equal angles
3—Formal Deduction Focus is on higher levels of geometry, using various theorems to teach how two triangles are congruent (e.g., side-angle-side (SAS) theorem).	**Learner is able to:** • Make deductions and support those deductions • Do high school–level geometry including construction of their own proofs involving quadrilaterals drawn on a sphere.
4—Rigor Rigor is associated with college-level geometry.	**Learner is able to:** • Compare different geometries at the proof level

Points, Lines, Angles, Lengths, and Distances

A fundamental concept of geometry is the notion of a **point**. A point is a specific location, taking up no space, having no area, and frequently represented by a dot. A point is considered to have no dimensions. In other words, it has neither length nor breadth (width) nor depth.

Through any two points there is exactly one **straight line**; lines are one-dimensional. **Planes** (think of flat surfaces without edges) are two-dimensional, meaning they have infinite length and width but no depth. From these foundational ideas one can move to some other important geometric terms and ideas.

- A **line segment** is any portion of a line between two points on that line. It has a definite start and a definite end, called the **endpoints**. The notation for a segment extending from point A to point B is $\overline{AB}$.

- A **ray** is like a line segment, except it extends forever in one direction. The notation for a ray originating at endpoint X through point Y is $\overrightarrow{XY}$.

An **angle** is formed when two rays (or lines) share an endpoint. Typically, a **degree** is the unit of measure of the angle created. If a circle is divided into 360 even pie-shaped slices, each slice has an angle measure of 1 degree. (Thus, a circle has 360 degrees.)

- If an angle has exactly 90 degrees it is called a **right angle**.

- Angles of less than 90 degrees are **acute angles**.

- Angles greater than 90 degrees but less than 180 degrees are **obtuse angles**.

- If two angles have the same size (regardless of how long their rays might be drawn), they are **congruent**. Congruence is shown by the symbol $\cong$ (e.g., $\angle m \cong \angle n$, which is read "angle m is congruent to angle n").

In addition, combinations of two angles can be classified as complementary and supplementary. The angles do not have to be adjacent (next to each other).

- **Supplementary angles** are two angles that add up to $180°$.

- **Complementary angles** are two angles that add up to $90°$.

If two lines intersect, they form two pairs of equal angles, called **vertical angles**. The measures of vertical angles (the angles across from each other) are equivalent; that is, vertical angles are congruent.

Parallel lines and **perpendicular lines** are important concepts in geometry. Parallel lines never cross. Consider the two parallel lines that follow, and a third line (a **transversal**) that crosses them. Note that among the many individual angles created, there are only two angle measures: $30°$ (noted in the figure) and the supplementary angle $150°$ ($= 180° - 30°$).

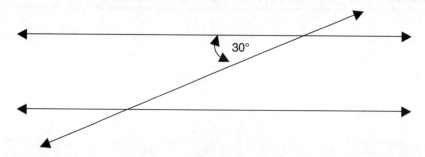

An example of perpendicular lines is shown in the figure below. When lines are perpendicular, the measures of the angles created at their intersection are all 90°, signified by the small square shown in the figure. We say *AB* is perpendicular to *CD*.

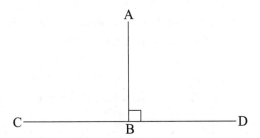

Polygons

A **polygon** is a many-sided plane (two-dimensional) figure bounded by a finite number of straight lines. An angle in a polygon is referred to as a vertex (plural is vertices).

Polygons are described based on the number of sides, which are equal to the number of vertices. Some of the most common are the following:

- Three-sided polygons are **triangles**.

- Four-sided polygons are **quadrilaterals**.

- Five-sided polygons are **pentagons**.

- Six-sided polygons are **hexagons**.

- Eight-sided polygons are **octagons**.

Triangles

Properties of Triangles

Triangles are three-sided polygons. There are three types of triangles classified according to their sides—isosceles, equilateral, and scalene.

- An **isosceles** triangle has two equal sides and two equal angles.

- If the measures of all sides of the triangle are equal, then the triangle is called an **equilateral** triangle (this means all sides are equal). This is also called an **equiangular** triangle (since all angles are also equal).

- A **scalene** triangle has three unequal sides.

Triangles can also be classified according to their angles:

- In an **acute** triangle, all three angles are acute.

- In a **right** triangle, one of the angles is a right angle.

- In an **obtuse** triangle, one of the angles is obtuse.

In the figure below, the base is b and the height, h, is the perpendicular distance from the base to the opposite vertex. Any side can be considered a base. Note that the height of a triangle is not necessarily the same as the length of any of its sides.

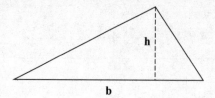

Using Triangles to Explore Geometric Relationships

A property of all triangles is that the sum of the measures of the three angles is 180°. If the measures of two angles are known, the third can be deduced.

Right triangles have several special properties. A chief property is described by the **Pythagorean theorem**, which states that in any right triangle with legs (shorter sides) a and b, and hypotenuse (the longest side) c, the sum of the squares of the legs will be equal to the square of the hypotenuse ($a^2 + b^2 = c^2$). Note that in the following right triangle, $3^2 + 4^2 = 5^2$.

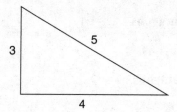

Sufficient evidence for congruence between two triangles can be shown through the following comparisons:

- **SAS** (Side-Angle-Side): If two pairs of sides of two triangles are equal in length, and the included angles are equal in measurement, then the triangles are congruent.

- **SSS** (Side-Side-Side): If three pairs of sides of two triangles are equal in length, then the triangles are congruent.

- **ASA** (Angle-Side-Angle): If two pairs of angles of two triangles are equal in measurement, and the included sides are equal in length, then the triangles are congruent.

- **AAS** (Angle-Angle-Side): If two pairs of angles of two triangles are equal in measurement and a pair of *corresponding* sides is of equal length, then the triangles are congruent.

Quadrilaterals

Parallelograms

A **parallelogram** is a four-sided polygon with two pairs of equal and parallel sides. In the figure below, one pair of parallel sides is designated as b and the height h is the perpendicular distance between the two bases. Note that, as with triangles, any side can be considered a base, the height of a parallelogram is not necessarily the same as the length of the other side. If it is, the figure is a rectangle.

A rhombus is a special type of parallelogram in which all the sides are the same length.

Rectangles

A **rectangle** is a type of parallelogram with four right angles. The sides are designated l, which is the same as the base b for parallelograms, and w, which is the height of the rectangle.

Squares

A **square** is a type of parallelogram with four right angles and four equal sides. The sides are designated s.

Circles

Circles are unique shapes in geometry because they have no angles. They are all the points that are equidistant from a point called the **center**. The **diameter** of a circle is a straight line segment that goes from one edge of a circle to the other side, passing through the center. The **radius** of a circle is half of its diameter (from the center to an edge). A **chord** is any segment that goes from one point on the edge of a circle to any other point on the edge. (All diameters are chords, but not all chords are diameters.)

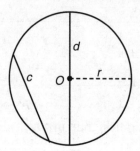

Formulas for Perimeter and Area

Finding the Perimeter

The **perimeter** of a two-dimensional (flat) shape or object is the distance around the object (think of a fence, for example). Perimeter is measured in linear units (e.g., inches, feet, and meters).

The **perimeter of a triangle** is found by adding the measures of the three sides of the triangle. This relationship can be represented by $P = s_1 + s_2 + s_3$, where s_1, s_2, and s_3 are the measures of the sides of the triangle. For example, if a triangle has three sides measuring 3 inches, 4 inches, and 5 inches, then the perimeter of the triangle is given by $P = 3$ inches + 4 inches + 5 inches = 12 inches.

The **perimeter of a rectangle** is found by adding twice the length of the rectangle to twice the width of the rectangle. This relationship is commonly given by the formula: $P = 2l + 2w$, where l is the measure of the length and w is the measure of the width. For example, if a rectangle has a length of 10 m and a width of 5 m, then the perimeter of the rectangle is given by $P = 2(10 \text{ m}) + 2(5 \text{ m}) = 30$ m.

The **perimeter of a square** is found by multiplying four times the measure of a side of the square. This relationship is commonly given by the formula $P = 4s$, where s is the measure of a side of the square. For example, if a square has a side of 5 feet, then the perimeter of the square is given by $P = 4(5 \text{ feet}) = 20$ feet.

The **circumference** of a circle can be thought of as the perimeter of the circle. It is the distance around the circle, and is given by the formula:

$$C = 2\pi r \text{ or } C = \pi d$$

where π, or pi, is defined as the ratio of a circle's circumference to its diameter. The value of π is the same for all circles; it is an irrational number, 3.14159 . . . The approximation 3.14 is adequate for most calculations. In the formulas for the circumference, the *d* represents the diameter and the *r* stands for the radius of the circle.

Finding the Area

The **area of a parallelogram** is found by multiplying the measure of the base by the measure of the height, or $A = bh$.

If a diagonal is drawn on any parallelogram, it is divided into two congruent triangles, so one half the area of the parallelogram, is the **area of a triangle**, or $A = \frac{1}{2}bh$.

The **area of a rectangle** is similarly found by multiplying the measure of the length (or base) of the rectangle by the measure of the width of the rectangle, which is also its height. This relationship is commonly given by $A = l \times w$, where l is the measure of the length and w is the measure of the width. For example, if a rectangle has a length of 10 m and a width of 5 m, then the area of the rectangle is given by $A = 10 \text{ m} \times 5 \text{ m} = 50 \text{ m}^2$.

The **area of a square** is found by squaring the measure of the side of the square. This relationship is commonly given by $A = s^2$, where s is the measure of a side. For example, if a square has a side of 5 ft, then the area of the square is given by $A = (5 \text{ ft})^2 = 25 \text{ ft}^2$.

The **area of a circle** can be found by squaring the length of its radius, then multiplying that product by π. The formula is given as $A = \pi r^2$. The value of π is approximately 3.14, as discussed above for the circumference of a circle. The approximate area of the circle with a radius of 6 can be found by squaring 6 (giving 36), then multiplying 36 by 3.14, giving an area of $A \approx 113$ square units (the symbol ≈ means "approximately equal to").

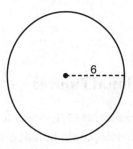

Similarity and Congruence

Geometric figures are **similar** if they have the exact same shapes, even if they do not have the same sizes. In the figure below, triangles A and B are similar. Corresponding angles of similar figures have the same measure, and the lengths of corresponding sides are proportional.

In the next figure, rectangles A and B are similar, but the corresponding sides are not only proportional, they are equal. Figures are **congruent** if they have the same shape *and* size. (Congruent figures are also similar, but similar figures are not necessarily congruent.)

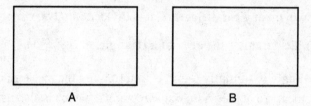

Three-Dimensional Figures

Three-dimensional figures have length, width, and height. Typical three-dimensional figures are

- a **rectangular solid** (think of a brick)

- a **cube** (a rectangular solid with all square sides)

- a **cylinder** (think of a can)

- a **prism**, a three-dimensional solid consisting of a collection of polygons, with two congruent, parallel faces (called bases) that are polygons and lateral (side) faces that are parallelograms

- a **sphere** (think of a ball)

Formulas for Three-Dimensional Figures

Volume refers to how much space is inside of three-dimensional, closed containers. It is useful to think of volume as how many cubic units could fit into a solid.

The **volume of a rectangular solid** is equal to the product of its length, width, and height; $V = l \times w \times h$. The **volume of a cube**, which has equal length, width, and height, is $V = s^3$.

The parts of a rectangular solid or cube are listed below and shown in the figure.

- A **vertex** is the union of two segments or point of intersection of two sides of a polygon.

- Each of the plane regions (sides) of a geometric body is a **face**.

- An **edge** is a line segment where two faces of a three-dimensional figure meet.

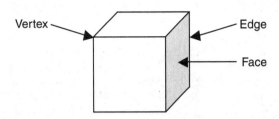

The number of faces, edges, and faces can be identified visually, or by the relationship among them: $F + V = E + 2$. A rectangular solid or cube has 6 faces, 12 edges, and 8 vertices.

The **volume of a prism** can be found by multiplying the area of the prism's base by its height. The volume of the triangular prism shown below is 60 cubic units. (The area of the triangular base is given as 10 square units, and the height is 6 units.)

A cylinder is like a prism in that it has parallel faces, but its rounded "side" is smooth. The formula for finding the **volume of a cylinder** is the same as the formula for finding the volume of a prism: the area of the cylinder's base is multiplied by the height, or $V = \pi r^2 h$. The volume of the cylinder shown below is $V = (5 \times 5 \times \pi \times 8) \approx 628$ cubic units.

Symmetry

Symmetry is the correspondence in size, form, and arrangement of parts on opposite sides of a plane, line, or point. For example, a figure that has line symmetry has two halves that coincide if folded along its line of symmetry.

Polygons may have lines of symmetry, which can be thought of as imaginary fold lines that produce two congruent, mirror-image figures. Squares have four lines of symmetry, and non-square rectangles have two, as shown in the following figures. Circles have an infinite number of lines of symmetry.

Tessellations

The arrangement of polygons that forms a grid is called a **tessellation**; however, other shapes may also tessellate. A tessellation is a pattern formed by the repetition of a single unit or shape that, when repeated, fills the plane with no gaps and no overlaps. Familiar examples of tessellations are the patterns formed by paving stones or bricks, and cross-sections of beehives, which are in the shape of hexagons. (See Math Forum at: *http://mathforum.org/geometry/rugs/symmetry/ grids. html.*)

| square grid | triangular grid | hexagonal grid |

Ordered Pairs

Ordered pairs comprise a set of numbers listed as x and y values that are used to locate a point on a coordinate plane. An ordered pair is written as (x, y), where the first number tells how far to move horizontally from 0 and the second number (y) tells how far to move vertically from 0.

Coordinate Plane

A coordinate plane is a grid made of two main perpendicular lines, the **x-axis** and the **y-axis**. The x-axis runs horizontally and the y-axis runs vertically. The point of intersection of the two axes is called the **origin**. The origin is defined by the ordered pair (0, 0). Sets of ordered pairs may be plotted on a coordinate plane to create different lines, rays, shapes, and so on.

Concepts of Measurement

Concepts and skills in the measurement strand of the math curriculum all deal with making comparisons between what is being measured and some suitable standard of measure. Measurement offers opportunities for interdisciplinary learning in social studies, geography, science, art, and music. Key to the development of skills in measurement is allowing for various types of measurement activities. Children need first-hand practice with measuring and making estimates in measurement.

The principles of measurement involve understanding the attributes of length, capacity, weight, area, volume, time, temperature, and angles. Being able to measure connects mathematics to the environment and gives children practical applications for computation skills. The ability to estimate by using measurement tools (e.g., rulers, thermometers, measuring cups, and scales) is a necessary skill for children to develop. According to Burns (2000), concepts in measurement include four stages in learning when developing classroom activities:

1. Comparing objects by matching—ordering items based on size.

2. Comparing a variety of objects for measuring—using body parts, blocks, cubes, etc.

3. Comparing objects using units in standard and metric systems.

4. Comparing using suitable units for specific measurements, taking into consideration the scale of the object being measured.

Time

The two basic kinds of clocks are **digital** and **analog**. The digital represents the time by using Arabic numbers, separating the hours from the minutes with a colon (12:45), which makes it relatively easy to read. The analog clock uses two hands to represent the hours and minutes based on 60 minutes for an hour and 60 seconds for a minute. Students must have a mathematical understanding of each of the numbers on a clock face when using analog clocks.

In addition, students should be aware of the time equivalents shown in Table 4-11.

Table 4-11. Time Equivalents

1 year = 365 days
1 year = 12 months
1 year = 52 weeks
1 week = 7 days
1 day = 24 hours
1 hour = 60 minutes
1 minute = 60 seconds

Temperature

Temperature is measured by using a thermometer, which is usually filled with mercury (a liquid metallic element that expands with heat). The **Fahrenheit** scale (°F) is used in the United States, whereas the **Celsius** scale (°C) is used in nearly every other country in the world. The Celsius scale is specifically useful in scientific experimentation. Water boils at 212°F or 100°C, and freezes at 32°F or 0°C.

Money

Teaching the concept of money involves understanding the concept of base ten. Children learn how to relate each denomination to pennies and understand the relationships among the other coins. Use real currency to introduce this concept. Children begin by observing the various coins and their attributes. They learn to associate the value for each of the coins and to make equivalences. Suggest that students begin by counting out a bag of coins and then trade out the various coins for larger denominations—for example, 5 pennies for one nickel.

Transformations: Translations, Rotations, and Reflections

Translation

Translation (also called a slide) simply means moving. Every translation has a direction and distance. This is known as a transformation that moves a geometric figure by sliding. Each of the points of the geometric figure moves the same distance in the same direction. This may be shown on a graph by moving the shape without rotating or reflecting it. The triangle in the following figure is translated down and to the left.

Rotation

Rotation (also called a turn) is known as a transformation that rotates or turns the shape around. Each rotation has a center and an angle for movement of a given number of degrees.

Reflection

Reflection (also called a flip) is known as a transformation that means to reflect an object or to make the figure/object appear to be backwards or flipped. It produces the mirror image of a geometric figure.

Conversions within and between Measurement Systems

Units of Measurement

TEKS requires that students in Kindergarten through Grade 6 become familiar with and apply knowledge of measurement using both U.S. customary (standard) and metric systems. The United States has supported the International System of Weights and Measures, as the metric system is formally known, since 1875. Russ Rowlett (2019) points out that the two systems have come to comfortably coexist in the U.S. "Americans," he says, "probably use a greater variety of units of measurement than anyone else in the world. Caught in a slow-moving transition from customary to metric units, we employ a fascinating and sometimes frustrating mixture of units in talking about the same things. We measure the length of a race in meters, but the length of the long jump event in feet and inches. We speak of an engine's power in horsepower and its displacement in liters. In the same dispatch, we describe a hurricane's wind speed in knots and its central pressure in millibars."

Customary Units

- **Linear** measurement: Customary units of length include inches, feet, yards, and miles.

- Measurement of **mass**: Customary units of weight include ounces, pounds and tons.

- **Volume** measurement: Customary units of capacity include teaspoons, tablespoons, cups, pints, quarts, and gallons.

Metric Units

- **Linear** measurement: Metric units of length include millimeters, centimeters, meters, and kilometers. The centimeter is the basic metric unit of length, at least for short distances. There are about 2.5 centimeters to 1 inch. The kilometer is a metric unit of length used for longer distances. It takes more than 1.5 kilometers to make a mile.

- Measurement of **mass**: Metric units of weight include grams and kilograms. The gram is the basic metric unit of mass (which for many purposes is the same as weight). A large paper clip weighs about 1 gram. It takes about 28 grams to make 1 ounce.

- **Volume** measurement: Metric units of capacity include milliliters and liters. The liter is the basic metric unit of volume. A liter is slightly larger than a quart, so it takes just under four liters to make a gallon.

Table 4-12 delineates the relationships within and between the customary and metric units of measurement.

Table 4-12. Customary and Metric Systems

Customary System	Metric System
Linear 12 inches (in.) = 1 foot (ft.) 3 feet (ft.) = 1 yard (yd.) 1,760 yards (yds.) = 1 mile (mi.) 5,280 feet (ft.) = 1 mile (mi.)	**Linear** 10 millimeters (mm) = 1 centimeter (cm) 100 centimeters (cm) = 1 meter (m) 1000 meters (m) = 1 kilometer (km)
Capacity and Volume 1 gallon (gal.) = 4 quarts (qt.) 1 gallon (gal.) = 128 fluid ounces 1 quart (qt.) = 2 pints (pt.) 1 pint (pt.) = 2 cups (C.) 1 pint (pt.) = 16 fluid ounces (oz.) 1 cup (C.) = 8 fluid ounces (oz.)	**Capacity and Volume** 1 liter (L) = 1000 milliliters (ml)
Mass and Weight 1 ton =-2000 pounds (lbs) 1 pound (lb.) = 16 ounces (oz.)	**Mass and Weight** 1 kilogram (kg) = 1000 grams (g) 1 gram (g) = 1000 milligrams (mg)

Logical Reasoning

The development of **logical reasoning** is closely related to children's language development. Elementary mathematics instruction should help students learn to organize ideas, understand what they are studying, and explain their thinking as they solve problems. Activities should provide students with opportunities to make generalizations and conclusions, to justify them with logical arguments, and to be able to communicate their reasoning to others. Mathematics is a way of thinking, rather than a body of facts. This is an important distinction for children to understand. Critical thinking and logical reasoning aid students in clarifying their thought processes, and they may apply this skill in all curriculum areas.

In the early grades through Grade 3, logical thinking should be introduced using an informal approach. There should be many opportunities for children to explore, manipulate, and experience concrete objects to identify their attributes, to make comparisons, to classify by their characteristics, and to make generalizations about their properties. The use of words such as *all, some, if, then,* or *not* helps children gain knowledge with the language used in logic. In upper elementary grades, students should be provided with learning activities involving deductive and inductive reasoning.

Deductive Reasoning

Deductive reasoning requires moving from an assumption to a conclusion. Deductive reasoning is reasoning from the general to the specific, and it is supported by deductive logic. Students use this type of reasoning in daily life, for example: "It is raining so I need to take my umbrella to school." Note that conclusions reached via deductive reasoning are sound only if the original assumptions are actually true.

An example of how deductive reasoning can be used to solve a geometry problem is the following.

The sum of the measures of the three angles of any triangle is 180° (a general proposition). The sum of the measures of ∠ K and ∠ L is 120°; therefore, the measure of ∠ J is 60° (a specific proposition).

Inductive Reasoning

Inductive reasoning involves examining particular instances to come to some general assumptions. This type of reasoning is informal and intuitive. When thinking inductively, students make hypotheses, extend thought patterns, use analogies, and make reasonable conclusions from examining what appears to be a large enough body of evidence. Students use this type of reasoning regularly in life situations; for example, "If I do my homework all this week, I think my mother will take me to the concert on Saturday."

With inductive reasoning, a general rule is inferred from specific observations (which may be limited). Moving from the statement, "All fish that I have ever seen have fins" (specific but limited observations) to "All fish have fins" (a general proposition) is an example of inductive reasoning. Conclusions arrived using inductive reasoning are not necessarily always true.

Axiomatic Structure

An **axiom** is a mathematical rule. This basic assumption about a system allows theorems to be developed. For example, the system could be the points and lines in the plane. Then an axiom would be that given any two distinct points in the plane, there is a unique straight line through them.

COMPETENCY 005: PROBABILITY AND STATISTICS

The teacher understands concepts related to probability and statistics and their applications.

Statistics is the science or study of data. Statistical methods are used to describe, analyze, evaluate, and interpret information. The information is then used for predicting, drawing inferences, and making decisions. Data analysis involves both probability and statistics. Probability gives a way to measure uncertainty and is essential for understanding statistical methods. It explains data sets to give a type of generalized statistic, to make a prediction, or to infer something beyond the specific data collected. Probability is used to create experimental and theoretical models of situations.

Counting Techniques for Solving Problems

Students use counting techniques to solve mathematics problems. Some of the techniques include the following.

- Use networks, traceable paths, tree diagrams, Venn diagrams, and other pictorial representations to find the number of outcomes in a problem situation. For example, suppose a motel has 4 different elevators that go from Joan's room to the pool and 3 different doors to the pool area. Use a tree diagram to show how many different ways Joan can get from her room to the pool.

- Use the fundamental counting principle to find the number of outcomes in a problem situation. For example, a student can choose from 6 shirts, 4 pairs of jeans, and 3 pairs of shoes to wear to school. Ignoring color coordination, construct a tree diagram or other pictorial representation to show how many different outfits the student could assemble.

- Use combinatorial reasoning to solve problems. For example, a gym locker combination contains the numbers 2, 4, 6, and 8, but the gymnast has forgotten the order in which they occur. What is the maximum number of combinations the gymnast needs to try before the locker can be opened?

- Use counting techniques to solve probability problems. For example, what is the probability that the gymnast's locker from the problem above opens with the first combination?

- Use simulations to solve counting and probability problems. For example, a panel of 12 jurors was selected from a large group that was 70% male and 30% female. The jury turned out to be 11 men and 1 woman. Suspecting gender bias, the defense attorneys asked how likely it is that this situation, or even 12 men and 0 women, would occur purely by chance. Simulate this situation by using a random number generator to select 12 numbers, letting 0, 1, and 2 represent women and 3, 4, 5, 6, 7, 8, and 9 represent men. Note the number of times that 11 or 12 men are chosen.

Research on Teaching Data Analysis

There is some general agreement with regard to six underlying facts about the learning and teaching of data analysis. These include the following:

1. A problem-solving approach to teaching is consistent with how learners develop data analysis knowledge. (Lajoie, Jacobs & Lavigne, 1995).

2. Concept knowledge must be developed first before developing procedural knowledge. This can then be further developed by using problem solving, for example, understanding the concept of sample before gathering data to analyze a problem/situation. (Horvath & Lehrer, 1998).

3. Concepts and procedures are interdependent. (Konold & Higgins, 2003)

4. Statistical representations can become more sophisticated using technology and as students have more experience with data (Friel, Curcio & Bright, 2001).

5. Data organization can be improved by using technology tools. (Konold, 2002; Lehrer & Romberg, 1996).

6. Teachers must sequence instruction based on developmental age-appropriate situations, so students may examine certain types of situations before other types. For example, students should study situations in which all outcomes are equally likely before studying situations in which all outcomes are not equally likely. (Horvath & Lehrer, 1998).

Probability

Learning probability and statistics provides real applications of arithmetic. When basic computation skills are used in context, students have the opportunity to see the advantages and limitations of their calculations. Most arithmetic is done with a degree of uncertainty. Examples include estimating costs, making calculations of needed building materials, approximating estimated time of arrival (ETA) on trips, and estimating time for baking or cooking food.

A set of data can be described by its range, mean, median, and/or mode.

The **range** of a set of data is the difference between the greatest and the least numbers in the data set. Subtract these numbers to find the difference, which is the range.

The **mean** of a set of data is the average of the data values. To find the mean, add all the data values and then divide this sum by the number of values in the set.

The **median** of a set of data is the middle value of all the numbers. To find the middle value, list the numbers in order from the least to greatest or from greatest to least. Cross out one value on each end of the list until you reach the middle. If there are two values in the middle, find the number halfway between the two values by adding them together and dividing their sum by 2 (taking the mean of the two numbers).

The **mode** is the value (or values) that appear in a set of data more frequently than any other value. If all the values in a set of data appear the same number of times, the set does not have a mode. It is possible, however, to have more than one mode.

Studying probability and statistics should involve real problems and/or simulations. A theoretical or abstract approach is not appropriate for students in elementary mathematics. The approach should be based on experiments that draw on children's experiences and interests. Children's intuition needs to be challenged. Once they understand or can say what "should happen" in a situation, then they may be able to conduct experiments to test their predictions. Basic to probability and statistics are the following steps:

1. Data collection

2. Sampling

3. Organizing and representing data

4. Interpreting data

5. Assigning probabilities

6. Making inferences

Probability is a way of describing the likelihood of a particular outcome. An event is random when a selection is made without looking. A fraction can be used to describe the results of a probability experiment in this way: (1) The numerator of the fraction is the number of *favorable* outcomes for the experiment. ("Favorable" outcomes just refers to the outcome of interest in the probability; it can even be unfavorable in a social sense, such as the probability of death due to a disease.) (2) The denominator of the fraction is the number of all the *possible* outcomes for the experiment.

> Gabrielle is randomly choosing a marble from a bag containing three marbles—1 red marble, 1 blue marble, and 1 green marble. What is the probability that she will choose a green marble on a single pull?
>
> - There is 1 green marble in the bag. There is 1 favorable outcome.
> - There are $1 + 1 + 1 = 3$ marbles in the bag. There are 3 possible outcomes.
>
> $$\text{Probability of choosing a green marble} = \frac{\text{Number of favorable outcomes}}{\text{Total number of possible outcomes}} = \frac{1}{3}$$
>
> The probability that Gabrielle will choose a green marble on a single pull is $\frac{1}{3}$, or 1 out of 3.

Students need to demonstrate an understanding of probability and statistics and be able to do the following: (1) use experimental and theoretical probability to make predictions; and (2) use statistical representations to analyze data. A **sample space** is the set of all possible outcomes of an experiment. For example, a coin is flipped, it will land either heads or tails. Students learn to list the sample space, or all the possible outcomes: heads or tails. Sample spaces may also be listed on a chart or tree diagram.

Jones, Langral, Thornton, and Mogill (1999) have developed a four-stage framework that attempts to explain the learning process for probability. Learners begin at the subjective level, at which they are easily swayed by personal experiences when making probabilistic statements. At the second level, transitional learners begin to recognize the importance of organizing information. At the third level, students become informal quantitative thinkers. At the final level, students work at the purely numerical level in which they understand the nuances of numerical argument and use sophisticated procedures to determine numerical facts.

Students should learn to read graphs, making quick visual summaries as well as further interpretations and comparisons of data through finding means, medians, and modes. Students can use tables, line graphs, bar graphs, circle graphs, line plots, and pictographs to organize and display data. This is a helpful strategy used in problem solving.

For example, a **line plot** represents a set of data by showing how often a piece of data appears in that set. This plot consists of a number line that indicates the values of the data set and marks placed above the corresponding number each time that value appears in the data set. For example, suppose the heights of ten 12-year-old girls were measured and recorded. Then a line plot can be used to record the data from a chart, and students may make comparisons of the range of height, find the tallest or shortest girl, and interpret the data found.

In real-world problems, students may sample a part of a population. Students need to learn the difference between random and nonrandom samples and the importance this difference makes in statistical studies. As an example, to determine the percentage of people who are left-handed, students would not poll only famous athletes as a random sampling.

For students to fully understand data analysis, all frameworks and researchers agree that students should generate their own data. They should work with simulations that model real situations. They should use dice, spinners, two-color counters, and coins. As students begin to understand how to gather their own data, they need to be consciously aware of any graphical representations they might choose to use, recognizing the difference between discrete and continuous situations. Technology is a highly useful tool in data analysis and in making sense of the data, so students should be made aware of what is available in the ever-changing digital world.

COMPETENCY 006: MATHEMATICAL PROCESSES

The teacher understands mathematical processes and knows how to reason mathematically, solve mathematical problems, and make mathematical connections within and outside of mathematics.

The National Council of Teachers of Mathematics (NCTM) and the Texas Essential Knowledge and Skills (TEKS) have emphasized the importance of teaching mathematical reasoning to children from Kindergarten through Grade 12. Teachers of the youngest students face a challenge because the ability to perform operations involving logical reasoning requires some level of cognitive maturity and the ability to think abstractly. From Kindergarten to Grade 2, children must understand the principles and patterns of the number system and the symbols used to represent numbers. Principles of measurement and basic geometry are also introduced early in the process. In Grades 1 and 2, children begin to use quantitative reasoning and basic algorithms for addition and subtraction. Beginning in Grade 3 and continuing throughout elementary school, students continue to improve their basic knowledge of the number system and the abstraction of mathematical reasoning and begin to explore basic algebraic, geometric, and spatial reasoning. They also master multiplication facts and division. Word problems and mathematical reasoning are heavily emphasized in preparation for TEKS, which is offered in Grades 3 to 12.

Logical Reasoning

Teachers must create opportunities to motivate children to engage in exploratory mathematics to develop logical thinking. For the early grades, this exploration can be done in **learning centers**, where children have the opportunity to work with blocks, shapes, and other manipulatives that are used to teach mathematical concepts in an indirect fashion through student-selected activities.

In addition to exposure to mathematics concepts in learning centers, teachers use instructional strategies to apply mathematics concepts in real-life situations. As an example, a role-play activity involving children ordering food in a restaurant on a given budget may be simulated in the classroom. This type of activity may guide children to understand basic mathematical concepts, including calculating sums of money, giving change, understanding percentages to determine an appropriate gratuity or sales tax, and the use of mathematics in daily life. Further extensions can be made with this scenario by teaching the students to understand the concept of budgeting and managing money based on a salary, including living within a budget and balancing a checkbook.

Solving mathematics problems involves logical reasoning, or thinking in a way that makes sense. Students can use logical reasoning to find patterns in a set of data and can then use those patterns to draw conclusions about the data that can be used to solve problems. They can identify characteristics that numbers or objects have in common, looking for patterns in different ways. For example, a group of geometric objects may have some property in common, such as all being quadrilaterals or all having right angles.

Problem-Solving Strategies

Solving problems involves more than just numerical computation; logical reasoning and careful planning also play important roles. Various methods can be used to solve word problems. Strategies may include, but are not limited to, acting the problems out, drawing a picture or graph, using logical reasoning, looking for a pattern, using a process of elimination, creating an organized chart or list, solving a simpler but related problem, using trial and error (guess and check), working backwards, or writing an equation. **Table 4-13** lists some of the steps used in solving problems.

Table 4-13. Steps in Solving a Problem

Understand the problem

Organize the given information and identify the question. Be aware that extraneous or irrelevant information may be given that is not needed to solve the problem.

Choose a strategy and/or make a plan

After you have organized the information, decide how to use this information to find an answer. Think about the math concepts that apply to the situation. Identify the order in which you will find new information and carry out your strategy.

Carry out the plan

After you have chosen a problem-solving strategy, use that strategy to work out the problem. Go step-by-step through your plan, writing down important information at each step.

Check your answer

Check your answer to see whether it answers the question. Is it stated in the correct units? Is it reasonable? Does it make sense? Estimate the solution and then compare the estimate to the computed answer. They should be approximately equal.

Developmental Considerations

Children in Pre-K and Kindergarten might have problems understanding basic number systems and how numbers are presented symbolically. They might have difficulties dealing with measurement activities that require them to master the principle of conservation. They might think that an apple split in half is more than a single apple, or a soda drink in a tall and narrow glass might be more than the same amount of liquid in a shorter and wider glass. These cognitive and reasoning limitations tend to disappear as children develop. By first grade, the principle of conservation is generally acquired.

Mathematics instruction in Kindergarten through Grade 6 involves not only knowing mathematical processes but also being able to determine when a given process is required.

Children must develop the ability to reason through word problems and understand the type of answer required. Most third graders can do addition, subtraction, multiplication, and even division. However, they might have difficulties with word problems and problem-solving activities that require them to identify the appropriate mathematical process. They might also have problems understanding questions involving multiple steps and deciding on the appropriate answer. The word problem that follows represents an example.

Joe can place a maximum of 5 apples in a paper sack. If he needs to put 32 apples in sacks, how many sacks does he need?

In this example, most students will know that the problem calls for division—32 divided by 5—which will yield the expected number of 6.4. Some students will provide 6.4 as the answer, but the real question is: "How many sacks does Joe need?" Children will have to reason that the number of paper sacks can be only whole numbers; thus, the answer cannot be 6.4 sacks but rather 7 paper sacks.

Mathematical reasoning is crucial for understanding and using mathematics. This type of contextual or situational reasoning is certainly important, and questions such as the preceding one have a solid place in the curriculum and on state tests. Logical reasoning is the foundation for understanding mathematics and its use in life.

Historical Development of Mathematics

Every culture has developed some form of functional mathematics concept. In most cases, accomplishments of these civilizations have been transmitted to and enhanced by other groups. This transmission of knowledge and its cumulative effects have resulted in the creation of the modern-day mathematics used around the world. Some of the key civilizations that impacted the development of mathematics in the Western world are discussed in the following sections.

Egyptians and Babylonians

The first mathematicians that impacted the development of modern-day mathematics were from the ancient civilizations of Babylon and Egypt around 3000 BCE. The ancient Egyptians wrote numbers using hieroglyphs to represents the numbers 1, 10, 100, 1,000, 10,000, and 1,000,000. They used numbers into the millions for practical purposes like managing resources and for building large-scale public structures such as temples and pyramids.

The Babylonians made great advances in science, math, and, specifically, in astronomy. They also developed tables for multiplication and division as well as square and cube roots. One of the greatest accomplishments of Babylonian civilization was the development of a number system with a base of 60. This number system constituted the foundation for the advanced mathematics evolution that followed the Egyptians and Babylonians.

Greeks

The Greeks built on the accomplishments of the Egyptians and Babylonians and further developed the field of mathematics. Most historians believe that the formal study of mathematics as a discipline began with the Athenian Greek school of Thales and Pythagoras. Some authorities identify Thales and Pythagoras as the founders of Greek mathematics. Thales (640–550 BCE) was a merchant who traveled extensively and became acquainted with Egyptian mathematics. Some of his contributions include the following facts: a circle is bisected by the diameter, angles at the base of an isosceles triangle are equal, and an angle inscribed in a semicircle is a right angle.

Pythagoras, a former pupil of Thales, followed his teacher's ideas and eventually became one of the leading figures of Greek mathematics. Pythagoras taught that there is a basic relationship between harmony and mathematics. He developed the relationship of the sides of a right triangle, later named the Pythagorean theorem. After the early Athenian Greeks, the Alexandrian Greeks emerged as the leaders in the study of science and mathematics. Around 300 BCE, Ptolemy founded the university at Alexandria in Egypt, which became the center of learning for the Western world. This institution became the leading force in the study of mathematics, contributing multiple discoveries and some of the greatest thinkers of the time. Two of the leading figures that emerged during this period were Archimedes and Euclid.

Archimedes calculated the distances of the planets from the Earth and constructed a spherical planetarium imitating the motions of the Sun, Moon, and the six then-known planets. He also made multiple discoveries with scientific and military applications. Euclid was one of the most influential Greek mathematicians in the world. He is believed to have learned geometry from the students of Plato. Euclid is famous for providing a complete record of the mathematics accomplishments of Ancient Greece. He wrote several books on the elements of geometry. His mathematics knowledge has served as the standard mathematics textbook for over two thousand years (Euclidean geometry).

The Greeks also discovered that rational numbers could not accurately express all mathematical values. Based on this need, they developed the concept of irrational numbers. An irrational number cannot be expressed as a fraction. In decimal form, irrational numbers do not repeat in a pattern or terminate; they continue to infinity. Some examples of irrational numbers are $\pi = 3.141592654\ldots$ and $\sqrt{2} = 1.41421356\ldots$

Hindus

Around the fifth century, the Hindus developed a system of mathematics that allowed for astronomical calculations. They developed a technique of computation that later influenced the development of modern-day algebra.

Arab Contributions

The Arabs were the first civilization to solve sophisticated algebraic equations such as those currently used in science and engineering (e.g., quadratic equations). They also developed and perfected geometric algebra. Arab mathematicians used the work of the Greeks in geometry and improved the development of the field. They founded non-Euclidian geometry and made advances in trigonometry. The greatest contributions of the Arabs were the development of the numeric system, which resulted in the spread of the cumulative knowledge of mathematics to the world.

The Concept of Zero

The concept of zero can be understood as nothing or a void, and as a number (0), that serves as a placeholder in a place-value mathematical system. Various ancient civilizations, including Egypt, Babylon, India, and perhaps the Olmec civilization in Mesoamerica, independently developed the concept of zero, understood as a void or nothing, but not all of these civilizations employed the number (0) as a placeholder, a numerical symbol, and in computational arithmetic. Indian mathematicians, perhaps as early as 600 CE united all these understandings of the concept zero. Indian numerals, including the zero, were rapidly adopted by Arab and Persian mathematicians and spread throughout the Islamic world, before being accepted in Western Europe, which had long struggled with the more unwieldy Roman and Greek number system.

The Number System

The **number system** used in modern days is described as a Hindu-Arabic numeration system. It uses numbers from 1 to 9 and 0. Historians seem to agree that the Hindus contributed to the development of the base-10 digit system and the Arabs perfected and spread it throughout the world.

The cumulative knowledge of the Babylonians, Egyptians, and Greeks was translated from Greek into Arabic. At the same time, the mathematical accomplishments of the Hindus were also translated into Arabic. The collective knowledge of these civilizations and the improvement and innovations developed in the Arab world became the mathematics of Western Europe and, over a period of several hundred years of further development, became the mathematics of the world.

Other Civilizations

Other civilizations, such as the Mayans and the Aztecs, made significant progress in mathematics. The Mayan civilization around 700 CE developed an elaborate calendar, and independently from the Arabs, the mathematical concept of zero. The Mayans also had highly advanced knowledge of astronomy, engineering, and the arts. Although the concept of zero was developed separately by the Mayans in 700 CE, there is no evidence to suggest that the Mayan notion of zero impacted the development of mathematics beyond the Maya empire in Central America.

The Aztec civilization flourished around 1325 BCE. The Aztecs were also skilled builders and engineers, accomplished astronomers, and mathematicians. Like the Egyptians, they used mathematical principles for functional purposes to build pyramids, palaces, plazas, and canals.

Mathematicians from other places in the world developed significant accomplishments in mathematics. China, Japan, and several kingdoms from Africa are examples of civilizations that made sizeable progress in mathematics; however, their accomplishments did not have a direct impact on the development of mathematics in the Western world. For a detailed analysis of the historical development of mathematics and the contribution of various civilizations, see the "History of Mathematics" website, maintained by David E. Joyce of Clark University in Worcester, Massachusetts (http://aleph0.clarku.edu/~djoyce/mathhist/).

Key Developments in Mathematics Education in the United States

Since the mid-20th century, the U.S. education system has made important changes in the teaching of mathematics. Some of the key changes are listed below.

1950s to 1960s

- Significant changes in content of elementary mathematics programs

- New content added

- Standard content taught at earlier grade levels

1970s

- Slowing down of content changes

- Attention and focus on "system of delivery" of content

Late 1970s, early 1980s

- Back-to-basics movement

- Heavy emphasis on drill and practice

Late 1980s

- Increased emphasis on teaching concepts and problem solving

1990s

- Increased use of computers and calculators for computation

- Increased emphasis on estimation, problem solving, and higher-level thinking

- Release of Professional Standards for Teaching Mathematics (1991), "a broad framework to guide" the teaching of mathematics from the National Council of Teachers of Mathematics

Early 2000s

- Increased emphasis on assessment, equity, technology, learning, and teaching and curriculum standards

- Use of literature and cultural connections with mathematics and its implication in teaching

- Increased emphasis on research-based instructional strategies

Sources

Burns, M. 2000. *About teaching mathematics: A K–8 resource.* Sausalito, CA: Math Solutions Publications.

Carpenter, T.M., Fennema, E., Franke, M.L., Levi, L., & Empson. S.B. (1999). *Children's mathematics: Cognitively guided instruction.* Portsmouth, NH: Heinemann.

Flavell, J.H. (1985). *Cognitive development.* 2nd ed. Upper Saddle River, NJ: Prentice Hall.

Fredericks, A.D., Blake-Kline, B., & Kristo, J.V. (1997). *Teaching the integrated language arts: Process and practice.* New York: Longman.

Friel, S.N., Curcio, F.R., & Bright, G.W. (2001). Making sense of graphs: Critical Factors influencing comprehension and instructional implication. *Journal of Research in Mathematics Education*, 32(2), 124–158.

Fuson, K.C., & Hall, J.W. (1983). The acquisition of early number word meanings: A conceptual analysis and review. In *The development of mathematical thinking,* ed. H.P. Ginsburg, pp. 49–107. Orlando, FL: Academic Press.

Fuys, D., Gedds, D., & Tischler, R. 1988. The Van Hiele model of thinking in geometry among adolescent. *Journal of Research in Mathematics Education Monograph #3.* Reston, VA: NCTM.

Horvath, J.K., & Lehrer, R. (1998). A model-based perspective on the development of children's understanding of chance and uncertainty. In S.P. Lajoie (Ed.), *Reflections on statistics: Learning teaching, and assessment in grades K–12,* (pp. 121–148). Mahwah, NJ: Lawrence Erlbaum Associates.

Jones, G.A., Langrall, C.W., Thorton, C.A., & Mogill, A.T. (1999). Student's probabilistic thinking in instruction. *Journal for Research in Mathematics Education*, 30(5), 487–519.

Kamii, C. (2000). *Young children reinvent arithmetic: Implications of Piaget's theory.* New York: Teacher College Press.

Konold, C. (2002). Teaching concepts rather than conventions. *New England Journal of Mathematics Education, 34(2),* 69–80. Retrieved from *http://researchgate.net/publication/266339257 Teaching concepts rather than conventions.*

Konold, C., & Higgins, T. (2003). Reasoning about data. In J. Kilpatrick, W.G. Martin, and D.E. Schifter (Eds.). *A research companion to principles and standards for school mathematics*, Reston, VA: NCTM.

Lehrer, R., & Romberg, T. (1996). Exploring children's data modeling. *Cognition and Instruction, 14(1),* 69–108.

Lejoie, S.P., Jacobs, V.R., & Lavigne, N.C. (1995). Empowering children in the use of statistics. *Journal of Mathematics Behavior, 14(4),* 401–425.

National Council of Teachers of Mathematics (NCTM). (2007). *Professional standards for teaching mathematics.* Retrieved from *http://toolkitforchange.org/toolkit/view.php?obj=1039&menu=i*

National Council of Teachers of Mathematics (NCTM). (2000). *Principles and standards for school mathematics.* Reston, VA: NCTM.

Pepper, C., & Hunting, R.P. (1998). Preschoolers' counting and sharing. Journal for Research in Mathematics Education, 29(2), 14–183.

Piaget, J., & Inhelder, B. (1969). *The psychology of the child.* New York: Basic Books.

Santrock, J.W. (2003). *Children* (7th ed.), Boston, PA: McGraw-Hill.

Sperry Smith, S. (2008). *Early childhood mathematics,* 4th ed. Boston, MA: Allyn and Bacon.

Texas Education Agency (TEA). (2008). Pre-kindergarten curriculum guidelines. Online: *http://tea.texas.gov/index2.aspx?id=2147495508&menu_id=214783718*

Texas Education Agency (TEA). (2007–2015). Texas Essential Knowledge and Skills by Chapter, online: *https://tea.texas.gov/about-tea/laws-and-rules/texas-administrative-code/texas-administrative-code-title-19-part-2*

Texas Education Agency (TEA). (2014–2015). STAAR released test questions. Available online at *http://tea.texas.gov/student.assessment/staar/math/*

U.S. Department of Labor. (2012). Bureau of Labor Statistics, U.S. Department of Labor Occupational Outlook Handbook, 2008–09 edition, Bulletin 2700. Washington, DC: Superintendent of Documents, U.S. Government Printing Office. Retrieved from. *https://www.bls.gov*

Van Hiele, P.M. (1986). *Structure and Insight.* Orlando, FL: Academic Press.

Vygotsky, L.S. (1986). *Thought and language* (new rev. ed.) Cambridge, MA: MIT Press.

Subject Test III: Social Studies (903)

COMPETENCY 001: SOCIAL SCIENCE INSTRUCTION

The teacher understands and applies social science knowledge and skills to plan, organize, and implement instruction and assess learning.

Social Studies Curricula

Social studies is an umbrella term encompassing the disciplines of history, geography, civics and government, economics, and psychology. All five components are intertwined with the standards shown in Figure 5-1, which were developed by the National Council for the Teaching of Social Studies in 1997 (NCTSS, 2006). The Texas Education Agency (TEA) used these curriculum standards as a foundation to develop the state social studies curriculum for Kindergarten through Grade 12. Educators have a crucial responsibility because they lay the foundation of American core values, citizenship, democracy, and patriotism. EC–6 teachers must learn to find ways to infuse their curricula with social studies lessons and recognize that social studies strongly supports literacy and other content areas. Understanding maps, diagrams, charts, and graphs as well as analysis of spatial patterns and relationships support students' spatial and mathematical reasoning capabilities.

Texas Essential Knowledge and Skills (TEKS) in Social Studies

The Texas Essential Knowledge and Skills (TEKS) is the state curriculum for Kindergarten to Grade 12. The TEKS organizes the social studies content inductively, from the known to the unknown. In this vertical alignment, children begin learning about the self in Kindergarten and

---

☞ To focus your study, go online to take the diagnostic test for this subject at *www.rea.com/studycenter*.

expand their knowledge with each, successive grade, eventually encompassing the community, the state, the nation, and the world.

The eight strands of the TEKS for social studies are history; geography; economics; government; citizenship; culture; science, technology, and society; and social studies skills. These eight strands are intended to be integrated for instructional purposes and provide a foundation for vertical alignment across grade levels from Kindergarten to Grade 12. Secondary grade-level social studies courses build and rely on the foundation laid by EC–6 teachers. A summary of the key components of the social studies curriculum covered in Kindergarten through Grade 6 follows.

Figure 5-1. National Curriculum Standards for Social Studies: The 10 Themes of Social Studies

This figure presents the National Curriculum Standards for Social Studies (National Council for the Social Studies, 2016). For additional information, go online: *https://www.socialstudies.org/standards*.

Kindergarten—Self, Home, Family, and Classroom

- The child as an individual and citizen

- Home and families as the foundations of culture and tradition

- State and national heritage and symbols

- Patriotic holidays and the contribution of historical characters

- Spatial awareness and locational terminology

- Physical and human characteristics of the child's world

- The difference between needs and wants; jobs and their functions

- Rules and their purposes; the role of authority and authority figures

- Gathering, organizing, and using information to communicate

- Basic chronological awareness and interpretation of images, maps, and other visuals

Grade 1—Child's Relationship to the Classroom, School, and Community

- The concept of chronology developed by distinguishing among past, present, and future

- Anthems and mottoes of Texas and the United States; customs, holidays, and celebrations of community, state, and nation

- Relationship among the classroom, school, and community

- Relationship between human wants and needs, goods and services, and market exchanges

- The value of work and the role of work in producing goods and services

- The role of rules and authority figures in establishing order, security and managing conflict

- Ethical dimensions of good citizenship and participation in civic life

- Importance of family and community beliefs, language and traditions

- The role of invention and impact of technological innovation on individuals, families, and communities

Using social studies skills to gather information, communicate in oral, visual, and written forms, and to problem solve individually and with others.

Grade 2—Local Community

- Impact of significant individuals and events in the history of the community, state, and nation

- Significance of community, state, and national celebrations as well as civic and patriotic symbols

- Concepts of time and chronology by measuring calendar time by days, weeks, months, and years

- Relationship between the physical environment and human activities; Functions of government and the services government provide

- Local, state, and national officials and their roles

- Relationships between work, income, production and consumer choices; Responsibilities of good citizenship and American beliefs and principles

- Social studies vocabulary and skills to express ideas, make decisions and problem-solve.

Grade 3—How Individuals Change Their Communities and the World

- Past and present heroes and their contributions as citizens, cultural icons, and entrepreneurs

- People who overcame obstacles to make technological or other breakthroughs

- Economic, cultural, and scientific contributions made by individuals

- Processes of community formation in the past

- Different physical environments and the ways humans have adapted to them

- Interpretation of maps and globes to determine distance, direction, and location

- How businesses operate within free enterprise systems

- Concepts of earning, spending, saving, and donating money

- Basic structures and function of local, state, and national government

- Characteristics of good citizenship (truthfulness, justice, equality, respect for oneself and others, participation in government, voting, and educating oneself about current issues)

- Individual acts of good citizenship and people who have exemplified good citizenship (such as Helen Keller, Clara Barton, and Ruby Bridges, for example) as well as organizations like the Red Cross that serve the common good

- Cultural differences and ethnic and/or cultural celebrations

- Application of critical thinking and social studies skills and vocabulary to communicate and solve problems.

Grade 4—History of Texas

- History of Texas from its beginnings to the present

- Events and individuals of the 19th and 20th centuries

- Human activity and physical features of regions in Texas and the Western Hemisphere

- Native Americans in Texas and the Western Hemisphere and their economic and cultural characteristics

- European exploration and colonization of Texas

- Types of Native American governments

- Characteristics of Spanish and Mexican colonial governments

- 19th century settlement of Texas; origins, key events, prominent figures and effects of the Texas Revolution

- Annexation of Texas to the United States, the Civil War, and Reconstruction in Texas

- 19th and 20th century political, social, and economic changes in Texas

- Physical regions of Texas and their characteristics

- Relationship of Texas geographic regions and patterns of settlement and urbanization in different time periods

- The development of the free enterprise system in Texas and the patterns of work and economic activity in the state

- Comparisons of Texas and U.S. governmental structures, institutions, and founding documents.

- Patriotic symbols, customs, and celebrations of Texas and key figures who have modeled active participation in the democratic process in Texas

- Contributions of people of various racial, ethnic, and religious groups in Texas

- Importance of scientific and technological innovation to Texas economic success

Grade 5—United States History

- History of the United States from colonization to the present.

- Significant events and individuals of the late 19th and 20th centuries, including contributions of important inventors and scientists

- Regions of the United States that result from physical features and human activity

- Characteristics and benefits of the free enterprise system

- Roots of representative government

- Important ideas in the Declaration of Independence

- Meaning of the Pledge of Allegiance

- Fundamental rights guaranteed in the Bill of Rights

- Customs and celebrations of racial, ethnic, and religious groups in the United States

Grade 6—People and Places of the Contemporary World

- This part of the curriculum is designed to introduce students to the concepts of cultural geography. The discipline of geography explores patterns, relationships, and processes at local to global scale.

- People and places of the contemporary world

- Societies from the following regions in the world: Europe, Russia and the Eurasian republics, North America, Middle America, South America, Southwest Asia-North Africa, Sub-Saharan Africa, South Asia, East Asia, Southeast Asia, Australia, and the Pacific Realm

- Influence of individuals and groups from different cultures on selected historical and contemporary events

- Different ways of organizing economic and governmental systems

Integration of Social Studies

The teaching of social studies necessitates integration of the eight strands of the essential knowledge and skills for social studies. However, teachers can go beyond this integration and add components from other content areas. A literature-based approach is an ideal way to integrate social studies with language arts. Through the use of authentic multicultural literature, teachers can expose children to quality reading as well as the cultures of the many ethnic and linguistic groups living in the United States. Social studies is strongly linked with English Language Arts and Reading. It not only requires strong reading and writing skills but also supports reading by providing an understanding of the history as well as the physical and cultural characteristics of a place.

The use of thematic units can also help teachers to integrate the eight strands of the essential knowledge and skills for social studies. In this approach, a teacher or teachers select a theme and organize content area instruction around it. Thematic instruction can be done in a self-contained classroom or in a departmental format in which several teachers teach the content. However, units may be organized by key time periods in history or regions of the world with key themes serving as "big ideas" or "guiding questions" to drive instruction. This method allows learners to "chunk" the material historically or geographically while simultaneously analyzing major themes or "big ideas" that connect to other units of instruction. Some educators may prefer this method because it divides content into units familiar to both the educator and the students.

Thematic instruction is ideal for English learners (ELs) because the use of a common theme in multiple content areas makes content more cognitively accessible for them. For example, in a unit on the **solar system**, the names of the planets and the terminology used to describe the system can be introduced and repeated in several subjects through the duration of the unit. The presentation and repetition of content in different subjects and under different conditions allow students the opportunity to develop English vocabulary while learning content.

Using Maps and Globes

Symbolic representation can pose challenges for children in Kindergarten through Grade 4 and occasionally in Grades 5 and 6. Maps and globes are tools for representing space symbolically. Globes are a mathematical model of the Earth and show correct, unaltered (not distorted) distance, size, and shape of continents and bodies of water. Maps are a flat representation of the world and distort the distance, size, or shape of continents and bodies of water. This distortion can confuse the young learner. In the early grades, the main purpose of globes is to familiarize children with the roundness of the Earth to help them develop a global perspective. Globes also can help in studying the proportion of land and water. In Kindergarten through third grade, teachers should use a simplified 12-inch globe that uses no more than three colors to represent land elevation and no more than two to represent water depth. For this age group, the globe should include only the largest rivers, cities, and oceans. In Grades 4 through 6, students can use a 16-inch globe containing additional details and usually seven colors to represent land elevation and three colors to represent water depth.

Activities for Students in Kindergarten through Grade 6

Teaching map concepts in Kindergarten through Grade 4 should include the following:

- Stress that the globe is a small representation of the Earth.

- Show how globes represent land and water.

- Identify major countries (e.g., the United States, Mexico, and Canada), their capitals and major cities.

- Identify major landforms and water bodies.

- Show and explain the location of the North Pole and the Northern Hemisphere, where most of the world's land is located.

- Show and explain the location of the South Pole and the Southern Hemisphere, where most of the world's water is located.

- Show the relationship and location of the Earth in the solar system.

- Use the globe to find the continent, the country, the state, and the city in which the children live.

- Encourage children to explore the globe to find places by themselves.

- Compare the size of the continents represented on a globe with their representation on a Mercator projection—the flat representation.

Teaching map concepts in fifth and sixth grade should include the following:

- Identify countries, capitals, and other major cities in the world

- Identify major landforms and bodies of water

- Create and interpret maps.

- Use maps and globes to pose and answer questions.

- Locate major historical and contemporary societies on maps and globes.

- Use maps to solve real-life problems, i.e., using road maps to plan a route to a specific destination.

Latitude and Longitude—Developmental Considerations

The concepts of **latitude** and **longitude** are generally covered in fourth grade and up. However, even fourth graders may have difficulty understanding the mathematics involved in the grid system. The Mercator projection favors shape and direction by distorting sizes the closer you get to the poles. To maintain the straight longitude lines on a Mercator map, the space between lines of latitude widens as you move away from the equator.

- Because the globe and Mercator projection look different, the length of the meridians of longitude and the parallels of latitude will therefore look different on a globe versus a Mercator projection. However, lines of longitude meet at the poles. Lines of latitude are measured in degrees based on the angle formed when measured from the equator, zero degrees latitude. Lines of longitude are measured in degrees based on time. (For more information on the history of measuring longitude, visit the *National Geographic* website at *https://www.nationalgeographic.org/encyclopedia/longitude.*)

Students also may have trouble conceptualizing and separating the hemispheres (Western, Eastern, Northern, and Southern). Teachers should define the term "hemisphere" and use a concrete example like a ball to represent these abstractions.

Using Technology Information in Social Studies

Research in social studies uses systematic inquiry. Engaging children in inquiry develops the ability to acquire and analyze information from sources. Inquiry also fosters the ability to design and conduct investigations, which helps students learn key content in social studies.

To gather information, students should learn about the sources used in social sciences research. They should learn to distinguish between primary and secondary sources as they become familiar with encyclopedias, almanacs, atlases, government documents, artifacts, and oral histories. Students should apply critical-thinking skills to organize and use information acquired from sources including electronic technology. Information about social studies is on the internet, but students should learn to evaluate the scholarship of the sources and then use those with credibility. Students also can use commercially developed programs like *Oregon Trails* and *Where in the World is Carmen San Diego?* Digital globes, such as Google Earth (*https://www.google.com/earth/*) or National Geographic's Map Machine (*maps.nationalgeographic.com/map-machine*) are **geospatial technologies** that provide a forum to analyze relationships and patterns at a local to global scale. These interactive programs expose students to problem-solving skills and social studies content in a fun and supportive environment.

Graphic Representations of Historical Information

Information in social studies can be presented in a visual form through the use of graphs and charts to make content accessible to all children, including ELs.

Graphs

The most common graphs are the pictorial graph, the bar graph, the pie or circle graph, and the line graph. The **pictorial graph** is the most concrete graph because it uses a picture of the object it represents. **Bar graphs** are more concrete than pie graphs. Although **pie graphs** appear simple enough for children in the elementary grades, students must understand percentages to interpret them, and percentages aren't studied until late in the elementary grades. Teachers first can use real situations to guide students in the construction of graphs. For example, teachers can create a simple graph showing information about students in the classroom, such as the number of boys and girls or their preferences for color or food. Figure 5-2 shows the results of a poll on the favorite foods of first-grade boys and girls. A common bar graph in social studies is the population pyramid, which shows the number of males and females for each age group in a community. The population pyramid is appropriate for upper elementary because it uses percentages as well as whole numbers. Learn more at the U.S. Census Bureau's website at *https://www.census.gov*. When possible, teachers should also incorporate such charts and graphs common to other disciplines as the dot plots in mathematics, to reinforce concepts and show that learning is continuous and can be applied in different ways.

Figure 5-2— Children's Food Preferences

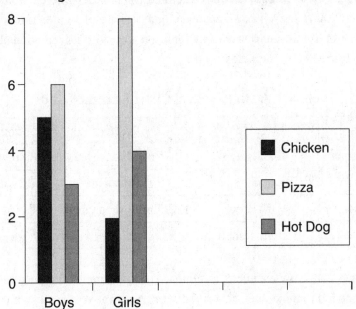

Figure 5-3. Pie Graph—Methods of Transportation

Teachers can use more sophisticated graphs like the pie to represent research information. For example, children can take five to 10 minutes a day to observe the transportation used by people in the neighborhood and prepare a graph similar to the one in Figure 5-3. Teachers can use this information to guide children to make inferences about the information contained in the graph. Why are so many people using pickup trucks for transportation? Why are few people walking?

Charts

Charts can record information and present ideas concisely. Charts are ideal for showing concepts concretely. **Data retrieval charts** can collect and track data gathered from research, observation, or experimentation. The chart allows easy comparison of two or more sets of data. For example, students could use the chart shown in Table 5-1 to record information about the foods of the ethnic groups represented in their classroom.

Table 5-1. Data Retrieval Chart—Ethnic Foods

Ethnic Group	Breakfast	Dinner	Special Days
Mexican American	Tortilla/eggs	Enchiladas/rice	Tamales/menudo
Puerto Rican	Bread/eggs	Pinto beans/rice	Roasted Pork/rice
African American	Grits/eggs	Collard greens/meat	Glazed smoked ham
Italian American	Frittata (omelet)	Spaghetti/meatballs	Special lasagna

Narrative charts can show events in a sequence. For example, students can develop charts showing the steps needed to make their favorite dishes. A narrative chart can also present a timeline of historical events. A simple timeline might show a child's personal history (See Figure 5-4a). Because children in Kindergarten through Grade 2 might have problems conceptualizing time, initial exposure to timelines should begin with what they did yesterday, what they are doing today, and what they will do tomorrow (See Figure 5-4b). Starting in third grade, children can introduce more challenging components from civics, economics, geography, and history such as researching the biography of a key figure in their hometown's history.

Figure 5-4a. A Timeline—My History

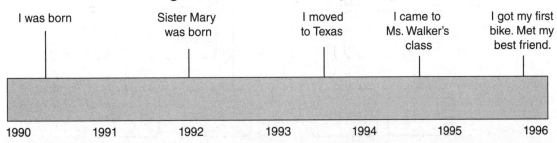

| I was born | Sister Mary was born | I moved to Texas | I came to Ms. Walker's class | I got my first bike. Met my best friend. |

| 1990 | 1991 | 1992 | 1993 | 1994 | 1995 | 1996 |

Figure 5-4b. A Timeline—My Day

Yesterday	Today	Tomorrow
I played with my dog. I went to school.	I went to school. I went to the library.	I will go to school. I am going to see a movie.

A tabulation or classification chart provides an orderly columnar display of information for comparison. For example, Table 5-2 compares data based on the 2020 United States census.

Table 5-2. Tabulation or Classification Chart— U.S. and Texas Populations by Group (2020)

Race/Ethnic Group Population	Percentage of U.S. Population	Percentage of Texas Population
Caucasian/not Hispanic	61.6%	39.7%
Black or African American	12.4%	11.8%
Asian	6%	5.4%
Hispanic or Latino	18.7%	39.3%
American Indian/Alaskan Native	1.1%	0.3%
Native Hawaiian/Pacific Is.	0.2%	0.1%

Source: U.S. Census Bureau

Using developmentally appropriate vocabulary, teachers can guide students to recall and infer data from the chart.

A **pedigree chart** shows the origin and development of something. Examples are a person's family tree, the pedigree line of a purebred dog, and the development of a political party. Figure 5-5 presents a family tree.

Figure 5-5. A Pedigree Chart—My Family Tree

An organizational chart shows the structure of an organization, such as a school or business. Figure 5-6 is a chart showing the typical organization of an elementary school.

Figure 5-6. Organizational Chart—Elementary School

A **flowchart** shows a process at certain points. For example, Figure 5-7 shows the process to complete an academic degree.

Figure 5-7. Flowchart for Program Completion

Addressing the Needs of English Learners

English learners (ELs) can find social studies instruction quite challenging. Teachers thus must modify instruction to make the content comprehensible for this group. Some textbooks have been written with ELs in mind. These books use numerous visual and graphic representations to make the content accessible to children learning English. For example, *Adventure Tales of America*, written by Jody Potts (1994), is an American history book that uses cartoons and illustrations to explain such complex concepts as electing the president and making a bill into law. It also uses concrete timelines to represent U.S. history. The illustrations give ELs the meaning of important concepts from which teachers can develop lessons.

Other books integrate language instruction with content to deliver both components in a contextualized format. One example is the English as a Second Language (ESL) series *Avenues*, published by Hampton Brown (Schifini et al., 2004). This set of books presents ESL lessons with content from other disciplines. The integration of content and language is one of the most effective strategies to promote content mastery as well as language development.

Cognates and Affixes

The Greek and Roman civilizations influenced the development of English and most Western languages. This association has resulted in the creation of multiple cognates—words that are similar in two or more languages. Most sophisticated English words in the content areas and, especially in social studies, are cognates of Spanish and other Western languages. Teachers can use these similarities to expand the students' vocabulary and enhance their understanding of content. Table 5-3 presents examples of the connection between English and Spanish words (Rosado and Salazar, 2002–2003).

Table 5-3. Common Greek and Latin Roots and Affixes

Roots/Affixes	Meaning	English/Spanish Cognates
Xeno Phobia	Fear of Foreigners or strangers	Xenophobia/Xenofobia
Phono Logy(ia)	Sound Study of	Phonology/Fonología
Photo Graphy	Light Graph, form	Photography/Fotografía
Homo Sapiens	Same, Man Able to Think	Homo sapiens/homo sapiens
Demo Cracy	People Government	Democracy/Democracia

Instructional Techniques to Support ELs

Teachers should use different activities to teach the state curriculum to ELs at the grade level and complexity required of native English speakers. Scaffolding was originally used to describe how adults support children's efforts to communicate in the native language (L1). The same concept can facilitate language and content development for ELs. The term *scaffolding* alludes to the provisional structure that provides support during the construction of a building. This support is eliminated when the structure is complete. Following this analogy, ELs receive language support to make content accessible to them until they achieve mastery in the second language (L2). When the mastery is accomplished, the language support is eliminated.

Graphic organizers are visuals that show relationships. These are the most common graphic organizers:

- A **semantic web** or **tree diagram** shows the relationship between main ideas and subordinated components.

- A **timeline** presents a visual summary of chronological events, and it is ideal for showing the events in a sequence.

- A **flowchart** shows cause-and-effect relationships and can show steps in a process, such as the process for admission to a school or program.

- A **Venn diagram** uses circles to compare common and unique elements of two or three distinct components, such as properties of numbers, elements of stories, or events or civilizations (like the Maya, Inca, and Aztec shown in Figure 5-8).

The **SQ4R** method, covered in Chapter 3: ELA and Reading, is a study strategy in which the learner engages in the entire reading process. The acronym stands for **survey**, **question**, **read**, **recite**, **record**, and **review**. During the **survey** part, readers examine the headings and major components of the text to develop predictions and generate questions. Through these **questions**, students establish the purpose for reading. As they **read**, students look for answers to the questions they generated. They monitor their comprehension as they **recite**, **record** (and thus **reflect**) by writing a summary of the content they have learned. Finally, they **review** to evaluate how much they learned about the content.

Figure 5-8. Venn diagram—Three Civilizations

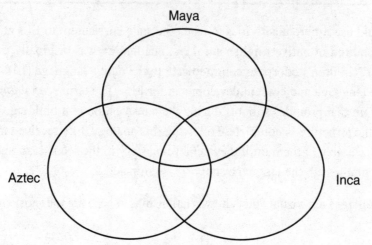

Strategies to Integrate Language Arts and Social Studies

Sheltered English

Sheltered English is an instructional approach designed to make content comprehensible for ELs (Echevarria, Vogt, and Short, 2012). Even though you will not spot the term in the Texas Administrative Code (TAC Chapter 89, Subchapter BB, 2018), elements of sheltered instruction are clearly entailed in meeting the needs of ELs. In such instruction, children are "sheltered" from the pressure of competing with native English learners. To deliver comprehensible input, content instruction is linguistically simplified through contextualized instruction, visual aids, hands-on activities, guarded vocabulary (i.e., minimize the "linguistic load"), and body language. Some strategies teachers can use to modify language to make it comprehensible are:

- Control the length and complexity of the sentences. Children respond better to short, simple sentences.

- Introduce technical vocabulary before beginning the lesson.

- Use repetition, restatement, and paraphrasing to clarify concepts.

- Control the speed of delivery and use a different type of intonation to emphasize important concepts.

- Supplement oral presentations with diagrams, graphic organizers, and manipulatives to make content easier to understand.

- Help students use drawings and graphic organizers to visualize word problems and experiments, and as tools for communication.

- Guide students in using role-play to represent important concepts.

- Use such linguistic modifications as repetition and pauses during speech (Parker, 2001).

- Make the presentation of content more interactive with comprehension checks.

- Use cooperative learning strategies.

- Organize content around thematic units.

- Use graphic organizers to simplify and chunk content.

- Emphasize the gist of concepts instead of details.

Sheltered English is most effective in a classroom with students from many language groups who are at least at the intermediate level of English language development (Schifini, 1985).

Academic Vocabulary in Social Studies

Academic vocabulary is the vocabulary needed to understand the concepts of school. In other words, it is the vocabulary of teaching and learning. Standardized assessments, such as state tests, use academic language. It is imperative that teachers use the appropriate terminology to prepare students for state and district exams. Marzano and Pickering (2005) emphasize the importance of teaching academic vocabulary to English learners and recommend a six-step systematic approach that includes direct instruction as well as practice and reinforcement. The steps to teach academic vocabulary are presented next.

- The teacher provides a description, explanation, or example of the new term.

- Students restate the description, example, or explanation in their own words.

- Students create a representation of the word by drawing a picture, symbol, or graphic.

- Students periodically participate in activities to add to their knowledge of terms.

- Students discuss terms with one another.

- Students participate in games and activities that reinforce the new term.

Cooperative learning is a teaching strategy designed to create a low-anxiety learning environment in which students work in small groups to achieve instructional goals. In cooperative learning, students with different levels of ability or language development collaborate to support each other to ensure that each member masters the objectives of the lesson. This approach can deliver content as well as language instruction. Traditionally, the strategy is delivered in specific steps (Arends, 1998):

1. **Present Goals**—The teacher goes over the objectives of the lesson and provides the motivation.

2. **Present Information**—The teacher presents information to students orally or with text.

3. **Organize Students into Learning Teams**—The teacher explains to students how to form learning teams and helps groups make an efficient transition.

4. **Assist Teamwork and Study**—The teacher-helps learning teams as they do their work.

5. **Test Students on the Content**—The teacher tests students' knowledge of learning materials as each group presents the results of their work.

6. **Provide Recognition**—The teacher finds ways to recognize individual and group efforts and achievements.

To emphasize the cooperative nature of the strategy, specific methods were developed to enrich the lessons such as Student Teams Achievement Division (STAD), Group Investigations, Think-Pair-Share, and Numbered Heads Together. These specialized methods are described in the sections that follow.

Student Teams Achievement Division (STAD)

1. The teacher presents new academic information to students.

2. Students are divided into four- or five-member learning teams.

3. Team members master the content and then help each other learn the material through tutoring and quizzing one another as well as conducting team discussions.

4. Each student gets an improvement score to show the growth he or she has made.

5. Daily or weekly quizzes are given to assess mastery.

6. Each week, through newsletters or a short ceremony, groups and individual students are recognized for showing the most improvement (Slavin, 1986).

Group Investigation

1. Students select a subtopic within a general area.

2. The teacher divides the class into groups of two to six students. Group composition should be ethnically and academically heterogeneous.

3. The students and the teacher plan specific learning procedures, tasks, and goals.

4. Students carry out the plan using sources. The teacher monitors the process and helps as needed.

5. The students analyze and evaluate information and plan to sum it in an interesting way for possible display or presentation to the class.

6. The students present their final product.

7. The teacher conducts individual or group evaluations (Thelen, 1981).

Think-Pair-Share

This activity was developed as a result of the wait-time research. Wait-time research suggests that pausing for a few seconds to allow children to reflect on the question can improve the quality of the response as well as the overall performance of children (Rowe, 1986).

1. **Think**—The teacher poses a question and asks students to spend a minute thinking alone about the answer. No talking or walking is allowed.

2. **Pair**—Students pair off and discuss what they have been thinking about, sharing possible answers or information.

3. **Share**—Students share their answers with the whole class. The teacher goes around the classroom from pair to pair until a fourth or a half of the class has a chance to report (Lyman, 1981).

Numbered Heads Together

This activity was designed to involve more students in the review of materials covered in class.

1. **Number**—The teacher divides the students into teams with three to five members each and assigns a number to each member.

2. **Question**—The teacher asks a question.

3. **Heads Together**—Students put their heads together to figure out the answer and to be sure everyone knows the answer.

4. **Answer**—The teacher calls a number, and students from each group with that number raise their hands and provide the answer (Kagan, 1985).

COMPETENCY 002: HISTORY

The teacher understands and applies knowledge of significant historical events and developments, multiple historical interpretations and ideas and relationships between the past, the present, and the future as defined by the Texas Essential Knowledge and Skills (TEKS).

World History

World historians differ often on how to periodize, or divide the history of the world into eras. The following scheme offers one useful periodization scheme, which is seen here alongside another common way of dividing the past for analytical purposes.

Pre-History   Beginnings of Human Society, 250,000 years ago to ca. 4000 BCE

Ancient History	Early Civilizations, ca. 4000–700 BCE
	Period of Classical Empires, ca. 600 BCE–500 CE
Middle Ages	Early Middle Ages, 500–1000
	Cross-cultural Interaction and Expansion, 1000–1500
Modern History	The First Global Age, 1450–1770
	Age of Industrial and Political Revolutions, 1750–1914
	Age of Crisis and Achievement 1914–present

Prehistoric Origins (250,000 Years ago to ca. 4,000 BCE)[2]

Study of early human society focuses on the evolution of the first humans from earlier hominids, the spread of humans from Africa to other world regions, the development of early hunter-gatherer societies, the emergence of symbolic thinking and problem-solving in early humans, the origins of early agriculture (known as the Neolithic Revolution) and the spread of techniques of plant and animal domestication.

Timeline of the Prehistoric Era

250,000 years ago	*Homo sapiens* evolves in Africa from earlier hominid species
200,000 years ago to 10,000 BCE	*Homo sapiens* migrates from Africa in a series of migratory waves and had settled across the globe.
75,000 years ago	*Homo sapiens* begin to develop ability to communicate complex ideas, stories, and use symbols to convey abstract ideas, including early religion
12,000 years ago	Beginning in the "Middle East" humans domesticate species of grains and animals, initiating the Neolithic or Agricultural Revolution. Other centers of early agriculture (Nile, West Africa, China, New Guinea, Andes, Mesoamerica) either learn or develop these techniques independently

---

[2] The terms "Before the Common Era (BCE)" and "Common Era (CE)" are used in place of the antiquated "Before Christ (BC)" and "Anno Domini (AD)". The years in the timeline decrease from 4000 BCE until the Common Era (CE) begins, after which time the years increase.

Early Civilizations and Pastoral Societies (4000 BCE–1000 BCE)

With the development of agriculture, urban civilizations emerged across the globe, beginning in Mesopotamia and the Nile River Valley, but also in the Indus River Valley, along the Yangtze and Huang He rivers in China. Later urban civilizations emerged in Mesoamerica, the Andes, and the American Southwest and along the Mediterranean. Early civilizations typically exhibited monumental architecture, irrigation systems, writing, legal and political institutions, polytheistic religions, markets, etc. Pastoral (nomadic) cultures also played a role as traders and raiders in spreading iron metallurgy, domestication of horses, and other technologies.

Timeline of the Era of Early Civilizations and Pastoral Societies

4000 BCE	Sumerian civilization introduces first written alphabet, and a system of irrigation.
3100 BCE	Upper Nile River Valley in modern Egypt unified under single Pharaoh.
3000 BCE	Norte Chico civilization develops in the Andes Mountains of Peru
2500 BCE	Nubian civilization develops alongside Egyptian in modern Sudan
2500 BCE	Indus River Valley civilization flourishes in South Asia
2000 BCE	Nomadic migrations of speakers of Indo-European languages originally from the Caucasus region of Central Asia begin to reach the Mediterranean, South Asia, and western Europe
1600–1046 BCE	First Chinese civilization, the Shang, thrives along Huang He River
1600–1100 BCE	Mycenaean precursor to Greek culture thrives along Aegean Sea
1200–400 BCE	Olmecs civilization develops in the Yucatan Peninsula

Classical Period of State Formation and Religious Development (ca. 1000 BCE–500 CE)

On the foundations of early civilization, the period from 1000 BCE featured the emergence of more complex states and political systems, often characterized by large multi-ethnic empires in which new religions, and legal and philosophical systems were developed. These included the Assyrian, Babylonian, and Persian Empires in the Middle East, the Han Empire in China, and the Mauryan Empire in South Asia. In Mesopotamia in this period religious developments included the origins of Judaism and Zoroastrianism. In India Buddhism, Jainism, and early Hindu belief systems emerged. In China, the philosophical thought of Confucianism and Daoism provided the intellectual foundations of Chinese political development. Along the Mediterranean, the ancient Greeks first established a system of city-states with a variety of political systems including Athenian democracy, in part supported by developments in Greek philosophical thought. In the western Mediterranean, the Roman Republic conquered vast territories and was transformed into an Empire. Christianity developed in this period and spread as it was adopted by Roman emperors. Each of the ancient empires of Eurasia experienced significant transformations at the end of this period.

Timeline of the Classical Period of Ancient History

1000–612 BCE	New Assyrian Empire's conquests of Fertile Crescent region
753 BCE	Date of the mythical foundation of Rome by Romulus and Remus.
509 BCE	Establishment of the Roman Republic.
605–562 BCE	King Nebuchadnezzar rebuilds the city Babylon
476–431 BCE	Golden age of Athenian philosophy, democracy and economic influence
336–323 BCE	Alexander "the Great" conquers eastern Mediterranean region and Persia, leading to the spread of Greek art, literature, language, and philosophy during the Hellenistic era
320–180 BCE	Mauryan Empire in India and spread of Buddhism in South Asia
221 BCE	The Chinese Empire is founded by Qin Shi Huangdi and continued from 210 BCE–220 CE under the Han Dynasty
27 BCE to 14 CE	Augustus rules as the first Roman emperor
6 or 4 BCE	Estimated date of birth of Jesus of Nazareth
70 CE	Roman armies defeat a Jewish rebellion in Palestine and the Jewish population is expelled from the city.
312 CE	The Roman Emperor, Constantine I, adopts Christianity
400–550 CE	Gupta Empire in India, high point of early Indian culture, art, and rise of Hinduism
476 CE	Western Roman Empire collapses and is replaced by Germanic kingdoms. The Roman Empire in the eastern Mediterranean persists as the Byzantine Empire until 1453 CE

The Middle Ages (500–1500 CE)

The "Middle Ages" designates a period between ca. 500 CE and ca. 1500 CE. The term signifies a period between the classical Greek and Roman period and the modern era, beginning with the European voyages of discovery in the 15th century. The first 500 years have often been imagined as a "Dark Age" and perhaps this might apply to conditions in western Europe. But, elsewhere it was a period of great creativity. This period features the restoration of the Chinese empire and then its flourishing under the Song Dynasty, the rise of Islam and the spread of Islamic culture across Afro-Eurasia, the high point of Mayan and other Mesoamerican societies, the development of empires in West Africa, as well as the Mongol conquests under Genghis Khan, which united much of the Eurasian continent under a single empire. In Europe, the successor states to the Roman Empire (the Byzantine in the east, and Germanic kingdoms in the west) struggled to compete with the wealth and vibrancy of the Islamic world and East and South Asia.

Timeline for the Middle Ages (CE)

527–565	Eastern Roman (Byzantine) Empire at its peak under Justinian I
300–650	Teotihuacán civilization classical period in central Mexico
581–907	Chinese Empire restored under Sui and Tang Dynasties.
610–661	Mohammad's revelations and the early spread of Islam under his successors
700	Mayan civilization at its height in Central America
750–861	Abbasid dynasty is founded and the Islamic Caliphate reaches its peak
800–1200	Empire of Ghana rules in West Africa, controlling trans-Saharan trade routes
800	Charlemagne crowned emperor of the Holy Roman Empire in Western Europe
843	Treaty of Verdun divides Western Europe by partitioning the Carolingian empire among the three surviving sons of the emperor Louis I (the Pious)
950–1150	Height of Toltec civilization in Mexico
990–1050	Vikings explore and briefly settle in North America
1096–1270	Crusades attempt to assert Christian control over Jerusalem and other cities in Middle East
1206–1270	Genghis Khan's campaigns across Eurasia establish empire extending from China to the Caspian Sea
1271–1295	Marco Polo travels to China from Italy
1280–1337	Mansa Musa I rules the Empire of Mali in West Africa

1325	Aztecs established Tenochtitlán on site of modern-day Mexico City
1346–1353	Black Death (Bubonic Plague) spreads across Eurasia and North Africa
1350	The "Renaissance," rebirth of classical knowledge and reason is said to begin
1368	Foundation of the Ming dynasty in China

The First Global Age (1450–1750)

Historians often date the beginnings of the "Renaissance" to the period ca. 1350–1500. Increasingly historians refer to this period as the "Early Modern Period" as well as the Renaissance, which strictly speaking refers to the belief that following the decadence of the Middle Ages, a "rebirth" of culture and society took place, initially modeled on the glories of classical Greece and Rome. The period beginning in the 15th century is often referenced as the "Age of Discovery" in many textbooks, but is increasingly described as the "First Global Age" as the two world hemispheres, are brought together through Spanish and Portuguese exploration and then conquest, and Europeans enter significantly into Indian Ocean trade circuits and trans-Eurasian trade circuits in a more systematic fashion than had been the case earlier. This period also is characterized by the expansion of European maritime empires, as well as the Russian, Ottoman, Mughal, and Qing Empires. In the Americas, the Inca and Aztec Empires rise to significance, and then are devastated by European conquest and disease. The period also features significant religious reform, most notably the Protestant Reformation, and important scientific discoveries, often characterized as the Scientific Revolution. Conflict in Europe, much of it resulting from religious differences, and the rise of monarchs who claimed absolute power by divine right, contributed to European expansion and technological innovation.

Timeline for the First Global Age

1441	Portuguese begin explorations down the coast of Africa in search of gold and trading partners. The Atlantic slave trade begins.
1453	Constantinople (last remnant of the Byzantine Empire) falls to Ottoman Turkish control.
1454	Johannes Gutenberg invents a mechanical moveable-type printing press
1488	Bartolomeu Dias, Portuguese mariner, sails to the southern tip of Africa
1492	Columbus sails from Spain to Americas
1492	Spain becomes unified under Ferdinand and Isabella, and the colonization of the Americas begins with Columbus's claim to the island of Hispaniola (Haiti and Dominican Republic)

1493	First Spanish settlement established on the island of Hispaniola, in modern Dominican Republic.
1498	Portuguese explorer Vasco da Gama establishes maritime trade route from Europe to India
ca. 1500	Aztec Empire in modern Mexico and Inca Empire in contemporary Peru at their peak.
1508	Second Spanish settlement established on island of Puerto Rico by Ponce de Leon
1517	Martin Luther begins the Protestant Reformation in Europe
1520–1566	Suleiman "the Magnificent" rules an Ottoman Empire that extends across eastern Europe, North Africa, and much of the Middle East
1522	Portuguese explorer Ferdinand Magellan's expedition circumnavigates the globe
1535	Spain completes the conquest of the Aztecs in Mexico and the Incas in Peru
1543	Copernicus suggests that the Sun, not the Earth, is the center of the universe
1571	Europeans defeat the Muslim Ottomans in the Battle of Lepanto
1588	England defeats the Spanish Armada and becomes the greatest naval power in the world
1607	England begins the colonization of North America
1609	Galileo uses a new invention, the telescope, to study the universe
1618	Thirty Years' War begins (The key participants in the war included: The Holy Roman Empire, Great Britain, the Dutch Republic, Denmark, Germany, Sweden, France, Spain, and Austria)
1642	Death of Galileo Galilei who confirmed the heliocentric theory and birth of Sir Isaac Newton
1644	Establishment of the Qing (Manchu) Dynasty in China (lasted until 1911)
1688	"Glorious Revolution" in England establishes limited constitutional monarchy

The Enlightenment—The Age of Reason

The Enlightenment refers to a period during the late 17th and 18th centuries when Europeans and their descendants in settler colonies like British North America, New Spain, and elsewhere emphasized scientific reasoning and rational thought and began to challenge many of the established dogmas of religion and traditional political ideals. These Enlightenment ideals, emphasizing liberty, equality, and the pursuit of happiness, form the core of classical liberalism. Often these challenges were justified by appeals to such things as abstract notions of liberty (freedom of religion, freedom of the press, rejections of inhumane forms of punishment, and challenges to the slavery). Some of the leading thinkers of this period were Jean-Jacques Rousseau, John Locke, Charles Montesquieu, Voltaire, Francis Bacon, and Adam Smith. Enlightenment ideas flourished in Europe and in their European colonies, including in British North America. Many leaders responsible for the writing of the Constitution were familiar with the leading Enlightenment thinkers and framed the Constitution to protect the natural rights of the individual and limit the power of the government.

Age of Industrial and Liberal Revolutions (1750–1900)

The ideals of the Enlightenment, coupled with technological innovations linked to new scientific knowledge, resulted in a period of extended political and social revolution coupled with the beginning of the Industrial Revolution and urban growth in Europe, the United States, and Japan. People in Europe and the Americas sought political independence from colonial governments and challenged traditional systems of government. For example, the quest for freedom led to the American War of Independence and the French Revolution. The American Revolution and turmoil caused by the French Revolution and Napoleonic Wars, contributed to the Spanish colonies in the Americas' efforts to gain independence. Similarly motivated, slaves in Haiti rose up and overthrew their French enslavers, the first successful slave revolt. These liberal ideas were also evident in the development of *laissez-faire* or free-market capitalism that developed at the same time and freed entrepreneurs and landowners to more efficiently exploit their resources. These political and economic changes enabled European, American, and Japanese states to become the core of the global economy, for the first time displacing China, India, and the Islamic world.

Timeline for the Age of Industrial and Liberal Revolutions

1682–1725	Peter the Great rules Russia; Frederick the Great becomes king of Prussia; expanded territory, strong military
1756–1763	Seven Years' War ensues, with France, Austria, and Russia clashing against Prussia and England
1768	James Cook visits regions in the Pacific
1776	Adam Smith publishes *Wealth of Nations*

1775–1783	American War for Independence ends with Treaty of Paris
1789	French Revolution begins with the fall of the Bastille in Paris
1791	As part of the Enlightenment, Thomas Paine publishes *The Rights of Man*
1804	Napoleon declares himself emperor of France, beginning the Napoleonic Era
1808	Wars for independence begin in Spanish America
1812–1815	War of 1812, termed by some historians as the "Second War for American Independence," fought between the U.S. (and its Indigenous allies) and the United Kingdom
1835–1836	Texas War for Independence ends with the Battle of San Jacinto
1836	Texas declares independence from Mexico
1837–1901	British Empire at its peak under Queen Victoria I
1845	Texas joins the United States as the 28th state
1848	Political revolutions across much of Europe
1861–1865	American Civil War
1869	Union Pacific Railroad links the East and West coasts of the United States
1898	Spanish-American War

The Age of Crisis and Achievement (1900–Present)

The 20th century witnessed the struggle for equal rights for women, the space race and the mass production of the automobile, as well as the end of European colonialism in Africa and Asia. It was also the century of the most bloody conflicts in human history: World War I and World War II, the Russian and Chinese revolutions, and such conflicts as the Korean and Vietnam wars. It was the century of the rise of America to world dominance, but also saw the world undergo the Great Depression, the rise of fascism, and the Holocaust, which involved the methodical state-sponsored murder of six million Jews along with millions of others by Nazi Germany and its collaborators during World War II. The second half of the century featured a Cold War between the United States and its allies and the Soviet Union and the Warsaw Pact nations. And, between 1989 and 1992, the Cold War came to a close, with the liberation of eastern European nations and the dissolution of the Soviet Union. While this appeared to promise a future of growing liberalization of trade, democratization, and peace, that peace was soon undermined by the threat of global terrorism, a renewed series of economic shocks, and the rise of authoritarian governments around the world.

Timeline for the Age of Crisis and Achievement

1910	Mexican revolution begins. Large numbers of Mexicans immigrate to the U.S.
1914	World War I begins when Austria declares war on Serbia and Germany on Russia
1917	The United States declares war against Germany and the Central Powers.
	Russian Revolution starts when the Bolsheviks, led by Lenin, seize power from Czar Nicholas II.
1918	World War I ends; Europe is in ruins, and Germany is heavily punished
1929	Great Depression begins in the United States
1933	Adolf Hitler achieves power in Germany
1936–1939	Spanish Civil War brings Francisco Franco to power
1939	World War II begins when Germany invades Poland and Czechoslovakia
1941	United States enters World War II following bombing of Pearl Harbor
1945	Germany surrenders to the Allied Forces, and Japan surrenders after the United States detonates two atomic bombs in Hiroshima and Nagasaki
1947	Pakistan and India obtain independence from Great Britain
1948–1949	State of Israel is founded in Palestine, and the Arabs declare war
1949	Communist Mao Zedong gains control of China
1959	Cuban Revolution; Communist Fidel Castro seizes power
1960–1974	Many countries in Africa gain independence
1965–1972	America participates in the Vietnam War
1969	American astronaut Neil Armstrong sets foot on the Moon
1973	U.S. pulls out of Vietnam; conflict ends
1974	U.S. President Richard Nixon resigns because of Watergate scandal
1975	Cambodian genocide begins; Pol Pot becomes Communist dictator in Cambodia
1976	First Ebola virus outbreaks in Sudan and Zaire
1978	John Paul II becomes the Catholic Pope
1979	Ayatollah Khomeini becomes leader of Iran following Iranian Revolution
1984	Indira Gandhi, Prime Minister of India, is assassinated
1986	Space Shuttle Challenger explodes
1989	Berlin Wall falls; Chinese military massacres students are protesting in Tiananmen Square

1990	Germany is reunited
1991	Soviet Union collapses, and the Cold War ends
1994	Free elections in South Africa and the end of apartheid
2001	9/11 terrorist attack in New York City, near Washington D.C., and over Shanksville, Pennsylvania
2001–2021	War in Afghanistan against the Taliban
2003	U.S. Space Shuttle *Columbia* disintegrates during re-entry on Feb. 1
	Iraq War (2003–2011) begins, led by combined forces of the U.S. and Great Britain.
2004	Boxing Day Earthquake Tsunami occurs on Dec. 26 in Indian Ocean, killing 230,000 people
2005	The Provisional Irish Republican Army ends its military campaign in Northern Ireland
2006	Ellen Johnson Sirleaf become president of Liberia, and thus Africa's first elected female head of state
2009	Barack Obama becomes the first African-American president of the United States
2010	A magnitude 7.0 earthquake in Haiti kills over 300,000 on Jan. 12
	Deepwater Horizon, the largest oil spill in U.S. history occurs in the Gulf of Mexico on April 20
2011	Wedding of Prince William and Catherine Middleton on April 29
	Osama bin Laden is shot dead by U.S. Navy SEALs in Pakistan on May 2
2012	Barack Obama wins second term as U.S. president
2013	Pope Benedict XVI resigns, the first pope to do so since 1415, and Pope Francis is elected, becoming the first pope from Latin America
2014	Worst Ebola epidemic on record history occurs in West Africa; first case of Ebola contracted in the United States.
2015	Greece announces bankruptcy, becoming the first developed country to default on its debt to the International Monetary Fund.
2015	Heads of China and Taiwan meet for the first time; the U.S. and Cuba resume diplomatic relations
2016	United Kingdom votes to leave the European Union (Brexit)
2016	Donald Trump becomes the 45th U.S. president, the first in U.S. history to ascend to the office with neither military nor government service
2017	Three massive hurricanes hit the United States: Harvey, Irma, and Maria
2018	Wildfires rage in northern California, the deadliest in the state's history
2019	U.S. President Donald Trump is impeached by the House of Representatives
2020	Death of George Floyd at the hands of police sparks #BlackLivesMatter protests across the U.S. and the world

2020   Covid-19 pandemic spreads from China to the rest of the world, killing 1.8 million people in the first year

2020   China National People's Congress grants itself sweeping powers to control civil liberties in Hong Kong

2020   Joe Biden is elected U.S. president, while the outgoing president, Donald Trump, leads an unprecedented effort to prevent official recognition of the newly elected president

2021   Covid-19 pandemic continues, infecting more than 220 million and killing at least 3.6 million people globally in its second year

U.S. ends military support in Afghanistan, and the Taliban quickly fills the void and takes control of the country

U.S. President Trump is impeached a second time on Jan. 13, one week before the end of his term, with 10 Republicans joining Democrats to charge the president with "incitement of insurrection" for his alleged role in the Jan. 6 attack on the U.S. Capitol; the vote was 232–197

2022   Russia invades Ukraine on Feb. 24

For details about these historical periods, go to these websites: Kidipede—History for Kids (*www.historyforkids.org*) and Ancient Mesoamerican Civilizations, created and maintained by Kevin L. Callahan of the University of Minnesota, Department of Anthropology (*www.angelfire.com/ca/humanorigins*).

The Industrial Revolution and Modern Technology

The Industrial Revolution began in England in the mid-18th century. Inventions that made mining fossil fuel (coal) easier provided the energy needed to expand and promote industrial development. Improvement on the steam engine and industrial machines led to the mass production of goods as well as a better distribution system. The economic growth motivated people to leave rural areas and move to the cities. The following timeline highlights inventions that supported the industrial revolution and modern life:

Timeline for Industrial and Technological Development

1769   Richard Arkwright patents the spinning machine powered by a waterwheel, which marks the beginning of industrial mass production of textiles

1793   Eli Whitney patents the cotton gin, speeding up the cleaning of raw cotton

1799   The invention of a continuous paper-making device known as the Fourdrinier machine makes mass production of paper possible

1831   An American, Cyrus H. McCormick, invents the mechanical harvester.

1836   Samuel Colt patents the first revolver in the U.S.

1837–1838	Samuel Morse invents the telegraph and the Morse code
1846	Ascanio Sobrero, an Italian chemist, invents nitroglycerin
1856	Louis Pasteur invents the process of pasteurization
1858	Jean Lenoir invents an internal combustion engine
1866	Albert Nobel invents dynamite
1876	Alexander Graham Bell patents the telephone
1885	Gottlieb Daimler invents the first gas-engine motorcycle
1900	Ferdinand von Zeppelin invents a rigid dirigible airship called the zeppelin
1903	The Wright brothers invent the first gas-powered airplane
1905	Albert Einstein publishes the theory of relativity: $E = mc^2$
1914	Henry Ford introduces the assembly line and begins building the first American cars
1928	Biologist Alexander Fleming discovers penicillin
1930	Vannevar Bush at the Massachusetts Institute of Technology invents the analog computer
1940	Peter Goldmark invents modern color television
1945	The atomic bomb is invented
1952	The hydrogen bomb is invented
1955	The antibiotic tetracycline is invented
1959	Jack Kilby and Robert Noyce invent the microchip
1969	The forerunner of the internet, known as ARPANET, is invented
1971	Ray Tomlinson invents internet-based email; engineer Ted Hoff develops the first microprocessor.
1974	Micro Instrumentation and Telemetry Systems (MITS) makes the Altair available, a mail-order personal computer building kit
1975	Paul G. Allen and Bill Gates form Microsoft
1985	Microsoft develops the Windows program
1988	Digital cellular phones are invented

1990	Tim Berners-Lee creates the internet protocol HTTP and the World Wide Web language HTML
1990	Hubble space telescope launched
1992	The first form of email becomes available to the public
1993	The European Organization for Nuclear Research (CERN) opens the World Wide Web to the public, a decision that profoundly alters how information is stored and shared, not to mention the very fabric of society.
	Global Positioning System (GPS) becomes commercially available
1994	The Channel Tunnel connecting England and France opens
1996	The first animal is successfully cloned (Dolly the sheep)
1997	Mars Pathfinder lands on the Martian surface
	A NASA Shuttle mission is commanded by a woman for the first time
	Toyota releases the Prius, the first mass-produced gasoline-electric hybrid car
1998	Construction begins on the International Space Station
	DVDs are introduced, revolutionizing data storage
2000	The first cellphone with a camera is introduced
	Bluetooth-enabled cellphones debut
	USB flash drive is made available in the U.S. by IBM
2003	Space Shuttle Columbia is lost on Feb. 1
2004	Facebook is founded
2006	The International Astronomical Union creates the first formal definition of a planet, making Pluto a dwarf planet
2007	iPhone comes to market on June 29
2011	The U.S. Space Shuttle program is officially ended
2019	Astronomers capture first photo of a black hole
2020	Crewed spaceflight resumes in the U.S.
	The U.S. Food and Drug Administration issues Emergency Use Authorizaton on Dec. 11 for the first Covid-19 vaccine, from Pfizer-BioNTech

Settlements, Building Communities, and Understanding Culture

Historically, communities have formed to provide for security and legal protection, material well-being, and to bring together religious believers. For example, peasants and townspeople during the Middle Ages offered their labor or surplus to a noble or ruler who promised to protect them. During the same period, Muslim, Buddhist, and Jewish communities were established across Europe, Africa, and Asia as merchants and missionaries from these faiths traded and settled. In United States history, communities of religious believers like the Quakers in Pennsylvania and the Puritans in Massachusetts came to British North America to practice their religion without persecution, but also to govern themselves and to prosper economically. As communities develop, they seek to meet their needs by educating their members, creating a system to govern and to protect the population, establishing communication and transportation systems, and providing recreation and entertainment. Community leaders include political and military leaders (e.g. mayors, governors, presidents, generals), police officers, firefighters, educators, doctors, inventors, entrepreneurs, scientists, business and labor leaders, athletes, artists, writers, activists, etc. Often these leaders become recognized as historical and patriotic figures. They help shape societies and can even contribute to the development of a state or nation. In the United States, many individuals have shaped communities as well as the nation. A short list of such individuals might include George Washington, Benjamin Franklin, Pierre-Charles L'Enfant, Harriet Tubman, Abraham Lincoln, Upton Sinclair, Susan B. Anthony, Ida Tarbell, Henry Ford, Steve Jobs, Franklin D. Roosevelt, Dwight Eisenhower, Harry Truman, Jonas Salk, Thomas Dewey, Mark Twain, Edward Hopper, Georgia O'Keeffe, Charlie Chaplin, Louis Armstrong, Billie Holiday, Booker T. Washington, W.E.B. DuBois, Martin Luther King Jr., Daniel K. Inouye, César Chávez, Jackie Robinson, and Lyndon Johnson (from Gillespie County, Texas). In Texas, many patriots and historical figures helped shape our communities and develop the state, for example, Sam Houston, Davy Crockett, Stephen F. Austin, Sarah Driscoll, José de Escandón, Captain Anthony F. Lucas, James Stephen Hogg, Molly Ivins, and Ann Richards, to name only a few.

Culture is "the sum total of knowledge, attitudes, and habitual behavior patterns shared and transmitted by the members of a society" (De Blij & Murphy, 1999). Cultures change and adapt for a number of reasons. For example, cultural attire can be a simple adaptation to account for cold or hot weather, mild or harsh climates. For example, a parka may be worn in Alaska while light jackets are worn in Texas during the winter. Native Americans exemplified adaptation when some groups used grease from animal fat to ward off mosquitoes. Cultures may also change through modifications. For example, the extreme heat and humidity in the South are better withstood through the invention of air conditioning. Modifications, such as roads and railroads as well as steel frames for buildings, etc., allowed cultures to develop and expand their population and their geographic area over time. Moving to a new location and interacting with communities can also impact groups of people. For example, in Texas, many cultural groups (e.g., Hispanic, Germans, Polish, Czech, African-American, etc.) have learned from each other through cultural diffusion. **Cultural diffusion** is "the process of dissemination, the spread of an idea or innovation from its source area to other cultures" (De Blij, Murphy, Alexander 1999). This can be seen in Texas through many foods (e.g., tacos, burritos, pork rinds, cornbread, sauerkraut, and sausage) and cultural traditions (e.g., Oktoberfest, Cinco de Mayo, festivals and state fairs, Kwanzaa, Christmas, Hanukkah, etc.). These are also examples of a **cultural exchange**, whereby groups of people take on some of the traits of other cultural groups.

Culture is also reflected in the arts. Artists like Kadir Nelson, an illustrator who visually captures elements of African-American culture, or Tomie DePaola, a children's author and illustrator, offer visual and written cultural influences. Carmen Lomas Garza, a graduate of Texas A&I in Kingsville, Texas, is known for art that illustrates her Mexican-American culture. Musicians also serve as cultural producers. Selena Quintanilla Pérez, who with her Tejano music, spread and influenced Mexican-American culture across the globe, both reflected and shaped Texas and American culture. Some authors offer portrayals of past cultures, as well, acting in a sense as historians. For example, Laura Ingalls Wilder's portrayals of American pioneer life on the Great Plains, offers a glimpse of the lives of settlers in the American Midwest. Rappers, jazz musicians, country music singers, bluegrass music, gospel and other musical genres provide important cultural reference points.

Ancient Civilizations of the Americas

Among the most developed ancient civilizations in the Americas were the Olmecs, Mayas, Toltecs, Aztecs, and Incas. The Olmec civilization flourished along the coast of the Bay of Campeche in modern Mexico beginning perhaps as early as 1500 BCE. The Olmec built urban centers, pyramid temples, and developed elaborate art styles, practiced ritual bloodletting and sacrifice, developed urban centers, and practiced settle agriculture. Many of the cultural features of later Mesoamerican societies were present in Olmec culture. Around the same time in the Andes Mountains, a precursor civilization to the Inca, the Chavin, developed in what is now Bolivia and Peru.

Mayas (1800 BCE to 900 CE)

One of the earliest civilizations of Mesoamerica was the Mayan, from regions of Mexico's Yucatán Peninsula, Guatemala, and Honduras. The Mayas developed a highly integrated society with elaborate religious observances for which they built stone and mortar pyramids. The center of the Mayan civilization was the city of Chichén Itzá and its religious centers, where human victims were sacrificed. The Mayas developed an elaborate calendar, a system of writing, and the mathematical concept of zero. They also had highly advanced knowledge of astronomy, engineering, and art. When the Spanish conquerors arrived, most Mayan religious centers had been abandoned, and the civilization was declining.

Zapotecs, Olmecs, and Toltecs

Farther north in Mexico, three highly sophisticated civilizations emerged: the Olmecs, Zapotecs, Teotihuacán, and Toltecs. Beginning with the Olmecs, who flourished around 1200 BCE and followed by the Toltecs and Zapotecs, these groups developed sophisticated civilizations. They used a ceremonial calendar and had built stone pyramids to perform religious observances. Teotihuacán is the best-known example of religious ceremonial sites built by these civilizations. They developed a partly alphabetic writing system and left codices describing their history, religion, and daily events. They also built pyramids starting in about 1000 BCE, which predates the pyramids in Egypt. Two of the most famous are the Pyramid of the Sun and the Pyramid of the Moon in Teoti-huacan, Mexico, between 1 and 250 CE.

Aztecs (ca. 1300 to 1525 CE)

The Aztec civilization achieved the highest development in Mexico. The Aztecs had a centralized government headed by a king and supported by a large army. They were also skilled builders and engineers and accomplished astronomers and mathematicians. They built the city of Tenochtitlan, with many pyramids, palaces, plazas, and canals. At the peak of their civilization, the Aztecs had a population of about 5 million. According to the Native Languages of America, Classical Nahuatl, the administrative language of the Aztec empire, is practically extinct. However, modern Nahuatl varieties are still being used in Mexico, and used in their bilingual education programs (Rosado, Hellawell, & Zamora, 2011). For more information on native languages go to *http://www.native-languages.org*.

Incas—Children of the Sun

The Inca civilization covered the modern countries of Ecuador, Peru, and central Chile. Although they were not as advanced in mathematics and the sciences as the Mayans and Aztecs, the Incas had a well-developed political system. They also built a monumental road system to unify the empire. Their civilization was at its peak when the Spanish conquerors arrived in Cuzco, the capital of the empire. The Quechua are descendants from the Inca and still live in large numbers in South America, mainly in the Andes Mountains.

Mound Builders in North America

In North America, two major groups, known as the Woodland and Mississippian peoples, lived in the Great Lakes and Mississippi area. These people built burial mounds dated as early as 500 CE. The Mississippian people built flat-topped mounds as foundations for wooden temples dating from 500 CE. The chiefs and the priests of these groups lived in residences built on the top of the mounds, while the rest of the population lived in houses below. These mound-building civilizations declined gradually and disappeared by the 14th century.

Inhabitants of the South and Southwest

In the southwestern United States and northern Mexico, two ancient cultures developed: the Anasazi and the Hohokam. The Anasazi developed adobe architecture consisting of individual apartments, storage areas, and a central plaza. They worked the land, developed a system of irrigation, and made cloth and baskets. The Hohokam built separate stone and timber houses around a central plaza. Neither group developed a written language. Drought and attacks from rival tribes contributed to the decline of these civilizations. Historians believe that the Anasazi built the cliff dwellings at Mesa Verde, Colorado, during the 14th and 15th centuries to protect against these attacks.

Pueblo Indians

Evidence suggests that the Anasazi settled along the Rio Grande and intermarried with the local population, leading to the emergence of the Pueblo people. The Pueblo culture improved on the architectural tradition and farming techniques of their predecessors. The Pueblos produced drought-resistant corn and squash, which became the foundation of their diet. The Pueblo Indians survived the Spanish conquest and colonization.

Iroquois

The Iroquois inhabited the area of Ontario, Canada, and upstate New York for at least 4,500 years before the arrival of Europeans. They hunted and fished, but farming became the main economic activity for the group. The Iroquois had a matrilineal line of descent, with women doing most of the farming to support the community. They developed the Iroquois Confederation to discourage war among the groups and to provide a common defense.

United States History

Colonization and European Settlement of North America

In 1565, the Spaniards established the first successful European settlement in North America—Saint Augustine—near what is now Jacksonville, Florida. Following the Spaniards, the English tried to establish their first permanent colony on Roanoke (1586), an island off the coast of North Carolina. This colony disappeared. Nearly 20 years later, the first permanent English settlement in North America was established on May 14, 1607, near present-day Williamsburg, Virginia. Further north, the Dutch settled colonies in the region of present-day New York and New Jersey. Following the Dutch, numerous private companies received royal charters, or patents, permitting them to begin colonization in North America. Three of the first and most successful were the Plymouth Company, the Massachusetts Bay Company, and the Virginia Company of London. The Virginia Company was the first to exercise this patent.

The English Colonies

Thirteen colonies were established on the Atlantic coastline. Three types of colonies developed and were based on three different charters: corporate colonies, royal colonies, and proprietary colonies. These were divided in three geographical regions: the New England Colonies, the Middle Colonies, and the Southern Colonies. The New England Colonies consisted of Massachusetts (including the northern portion that would become the State of Maine in 1820), Connecticut, Rhode Island, and New Hampshire. Their economy was based on farming and such small industries as fishing, lumber, and crafts as well as the triangular trade between West Africa, the Caribbean, and New England. The Middle Colonies consisted of New York, New Jersey, Delaware, and Pennsylvania. Their economy was based on farming, shipping, fishing, and trading. The Southern Colonies were Maryland, Virginia, North Carolina, South Carolina, and Georgia. Their economy, which was centered around plantation agriculture, was based on tobacco, rice, and indigo. Plantations produced agricultural crops in large scale and exploited enslaved Africans and indentured servants, as well as the environment. Each colonial region had unique cultures, communities, and geographical settings that affected their political and economic development.

Virginia (1607)

The Virginia Company established the first English colony in Jamestown, Virginia. After a period of extreme hardship and uncertainty, the colony was able to succeed largely by producing tobacco. In 1619, the colony of Virginia established the first European-style form of government in North America, the **House of Burgesses**. Additionally, in 1619, the first African slaves were acquired in Jamestown, though early tobacco plantations were initially dependent on **indentured servants**, who agreed to work for a period of time in exchange for passage across the Atlantic.

Massachusetts (Plymouth Colony, 1620), (Massachusetts Bay, 1630)

Protestant reformers known as Puritans were the first English settlers to establish a presence in New England. The Pilgrims, who fled England to avoid religious persecution, founded Plymouth in 1620 as the first permanent colony in New England. The Pilgrims were separatists, a radical faction of Puritans who wanted to separate from the Church of England rather than merely purify it. The ship used for the journey was called the *Mayflower*. In 1629, a second charter was granted to another group of Puritans, led by John Winthrop, to establish a colony near Plymouth, known as the Massachusetts Bay Company.

New Hampshire (1623)

Two groups founded the New Hampshire colony. The first group was led by London merchant Capt. John Mason, who established a fishing village in 1623. Mason was one of several proprietors, but never lived in the colony. He acquired a charter for the colony of New Hampshire in 1622 and named the territory after his home county of Hampshire. But the first settlers were fishermen led by a David Thompson who settled near Portsmouth in 1623. Later villages were founded by other arrivals. In 1638, a group led by John Wheelwright founded a second settlement called Exeter. That colony began as a proprietorship but became a royal colony.

Maryland (1634)

In 1632, King Charles I granted to Lord Baltimore (Cecil Calvert) a charter establishing the colony of Maryland under Lord Baltimore's proprietorship. The colony was established as a refuge for Roman Catholics.

Rhode Island (1635)

Roger Williams founded the Rhode Island colony in 1636, and in 1637 Anne Hutchinson settled an additional part of the colony after being expelled from Massachusetts. Both Williams and

Hutchinson had been banned from Massachusetts for their religious and political views and were looking for sanctuary. The colony was granted a corporate charter (or legally founded) in 1640.

Connecticut (1635)

Dutch fur traders explored the region that would become Connecticut as early as 1614 and settled in the Hartford area as early as 1623. The earliest English settlers were Puritans from Massachusetts who began to settle in the region as early as 1635. The largest contingent of English early settlers were led by Thomas Hooker and arrived in 1636 after falling out with the Puritans in Massachusetts. In 1662, Connecticut obtained a royal charter under the leadership of John Winthrop Jr.

South Carolina (1663)

In 1663, King Charles II created the colony of Carolina by granting the territory of what is now North Carolina, South Carolina, and Georgia, to loyal supporters. It began as a proprietary colony and became a royal colony in 1719. The colony quickly became a supplier of rice (grown on plantations reliant on slave labor), indigo, and cattle hides.

New York (1664)

The British colony of New York began as the Dutch colony called New Netherlands. The town today known as New York City was originally called New Amsterdam, after the Dutch city of the same name. In 1664, the English took control of New Netherlands, renaming it New York in honor of its new proprietor, the brother of King Charles II, the Duke of York. The colony remained a proprietary colony until 1685 when it became a royal colony.

New Jersey (1664)

The Dutch founded the New Jersey colony in 1623, though the Swedes also claimed part of southwestern New Jersey. After taking over the Dutch territory between Virginia and New England in 1664, King Charles II of England gave it to his brother, the Duke of York. The duke then gave the territory as a proprietary grant to Sir George Carteret and Lord Berkeley. In 1702, New Jersey became a royal colony.

Pennsylvania (1681)

As early as 1638, Swedish, Dutch, and English settlers tried to establish permanent settlements in Delaware, part of which would be incorporated into Pennsylvania. In 1681, William Penn was granted the larger territory now known as Pennsylvania. He was a Quaker, a religion persecuted in England. He made Pennsylvania a safe haven for Quakers. In 1682, Penn established the city of Philadelphia. Though Quakers were the most prominent group to settle in Pennsylvania, large numbers of German Mennonites also came to Pennsylvania. These "Pennsylvania Dutch," from the word *Deutsche* (or "German"), established the city of Germantown near Philadelphia in 1683.

Delaware (1701)

Dutch, Swedish, and Finnish settlers first settled the colony between 1631 and 1638. The region was claimed by both Cecil Calvert, Lord Baltimore, and by the Duke of York, but was granted to William Penn in 1681. The colony became self-governing in 1701.

North Carolina (1712)

By 1653, Virginia colonists had begun moving south and settling in the North Carolina region. In 1663, King Charles II rewarded key allies with proprietorship of the colony of Carolina, which included North Carolina, South Carolina, and Georgia. Disputes over how the colony was to be governed resulted in the division of North and South Carolina in 1712. In 1729, most of the proprietors of North Carolina ceded their ownership to the crown and the colony became a royal colony.

Georgia (1732)

Georgia was founded as both a haven for the English poor and as a buffer between England's more profitable colonies and Spain's territories in Florida. English settlement of the region began after James Oglethorpe, a social reforming member of parliament, proposed that a colony be founded to house England's poor and those jailed for their inability to pay their debts. He and other reformers acquired a charter for their colony in 1732. In 1752, Georgia became a royal colony and soon was increasingly settled by plantation owners and their slaves.

Representative Government in Colonial America

The United States was settled by Englishmen and women who claimed the rights and freedoms of English subjects including a degree of self-government. Among the documents of the English constitution which supported this belief were the Magna Carta and English Bill of Rights of 1688. The colonists based their own institutions (like the Virginia House of Burgesses and the Massachusetts General Assembly) and documents (like the Mayflower Compact and Fundamental Orders of Connecticut) on these English traditions of rights and self-rule. In the late eighteenth-century, the influence of Thomas Hobbes, John Locke, and Enlightenment thinkers like Montesquieu, Rousseau, and Thomas Paine also contributed to American notions of representative government. The American colonies differed from many later colonies because they were settled by English citizens who chose to move to the New World. The colonists thus brought with them ideals of individual liberty and representative government that reflected English traditions. They believed in the right to elect representatives to decide such important issues as taxation. The Virginia House of Burgesses was the first colonial assembly of elected representatives. Other colonies similarly established representative assemblies.

The Mayflower Compact was drawn and signed by the Pilgrims aboard the Mayflower. They pledged to consult one another to make decisions and act by the will of the majority. It is one of the earliest agreements in the Americas to establish a political body and to give that body the power to act for the good of the colony.

Indentured Servants

The indentured servant system of contracted labor was used to bring workers to the New World. In practice, the indentured servant would sell his or her labor to an agent or ship captain before leaving England. In turn, the contract would be sold to a buyer in the colonies to recover the cost of passage. The labor of criminals and debtors could be sold for life or until they paid their debts. In some cases, at the end of the service, servants remained as salaried workers, or in the best situations, the servants were given a piece of land for their services. This system of provisional servitude was not applied to Africans. Instead, lifetime slavery was instituted, and indentured laborers gained protections and rights that were denied the enslaved, who were ultimately defined as property or chattel.

The French and Indian War

The French and Indian War, the North American part of the Seven Years' War, began in 1754 as part of a larger imperial war in Europe between France and Britain. Both countries sought to expand their control in the Americas. Their poorly defined borders and attempts to militarily strengthen their claims caused increased tensions that led to war. The war officially ended with the Treaty of Paris in 1763 and a solid British victory. However, the conflict was expensive. Therefore, the British government levied heavy taxes on the American colonists to help pay for the war, adding to the rising tensions in the colonies. Coupled with limitations on colonists' westward expansion and increased war with the Indians, the aftermath of the French and Indian War has often been seen as a contributing factor to the coming of the American Revolution.

American Revolution

The causes of the War of Independence, or the American Revolution, were largely economic. England, like other European powers, saw its colonies primarily as existing for the benefit of the mother country, as a source for exports that would benefit its balance of trade with other powers, increasing the mother country's supply of gold and silver. This system, known as **mercantilism**, had benefited both the colonies and England during the first century and a half of colonial rule. But, as England attempted to tighten its control over its colonies worldwide and to govern them more efficiently for its purposes, tensions between American colonists and the British government grew more intense after the French and Indian War.

The war had resulted in a debt crisis, and the British Crown needed to rapidly increase revenues by instituting more effective taxation. The taxation system that followed the French and Indian War was strongly opposed by the colonies. They responded with civil disobedience, often led by such groups as the **Sons of Liberty**, against royal officials and by boycotting British goods. In response to civil disobedience, the British sent troops to Boston, where soldiers and Boston workers clashed, and several colonists were killed in 1770, in an incident that rapidly became known as the **Boston Massacre**. British court decisions, like the **Somerset Decision** in 1773, which outlawed slavery in the British Isles, as well as the deployment of Black soldiers to Boston, also contributed to tensions between the colonists and the British. In one of the most infamous acts of civil disobedience, the **Boston Tea Party**, the colonists in 1773 dumped tea into Boston harbor to protest taxation. In response, the British parliament closed Boston's harbor, shuttered its General Assembly, and effectively declared martial law.

Continental Congress

Following the events in Massachusetts, representatives of the colonies met in Philadelphia in the fall of 1774 to discuss the political and economic situation in the colonies, but not to seek independence. No clear solutions were reached at this First Continental Congress. But, after the Battles of Lexington and Concord and Bunker Hill in the spring of 1775, a Second Continental Congress met to discuss preparations for war and to demand independence. George Washington was elected commander of the American forces, and war was declared against the British. The Congress named a committee to draft a constitution for union of the states, the **Articles of Confederation**, and a second committee, led by Thomas Jefferson, to prepare a Declaration of Independence, which was officially signed (primarily) on August 2, 1776.

The Declaration of Independence

The **Declaration of Independence** pronounced the colonies free and independent states. It was written largely by Thomas Jefferson. It consists of a preamble, or introduction, followed by three main parts. The first part, reflecting the thought of John Locke and eighteenth-century Enlightenment philosophy, stresses **natural unalienable rights and liberties** that belong to all people from birth. It also asserts the view that governments are established through the **consent of the governed**, rather than by divine right and that when governments fail to secure the natural rights of citizens, the people have the right to rebel against it. The second part consists of a list of specific grievances and injustices committed by Britain, which justified the rebellion of the colonies. The third part announces the establishment of a new nation, the independent United States of America. This document provided the foundation to later establish the principle of equal rights for all people. By signing this document, the colonists formally declared they were independent from English rule, thus officially beginning the American Revolution.

Revolution

The **American Revolution** began in Massachusetts in the outskirts of Concord and Lexington. In 1775, while Massachusetts' colonial militia was stockpiling weapons and ammunition, hundreds of British soldiers marched to disarm them. Paul Revere warned the colonists of British troop movements, and the militia (the Minute Men) resisted their advance. At Concord, the British were repelled and forced back to Boston. American sharpshooters ambushed and killed hundreds of British soldiers on their way back to Boston. After this colonial victory, the Battle of Bunker Hill was fought near Boston. The British experienced many casualties but managed to defeat the colonial troops. Nonetheless, the British contingent in Boston withdrew to prepare a larger assault on New

York, with the aim of isolating New England from the other colonies and controlling the Middle Colonies. In Virginia, after patriots sought to keep the royal governor from removing ammunition and weaponry, the governor, Lord Dunmore, offered enslaved Virginians their freedom if they joined the British force. In 1778, after American success at the Battle of Saratoga in New York, the French joined the war in support of the Americans, thanks largely to the diplomatic efforts of Benjamin Franklin. With the war entering a stalemate in the North, the British directed their efforts on the South after 1778. There, with the support of the French, the American troops defeated the British forces at Yorktown, Virginia, in 1781. **The Treaty of Paris**, officially signed in 1783, ended the war and gave independence to the new nation. For additional details about the American Revolution, go to the web page of HistoryCentral.com at *http://www.historycentral.com/Revolt*.

Establishing a New Nation

Articles of Confederation

During the Revolutionary War, the **Second Continental Congress** ran the government, under the Articles of Confederation, the nation's first constitution which was ratified in 1781. The new government, which had limited power, was composed of representatives from each of the 13 independent states. The Congress could not declare war or raise an army. It could ask the states for money or for soldiers, but the states had to agree to provide them. Under this government, each state printed its own money and taxed imports from other states. There was no executive branch or national court system.

The new government did provide common citizenship to most residents of the United States. It organized a uniform system of weights and measurements as well as a postal service. It also became responsible for issues related to Native Americans living within and along the borders of the new nation. The confederation served as the official government of the young republic until 1789, when the ratified United States Constitution went into effect.

United States Constitution

After six years under the **Articles of Confederation**, many national leaders realized that the American government needed revision to bolster its strength and to improve its governing capabilities. To accomplish this goal, a constitutional convention was held in Philadelphia in 1787. The leaders of this initiative were George Washington, James Madison, Benjamin Franklin, and Alexander Hamilton. From this convention, a new form of government emerged. The **Constitution of the United States** was officially ratified in 1788, and in 1789 George Washington was selected to be the first president of the United States. The republic defined by the Constitution was composed of three branches—executive, judicial, and legislative—and included a system of checks and balances to regulate each branch.

To learn more about historical American documents, go to "A Chronology of U.S. Historical Documents," a website created and maintained by the University of Oklahoma Law Center, at *www.law.ou.edu/hist*.

Policies of the New Nation

The First National Bank of the United States

One of the controversial decisions made during George Washington's presidency was the establishment of a national bank, which served as the bank for the federal government, provided stability to the nation's monetary supply and provided capital for improvement projects and businesses. It was controversial because Jeffersonians objected that Congress did not have the power to authorize its establishment, while Alexander Hamilton and the Federalists argued that the power was implied in the Constitution.

George Washington's "Farewell Address"

George Washington's presidency set in place many of the principles by which executive power would be exerted over the course of American history. Rather than seek a third term of office, for example, Washington resigned and handed over power to his elected successor through a peaceful transfer. This set the precedent that American presidents (with the exception of Franklin D. Roosevelt) would serve only two terms. In his farewell address, Washington cautioned against the "spirit of faction," or partisan politics, that was already evident. Political parties were not planned for in the U.S. Constitution and Washington objected to the jockeying for power taking place as his retirement neared. Washington also warned against "foreign entanglements" which might lead the United States into wars in Europe. This warning has contributed to continued to a strong strain of American suspicion of international involvement, most notably seen in the interwar period of the 1920s and 1930s.

Washington, D.C.

Congress was authorized under the U.S. Constitution to establish a federal district of up to 10 square miles for a new capital city. Before the new capital was in place, the seat of government had been in Philadelphia. Not until 1790 did Congress settle on a site on the shores of the Potomac River between Virginia and Maryland. In 1791, Pierre Charles L'Enfant, a French military officer and engineer who had served in the Continental Army during the American Revolution, was chosen to plan the new capital. Among the surveyors to lay out the streets and avenues of the city was Benjamin Banneker, a free Black man known for his skill as an astronomer, mathematician, and author.

Louisiana Purchase

In 1803, Thomas Jefferson sent negotiators to Paris to meet with Napoleon I of France about purchasing the city of New Orleans, thereby giving the United States access to a port on the Mississippi River through which the products of the nation's interior could be sent to global markets. Napoleon instead offered to sell the entirety of France's vast territories extending up the Mississippi and Missouri rivers. This also proved controversial, as Federalists contended that such purchases were not constitutional and that they threatened to undermine the balance of political power. The acquisition, spanning over 828,000 square miles and obtained for a sum of only $15 million, nearly doubled the nation's size. Shortly after the signing of the treaty, Jefferson sent Merriwether Lewis and William Clark to survey the land in the Louisiana Territory. This expedition lasted for three years as Lewis and Clark, with their team, made their way through Indian-controlled territory, laying claim to the land and exploring its features.

War of 1812

In 1812, the United States, under President James Madison, was drawn into the wider conflict between Napoleonic France and England. Madison, like his predecessor, Thomas Jefferson, had favored France in this conflict. England had also angered Americans by boarding American ships trading with France, blockading vessels destined for the European continent, impressing (drafting) American sailors into the British navy, and by supporting Indian nations who were endeavoring to keep American settlers out of their territories. Washington, D.C., was momentarily captured and burned by the British. The final battle of the War of 1812 in the United States occurred in 1815, after the Treaty of Ghent, which ended it, had been signed. The Battle of New Orleans catapulted Andrew Jackson into the political consciousness of the American public.

Monroe Doctrine

In 1823, President James Monroe made clear to European countries that the United States would not permit the establishment of colonies in the Western Hemisphere. Monroe also banned European countries from attacking the new American republics that were just becoming established in the early 19th century. Monroe also committed the U.S. not to involve itself in European affairs. This concept of "America for Americans" is known as the **Monroe Doctrine**. It has justified both U.S. opposition to European intervention in the hemisphere, but also frequent American interference in the affairs of Latin American and Caribbean nations.

Manifest Destiny

In 1844, President James K. Polk declared to the world that the United States would eventually become a world power and expand to its natural borders. Some of the borders mentioned were the Pacific to the west and Mexico to the south. Eventually, Polk's expectations became a reality as a result of the war between Mexico and the United States from 1846 to 1848. This prevailing nationalistic attitude in the 1800s was called **Manifest Destiny**, a term coined by newspaper editor John O'Sullivan in 1845 to describe this way of thinking. It was initially used as a Democratic slogan. Many Americans believed it was the country's destiny to stretch from the Atlantic Ocean to the Pacific Ocean. This belief helped fuel and justify westward expansion, wars, land purchases, mistreatment of the Native Americans, and economic development. Yet, it was not a conviction everyone supported. Some Americans, most notably the Whig party, did not believe that it was Americans' divine right to expand, but rather that the U.S. should be a virtuous example of democracy.

As America grew in the 19th century, so did its need for resources, land, and desire to expand. European settlers had originally claimed much of the terrain, although Native Americans had long established territories of their own. Therefore, when land was acquired through agreements (e.g., the **Louisiana Purchase** from the French), annexation (e.g., Texas), and war (e.g., with Mexico), the American people expected that they had a right to the land. Acquiring more land made the country stronger economically. A powerful impulse for westward expansion from the beginning of the republic was the demand for land on which to grow cotton, the nation's primary export, and to produce the food and other resources needed in industrializing cities. The **Transcontinental Railroad** was built to move resources and people across the nation, linking the East Coast to the West Coast. The railroad was pivotal to the economic growth and development of the United States and to the rapid settling of the West.

However, this expansion came at great cost to the Native Americans. Some Native Americans might have coexisted peacefully with settlers if peace agreements had been made and kept. Other groups, such as the Comanche and Apache, were more resistant. The expansion of American settlements in the 1800s caused tensions between Native Americans and settlers. In the end, Native Americans were forced to give up their lands and eventually their way of life. The American government set aside reservations, land specifically for these groups. However, this land was typically of poor quality and unwanted by both settlers and Native Americans. This forced Native Americans into a state of dependency and poverty. If life on the reservation was refused, war ensued to compel them to comply. In many cases, Native Americans were killed in raids or in war. Native Americans also attacked settlers, which added to the distrust and increased military action. One of the most controversial actions occurred in 1830 when Andrew Jackson signed the **Indian Removal Act**, which forced Native Americans out of the southern cotton-producing lands in the South, east of the Mississippi. Although this action did not follow the legal process of negotiating fairly, Andrew Jackson's administration wanted all Native Americans out of the economically productive eastern part of the country. The Indian removal process, also known as the **Trail of Tears**, forced Native Americans to vacate their homes in the southeastern part of the United States to lands in the West, mainly in what is now Oklahoma.

As the nation grew, so did political controversy over slavery. Agreements were made to limit the number of states that did or did not allow slavery. Expanded territories became states as the population increased, thereby adding to the number of members of Congress in the Senate and House of Representatives. The influx of legislators affected laws and policies. These legislative decisions included laws about Native Americans, slavery, and big business (e.g., railroads, steel, meat-packing plants, etc.).

Slavery in the United States

Dutch merchants brought the first African slaves to Virginia in 1619 to work on plantations. From 1640 to 1798, perhaps 300,000 slaves were brought to the United States. Before the 1790s, most enslaved people worked growing tobacco, rice, sugar, and indigo and as cattle herders. With the invention of Eli Whitney's cotton gin, cotton became the economic mainstay of the South, and the demand for labor increased the slave trade. From 1798 to 1808, more than 200,000 African slaves were brought to America, mostly to the South. After the ending of the African slave trade in 1808, another 50,000 estimated enslaved people were imported into the United States illegally.

Beginning in 1774, the North began regulating and eventually prohibiting slavery. By 1804, New York and New Jersey had passed gradual emancipation laws. Meanwhile, the internal slave trade in the South grew to meet the economic needs of the area. Eventually, slavery, along with other economic and ideological differences between the regions, resulted in the American Civil War. In 1862, Abraham Lincoln issued the **Emancipation Proclamation**, granting freedom to slaves in the South. After the war, the Thirteenth Amendment to the Constitution officially abolished slavery. Additionally, in 1866 the Fourteenth Amendment gave African Americans full citizenship, and the Fifteenth Amendment granted voting rights to Black men.

Civil War

The expansion of the United States brought additional problems for the young nation. Slavery divided the nation. By the 1800s, slavery had been virtually abolished in the North. The northern states' reasons for turning against slavery were primarily economic: the North had become more urban and industrialized than the South, and northern states received large numbers of immigrants who provided the necessary labor. Southern states remained mostly rural and received few immigrants, making slavery the foundation of their economy. With the nation's expansion west and the addition of new states, slavery became a contentious issue. Any new state would affect the balance between the free and slave states.

Slavery became the main topic of the presidential election of 1860. The candidates were clearly aligned either for or against slavery. The southern Democrats backed a strong proslavery candidate, John C. Breckinridge of Kentucky, while the new Republican Party selected a strong antislavery candidate in Abraham Lincoln. Lincoln's election resulted in the secession of the southern states from the union, the creation of the Confederacy, and the start of the American Civil War. The southern states created the Confederate States of America and selected Jefferson Davis as president.

The American Civil War in Texas

Initially Texas was divided about entering the war. Texas had fought hard to get into the Union, but many Texans did not like the northern legislators' control of the government. Texans also did not like the antislavery sentiment, although only about one-fourth owned slaves. Once in the war, the state provided many troops and was essential to westward expansion, protecting the Gulf Coast and supporting major battles in the Deep South. For more information visit the Texas State Historical Association, *https://www.tshaonline.org/handbook/online/articles/qdc02*.

Battle of Gettysburg

There were many battles fought during the Civil War, but none was as critical to the outcome of the war as the Battle of Gettysburg. Fought in 1863, this three-day battle resulted in more casualties than any other single battle in the history of the United States. At Gettysburg, more than 50,000 soldiers from the North and the South lost their lives. In a speech delivered on the battlefield in November 1863 to dedicate the battlefield cemetery, President Lincoln eulogized the fallen Union soldiers in a speech known as the **Gettysburg Address**.

After five years of fighting and the loss of thousands of lives and millions of dollars in property, in 1865 the commander of the Confederate army, General Robert E. Lee, surrendered at Appomattox Court House to General Ulysses S. Grant, commander of the Union forces.

Reconstruction Era (1865–1877)

Because the war was fought primarily in the South, the region was devastated. Therefore, physical reconstruction focused on the South. However, the emotional reconstruction as well as the reconstruction of American unity had to be done nationwide, and admission of rebel states back into the Union was not automatically granted. The Reconstruction period was characterized by hatred and violence. Lincoln was assassinated shortly after the end of the war in 1865, and leadership of the reconstruction effort fell to Andrew Johnson, a southerner who was disliked by the North as well as the South. He was impeached and almost removed from power.

A major obstacle to the reunification of the nation resulted from the Black Codes. These restrictive laws were passed by southern legislatures to control former slaves. Some Black codes restricted free assembly, while others restricted the jobs that former slaves could do. In 1867, the U.S. Congress, still composed entirely of northerners, passed legislation to eliminate the Black Codes. Additionally, Congress required southern states to ratify the **Fourteenth Amendment** of the Constitution prior to being allowed back into the Union. The Fourteenth Amendment gave citizenship to Blacks. Finally, in 1870, the last two states (Texas and Florida) were allowed back into the Union.

Reconstruction in Texas

Reconstruction in Texas caused much political, economic, and social tension. The Union first moved federal troops throughout the state to aid in the transition and to enforce Union rules. However, within a year most of the troops were sent to the frontier, allowing more former secessionists to have political power. After much turmoil and the removal of key state and local legislators throughout the state, Texas ratified the new constitution, established the Bureau of Refugees, Freedmen, and Abandoned Lands (the Freedmen's Bureau), and accepted the Thirteenth, Fourteenth, and Fifteenth amendments. However, violence broke out as some areas developed so-called Black Codes, laws designed to control the African-American population. Additionally, Reconstruction witnessed the rise of the Ku Klux Klan (KKK) which used terroristic violence to intimidate African Americans and control their labor. Other issues facing Texas included economic change as well as ongoing tensions with state's Native American population. Railroads were a major part of economic development in Texas because they would allow quick access to agriculture and textile markets. This industry needed financial support after the war, which caused tension within and between political parties. Additionally, the influx of immigrants as well as migrants from the Deep South who came to Texas for a better life taxed the ability of already overburdened systems to support the increase in population. For more information go to *https://www.tshaonline.org/handbook/online/articles/mzr01.*

Ku Klux Klan

The **Ku Klux Klan** was among a number of secret societies established during Reconstruction to enforce the implementation of the Black Codes and to terrorize African Americans. Klan members warned Blacks not to vote or exercise individual freedoms. The Klan divided the South based on color lines. More subtle legislation was passed in the South to control the progress of African Americans. These new laws were known as Jim Crow laws. Racial separation characterized life in the South and in other parts of the nation for most of the 19th century and the first two-thirds of the 20th century. The Ku Klux Klan experienced a revival in the 1920s, both across the South, but also in many northern states. The 1920s Klan promoted religious fundamentalism and devout patriotism, claiming to represent real Americans and clean living. They targeted Blacks, but also Catholics, Jews, and immigrants. They also sought to control electoral politics and, with a membership that may have reached 8 million, entered into the American mainstream. In fact, so successful was the Klan that in the mid-1920s, it managed to control the state governments of three states: Colorado, Oregon, and Indiana.

Economic Development

After the reunification of the country, energy was redirected to the economic development and growth of the nation. Inventions as well as the development of the railroad paved the way to economic recovery. The reconstruction that followed the war also played a vital role in the development of the United States as a solid economic and industrial nation.

In the late 19th and early 20th centuries, Americans recognized opportunities in cities. Migration to urban areas caused the cities to grow exponentially in size and population as well as population density. This is called **urbanization**. The fast growth caused issues with housing, transportation, sanitation, and employment (De Blij & Murphy, 1999). People from diverse backgrounds were forced to live and work in proximity. The surrounding countryside was absorbed as an area grew. Poor areas, called **shantytowns**, sometimes developed on the periphery of the cities. The rapid increase in population provided more workers than needed for manufacturing, resulting in a surplus of labor. In Texas, the greatest examples of urbanization occurred in cities that serve as major transportation and economic centers. They include Galveston, Houston, Corpus Christi, El Paso, San Antonio, Austin, Dallas, Fort Worth, and Amarillo. Urbanization also led to urban sprawl, the multidimensional expansion of a city. Urban sprawl may not always coincide with proper coding and planning.

In the 19th and 20th centuries, American farmers used exploitive agricultural methods that rarely conserved the soil. Overgrazing as well as expanding farmland and using new mechanized practices increased production but created a problem. The land could not replenish the nutrients at the same rate they were used. In the 1930s, the area encompassing the Texas and Oklahoma panhandles as well as parts of Kansas, Colorado, and New Mexico suffered from a strong drought. The thin, dry soil did not have enough plants to anchor the topsoil. Strong winds blew the topsoil into dust storms. The affected region was called the Dust Bowl.

Civil Rights Movement

Civil Rights for Freed Slaves

Civil rights are legal and political rights of the people in a particular country. In the United States, the Constitution and its Bill of Rights guarantee civil rights to American citizens and residents. The first 10 amendments to the U.S. Constitution are known as the Bill of Rights. As a result of the Civil War, three additional amendments were added. The Thirteenth, Fourteenth, and Fifteenth amendments were passed during Reconstruction. The **Thirteenth Amendment** freed the slaves without compensation to slave owners. The **Fourteenth Amendment** declared that all people born in the U.S. were citizens (except Native Americans), that all citizens were entitled to equal rights, and that their rights were protected by due process. The **Fifteenth Amendment** granted Black men the right to vote.

The civil rights movement sought equality for African Americans. Even after the Thirteenth, Fourteenth, and Fifteenth amendments were added to the Constitution, Blacks were denied full civil rights. Discrimination existed throughout the nation. Jim Crow laws enforced strict separation in the South. They were also kept from voting by poll taxes and literacy tests. In the North many qualified African Americans could not find good jobs. Segregation rules restricted Blacks to separate facilities in public places such as theaters, restaurants, buses, restrooms, and schools. Discrimination also affected other minorities such as Latinos, Asians, and Native Americans. In 1896, *Plessy v. Ferguson* legalized segregation, allowing "separate but equal facilities" for Black and white students.

The African-American Civil Rights Movement

Several historic events marked the beginning of what is known as the **Civil Rights Movement**. In 1947, Jackie Robinson became the first African American to play baseball on a major league team. In 1948, President Truman ordered the integration of the armed forces and introduced civil rights legislation in Congress. The National Association for the Advancement of Colored People (NAACP) challenged the laws of segregation with the *Brown v. Board of Education of Topeka* case, and in 1954 the Supreme Court ruled that racial segregation in public schools was unconstitutional. Thurgood Marshall, who helped argue the case before the Supreme Court, would become the first African-American Supreme Court justice in 1967.

Another important event in the civil rights movement was the Montgomery bus boycott. In December 1955, Rosa Parks, a 42-year-old Black activist and respected resident of Montgomery, Alabama, refused to give up her seat on the bus to a white man as the state's Jim Crow laws required. She was arrested and sent to jail. Her actions prompted local community leaders of the NAACP to form the Montgomery Improvement Association.

The association chose a young Baptist minister, Dr. Martin Luther King Jr., to lead the organization and to direct a boycott of the Montgomery bus company. The boycott began in December 1955 and ended about a year later when the U.S. Supreme Court ruled segregation on buses unconstitutional. This victory gained national attention, and King became the most prominent figure of the civil rights movement. He founded the Southern Christian Leadership Conference (SCLC) with other African-American leaders. The SCLC favored such nonviolent forms of protest as sit-ins, boycotts, and protest marches. King's "I Have a Dream" speech, delivered Aug. 23, 1963, took place during the march on Washington in support of the Civil Rights Act of 1964. The eloquent speech and orderly demonstration gained more supporters for the cause. King's work resulted in the Civil Rights Act in 1964. He was assassinated in 1968 in Memphis, Tennessee.

President John F. Kennedy proposed new civil rights laws as well as programs to help the millions of Americans living in poverty. After his assassination in Dallas in 1963, President Lyndon B. Johnson urged Congress to pass the laws in honor of Kennedy. Johnson persuaded the majority of Democrats and some Republicans. The **Civil Rights Act** passed in 1964 prohibited segregation in all public facilities and discrimination in education and employment.

The Mexican-American Civil Rights Movement

During the 1960s Mexican Americans were engaged in the struggle for human rights, and Mexican-American leaders started the Chicano Movement as part of that struggle. This movement was cultural as well as political (Rosales Castañeda n.d.). It embraced four main goals: the restoration of land grants, farm workers' rights, education, and political rights (Mendoza, 2001). The movement also sought to rescue the cultural and linguistic identity of Mexican Americans. Activist Reies Tijerina started the Chicano Movement in New Mexico with the *land grant movement*, which sought to recover the land taken from the Mexican Americans as a result of the Guadalupe Hidalgo Treaty of 1848 and the eventual annexation of the American Southwest. In Colorado, Rodolfo "Corky" Gonzales founded the *Crusade for Justice* as a platform for the political movement (Mendoza, 2001). He also defined the movement through his epic poem "Yo Soy Joaquín/I am Joaquin." His poem described the historical development of Mexican-American identity and described the struggles of Mexican Americans in the United States.

To support the rights of farm workers, human rights leaders César Chávez and Dolores Huerta founded the United Farm Workers (UFW) union. Through the UFW they fought for better working conditions and fair compensation for agricultural workers.

In Texas, the movement focused its attention on the educational and political rights of Mexican Americans. World Wars I and II and the experiences of Hispanics who had served in these wars served as important sparks for the movement. The Mexican-American Civil Rights movement in Texas began in 1929 with the formation in Corpus Christi, Texas of the League of United Latin American Citizens (LULAC) whose organization and activism mirrored that of the National Association for the Advancement of Colored People (NAACP), which sought to end discrimination against African Americans. The Mexican-American Civil Rights movement took off in earnest after World War II with the return of many Hispanic GIs from the war. Having fought against racism and discrimination in Europe, Hispanic veterans returned home to Texas only to face segregation and discrimination against Mexican Americans. Hector P. Garcia and other GIs established the American G.I. Forum in 1948 with the goal of ending segregation, ensuring Mexican-American veterans' access to the G.I. Bill, and with ending anti-Mexican discrimination more generally. In the 1960s, with the increased involvement of a next generation of Mexican-American activists, the Mexican Civil Rights Movement began to concentrate on greater political power for Hispanic residents of Texas. In Crystal City, students took a leadership role organizing Mexican-American voters and joining the political process. As part of this, the Mexican American Youth Organization (MAYO), under the leadership of José Ángel Gutiérrez and Mario Compean founded the Raza Unida Party (RUP) in 1970. Through the RUP, they sought to bring greater economic, social, and political autonomy to Mexican Americans (Acosta, 2009). As a result of this movement, the RUP nominated candidates for mayor, city councils, and school boards in three South Texas cities— Crystal City, Cotulla, and Carrizo. The RUP won seats in those communities. This political awakening of the Mexican-American voters in Texas paved the way for better schools and programs for Mexican-American and minority children in general.

With Mexican-American voters' increased activism, Hispanic citizens began to experience greater representation in Texas government. Between 1900 and 1953, only two Hispanic representatives, José T. Canales and Augustine Celaya, had served in the Texas legislature. Henry B. Gonzalez was the first Mexican-American elected to the Texas Senate. In 1977, Irma Rangel, became the first Mexican-American woman to serve in the Texas legislature.

Civil Rights in Texas

Texas civil rights issues center mainly on African Americans and Mexican Americans, the largest ethnic minority groups. Although both groups have fought for equal treatment since the mid-1800s, true change did not occur until the 20th century. This change was fraught with violence and intimidation from such factions as the Ku Klux Klan, the White Caps, community leaders, law officials, and the Texas Rangers. Such actions as the poll-tax and Jim Crow laws limited African-American and Mexican-American involvement in politics and society. Schools and communities were segregated by ethnicities until the *Brown v. Board of Education* (1954) decision started a shift to integrated schools. Civil rights transformation was a long, arduous process. It required laws to change, and communities had to modify their cultural customs, traditions, and mindsets. Much support for civil rights came from the middle class. After World War II, many Mexican- or African-American men pushed for equal treatment, which influenced the tumultuous 1960s when many men and women spoke out against inequalities. These ethnic groups have made gains in their struggle for civil rights and continue to work to ensure that they are treated equally by the law and within their Texas communities. To learn more, read the information contained in the following link: *https://www.tshaonline.org/handbook/online/articles/pkcfl*.

Women's Rights

While the Nineteenth Amendment to the Constitution guaranteed women the right to vote in 1920, women remained subject to discrimination. The civil rights movement and the introduction of the birth control pill provided the impetus for the women's movement of the 1960s. The women's movement sought better employment and professional opportunities for women. The Equal Pay

Act of 1963 and the Civil Rights Act of 1964 prohibited discrimination based on gender. In 1966, Betty Friedan, author of *The Feminine Mystique*, and other leaders founded the National Organization for Women (NOW). This organization adopted the activist approach used by the African-American leaders of the civil rights movement. In 1972, the Equal Rights Amendment was passed by Congress to guarantee women's equal rights. But it came up three states shy of the 38 needed for ratification as part of the Constitution.

The Woman Suffrage movement in Texas was a long struggle that began in the 1860s. Although women worked and paid taxes like men, they did not have the right to vote for leaders and rarely participated in government and politics. Opponents of woman suffrage feared that allowing a change in women's status would challenge cultural customs and traditions. In fact, recent male immigrants could vote before women could. Women not only had to convince political leaders to stop the disenfranchisement of women. They also had to persuade people, including other women, that women's roles at home, in the community, and at work would not change simply because they could vote. The Texas legislature considered and/or voted on woman suffrage multiple times from the 1860s to the early 1900s. In June 1919, the Nineteenth Amendment, giving women the right to vote nationally, was submitted to the states for ratification. On June 28, 1919, Texas became the ninth state to ratify it. To learn more, read the information contained in the following link: *https:// www.tshaonline.org/handbook/online/articles/viw0.*

Temperance Movement—Prohibition

The temperance movement sought to prohibit alcohol sales and consumption in the United States. This movement began in the 1830s, and by 1855 13 states had enacted legislation to prohibit the use of alcohol. In 1919 the U.S. Constitution was amended to prohibit alcohol sales at the national level. This marked the adoption of the Eighteenth Amendment. Battles between law enforcements agents and organized crime characterized the Prohibition era. After 14 years of Prohibition, it was repealed in 1933 with the Twenty-first Amendment.

Texas politics was affected by the Prohibition movement for nearly a century (1840s–1930s). Initially, Prohibition resonated with fundamentalist Christians and later gained local and state support. Local communities determined whether they would be "dry" (that is, prohibit the production and sale of alcohol) or not. The Legislature passed laws limiting and disallowing alcohol before the Eighteenth Amendment to the U.S. Constitution, which prohibited alcohol in the United States. After the repeal of the Eighteenth Amendment, Texas reverted to allowing local governments to determine whether to allow the sale of alcohol in their communities. Texas still has some dry counties and cities. Since the 1980s, laws have dictated the legal drinking age, and warning labels are required on alcohol products. For more information, visit the Texas State Historical Association, *http://www.tshaonline.org/handbook/online/articles/vap01.*

Conflicts and Wars

Spanish-American War of 1898

The outbreak of war in 1898 between Spain and the United States would signal that the U.S. had consolidated a unique leadership position both militarily and diplomatically. Setting the tone for the **Spanish-American War** were blaring headlines accompanied by sensationalized reporting of the sinking of the *USS Maine*. This served as a springboard for the United States to establish itself as a global power with strong spheres of influence in the Caribbean Sea and Pacific Ocean. This would also shape America's role in future European affairs. The U.S. helped Cuba gain its independence, and acquired control of the Philippines, Guam, and Puerto Rico. Eventually, the Philippines became an independent nation, while Puerto Rico and Guam remained U.S. territories. In Cuba the United States took control of Guantánamo Bay and established a naval base. Five years later, Cuba signed a lease to allow the naval base to remain in place. In 1934 Cuba gave the United States a perpetual lease to the area. Eventually, the people of Guam and Puerto Rico became American citizens.

World War I

The first global war, which came to be known as **World War I**, began in Europe and involved two alliances: the **Allies** and the **Central Powers**. The Allies included the countries of England, France, Russia, and Italy, and toward the end of the war, the United States. The Central Powers included the countries of Germany, the Austria-Hungary Empire, Turkey, and Bulgaria. Initially, America remained neutral and benefited from trading with the Allies. America's neutrality was challenged, however, when the Germans developed the submarine, and used it to destroy Allied ships and to sink American merchant ships. In 1915, the Germans sank a British liner, the *Lusitania*, killing more than 1,100 passengers, including 128 Americans. Additionally, American cargo ships were sunk. This forced President Wilson to ask Congress to declare war against Germany and the Central Powers April 6, 1917. The influx of fresh American forces fostered the Allies' victory in 1918.

With the **Treaty of Versailles**, the war officially ended. In this treaty, the Central Powers were punished and forced to pay for the war. Additionally, the Austria-Hungary Empire was dismembered, and new countries were created. The punitive conditions of the Treaty of Versailles created resentment among the German population. This resentment helped lead to the second global confrontation, **World War II**.

The Bolshevik Revolution in Russia

In 1917, the Communists, led by Vladimir Lenin, took over the Russia Empire in what was called the **Bolshevik Revolution**. To address the unrest at home, Russia withdrew from World War I. As a result of this revolution, or civil war, the Russian Empire ceased to exist and the Union of Soviet Socialist Republics (USSR) was established (1922). The USSR underwent a period of governmental reconstruction to incorporate the communist philosophy. As a result of this revolution, Russia experienced a period of governmental reconstruction to incorporate the communist philosophy.

The Great Depression

After World War I, the United States enjoyed a period of prosperity during the 1920s, though the farm sector did not fare as well as urban manufacturing. But it all ended abruptly October 29, 1929, when the stock market crashed, starting what was called the **Great Depression**. During the Depression, millions of people lost their capital and their jobs. Between 1933 and 1937, President Franklin D. Roosevelt implemented a series of government-sponsored programs, called the **New Deal**, designed to revitalize the economy and alleviate the poverty and despair caused by the Depression.

World War II

The emergence of totalitarian countries like the USSR, Germany, and Italy created instability in Europe and led to war. The Communist Soviet Union under Joseph Stalin became a threat to European countries. Italy was a fascist, belligerent state where individual liberties were ignored. Germany under Adolf Hitler was ready to avenge the humiliating treatment it suffered as a result of World War I. In the Pacific, Japan was building an empire that had already conquered parts of China. These conditions promoted the creation of military alliances that led to World War II. Germany, Italy, and Japan created the **Axis Powers**, and the USSR, France, and England became the Allies. The war started with the German invasion of Poland in 1939. Two days later, France and England declared war against Germany. Hitler conquered most of Europe in a short time. France was occupied, and England was brought close to submission. The United States supported the Allies with supplies and weapons but did not send troops. Although it remained neutral for the first few years of the war, the United States joined the Allies when Japan attacked its naval base in Pearl Harbor, Hawaii, in 1941. Three days later, Hitler declared war on the United States. Believing Germany to be the greater threat, the United States concentrated on the war in Europe before turning its attention to Japan.

On the U.S. domestic front, the war fought to secure liberties of many in Europe, also opened the door to wider opportunities for minorities and women. Women were needed in American industries. African-American soldiers and pilots, like the Tuskegee Airmen, served with distinction, and afterward were less likely to accept a return to Jim Crow segregation. Japanese Americans, even as their families were being detained in internment camps, volunteered for the 442nd Regimental Combat Team, a segregated unit composed only of *Nisei*, second-generation Japanese-Americans. This unit was the most decorated one of its size in the war.

D-Day

With Hitler in full control of Europe, the United States joined England and representatives of the French government to plan and execute the invasion of Europe in 1944. On June 6, Gen. Dwight D. Eisenhower, with a quarter of a million Allied soldiers, crossed the English Channel into France and launched one of the largest offensives against the German occupying forces. This large attack on Germany was known as D-Day. As a result of the collective effort of the Allies, France was freed from German occupation. With the combined forces of England, Russia, Canada, and the United States, Hitler and the Axis forces were defeated.

Yalta Conference

The Allies met in Yalta, Russia, to discuss the terms of the treaty to end the war. The Allied leaders—Winston Churchill, Joseph Stalin, and Franklin D. Roosevelt—discussed the peace. Under the terms of peace agreed to at Yalta, Germany was to be divided into four sections, each controlled by an Allied country—Britain, France, Russia, and the United States. The Germans were to pay the Russians for war reparations in money and labor. Poland was divided, and the Russians received control of one section (later they took full control of the nation). Finally, plans were set to organize the United Nations to prevent future conflicts in the world.

Hiroshima and Nagasaki

The United States was fighting the war on two fronts, and the Japanese appeared to be invincible. An island nation, Japan had gained control of much territory in the Pacific, most of it islands. Securing each island would take much time and cost many American soldiers' lives. The best available option was determined to be the atomic bomb. After asking for the Japanese to surrender, the United States by the order of President Harry Truman dropped two atomic bombs, one each on the cities of Hiroshima and Nagasaki. The death and destruction caused by these two bombs forced the Japanese government to surrender in 1945, which officially ended World War II.

Marshall Plan

The Marshall Plan was a U.S.-supported program to rebuild the economic infrastructure in Europe. The United States provided money and machinery for the reconstruction of the continent.

The Holocaust and Creation of Israel

During World War II, Hitler devised a "master plan" to exterminate the Jewish population. Germany placed European Jews in concentration camps and systematically killed millions. This act of genocide is known as the Holocaust. At the end of the war, under the leadership of Great Britain, the United States, and the United Nations, the State of Israel was created in Palestine on May 14, 1948. On that same day, the Arab Liberation Army (ALA) was created to fight the Jewish state and defend Palestinians from dispossession of their land. This liberation movement has resulted in several wars between Israel and the Arabs.

Truman Doctrine

In response to the threat of the Soviet Union, President Truman issued a proclamation warning communist countries that the United States would help nations in danger of falling under communist control. This declaration was called the Truman Doctrine and sought to "contain" Communism in the Soviet Union and in the nations which had fallen to the Soviet Union during World War II. In 1949, China became a Communist nation, under the leadership of Mao Zedong. The spread of communism threatened the spread of American influence and access to world markets. As a result of this doctrine, the United States fought two major military conflicts: the Korean War and the Vietnam War.

Cold War

As a result of the Yalta agreement, the Soviet Union became the most powerful country in Europe and Asia. Following Russia's taking over Poland and other eastern European nations, and its building in East Berlin of the Berlin Wall, a new war emerged between the Soviet Union and the United States—the Cold War. Although war was never formally declared between the two nations, confrontations were periodically sparked from 1945 to 1991. In 1963, the two nations were on the verge of nuclear war after Premier Nikita Khrushchev ordered the deployment of nuclear missiles to Cuba. An intense negotiation between Premier Khrushchev and President Kennedy avoided war between the two countries. This intense confrontation was called the Cuban Missile Crisis.

The Cold War ended with the fall of the Soviet Union under the leadership of Mikhail Gorbachev. The fall of the Soviet empire resulted in the reunification of Germany and the independence of the many of the republics that made up the Union of Soviet Socialist Republics (USSR).[3] Three decades later, in February 2022, Russia would invade Ukraine, part of the former USSR, accusing the neighboring country of committing genocide against ethnic Russians and Russian speakers in Ukraine. The invasion was widely condemned. In March, the International Court of Justice ruled that Russia must halt all military operations in Ukraine, but Russian President Vladimir Putin did not accede to the ruling.

War on Terrorism

On September 11, 2001, terrorists from Saudi Arabia who were part of the Al-Qaeda organization attacked Americans on American soil in a series of murderous events. The assailants hijacked four domestic aircraft and used two of them as missiles to crash into the twin towers of the World Trade Center in New York and a third to strike the Pentagon just outside Washington, D.C. A fourth plane crashed in Shanksville, Pennsylvania, as passengers tried to wrest control of the plane from the hijackers. The attacks killed nearly 3,000 people. The Taliban, an Islamic fundamentalist party in Afghanistan, had harbored the terrorist group that planned the 9/11 attacks. Al-Qaeda's leader, Osama bin Laden, the mastermind of the 9/11 attacks, was hunted for nearly a decade and was killed by U.S. special forces on May 2, 2011, in his Pakistani compound.

As a result of the attacks, the United States, under President George W. Bush, declared war on terrorism and attacked and ultimately toppled the ultraconservative Taliban regime early in the course of the Afghanistan War (2001–2014). Though the U.S. (and NATO) combat mission in Afghanistan formally ended on December 28, 2014, a reduced footprint of about 13,000 troops continued to support and train Afghan troops until a drawdown was initiated in 2020. The last American troops were withdrawn from Afghanistan in 2021.

---

[3] Often *Russia* and *USSR* are used interchangeably. Teachers should be aware of this misconception and use these terms correctly.

Concerned that other attacks, possibly using chemical or other "weapons of mass destruction" (WMDs) might be imminent, the Bush administration in 2003 also ordered a search for WMDs. Allegations that Iraq had stockpiled WMDs, later acknowledged to be based on faulty intelligence, resulted in a U.S. invasion of Iraq beginning in 2003. This second Iraq War resulted in the toppling of the Iraqi ruler, Saddam Hussein, the death of possibly 450,000 Iraqis, and 4,431 American deaths. While the war concluded in 2011, the American presence in Iraq continued as the Obama administration sought to extricate the nation from the conflict without further destabilizing the region. In reaction to the United States presence in Iraq and exacerbated by the eruption of civil war in Syria, another terroristic threat emerged in the Middle East, the Islamic State in Iraq and Syria (ISIS), also known as the Islamic State in Iraq and the Levant (ISIL). ISIS had as its goal the recreation of the Islamic Caliphate, a unified Islamic state. Al-Qaeda, rather than seeking to reunite the Islamic community under one nation, has sought to expel Western and most specifically United States influences from Islamic countries, most specifically from the Arabian Peninsula. Both organizations have now branched out to parts of Africa and Asia and together, though not a unified threat, have targeted U.S. and other Western interests across the world through the use of terroristic means.

January 6, 2021, Assault on the U.S. Capitol

Following Democrat Joe Biden's victory in the 2020 presidential election, in which Biden won the popular vote by a seven million-vote margin and the electoral college by a margin of 306 to 232, President Donald J. Trump, a Republican, refused to accept the result. Trump alleged fraud in a number of key states, though numerous court decisions and investigations found no credible evidence of electoral irregularities. Trump and many of his supporters, however, continued to contest the election and refused to acknowledge Biden's victory. In an effort to challenge the results, a march on Washington was called for January 6, 2021, the day that the electoral college results would be certified by the United States Congress. In remarks by President Trump and others at the Ellipse, just south of the White House, demonstrators were encouraged to march on the capitol to express their outrage at the electoral results and to urge Vice President Mike Pence and Congress to decertify the electoral college vote count and return the election to state legislatures to choose electors favorable to Trump. The demonstrators turned violent and invaded the Capitol building, threatening the lives of Democratic leaders and even Vice President Pence. After seeking shelter during the attack, Congress reconvened with Pence presiding over the count, and the election was certified, ending Trump's efforts to overturn the election. Investigations in the House of Representatives and by the U.S. Department of Justice sought to determine the degree to which the assault on the capitol was part of a coordinated, criminal conspiracy to undermine the institutions of electoral democracy.

History of Texas

Before European Colonization

Texas was only sparsely populated by Native Americans before the 16th century, with populations centered in the coastal plains and East Texas where resources were more abundant, but also in the watersheds of the Rio Grande and Nueces rivers in the west. The settlement of populations of horse nomads, like the Comanche and Lipan Apache, in the grasslands of the Great Plains region would develop only after the horse had been widely introduced in the 17th century.

The three groups living in the coastal plains—the Coahuiltecans, Karankawas, and Caddos—were food gatherers, fishermen, and farmers. When the Spanish arrived in Texas, they made first contact with these groups. The name Texas came as a result of contact with the Caddos. Trying to communicate to the Spaniards that they were not hostile, some Caddos identified themselves with the word *taysha*, which in their language meant "friend" or "ally" (Fry n.d.). When the Spaniards heard the word *taysha*, they thought the Caddos were identifying the name of the region. From that exchange, the name Texas and the state motto, "Friendship," emerged. A fourth group, the Jumanos, lived in the mountains and basins of West Texas. They settled in small agricultural settlements like the pueblos of New Mexico but were also often middlemen in trading goods from northern Mexico to the Indians of east Texas. The last two groups are the Comanche and the Apache. Both developed as horse nomads who competed with one another for grasslands and hunting grounds, and both coexisted with European settlement, trading with and raiding European outposts, while strongly resisting European encroachment on their territories which had been introduced by the Spanish, the Comanche and Apache became fierce warriors and successful buffalo hunters. The domestication of the horse allowed the development of the culture of the buffalo. When buffalo were later annihilated in the area, these two groups became practically extinct. Table 5-4 presents a summary of Native American groups from Texas.

European Colonization

Cabeza de Vaca

The Spanish exploration of the territory that became Texas began in 1528, when Álvar Núñez Cabeza de Vaca and three companions landed. The four Spaniards made contact with the Caddo in the southeastern part of the state, near modern-day Houston. In his account of the meeting, de Vaca described the Caddo as a sophisticated Native American group. From there, de Vaca continued exploring the area that became New Mexico and Arizona (Sheppard n.d.). Spanish interest in the area was only renewed in 1541, when Francisco Vázquez de Coronado explored the region that became Texas.

Francisco Vázquez de Coronado

In response to reports of the mythical Seven Cities of Cibola, Coronado led an expedition of almost a thousand men in search of the golden cities. The expedition left Mexico City and explored the southwestern United States and northern Texas. In 1542, Coronado returned to Mexico empty-handed. For the next 140 years, the Texas region remained isolated, and no other attempts were made to colonize it.

Table 5-4. Native American Groups from Texas

Regions	Native Group
Coastal plains, flatland	**Coahuiltecan** (Rio Grande Valley) **Economic Activity:** Food gatherers and hunters—roots, beans of the mesquite tree, rabbit, birds, and deer **Features:** Lived in family groups
	Karankawa (Southeastern Texas) **Economic Activity:** Fishing and food gathering **Features:** Lived as nomads and used canoes for fishing
	Caddo (East Texas, Piney Woods) **Economic Activity:** Farming—squash, pumpkins, tobacco, and corn (good food supply) **Features:** Built villages and lived in groups
Central plains, flatland, and hills	**Apache** (Central and western Texas) **Economic Activity:** Farming and hunting **Features:** Lived as nomads, built portable housing called tepees, domesticated horses, and hunted bison
Great Plains, flatland, and hills	**Comanche** **Economic Activity:** Hunters **Features:** Lived as nomads and built portable housing; also domesticated the horse and hunted the buffalo
Mountains and basins	**Jumano** (West Texas) **Economic Activity:** Farming and hunting **Features:** Mostly sedentary and built homes of adobe

Juán de Oñate

In 1595, Juán de Oñate received permission from King Philip II of Spain to colonize New Mexico. In 1598, he founded the first European settlement west of the Mississippi in New Mexico. However, Spanish interest in Texas, which seemed to have little economic value, was minimal.

First Mission in Texas

In 1682, the Spanish established the first permanent settlement in Texas—the mission of Ysleta del Sur near what is now El Paso. After this mission, no serious efforts were made to colonize the area until the French threatened the Spanish hegemony in East Texas.

French Influence in Texas

In 1682, René Robert Cavelier, Sieur de la Salle, established a French settlement in Fort Saint Louis in East Texas. A few years later, the Spaniards expelled the French and established a series of missions in East Texas to control the French threat in the region.

San Antonio

In 1718, the Spanish established a mission and a fort—San Antonio de Valero and Fort San Antonio de Bexar—near what is now San Antonio. These settlements were established to provide protection and support to settlements in East Texas.

Mexican War for Independence

During the first part of the 19th century, punctuated by bloodshed to break away from three centuries of Spanish rule, the Spanish empire began crumbling. Mexico obtained its independence in 1821 and took control of the colony of Texas.

Anglo-American Presence in Texas

In 1820, Moses Austin received permission from the Spanish government to bring 300 Anglo-American families to settle in Texas. On Austin's return trip to Missouri to recruit settlers, Austin contracted pneumonia and did not live to see his colony in Texas established. Austin's son, Stephen, later negotiated with the Mexican government and obtained a similar agreement to let Anglo-Americans settle in Texas between the Brazos and Colorado rivers. By December 1821 Austin and fellow Anglo-American settlers had begun to establish themselves in the region. Austin and other *empresarios*,or land agents, including Martín de Léon, secured agreements with the Mexican government to bring a specified number of settlers to Texas in exchange for titles to land grants By 1835, the settlers, most of the from the United States, were the majority in the region, which increased tensions with the Mexican government.

Texas War for Independence

Conflicts between Texans and the Mexican government started as early as 1830. The colonists felt that the government was not providing adequate support and protection to Texas. Additionally, the government of Santa Anna sought to centralize administration, reducing the power of the states in Mexico's federal system. This led to conflict between Mexico City and the nation's northern states. Finally, between Mexican independence and the Texas Revolution, the government of Mexico had instituted efforts to regulate and even abolish the practice of slavery. These factors contributed to the eventual outbreak of war between Texans and the Mexican government. Attempts to negotiate with President Santa Anna failed. Even sending Stephen Austin to Mexico City to represent the colony only led to further misunderstanding as the Mexican government was not willing to negotiate and jailed Austin for a year.

First Battle in Gonzales

Following Santa Anna's order to disarm state militias across Mexico, the military commander of San Antonio ordered the Texans living at Gonzales to return a small cannon issued to it by the Mexican government to protect the colonists from Native American attack. By order of the government, Mexican soldiers came to take the cannon from the colonists in October 1835. The Texans refused to relinquish their weapon and fired it against the Mexican soldiers. The incident in Gonzales began the war for Texas independence.

Sam Houston

Sam Houston, a former governor of Tennessee, and United States Congressman from Tennessee had moved to Texas in 1832 and become embroiled in the debate over Texas independence. Following the disasters at the Alamo and Goliad, Houston would be named the commander of the Texas army. He would later serve as the President of the Republic of Texas, governor of the state of Texas, and as one of the state's first two United States Senators.

The Alamo and Goliad

The first meaningful battle of the Texas war for independence took place near what is now San Antonio in a small mission and fort called the Alamo. When the war began, fewer than 200 men, led by Col. William Travis, defended the Alamo. Such historical figures as James Bowie and Davy Crockett joined Travis in defending the Alamo, bringing the total number to nearly 260 men. In 1836, Gen. Antonio López de Santa Anna and the Mexican army took the fort and killed all but a handful of those inside. Among the survivors was Enrique Esparza, a child just 6 years of age whose father Gregorio died defending the Alamo, and Susanna Dickinson, whose husband was also a casualty of the battle. Santa Anna, despite losing as many as 400 killed and wounded, continued marching against the rebels and took Goliad, where more than 300 rebels were killed. These two battles provided the patriotic emotion that resulted in the creation of an army and led to victory against Mexico.

Texas Declaration of Independence

A few days before the Battle of the Alamo, a group of Texans met at Washington-on-the-Brazos to issue a declaration of independence and to form the new government. An interim government for the Republic of Texas was established, with David G. Burnet as president and Lorenzo de Zavala as vice president.

The Runaway Scrape

Following the tragic results of the Battles of the Alamo and Goliad, Sam Houston was given command of the Texan troops, now vastly outnumbered by Santa Anna's army. Houston led a strategic retreat toward Louisiana that led to a chaotic flight of Anglo-American settlers with their slaves, in fear of Mexican reprisals or Indian attacks on unprotected farmsteads. Bad weather made matters worse. This flight has been remembered as the "Runaway Scrape."

Battle of San Jacinto

While the colonists were fighting the Mexican army at the Alamo and in Goliad, Gen. Sam Houston was strengthening the army of the new republic. The Texan army continued retreating ahead of the Mexican forces until they reached the San Jacinto River, near the city of Houston. In a battle that lasted less than 20 minutes, Houston's troops defeated the Mexican army and captured Gen. Santa Anna. Texas President Burnet and Mexican President Santa Anna signed the Treaty of Velasco, with Santa Anna agreeing to withdraw his troops from Texas in exchange for safe conduct back to Mexico, where he would lobby for recognition of Texas independence. Santa Anna's commitment never materialized, and the Mexican government refused to recognize Texas as an independent republic. Nevertheless, Sam Houston became the president of the new republic, and from 1836 to 1845, Texas was an independent nation. However, the Mexican government still considered it a rebellious province that it could reclaim (Barker & Pohl, 2009).

Tejano Revolutionaries

In addition to the sacrifice of William Travis, James Bowie, and David (Davy) Crocket at the Battle of the Alamo, and the successes of Sam Houston at the Battle of San Jacinto, many Texas revolutionaries of Mexican or Tejano descent served the cause. Juan N. Seguín, a prominent San Antonio figure before the outbreak of revolution, supported Texas independence. He was then elected to the Texas Senate and served three terms. Like Seguín, Lorenzo de Zavala sided with the Texas rebels against Santa Anna, arguing that Santa Anna's centralizing reforms violated the Mexican constitution. He then served as the first vice president of the Republic of Texas. José Francisco Ruiz, a prominent San Antonio politician and military leader, who had served in the Mexican War for Independence, in 1836 joined the cause of Texas independence. He and his nephew, José Antonio Navarro, were among the signers of the Texas Declaration of Independence. Plácido Benavides was another opponent of Santa Anna who served vital roles in the success of the Texas Revolution. However, like Seguín, De Léon, and other Tejano rebels, after the Battle of San Jacinto, he was accused of not being sufficiently loyal to the new Texas Republic and was forced to flee, living out his life in exile.

Republic Period

After gaining their independence, many Texans supported immediate annexation of the area to the United States, but this was not to be. Instead, the Republic of Texas, under the Constitution of 1836, establishing a system of government modeled on that of the United States. It called for a powerful executive, a bicameral legislature, and a judicial branch. Adult white males monopolized the right to vote, and protections of slavery (largely unstated in the United

States Constitution) were made clear. The new Republic of Texas faced difficulties funding its government and maintaining financial independence as it fell further into debt. Sam Houston and Mirabeau Lamar, the republic's second president, managed with difficulty to secure international recognition for the new country, prosecute ongoing wars with Indian nations on its frontiers, and confront Mexican efforts to regain the state. One of the lasting institutions established by the republic was the Texas Rangers, a force originally established to confront threats from the Comanche, Cherokee, and other Indian nations. Despite the economic hardship typical of new nations, Texas remained independent for 10 years and was recognized by several nations, including the United States. However, with the republic unable to secure its borders and reverse its financial fortunes, the key leaders in Texas sought annexation by the United States. The last president of the Republic of Texas, Anson Jones, nonetheless negotiated a settlement with Mexico, despite both Texas congressional houses voting in favor of annexation by the United States. The Texas Congress repudiated Jones's effort, and in December 1845 Texas was annexed to the United States, while Jones retired to a life on his Texas plantation.

Texas Joins the United States

In 1845, Texas became the 28th state of the American union. The U.S. government immediately sent troops to the north bank of the Nueces River, near present-day Corpus Christi, in order to make good on the Texan—and now United States claim—to the Nueces strip, which Mexico considered its territory. The ensuing clashes between Mexican and U.S. forces resulted in Congress declaring war in May 1846. These confrontations provided the pretext for a U.S. war on Mexico intended as a war of imperial expansion, justified by the ideas of Manifest Destiny.

Mexican-American War

Between 1846 and 1848, Mexico and the United States waged a war that ended with a decisive victory and tremendous land acquisitions for the United States. As a result of the Treaty of Guadalupe Hidalgo, Mexico withdrew its claim over Texas and established the Rio Grande, or Rio Bravo, as it is known in Mexico, as the official border between the two countries. Mexico also ceded California and the territory known today as the American Southwest to the United States. Figure 5-9 presents a timeline of important events in Texas from 1528 to 1861. With this victory, Texas claimed territories bordering the Rio Grande that included much of New Mexico, and parts of contemporary Colorado, Kansas, Oklahoma, and even Wyoming. The current boundaries would not be finally settled until 1850.

Confederacy Period (1861–1865)

At the onset of the American Civil War, Texas left the Union and joined the Confederacy as a proslavery state. Perhaps as many as 90,000 Texans served in the Confederate Army, though most spent the war years defending the state from incursions by United States naval and infantry forces along the Gulf Coast or fighting against the Plains Indians. Texans, nonetheless, did play important roles in the fighting elsewhere, most notably in John Bell Hood's Texas Brigade. After five years of war, the Confederate army, led by Gen. Robert E. Lee, surrendered to Gen. Ulysses S. Grant, the leader of the Union forces. After the war, the Union forces occupied the South for 12 years (1865–1877) during Reconstruction.

Figure 5-9. Texas Timeline, 1528 to 1861

1528	1541	1682	1682	1690	1718	1820
Cabeza de Vaca lands in Texas	Coronado explores Texas	Mission founded in El Paso	La Salle (French) lands in Texas	First mission in East Texas San Francisco de los Tejas	Mission and fort founded in San Antonio	Austin arrives in San Antonio

1861	1848	1846	1845	1836	1835	1833
Texas secedes from the union	Treaty of Guadalupe Hidalgo	Mexican-American War begins	Texas becomes the 28th state in the union	Battle of San Jacinto; Texas declares independence	Battle of Gonzales marks beginning of Texas revolution	Santa Anna becomes president of Mexico

Juneteenth

Official notification that the approximately 250,000 enslaved Texans had been emancipated was not officially announced in Texas (by the Union General Gordon Granger) until June 19, 1865, two and a half years after President Lincoln had proclaimed it so. First celebrated in 1867, under the aegis of the Freedmen's Bureau, Juneteenth then became a state holiday, called "Emancipation Day in Texas," in 1980. During the era of the Civil Rights movement, African Americans who had migrated from Texas over the previous decades spread Juneteenth celebrations across the country. On June 17, 2021, President Joe Biden signed the Juneteenth National Independence Day Act, making Juneteenth a federal holiday.

Reconstruction Period

Under Reconstruction, Texas was briefly occupied by U.S. troops. Texas was allowed to rejoin the union in 1870, with the adoption of a new constitution, renunciation of secession, and the ratification of the 13th Amendment that had abolished slavery. During Reconstruction, despite efforts to reinstitute discriminatory Black Codes and despite the violence of the Ku Klux Klan terrorizing African Americans across the state, 19 African Americans were elected to the Texas legislature. One feature of Reconstruction in Texas, as elsewhere across the South, was the development of a system of sharecropping used on cotton plantations that had formerly relied on enslaved labor. In this system, former slaves worked the land and received a share of the crop, often between a quarter and half of the harvest, while the landowner took the rest. As a result, former slaves often found themselves indebted and bound to the land in a new form of coerced labor system. Reconstruction also saw increased efforts to expel Comanche, Kiowa, Apache, and other Indians from the state. During this period, buffalo hunters decimated the herds on which the Plains Indians depended. To secure the frontier, federal troops, often including African American soldiers, known as "Buffalo Soldiers" garrisoned forts along the frontier. In reaction to settler incursions on their hunting grounds, in the Red River War, Comanche and other Indian groups led by Quanah Parker, fought a series of battles in central and west Texas, before they were defeated by the superior firepower of federal frontier soldiers.

Economic Development after Reconstruction

After Reconstruction, the Texas economy flourished, largely based on the growth of the cattle industry and the sharecropping system of cotton production that replaced plantation slavery. Initial growth in ranching depended upon open range cattle herding in the grasslands of south and central Texas. Ranchers like Charles Goodnight then drove herds northward to supply army posts and Indian villages in New Mexico and Colorado. The Goodnight-Loving trail along which cattle were driven reached later to the stocking ranges of Wyoming and Montana. Other ranchers drove cattle along the Western, Chisolm, and Sedalia trails to railheads in Kansas and Missouri for shipment to eastern urban markets. Among the colorful figures from this era in Texas ranching was Elizabeth "Lizzie" Johnson, a "cattle queen" who is thought to be the first woman in Texas to ride the Chisholm Trail. The days of open-range ranching, however, were not long-lived. Barbed wire was introduced in 1880, and ranchers gradually abandoned the open range system and relied on scientific cattle breeding and ranch management to increase production and improve the quality of meat. Richard King and Mifflin Kenedy, who before the Civil War had begun amassing land in South Texas, took the lead in many of the ranching innovations that changed the landscape of cattle herding in the state, fencing in their grazing lands and water resources, and acquiring legal protections and financial capital to dominate the Texas grasslands.

Railway construction in Texas would contribute to the state's economy after Reconstruction as well. Rail construction in Texas before the Civil War lagged behind the rest of the country. In 1860, Texas had only 400 miles of track. In 1876, United States government land subsidies were used to encourage rail construction. Through this approach, some 40 railroads received 32 million acres of land, on which to build the state's rail infrastructure. Railroads made possible the growth of many small towns across the state, encouraged settlement, and opened up farm and ranch land to produce the foods and raw materials needed in Texas's urban centers.

Boom or Bust Economic Cycles in Texas

As Texas developed in the latter part of the 19th century and into the 20th, it experienced a number of "boom or bust" economic cycles. A "boom or bust" economy undergoes sharp fluctuations from boom, a period of rising prices and job growth, to bust, a period of price stagnation and unemployment. These variations affect the stability of the economy and the ability for the state to plan its future. Often booms are fueled by discoveries or technical innovation in leading industries. For example, in 1901, oil was discovered in the Spindletop Oil Field near Beaumont, in part due to the efforts of an eccentric entrepreneur named Patillo Higgins. The development of the oil industry made Texas the leading producer of oil in the United States. Because of this boom, cities like Houston and Dallas became large urban and industrial centers. "Busts" are often the result of overproduction in leading industries. Cattle markets, for example, boomed from the 1860s to the 1880s, flourishing with the spread of rail connections. However, overgrazing and destruction of plains grasslands, coupled with harsh weather conditions, contributed to a bust in cattle production in the mid-1880s.

The most significant "bust" in the 20th century was the Great Depression, which hit Texas hard. Depressed agricultural prices in the 1920s and 1930s undercut the prosperity of Texas farmers and ranchers, while drought and dust storms (the Dust Bowl) devastated the wheat and cotton growing regions of the Texas Panhandle. A farm exodus ensued, as Texas migrants fled to California and elsewhere seeking work as migrant labor. Many sharecroppers and tenant farmers also fled to Texas cities, making Texas a majority urban state for the first time.

World Wars and Beyond

World War I saw nearly 1 million Texans register for the draft with nearly 198,000 serving in the war effort. As a result of World War I, Texas emerged as a leading military training center. Several military bases were established, bringing economic growth. The rapid development of the aircraft industry and highly technological businesses led to rapid industrialization. World War II saw similar personal sacrifices and economic growth in Texas. Nearly 830,000 Texans served in the U.S. military. Texans like Lt. Audie Murphy (awarded the Medal of Honor for single-handedly holding off a squad of German soldiers) and Commander Sam Dealey (the most decorated American naval officer) stand out as Texas war heroes. Cleto Rodriguez, another Medal of Honor winner for his bravery during the Battle of Manila in 1945, was one of many Texans of Mexican descent who played important roles in the fighting. But Texas's role in producing fighter planes like the P-51 Mustang or bombers, like the B-24 Liberator, or producing the oil that fueled the war effort, and even housing prisoners of war in camps across the state, demonstrated a much wider contribution to the war effort. By World War II, Texas was a leading state in the defense industry, and while still reliant on agriculture, ranching, cotton, and oil production, after World War II, Texas became increasingly a center for new high-technology industries and defense production.

Six Flags over Texas

The phrase "Six flags over Texas" describes the different countries that have exerted control in Texas since 1519. It was in that year that Alonso Álvarez de Pineda led a Spanish expedition that sailed along the Gulf of Mexico coastline from Florida to Cabo Rojo, Mexico. Álvarez de Pineda and his men became the first Europeans to explore and map the Gulf littoral between the areas that had been surveyed by Juan Ponce De León and Diego Velázquez.

- Spain (1519–1821)
- France (1685–1690)
- Mexico (1821–1836)
- Republic of Texas (1836–1845)
- United States (1845–1861)
- Texas in the Confederacy (1861–1865)
- Back to the American union (1870–present)

State Almanac

Here's a snapshot of symbols, iconography, and the geographical context of Texas:

- State flower   Bluebonnet
- State bird   Mockingbird
- State tree   Pecan
- State motto   Friendship
- Border states   Oklahoma, Louisiana, Arkansas, and New Mexico
- State song   "Texas, Our Texas," by William J. Marsh and Gladys Yoakum Wright

Here are the lyrics to "Texas, Our Texas":

Texas, our Texas!
All hail the
mighty State!
Texas, our Texas!
So wonderful so
great!

Boldest and grandest, withstanding ev'ry test;
O Empire wide and glorious, you stand supremely blest.

[Refrain]
God bless you Texas!
And keep you brave and
strong, That you may grow
in power and worth,
thro'out the ages long.

COMPETENCY 003: GEOGRAPHY AND CULTURE

The teacher understands and applies knowledge of geographic relationships involving people, places, and environments in Texas, the United States, and the world; and also understands and applies knowledge of cultural development, adaptation, diversity, and interactions among science, technology, and society as defined by the Texas Essential Knowledge and Skills (TEKS).

Geography

Geography studies the Earth's surface, the organisms that populate it, and their interaction within the ecosystem by examining spatial patterns, processes, and relationships from a local to global scale. Geography can be divided into two main areas: physical and cultural. *Physical geography* refers to the physical characteristics of the surface of the Earth and how those features affect life (e.g., plate tectonics, landforms, bodies of water, climate, biomes, weathering, erosion, etc.). *Cultural, or human, geography* deals with the interaction of humans with their environment and how that interaction produces changes. Humans can alter the physical environment of the Earth, but the physical environment can also shape humans and their culture. For example, the Incas built the capital of their empire, Cuzco, in the Andes Mountains in what is now Peru. This city has an altitude of 11,152 feet above sea level, where oxygen is scarce and agriculture is a challenge. However, the Incas managed to live and flourish. They carved the land for agriculture and built roads and cities. In turn, the environment changed the Incas, who had to evolve to tolerate the low levels of oxygen. Studies conducted on the Indians from Peru suggest that people of the Andes developed genetic adaptations for high-altitude living (Discovery Channel, March 10, 2004). By adapting to environmental conditions, the inhabitants not only survived but also flourished in less-than-ideal conditions.

How Physical Geography Influences Settlement Locations

People typically settle where there is good land, good climate, and good, clean water. The location of such renewable and nonrenewable natural resources as fresh water, fossil fuels, fertile soils, and timber affect decisions about where to build a community. For example, the settlement patterns in Texas and in the United States show that people did not simply settle where the climate was good for crops or along the coast where land was easily accessed. People also settled away from the coast along waterways. This provided a fresh source of water as well as a resource for food and transportation. However, settlement decisions can also cause stress on the natural resource. For example, in San Antonio the Edwards Aquifer is one of the most prolific underground sources of water in the world. The demand for the water may become greater than the capacity of the aquifer, which will affect the livelihood of the people as well as the potential development of urban areas in the region.

Locating Places and Regions on a Map

Maps have two categories: reference and thematic. *Reference maps* show the locations of places, boundaries of countries, states, counties, towns, landforms and bodies of water. They are sometimes referred to as political and physical maps. A *physical map* shows the topography of the Earth, including land features and elevations. A *political map* shows how a country is organized. Atlases are examples of reference maps. *Thematic maps, or special purpose maps,* show such specific topics as population density or distribution of world religions as well as physical, social, economic, political, agricultural, or economic features. An *economic map* shows the important resources of a country or region. A *historical map* shows the location of historical events. *Population maps* show where people live.

A globe is a scale model of the Earth shaped like a sphere. Because a globe models the shape of the Earth, it shows sizes and shapes accurately. The Mercator projection map is a flat representation of the Earth, and it thus distorts the shape, size, and/or distance in some way. This projection, used initially for shipping, is most accurate nearest the equator. The portability of maps makes them more useful than globes. The position of people, places, and things can be identified using relative or absolute location. **Relative location** uses references to help describe where something is. For example, a house may be located next to a big soccer field. **Absolute location** provides the exact position of the destination. This could be as simple as an address for a house or the coordinates of the location using latitude and longitude. It is important to say "latitude and longitude" in that order because the coordinate system identifies latitude first. For example, Dallas is located at 33° N, 97° W.

The Grid System

A grid system is a network of horizontal and vertical lines used to locate points on a map or chart by coordinates. This grid shows the location of places. In this grid system, latitudinal and longitudinal lines form divisions that consist of geometrical coordinates used to designate the location of places on the surface of the Earth on a globe or map. The lines measure distances in degrees.

Latitudinal lines are horizontal and run parallel around the Earth measuring the distance north and south of the equator. The equator is identified as the 0 degree line of latitude, and it divides the Earth into the Northern and the Southern hemispheres. The United States is located in the Northern Hemisphere, while Brazil is located in the Southern Hemisphere. Longitudinal lines are vertical and run north and south going east and west. The 0 degree line of longitude is the first meridian known as the prime meridian. It goes through Greenwich, England, and it divides the Earth into the Eastern and Western hemispheres. The United States is in the Western Hemisphere, and Japan is in the Eastern Hemisphere.

Geographic Symbols

A compass rose is a design printed on a chart or map for reference. It shows the orientation of a map on Earth and shows the four cardinal directions (north, south, east, and west). A compass rose may also show intermediate directions (southeast, northeast, northwest, and southwest). Maps use symbols to contain a lot of information that can be easily understood. Common map symbols include dots, stars, and small pictures to represent cities or places. Some maps use different colors to represent such features as elevations and divisions. These symbols and colors are defined in the map's key, or legend. A map scale shows the distance between two places in the world. The scale to which a map is drawn represents the ratio of the distance between two points on the Earth and the distance between the two corresponding points on the map. When teaching cardinal and intermediate directions, teachers sometimes label walls with *N*, *S*, *E*, *W* to aid students when giving directions. Teachers need to take precautions to assure that each wall is labeled accurately. This means that the wall that faces north is labeled "North." If North is in a corner, label the corner North. The wall then can have a sign for the correct intermediate direction.

Time Zones

Time zones are established based on the lines of longitude, or meridians. These lines run from north to south. The prime meridian, or the meridian at 0 degrees, has been set in Greenwich, England. On the other side of the globe is the 180th meridian along which the International Date Line generally follows. The prime meridian divides the Earth into the Western and Eastern hemispheres. Following the sunlight as it travels along the rotating Earth, the time decreases moving from east to west. When people travel from China (east) to the United States (west), they save a day; that is, they might spend a day traveling but still arrive on the same calendar day.

The United States has six time zones of one hour difference each—Eastern, Central, Mountain, Pacific, Alaska, and Hawaii. Figure 5-10 represents the six time zones in the United States, with a key city pinpointed for each zone. Technically, the United States has four time zones in the contiguous 48 states, five in the continental U.S. (America) with the addition of Alaska, and when we include Hawaii, the sixth time zone is accounted for. For more information about time zones, go to the website provided by the National Institute of Standards and Technology (an agency of the U.S. Department of Commerce) and the U.S. Naval Observatory at *http://time.gov/aboutB.html*.

Figure 5-10. Times Zones in the United States

West ←					→ East
Hawaii	Alaska	Pacific	Mountain	Central	Eastern
1:00 PM	2:00 PM	3:00 PM	4:00 PM	5:00 PM	6:00 PM
Honolulu	Anchorage	Los Angeles	Phoenix	Dallas	New York City

Regions of the World

A world region is an area of the world that shares similar, unifying cultural or physical characteristics different from those of surrounding areas. The physical features refer to such topographic characteristics as elevation, rivers, and mountains. The cultural features include all the features that distinguish different groups of people. Examples of these features include language, religion, government, economics, food, architecture, shared values, and family life.

Geographers have divided the world into 10 common regions: North America, Central and South America, Europe, Central Eurasia, the Middle East, North Africa, Sub-Saharan Africa, South Asia, East Asia, and Australasia. These divisions are based on physical and cultural similarities. North America consists of Canada, the United States, and Mexico. The Europeans colonized the North American region. Table 5-5 presents an overview of the world regions by physical and cultural features. World region names and scope can vary depending on the purpose of those defining the area. For example, when discussing North America and Latin America, North America in this instance only refers to Canada and the United States, while Latin America consists of everything south of the United States (Mexico, Central America, the Caribbean, and South America).

Table 5-5. World Regions

World Region	Physical Features	Cultural Features
North America	• Consists of Canada, the United States, and Mexico. • The United States is the fourth largest country in the world. • Oil is an important resource in the U.S. • Most of the U.S. has a humid-continental or humid-subtropical climate • Most of Canada has a subarctic or tundra climate. • Over 75% of Canadians live along the Southern border. • The areas of greatest concentration of population in the U.S. are along the East Coast and California. • The climate of Mexico ranges from humid tropical and subtropical to desert and highland. • Mexico has rich mineral resources including oil.	• Europeans colonized this region. • Languages spoken are predominantly English, Spanish, and French. • Most people hold Christian beliefs.

(continued)

World Region	Physical Features	Cultural Features
Central and South America	• Includes the countries of Central America, the Caribbean islands, and South America. • The majority of this continuous mass of land is south of the equator. • South America extends from Point Gallinas in Colombia to Cape Horn. • Part of South America lies closer to the South Pole than any other land mass of this size. • Venezuela is one of the world's leading exporters of oil. • Most of Eastern Central America and equatorial South America have a humid tropical climate.	• Most people speak Spanish, but many other languages are spoken: Portuguese, French, Dutch, English, and several Native American languages and dialects. • Christian beliefs, the Roman Catholic religion is predominant. • Architecture, law, religion, traditions, and language are strongly influenced by Europe's colonial rule of this region. • The many ethnic groups in this region are separated by geographical barriers such as the Andes and the Amazon.
Europe	• Western section of the Eurasian continent • Shares a mountain chain, the Alps. • Most of Europe has a temperate climate. • Europe's irregular coastline has many harbors that are important manufacturing and trade centers. • The rivers of Europe are important resources for trade, water, and hydroelectricity. • European population growth rates are the smallest in the world.	• Shares a common history in the Roman Empire and later the Catholic Church and Latin language. • English is the most spoken language in Europe, German and French are also widespread. • Cultural diffusion or shared cultural traits spread throughout Europe. • Ninety percent of all adults ages 15–24 speak a second language and some countries are considered multilingual. • Europeans practice many different religions. • Roman Catholicism is the predominant religion of many European countries. • Most of Northern and Central Europe is Protestant. • Jews live in many parts of Western Europe.
Central Eurasia	• Central Asia and Eastern Europe • United around one continuous mass of land located in the middle of the continent. • Little access to the sea • The borders of Eastern European countries have changed many times. • From WWII to the late 1980s, the Soviet Union controlled Eastern Europe and introduced communism to the region.	• Conquered at different times by the Persians, Mongolians, Tartars, the French, the Germans, and the Russians. • Slavic languages are predominant. • Most people in the Eastern part of the region follow the Eastern Orthodox church; people in the Northern area are mostly Roman Catholic.

(continued)

World Region	Physical Features	Cultural Features
Middle East	• Consists of the area of southwest Asia and North Africa. • Access to sea water • The majority of the land is desert. • Rich in oil	• While the majority of people follow the religion of Islam, there are also groups that follow Christianity and Judaism. • The religion defines the law in many places. • The most ancient of human civilizations—Egyptians, Assyrians, Babylonians, Persians, Greeks, and Romans—have left their mark in this region. • This region has been the fighting ground for many religious battles.
North Africa	• Part of the African continent • Includes Egypt, Libya, Tunisia, Algeria, and Morocco • Extensive coastline • The Sahara Desert and the Nile River are two important physical features of this area • Rich in oil • Egypt is undergoing rapid growth, urbanization, and industrialization	• The majority of people follow the religion of Islam. • People speak Arabic predominantly. • Religious issues influence the politics of this area.
Sub-Saharan Africa	• Consists of Africa south of the Sahara • Most of the area is a savanna • Has abundant rain • Extensive coastline • Fertile land • Most people live in the forest zone and the dry savannas • Agriculture is the predominant activity in West Africa • Livestock is the predominant economic activity in the northern area	• Cultural diversity reflects indigenous, Arab, and European influences. • Majority follows tribal beliefs, Christianity, or a combination of both. • Most people speak native African or European languages. • Over 500 ethnic groups live in this region.
South Asia	• Consists of a large Indian peninsula that extends into the Indian Ocean. • Abundant rainfall • Strong seasonal winds called monsoons • Rice is an important crop. • One of the most populated regions in the world. • The world's highest mountains are located in the northern area of this region. • Many major manufacturing and trade centers are located along the coast.	• People in South Asia speak many languages. • Predominant beliefs are of Eastern origins such as Buddhism and Hinduism. • Many South Asians are farmers who live in small villages. • Many cultural influences • Through the efforts of Mohandas Gandhi the region gained its independence from Britain in 1947.

(continued)

World Region	Physical Features	Cultural Features
East Asia	<ul><li>Consists of China, Korea, Taiwan, and Japan.</li><li>It is the most densely populated region in the world.</li><li>Large expanse of coastline.</li></ul>	<ul><li>Buddhism and Taoism are predominant religions.</li><li>Confucian philosophy</li><li>People speak Chinese, Japanese, Korean, Mongolian, and many other languages.</li><li>Chinese Script or characters influence many of the writing systems of these languages.</li><li>Culturally, China has had a major influence in this region.</li></ul>
Australasia	<ul><li>It is composed of the Australian continent and surrounding islands.</li><li>South of the equator</li></ul>	<ul><li>English is the predominant language of most of the nations in this region</li><li>Population is a large Christian majority.</li></ul>

Regions of the United States

The concept of regions facilitates the examination of geography by providing a convenient and manageable unit for studying the Earth's human and natural environment. The continental United States can be divided into eight broad physical geographic divisions:

- **Laurentian Highlands** are part of the Canadian Shield that extends into the northern United States and the Great Lakes area. This area has a hard winter, and agriculture is limited.

- **Atlantic–Gulf Coastal Plains** are the coastal regions of the eastern and southern states. It includes New York City in the North, the Mid-Atlantic states to Florida in the South, and all the way west to Texas on the Gulf Coast. It is sometimes referred to as two regions: Coastal Plains and Gulf Coastal Plains.

- **Appalachian Highlands** covers the Appalachian Mountains, the Adirondack Mountains, and New England—Connecticut, Maine, Massachusetts, New Hampshire, Rhode Island, and Vermont.

- **Interior Plains and the Great Plains** covers the interior United States. Included in this area are the states west of the Appalachians, south of the Great Lakes, and as far west as Montana, Wyoming, Colorado, New Mexico, and northwestern Texas. Most of the nation's wheat, corn, and feed crops are grown in this area.

- **Interior Highlands** is also part of the interior continental United States. This area includes the Ozark Mountains and Missouri, Arkansas, and Kentucky as well as part of Oklahoma and Kansas.

- **Rocky Mountain System** is in the western United States and Canada extending from British Colombia to Montana, Utah, Colorado, and New Mexico. The mountain range is called the **Continental Divide**, because it separates the eastward-flowing rivers from the westward-flowing rivers. The waters that flow eastward empty into the Atlantic Ocean, and those that flow westward empty into the Pacific Ocean.

- **Intermontane Plateaus** is a large region that includes the Pacific Northwest, the Colorado Plateau, and the basins of the southwestern United States. This area covers Washington, Oregon, Idaho, part of Utah, New Mexico, and Arizona. It also covers the Grand Canyon and Death Valley.

- **Pacific Mountain System** covers the West Coast. This area extends from the Cascade Mountains in the north down the entire West Coast through Washington, Oregon, and California.

Texas Regions and Economic Activity

Texas is the second-largest state in the United States, behind Alaska. Covering 268,601 square miles, the state contains five geographic regions within its boundaries. Table 5-6 lists the regions and the key cities and main economic activities of each.

Largest Rivers in the World

These are the three largest rivers in the world:

- The Nile (North and East Africa) is the longest river in the world. It originates in Lake Victoria, which is shared by Uganda, Kenya, and Tanzania. It flows north[4] following the downward slant of the land to its mouth at the Mediterranean Sea.

- The Amazon (South America) is the second-largest. The widest river in the world, it originates in Perú, and its mouth is at the Atlantic Ocean off the coast of Brazil.

- The Chang Jiang or Yangtze (China) is the third-largest river. Its source is the Tibetan Plateau, and its mouth is at the East China Sea.

For more information about the world's largest rivers, go to the Social Studies for Kids website at *www.socialstudiesforkids.com/articles/geography/longestriverstable.htm.*

Table 5-6. Regions and Economic Activity in Texas

Region	Key Cities	Main Economic Activities	Key Statistics
Coastal plains, flatland	Dallas, Houston, San Antonio, Austin, Corpus Christi, Laredo	Lumber—East Texas (Piney Woods) Oil—Refineries in Houston Farming—Rice, oranges, cotton, wheat, milo Ranching—Cattle in Kingsville Shipping—Houston	Population—High: 1 of 3 Texans Rainfall—High Distinguishing Mark—Hurricanes

---

[4] Students may have a misconception that rivers only run south. Due to gravity, rivers run downhill. This means that they can flow in a cardinal or intermediate direction, as long as it is toward lower levels of land.

North Central plains, flatland and hills	Fort Worth, Arlington, San Angelo, Abilene	Ranching—Cattle, wool (mohair), sheep Farming—Grains	Population—High Rainfall—Medium Distinguishing Marks—Tornadoes, northerlies (cold winds), hailstorms; large ranches
Great Plains Flatland and hill country	Midland, Odessa, Lubbock, Amarillo, Texas Panhandle	Ranching—Cattle, sheep Minerals—Graphite Oil—Odessa and Midland Farming—Wheat	Population—Average Rainfall—Medium Distinguishing Marks—Snowstorms, dust storms, windmills, use of aquifers
Mountains and basins, Rocky Mountains, Davis, Chisos, and Guadalupe, Chihuahuan Desert	El Paso	Ranching—Limited large ranches Mexico-U.S. border economy based on trading of goods produced by the industries established in Mexico—maquiladoras.	Population—Low Rainfall—Low; hard rain wears out the rocks and land Distinguishing Mark—Big Bend National Park

Rivers in the United States

These are the largest and most important rivers in the United States:

- The Mississippi is the longest river in the United States and the 14th longest in the world. It begins in Minnesota and ends in the Gulf of Mexico.

- The Ohio River begins near Pittsburgh and runs southwest, which becomes a tributary of the Mississippi River just south of Cairo, Illinois.

- The Rio Grande begins in the San Juan Mountains of southern Colorado and ends in the Gulf of Mexico. The river is the official border between the United States and Mexico, where it is known as the Rio Bravo.

- The Colorado River begins in the Rocky Mountains and ends in California.

- The Missouri River begins in the Rocky Mountains, flowing north first and then generally southeast across the central United States, ending at the Mississippi River, just to the north of St. Louis.

For information about the most significant rivers of the continental United States, visit *https://www.worldatlas.com*.

Mountains in the World

With notable exception of the peak known as K2, which is part of the Karakoram Range, the tallest mountains in the world are located in the Himalayas, ranging across the countries of China,

Pakistan, Nepal, and Tibet. Table 5-7 lists the top 10 tallest mountains. Compared with the world's tallest peaks, those within the U.S. are small. The highest mountain is Denali, formerly known as Mt. McKinley, in Alaska. Alaska has 16 of the highest peaks in the United States. A list of the mountains with 16,000-foot altitudes or above is presented in Table 5-8. For additional information about the world's mountains, go to *www.infoplease.com/ipa/A0001771.html*.

Deforestation

Deforestation can increase soil erosion and can lead to tragedies like the mudslides that occurred in 2006 in the Philippines, where thousands of people were buried alive. The rate of soil erosion is most likely to exceed the rate of soil formation in areas like Brazil, where people have cut forests to clear land for farming.

Table 5-7. Tallest Mountains in the World

Mountain	Location	Height (feet)
Everest	Nepal/Tibet	29,035
K2	Pakistan/China	28,250
Kanchenjunga	India/Nepal	28,169
Lhotse I	Nepal/Tibet	27,940
Makalu I	Nepal/Tibet	27,766
Cho Oyu	Nepal/Tibet	26,906
Dhaulagiri	Nepal	26,795
Manaslu I	Nepal	26,781
Nanga Parbat	Pakistan	26,660
Annapurna	Nepal	26,545

Table 5-8. Tallest Mountains in the United States

Mountain	Location	Height (feet)
Denali[5]	Alaska	20,310
Mt. St. Elias	Alaska	18,008
Mt. Foraker	Alaska	17,400
Mt. Bona	Alaska	16,500
Mt. Blackburn	Alaska	16,390
Mt. Sanford	Alaska	16,237

[5] Also known as Mt. McKinley. Denali's official elevation, the highest in North America, was established by the U.S. Geological Survey in 2015.

Deposition

Deposition is the carrying of soil from one place to another, usually by water or wind. This process is responsible for the creation of beaches as well as the sand dunes found in desert areas and the landforms created by glaciers.

Geographical Tools

Social scientists (e.g., geographers, historians, political scientists, and economists) use an assortment of geographical tools to help examine physical and cultural geographic data. First, the globe is recognized as a mathematical model of the world and is important to students' development of spatial thinking. It shows accurate distance, shape, and size of continents and bodies of water. As will be discussed, colors are used to symbolize elevation or other concepts. The complexity of the globe increases with the grade level. Maps are a flat representation of the world or a region of the world. As with globes, the complexity of maps increases developmentally with the grade level. Charts, graphs, and diagrams are also used to analyze data. Some mathematical representations, such as Dot Plots, offer an opportunity to reinforce mathematical concepts while examining cultural and historical data sets. Digital geospatial tools can offer teachers an alternative to paper maps and allow for more depth and rigor when used appropriately. These tools can provide an easy way to explore data spatially, such as in the Annie E. Case Foundation "Kids Count" website (*http://datacenter.kidscount.org/*) and the Census Bureau webpage for kids (*http://www.census.gov/schools/census_for_kids*). Others provide interactive online maps such as *http://mrnussbaum.com/united-states/amwest/* or *http://mrnussbaum.com/united-states/southwest/*. A popular digital globe is Google Earth *https://www.google.com/earth/*), which allows users to add data layers and to spatially analyze data from a local to global scale. Finally, ArcGIS Online (*http://www.arcgis.com/features/*) offers an online tool that facilitates inquiry-based discussions and lets students and teachers explore data and create maps.

Map Skills by Grade—Scope and Sequence

Kindergarten

Students should create and interpret maps of places and regions of the world that contain developmentally appropriate map elements and symbols. A compass rose and grid system should be used to locate places on maps and globes as well. Place location, or memorizing countries, cities, bodies of water, and landforms on a map, is critical to learning geography and other social studies. It lays the foundation on which content about Texas, the United States, and the world can be built. Its importance is akin to the multiplication tables in mathematics. Maps may be provided through an online or desktop digital source or on paper. Paper maps may already have an outline of a region or require students to sketch the area. Sketch maps are important because they require students to create a mental image, or map, of the area. Doing so will help them visualize the region when learning about social studies, and it will also help them to make connections to other content, including literature and science.

In addition to the knowledge required in the Texas Essential Knowledge and Skills (TEKS), each student in Kindergarten through Grade 6 should learn the following geography skills and concepts.

- Understands and uses terms related to location, direction, and distance (*up, down, left, right, here, near, far*).

- Recognizes a globe as a model of the Earth.

- Recognizes and uses terms that express relative size and shape (big, little, large, small, round, square).

- Identifies school and local community by name.

- Recognizes and uses models and symbols to represent real things.

- Identifies bodies of water—oceans, seas, lakes, rivers, ponds, and bayous (TEKS).

- Identifies landforms—plains, mountains, deserts, hills, and canyons (TEKS).

- Identifies natural resources—water, soil, trees, metals, and fish (TEKS).

Grade 1

- Makes and uses simple classroom maps to locate objects.

- Knows geographical location of home in relation to school and neighborhood.

- Knows the layout of the school campus.

- Identifies state and nation by name.

- Follows and gives verbal directions (here, there, left, right, below, above).

- Distinguishes between land and water symbols on globes and maps.

- Relates locations on maps and globes to locations on the Earth.

- Observes, describes, and builds simple models and maps of the local environment.

- Knows the four cardinal points (TEKS).

- Identifies the physical characteristics of places—precipitation, body of water, landforms, types of vegetation, and climate (TEKS).

Grade 2

- Makes and uses simple maps of the school and neighborhood.

- Interprets map symbols using a legend.

- Knows and uses cardinal directions.

- Locates community, state, and nation on maps and globes.

- Identifies local landforms.

- Differentiates between maps and globes.

- Locates other neighborhoods studied on maps.

- Knows the continents of the world (TEKS).

- Identifies important landmarks—Statue of Liberty, Washington Monument, etc. (TEKS).

- Identifies natural resources (TEKS).

- Identifies aspects of the physical environment, from organisms to communities (TEKS).

Grade 3

- Uses distance, directions, scale, and map symbols.

- Compares own community with other communities.

- Compares urban and rural environments.

- Uses charts to record and present information (TEKS).

- Understands climate and such influences on climate as wind velocity, precipitation, and proximity to bodies of water.

- Uses the compass rose as a means of orientation on a map of the Earth (TEKS).

- Uses graphs (TEKS).

- Uses graphic organizers and diagrams to arrange items in meaningful way (TEKS).

- Understands that landforms change through erosion and deposition (TEKS).

- Understands that regions are areas of the Earth's surface (TEKS).

- Uses scale to represent distances (TEKS).

- Uses timelines to list events chronologically.

Grade 4

- Interprets pictures, graphs, charts, and tables.

- Works with distance, directions, scale, and map symbols.

- Relates similarities and differences between maps and globes.

- Uses maps of different scales and themes.

- Recognizes the common characteristics of the map grid system.

- Compares and contrasts regions on a state, national, or world basis.

- Understands such concepts of adaptation and modification as changing the landscape to meet survival needs and building to adjust to a new environment (TEKS).

- Identifies elements that affect the climate (TEKS).

- Uses a compass rose to find true directions.

- Identifies key explorers and their achievements (TEKS).

- Identifies how geography affects the settlement and development of places.

- Understands the connection between climate and vegetation.

- Identifies global divisions, like the prime meridian, the equator, and the four hemispheres (TEKS).

Grade 5

- Uses geographic tools to collect, analyze, and interpret data (TEKS).

- Applies such geographic tools as grid systems, legends, symbols, scales, and compass roses to make and interpret maps (TEKS).

- Translates geographic data into such formats as graphs and maps (TEKS).

- Understands the concept of regions and can describe regions in the U.S. that result from patterns of human activity, including political, population, and economic regions as well as from physical characteristics, including landform, climate, and vegetation regions (TEKS).

- Locates the 50 states on a map and identifies regions made by groups of states, such as New England and the Great Plains (TEKS).

- Understands and describes location and patterns of settlement as well as their distribution (TEKS).

- Analyzes the location of U. S. cities, including state capitals (TEKS).

- Understands how people adapt and modify their environment to meet human needs (TEKS).

- Analyzes the consequences of human modification of the environment in the United States (TEKS).

Grade 6

- Uses maps, globes, graphs, charts, models, and databases to answer geographic questions.

- Creates maps, graphs, models, and databases (TEKS).

- Poses and answers questions about geographic distributions and patterns from selected world regions and countries (TEKS).

- Compares selected world regions and countries by using data from maps, graphs, charts, databases, and models (TEKS).

- Understands the characteristics and relative locations of major historical and contemporary societies (TEKS).

- Locates major historical and contemporary societies on maps and globes (TEKS).

- Identifies and explains how geography affects patterns of population in places and regions (TEKS).

- Understands how geography influences the economic development, political relationships, and policies of societies (TEKS).

- Understands the impact of physical processes on patterns in the environment (TEKS).

- Understands the impact of interactions between people and the physical environment on the development of places and regions (TEKS).

Culture

The culture of a group is reflected in what its people write, create, and wear as well their government, decisions, customs and ceremonies, way of life, and dwellings. Humans share their culture through oral traditions, stories, real and mythical heroes, music, paintings, and sculptures. Significant historical periods represent cultural ideals at a given time and may continue to influence following generations as well as other regions of the world. For example, the Renaissance, Baroque, Classicism, Neoclassicism, and Romanticism are key historical periods that gave birth to influential literature, art, and music. The Renaissance, or "rebirth," was a time of great creativity. William Shakespeare's plays explored humanity in plays that are still read and performed. Leonardo da Vinci created inspiring painting and sculptures. He also was known as the "Renaissance Man" who learned about and pursued different disciplines that enabled him to pursue his interest in science and inventions as well. Literature and art often also reflect their time as well as the societies in which they were produced. The Renaissance also reflected reformation of attitudes toward political authority, which was mainly embodied in the church and monarchs. Society questioned and challenged decisions made by the church – as well as the monarch's rule. (For more information, go to *http://www.britannica.com/EBchecked/topic/497731/Renaissance*.) In the United States, the American Renaissance occurred in literature from the 1830s through the Civil War and into the 1880s. As with the European renaissance, literature and the arts explored humanity and challenged current beliefs in the church, politics, and society. It was a period of time that was greatly governed by Transcendentalism. American Transcendentalism, a term derived from the philosopher Kant, was heavily influenced by the great minds of England and Germany. In America this philosophy, or belief, was idealistic in nature, rooted in faith, and had a visionary bent. It was a collection of complex beliefs that held "that the spark of divinity lies within man; that everything in the world is a microcosm of existence; that the individual soul is identical to the world soul, or Over-Soul, as Emerson called it. … By meditation, by communing with nature, through work and art, man could transcend his senses and attain an understanding of beauty and goodness and truth." (*http://www.pbs.org/wnet/ihas/icon/transcend.html*) This philosophy permeated American life through literature, poetry, art work (e.g., painting, sculpture), architecture, and music. Key transcendentalist authors include Emerson, Thoreau, Hawthorne, Whitman, and Dickinson, just to name a few. The Renaissance is just one example of how creative expression can both be influenced by and transcend societal boundaries to explore such universal ideas as religion, justice, and the passage of time.

Culture can also be viewed through the lens of race, gender, ethnicity, socioeconomic class, and other sociological perspectives. Historically, individuals differentiate themselves, and this affects their societies. For example, race has been used as a way to segment society and to allow certain groups to achieve status or some reward over another group. Race groups people according to such common features as hair, eye, or skin color. Ethnicity identifies a group of people by cultural traits. During World War II, Adolf Hitler, the leader of Nazi Germany, scapegoated Jews as the reason for the economic and social crisis Germany was facing. He drove a wedge that separated Jew from non-Jew. Although he referred to the ethnic group, Jews were recognized by characteristics that Hitler identified as the Jewish race. In the United States, race has been viewed as both unifying and divisive. For example, enclaves developed in cities where people with similar ethnic backgrounds lived. In this way, the immigrants felt at home and could ease into American culture. However, cultural differences sometimes have divided people. After a series of potato famines in Ireland, Irish immigrants moved to America to find a new life—and were met with derisive depictions that included, for example, newspaper classified ads that said, "Irish Need Not Apply." Texas was settled by cultural groups who created towns to reflect their German, Polish, Mexican, and other heritages. At the same time, society was often stratified by race, gender, and socioeconomic class.

Cultural Diffusion

Cultural diffusion describes the exchange or transmission of cultural information and lifestyles among people worldwide. For example, most people use cotton, a fabric developed in India, and silk, developed in China. Chickens and pigs were originally domesticated in Asia, but because of cultural diffusion, these animals are common in most countries. Many countries are predominantly Christian today, but Christianity was born in the Middle East, where most people are Muslim. The Romans facilitated the cultural diffusion of Christianity around the ancient world. Travelers visiting Morocco, a Muslim country in North Africa, may be surprised to hear Puerto Rican salsa and Jamaican reggae music played in local nightclubs. The popularity of Latin and Caribbean rhythms in a predominantly Muslim country is an example of the powerful effect of cultural diffusion.

Cultural diffusion influences the development of multicultural societies, which may have unifying and divisive qualities. The influx of people can aid the social and economic development of a nation. All cultures have unique characteristics and knowledge that can add to a society. These include inventions, art, music, and technology as well as production techniques. However, tensions can rise when people compete for housing, jobs, and land. Large cultural groups also may seek to dominate and exploit smaller, weaker cultural groups. Conflict also may occur if cultural groups try to force their way of life on others.

Relationships among cultural groups are dynamic. The relationships are influenced by conflict, cooperation, and change and are based on such factors as race, ethnicity, and religion. For example, in the 1960s tensions among the Caucasian and African-American races in the United States brought about much change. Although in the South some conflicts occurred in the form of riots, protests, and attacks, both races also cooperated through marches, speeches, peaceful demonstrations, and, eventually, new laws. Religion can also engender tension and conflict. For example, in Northern Ireland, Catholics and Protestants fought for many years. Although both groups are Christian, sectarian violence continued for decades until a power-sharing agreement was reached in 1998.

Improved communication, transportation and economic development can also impact cultural change. For example, the country of Malawi, on the continent of Africa, has a poor infrastructure resulting in a few people owning a telephone in their house or village. Telephones with landlines require electricity, wiring under or above ground, and other infrastructure. However, satellites allow farmers in this country to operate satellite mobile telephones that need little infrastructure. The people in Malawi, like many African cultures, have a strong oral tradition, meaning they learn by listening as experienced elders pass knowledge and traditions. Many cannot read and write. Satellite phones let members of this society gain new knowledge to improve their agriculture by using their oral traditions rather than written language.

COMPETENCY 004: ECONOMICS

The teacher understands and applies knowledge of economic systems and how people organize economic systems to produce, distribute, and consume goods and services.

Basic Principles of Economics

Economics is a social science that analyzes the principles that regulate the production, distribution, and consumption of resources in society. It emphasizes how these principles operate within the economic choices of individuals, households, businesses, and governments. Economics can be divided into two main areas: macroeconomics and microeconomics. *Macroeconomics* studies the economy at the world, regional, state, and local levels. The topics include reasons and ways to control inflation, causes of unemployment, and economic growth. *Microeconomics* deals with specific issues related to decision-making.

Theory of Supply and Demand

This theory of supply and demand maintains that prices vary based on balance between the availability of a product or service at a certain price (supply) and the desire of potential buyers to pay that price (demand). This balance of supply and demand can occur naturally or be created artificially. An example of an artificially created balance is the intentional destruction of a surplus of a given product on the world market to maintain the price. Another way is to control the production and availability of the product to create a scarcity situation. Cartels like the Organization of Petroleum Exporting Countries (OPEC) can keep prices artificially high.

Goods and Services

Machines increase the availability of goods and services. Machine, or industrial, production can decrease the cost of making the goods and consequently their price. For example, as a result of the division of labor and the use of assembly lines by Henry Ford at his Highland Park Ford Plant in Michigan in 1913, production costs of manufacturing the Model T decreased and productivity increased. The price of the Model T Ford then dropped from $950 in 1908 to $290 in 1924, or the equivalent of 22 months of work to purchase to the equivalent of three months. Mass production that resulted from the Industrial Revolution made contemporary families and children more likely to become consumers rather than producers. Before the Industrial Revolution, especially in colonial America, children produced goods and contributed to household incomes and manufacturing.

Economic activities are categorized into five major categories: primary, secondary, tertiary, quaternary, and quinary. Primary economic activities directly use natural resources by such activities as farming, mining, logging, and so on. Secondary economic activities take the primary goods and change, or manufacture, them in some way. For example, fresh vegetables are canned or put into a frozen dinner. Tertiary activities typically refer to the service industry. To carry the previous examples further, the grocery store where canned and frozen foods are bought is considered part of the tertiary sector. Quaternary activities typically require specialized knowledge or technical skills and refer to the "collection, processing, and manipulation of information and capital (finance, administration, insurance, legal services, computer services, etc.)" (de Blij & Murphy 1999, 320). Finally, the quinary sector "denotes activities that facilitate complex decision making and the advancement of human capacities (scientific research, high-level management, etc.)" required for jobs like "research professors, the heads of corporations, and top government officials" (de Blij & Murphy 1999, 320).

Major Economic Systems

The three main economic systems are: free enterprise (also known as market economy and/or capitalism), communism, and socialism.

Free Enterprise

Free enterprise is an economic and political doctrine of the capitalist system. The concept is based on the premise that the economy can regulate itself in a freely competitive market through supply and demand and with minimum governmental intervention. This economic system allows entrepreneurship, or individually owned and operated businesses. One of the main benefits of free enterprise is the competition among businesses. This results in a greater choice and better prices for consumers as well as in increased specialization and trade. Americans believe strongly in equal opportunities for all. All citizens are to be given an equal chance to succeed. Individual ownership and engagement in the free-market system comes with the responsibility and importance of employing moral and ethical business practices. The federal government is sometimes needed to protect workers, small businesses and the consumer. For example, business cannot discriminate, or treat someone differently, based on such things as skin color, ethnicity, and gender. The United States government is also supposed to safeguard small business by preventing monopolies, which occur when one business controls part of the market. The U.S. government tries to encourage small businesses to flourish. Additionally, regulations are laws that require businesses to use safe practices. For example, in the early 20th century, President Theodore Roosevelt pushed through a meat inspection act to make sure that meat is packaged properly to prevent people from getting sick. The Food and Drug Administration now requires such additional information as the expiration date to inform consumers about a product.

Free enterprise has greatly influenced globalization. *Globalization* can be defined as a continuous increase of cross-border financial, economic, and social activities. It implies some level of economic interdependence among individuals, financial entities, and nations. Because of globalization, trade barriers have been lessened and in some cases eliminated, and tariffs on imported products have been largely discontinued. In a global market, it is difficult to determine the origins of products. For example, Japan-based Toyota Motor and U.S.-based Ford Motor joined forces to build cars using parts and labor from Mexico.

The concept of *economic interdependence* describes a close connection between producers and consumers of goods and services within a nation or across nations. This economic interdependence has guided nations to establish large markets of free trade zones like the European Union (EU) trade agreements and the North American Free Trade Agreement (NAFTA) for Canada, Mexico, and the United States. NAFTA was succeeded by the United States-Mexico-Canada Agreement (USMCA), which took effect on July 1, 2020. The USMCA kept key provisions of NAFTA in place. The European Union went a step further than just a trade pact by adopting a common currency—the euro—in 2002. This alliance has resulted in the euro's ranking as one of the strongest currencies in the world. (Following a 2016 referendum, the United Kingdom withdrew from the EU on Jan. 31, 2020. The move came to be known as "Brexit," a portmanteau of "British exit from the EU." The UK is the only sovereign country to have left the EU.)

Communism

Communism[6] is a system in which the state controls economic activity in the nation. The state rejects free enterprise and capitalism. Private ownership thus is discouraged and often prohibited. Usually the nation is ruled through a one-party system. In theory, communism maintains that the country should not have social classes as a way to avoid the oppressor–oppressed dichotomy. In reality, a small, elite, wealthy class controls the country. Typically, a large gap emerges between the

---

[6] Note: Although Communism is technically an economic term, it may be used to describe both an economic and political system in the context of strong government control, meaning that the government gives little power to the citizens of the country. This can be confusing for students. Be sure to be clear how you phrase your discussion with students.

rich and poor classes in this type of economic system. The middle class in this system is not well defined or large in size. In some cases, it is possible that a middle class may not exist.

Socialism

Socialism is a system of government in which the government to varying degrees owns important elements of the productive capacity of a nation, and to varying degrees, in combination with the private sector, allocates resources in order to encourage the priorities of equality, wealth distribution, social welfare, and other societal objectives rather than prioritizing the rights of individual households or businesses to make these choices and to profit individually. It is thus a form of mixed economy with a degree of private ownership restrained for the public good. The central government controls the production and distribution of goods, services, and labor. Different socialist countries have offered very diverse answers as to how much government intervention is permitted in the economy. Most Western European nations that have espoused socialist principles have been democratic socialist, combining liberal-democratic traditions in governance.

Money and Banking

Under the presidency of Woodrow Wilson, the Federal Reserve System was established in 1913. The main purpose of this institution is to keep the banking industry strong to ensure a supply of currency. The Federal Reserve is run by the Federal Reserve Board of Governors, a seven-member body appointed to a four-year term, with the option of being reappointed to a maximum of 14-year terms. The main function of the Federal Reserve Bank is to promote fiscal stability and economic growth and to regulate inflation and deflation. The Board of Governors controls the flow of money and sets the interest rate that banks use to lend money. The board increases the interest rate to control inflation and lowers the interest rate when business slows. To learn more about the Federal Reserve System go to (*http://www.federalreserve.gov*).

Economic Indicators

The health of an economy is determined by assessing indicators. An indicator is a statistic used to evaluate the strength of an economy to make economic predictions about the country or state. For example, a country's gross national product (GNP) or gross domestic product (GDP) describes the monetary value of its goods and services. Other indicators may include unemployment, number of doctors, life expectancy, number of imports and exports, inflation and deflation.

Inflation and Deflation

Inflation reduces the purchasing power of money, which technically affects the value of the currency. Countries devalue their currency to keep up with inflation. Deflation is the opposite: the purchasing power of money increases, thereby lowering the prices of goods and services. In deflation, consumers benefit, but industry suffers. The Federal Reserve controls the flow of money and keeps a balance between inflation and deflation.

Government Regulations and Taxation

City, state, and national governments regulate businesses to ensure safe, fair, and consistent practices and create a framework for standardizing production of certain products. Taxes support regulations by providing the money to pay people to inspect products and practices as well as to enforce sanctions. Regulations are important to build consumer trust. For example, children's toys are not allowed to use lead-based paint because a child may put a toy in his or her mouth and become sick. Taxes pay for inspectors to monitor toy manufacturers as well as the people who take these cases to court. Buildings are also examined during construction to check that the frame and materials are up to code. When businesses fail to comply with regulations, the owners are fined or in some cases put in jail. However, if the regulations are viewed as burdensome to businesses, it can be said that the regulations will negatively affect business development or be too great of a tax burden for the community. There must be a careful balance between providing a safe, consistent product and being too restrictive and thereby cause a negative impact on businesses.

American Federal Income Tax System

In 1913, the Sixteenth Amendment of the U.S. Constitution allowed the imposition of direct taxation of citizens. This direct taxation is known as the federal income tax.

Interdependence of State, National, and World Economies

The economy of Texas is based primarily on telecommunications, software, financial services, business products and services, semiconductors, biotechnology, and oil and coal. Agriculture and ranching are still viable economic activities, but they no longer carry the economy. A large percentage of these products is exported to Mexico and Canada and other world markets. According to the Texas Economic Update, if Texas were a nation, it would rank as the ninth-largest economy in the world.

The Texas economy relies heavily on exports of goods and services. From 2002 through 2020, Texas was ranked as the No. 1 state in export revenues (TFB, 2020). Without its exports, the Texas economy could not sustain its growth. Because of the interdependence of state and global economies, political turmoil and economic problems in the world affect the Texas economy. For example, because part of Texas's economy is based on petroleum, the OPEC cartel's decisions directly affect the state's economy.

COMPETENCY 005: GOVERNMENT AND CITIZENSHIP

The teacher understands and applies knowledge of concepts of government, democracy, and citizenship, including ways that individuals and groups achieve their goals through political systems.

Forms of Government

The U.S. Department of State identifies 26 forms of governments in the world (CIA, n.d).

Three of the most common forms of government are democracy, monarchy, and totalitarian. A description of these types of government follows:

1. **Democracy** is a form of government in which the majority rules. The governments' power is limited, meaning that a constitution, or agreement with the people, delineates the authority that the government is allowed. Citizens in this government enjoy an abundance of civil liberties. In the United States, these civil liberties are unique because they are called "inalienable rights," meaning that they cannot be ever taken away from the citizens by the government or any other entity. Although rare, pure democracies, a form of government where each individual votes on all decisions, exist in some places. In the United States, pure democracies are still used in some town hall meetings, where people meet to make decisions for their town. In practice, it becomes a representative democracy, in which the people elect candidates to represent them in the government. Democratic governments typically have either free enterprise or socialist economies.

2. **Monarchy** is a system in which a king or queen leads the nation. The monarch gains power by inheriting it from his or her parents. The monarch can have supreme powers and control the entire government, or he or she can have limited or ceremonial powers circumscribed by a parliament or a constitution, which occurs in a constitutional monarchy.

3. **Totalitarian** is a form of government in which one person or a few people have all of the governing power and authority. The central government controls nearly all aspects of its citizens' political, social, cultural, and economic lives, including education, employment, housing, reproduction, and movement. This form of government typically has either a communist or socialist economic system. Additionally, citizens have few individual rights, while the government has unlimited rights. Incidences of human rights violations, or abuses, are typically more frequent under this government.

The three main classifications for these forms of government are based on the number of people in power—government by one person, a group, or by many people:

CHAPTER 5

TExES CORE SUBJECTS EC–6

Rule by One

In this government, one person becomes the supreme leader of the nation.

Some of the terminology and concepts linked to this type of government are:

- **Autocracy:** Ruler has unlimited power and uses it arbitrarily.

- **Monarchy:** A king or queen rules and holds complete control over the subjects. Ruler sometimes claims birth and divine rights. This does not refer to a constitutional monarchy.

- **Dictatorship:** The ruler holds absolute power to make laws and command the army.

Ruled by a Few

In this system, a group of influential people controls the government. Traditionally, they appoint one of their own to function as the supreme leader of the government. Some examples of this government are:

- **Theocracy:** Ruled by a group of religious leaders, such as the Taliban in Afghanistan.

- **Aristocracy:** A group of nobles controls the economy and the government.

- **Oligarchy:** A small group of powerful and wealthy people rule the nation with the support of the military.

- **Military:** A committee of military officers or a *junta* rules.

Rule by Many

In this government, the citizens technically are the government because they make the decisions for the community being governed (e.g., cultural group, town, state, or nation). This is called a democracy. In its purest form, each person participates in voting on each decision made for the community. In practice, the citizens elect members to represent them and elected officials become the government. This is called a representative democracy. Today, most democracies are also a constitutional democracy, meaning that they are regulated by a constitution. Examples of representative governments include constitutional democracy and parliamentarian (or constitutional) monarchy.

The historical origins of democratic governance can be found in Ancient Greece where the cultures participated in pure and representational democracy and developed a court system with a jury. More information about Ancient Greece and the roots of democracy can be found online at *http://www.history.com/topics/ancient-history/ancient-greece-democracy*.

Some examples of this government are:

- **Democracy:** The citizens of the nation directly or through elected members make important decisions and become part of the government.

- **Republic:** A representative democracy is led by someone who is not a monarch, such as a president. Example: the United States of America.

- **Constitutional Democracy:** It is a democratic government regulated by a constitution. This form of government can be led by either a president or prime minister and is also referred to as a "constitutional republic."

- **Parliamentarian Monarchy:** The monarch shares the power with the parliament. Often, the powers of the monarch are ceremonial in nature, as they are in Great Britain. This government is also referred to as a "constitutional monarchy."

Government Power Structure

The structure of the governmental power can be designed so that either almost all of the decision-making capabilities are held within the centralized government (unitary government) or the power is shared between the central and local governing bodies (federal government).

- **Federal Republic:** A constitutional government in which the powers of the central government are restricted to create semi-autonomous bodies (states or provinces) with certain degrees of self-governing powers, as in the United States.

The American Government

The U.S. governmental system has been identified as a federal republic, constitutional republic, and constitutional democracy. These terms describe types of representative governments. The terms "constitutional republic" and "constitutional democracy" can be used interchangeably. The term "constitutional" implies that it is governed by a constitution that delineates the power of the government and its people. It is a federal republic because the U.S. government is a representative democracy that shares between a central, or national, government, and smaller units of power, such as that of the states. The U.S. is a representative democracy because the citizens elect senators and representatives to Congress.

In the U.S. the national government makes decisions for the benefit of the country as a whole (e.g., laws, coin money, regulate trade and commerce, protection of rights, foreign affairs, declaration of war, banking regulations, education, taxation, postal services, etc.). The state government makes decisions pertaining to the people and businesses within its borders. These include elections, business regulations, education, taxation, transportation and communication, and so on. The national, or federal, government's powers are delineated in the U.S. Constitution. All powers not mentioned belong to the states. Local governments provide direct governance of the people in an immediate area. Many local government duties mirror those of the state (taxation, communication & transportation, education, business regulation, etc.) on a smaller scale. State legislatures determine local governments' power. The official White House website (*http://www.whitehouse.gov/ our-government/executive-branch*) provides more details about the federal government. Government responsibilities and programs are largely funded by taxes. Most Americans contribute a portion of their paycheck to the federal income tax. They also contribute to a variety of social insurance programs, like Social Security, Medicare, Medicaid, and unemployment insurance, through their paycheck. Each state decides how to distribute the state and local tax burden, dividing the burden between income taxes, both corporate and individual, sales and excise taxes, property taxes, and other fees. Texas has no state and local income tax and relies heavily on sales and property taxes. Local government in Texas is funded largely by sales taxes, property taxes, and fees. Governments can also issue bonds, which are a mechanism to allow the government to borrow money from its citizens or from other countries.

The Constitution is the supreme law of the nation. It contains a description of the government and the rights and responsibilities of its citizens. The document can be amended with the approval of two-thirds of the House and the Senate and the ratification of individual state legislatures. The amendment process is deliberately difficult to ensure that a wide consensus exists before significant changes to the Constitution are introduced. Amendments to the U.S. Constitution have made it more democratic than the original document.

Effective leadership in a constitutional republic is critical for the success of the country. The leader must collaborate with opposing parties to make the best possible decisions for the nation. The following links list U.S. presidents and Texas governors and describes their term in office *http://www.whitehouse.gov/about/presidents* and *https://www.tsl.texas.gov/ref/abouttx/governors. html.* To develop a better understanding of effective leadership, teachers can ask students to compare and contrast leaders, the decisions they made, and the long-term impact of those decisions.

Executive Branch

The executive branch of the U.S. government is composed of a president and a vice president elected every four years by electoral votes based on each state's popular vote. The president is the commander-in-chief of the armed forces. He or she appoints cabinet members, nominates judges to the federal court system, grants pardons, recommends legislation, and has the power to veto legislation.

Judicial Branch

The judicial branch is composed of a federal court system that includes the Supreme Court and a system of lower courts—district courts, appeals courts, bankruptcy courts, and special federal courts. Federal judges are nominated by the president of the United States and confirmed by the Senate. All federal judges are appointed for life. The Supreme Court is composed of nine judges, and their ruling is considered final. Some of the major responsibilities of this body are to interpret the Constitution, resolve conflicts among states, and interpret laws and treaties.

Legislative Branch

The legislative branch is composed of Congress, which is divided in two parts—the Senate and the House of Representatives. The Senate comprises two senators from each state, while the composition of the House is based on the population of each state. Congress makes the laws of the nation, collects taxes, coins money and regulates its value, controls appropriations, and regulates the jurisdictions of federal courts. Congress can also declare war, impeach public officials, and override presidential vetoes.

System of Checks and Balances

The U.S. Constitution provides for a system of checks and balances among the three branches of the government. In this system, individual branches check the others to be sure that no one assumes full control of the central government. The legislative branch can check the executive branch by passing laws over presidential veto by a two-thirds majority in both houses. This branch exerts control over the judicial branch by refusing to confirm the president's judges. The executive can check the legislative branch by the use of the veto and the judicial branch by appointing federal judges. The judicial branch can check the other two branches through the process of judicial review, which can declare legislation unconstitutional or illegal. For example, on June 26, 2015, the U.S. Supreme Court ruled that states cannot ban same-sex marriage. With this ruling the U.S. became the 21st country to legalize gay marriage.

Judicial Review Process—*Marbury v. Madison*

A dispute that occurred as the Thomas Jefferson administration came into power fundamentally altered the system of checks and balances of the American government. In this case, the judicial branch confirmed its power to review and assess the constitutionality of the legislation passed by Congress and signed by the president. This process is now called the *judicial review.*

Bill of Rights

After the U.S. Constitution was enacted in 1783, the founders believed that additional measures were necessary to preserve basic human rights. The first 10 amendments to the U.S. Constitution came to be called the Bill of Rights. A summary of those amendments follows:

First Amendment—separation of church and state; freedom of religion, speech and press; and the right to peaceful assembly

Second Amendment—rights to keep and bear arms

Third Amendment—made it illegal to force people to offer quarters to soldiers in time of peace

Fourth Amendment—rights to privacy and unreasonable searches or seizures

Fifth Amendment—rights of due process, protection against self-incrimination, and protection from being indicted for the same crime twice (double jeopardy)

Sixth Amendment—rights to speedy public trial by an impartial jury and to counsel for one's defense

Seventh Amendment—guarantees right to jury trial in most civil court cases

Eighth Amendment—protection against cruel and unusual punishment

Ninth Amendment—enumeration of specific rights in the Constitution cannot be taken as a way to deny other rights retained by the people

Tenth Amendment—rights not delegated to the federal government by the Constitution are reserved to the states or to the people

Additional Key Amendments to the U.S. Constitution

Thirteenth Amendment—Slavery abolished

Fourteenth Amendment—Citizenship and rights—Citizenship bestowed upon African Americans including former slaves; Reaffirmed privileges and rights for all citizens

Fifteenth Amendment—Race is no bar to voting rights—Right to vote for African-American males

Sixteenth Amendment—Ratified in 1913, it gives the federal government the power to levy taxes

Nineteenth Amendment—Women's suffrage

Twenty-fifth Amendment—Presidential disability and succession

Twenty-sixth Amendment—Right to vote granted to American citizens aged 18 or older

For a detailed analysis of the U.S. Constitution and the 27 amendments, see the U.S. Constitution online at *http://www.usconstitution.net/const.html*.

Power Sharing Between State and Federal Governments

One of the most significant principles of the U.S. Constitution is the concept of power shared between the federal and state governments. Some of the powers reserved to the federal and state governments follow.

Powers Reserved for the Federal Government

- Regulate interstate and foreign commerce

- Print money and regulate its value

- Establish the laws for regulation of immigration and naturalization

- Regulate admission of new states

- Declare war and ratify peace treaties

- Establish a system of weights and measures

- Raise and maintain armed forces

- Conduct relations with foreign nations

Powers Reserved for State Governments

- Conduct and monitor local, state, and federal elections

- Provide for local government

- Ratify proposed amendments to the Constitution

- Regulate intrastate commerce

- Provide education for its citizens

- Establish direct taxes like sales and state taxes

- Regulate and maintain police power over public health and safety

- Maintain control of state borders

In addition to the powers reserved to the states, the Tenth Amendment of the U.S. Constitution provides additional powers to the state. In this amendment, the powers not specifically delegated to the federal government are reserved for the states.

Local and State Governments

Most states follow the type of government established in the U.S. Constitution. State governments have three branches—executive, legislative, and judicial. The main difference is that the executive branch is led by a governor and the judicial branch is composed of a state court system subordinate to the federal court system. The city government is typically headed by a mayor or city manager with the support of a city council.

Citizenship

The development of civic ideas and practices is a lifelong process that begins in school by observing national holidays, learning about the contribution of historical figures, and pledging allegiance to the American and Texas flags each day. Students should develop foundational knowledge about what each pledge means as well as the history of their development and why the pledges are important to American citizens. In this way, saying the pledge will be meaningful rather than rote memorization and recitation of words that students do not understand. In first grade, encouraging good citizenship continues with the introduction of the American anthem and the mottoes of Texas and the United States. Civic education and the principles of democracy are infused through active participation in community activities. To promote civic responsibility, students can get involved in discussions about issues that affect the community. Teachers should guide students to suggest possible solutions to community problems and then to listen and analyze contribution from other students. Through this exchange, students are guided to practice principles of democracy and to value individual contributions to solve community problems.

Additionally, students should define what is a "good citizen" and to connect their definition with historical and contemporary examples from the community, state, and nation. Americans value such things as recognizing social responsibilities, helping each other, making sure everyone has food, shelter, and clothing, caring for the elderly, keeping the land clean, using things wisely, caring for others, being patriotic, respecting our men and women in uniform (e.g., military, police, firefighters), respecting our state and country flags and what they symbolize, and so on. Teachers can invite speakers from such organizations as food pantries, the Red Cross, Boy Scouts, Girl Scouts, the League of Women Voters, and Meals on Wheels to show examples of good citizenship. Interdisciplinary service learning can be developed to help students explore this topic in-depth. Students can investigate ways that good citizens keep the land clean via recycling as well as with larger projects. For example, Chad Pregracke was concerned about the trash in the Mississippi River as a teenager. Realizing no one else was going to clean up the river, he began to fill his little boat with trash and haul it away. He developed an organization that now has over 70,000 volunteers who work to clean the rivers (see *http://livinglandsandwaters.org/* for more information). Inspiring stories help students realize they can be good citizens as well. Clara Harlowe Barton was a teacher who risked her life to help soldiers during the Civil War. She later founded the American Red Cross. Teachers should help students recognize the values that made these people good citizens and show students how they can also be good citizens (For more information go to *https://www. redcross.org/about-us/who-we-are/history.html.*).

In Grades K–6 students should learn the meaning and importance of national holidays. Holidays with historic significance include Memorial Day, Labor Day, Columbus Day, Independence Day, Constitution Day, Thanksgiving Day, Veterans Day, and Martin Luther King Jr. Day. Other days of commemoration include Indigenous Peoples' Day and Cinco de Mayo. Memorial Day honors members of the military who died in war. Labor Day recognizes the importance of workers and labor unions. Columbus Day commemorates the arrival of Christopher Columbus to the Americas. Independence Day commemorates the adoption of the Declaration of Independence. Constitution Day celebrates the signing of the United States Constitution. Veterans Day celebrates those who have served in the country's armed forces. Thanksgiving Day is celebrated across the United States, in part in remembrance of the day of thanksgiving observed by the Pilgrims in thanks for having survived their harsh first winter in New England. Martin Luther King Jr. Day honors the leader of the civil rights movement. Indigenous Peoples' Day, begun as a counter-celebration to Columbus Day stemming from the impact of European colonists on Native Americans, was formally recognized by presidential proclamation in 2021, celebrates and honors Native American peoples. Cinco de Mayo commemorates Mexico's unexpected victory over France in the Battle of Puebla on May 5, 1862; it traditionally provides an opportunity to celebrate Mexican-American culture.

Children as early as prekindergarten can be guided to develop civic responsibility. Teachers can promote this responsibility by involving students in situations in which they practice civic responsibility. For example, teachers can make children aware of how producing trash can affect the environment. Students can be guided to examine the amount of trash they produce daily and explore ways to reduce it. Promoting a sense of responsibility to the common good constitutes the main principle in developing responsible citizenship.

American Symbols

American Patriotic Symbols

In Grades EC–6, children learn what Americans value as a nation and expect from the citizenry. Patriotic symbols are visible signs of national pride. The U.S. National Flag, the Pledge of Allegiance, the Statue of Liberty, the Liberty Bell, and the White House are important examples of patriotic symbols.

- The United States of America National Flag has 50 stars representing the 50 states of the Union. The color red represents hardiness and valor, the white symbolizes purity and innocence, and the blue symbolizes vigilance, perseverance, and justice. Congress approved a new flag with 13 red and white alternating horizontal stripes and 13 stars representing the original colonies in 1777. A star was added to the flag each time a state entered the union. The Flag Act of 1818 set the number of stripes at thirteen and provided that a star be added for each new state admitted into the Union.

- The Pledge of Allegiance is a declaration of patriotism. It was first published in 1892 in *The Youth's Companion* and is believed to have been written by the magazine's editor, Francis Bellamy. The original purpose was that the pledge was to be used by schoolchildren in activities to celebrate the 400th anniversary of the discovery of America. The pledge was widely used in morning school routines for many years and received official recognition by Congress in 1942. The phrase "under God" was added in 1954, and a law indicating the proper behavior to adopt when reciting the pledge, which includes standing straight, removing hats or any other headgear, and placing the right hand over the heart.

- The "Star-Spangled Banner" is the national anthem of the United States. It was originally a poem written by Francis Scott Key during the Battle of Baltimore in the War of 1812 against the British. In 1931, it was made the official national anthem of the United States.

- The Statue of Liberty was a gift of friendship from the people of France to the people of the United States commemorating the United States' 100th anniversary. It is a universal symbol of freedom, democracy, and international friendship.

- The Liberty Bell is a symbol of freedom and liberty. The Pennsylvania Assembly ordered the Liberty Bell to commemorate the 50th anniversary of Pennsylvania's original constitution,

William Penn's Charter of Privileges. It is traditionally believed that it was rung to summon the people of Philadelphia to hear the Declaration of Independence. It became an icon when the abolitionists adopted it as a symbol of freedom. The abolitionists changed its name from the State House Bell to the Liberty Bell.

- The White House was originally planned by President George Washington in 1791 and was completed in 1800 when its first resident, President John Adams, moved in with his wife, Abigail. It was originally called the President's House. President Theodore Roosevelt christened it with the name the White House in 1901, and for over 200 years it has been the home of the U.S. presidents and their families. It is recognized as a symbol of the U.S. presidency throughout the world.

- The Great Seal of the United States consists of a bald eagle holding an olive branch and a bundle of arrows. The olive branch represents peace and the arrows represent military strength. The eagle holds a scroll in its beak with the nation's motto: "*E Pluribus Unum*" which means "Out of many, one."

For additional information about symbols of the United States, go to *www.statesymbolsusa.org*.

Texan Symbols

Texas Patriotic Symbols

Patriotic symbols are also signs of state pride. The Texas Flag, the Texas Pledge of Allegiance, bluebonnets, longhorns, oil rigs, and the state capitol are important symbols of Texas state pride. Such places such as King's Ranch, the Alamo, cattle trails, the Capitol, Gruene Hall, and the San Jacinto battlegrounds are examples of landmarks that are meaningful symbols. For additional information about symbols of Texas, go to *http://www.statesymbolsusa.org/Texas/state_symbols. html*. For additional information about national monuments and landmarks in Texas, go to *http:// texastimetravel.com/node/28774*.

Sources

Acosta, T.P. (2009). Raza Unida Party. *The Handbook of Texas Online. Texas State Historical* Retrieved from *Association.* Retrieved from *http://www.tshaonline.org/handbook/online/ articles/RR/war1.html*

Arends, R. (1998). *Learning to Teach.* (4th ed.) Boston: McGraw-Hill.

Barker, E.C. & J.W. Pohl. (2009). Texas Revolution. *The Handbook of Texas Online. Texas State Historical Association. https://www.tshaonline.org/about*

BIDC—Business and Industry Data Center. 2006. Overview of the Texas Economy. *Office of the Governor, Economic Development and Tourism.* Retrieved from *http://governor.state.tx.us/ ecodev/business_research/texas_economy*

CIA World Fact Book. Central Asia: Russia. Retrieved from *https://www.cia.gov/resources*

CIA World Fact Book. Nations: Forms of Government. Retrieved from *http://www.historyguy.com/nations/government_types.html*

De Blij, Harm J. & Murphy, A.B. 1999. *Human Geography: Culture, Society, and Space.* (7th Ed.) Wiley: New York.

Echevarria, J., M. Vogt, and D. Short. 2000. *Making content comprehensible for English language learners: The SIOP model* (4th ed.). Needham Heights, MA: Allyn and Bacon.

Fry, P.L. "Origin of Name." *The Handbook of Texas Online. Texas State Historical Association.* Retrieved from *https://www.tshaonline.org*

Ganeri, A., H.M. Martell, and B. Williams. 1999. *The World History Encyclopedia.* Bath, UK: Parragon.

Kagan, S. 1985. *Cooperative learning resources for teachers.* Riverside, CA: Spencer Kagan.

Kerr, A. 2006. Temperance and prohibition. History Department, Ohio State University. Retrieved from *http://prohibition.osu.edu*

Lyman, F.T. (1981). The responsive classroom discussion: The inclusion of all students. In *Mainstreaming Digest,* ed. A.S. Anderson, 109–113. College Park: University of Maryland Press.

Marzano, R., and D. Pickering. (2005). *Building academic vocabulary: Teacher's manual.* Alexandria, VA: ASCD.

Mayell, H. (2004). Three high-altitude peoples, three adaptations to thin air. *National Geographic.* Retrieved from *https://www.nationalgeographic.org/society*

Mendoza, V. (2001). Video review of *Chicano! History of the Mexican American Civil Rights Movement. The Journal for MultiMedia History,* Volume 3. Retrieved from *www.albany.edu/jmmh/vol3/chicano/chicano.html*

National Council for the Teaching of Social Studies (NCTSS) (2006). Expectations of Excellence: Curriculum Standards for Social Studies—Executive Summary. Retrieved from *www. socialstudies.org*

Parker, W.C. (2001). *Social Studies in Elementary Education.* 11th ed. Columbus, OH: Merrill Prentice-Hall.

Potts, J. (1994). *Adventure Tales of America.* Dallas, TX: Signal Media.

Rosado, L., and D. Salazar. 2002–2003. La Conexión: The English/Spanish connection. *National Forum of Applied Educational Research Journal* 15(4): 51–66.

Rosado, L., Hellawell, M. & Zamora, B.E. (6/16/2011). An Analysis of the Education Systems in Mexico and the United States from Pre-Kinder to 12 Grade. Educational Resources Information Center (ERIC #ED520900).

Rosales Castañeda, O. (2006). *The Chicano Movement in Washington State* Retrieved from http://depts.washington.edu/civilr/mecha_intro.htm

Rowe, M.B. 1986. *Wait Times: Slowing Down May Be a Way of Speeding Up. Journal of Teacher Education,* 37, 43–50.

Schifini, A. (1985). *Sheltered English: Content area instruction for limited English proficiency students.* Los Angeles County Office of Education.

Seattle Civil Rights and Labor History Project. (2006). Retrieved from *http://depts.washington. edu/civilr/index.htm*

Sheppard, D.E. (n.d.) *Cabeza de Vaca in North America.* Retrieved from *http://www.floridahistory. org*

Slavin, R. (1986). *Student Learning: An Overview and Practical Guide.* Washington, DC: Professional Library National Education Association.

Subject Test IV: Science (904)

The National Science Teachers Association (NSTA) supports the idea that scientific inquiry should be a basic component of the curriculum in every grade in American schools (NSTA, 2002). A position paper of the organization published in 2002 emphasizes the importance of offering students early experience in problem solving and scientific thinking. The report suggests that children learn science best under the following conditions:

- Students are actively involved in firsthand exploration of scientific concepts.

- Instruction is related and built on the abilities and experiences of the learners.

- Instruction is organized thematically.

- Mathematics and communication skills are integrated.

The report also indicates that the curriculum should emphasize the contributions of people from a variety of cultures. Finally, the NSTA (2002) states that science education can be successful if teachers receive adequate professional development and school administrators show a genuine interest in science education.

☞ To focus your study, go online to take the diagnostic test for this subject at *www.rea.com/studycenter*.

COMPETENCY 001: LABORATORY PROCESSES, EQUIPMENT, AND SAFETY

The teacher understands how to manage learning activities, tools, materials, equipment and technologies to ensure the safety of all students.

Classroom and Laboratory Health and Safety

Teachers must create a safe environment for children involved in scientific inquiry. Here are some of the principles and practices that teachers can follow to reduce risks and protect children:

- Require students to use appropriate personal protective gear such as goggles, laboratory coats, and gloves.

- Use appropriate procedures for cleaning and disposing of materials.

- Adhere to appropriate disciplinary procedures to avoid accidents. For example, do not allow children to play with water or other lab materials.

- Substitute less hazardous equivalent materials when possible. For example, use cleaning products instead of chemicals in their pure form.

- Use polyethylene or metal containers in place of glass.

- Advise children to avoid tasting or ingesting substances or materials.

- Label containers appropriately to avoid confusion.

- Control the use of sharp objects that can puncture the skin.

- Supervise the use of living organisms and the cleaning of instruments.

- Avoid experimenting with human cells and bodily fluids.

- Share the responsibility for the safety of the students with the whole group; in a well-managed science lab, students should motivate each other to follow safety procedures.

- Make provisions for the movement and handling of equipment and materials for students with special needs.

- Prepare, review, and send home an age-appropriate safety contract requiring parent/guardian signature.

- Organize all materials to be used in class by placing them in separate bins for a member of each student group to pick up for use for the lab activity and for returning materials after the lab activity.

- Prepare and practice an emergency plan with students should an accident occur.

- Clearly label and demonstrate the use of safety equipment with students, such as the eyewash station and fire blanket.

- Document all accidents, regardless of how minor, and have another teacher sign as witness if possible.

- Clearly write and read to students the safety precautions for the laboratory before beginning the activity.

- Place posters around the room emphasizing the safety rules of the classroom and laboratory.

- Keep all chemicals and glassware in locked cabinets.

- Maintain regular inventory of all laboratory materials and chemicals.

- Store acids and other caustic chemicals in cabinets close to the floor in case they fall when retrieved for use.

- When using an open flame, such as lit candles, students must tie long hair back and tape or roll up loose sleeves to avoid contact with the fire.

The use of dangerous chemical substances in the elementary classroom is limited in scope. Many laboratory chemicals can be substituted with household products. However, care needs to be taken even when handling household chemicals. It is important to demonstrate safe laboratory procedures for the classroom because household products are still chemicals and pose some level of risk to students. Safety management of chemicals in the classroom requires teachers to have knowledge of those chemicals and their properties. For example, teachers need to be aware that a simple tool such as a mercury thermometer can break and pose a danger to children. In general, maintaining safety requires teachers to take the following steps:

- Assess the relative danger of each chemical used in the classroom.

- Label and store chemicals appropriately.

- Implement safety procedures for the use and handling of materials and equipment.

- Follow appropriate procedures for cleaning containers and disposing of chemicals.

Animal and animal specimens must be treated with care and respect. In keeping live animals, it is imperative that the feeding and handling of the animal is clearly understood. Students must learn to handle the animals in a caring and humane manner. Animals found in nature should not be kept in the classroom as they pose a risk of disease and possibly a greater risk of attack such as biting, compared to those used to human interaction. Humane treatment is expected of all creatures, from mealworms to butterflies, and to rabbits and hamsters. A plan to care for the animals must be made in advance of school holidays and vacations. If hatching eggs in the classroom, be sure a farm agrees to take the chicks once hatched. Specimens of once living organisms also must be handled with care and respect. Do not allow students to take dissected organs or tissues out of the classroom or laboratory. Wash and disinfect hands and laboratory surfaces after handling live animals and/or specimens of once living organisms. Teaching the students responsibility in caring for living things is an excellent learning experience for them, and thus important for teachers to serve as models for expected behaviors.

CHAPTER 6

TExES CORE SUBJECTS EC–6

Scientific Tools and Equipment for Gathering and Storing Data

Various tools or instruments are used in scientific experimentation in Kindergarten through Grade 6. The classroom can be equipped with measuring devices like graduated cylinders, beakers, scales, dishes, thermometers, meter sticks, and micrometers. They might also have anatomical models showing the body systems. Teachers need to learn to use these tools and equipment properly in order to help their students know how to use them and to collect accurate data in their inquiry investigations.

The TEKS requires students to gather information using specific equipment and tools. Examples of the tools required in K–6 are presented in Table 6-1 (TEA 2019 mod.).

Table 6-1. Tools and Equipment Required in the TEKS, by Grade

Tools and Equipment	K	1st Grade	2nd Grade	3rd Grade	4th Grade	5th Grade	6th Grade
Nonstandard measurements	✓	✓	✓				
Hand lenses	✓	✓	✓	✓	✓	✓	✓
Computers	✓	✓	✓	✓	✓	✓	✓
Balances	✓	✓	✓	✓	✓	✓	✓
Cups and bowls	✓	✓	✓	✓	✓	✓	✓
Thermometers		✓	✓	✓	✓	✓	✓
Clocks			✓	✓	✓	✓	✓
Meter sticks			✓	✓	✓	✓	✓
Microscopes				✓	✓	✓	✓
Safety goggles				✓	✓	✓	✓
Magnets				✓	✓	✓	✓
Compasses				✓	✓	✓	✓
Timing devices					✓	✓	✓
Calculators					✓	✓	✓
Sound recorders					✓	✓	✓
Hot plates						✓	✓
Burners						✓	✓
Beakers						✓	✓
Graduated cylinders						✓	✓
Flasks (Erlenmeyer and Florence)						✓	✓
Test tubes and holders						✓	✓

Proper Laboratory Procedures and Precision

Scientific experimentation cannot rely solely on our senses to record information. People need to extend what can be observed with their senses by using scientific instruments such as balances, microscopes, beakers, and graduated cylinders to make precise observations and measurements. Science requires the use of standard measuring devices to be sure that the information is clear, accurate, and able to be replicated in experimental settings. The metric system of measurement used by most scientists is the International System of Units, also known as Standard Units, or SI Units because it is used in most countries to maintain consistency in measurements. These SI units are based on the metric system, such as meters and kilometers to measure length, grams and kilograms to measure mass, and milliliters or liters to measure liquid volume and cubic centimeters to measure solid volume. The United States uses a combination of what is known as a non-standard unit system of measurement, or non-SI Units, along with the SI unit metric system. In fact, the United States is the only technologically developed country in the world that uses non-standard units for business transactions and for day-to-day activities. However, for international business, engineering, and natural sciences, all countries use a more standardized, precise system of weights and measurement, the SI unit metric system. The English or non-SI system uses units such as inches, feet and yards to measure length, ounces and pounds to measure mass, and fluid ounces, quarts and gallons to measure liquid amount or volume, with inches and meters used for solid amounts or volume. The SI units are a system of fractions and multiples of units related to each other by powers of 10, allowing conversion and comparison of measures simply by shifting a decimal point, and avoiding the lengthy arithmetical operations required by the non-SI English system. The TEKS requires the teaching of both the SI metric and the non-SI English systems; however, all scientific data are to be reported using the metric system.

COMPETENCY 002: HISTORY AND NATURE OF SCIENCE

The teacher understands the history and nature of science, the process and role of scientific inquiry and the role of inquiry in science instruction.

History and Nature of Science; Diversity and Equity in Science

The history and nature of science provides an important framework for student learning. By learning the history of science, students will come to understand that science is changing and dynamic rather than fixed and tentative. Furthermore, they will discern that their own conceptions and understandings of science can change in light of new experimental observations and evidence. Therefore, it is important to use the history and nature of science as a tool to promote students' learning. For example, the students can learn about the Earth-centered model of the solar system that prevailed for hundreds of years before Copernicus and then Galileo supported a new model, which is now the accepted view of a Sun-centered (heliocentric) model of the solar system. With better tools developed through time and the extension of findings through observations and experiments, our scientific knowledge constantly shifts and changes.

It is important for students to understand the struggle of scientists in the past in conducting experiments and arriving at meaningful conclusions. These struggles are similar to those that students themselves may experience in arriving at sound conclusions, including errors in measurement, misunderstandings of information, and difficulties with interpretation. In addition, teachers must know and highlight for students contributions from both males and females as well as people of varied cultural and ethnic backgrounds who have contributed to scientific progress and discovery throughout history. Teaching the history of science helps students better understand how to use what has been learned to build new conclusions and make new discoveries today, and help them realize that they are the scientists of the present and future.

Important history-of-science topics for teachers to understand and to incorporate into their teaching are shown in Table 6-2.

Table 6-2. History of Important Science Concepts to Use in Classroom Teaching

Concept	Description	Who	Timeframe	Resource
Cell theory	All living things are made up of cells and all cells have arisen from other existing cells.	Robert Hooke Henri Dutrochet	1635–1703 1776–1847	*http://www.biologyreference.com/Gr-Hi/History-of-Biology-Cell-Theory-and-Cell-Structure.html*
Plate Tectonics	Continents on Earth today were long ago formed together in a single landmass.	Alfred Wegener	1880–1930	*http://www.scec.org/education/k12/learn/plate2.htm*
Laws of Motion	1. An object at rest will remain at rest unless acted on by an unbalanced force. An object in motion continues in motion with the same speed and in the same direction unless acted upon by an unbalanced force. This is known as the law of inertia. 2. Acceleration is produced when a force acts on a mass. The greater the mass, the greater the amount of force needed (to accelerate the object). 3. For every action there is an equal and opposite reaction.	Sir Isaac Newton	1643–1727	*http://teachertech.rice.edu/Participants/louviere/Newton/index.html*

(continued)

Concept	Description	Who	Timeframe	Resource
Universal Gravity	Every object in the universe attracts every other object with a force directed along the line of centers for the two objects that is proportional to the product of their masses and inversely proportional to the square of the separation between the two objects.	Sir Isaac Newton	1643–1727	*http://csep10.phys. utk.edu/astr161/ lect/history/ newtongrav.html*
Technology	The invention and development of systematic techniques and/or tools for making and doing things.	Various Scientists and Inventors	2.5 Million Years Ago to the Present	*http://www. historyworld. net/wrldhis/ PlainTextHistories. asp?historyid=ab11*

Planning and Implementing Scientific Inquiry

Scientific inquiry is promoted through students engaging in hands-on activities and experimentation. From their experiences conducting scientific experiments, students acquire information firsthand and develop problem-solving skills. Children in Grades EC–6 are inquisitive and want to understand the environment around them. Teachers can use this interest to provide students with opportunities to use electronic and printed sources to find answers to their questions and to expand their knowledge about the topic. It is important for children to develop inquiry skills. This can only be accomplished by allowing them to experience science for themselves in hands-on investigations. By doing so, children develop important science inquiry and thinking skills (Table 6-3).

Table 6-3. Science Thinking Skills (FOSS, 2000)

- **Observing:** Using the senses to obtain information from the environment
- **Communicating:** Talking, drawing, electronic information sharing (e.g., email, texts, blogs) and acting
- **Comparing:** Pairing, judging similarities and differences, and seeking one-to-one correspondence
- **Organizing:** Grouping, seriating, and sequencing
- **Relating:** Determining cause-and-effect, connecting concepts, and grouping information
- **Inferring:** Using super-ordinate/subordinate classification, using data to make assumptions, employing if/then reasoning, and developing scientific laws
- **Applying:** Using knowledge to develop strategic plans, invent new concepts and processes

The model of inquiry that best supports science learning is a model known as the **learning cycle**, consisting of three phases: **exploration**, **concept invention**, and **application** (Lawson, Abraham, & Renner, 1989; Marek & Cavallo, 1997). Over time the learning cycle was extended with the addition of two new phases becoming what is known as the 5-E model (Bybee, 1989). What follows is some history on the development of inquiry-based teaching via the learning cycle and 5-E model.

The original three-phase learning cycle model developed by Robert Karplus in the early 1960s was based upon the following theoretical foundation:

1. Science must be taught in a way that is *consistent with the nature of science*. Science is discovery and investigation, and that means science must be taught as an active process—as something we *do*. The children need to have the opportunity to experience the true nature of science by doing science exploration for themselves through direct experiences and hands-on investigations.

2. Science teaching must be focused on promoting the main purpose of education, namely, to promote the development in our students the *ability to think*—to be critical and independent thinkers. Science must be taught in a way that promotes the students use of independent, critical, and higher-level thinking abilities (e.g., logic). Promoting this purpose of education is best accomplished by *not* giving or telling students the "answers" or information (e.g., as in giving a lecture). Instead students should be afforded hands-on, direct experiences in which they use logic and reasoning to find "answers" or explanations for themselves; further discussion and teacher guidance can follow the students' direct experiences.

3. Science must be taught in a way that *matches how students learn,* which has been described as the **mental functioning** model by Piaget (1964). How individuals learn is through mentally experiencing the following three-phase mental process: (1) **Assimilation (with disequilibrium)**, (2) **Accommodation**, and (3) **Organization**. According to the model, in learning, individuals first *assimilate* or "take in" information with our senses from our environment and from what we are experiencing in our environment. During assimilation, we may have a sense of "disequilibrium," which is confusion or "cognitive conflict," as we try to make sense of our experiences. When in disequilibrium, we need to go back and *assimilate* more information—make more observations and gather more data. When we have assimilated enough information and made sense of the information we have gathered, our minds experience *accommodation*. That is the "aha!" moment, the point when we ultimately feel "cognitive relief" — we figured it out, or what we have observed/experienced now makes sense! Third, our minds take that newly accommodated information and we *organize* it into our mental structures. That is, we connect the new idea or what we have just figured out/made sense of to what we already know, what we experience in everyday life, and/or to new and related concepts.

The three phases of learning described by Piaget, assimilation-accommodation-organization, match the original learning cycle's three phases: Exploration-Concept Invention-Application. The logic in developing the learning cycle in these three phases was that, given what educators know about how children (people) learn, teachers should be teaching in a sequence or way that matches this learning pattern. To do so, teachers should first provide students with an **Exploration** phase in which students can assimilate information using their senses. The students may or may not experience disequilibrium, but, as teachers, we should guide them (not tell them!) through the sense-making process. Teachers should then carry out a discussion in the **Concept Invention** phase in which students share their observations and findings. With careful questioning, teachers guide students to review their data/observations toward helping them reach the "aha!" moment or accommodation. In this second phase, students write a summarizing *statement of the concept* and post it on the board, and/or read their concept statement aloud to others. In writing and stating the concept in this second phase students accommodate or gain understanding of the concept. In the final phase of the learning cycle, the teacher then helps students organize the new concept by providing experiences where they apply the concept in new contexts. In this phase, known as the **Application phase** students connect the concept with what they observe in everyday life, or what they already know.

Furthermore, by teaching via the learning cycle, teachers are teaching in a way that is consistent with the nature of science—as an active, hands-on process characterized by investigation and discovery—and teachers are teaching in a way that supports the purpose of education; that is, teachers are promoting children's development of higher-level thinking abilities. The learning cycle and its origins and theory base is more fully described in a book by Marek and Cavallo (1997) titled *The Learning Cycle: Elementary School Science and Beyond.*

Over time, science educators added some additional phases to the learning cycle, namely, the **Engage** phase, with the idea that teachers need to do something that will gain the students' attention before beginning the exploration phase. Engage can be a demonstration (without explanation) or simply posing a question, challenge, or problem. So the original learning cycle model's first phase, **Exploration**, became two phases, **Engage** and **Explore**. Though identical, the **Concept Invention** phase's name was changed to **Explain** and **Application** phase had the name changed to **Elaborate**, to sustain the alliteration. Assessment or the measurement of learning in the original three-phase model was to take place throughout the learning cycle. However, science educators at the time preferred to have assessment articulated as an additional phase labelled **Evaluate**, which was so named to keep the "E" pattern in each phase of the model. So the three-phase **learning cycle** model was expanded into a **5-E Model**: *Engage, Explore, Explain, Elaborate, Evaluate.*

The two models are basically the same and grew out of the same underlying philosophy and theoretical foundation. However, the three phases more closely follow the model of learning—assimilation, accommodation and organization—as first described by Piaget, whereas the 5-E incorporates two additional essentials of classroom teaching, namely gaining students focus and attention, and measuring student learning.

Most importantly, in both models, the learning cycle and 5-E, students are *not told* the science concept or information before beginning the inquiry, but must discover the concept themselves through hands-on investigation, observation, and collection of data. In using the *Engage* phase (from 5-E) the students' learning experience begins with the teacher posing one or more questions, giving an interesting demonstration, or providing a laboratory guide; but in all of these, this phase captures their curiosity and motivates them to learn. Whether or not an *Engage* phase is used, students next (or first) experience an *Exploration* phase—and it must be a student-centered hands-on activity, investigation, or experiment. In the *Exploration* phase, students make observations and gather data on a science idea or topic area. In this phase, students can determine the experimental design or it can be pre-determined by the teacher. The main aspect, however, is that students are doing the lab activity themselves, and have not been told the expected outcome beforehand. For example, students may grow plants in the light and in the dark, and make observations, draw and/or take photos, and measure the plants grown under the two differing conditions over a period of time. All other variables are controlled (soil, water, air); only the light received by the plants is different, which is the variable.

After the observations have been made and data has been gathered by students, the teacher begins the next instructional phase called *Concept Invention*, or in the 5-E model, the *Explain* phase. In this phase the students present and share data with their classmates in a teacher-guided discussion of findings. The teacher uses questions to guide students' thinking and encourages the use of logic and reasoning as they interpret their data. For example, students may post the photos or drawings of plants grown in the dark and in the light, make line graphs of plant height over time, or share qualitative information about how the plant appeared after grown under the two conditions (e.g., plants in the light were green, whereas plants in the dark were yellow and pale). At the end of this phase, the students construct an overall statement that summarizes their data and observations, which is the central science *concept*. The science vocabulary is then linked to the concept students "invented."

Next the teacher helps students through the *Application* (from the learning cycle) or *Elaborate* (from the 5-E model) in which students use the new concept they have learned as it is applied in new contexts. For example, students can create new questions to investigate or hypotheses to test, based on what they have just learned (the concept) and develop a way to answer their questions or test their hypotheses (e.g., what color of light is best for plants to grow?). They can also go to the internet to learn more about the concept they have just invented. In this phase the teacher can engage students in additional hands-on laboratories, readings, discussions, field trips, and/or writing activities that extend and expand upon the concept. These models of inquiry science teaching and learning are endorsed by NSTA (NSTA, 1998, 2003).

The diagram in Figure 6-1 shows the inquiry-based learning cycle model as it corresponds to the 5-E model of science teaching. The template shown in Table 6-4 explains each phase of the learning cycle as it relates to the 5-E Model for structuring inquiry-based science teaching for all students.

Figure 6-1. The Learning Cycle and 5-E Model

Interpreting Findings in Science Inquiry

In planning and conducting experiments, teachers should guide children to develop an appropriate procedure for testing hypotheses, including the use of instruments that can yield measurable data. Even at the early stages of scientific experimentation, the procedure must be clear and tangible enough to allow replication by other students or scientists. Help students understand the concept of controlling variables and testing only one variable at a time. Students need to learn to be precise in the collection of data and measurements. Ensure the use of the metric system in obtaining all measurement data.

The best way to promote students' critical and logical thinking abilities is to allow them to gather their own data and observations for interpretation. It also gives them experience with using appropriate tools, resources, and technology of science that will lead to accurate organization and analysis of data. The students will be able to experience and practice science skills by verifying their findings, basing findings on evidence, and analyzing sources of error. Having students collect and report their own data also brings the teacher opportunities to discuss scientific ethics with students.

In explaining data collection procedures and display of findings to English learners, the teacher needs to demonstrate and provide a model of what the final results should look like. In using inquiry, students work in groups, which is particularly helpful for second language learners as they interpret and exchange ideas about data and scientific reasoning.

When students complete their experiments, teachers need to engage them in the process of analyzing their own, and other groups' data for similarities, differences, and variations including error. This occurs in the concept invention or "explain" phase of the learning cycle and 5-E model, and again in any application or "elaborate" activities in which data has been collected. After data

Table 6-4. The 5-E Model of Instruction

5-E Definition	Teacher Behavior	Student Behavior
Engage		
• Generate interest • Access prior knowledge • Connect to past knowledge • Set parameters of the focus • Frame the idea	• Motivates • Creates interest • Taps into what students know or think about the topic • Raises questions and encourages responses	• Attentive in listening • Asks questions • Demonstrates interest in the lesson • Responds to questions demonstrating their own entry point of understanding
Explore		
• Experience key concepts • Discover new skills • Probe, inquire, and question experiences • Examine their thinking • Establish relationships and understanding	• Acts as a facilitator • Observes and listens to students as they interact • Asks good inquiry-oriented questions • Provides time for students to think and to reflect • Encourages cooperative learning	• Conducts activities, predicts, and forms hypotheses or makes generalizations • Becomes a good listener • Shares ideas and suspends judgment • Records observations and/or generalizations • Discusses tentative alternatives
Explain		
• Connect prior knowledge and background to new discoveries • Communicate new understandings • Connect informal language to formal language	• Encourages students to explain their observations and findings in their own words • Provides definitions, new words, and explanations • Listens and builds upon discussion from students • Asks for clarification and justification • Accepts all reasonable responses	• Explains, listens, defines, and questions • Uses previous observations and findings • Provides reasonable responses to questions • Interacts in a positive, supportive manner

Extend/Elaborate		
• Apply new learning to a new or similar situation • Extend and explain concept being explored • Communicate new understanding with formal language	• Uses previously learned information as a vehicle to enhance additional learning • Encourages students to apply or extend the new concepts and skills • Encourages students to use terms and definitions previously acquired	• Applies new terms and definitions • Uses previous information to probe, ask questions, and make reasonable judgments • Provides reasonable conclusions and solutions • Records observations, explanations, and solutions
Evaluate		
• Assess understanding (Self, peer and teacher evaluation) • Demonstrate understanding of new concept by observation or open-ended response • Apply within problem situation • Show evidence of accomplishment	• Observes student behaviors as they explore and apply new concepts and skills • Assesses students' knowledge and skills • Encourages students to assess their own learning • Asks open-ended questions	• Demonstrates an understanding or knowledge of concepts and skills • Evaluates his/her own progress • Answers open-ended questions • Provides reasonable responses and explanations to events or phenomena

Based on the 5-E Instructional Model presented by Dr. Jim Barufaldi at the Eisenhower Science Collaborative Conference in Austin, Texas, July 2002.

has been collected from students' explorations, they display their data in charts and graphs, for example, and communicate their observations and, ultimately, concept statements to the class by posting them on the board and/or through an oral presentation. The data helps them develop conclusions and form new research questions or hypotheses as they evaluate their findings, setting the foundation for new explorations. Students should be able to present pertinent data by using graphic representations, and communicate their findings in written and oral forms to their peers.

In using scientific inquiry as in the learning cycle and 5-E model, scientific vocabulary is introduced *after* students have had hands-on experiences in the (engage and) exploration phase *and* have used their observations and data to construct meaning from their experiences in the *concept invention* or "explain" phase. Once students have had the hands-on direct experience with the concept, and have stated the meaning of their observations, the scientific vocabulary or terms that label the concept can be introduced by the teacher. In the application or elaborate phase, the teacher and students use the new vocabulary in extended experimentation, discussion, readings, writing, and other learning activities. Introducing terms after students have directly experienced the science inquiry and constructed meaning from their experiences by making a concept statement is especially important for second language learners in facilitating the development of understanding of science concepts. For all students, but especially for second language learners, this helps them understand concepts when terms are later *re-introduced*. By giving students the experience—something they *do*—and then allowing them to form meaning from their experience in ways that make sense to them, then when the term that labels what they learned is introduced, they are able to link it to prior knowledge and learning experiences in their minds. The terms are now able to build their background knowledge, which is critical for second language learners to understand the language of science. Making a connection between the hands-on activities and scientific vocabulary is beneficial to all students but especially to ELs, who can link the actions with the appropriate concept and vocabulary words without engaging in translations.

Promoting Logical Thinking and Scientific Reasoning

Interpreting results is one of the most challenging phases of scientific inquiry for children in EC–6. Students can easily discuss the observable results but might have difficulty interpreting their meaning. Teachers have to use developmentally appropriate practices to guide students to make extrapolations and infer information from the data, which involves the teachers' use of questioning.

Questioning

The use of good questions by the teacher is critical to promoting logical thinking and scientific reasoning among students. Good questioning causes students to reflect upon the logic of their data and observations with confidence and also identify possible misinformation or misunderstanding of important concepts. Through good questioning, students learn to carefully analyze their findings and prepared with experimental evidence, they can effectively use scientific argumentation and respond to questions and challenges to their findings in order to support their conclusions. In teaching science, probing questions are most effective. Probing questions are framed in a way that asks students to reveal their thinking and explain their rationale for conclusions they may draw from their experiences. Probing questions may be simple, such as "What do you think?" and "Why do you think that may be true?" as examples. Overall, it is vital for teachers to use good questioning to reveal student learning and assess their progress in forming sound scientific frameworks of understanding. Questioning is clearly the hallmark of science inquiry and should be used throughout inquiry instruction. In the learning cycle/5-E model, questioning must be designed to lead students toward being able to state the concept, so it is especially critical in the concept invention or "explain" phase.

Teachers can guide students at various levels of development to observe events; and through questioning, teachers can help students develop higher-order thinking skills. For example, a teacher can lead children to make predictions while conducting experiments with objects that float or sink in water. By asking students to predict and explain why an object might sink or float, the teacher is leading students to analyze the properties of the object and the water to make an evaluative decision; that is, the children are using analysis and evaluation to complete that simple task. The following guide will help teachers best promote and elevate logical thinking abilities among students.

Taxonomy of the Cognitive Domain

Use key questioning terms aimed at the full range of the cognitive domain. (Bloom & Krathwohl, 1956; Anderson & Krathwohl, 2001).

LEVEL 1: Knowledge

Recall factual information on command.

Examples

List the five Kingdoms.

Label the parts of the cell in the diagram provided.

Write the formula for density.

LEVEL 2: Comprehension

Communicate an idea in a different form.

Examples

Explain heat transfer through conduction.

Restate what a habitat is in your own words.

Submit a definition of photosynthesis in your own words.

LEVEL 3: Application

Use what is known to find new solutions or apply in new situations.

Examples

Relate the concept of convection to lake turnover.

Utilize your understanding of burning to explain why sand works to put out a fire.

Making use of the clothes you are wearing, how can you stay afloat for several hours?

LEVEL 4: Analysis

Break things and ideas down into component parts and find their unique characteristics.

Examples

Examine blueprints of the electrical circuitry of your school building and explain how it works to bring electricity to your laboratory station.

Study the diagram of human digestion and *reason* what the organ marked #7 might be and explain its function.

Using the given laboratory materials, *deduce* the identities of the substances labeled "A," "B," and "C."

LEVEL 5: Synthesis

Use what is known to think creatively and divergently; make something new or original; pattern ideas or things in a new way.

Examples

Create a burglar alarm system for the classroom.

Build a telescope for classroom use.

Develop a plan for cleaning the pollutants in the Trinity River.

LEVEL 6: Evaluation

A. Use what is known to make judgments and ratings; accept or reject ideas; determine the worthiness of an idea or thing.

Examples

Decide whether you agree with the production of more nuclear power plants and provide justification for your decision.

Make a ruling you would give to car manufacturers on global warming and provide support for your ruling.

Rank the top five greatest discoveries in scientific history and *explain* why you have chosen those discoveries and ranked them the way you did.

B.   Avoid yes/no questions (unless part of a game) and questions with obvious answers.

Examples

Showing a picture of a cell
Not so good

Is this a cell?
Better

What is this structure and how do you know?
(Students watching a chemical reaction in which the solution turns blue)
Not so good

Did it turn blue?
Better

What happened? What did you observe? Why did this happen?

C.   Use questions beginning with the words *Why, How, What, Where,* and *When* that probe students' thinking.

Examples

How do you know? Why do you think that?

Where did you see a change?

What is your explanation for this observation? When did you notice the change occur?

What do you think?

COMPETENCY 003: IMPACT ON SCIENCE

The teacher understands how science impacts the daily lives of students and interacts with and influences personal and societal decisions.

Science in Daily Life

Students need to be aware of how science is present and plays a role in their daily lives. The functioning of their bodies, the natural environment that is around them, and their everyday use of electrical appliances, bicycles, computers, and cellphones are examples of biological and physical science in their lives. However, students tend to keep the science they learn in school separate from the science they experience in everyday life! It is important that teachers help students connect the science they are learning in school to the world around them to broaden their understandings and promote the usefulness, value, and applicability of science. In the learning cycle and 5-E models, the best time to help students make these connections is in the application/elaboration phase. After students have experienced a hands-on lab activity and constructed an understanding of the concept, the teacher should help them relate that new concept to their everyday lives and see how the concept works in differing contexts. Connecting newly-learned concepts to the students' life experiences makes the learning more meaningful for students and helps them retain understanding of the concept for later use. Relating science to what students already know and experience in life helps bridge the disconnections between "school science" and science they observe and experience in everyday life.

Science has brought society many advantages that have served to increase the health and longevity of humans, and to improve the quality of life for all. However, there may be consequences, often unforeseen, to scientific discovery and invention that impacts society and the natural environment, as well as the habitats and survival of the living organisms that share this planet. To better understand these issues, students need to gain scientific knowledge and evidence of what is known. Armed with appropriate background knowledge, students will be in the position to weigh the pros and cons of various scientific discoveries and debate issues that prevail in our global community. Students should be apprised of issues such as global warming, for example, but before taking a position on the topic, they must be prepared with accurate scientific information on the topic. When students are given opportunities to use scientific concepts as support for sound logic and reasoning to debate or evaluate a scientific issue, they are operating at a high cognitive level important to their intellectual development. Equally important is student awareness of the ethical, personal, societal, and economic implications of science, from both positive and negative perspectives. Students need to realize the trade-offs often inherent in scientific discovery and experimentation—for example, laboratory testing on animals. Many new and important discoveries have improved the quality of life at the cost of animals' lives. In order to best understand the complexity of how science interfaces with personal and societal issues, students need to be engaged in electronic and library research on impactful science topics and in discussion with peers and experts in the science fields. Topics such as cloning, global warming, alternative and fossil fuels, and acid rain are just a few additional topics tied to ethical, personal, societal, and economic concerns. It is important that students fully understand the scientific knowledge that underlies all such complex issues, and can formulate decisions based on the related knowledge.

Energy as a source of fuel and electricity is a major issue threatening the economic, environmental, and personal status of living in the U.S. and global society. It is important to be able to identify and know about fossil fuels, their origin, how they are obtained, and how they are used for energy consumption. These fossil fuels include coal, oil, and natural gas. These fossil fuels are nonrenewable and will one day be expended. Therefore, science must continue to develop and improve upon alternative sources of energy such as wind, hydroelectric, solar, and geothermal. Teachers must be able to identify and understand these other sources of energy and be able to guide students toward understanding how these alternative, renewable energy sources are used and how they impact our society's energy needs.

A significant impact of science on daily life relates to student fitness and health.

Childhood obesity is a serious problem in the U.S., and teachers can play an important role in educating children on the negative health issues associated with poor nutrition and a lack of exercise. Students need to learn about factors that impact physical and psychological health and about how to make good choices on such factors, including nutrition, hygiene, physical exercise, smoking, drugs, and alcohol. Understanding human biology, therefore, is important for students to realize how obesity and other factors such as substance use/abuse affect their physical and mental health. The topics of heart disease, diabetes, and cancer should be included in the curriculum as ways to help students understand the detrimental effects of unhealthy life choices.

COMPETENCY 004: CONCEPTS AND PROCESSES

The teacher knows and understands the unifying concepts and processes that are common to all sciences.

Explanatory Framework across Science Disciplines

Science is a way of knowing, a process—it is a systematic way of looking at the world and how it works. This competency focuses on how science uses a regular, consistent method of collecting and reporting data about scientific phenomena. Science is a way of organizing observations and then seeking patterns and regularity in order to make sense of the world. In science we organize evidence, create models, and explain observations in a logical form. We make predictions and hypotheses and test our predictions and hypotheses through controlled experimentation, meaning all variables of the experiment remain constant except for the variable being tested. We repeat experiments multiple times and seek constancy in our laboratory findings and in real life experiences in both form and/or function. Repeating experiments many times increases reliability of the findings. Reliability is established when the same or closely similar findings occur each time the experiment is repeated. Consistent findings from repeated experiments provide strong support for conclusions made. These patterns and consistencies in our observations and data are important for constructing evidence-based explanations and making new predictions.

Science embraces a broad spectrum of subject matter, such as life science, physical science, and earth science, all of which is interrelated. For example, in studying the ecosystem, teachers must understand the biological aspects (e.g., the living organism) and how they interact, as in predator–prey relationships and symbiotic relationships (e.g., parasitism, commensalism), as well as the chemical aspects of the ecosystem (e.g., nitrogen cycle), the geologic or earth science aspects (e.g., the landscape, the water, and the climate) and the physics aspects (e.g., energy transfer, motion). Ecosystems, for example, regardless of location on earth, share unifying components and characteristics, and teachers must understand this unity. In life science, there is unity of what makes organisms "living"—they all must carry on life functions and are composed of one or more cells. These are the criteria that unify life forms and classify something like a virus, for example, as non-living (it does not carry on the life functions and is not composed of cells).

All scientific observations can be described by their characteristics or "properties." These properties organize the observations according to commonalities, or classification. Observed properties and patterns are centered on space, time, energy, and matter.

Scientific Models

Models are representations of the natural world and universe in order to help better understand how something appears, its form and/or its function. For example, we may make models of the solar system, cells, or an atom to help us better explain its form and function and interactivity with other structures. Such models can be helpful to us in understanding the actual concept the model represents, and scientists often make models for this purpose. However, it is important to understand that, although it represents the actual science phenomena or concept and provides explanatory power, it is not the same as the actual science concept and is limited. Models in science may be physical, as in a physical model of a cell; conceptual, as in a concept map or an analogy; and/or mathematical as in a formula showing relationships, such as $d = m/v$ (formula for density).

COMPETENCY 005: STUDENTS AS LEARNERS AND SCIENCE INSTRUCTION

The teacher has theoretical and practical knowledge about teaching science and about how students learn science.

Developmentally Appropriate Practices

Exposing children to scientific inquiry can begin as early as age three or four. However, teachers must be aware of the stages of cognitive, social, and emotional development of children to appropriately introduce children to science concepts. For example, observing and experimenting with water and colors can easily be done by three- or four-year-olds, but using microscopes to observe and analyze animal or vegetable cells might be more appropriate for children in third and fourth grades. Students in EC–6 need direct experiences in order to understand concepts. According to Piaget (1964), children transition through stages of development that require direct involvement to make sense of their experience. The model of teaching described earlier, the learning cycle and 5-E model, are based upon promoting the intellectual development of children. Thus, these models of teaching were designed to be consistent with the nature of science—and importantly, to match how children naturally learn (Marek and Cavallo, 1997; Renner and Marek, 1990). It is important that teachers understand the theory and research that underlie such models, as well as know how to use these models in teaching.

Misconceptions or alternative conceptions are a pervasive problem in science teaching and learning. Children tend to view the world from their own perspectives and draw conclusions based on their limited experiences. Once misconceptions are established in learners' minds, they are difficult to change. Therefore, teaching needs to allow children the opportunity for direct experience and collecting evidence. Teaching science also must begin with the teacher understanding what the students already know, and incorporate the students' every day experiences. Learning this information from students will guide instructional planning, toward designing culturally relevant, meaningful learning experiences for the students. The learning cycle has been established as a teaching model that allows teachers to learn the students' prior knowledge, promotes conceptual change, helps students resolve misconceptions, and leads to more scientifically accurate and meaningful understandings (Sandoval, 1995).

Teachers need to begin lessons with direct, concrete activities giving students experience with objects. After conceptual understandings are established in learners, then teachers can move them from the concrete to more abstract reasoning. For example, in learning the concept of density, it is important that students have objects to touch, feel, weigh (take the mass of) and measure first, as in the exploration phase of the learning cycle. From direct experience with the objects, students should construct the concept that "a certain amount of matter (mass) is packed into a given amount of space (volume)." The term that labels this concept is "density." As application, teachers help students develop their abstract-thinking abilities by having them solve problems using the formula for density, $d=m/v$. Teachers need to select instruction appropriately such that concrete experiences are used first, leading the students to later use abstract reasoning. Teachers need to select learning experiences that will promote the students scientific knowledge, skills, and use of inquiry. Further, the students are able to use the prior knowledge they have formed about density to learn more extended, related concepts such as buoyancy. This example demonstrates the instructional knowledge and skills teachers need to have to prepare the best possible science learning experiences for students. The learning cycle or 5-E model are consistent with the goals of this competency.

Science for all has long been the theme of science education's guiding documents such as Project 2061, a long-term initiative of the American Association for the Advancement of Science created in 1989, and the National Science Education Standards, published by the National Research Council in 1996. *Science for all* means that teachers need to help their students abandon stereotypes they may hold of science and scientists. For example, that science is a male-dominated profession. Teachers should help students to more appropriately view science as a field for males and females and for all cultures and ethnicities. To accomplish this goal, teachers need to be aware of their own potential, often not intentional, bias toward science and scientists that may be exclusionary. For example, teachers need to be aware of utilizing both, or alternating between "he" and "she" in examples. If discussing astronauts and doctors, for example, teachers (owing to misleading stereotypes) tend to inadvertently refer to them as "he," whereas nurses and teachers are often only referred to as "she." Teachers need to be aware of any possible gender-biased habits and regularly change the gender they may attribute to stereotypically male or female careers to the opposite gender. Likewise in using names in teaching examples given to students or in word problems. Teachers need to use names common in a variety of cultures to broaden the perception of who may be a scientist.

Teachers should design instruction to allow students of different cultures, genders, and ethnicities to work together in mixed collaborative groups. Doing so allows students to share experiences that will help broaden their understanding of differing perspectives. Vocabulary in science is particularly difficult and new to students, and should only be introduced after students have had direct laboratory experiences with particular concepts that they can later label with science terminology. This process is beneficial to English learners because it allows them to have a physical experience of the concept before learning its scientific label. Posters of scientists displayed in the room should represent male and female scientists of diverse ethnicities and cultures while also showing the many distinct fields of science, such as environmental science, veterinary medicine, geology, engineering, and architecture, as well as the more traditionally represented physics and chemistry. Likewise, discussions of science and scientific discovery should include contributions from a diverse range of scientists. Using these measures will broaden the students' views of "who can be a scientist," with the goal that they see *themselves* as scientists. In laboratory activities it is important that all group members have the opportunity to handle the materials and perform the experiment, and that the same students are not relegated to note-taking. Varying laboratory responsibilities can be accomplished by assigning group members roles to perform when they are conducting a laboratory activity. Such roles may include materials collector, record keeper, reporter, and lab facilitator. Be sure to rotate these roles from one laboratory activity to the next to ensure all students have an opportunity to work in the various roles.

COMPETENCY 006: SCIENCE ASSESSMENT

The teacher knows the varied and appropriate assessments and assessment practices for monitoring science learning in laboratory, field and classroom settings.

Measuring Student Learning

Teaching cannot occur without student *learning*, and in order to determine that learning is occurring, student progress needs to be assessed on a regular basis. Assessment of learning should occur on some scale, large or small, every class day, and as students move through the learning of concepts, as in the learning cycle and 5-E models. Measuring learning as it is occurring is "authentic assessment" and allows teachers to adjust the instruction according to student learning and potential difficulties in learning. Alternative assessment methods, in addition to the more traditional testing formats (e.g., multiple-choice) should be used to obtain a full picture of what students know and do not know or can and cannot do. Alternative assessments include techniques such as verbal reports, laboratory practical exams, story writing, developing advertisements or brochures, constructing a concept map, writing essays, creating drawings or models, and developing a play or skit. In each assessment, the concepts to be learned are represented in alternative ways—yet clearly communicate what students have learned and understand.

It is essential that teachers monitor and assess students' understanding of concepts and skills on a regular, consistent basis and use this information to adjust instruction. The results of frequent informal and formal/traditional and alternative assessments should be used as a tool for planning subsequent instruction. Teachers must communicate progress to students so they can learn to self-monitor their own learning and understand what is needed to achieve learning goals.

Assessing the Science Curriculum

As part of the accountability system, Texas has a comprehensive assessment system to measure the state uniform curriculum—the Texas Essential Knowledge and Skills (TEKS). In this system, students take the State of Texas Assessments of Academic Readiness (STAAR) test in Grades 3 through 12. However, the science component of TEKS is assessed only in Grades 5, 8, and 10. The fifth-grade science test is available in Spanish; thus, Spanish-speaking ELs can take the test in Spanish. In addition to the required science STAAR examinations, students are assessed through teacher- and district-developed tests in Kindergarten through Grade 12.

COMPETENCY 007: FORCES AND MOTION

The teacher understands forces and motion and their relationships.

The key universal forces included in this section are gravity, electricity, and magnetism.

Magnetism and Gravity

Magnetism is the force of attraction or repulsion between objects that results from the positive and negative ionic charges of the objects. Usually, the objects are metals, such as iron, nickel, and cobalt. Magnets have two poles that have opposing charges or forces: north (+) and south (–). When the north pole of a magnet is placed close to the north pole of a second magnet, repulsion occurs. When poles of different kinds (north and south) are placed in close proximity, they attract one another. The strength of the forces depends on the size and the proximity of the magnets. The charged area around a magnet is called a magnetic field. The Earth is like a large magnet, with opposing forces—the North Pole and South Pole, and the magnetic field of attraction of Earth. We know that magnetic field as gravity. Without gravity, all objects on Earth, including the atmosphere, would not be held onto its surface. Planets and other celestial objects that are more massive than Earth, such as Jupiter, have stronger gravitational forces, and those that are less massive and/or dense, such as our Moon, have weaker gravitational forces.

Force and Motion

Force is defined as the action of moving an object by pulling or pushing it. Force can cause an object to move at a constant speed or to accelerate. When force is applied over a distance, work is done. **Work** is the product of the force acting in the direction of movement and causing displacement. **Energy** is defined as the ability to do work; when a tow truck uses force to pull a car and move it to a different location, energy is used and work is accomplished. Newton's laws of motion are important to understand in mastering this competency. Newton's first law is that an object at rest will remain at rest unless acted upon by an (unbalanced) force, and an object in motion will continue to stay in motion with the same speed and in the same direction unless acted upon by an (unbalanced) outside force. This first law is also called *inertia*. Newton's second law is that acceleration is produced when a force acts on mass and the greater the mass of the object being accelerated, the greater the amount of force needed to accelerate that object. Newton's third law of motion is that for every action there is an equal and opposite reaction (see *https://www.teachengineering. org/lessons/view/ucd_newton_lesson03#*).

Force and motion, as well as changes in motion, may be measured through hands-on activities in which variables such as time, speed, distance, and direction can be recorded and graphed, and teachers need to know how to do so. For example, teachers can have students experience and record what happens when an object with higher mass (such as a large marble or ball bearing), collides with an object with less mass (e.g., a small marble or ball bearing). Teachers should also know what happens when the rate of speed is high when the objects collide compared to when the rate of speed is low. The game of pool or billiards is a good example. When forces are unbalanced, it may cause the object to change its motion or position.

Relationships between Force and Motion: Machines, Space, and Geologic Processes

A machine is something that makes work easier. Machines can be as simple as a wedge or a screw or as sophisticated as a computer or gas engine. A **simple machine** has few or no moving parts and can change the size and direction of a force. A screw, hammer, wedge, and incline plane are examples of simple machines. Simple machines are part of our daily activities. For example, children playing on a seesaw are using a simple machine called a **lever**. Thus, teachers and their students should know the practical use of these simple machines in everyday life. A **complex machine** is two or more simple machines working together to facilitate work. Some of the complex machines used in daily activities are a wheelbarrow, a can opener, and a bicycle.

Force and motion is what keeps the Sun, Earth, Moon, and planets in their orbits and explains the structure and changes of the universe. On Earth, force and motion are found in all geologic processes, explaining phenomena such as tides and tsunamis.

COMPETENCY 008: PHYSICAL AND CHEMICAL PROPERTIES

The teacher understands the physical and chemical properties of and changes in matter.

Matter

Matter is anything that takes up space and has mass. The **mass** of a body is the amount of matter in an object or thing; **volume** describes the amount of space that matter takes up. Mass is also the property of a body that causes it to have weight. **Weight** is the amount of gravitational force exerted over an object. It is important not to confuse mass and weight. What students are measuring on their balances in the laboratory is an object's *mass*. Weight changes as an object goes from one level of gravitational force to another, for example, from Earth to the Moon, because the amount of "pull" on that object is different; but the mass of the object—how much matter or material is in the object—does not change unless we do something to actually take away or add matter to that object.

There are 118 basic kinds of matter, called **elements**, which are organized into the **periodic table**. An element is composed of sub-microscopic components called **atoms**. An element is made up of one kind of atom as listed on the periodic table. For example, Fe is the element iron, and if you had an item composed of iron, it would be composed of only iron (Fe) atoms. Atoms are made up of particles called **electrons, neutrons,** and **protons**. The mass of the atom is located mostly in the nucleus, which is made up of protons and neutrons. The electron contains little mass and follows an orbit around the nucleus. **Molecules** are two or more atoms bonded together in a chemical bond. The atoms of a molecule can be more than one of the same *kind* of atom, as in the naturally occurring oxygen molecule, O_2, or a molecule can be two or more different atoms as in carbon dioxide, CO_2, ammonia, $NH3$, and glucose, $C_6H_{12}O_6$. **Compounds** are when you have two or more *different* kinds of atoms in the molecule and you have a given amount of that substance. In other words, compounds consist of matter composed of atoms that are chemically combined with one another in molecules in definite weight proportions. An example of a compound is water; water is oxygen and hydrogen combined in the ratio of two hydrogen molecules to one molecule of oxygen H_2O. So, you can also call it *one* H_2O a molecule.

Properties of Matter

Matter has physical, thermal, electrical, and chemical properties. These properties are dependent upon the molecular composition of the matter.

Physical Properties

The physical properties of matter are the way matter looks and feels. It includes qualities like color, density, hardness, and conductivity. **Color** represents how matter is reflected or perceived by the human eye. **Density** is the mass that is contained in a unit of volume of a given substance; it is a measure of how much *matter* is packed into a certain *amount of space*, or mass divided by volume $(D = M/V)$. **Hardness** represents the resistance to penetration offered by a given substance. **Conductivity** is the ability of substances to transmit thermal or electric current.

Thermal Properties

Matter is sensitive to temperature changes. Heat and cold produce changes in the physical properties of matter; however, the chemical properties remain unchanged. For example, when water is exposed to cold temperature (release of heat), it changes from liquid to solid; and when water is exposed to heat, it changes from solid to liquid. With continued heat, the water changes from liquid to gas (water vapor). Water vapor can be cooled again and turned back into liquid. However, through all these states, water retains its chemical properties—two molecules of hydrogen and one molecule of oxygen or H_2O.

Electrical Properties

Matter can be classified as a conductor or nonconductor of electricity. Conductive matter allows the transfer of electric current or heat from one point to another. Metals are usually good conductors, while wood and rocks are examples of nonconductive matter.

Chemical Properties

The chemical properties of one type of matter (element) can react with the chemical properties of other types of matter. In general, elements from the same groups will not react with each other, while elements from different groups may. The more separated the groups, the more likely they will cause a chemical reaction when brought together. A type of matter can be chemically altered to become a different type of matter; for example, a metal trash will rust if left out in the rain.

States of Matter

Matter can exist in four distinct states: solid, liquid, gas, and plasma. Most people are familiar with the basic states of matter, but they might not be familiar with the fourth one, plasma. Plasmas are formed at extremely high temperatures when electrons are stripped from neutral atoms (University of California, 2006). Stars are predominantly composed of plasmas. Solids have mass, occupy a define amount of space or *volume* or have a definite shape, and are more dense than liquids. Liquids have mass, occupy a definite volume, do not have a definite shape, but instead take the shape of their container. Gases have mass, do not have a definite volume, have no definite shape but take the shape of their container, and are the least dense of the three states of matter. Plasma has no definite shape or volume, and is a substance that cannot be classified as a solid, liquid, or gas. When substances change from one state of matter to another, such as ice melting, it is a physical change, and not a chemical change.

Mixtures and Solutions

Mixtures are combinations of two or more substances, where each substance is distinct from the other; that is, made up of two or more types of molecules and not chemically combined. The two substances in the mixture may or may not be evenly distributed, so there are no definite amounts or weight proportions. Mixtures may be *heterogeneous*, which means an uneven distribution of the substances in the mixture throughout. A mixture may be *homogeneous,* which means the components are evenly distributed throughout. Examples of mixtures include milk, which is a heterogeneous mixture of water and butterfat particles. The components of a mixture can be separated physically. For example, milk producers and manufacturers remove the butterfat from whole milk to make skim milk.

Solutions are *mixtures* that are *homogeneous*, which means that the components are distributed evenly and there is an even concentration throughout. The solute is the substance in the smaller amount that dissolves and that you add into the substance that is in the larger amount—the solvent. Water is a common solvent. Solids, liquids, and gases can be solutes. Examples of solutions are seawater and ammonia. Seawater is made up of water and salt, and ammonia is made up of ammonia gas and water. In these examples, the salt and the ammonia (NH_3) are the solutes; water is the solvent.

Physical and Chemical Changes in Matter

A **physical change** is a change in a substance that does not change what that substance is made of. Examples of physical changes are melting ice (boiling water), tearing paper, chopping wood, writing with chalk and mixing sugar and water together. In the mixing of sugar with water, or salt with water, even though the sugar or salt may not be visible to the naked eye in the water, it is still there and still has the same composition—that is, the molecules that make up the sugar or salt and water are still the same as when you mixed them. You can evaporate the water and you will recover your sugar or salt crystals.

A **chemical change** is when the substances that were combined are no longer the same molecules—they have changed to new substances. For example, burning wood, mixing baking soda and vinegar, or a rusting nail, which is when the iron of the nail (Fe) combines with oxygen (in the presence of water) to form a new substance—that is, a new molecule is formed, iron oxide Fe_2O_3.

Physical changes can be reversed, whereas chemical changes generally cannot. Evidence of a chemical change includes that the combination of the substances gives off a gas (bubbles are observed), it changes color (change of color alone does not always indicate a chemical change, but may signify a chemical change if the other evidences are also present), gives off heat and becomes warmer, or absorbs heat and becomes colder (temperature change), and forms a precipitate (a solid substance). When heat is given off in a chemical change, it is an **exothermic** reaction; and when heat is absorbed in a chemical change (the combination becomes colder), it is an **endothermic** reaction. Everyday examples of exothermic reactions are firewood burning or the use of a hand warmer that many mountain climbers and snow skiers use, and examples of endothermic reactions are a cold pack used in sports injuries or the combination of baking soda and vinegar. Try it with a thermometer in the vinegar during the reaction and see!

Chemical Reactions in Everyday Life

Chemical reactions occur in everyday life and are an essential part of our physical and biological world. The burning of gasoline in automobiles is a chemical change—and burning of any kind for that matter. Burning is the combination of oxygen from the atmosphere with substances containing the carbon atom. The proper temperature has to be reached in order to begin this exothermic reaction, but once started, the chemical reaction can continue until the oxygen is used up or is prevented from entering into the reaction. When oxygen comes in contact with carbon substances at the right temperature or "activation energy" to produce a reaction, the chemical reaction we see is burning, and the reaction itself gives off heat (exothermic). So since gasoline is a fossil fuel (a once living organism), it contains carbon. When we provide the energy it needs to begin the reaction (activation energy), as long as oxygen is present, the carbon substance will burn. Burning is a chemical reaction because the carbon and oxygen combine to form new substances such as carbon monoxide (CO) and carbon dioxide (CO_2). The same reaction occurs in burning wood, candles, and even in cell respiration—the oxygen we breathe and carry through our bloodstream is combined in our cells with carbon-containing glucose molecules in a type of "controlled" burning. Our bodies give off heat from this reaction, which is why we are able to maintain a fairly high temperature of about 98.6 degrees Fahrenheit. Other examples of chemical reactions in everyday life include chemical batteries, the digestion of food, and cooking/baking. Moreover, the process of photosynthesis, where plants use sunlight to convert carbon dioxide gas and water into food for the plant known as glucose (a simple sugar), is also an important chemical reaction responsible for providing food for and sustaining all life on Earth.

COMPETENCY 009: ENERGY AND INTERACTIONS

The teacher understands energy and interactions between matter and energy.

Principles of Energy

Energy is available in many forms, including heat, light, solar radiation, chemical, electrical, magnetic, sound, and mechanical energy. It exists in three states: potential, kinetic, and activation energies. An object possessing energy because of its ability to move has **kinetic energy**. The energy that an object has as the result of its position or condition is called **potential energy**. The energy necessary to transfer or convert potential energy into kinetic energy is called **activation energy**. All three states of energy can be transformed from one to the other. A vehicle parked in a garage has potential energy. When the driver starts the engine using the chemical energy stored in the battery and the fuel, potential energy becomes activation energy. Once the vehicle is moving, the energy changes to kinetic energy. An object with high potential energy will produce high kinetic energy once it is transformed and releases this potential energy (as kinetic energy). For example, a small firecracker has lower potential or stored energy compared to professional fireworks. This is evidenced by the amount of kinetic or released energy when it is fired off. A bicycle with its rider has more potential energy at the top of an incline than it does on a flat surface. When potential energy of the bicycle on the incline is transformed to kinetic (riding down the hill) it will have more energy released compared to the bicycle on the flat surface.

Heat and Temperature

Heat is a form of energy. Temperature is the measure of heat. The most common device used to measure temperature is the thermometer. Thermometers use heat-sensitive substances—mercury and alcohol—that expand when heated.

Heat and Light

The most common form of energy comes from the Sun. Solar energy provides heat and light for animals and plants. Through **photosynthesis**, plants capture radiant energy from the Sun and transform it into **chemical energy** in the form of glucose. This chemical energy is stored in the leaves, stems, and fruits of plants. Humans and animals consume the plants or fruits and get the energy they need for survival. This energy source is transformed again to create kinetic energy and body heat. **Kinetic energy** is used for movement and to do work, while **heat** is a required element for all warm-blooded animals, like humans. Cold-blooded animals also require heat, but rather than making it themselves through the transformation of plant sugar, they use solar energy to heat their body. Energy transformation constitutes the foundation and the driving force of an ecosystem. In addition to heat and solar radiation, energy is available in the forms of electricity and magnetism.

Heat Transfer

The transfer of heat is accomplished in three ways: conduction, radiation, and convection. **Conduction** is the process of transferring heat or electricity through a substance. Conduction occurs when heat makes the molecules move quickly; the heat is transferred from one molecule to the next and so on through the substance. Conduction occurs in solid materials, such as a metal spoon. It occurs when two objects of differing temperatures are placed in contact with each other and heat flows from the hotter object to the cooler object. A common example is leaving a spoon in a cup of hot tea. The spoon is cool, but the part in the hot tea is warmed. Eventually, the part of the spoon not itself in the hot tea (the handle) will also become warm. The transfer of heat through the spoon is an instance of conduction. As another example, in the cooling system of a car, heat from the engine is transferred to the liquid coolant. When the coolant passes through the radiator, the heat transfers from the coolant to the radiator, and eventually, out of the car. This heat transfer system preserves the engine and allows it to continue working.

Radiation describes the energy that travels at high speed in empty space (that is, where there are no atoms or molecules) in the form of light or through the decay of radioactive elements. Radiation is part of our modern life. It exists in simple states as the energy emitted by microwaves, cellphones, and sunshine—or as potentially dangerous energy as X-ray machines and nuclear weapons. The radiation used in medicine, nuclear power, and nuclear weapons has enough energy to cause permanent damage and even death.

Convection describes the flow of heat through the movement of liquid or gaseous matter from a hot region to a cool region. In its most basic form, the concept of convection is that warm air rises and cold air sinks, and warm liquid rises and cold liquid sinks. The colder air or liquid contracts and so is denser, thus it sinks; the warmer air spreads out or expands, and so is less dense and rises. Thus, convection occurs when the heating of a substance changes its density. A good example is the heating of air over land near coastal areas coupled with the influx of cooler offshore sea breezes. The heated air inland expands and thus decreases in density, causing the cooler, more dense air to rush in to achieve equilibrium. The cold air moves underneath the warm air, causing the warm air that was over the land to rise, where it cools and sinks again. Typically the air was also holding moisture, and so a storm may occur as a result. A more common example of convection is the process of heating water on a stove. In this case, heat is transferred from the stove element to the bottom of the pot to the water. Heat is transferred from the hot water at the bottom to the cooler water at the top by convection. At the same time, the cooler, denser water at the top sinks to the bottom, where it is subsequently heated. This circulation creates the movement typical of boiling water. Convection currents created by the combining or colliding of cold and warm air masses is one factor responsible for storms and circular rotation of the air in tornados and hurricanes. Ocean currents are also caused by the collision of cold water and warm water masses in the oceans (Cavallo, 2001). See also: *http://www.physicstutorials.org/home/heat-temperature-and-thermal-expansion/heat-transfer-via-conduction-convection-and-radiation.*

Electricity and Magnetism

When you arrange an energy source, such as a battery, a wire, and a light bulb (or motor, or bell, or any electrical device) such that all *metal* parts are touching (metal is a good conductor of energy) in a *circle*—the bulb will light (the motor will run, the bell will ring, and so on). Arranging the items in this circle creates an "*electric circuit.*" The energy from the battery or other energy source is able to "flow" or be transferred through the metal wires and parts of the circuit. A **closed circuit** is when all metal parts are touching and the electrical charge is able to continue to be transferred through the circuit. A light switch or other "on button" closes the circuit and allows the electricity to flow. An **open circuit** is when there is a break someplace in the flow of electricity through the circuit. A switch or "off button" opens the circuit and stops the electricity flow. When you ring a doorbell, you are closing the circuit or allowing all metal parts to touch and send electricity through it to make the bell ring; when you let go of the doorbell button, the circuit is open, and so the flow of electricity stops and so does the bell's ringing.

Lightning is a form of *static* electricity which means it is not "flowing" or being transferred in the way it is through a metal wire, but is caused by friction, much the same as walking across a carpet in socks and getting a shock when a metal doorknob is touched. In both kinds of electricity, the electrons in the atoms of the substance, which are negatively charged, are pulled away from their atom's nucleus, giving the object, or cloud, a negative charge. The negative charge is quickly attracted to a positive charge—in the case of lightning, that positive charge could be something (or someone!) on the ground. The positive charge quickly jumps toward the negative charge and the negative charge quickly jumps toward the positive charge, and a flash of lighting is seen and clap of thunder is heard; or in the case of the doorknob, a spark and a snap sound. Electric circuits are just a way to channel the electricity and the opposing charges through a conductor such as metal wires to allow us to use the energy to do work and to transform the energy into different forms such as sound (a radio), light (light bulbs), mechanical (machinery), and/or heat energy.

There is a difference between magnetic fields and electric fields. A field occurs around an object known as a magnet, which attracts and repels other magnetic objects. The strength of a magnet and its magnetic field is due to the material it is made of. In a magnet, as we mentioned, the particles (atoms, molecules) are lined up in the same direction (imagine a marching band), which creates the north and south "poles" of the magnet. Gravity is different in that its strength depends on the mass of the object (Earth, the Moon); however, the particles are still lined up in the same direction at any given time in history such to create a gravitational field with its north and south poles. The magnetic field on Earth is due to its iron core. The gravitational field surrounding Earth protects it from radiation that may bombard our planet from space, such as solar winds.

The current that moves through a wire in an electric circuit also acts like a magnet. It creates a negative and positive side to objects within the field, as in an **electromagnet.** A classroom electromagnet is created by attaching the ends of a wire to the positive and negative ends of a battery, and winding the wire on an iron nail. The nail will become an electromagnetic and be attracted to metal objects (e.g., paper clips). The more coils around the nail, the stronger the electromagnet. For more information see: *http://www.physics4kids.com/files/elec_magneticfield.html.*

Light Energy

Light energy, and all energy for that matter, travels in waves and in a straight-line path. The electromagnetic spectrum shows the different wavelengths and frequencies of energy, including the small portion that is visible light. The electromagnetic spectrum includes, for example, microwaves, X-rays, radio waves, infrared radiation, visible light waves, and ultraviolet radiation, all of which have different wavelengths and frequencies that distinguish one type of wave from another (See: *http://imagine.gsfc.nasa.gov/docs/science/know_l1/emspectrum.html* and *http://missionscience.nasa.gov/ems/01_intro.html*).

Visible light is the wavelength of light we can see, which our eyes see as white light. However, this white light is composed of a host of other wavelengths of light that our eyes cannot always distinguish, which we know as the visible light spectrum, or a rainbow. The colors of white light include red, orange, yellow, green, blue, indigo, and violet (although some sources now eliminate indigo as separate from violet), or ROYGBIV. When light, again, traveling in a straight line, hits an object or substance and is *bent*, it is called **refraction**. The bending of light waves may result in the colors of light in the spectrum becoming visible, as when we see a rainbow in the sky (the water molecules in the air bend the light) or when light travels through cut glass such as with a prism. **Reflection** is when light waves bounce back, as when looking in a mirror. The principles of reflection and refraction are used in periscopes and telescopes in order to be able to see objects we may otherwise not be able to see. They are often popular in magic shows when objects are said to "disappear." In actuality, the light of the object has been refracted or reflected to a place away from our eyes so that we can no longer see it.

Refraction is also used to our advantage through concave and convex lenses. Concave or convex lenses work such that when light passes through, the lenses change the focal point. The eye contains a lens, but when light passing through the eye cannot properly focus on the "screen" known as the retina, the object being viewed may be blurred. Concave or convex lenses are used in eyeglasses to adjust and correct the focal point. These lenses are also used in cameras, microscopes, and telescopes. A spoon is an example of both a concave and a convex lens—if you look into the concave side, you will see yourself upside down. If you look into the convex side of the spoon, you will see yourself right side up. This is due to refraction (and reflection) of light. For more on this topic, see *http://www.myschoolhouse.com/courses/O/1/36.asp.*

Sound Energy

Sound also travels in waves. Sounds are caused by vibrations, such as a guitar string (or a rubber band), or banging on a drum or cymbal. Sound has a certain wavelength, frequency, pitch, and amplitude (loudness). Sound waves must travel through a medium, which may be solid, liquid, or gas. Sound travels best through solids because there are more molecules (particles) to vibrate, and least well through gases.

The types of sound waves are longitudinal and transverse. **Longitudinal waves** move parallel to the direction the wave moves, and **transverse waves** move perpendicular to the direction of the wave. For more information and animations on sound waves, see *http://www.acs.psu.edu/drussell/demos/waves/wavemotion.html.*

COMPETENCY 010: ENERGY TRANSFORMATIONS AND CONSERVATION

The teacher understands energy transformations and the conservation of matter and energy.

Electricity

Electricity is the flow of electrons or electric power or charge. The basic unit of charge is based on the positive charge of the proton and the negative charge of the electron. Energy occurs naturally in the atmosphere through light. However, it is not feasible to capture that type of energy. The electricity that we use comes from secondary sources because it is produced from the conversion of primary (natural) sources of energy like fossil fuels that are **nonrenewable** (natural gas, coal, and oil) and nuclear, and **renewable** resources such as wind and solar energy. All sources of energy are used to produce a common result—to turn a turbine that generates electricity (see: *http://www. energyquest.ca.gov/story/chapter06.html*). Electricity that is generated can then be sent through wires for human use, and can be transformed into other forms of energy, including sound, light, heat, and force.

Conservation of Energy

The main principle of energy conservation states that energy can change form but cannot totally disappear. For example, the stored energy in a battery can be used to turn on a flashlight. In this case, chemical energy stored in the battery (potential energy) is transformed into light energy being emitted from the bulb (kinetic energy). Another example of energy conservation is placing merchandise on shelves. Energy was used to do the work (placing merchandise on a shelf) and it was stored as potential energy. Potential energy in turn can be converted to kinetic energy when the merchandise is pushed back to the floor. In this case, work was recovered completely, but often the recovered energy is less than the energy used to do the work. This loss of energy can be caused by friction or any kind of resistance encountered in the process of doing the work. For example, as a vehicle's tires roll across the pavement, doing the work of moving forward, they encounter friction. This friction causes heat energy to be released, as well as kinetic energy.

In essence, energy cannot be created or destroyed, only changed in form. Likewise, matter cannot be created or destroyed, only changed in form. Thus, energy from the Sun is changed, for example, to chemical energy when plants use the energy to make glucose in photosynthesis. The energy from the Sun is stored in the chemical bonds of the glucose molecule and will be released for use by the organism—the plant itself, or any organism that eats the plant and its glucose—when the molecule's chemical bonds are "broken" by oxygen in cell respiration and/or stored in another chemical form known as ATP. Likewise, electrical energy comes from burning, or breaking the bond of carbon-based molecules as in fossil fuels. This electricity generated is then transformed to another form by first capturing and sending that electrical energy through metal wires originating at the power-generating plant, and sending it in a complete, closed circuit to homes, businesses, and industries. There the electrical energy may be transformed to sound, heat, light, and/or mechanical energy. In all cases, the energy is not lost, it is changed in form.

It is important to conserve matter and energy generated from fossil fuels as these are non-renewable sources and will one day be expended. It is also important to continue exploring alternative, renewable forms of energy and electricity generation to meet our society's energy demands and maintain our Earth's clean air and water supplies.

Key Principles of the Physical Science Competencies

Following are key principles of the physical science competencies for EC–6:

- To help students develop higher-order thinking skills, teachers need to guide students to analyze research data and make extrapolations or inferences based on data analysis.

- Matter is anything that has mass and takes up space.

- Mass is the amount of matter something contains.

- Volume refers to the amount of space taken up by an object.

- The states of matter are solid, gas, liquid, and plasma.

- There are 118 basic kinds of matter called elements.

- Elements are made up of atoms. An atom is the smallest part of matter.

- A compound is a kind of matter made up of two or more elements. A chemical formula describes the kinds of elements present in a compound. The chemical formula of water is H_2O because it has two molecules of hydrogen and one molecule of oxygen.

- Physical properties of matter are the characteristics that can be seen or measured without changing the material.

- Chemical properties of matter are the characteristics that can only be seen when the material changes and new materials are formed; for example, wood burns and turns into ashes. A chemical property of wood is its ability to burn.

- Water boils at 212 degrees Fahrenheit or 100 degrees Celsius, and it freezes at 32 degrees Fahrenheit or 0 degrees Celsius.

- Weight is the amount of gravitational force exerted over an object.

- When measuring dry chemicals on a balance scale, teachers should follow these steps: (1) Place and weigh a watch glass or dish, (2) place the dry chemical inside the watch glass or dish, and (3) subtract the weight of the glass or dish from the total to obtain the real weight of the chemical.

- Energy and matter may be changed from one form to another but are not lost.

- Heat is transferred by conduction, convection, and radiation.

- Electric circuits may be open or closed.

- Potential energy is stored energy; kinetic energy is energy in motion or actively being used. Activation energy is the energy it takes to change potential energy into kinetic energy.

- Light travels in waves and in a straight line; light may be refracted or bent and/or reflected.

- Sound is caused by vibrations.

COMPETENCY 011: STRUCTURE AND FUNCTIONS OF LIVING THINGS

The teacher understands the structure and function of living things.

Structure and Function

All living things carry on life functions such as respiration, nutrition, response, circulation, growth, excretion, regulation, and reproduction, all of which characterize them as *living* as opposed to nonliving. In addition, all living things are composed of the basic unit of life known as *cells*. Organisms, as well as individual cells of an organism and single-celled organisms, carry on these life functions using specialized structures. For example, earthworms carry on respiration through their moist skin; plants excrete gases from tiny pores on the underside of leaves called stomata; a single-celled amoeba ingests food by use of a "false foot" or pseudopodia; and insects respond to chemical attractants, called pheromones, of the opposite-sex insect for mating.

Animal and Plant Cells

Animal and plant cells are similar in appearance. Animal cells contain mitochondria, small round or rod-shaped bodies found in the cytoplasm of most cells. The main function of mitochondria is to produce the enzymes for the metabolic conversion of food to energy. This process consumes oxygen and is termed **aerobic respiration**.

Plants cells contain mitochondria, which allows them to carry on respiration where they use oxygen (O_2) to burn glucose ($C_6H_{12}O_6$), and excrete carbon dioxide (CO_2) and water (H_2O) just like animals. However, plants also have specialized organelles called chloroplasts used for capturing sunlight and use this energy, along with CO_2 taken into leaves from the atmosphere and H_2O taken up from the roots, to make glucose ($C_6H_{12}O_6$), a simple sugar (food), and excrete O_2. (The $C_6H_{12}O_6$ is then burned by O_2 in respiration as already described.) Chloroplasts contain chlorophyll in the food-making process, called **photosynthesis**. Photosynthesis is the process by which chlorophyll-containing organisms convert light energy into chemical energy.

Cell System

The cell is the basic unit of living organisms and the simplest living unit of life. Living organisms are composed of cells that have the following common characteristics:

- Have a membrane that regulates the flow of nutrients and water that enter and exit the cell

- Contain the genetic material (DNA) that allows for reproduction

- Require a supply of energy

- Contain basic chemicals to make metabolic decisions for survival

- Reproduce and are the result of reproduction

Eukaryotic and Prokaryotic Cells

There are two kinds of cells—prokaryotic and eukaryotic. **Prokaryotic cells** are the simplest and most primitive type of cells. They do not contain the structures typical of eukaryotic cells. Prokaryotic cells lack a nucleus and instead have one strand of deoxyribonucleic acid (DNA). Some prokaryotic cells have external whip-like flagella for locomotion or a hair-like system for adhesion. Prokaryotic cells come in three shapes: cocci (round), bacilli (rods), and spirilla or spirochetes (helical cells). Bacteria (also called Monera) are prokaryotic cells. For more information and animated illustrations of prokaryotic cells see *www.cellsalive.com/cells/bactcell.htm*.

Eukaryotic cells evolved from prokaryotic cells and in the process became structurally and biochemically more complex. The key distinction between the two cell types is that only eukaryotic cells contain many structures, or organelles, separated from other cytoplasm components by a membrane. The organelles within eukaryotic cells are the nucleus, mitochondria, chloroplasts, and Golgi apparatus. The nucleus contains the deoxyribonucleic acid (DNA) information. The mitochondria have their own membrane and contain some DNA information and proteins. They generate the energy for the cell. The chloroplast is a component that exists in plants only, allowing them to trap sunlight as energy for the process of photosynthesis. The Golgi apparatus secretes substances needed for the cell's survival. For information and animations on eukaryotic cells, see *www.cellsalive.com/cells/3dcell.htm*.

Classifications of Living Things

Living things are divided into five groups, or **kingdoms**: Monera (bacteria), Protista (protozoans), Fungi, Plantae (plants), and Animalia (animals).

Monera consists of unicellular organisms. It is the only group of living organisms made up of prokaryotic cells—the cells with a primitive organization system. Some examples of this organism are bacteria, blue-green algae, and spirochetes.

Protista contains a type of eukaryotic cell with a more complex organization system. This kingdom includes diverse, mostly unicellular organisms that live in aquatic habitats, in both freshwater and saltwater. They are not animals or plants but unique organisms. Some examples of Protista are protozoans and algae of various types. The Amoeba, Paramecium, and Euglena are in the Protista Kingdom.

Fungi are multicellular organisms with a sophisticated organization system—that is, containing eukaryotic cells. Fungi exist in a variety of forms and shapes. Because they do not have chlorophyll, they cannot produce food through photosynthesis. Fungi obtain energy, carbon, and water from digesting dead materials. Some examples of these types of organisms are mushrooms, mold, mildews, and yeast.

Plants are multicellular organisms with a sophisticated organization system. In addition to more familiar plants, moss and ferns also fall under this category. Plant cells have chloroplasts, a component that allows them to trap sunlight as energy for the process of photosynthesis. In photosynthesis, plants use carbon dioxide from the atmospheric environment and as the by-product of this process, supply the oxygen needed for the survival of animals.

Animals are also multicellular with multiple forms and shapes, and with specialized senses and organs. The Animalia kingdom is composed of organisms such as sponges, worms, insects, fish, amphibians, reptiles, birds, and mammals. Animals are the most sophisticated type of living organisms and represent the highest levels of evolution. Animals live in all kinds of habitats, and they are as simple as flies or as sophisticated as humans.

For additional information about living things, go to the website of the Behavioral Sciences Department of Palomar College, San Marcos, California, at *https://www2.palomar.edu/anthro/animal/default.htm*.

There are relationships between the characteristics, structures, and functions of organisms and corresponding taxonomic classifications. **Homologous** structures refer to different living organisms with structural or anatomical features that look or function in a similar way. The explanation is because the organisms were inherited from a common ancestor. **Non-homologous** structures between two organisms are similar in structure and function, but arose independently and not from a common ancestor. **Parallelism** is when there are similar structures between two organisms in different species that arose after diverging from a common ancestor. The common ancestor did not have the structure, but had the beginning features of that structure. **Convergence** is when similar structures developed after diverging from a common ancestor, but the common ancestor did not have the trait or the beginnings of the trait. **Analogous** structures have the same structure or function but arose from different ancestors, for example the wings of a bird and butterfly. For more detailed information see: *https://www.majordifferences.com*.

Life Cycles

Life traditionally begins with a seed or a fertilized egg, which goes through metamorphosis until the organism is fully formed. The development and growth of organisms can take days, months, or years, but eventually they all go through similar stages: creation, short cycle, reproducing once and then dying. Others, like vertebrates, spend more time in the reproductive stage.

Different living organisms may go through either **complete** or **incomplete** metamorphosis in the transformation to adult. Complete metamorphosis has four different life stages: egg, larva, pupa, and adult. Butterflies and darkling beetles go through complete metamorphosis. Incomplete metamorphosis has three different life stages: egg, nymph, and adult. A nymph is a smaller version of the adult but does not have wings. Grasshoppers go through incomplete metamorphosis.

Some examples of living organisms and the changes that they go through are presented in Table 6-5.

Table 6-5. Life Cycles of Common Organisms

Organism	Stage 1	Stage 2	Stage 3	Stage 4	Stage 5
Darkling Beetle	Egg (fertilized by male sperm)	Larva—called "mealworm" though not a true worm	Pupa—mealworm curls up into a pupated or sleeplike state	Darkling Beetle	Reproduction—organisms lay eggs Death of the adult
Butterfly	Egg (fertilized by male sperm)	Larva—called caterpillar	Pupa—caterpillar forms a cocoon or chrysalis	Butterfly	Reproduction—organisms lay eggs Death of the adult
Frog	Egg (fertilized by male sperm)	Embryo	Tadpole	Frog	Reproduction—organism lays eggs Death of the adult
Human	Egg (fertilized by male sperm)	Embryo/Fetus	Child through adolescent	Human adult	Reproduction—organisms have live birth of offspring Death of the adult
Tree	Seed with embryo or "baby plant" inside (egg or ovule inside of flower, ovary fertilized by male sperm, nuclei inside of pollen grains)	Sprout	Growing plant	Mature tree	Reproduction—Tree produces flowers with new seeds that are dispersed Death of the adult

Some of the most spectacular metamorphoses, which is described as changes in the organism from one stage of life to another, are experienced by insects, amphibians, and humans. Insects such as the darkling beetle and the butterfly go through drastic changes in a period of weeks. Frogs go through similar transmutations that allow them to move from an aquatic environment to land. Humans, on the other hand, begin life as microscopic beings and after nine months develop into a six- to nine-pound physically functional individual. The TEKS emphasize that during the elementary school grades, students should be exposed to the concept of life cycles for plants and animals, including humans.

Life Cycle of Plants

The life cycle of plants generally begins with seeds. Mature plants produce the seeds, which are transported through various means: wind, water, hitchhiking on animals, or ingested as food and released as droppings or waste. For the seeds to germinate, they need air, the right amount of heat or proper temperature specific for that seed, and water. They do not need light to *germinate* or initially sprout, but do need light to grow since they need to carry on photosynthesis for their source of food, and to mature into an adult plant that can reproduce new seeds. Growing plants also need the right kind of soil, sufficient water, and heat/light from the Sun. As part of the growth process, plants develop a root system for support and to extract the water and minerals they need from the soil. It is important to understand that fertilizers are *not* food for the plant—they only provide vitamins and minerals for the plant to help it remain healthy. The only food the plant has is what it makes for itself through photosynthesis.

Through the process of **photosynthesis**, a plant containing chlorophyll captures energy from the Sun and converts it into chemical energy. Part of the chemical energy is used for the plant's own survival, and the rest is stored in the stem and leaves. As part of the growth process, some plants produce flowers, which are pollinated by insects or through the wind. That is, the pollen, which contains sperm nuclei, is transferred from the male part of the flower, the stamen, to the female part of the flower, the pistil. Once pollination occurs, the sperm leaves the pollen and travels to the ovules or eggs inside the ovary of the pistil and fertilizes the ovules. The fertilized ovules become the seeds. The ovary swells to become the fruit, and the flower itself dies because it has now served its purpose. The fruits contain, carry, and protect the seeds until they are dispersed to a place where they can sprout, and the cycle of the plant continues.

For information on how this process can be presented to children in the elementary school grades search: "The Life Cycle of Plants" ("Science Lesson for 2nd Graders") at *www.youtube. com*. An inquiry-based curriculum on the life cycle of plants can also be found in the NSTA publication "Science and Children" by Cavallo (2005) titled *Cycling Through Plants*.

Life Cycle of Animals

Many animals come from eggs. For some animals, the egg grows inside the female animal and is fertilized by the male. For others such as most fish species, the eggs are fertilized by the male after they have been expelled from the female's body. When fertilized internally, the fertilized egg may be laid externally from the female as in many insects, reptiles, and birds, or it may remain in the body of the female until birth. The egg has an outer lining to protect the animal growing inside. Bird eggs have hard shells, while the eggs of reptiles, like the turtle, have hard but flexible coverings. With the appropriate care and heat, an egg will hatch. After hatching, in some species, the parents protect and feed the newborn until it can survive on its own; in other species, the eggs are left on their own to survive. On reaching adulthood, females begin laying eggs, and the cycle of life continues. Mammals are also conceived through egg fertilization, but the resulting embryo is kept inside the mother until it is mature enough for life outside the womb.

Needs of Living Organisms

Living organisms like plants and animals need to have ideal conditions for their survival. They need nutrients, the appropriate temperature, and a balanced ecosystem to survive and reproduce. A healthy ecosystem must contain an appropriate system for energy exchange or a food chain. The right combination of herbivorous and carnivorous animals is necessary for a healthy ecosystem. The food chain generally begins with the primary source of energy, the Sun. The Sun provides the energy for plants; plants in turn are consumed by animals; and animals are consumed by other animals. These animals die and serve as food sources for fungi and plants. When this balance is disrupted either by the removal of organisms or the introduction of nonnative species, the ecosystem is affected, forcing animals and plants to adapt or else die. Thus, the common basic needs of all living organisms for survival are *air, water, food,* and *shelter.*

Body Structure and Function

Cells are the basic unit of all living organisms. Within cells are specialized organelles that carry on all of the life functions at a microscopic/chemical level. For example, the mitochondria carry on cell respiration, and ribosomes assemble proteins for use both inside the cell and out. Teachers should know the parts of the cell, called organelles, and their functions, particularly, the nucleus, mitochondria, chloroplasts (plants only), ribosomes, Golgi, endoplasmic reticulum, vacuoles, and cell membranes. An explanation of organelles may be found at *https://www.cellsalive.com.*

Moving outward from the *cell*, it is important to know that cells communicate with one another on a chemical level and work together to perform specific functions. The shape of these groups of cells and activity levels differ according to their particular function in the body; for example, muscle cells are long and narrow so they may better respond to stimuli and contract. Groups of cells with similar functions are called *tissues.* Tissues are organized together to perform a specific life function. A complex system of tissues working together to carry on one of the body's life functions is an *organ.* A group of different organs working together to support and help carry out a life function and keep the organism alive is called an *organ system.* Examples of systems include the digestive system, the respiratory system, the immune system, the muscular system, the skeletal system, the nervous system, and the circulatory system. Organ systems are organized into an *organism.* The order of organization is as follows:

Cells → Tissues → Organs → Systems → Organ Systems → Organism

For more information on the structure and function of organisms, see *https://www.neok12.com/ Cell-Structures.htm.*

Systems of the Human Body

Musculoskeletal System

The human skeleton consists of more than 200 bones held together by connective tissues called ligaments. Movements are effected by contractions of the **skeletal muscles**, and skeletal muscles are arranged in pairs, such as the biceps and triceps of the upper arm. When one of the pair contracts, it causes a certain movement of the bones; in the meantime the opposing muscle relaxes. When the opposing pair of muscle contracts, a different movement of the bones occurs, and the original muscle of the pair relaxes. For example, when the biceps (the muscle on top of the upper arm) contracts, the arm bends upwards; when the opposing muscle of the pair, the triceps, contract, the arm extends. Skeletal muscles are attached to bones with specialized connective tissue called tendons.

The specialized connective tissue that attaches bones to other bones is called ligaments. The soft spongy tissue on the ends of bones is called **cartilage**. Muscular contractions are controlled by the nervous system.

In addition to skeletal muscle, the body also has muscles that are not part of the musculoskeletal system, thus not attached to bones. One such muscle type is called **smooth muscle**. Smooth muscle forms the inner linings of our digestive system and is controlled involuntarily by our autonomic (automatic) nervous system. A third type of muscle is **cardiac muscle**, which is the muscle of the heart, and is also controlled by our autonomic nervous system.

Nervous System

The nervous system has two main divisions: the somatic and automatic. The somatic allows the voluntary control of skeletal muscles, and the automatic, or involuntary, controls cardiac and glandular functions. **Voluntary movement** is caused by nerve impulses sent from the brain through the spinal cord to nerves to connecting skeletal muscles. **Involuntary movement** occurs in direct response to outside stimulus. Involuntary responses are called reflexes. For example, when an object presents danger to the eye, the body responds automatically by blinking or retracting away from the object.

Circulatory System

The circulatory system follows a cyclical process in which the heart pumps blood through the right chambers of the heart and through the lungs, where it acquires oxygen. From there it is pumped back into the left chambers of the heart, where it is pumped into the main artery (aorta), which then sends the oxygenated blood to the rest of the body using a system of veins and capillaries. Through the capillaries, the blood distributes the oxygen and nutrients to tissues, absorbing from them carbon dioxide, a metabolic waste product. Finally, the blood completes the circuit by passing through small veins, which join to form increasingly larger vessels. Eventually, the blood reaches the largest veins, which return it to the right side of the heart to complete and restart the process.

Immune System

The main function of the body's immune system is to defend itself against foreign proteins and infectious organisms. The system recognizes organisms that are not normally in the body and develops the antibodies needed to control and destroy the invaders. When the body is attacked by infectious organisms, it develops what we know as a fever. Fever is the body's way of fighting invading molecules. The raised temperature of a fever will kill some bacteria. The major components of the immune system are the thymus, lymph system, bone marrow, white blood cells, antibodies, and hormones.

Respiratory System

Respiration is carried out by the expansion and contraction of the lungs. In the lungs, oxygen enters tiny capillaries, where it combines with **hemoglobin** in the red blood cells and is carried to the tissues through the circulatory system. At the same time, carbon dioxide passes through capillaries into the air contained within the lungs.

Animals inhale oxygen from the environment and exhale carbon dioxide. Carbon dioxide is used by plants in the process of photosynthesis, which produces the oxygen that animals use again for survival.

Digestive and Excretory Systems

The energy required for sustenance of the human body is supplied through the chemical energy stored in food. To obtain the energy from food, it has to be fragmented and digested. Digestion begins at the moment that food is placed in the mouth and makes contact with saliva. Fragmented and partially digested food passes down the esophagus to the stomach, where the process is continued by the gastric and intestinal juices. Thereafter, the mixture of food and secretions makes its way down the small intestine, where the nutrients are extracted and absorbed into the bloodstream. The unused portion of the food goes to the large intestine and eventually is excreted from the body through defecation. For a detailed analysis of each component of the body system go to the Human Anatomy Online website at *www.innerbody.com/htm/body.html*.

Reproductive System

Students in the upper elementary grades (5 and 6) should know some basic biological facts about human reproduction. They should know that the body matures and develops in order for child-bearing to occur. The menstrual cycle should be understood by students, including what occurs in ovulation to prepare the egg cell, namely, the process of meiosis. In males, the process of meiosis occurs to produce the sperm cell. Students should know that these specialized cells, called gametes (egg and sperm), unite to form a fertilized egg, which grows and develops in distinct stages to produce new offspring.

COMPETENCY 012: REPRODUCTION AND THE MECHANISMS OF HEREDITY

The teacher understands reproduction and the mechanisms of heredity.

Reproduction

An organism may consist of only one cell, or it may comprise many billions of cells of various dimensions. For example, cells are complete organisms, such as the unicellular bacteria; others, such as muscle cells, are parts of multicellular organisms. All cells have an internal substance called cytoplasm—a clear gelatinous fluid—enclosed within a membrane. Each cell contains the genetic material containing the information for the formation of organisms. Cells are composed primarily of water and the elements oxygen, hydrogen, carbon, and nitrogen.

Growth in most organisms is caused by nuclear cell division (**mitosis**.) In mitosis the chromosomes (containing DNA, which is the genetic material of the cell or blueprint) first replicate—in humans the 46 chromosomes in the cell double. The cell then divides through a series of steps resulting in 2 new cells that each has the original 46 chromosomes, or the exact copy of the original. Through mitosis, new cells are made. Mitosis occurs in growth as well as the formation of scars, new bone cells, muscle cells, blood cells—in fact, any cell in the body throughout life.

However, in single-celled organisms, mitosis is the cell's form of reproduction—making exact copies of the DNA in each of the two "daughter" cells, and is often called binary fission. This type of reproduction is also called **asexual reproduction** because only one organism (the single cell) is involved and there is no exchange of genetic material or DNA. Thus, the two offspring cells, or daughter cells, are identical to the original or parent cell.

In humans and many other organisms, particularly mammals, another form of cell division occurs only in the reproductive organs (in most called the female ovaries and male testicles) where the DNA is replicated/copied; however, the cell divides *twice* in a process called **meiosis**. Meiosis is how sperm and egg cells are formed through a series of steps. The original cell in the female ovary or male testicle first duplicates (replicates) its 46 chromosomes (containing the genetic blueprint material, DNA) and then divides *twice,* the result is four cells with half the number of chromosomes, or 23 chromosomes each. In forming the egg cell, only one is a viable egg that can be fertilized and the remaining three are polar bodies that eventually dissolve. In the male, all four sperm cells that were formed by meiosis of the original cell are viable and capable of fertilizing the egg. The process is similar in other organisms; however, the number of chromosomes may be different, depending on the particular species—a similar process even occurs in plants, where the flower is the reproductive organ—the ovules are the egg cells, and the pollen contains the sperm.

This form of reproduction is known as **sexual reproduction**, because it requires the combination of DNA between two organisms of the same species (male, female). The fertilization of the egg by sperm cells occurs through copulation in vertebrates, and for fish and some amphibians it occurs through cross-fertilization. Cross-fertilization occurs outside the body; the female lays the eggs (ovum), and the males spray them with sperm to fertilize them.

Plant Reproduction

The reproduction of plants can also be divided into asexual and sexual mechanisms. Asexual reproduction of plants takes place by cutting portions of the plant and replanting them. Sexual reproduction involves seeds produced by female and male plants, which are then cross-pollinated with help from insects or other animals. As mentioned, the flower is the reproductive organ of the plant. The flower consists of several parts that are the male and female reproductive organs. Some flowers may have only the male part, and likewise, some flowers contain only the female part of the same species of plant/tree. So there actually can be a "male" tree and a "female" tree, for example. In the flower, the male reproductive organ is the stamen, which is divided into filament and anther. The filament simply holds up the anther, and the anther contains the pollen and in the pollen are the sperm nuclei. Flowers may also contain the female reproductive organ, or pistil, which consists of the ovary, style, and stigma. The ovary contains the egg cells, which in the flower are called ovules. The style is the tube above the ovary, and the stigma is the top of the style which has a sticky substance. The pollen needs to either be manually placed on the stigma, or blown there by the wind, or what usually happens, it needs to stick to the body of a bee or butterfly (who are actually in search of sugary nectar in the flower and not the pollen). When the pollen sticks to the body of the insect, it may then be transferred from the anther (male part) to the stigma (female part). In essence, the sperm nuclei then travel down the style until it reaches the ovules, where fertilization occurs. The fertilized egg then becomes the seed. The ovary of the flower may swell and become the fruit (as in a peach or apple). This process helps protect the seeds and also helps with seed dispersal (animals eat the fruit, the seed has a seed coat that protects it and is indigestible, the animals excretes the seed, unharmed, in its fecal matter). Seed germination—where the seed sprouts into a plant—requires the appropriate quantity of air, water, and heat.

Hereditary Material

DNA is the hereditary material of living organisms. It has as its smallest complete component what is called a nucleotide. A single nucleotide consists of the sugar deoxyribose, a phosphate molecule, and a nitrogen base molecule. There are four nitrogen bases that are paired in the double-helix structure of DNA. These nitrogen bases are adenine, thymine, guanine, and cytosine. In DNA, adenine always pairs with a nucleotide having thymine as its nitrogen base (A-T); and guanine always pairs with a nucleotide having cytosine as its nitrogen base (G-C), and vice versa (T-A; C-G).

In bacteria, also called monera or prokaryotic cells, DNA is in a single strand. In more complex organisms including protista, fungi, animals and plants, which are all composed of eukaryotic cells, the DNA is arranged in **chromosomes**, and these chromosomes are located in the nucleus (though new evidence has emerged in recent years that DNA is present in other cell organelles, particularly the mitochondria). The number of chromosomes in the cells of organisms varies from one species to another—but it is the same for all members of that species. Along the strands of DNA that exist inside of chromosomes, there are certain locations that direct specific functions of cells, including hereditary traits, called **genes**. Certain genes give the cell directions, in the developing embryo, for example, for the expression of traits such as eye color, hair color, and leg shape and size. In already developed organisms, such as the human adult, other genes (sections of DNA) direct the production of substances and control specific activities and functions. The production of insulin in pancreatic cells, for example, is controlled by certain genes in the chromosomes in the cells of the organ known as the pancreas. In inheritance and cell functions, traits can be controlled or determined by more than one gene, located on the same, or even on different chromosomes. Likewise, there may be several traits influenced by one single gene.

As discussed earlier, the fertilized egg that eventually grows into the organism that then goes through its respective life cycle to adult contains half the number of chromosomes from the female egg (mother) and half the number of chromosomes from the male sperm (father). In the human, there are 23 chromosomes in the egg and 23 in the sperm, so the fertilized egg and, therefore, the offspring (baby) has 46 chromosomes—which is the normal number for all cells in all organisms of the human species. The 23 chromosomes of the egg have an exact pair or match in the sperm. That matching chromosome contains genes with DNA that direct the same traits. So along the length of chromosome number 20, for example, in the egg cell, you will find it controls the same traits that are along the length of chromosome number 20 in the male sperm. However, the 23 chromosomes in the egg contain the specific qualities or characteristics of the mother; whereas, the 23 chromosomes in the sperm contain the specific qualities or characteristics of the father. Though more than one chromosome controls eye color—we will use one chromosome as an example. In one of the egg cell's chromosomes, there is a gene that controls eye color, and in the egg this eye color could be "blue." In the corresponding chromosome in the same location in the sperm cell, there will also be a gene for eye color, but the characteristic of that eye color may instead be "brown." So traits are located on the same number chromosome whether that chromosome originated from the egg or the sperm; however, the quality or characteristic may differ (that is, the pigment color that section of DNA or gene directs the cell to make). The gene for eye color and other traits that are the paired chromosomes in the same location are called **alleles**. When the egg is fertilized, the directions coded in the DNA alleles are set. In many alleles, one of the traits directed by the gene on one chromosome is **dominant**, and the other is **recessive**. The dominant trait is the one that typically "shows" or is *expressed* in the offspring. In the case of eye color, brown is usually dominant over blue eye color, so if one of the alleles is for "blue" eyes and the other allele from the other parent is for "brown" eyes, the offspring will show the dominant trait and have brown eyes. Again, it must be cautioned that many genes may direct eye color especially in an organism as complex as humans, but it is simply used as an example here. In addition, it is important to note that **environmental factors** play an important role in the expression (showing up) of traits in the offspring as they grow and develop. Sometimes environmental stressors, for example, can cause a genetic change in an organism that otherwise may not have been expressed, such as certain food allergies or intolerances.

For more genetics information and activities go to the U.S. National Library of Medicine website at *https://www.nigms.nih.gov/education/genes*.

COMPETENCY 013: ADAPTATIONS AND EVOLUTION

The teacher understands adaptations of organisms and theory of evolution.

Adaptations

Genetics plays an important role in the ability of organisms to be able to survive and thrive in their environment and, ultimately, produce new offspring where they can pass on similar genetic material, like that which allowed *them* to survive and thrive, and maybe survive and thrive even better. Some inherited traits, called **adaptations**, allow the organisms to best survive in their environment and others do not, and may even lead to their demise (and those prevent the prospect of future offspring). Adaptations do not suddenly arise or develop in the lifetime of organisms. They occur gradually in the species over time. For example, if a certain deer-like animal thousands of years ago was particularly fast—that is, it was born with stronger muscle tissue than most, and a better bone and muscle physical structure—perhaps it was better able to run away from predators and survive. Therefore, this deer-like animal was able to survive long enough for it to have offspring with similar genetic material. At the same time, those deer-like animals that were not born with the same muscular and structural soundness as this one were killed as prey before they could reproduce. The animal that was best adapted to its environment (needing to run from predators) was the first deer-like animal. In time, those animals that are best suited in this, as well as in other ways, are the organisms that survive, as do their offspring. Those not well adapted perish. It is also the case that the organism that survives will breed with another that also has better adapted characteristics, and was also able to survive in the natural environment. A change or **mutation** in the genetic material—that is, the genes that direct the development of a trait—may give rise to a new characteristic that either is or is not better suited for the environment. In the case that it is better suited, the organism will survive and produce offspring with this same mutation. Over the years, mutations that are better suited to the environment may make the organism appear quite different than it did hundreds, thousands, and millions of years earlier. If the environment itself changes, however, organisms that were able to survive under the previous conditions (climate, water supply, vegetation, landscape) may be unable to survive in the new environmental conditions. Thus, a catastrophic event, such as perhaps a large asteroid striking the Earth, could change the environmental conditions and leading either to the extinction of organisms, or the survival of organisms that would not have survived under the conditions before the strike. Likewise, selective breeding, which is human selection of which organisms breed with another, and thus, control of the genetic material that is passed onto offspring, also effects the change over time of organisms. The combination of genetics, adaptations, changes over time, mutations, selective breeding, and environmental conditions/changes contribute to the concept known as evolution. For more detailed information on evolution see: *https://evolution.berkeley.edu/evolution-101.*

COMPETENCY 014: ORGANISMS AND THE ENVIRONMENT

The teacher understands the relationships between organisms and the environment.

Ecology

Ecology studies the relationship of organisms with their physical environment. The physical environment includes light, heat, solar radiation, moisture, wind, oxygen, carbon dioxide, nutrients, water, and the atmosphere. The biological environment describes living and nonliving organisms in the ecosystem. There are three main components of an ecosystem:

- **Producers** are green plants that produce oxygen and store chemical energy for consumers.

- **Consumers** are animals, both herbivores and carnivores. The herbivores take the chemical energy from plants, and carnivores take the energy from other animals or directly from plants.

- **Decomposers**, like fungi and bacteria, are in charge of cleaning up the environment by decomposing and freeing dead matter for recycling back into the ecosystem.

Maintaining a Healthy Balance

A successful ecosystem requires a healthy balance among producers, consumers, and decomposers. This balance relies on natural ways to control populations of living organisms and is maintained mostly through competition and predation.

Competition

When a shared resource is scarce, organisms must compete to survive. The competition, which occurs between animals as well as between plants, ensures the survival of the fittest and the preservation of the system.

Predation

Predation is the consumption of one living organism, plant or animal, by another. It is a direct way to control population and promote natural selection by eliminating weak organisms from the population. As a consequence of predation, predators and prey evolve to survive. If an organism cannot evolve to meet challenges from the environment, it perishes.

Adaptation for Survival

Changes in the environment create a situation where only those organisms with structures and functions suited to that particular environment survive and produce offspring with those same structures and functions, and those that do not have features that enable them to survive will perish before they are able to reproduce. If the environment changes, whether gradually or suddenly (e.g., a volcanic eruption that darkens the sky for a long period of time), then it may be the case that species that once could survive in the former environment can no longer survive in the current environmental conditions. Thus organisms with different structures and features are present in today's environment where they would not have survived in an earlier environment, and vice versa. For example, over thousands of years, the anteater species and its offspring were able to survive better if they had a long snout to be able to reach for ants, and frogs with a long, sticky tongue to catch flies were better able to survive and produce offspring with the same characteristics. Adaptation for animals, plants, and even humans is a matter of life and death.

Changes in the food chain of animals is another occurrence that may lead to a change in behaviors and adapt to new conditions. For example, because their habitats are destroyed when land is developed by humans, raccoons and opossums have learned to coexist with humans and to get new sources of food. Bears have managed to successfully adapt to colder climates by hibernating during the winter and living on the fat they accumulate during the rest of the year. Other animals, like the chameleon or the fox, have developed camouflage to hide from predators. Humans are not exempt from the need to adapt to new situations. For example, humans have had to adapt and use tools to produce, preserve, and trade the food supplies they needed to sustain them. All these examples represent ways in which organisms adapt to deal with challenges in their ecosystem.

One adaptation of living organisms is the ability to live together forming different kinds of relationships to one another. Living and interacting in a long-term way that in some way impacts the survival and/or well-being of one or more organism in the relationships is called **symbiosis**. There are different kinds of symbiotic relationships between organisms. When both species benefit from the relationship, the interaction is called **mutualism**. An example of mutualism is the presence of a certain kind of protozoan that lives in the guts of termites – the termites benefit by having assistance in digesting wood, and the protozoans have a living environment and food source. **Parasitism** is a symbiotic when one organism benefits but the other organism is harmed. Examples are bacteria or other organisms that cause illness or even eventual death in a living organism, such as staphylococcus bacteria invading the bloodstream or tapeworms in the intestines of animals or humans. **Commensalism** is a third type of symbiosis in which one organism species benefits and the other is neither harmed nor benefitted, basically unaffected. An example is the barnacles that attach to sea organisms, such as turtles. The barnacles have a place to anchor, yet the turtle is essentially unharmed by their presence. For more information see: *https://study.com/academy/lesson/symbiotic-relationships-mutualism-commensalism-amensalism.html.*

Key Principles of the Life Science Competencies

Following are key principles of the life science competencies for EC–6:

- When working with animals, teachers are ethically responsible for their well-being. Teachers need to provide an adequate environment for the survival and development of animals under their care.

- By observing the development of frogs and butterflies, students directly acquire information on the life cycles. Students can also observe how organisms adapt to their environment.

- Fungi obtain energy, carbon, and water from dead material. Fungi do not have chlorophyll, so they cannot produce food through photosynthesis.

- Chromosomes contain the genetic code, or DNA.

- Mitosis describes the process of a cell splitting to create two identical cells.

- Meiosis is the process of cells dividing to produce the egg and sperm cells, each with half the number of chromosomes as the parent cell so they are ready to restore the normal number of the species upon fertilization.

- Photosynthesis is the process of capturing, storing, and converting solar energy. It is also the source of oxygen in the atmosphere.

- Insects have three main parts: head, thorax, and abdomen.

- Humans have several body systems, including the musculoskeletal, nervous, circulatory, immune, respiratory, and digestive/excretory systems.

- Adaptations are features or characteristics of an organism that best help it survive in its environment.

- Organisms in the environment depend upon one another for survival and are inextricably linked in the ecosystem.

COMPETENCY 015: STRUCTURE AND FUNCTION OF EARTH SYSTEMS

The teacher understands the structure and function of Earth systems.

Structure and Composition of the Earth (Geology)

Landform Characteristics

The formation of deserts, mountains, rivers, oceans, and other landforms can be described in terms of geological processes. Mountains are formed by colliding plates. For example, the Appalachian Mountains in the United States were formed 250 million years ago when the tectonic plate carrying the continent of Africa collided with the plate carrying the North American continent (Badder et al., 2000). Rivers and natural lakes form at low elevations where rainfall collects and eventually runs down to the sea. The sediment gathered by the rivers in turn accumulates at river mouths to create deltas. These are both constructive and destructive processes that form the Earth. Constructive processes include those that build mountains, such as the gradual (over millions of years) collision and crushing together of the Earth's tectonic plates. Destructive processes include weathering and erosion — the wearing down of mountains and rock by forces such as water, wind, and ice.

Layers of the Earth

The average circumference of the Earth at the equator is 25,902 miles, and its radius is about 3,959 miles. The Earth is divided into three main parts:

- The **crust** is the outer portion of the Earth where we live. The thickness of the crust varies from about 3 miles to 40 miles, depending on the location. It contains various types of soil, metals, and rocks. The crust is broken down into several floating tectonic plates. Movements of these plates cause earthquakes and changes in landforms.

- The **mantle** is the thickest layer of the Earth located right below the crust. It is composed mostly of rocks and metals. The heat in the mantle is so intense that rocks and metals melt, creating magma and the resulting lava that reaches the surface.

- The **core** is the inner part of the Earth. It is composed of a solid **inner core** and an **outer core** that is mostly liquid. The inner core is made of solid iron and nickel. Despite temperatures in the inner core that resemble the heat on the surface of the Sun, this portion of the Earth remains solid because of the intense pressure there.

For more information about the layers of the Earth, go to the following website: *www.scec.org/ education.*

Continental Drift

In 1912, the German scientist Alfred Wegener proposed that all the continents were previously one large continent but then broke apart and drifted through the ocean floor to their present locations. Wegener's theory of continental drift is the basis of today's concept of plate tectonics.

Tectonic Plates

According to the theory of plate tectonics, the surface of the Earth is fragmented into large plates. These plates are in continuous motion, floating on the liquid mantle and always changing in size and position. The edges of these plates, where they move against each other, are sites of intense geologic activity, which results in earthquakes, volcanoes, and the creation of mountains. The generator for the movement of the continents and the Earth's plates is the mid-Atlantic ridge— a huge volcanic mountain range on the floor of the Atlantic Ocean that is continuously erupting and pushing the plates apart in opposite directions from each other. The plates that cover the surface of the Earth are constantly colliding because of the ocean floor spreading initiated at the mid-Atlantic ridge. The boundaries of the plates may be **convergent** or **divergent**. Convergent plates are coming together, whereas divergent plates are moving apart. When one convergent plate moves underneath another plate, it is called subduction or a **subduction zone**. A subduction zone creates a deep trench, such as that the oceanic trench located of the western coast of South America. When one convergent plate cannot move beneath another, the plates still collide, but in this case uplift occurs, which forms mountain ranges. This type of convergent zone is a **collisional boundary** and can be found, for example in Nepal where the Himalayan Mountains are the result of two plates converging/colliding. The mid-Atlantic ridge, where ocean floor spreading is occurring, is a divergent zone. For more information go to *https://www.nationalgeographic.com/science*.

Forces That Change the Surface of the Earth

Three main forces and processes change the surface of the Earth: weathering, geological movements, and the creation of glaciers.

Weathering

Weathering is the process of breaking down rock, soils, and minerals through natural, chemical, and biological processes. Two of the most common examples of physical weathering are exfoliation and freeze thaw.

- **Exfoliation** occurs in places like the desert when the soil is exposed first to high temperatures, which causes the soil to expand, and then to cold temperatures, which makes the soil contract. The stress of these changes causes the outer layers of rock to peel off.

- **Freeze-thaw** breaks down rock when water gets into rock joints or cracks and then freezes and expands, breaking the rock. A similar process occurs when water containing salt crystals gets into the rock. Once the water evaporates, the crystals expand and break the rock. This process is called salt-crystal growth.

Weathering can be caused by chemical reactions. Two of the most common examples of chemical weathering are acid formation and hydration. Acid is formed under various conditions. For example, sulfur and rain are combined to create acid rain, which can weather and change the chemical composition of rock. Hydration occurs when the minerals in rock absorb water and expand sometimes changing the chemical composition of the rock. For example, through the process of hydration, a mineral like anhydrite can be changed into a different mineral, namely gypsum.

Erosion

After weathering, a second process called erosion can take place. **Erosion** is the movement of sediment from one location to the other through the use of water, wind, ice, or gravity. The Grand Canyon was created by the processes of weathering and erosion. The water movement (erosion) is responsible for the canyon being so deep, and the weathering process is responsible for its width (Badder et al., 2000).

Earthquakes and Geologic Faults

The movement of the Earth's plates has forced rock layers to fold, creating mountains, hills, and valleys. This movement causes **faults** in the Earth's crust, breaking rocks and reshaping the environment. When forces within the Earth cause rocks to break and move around geologic faults, earthquakes occur. A fault is a deep crack that marks the boundary between two plates. The San Andreas Fault in central California is a well-known origin of earthquakes in the area. The epicenter of an earthquake is the point on the surface where the quake is the strongest. The **Richter scale** is used to measure the amount of energy released by the earthquake. The severity of an earthquake runs from 0 to 9 on the Richter scale. Small tremors occur constantly, but every few months, a major earthquake occurs somewhere in the world. Scientists are researching ways to predict earthquakes, but their predictions are not always accurate.

Volcanoes

Volcanoes are formed by the constant motion of tectonic plates. This movement creates pressure that forces magma from the mantle to escape to the surface, creating an explosion of lava, fire, and ash. The pressure of the magma and gases creates a monticule, or a small cone, that eventually grows to form a mountain-like volcano. Volcanic activity can create earthquakes, and the fiery lava can cause destruction.

Gravity

Gravity is the force of attraction that exists between objects. Gravity keeps the Earth in its orbit by establishing a balance between the attraction of the Sun and the speed at which the Earth travels around it. However, gravity is also responsible for many of the Earth's forces that change the land. For example, when ice melts on the tops of mountains, it is because of gravity that the water will form streams and rivers that flow down the mountain, eventually making its way to the lowest point. Some of the main functions of gravity are listed here:

- Keeping the Earth's atmosphere, oceans, and inhabitants from drifting into space

- Pulling the rain to the rivers and eventually to the sea

- Guiding the development and growth of plants

- Affecting the way that our bones and muscles function

For information about the Earth and space, go to the official website of the National Aeronautics and Space Administration (NASA) at *www.nasa.gov*. This site includes special sections for children, K–12 students, and teachers.

Surface Water and Groundwater

Surface water is the water in streams, lakes and rivers, and all water that is on the surface of the land. Groundwater is water that seeps beneath the surface of the land and forms an underground "river" of water. The groundwater seeps into the soil until it reaches an impermeable layer of rock. The water stays on top of this layer and is a source of drinking water. This water may be tapped into via aquifers and wells. For more information, visit the U.S. Geological Survey at *http://water. usgs.gov/ogw/gwsw.html.*

The Earth's Atmosphere

The Earth is surrounded by a large mass of gas called the **atmosphere**. Roughly 348 miles thick, atmosphere supports life on the Earth and separates it from space. Among the many functions of the atmosphere are these:

- Absorbing energy from the Sun to sustain life

- Recycling water and other chemicals needed for life

- Maintaining the climate, working with electric and magnetic forces

- Serving as a vacuum that protects life

The atmosphere is composed of 79 percent nitrogen, 20 percent oxygen, and 1 percent other gases. These other gases include argon, and also water, greenhouse gases like ozone, and carbon dioxide. The Earth's atmosphere has five layers. The layer closest to the Earth is called the troposphere, and the weather we experience occurs in this layer. For more information on the atmosphere, NASA's Space Place at *https://spaceplace.nasa.gov/atmosphere/en/.*

Natural and Human Influences on Earth Systems

It is important to understand that many natural processes on Earth can change its systems. For example, earthquakes and volcanoes can be destructive and change the structure and composition of the landscape. Tsunamis, an enormous wall of water that crashes into shorelines caused by earthquakes under bodies of water such as oceans, can create a dramatic change in that shoreline. However, human influences may also change Earth systems. The destruction of the rainforests, called deforestation can change the structure and composition of the land, and on a larger scale, affect the balance of atmospheric gases including carbon dioxide and oxygen levels. Carbon dioxide emissions from factories, automobiles, and airplanes, as examples, may play a role in changing the atmospheric composition as well. Carbon dioxide, considered a "greenhouse gas," tends to trap heat energy and result in an overall warming of the atmosphere, which has an impact on climate and plant growth that in turn affects all living organisms on Earth. There are many natural and human influences that contribute to the increase of greenhouse gases in the atmosphere, producing what is known as "global warming." Other greenhouse gases include methane (CH_4) and ozone (the molecule O_3), which are components of smog when at the surface of the Earth.

It is important to distinguish global warming and the ozone that is in smog from the destruction of the ozone layer (hole in the ozone layer), which are two entirely distinct phenomena. Ozone forms a layer at the top of the atmosphere that blocks harmful ultraviolet rays from the Sun from reaching the Earth's surface ("good ozone"). The "hole" in the ozone layer means there is a destruction of this ozone layer, and now harmful ultraviolet radiation is reaching Earth's surface where this hole is present. Chlorofluorocarbons, which are found in aerosols, contribute to the destruction of the ozone layer. For more information on greenhouse gases and ozone, go to *http://hvo.wr.usgs.gov.*

COMPETENCY 016: CYCLES IN EARTH SYSTEMS

The teacher understands cycles in Earth systems.

Rock Types

The hard, solid part of the Earth's surface is called rock. Rocks are made of one or more minerals. Rocks like granite, marble, and limestone are extensively used in the construction industry. They can be used in floors, buildings, dams, highways, or the making of cement. Rocks are classified by the way they are formed. Here are descriptions of the three types of rock:

- **Igneous** rocks are crystalline solids that form directly from the cooling of magma or lava. The composition of the magma determines the composition of the rock. **Granite** is one of the most common types of igneous rocks and is created from magma (inside the Earth). Once magma reaches the Earth's surface, it is called lava. The cooling lava forms different rocks depending on composition and the rate of cooling. A rock that has cooled quickly, for example, may have a glassy look, and is called **obsidian**. *https://www.msnucleus.org/membership/slideshows/volcano.html.*

- **Sedimentary** rocks are called secondary rocks because they are often the result of the accumulation of small pieces broken off from preexisting rocks and then pressed into a new form. Sedimentary rock is usually formed when sediments in water settle to the floor of that body of water, and are pressed as more layers on top, compacting the sediments into different rock types according to the level of compaction and pressure applied (e.g., sandstone, shale, slate). See: *https://www.sciencekids.co.nz/sciencefacts/earth/sedimentaryrocks.html.*

- **Metamorphic** rocks are also secondary rocks formed from igneous, sedimentary, or other types of metamorphic rock. When hot magma or lava comes in contact with rocks or when buried rocks are exposed to pressure and high temperatures, the result is metamorphic rocks. For example, exposing limestone to high temperatures creates marble. The most common metamorphic rocks are slate, gneiss, and marble. For more information on rocks and the rock cycle (next section), go to *https://www.learner.org/series/interactive-rock-cycle/.*

There are three types of sedimentary rocks (for greater detail and illustrations, visit Geology.com at *https://geology.com/rocks/sedimentary-rocks.shtml*):

- **Clastic** sedimentary rocks are made when pieces of rock, mineral, and organic material fuse together. These are classified as conglomerates, sandstone, and shale.

- **Chemical** sedimentary rocks are formed when water rich in minerals evaporates, leaving the minerals behind. Some common examples are gypsum, rock salt, and some limestone.

- **Organic** sedimentary rocks are made from the remains of plants and animals. For example, coal is formed when dead plants are squeezed together. Another example is a form of limestone rock composed of the remains of organisms that lived in the ocean.

Rock Cycle

The formation of rock follows a cyclical process. For instance, rocks can be formed when magma or lava cools down, creating igneous rocks. Igneous rocks exposed to weathering can break into sediment, which can be compacted and cemented to form sedimentary rocks. Sedimentary rocks are exposed to heat and pressure to create metamorphic rocks. Finally, metamorphic rocks can melt and become magma and lava again (Badder et al., 2000). An animation of the rock cycle and forces causing the changes in rock can be found at *https://serc.carleton.edu/NAGTWorkshops/ petrology/visualizations/rock_cycle.html*.

Minerals

Minerals are the most common form of solid material found in the Earth's crust. Even soil contains bits of minerals that have broken away from rock. To be considered a mineral, a substance must be found in nature and must never have been a part of any living organism. Minerals can be as soft as talc or as hard as emeralds and diamonds. Dug from the Earth, minerals are used to make various products:

- **Jewelry**—Gemstones such as amethysts, opals, diamonds, emeralds, topazes, and garnets are examples of minerals commonly used to create jewelry. Gold and silver are another type of mineral that can be used to create jewelry.

- **Construction**—Gypsum boards (drywall) are made of a mineral of the same name—gypsum. The windows in homes are made from another mineral, quartz.

- **Personal Use**—Talc is the softest mineral and it is commonly applied to the body in powder form.

Water Cycle

The hydrologic cycle describes a series of movements of water above, on, and below the surface of the Earth. This cycle consists of four distinct stages: storage, evaporation, precipitation, and runoff. It is the means by which the Sun's energy is used to transport water from the rivers and oceans to land masses, and through the atmosphere. The heat of the Sun evaporates the water and takes it to the atmosphere from which, through condensation, it falls as precipitation. As precipitation falls, water is filtrated back to underground water deposits called aquifers, or it runs off into storage in lakes, ponds, and oceans.

Tides

The word *tides* is used to describe the alternating rise and fall in sea level with respect to the land, produced by the gravitational attraction of the Moon and the Sun. Additional factors such as the configuration of the coastline, depth of the water, the topography of the ocean floor, and other hydrographic and meteorological influences may play an important role in altering the range, interval, and times of the arrival of the tides.

Nutrient Cycling

Nutrient cycling is among the most critical processes in an ecosystem. Nutrient cycling includes carbon and nitrogen cycles.

The **carbon cycle** is the capture of carbon from carbon dioxide in the atmosphere by plants to make glucose. When this glucose is used as food for the plant or other organisms, it is digested, then by respiration, broken apart again into carbon dioxide and returned to the atmosphere. The process continues in a life-sustaining process. More information on the carbon cycle can be found at *https://eo.ucar.edu/kids/green/cycles6.htm.*

For the **nitrogen cycle** it is important to recognize that most of the air we breathe is nitrogen, but it is not useful to us in that form, so it is exhaled. Lightning causes nitrogen in the air to combine with oxygen. Certain bacteria that live on the roots of certain plants, called nitrogen-fixing bacteria, are able to take nitrogen in this combined form with oxygen and make it available for use by plants. The plants can incorporate the nitrogen into their plant structure, and when eaten by animals and other organisms, this nitrogen becomes available for use. The nitrogen returns to the soil when the plant or other living organism dies and decays, releasing nitrogen gas back into the atmosphere. Nitrogen is important to all living things because it is a major component of DNA, RNA, and amino acids, which are the building blocks of proteins. A good animation of the nitrogen cycle can be found at Australia's Agriculture Victoria website at *http://vro.agriculture.vic.gov.au/dpi/vro/vrosite.nsf/pages/soilhealth_nitrogen-cycle.*

COMPETENCY 017: ENERGY IN WEATHER AND CLIMATE

The teacher understands the role of energy in weather and climate.

Weather

The elements of weather include interactions between wind, water (precipitation), wind speed and direction, air pressure, humidity, and temperature. Wind is caused by air masses that have different amounts of heat (temperatures), where there may be a warm air mass that is moving toward a cold air mass. Air pressure is related to both the amount of water in the air mass and its temperature (heat content), in that warm air has higher pressure than cold air—warm, high pressure air masses move toward cold, low pressure air masses. One simple rule is that energy always moves from *warmer to colder*. So, if you open a window on a hot summer day when your air conditioning is on, the cold does *not go out*—the warm air comes in. The same is true on a larger scale with warm and cold air masses.

Humidity is a measure of the percentage of water that is in the air. Dew point is the temperature at which the air needs to be for the water to condense out of the air in liquid form as precipitation; or it may be observed as "dew." In other words, air has a certain amount of water vapor (water in the gas state) in it (the percent is measured as humidity). That water vapor will turn to liquid water as temperatures drop overnight, in which we observe dew, or when a cold front moves in that lowers the temperature, which can result in a rain or snow storm. For resources and information on weather, go to the National Weather Service education website at *www.nws.noaa.gov*.

Wind is measured by an instrument called an **anemometer**. Air pressure is measured by a **barometer**; **rain gauges** and other instruments measure precipitation. Temperature is measured by a **thermometer**. Relative humidity is measured by a **psychrometer**. For more information on these instruments, see *http://www.weatherwizkids.com/weather-instruments.htm*.

Climate

Weather is the conditions of the atmosphere at a given, relatively short period of time. Climate, however, is the weather conditions in an area on a continuous, seasonal basis. The climate is more complex and can be measured by the average variety of weather conditions, such as temperature and precipitation, that occur seasonally in that geographic region of the world over a long period of time. More information, including the contrast between weather and climate, can be found at *www. nasa.gov/mission_pages/noaa-n/climate/climate_weather.html*.

Predicting Weather

Weather can be predicted by tracking weather patterns using maps and charts. These maps have special symbols that indicate, for example, warm and cold air masses, air pressure, and relative humidity in a region. By knowing how air behaves, such as cold air goes down and warm air rises, warmer air always moves toward colder air, and high pressure always moves outward toward lower pressure, we can track the weather and make predictions. Clouds are also an indication of the type of weather occurring in an area. For a summary of predicting cloud types see: *http://scied. ucar.edu/webweather/clouds/cloud-types*. For information on predicting weather with associated cloud types, see *http://sectionhiker.com/predicting-the-weather-using-clouds/*. Interpreting weather maps is an important skill for weather prediction. Symbols that can be found on a weather map include those indicating cold fronts, warm fronts, occluded fronts, isotherm lines, high and low pressure, and wind speed and direction. It is important to know these symbols and their meanings in predicting weather. The symbols and their meanings can be found at *http://www.wikihow.com/Read-a-Weather-Map* and *http://www.weatherwizkids.com/weather-forecasting.htm*.

The Earth's Surface and Position as a Factor in Weather and Climate

The Earth's surface is primarily water, and bodies of water affect the weather and climate of an area. Water has a high specific heat, which means that it takes longer to take in heat and longer to release the heat it has absorbed than any other material on Earth. Therefore, coastal areas tend to be warmer than areas inland or away from water, because the water moderates the temperature, even if the locations are at the same latitude. In the U.S., for example, areas in the middle of the country will have greater extreme differences in the cold temperatures in the winter and warm temperatures in the summer compared to a location at the same latitude near the ocean.

Large lakes, such as the Great Lakes also create a situation called "lake effect" in the winter—the air over the lake is relatively warm, and so can carry water vapor (evaporation). As soon as that air carrying water moves over land, however, it rapidly cools and releases its water (precipitation) in the form of snow over the land. Mountains and other landforms also have an effect on the weather. When air holding water hits a mountain side, it is forced upward which makes the air cool and therefore rain (or snow) on that side of the mountain. This is typically the western side of the mountain in the U.S. as in the mountain ranges of the Rocky Mountains. Once the precipitation is gone from that air mass and the air mass crosses the mountain to the other side, it drops back down and warms, but now it is dry air and so may result in an arid region or desert. The Gobi Desert, in Asia, is a result of this phenomenon.

On a much larger scale, the tilt of the Earth itself—as a planet—is responsible for weather and climate. The Earth is on a 23° tilt on its axis in space. This tilt means the Earth's North Pole is pointed *away* from the Sun when it is in one location in its orbit (path around the Sun), and *toward* the Sun when it is in the opposite orbital location. This tilt of the Earth results in the seasons, with extreme changes being in locations closer to the North and South poles. See more information on this topic at *https://www.windows2universe.org/kids_space/qearth_motion.html*.

COMPETENCY 018: SOLAR SYSTEM AND THE UNIVERSE

The teacher understands the characteristics of the solar system and the universe.

Properties and Characteristics of Objects in the Sky

Galaxies

Galaxies are large collections of stars, hydrogen, dust particles, and other gases. The universe contains countless galaxies. The solar system that includes Earth is part of a galaxy called the Milky Way.

Stars

Stars like the Sun are composed of large masses of hydrogen pulled together by gravity. The hydrogen, with strong gravitational pressure, creates fusion inside the star, turning the hydrogen into helium. The liberation of energy created by this process causes solar radiation, which makes the Sun glow with visible light, as well as forms of radiation not visible to the human eye.

The Earth-Sun-Moon System

Movements of Planet Earth

Earth performs two kinds of movement: rotation and revolution. **Rotation** describes the spinning of Earth on its axis. Earth takes approximately 24 hours to make a complete (360°) rotation, which creates day and night. The length of daylight hours varies from 9 to 15 hours, depending on Earth's location in its Revolution around the Sun. Thus, Earth spins on its axis or rotates, which causes day and night, and revolves in an orbit around the Sun, which causes seasons with differing hours of day and night. In the winter, and particularly at the winter solstice (around December 21), the ratio is close to 9 hours of daylight and 15 hours of darkness (night). In summer, at the Summer Solstice (around June 21) the ratio is reversed, with 15 hours of daylight and 9 hours of night. In the fall and spring seasons, the daylight and nighttime hours are closer to equal at 12 daylight hours, and 12 nighttime or darkness hours. The fall or "autumnal" equinox is near September 22, and the spring or "vernal" equinox is typically near March 21. For more information, visit the National Weather Service at *http://www.weather.gov/cle/Seasons.*

While Earth is rotating on its axis, it is also following an orbit around the Sun. This movement is called **revolution**. It takes a year, or 365¼ days, for Earth to complete one revolution. The tilt of Earth as it moves around the Sun and its curvature create **climate zones** and seasons. The zones immediately north and south of the equator are called the tropics— Cancer (north) and Capricorn (south). The Arctic Circle (North Pole) and Antarctic Circle (South Pole) are the area surrounding Earth's axis points. Latitude lines are imaginary horizontal lines around Earth, and longitude lines are likewise vertical lines around the Earth from the North to the South Poles. These lines form a grid that helps us locate an object (lake, mountain, city) by its position on Earth as determined by its specific latitude and longitude.

Phases of the Moon

During each lunar orbit around Earth (about 28 days), the Moon appears to go through several stages based on the portion of the Moon visible from Earth. The Moon does not have its own source of light but reflects the light from the Sun. The shape of the Moon varies from a full moon, when Earth is between the Sun and the Moon, to a new moon, when the Moon is located between the Sun and Earth. A description of the major stages of the Moon follows:

- **New Moon**—The Moon is not visible to Earth because the side of the Moon facing Earth is not being lit by the Sun.

- **Crescent Moon**—At this stage between the half moon and the new moon, the shape of the Moon is often compared to a banana.

- **Half Moon, or First Quarter**—During this stage, half of the Moon is visible.

- **Gibbous Moon**—In this stage, about three quarters of the Moon is visible.

- **Full Moon**—The whole Moon is visible from Earth.

- The term **blue moon** describes the appearance of two full moons in a single calendar month. Because this phenomenon happens relatively seldom, the expression "once in a blue moon" represents an infrequent event.

Components of Our Solar System

Solar System

The Sun is the center of our solar system, which contains eight planets, five dwarf planets, 200-plus satellites, or moons, that orbit the planets, and a large number of smaller bodies like comets and asteroids. Short definitions of these terms follow:

- **Planets** are large bodies orbiting the Sun.

- **Dwarf planets** are small bodies orbiting the Sun. For further explanation of the distinction between planets and dwarf planets, see *https://solarsystem.nasa.gov/planets/overview/*.

- **Satellites** are moons orbiting the planets. Earth has one moon whereas other planets may have no moons (Mercury, Venus) or many moons (Jupiter, Saturn).

- **Asteroids** are small dense objects or rocks orbiting our star, the Sun. The Asteroid Belt of our own solar system is located between Mars and Jupiter. Some theorize that the asteroids could be the remains of an exploded planet.

- **Meteoroids** are fragments of rock in space, most originating from the debris left behind by comets that burn up/vaporize upon entering Earth's atmosphere due to friction from the air molecules.

- **Comets** are small, icy objects traveling through space in an elongated, elliptical orbit around the Sun.

Planets

The objects in our solar system revolve around our star, which we call the Sun. The **inner solar system** contains the planets Mercury, Venus, Earth, and Mars, in this order. The **outer solar system** comprises the planets Jupiter, Saturn, Uranus, and Neptune, and a number of dwarf planets, including Pluto, Ceres, Eris, Haumea, and Makemake, with likely more yet to be found (see Table 6-6). More information about our solar system can be found at *http://starchild.gsfc.nasa.gov*.

Table 6-6. Planets and Dwarf Planets of Our Solar System

Inner Planets	Mercury, Venus, Earth, Mars
Outer Planets	Jupiter, Saturn, Uranus, Neptune
Dwarf Planets	Pluto, Ceres, Eris, Haumea, Makemake

Key Principles of the Earth Science Competencies

- Our solar system is part of the Milky Way, one of many galaxies in the universe.

- Minerals and rocks are commonly used in our daily life.

- The movement of tectonic plates creates intense geologic activity that results in earthquakes and volcanic activity.

- The Earth's atmosphere protects and preserves life.

- The water cycles are the movement and distribution of water within the Earth's atmosphere.

- The tilt of the Earth causes the seasons, and not the distance it is in its orbit away from the Sun.

- Human activities as well as natural processes impact the landscape and processes on Earth.

- Weather is the interaction of many factors, including air temperature, air pressure, and humidity. Weather is the conditions in the atmosphere at a given location and time.

- The solar system consists of the Sun, inner planets, outer planets, dwarf planets, satellites, asteroids, comets and meteoroids.

Sources

American Association for the Advancement of Science (1989). *Science for all Americans: A Project 2061 report on literacy goals in science, mathematics, and technology.* Washington, DC.

Anderson, L.W., Krathwohl, D.R., et al. (Eds.) (2001). *A Taxonomy for Learning, Teaching, and Assessing: A Revision of Bloom's Taxonomy of Educational Objectives.* Boston, MA: Allyn & Bacon (Pearson Education Group)

Badder, W., Peck, D., Bethel, L.J., Sumner, C., Fu, V. & Valentino, C. (2000). *Discovery works.* (Texas ed.). Boston: Houghton Mifflin.

Bloom, B.S. & Krathwohl, D.R. (1956). *Taxonomy of Educational Objectives: The Classification of Educational Goals, by a committee of college and university examiners. Handbook I: Cognitive Domain.* New York: Longmans, Green

Bybee, R., Buchwald, C.E., Crissman, S., Heil, D., Kuerbis, P., Matsumoto, C. & McInerney, J.D., (1989). *Science and technology education for elementary years: Frameworks for curriculum and instruction.* Washington, DC: The National Center for Improving Science Education.

Cavallo, A.M.L. (2001). Convection connections: Integrated learning cycle investigations that explore convection—the science behind wind and waves. *Science and Children, 38*, 20–25.

Cavallo, A.M.L. (2005). Cycling through plants. *Science and Children, 4, 22–27.*

Full Option Science System (FOSS). (2000). Lawrence Hall of Science, University of California, Berkeley, CA.

Lawson, A.E., Abraham, M.R., & Renner, J.W. (1989). *A theory of instruction: Using the learning cycle to teach science concepts and thinking skills.* NARST Monograph No. 1.

Marek, E.A., & Cavallo, A.M.L. (1997). *The learning cycle: Elementary school science and beyond* (Rev. ed.). Portsmouth, NH: Heinemann.

National Research Council (1996). *National Science Education Standards.* Washington, DC: National Academy Press.

National Science Teachers Association. (2003). *Standards for science teacher preparation: Skills of teaching* (Revised Version). Washington, DC: National Science Teachers Association.

National Science Teachers Association (NSTA). (2002). Elementary school science. Position paper. Retrieved, from *http://www.nsta.org/about/positions/elementary.aspx.*

National Science Teachers Association (1998). *Standards for Science Teacher Preparation: Skills of Teaching.* Washington, DC: National Science Teachers Association.

Piaget, J. (1964). Cognitive development in children: Piaget, development and learning.

Journal of Research in Science Teaching, 2, 176–80.

Renner, J.W., & Marek, E.A. (1990). An educational theory base for science teaching.

Journal of Research in Science Teaching. 27(3): 241–46.

Sandoval, J.S. (1995). Teaching in subject matter areas: Science. *Annual Review of Psychology,* 46, 355–74.

TEA (2013 mod.) *Texas Essential Knowledge and Skills by Chapter*, online: *https://tea.texas.gov/academics/curriculum-standards/teks/texas-essential-knowledge-and-skills.*

University of California, Lawrence Livermore National Laboratory (2006). Plasma: The fourth state of matter. Retrieved from *https://lasers.llnl.gov/science/discovery-science/plasma-physics.*

Subject Test V: Fine Arts, Health, and Physical Education (905)

COMPETENCY 001: VISUAL ARTS

The teacher understands concepts, processes, and skills involved in the creation, appreciation, and evaluation of art and uses this knowledge to plan and implement effective and engaging visual arts instruction.

Fine Arts or Visual Arts?

Fine arts is an umbrella term used to describe artworks that appeal to people's aesthetic perceptions. The fine arts include music, theater, sculpture, painting, printmaking, and other traditional forms of art. However, the fine arts exclude applied arts or craftwork like basket weaving, ceramics, and textiles. To include more forms of artistic expression, the term **visual arts** was coined. Visual arts refers to such artistic expressions as sculpture, painting, and printmaking, but it also includes less familiar art forms. These include textiles, basket weaving, ceramics, metalworking, and jewelry-making as well as more recent art forms, such as photography and filmmaking.

Visual arts is a more inclusive term that better describes arts produced and appreciated in modern society.

Children's Artistic Development

Children's earliest experiences with visual arts are more scientific than artistic. A child making marks by moving a crayon or marker across a surface is concentrating on the sensory experience more than on self-expression or symbolism. The child is most interested in the texture of the sur-

☞ To focus your study, go online to take the diagnostic test for this subject at *www.rea.com/studycenter*.

face, the colors that appear, and the shapes that emerge. By age three or four, however, the child may notice a similarity between an actual object and a mark that he or she has made. At this point, the child artist realizes that the colors and shapes can symbolize people, objects, and events in real life (Shirrmacher and Fox, 2009).

Drawing is one of the most basic forms of communication used across cultures. Children from diverse cultural backgrounds use a similar style and content in their attempts to express ideas graphically. Around age five, children move into drawing symbols to represent people and objects. A house, for example, may be consistently represented as a square with a triangle on top, regardless of the appearance of the house in reality. The use of symbolized drawings continues through the early elementary years, when children typically become enamored with repeating a particular theme in their drawings. A scene with a house, a tree, and hills in the background, or one with a spaceship, a planet surrounded by rings and a quarter moon may be repeated often and with little variation as the child artist works toward his or her ideas of perfection. As children move into the middle and later elementary years, they strive increasingly to achieve photographic realism in their art. They may experience frustration at this point, and this frustration may convince some children that they do not have artistic abilities. They then might become reluctant to participate in art activities.

Goals in Art Education

The goals of art education include developing children's aesthetic perception and providing experiences with many art forms. Art education also aims to facilitate children's reflections on and discussions of how they observe and respond to art. Education in the arts also provides opportunities for children to develop and extend their own artistic abilities, and it exposes children to characteristics and objects of art. Art education empowers children to analyze diverse forms of the visual arts by using informed judgment. Because of these important benefits and life skills, art education is a vital component of the Texas Essential Knowledge and Skills for Grades K–12.

Texas Essential Knowledge and Skills

The state curriculum for fine arts and visual arts is organized around four main strands—**perception, creative expression, historical/cultural heritage,** and **critical evaluation**. A summary of the key elements required for children in Grades K–6 is presented in Table 7-1 (TEA, 2013 mod.). Traditionally, an art teacher collaborates with EC–6 teachers to deliver these curriculum components. EC–6 teachers should understand the visual art curriculum components and know how to integrate them throughout their grade-level curriculum.

Table 7-1. Visual Arts Strands for K–6 in Texas

Grade	Perceptions	Creative Expressions	Historical/Cultural	Critical Evaluation
Kinder-garten	Identify colors, textures, and forms in the environment.	Create artwork using colors, forms, and line.	Share ideas about personal artworks and show respect for different opinions.	Express ideas about personal artworks, and the artworks of peers or professional artists.
1	Identify such art elements as color, texture, form, and line with emphasis on nature and human-made environments.	Invent images that combine color, form, and line and organize forms to create designs.	Show a basic understanding of art history. Select artwork that shows families and groups.	Make informed judgments about their own creations and the work of peers.
2	Continue using color, texture, form, line, space as well as such art principles as emphasis, patterns, and rhythm to create artworks.	Produce drawings, paintings, prints, constructions, and modeled forms using different art materials.	Develop respect for the artistic traditions and contributions of diverse groups.	Define reasons for preferences in artworks.
3	Continue emphasizing such art principles as emphasis, patterns, rhythm, balance, proportion, and unity in artworks.	Express ideas through original artworks using different media. Develop compositions using design skills; and produce drawings, print constructions, and ceramics.	Compare artworks from different cultures and link them to different occupations.	Apply simple criteria to identify main ideas in original artworks.
4	Communicate ideas about self, family, school, and community using sensory knowledge and experiences.	Invent ways to produce artworks and to explore photographic imagery using different media and materials.	Compare artworks from different groups; identify the role of art in American society.	Interpret ideas and moods in original artwork.
5	Identify in artworks basic arts elements like color, texture, form, line, space, and value.	Express ideas through original artworks, using different media with appropriate skill.	Show an understanding of art history and culture as records of human achievement.	Make informed judgments about their own creations and the artworks of others.
6	Use art vocabulary to describe the interdependence of the art elements, value and principles such as emphasis, pattern, rhythm, balance, proportion, and unity.	Express ideas through original artworks, using different media with appropriate skill.	Show an understanding of art history and culture as records of human achievement.	Make informed judgments about their own creations and the artworks of others.

Art Techniques and Materials

Painting and drawing are familiar activities to most elementary teachers, but other techniques and materials in the visual arts curriculum may be foreign to them. Some less familiar activities are:

1. **Printmaking:** This artistic process makes a print in which color (paint or ink) is applied to an object, and the object is then pressed onto a surface. When the object is lifted, a print remains on the surface.

2. **Ceramics:** The use of clay to create ceramics is one of the oldest art forms. Ceramics requires the use of a special oven to treat fresh clay with heat until it hardens. Traditionally, a special paint is used to create the desired color as well as the shine that typifies ceramics.

3. **Textiles:** The textile arts use plant, animal, or synthetic fibers to make practical or decorative objects, including stitchery, weaving, dyeing, printing, lace making, knitting, crocheting, and embroidery.

4. **Basket weaving:** This ancient art uses unspun fibers (pine straw, animal hair, hide, grasses, thread, or wood) to create baskets or other forms for artistic or practical purposes.

5. **Metalworking:** Traditional metalworking is the artistic process that shapes metals to produce individual pieces, assemblies, or structures, including jewelry.

6. **Photography and filmmaking:** This relatively recent art creates still or moving pictures by recording images on a sensitive medium, such as photographic film or an electronic sensor.

7. **Sculpture:** A sculpture is a three-dimensional artwork made by shaping or combining such hard material as marble, rock, glass, wood, or metal. Some sculptures are created directly by carving a solid material; others are assembled, built together and fired, welded, molded, or cast.

8. **Computer-generated art:** This relatively new form of art is created through the manipulation of pixels, either through drawing and painting software or through electronic images stored in the computer. The computer screen serves as the canvas, and colored light is the medium.

The Art Classroom

Whether art activities happen in an art room or the regular class, the room should allow for individual seating as well as small-group and large-group arrangements. In addition to space for learning centers, the teacher should have space to lecture and display students' work. The room also needs areas for drawing, painting, and printmaking as well as for creating computer graphics. The room also should have space for modeling and for assembling crafts. The room should have natural and artificial light, and materials should be stored in cabinets, with teachers controlling access. Safety guidelines are critical, and following them should be mandatory. Easy maintenance is a must, so sinks and surfaces must be durable and have cleanable finishes.

Visual Arts Activities for K–6

Throughout the elementary grades, students engage in such art activities as drawing, painting, designing, constructing, crafts, sculpting, weaving, and finger-painting. In Grades 3 and 4, students continue developing the skills from K through 2 and work with such new techniques as printmaking, sponge painting, graphics, film animation, and environmental design. In Grades 5 and 6, students should show technical skills and be able to make art based on personal experiences and direct observation.

The elementary curriculum encourages the integration of visual arts in the regular classroom with special activities in the art room. Appropriate art activities should focus first on self-expression. Because the fine motor and perceptual skills of children are still developing, their creative work may have little resemblance to reality. That's not the aim of artistic activities with children. The important goal is to encourage children to experiment, explore, and express their own ideas through their own artistic efforts. A list of strategies to engage students in art follows.

Activities to Engage Student in the Arts

1. **The Colors of the Rainbow.** Guide students to observe a rainbow and identify the colors it shows.

    - After they identify the colors of the rainbow—red, orange, yellow, green, blue, indigo, and violet—use the same activity to introduce the concept of primary and secondary colors.

2. **Experimenting with Colors.** Guide children to experiment mixing colors to discover the three secondary colors. Students can be guided later to combine colors to create tertiary colors. Use this table to guide their experimentation.

Primary Color 1	Primary Color 2	What color will result?	Actual results
Yellow	Blue		Green
Yellow	Red		Orange
Blue	Red		Purple

3. **Printmaking.** Ask children to bring artifacts that can be used in printmaking. Some common examples are leaves, pieces of fruits or vegetables, butterflies or pieces of fabrics. Establish a connection between printmaking and the concept of fossils.

4. **Art Critics.** Present paintings from different artists, and guide students to examine them based on the elements of art (line, space, value, color and texture). Guide more advanced students to analyze the artworks based on the principles of art (emphasis, balance, rhythm, contrast, movement and harmony).

5. **The Arts in Occupations.** Provide a list of occupations and guide students to determine how these occupations use the visual arts. Some of the occupations with clear connection with visual arts are: architects, plastic surgeons, engineers, advertisements, fashion designers, and photographers.

6. **Colors in Advertising and Branding.** Guide students to study the color wheel and determine how advertisers and designers use complementary colors in advertising, website development, and car designs as well as in decorating offices and buildings.

Materials for the elementary art program include scissors, wet and dry brushes, fabrics, wrapping papers, film, computers, clay, glue, construction paper, crayons, beads, and multiple household items. Safety is a primary concern, and toxic substances or potentially dangerous tools should not be allowed in the classroom. Rotating familiar materials for use in classroom art projects should help encourage artistic engagement.

Assessment in the visual arts is based on the child's attitudes and dispositions toward engaging in activities to produce and appreciate art:

- Does the child engage in art-production activities willingly and enthusiastically?

- Is the child willing to try new materials and techniques?

- Does the child express original ideas in his or her artwork?

- Does the child thoughtfully consider the art products of others and discuss the elements and principles of the exhibited art?

The EC-6 teacher and the arts specialist should consider these questions carefully during the assessment. By relating art production in the elementary curriculum to art products created by artists from other historical eras and cultures, children are introduced to art appreciation and the elements and principles of art. An analysis of the elements and principles of art follows.

Elements and Principles of Art

Art communicates and expresses ideas, emotions, and experiences. To communicate their own ideas and to understand the ideas of other artists, children must know the elements of art. Young artists use the elements and principles of art to create paintings, drawings, and designs.

Elements of Art

The seven elements of art are the individual components (i.e., color, texture, shape, form, line, space, value) that may be combined to create original artwork (Texas Education Agency, Preparation Manual for Core Subjects EC–6 [391], 2020). Most works of art have at least some aspect of each. A description of the elements follows.

1. **Color** represents reflected light and the way it bounces off objects. The three primary colors are red, yellow, and blue. They cannot be created through combinations of other colors. The secondary colors are created through the combination of primary colors. The three secondary colors are green, orange, and violet. There is an unlimited number of tertiary colors. The tertiary colors fall between the primary and secondary colors. The compound colors contain a mixture of the three primary colors. There also warm colors (such as yellow, orange, and red) and cool colors (such as blue, green, and purple). There are also complementary colors. These colors go well in combination. For example, complementary colors are used to develop websites and to create PowerPoint presentations. Figure 5.1 shows the complementary colors (Ryan, 2002–2009). Artists use all these color combinations to create the environment of a painting.

2. **Texture** describes the surface quality of a figure or shape. A shape can appear to be rough, smooth, soft, hard, or glossy. Texture can be physical (felt with the hand—for example, a buildup of paint) or visual (giving the illusion of texture—for example, the paint gives the impression of texture, but the surface remains smooth and flat).

3. **Shape** represents a self-contained, defined area of a two- or three-dimensional area creating a form. The two basic types of shapes are geometric and organic. *Geometric shapes* refer to squares, triangles, circles, and rectangles. *Organic shapes* describe more natural shapes like leaves, animals, and clouds.

4. **Form** refers to the forms and materials used to create sculptures. Students can work with line in two and three dimensions to discover how shapes become forms.

5. **Line** refers to marks from a pen or brush used to highlight a specific part of a painting or structure. More subtle lines can be used to accomplish the opposite effect.

6. **Space** describes the emptiness around or within objects. Space can be used to create perspective, to create objects or people in different planes, and to create a sense of depth. Positive space is the main area or object of focus in an artwork. Smaller objects in a painting seem farther away, while larger objects appear to be closer.

7. **Value** refers to the darkness or lightness of an artwork. Values are commonly used to create the two-dimensional quality of artwork. Values also indicate the source of light in a work and provide a three-dimensional view of figures by suggesting shadows. Values can also represent the tone of the artist and the artwork. Darker values show sadness, mystery, or formality, while lighter values usually indicate contentment and relaxation.

Figure 7-1. Complementary Colors

Color Wheel

The complementary colors are those that appear opposite each other on the color wheel in Fig. 7-1. For example, purple is a complementary color of yellow.

Principles of Art

The principles of art describe the guidelines that artists follow to create art and to deliver their message. Artists use the elements of art to communicate the principles in their creations. The principles of art include emphasis, balance, rhythm, contrast, movement, and harmony (National Gallery of Art, n.d.). A description of these principles follows.

1. **Emphasis** is the technique of making one part of a work stand apart from the rest. It guides viewers to pay attention to specific details or components of the artwork. The lines and texture often lead viewers to the target feature. Lines in paintings and sculpture can point or lead to where to focus the attention. By making texture different from the rest of the work in one area, the artist can also make the target area stand out.

2. **Balance** refers to the positioning of objects in such a way that none of them overpower other components of the artwork. Size, space, color, shape, and lighting can be used to create balance. For example, a large shape close to the center can be balanced by a smaller shape close to the edge. A composition with a large light-toned shape can be balanced with a small dark-toned shape. The two main kinds of balance are symmetrical and asymmetrical. Symmetrical balance occurs when the two halves of a figure coincide to create a mirror image. The line of symmetry is the line that divides the figure in two. The easiest way to identify symmetrical figures is to fold the figure in half. If these two halves are identical, we can say that the figure is symmetrical. Asymmetrical balance occurs when two sides of an artwork are different. For example, the artwork of the American flag—horizontal lines of different sizes and a smaller rectangle in the upper left corner with stars—makes it asymmetrical.

3. **Rhythm** describes the patterns used in the artwork. For example, placing a repetition of objects evenly spaced presents a regular type of rhythm. Elements increasing or decreasing in size in an artwork present a progressive rhythm.

4. **Contrast** creates interest through the combination of elements. Contrast can break the monotony or repetitious pattern in a work of art. Rembrandt's paintings are known for using value (lightness and darkness) to create contrast. He also used lighter values to highlight portions of the paintings.

5. **Movement** refers to how artists produce the illusion of motion. In painting, artists use line to simulate the movement of wind or water. This technique leads viewers to perceive the effects of motion and action through the artwork.

6. **Harmony** represents a sense of completeness in the artwork. It shows the unity of the artwork. For example, texture and color can be combined to provide a sense of balance and harmony.

While the elements and principles of art provide the foundations of artwork in all media and styles, they also apply to other disciplines and contemporary occupations. **Line**, **shape**, **space**, and **balance** have parallel meanings in the mathematics, while **texture** and **color** are also basic in scientific observation. Similarly, **rhythm** and **harmony** describe synonymous concepts in both art and music. Such mathematical concepts as symmetry, angle, distance, and convergence appear in artwork and must be understood by artists. Similarly, artists explore science concepts related to light, water, and temperature in their work. Engagement in art also requires artists, whether adults or children, to problem-solve and think. Artists must consider how to communicate emotions and ideas in their work, how to convey change and movement, and how to use symbolism. Artists of all ages must also learn to evaluate their own creative work and that of others.

For an analysis of strategies and lesson plans to teach the elements and principles of art, see the website of the National Gallery of Art at *http://www.nga.gov/content/ngaweb/education/teachers.html*.

Application of Art Principles in Other Fields

The skills and dispositions required of artists apply to multiple fields and occupations. For example, architects and interior designers draw upon the elements and principles as well as other technical skills of art to create aesthetically pleasing designs for buildings, landscaping, and interior spaces. Commercial artists apply their abilities to advertising as well as to the animation of comics or cartoons and the illustrating of print media. Teachers should show students how the visual arts are present throughout daily life and guide them to identify and enjoy these artworks wherever they appear.

Identifying Characteristics of Style in Works of Art

A **style** is an artist's manner of expression. When a group of artists during a specific period, which can last a few months, years, or decades, have a common style, it is called an **art movement**. These movements are found predominantly in Western cultures and occur in both visual art and architecture.

There are eight main historical periods, each with artistic styles and art movements within each. Although some periods have only one or two unique art styles, the 20th century has produced 36 unique styles. Descriptions of some of the widely known styles throughout history follow (Witcombe, 1995).

The **Prehistoric** period is characterized by paintings that represent the daily activities of a group of people. The best-known representation of this type of art is the Caves of Altamira in modern Spain. The Paleolithic peoples of Europe produced small, stylized stone carvings of women as symbols of fertility. These small statues have been found most often in modern France, Italy, and Austria. Some of the world's most prominent prehistoric art is spread across the African continent.

The **Ancient** period produced a large number of masterpieces from such varied civilizations as the Sumerians, Babylonians, Assyrians, Egyptians, Greeks, and Romans. These civilizations carved even the hardest rocks, such as granite and basalt, into battle narratives and historical records. As they did with their architectural monuments the pyramids, the Egyptians made their statues colossal to exalt the power of their society's leaders and gods. Ancient Greek art has its roots in the Minoan civilization on the island of Crete, which flourished about 2500 to 1400 BCE. The palace at Knossos held characteristic wall paintings revealing a civilization interested in games and leisure as well as the beauty of the sea.

Mainland Greeks of the **Classical** period, which occurred about 1,000 years after the ancient period, were fascinated by physical beauty. The Greeks fashioned their Olympian gods in the human image, with a universal ideal of perfection and guided by a master plan, recreating them in idealized and gracefully proportioned sculptures, architecture, and paintings. The populace in the **Hellenistic** period (330–31 BCE) was fascinated by physical beauty and appreciated these objects of art for their beauty alone. Roman culture excelled in engineering and building, skills intended to organize a vast empire and provide an aesthetic environment for private and public use. The Romans built temples, roads, bathing complexes, civic buildings, palaces, and aqueducts. One of their greatest artistic and engineering accomplishments was the Pantheon, the massive-domed temple of all the gods. The Pantheon is one of the best preserved of all buildings from the classical period.

The **Medieval** period (500–1400 CE) also produced numerous artistic masterpieces. The Romanesque style of art and architecture was preeminent about 800 to 1200 CE. By then, many local styles, including the decorative arts of the Byzantine Empire and the German and Celtic tribes, were contributing to European culture. Common features of Romanesque churches include round arches, vaulted ceilings, and heavy walls that are ornately decorated, primarily with symbolic figures of Christianity. Gothic architecture flourished during this period with the creation of magnificent ribbed vaulting and pointed roofs. The cathedrals in this style represent some of the purest expressions of an age. They combine a continued search for improvements in engineering and structure al with stylistic features that convey a relentless verticality, a reach toward heaven, and the unbridled adoration of God. Soaring and roomy, the construction of the Gothic cathedrals employed such elements as flying buttresses (structure to reinforce a wall) and pointed arches and vaults. They also included a number of sculptures and stained-glass windows that for the worshippers were visual encyclopedias of Christian teachings and stories

Renaissance (14th to 16th century) artists developed new forms and revived classical styles and values, with realism and the belief in the importance of the human experience on Earth. Great sculptors approached true human characterization and realism as they revived elements of Greek architecture. Like the painters of the period, Renaissance architects took a scientific, ordered approach and emphasized perspective and the calculated composition of figures in space. Art became more emotional and dramatic. Because of this, the use of color and movement increased, and the compositions were more vigorous. The references to classical iconography and the pleasures of an idyllic golden age also increased. Typifying this emotional, dramatic art are Michelangelo's magnificent Sistine Chapel frescoes and his powerful sculptures of David and Moses; Leonardo da Vinci's *Mona Lisa*; Raphael's *School of Athens* fresco; and the increasingly dramatic and colorful works of the Venetian and northern Italian masters Titian, Correggio, Giorgione, and Bellini.

Baroque style emerged in the 17th century in Europe. This style used exaggerated motion and elaborate artwork. The movement produced drama, tension, exuberance, and grandeur in sculpture, painting, literature, and music.

Rococo art characterizes the art of the early 18th century. Artists of the Rococo era turned the agitated drama of the baroque style into light, pastel-toned, swirling compositions that seem placed in an idyllic land of a golden age.

Nineteenth-century art was characterized by three elements—romanticism, realism, and impressionism. In the first half of the 19th century, landscape painting in England reached a zenith with the works of John Constable and Joseph Mallord William Turner. Turner's awe-inspiring landscapes form a bridge between the spirit of romanticism and the expressionistic brushwork and realism of the Barbizon School in France, whose chief painters were Charles-Francois Daubigny and Jean-Baptiste-Camille Corot. Beginning with Barbizon, the French painters of the 19th century concentrated increasingly on the journalistic depiction of everyday life and the natural environment in a free, painterly (gesture and brushwork) style.

Realism rejected traditional means of composing a picture, academic methods of figure modeling and color relations, and accurate and exact rendering of people and objects. Realism instead emphasized quickly observed and sketched moments from life, the relation of shapes and forms and colors, the effects of light, and the act of painting itself. The realist pioneers were Gustave Courbet (*The Stone Breakers, A Burial at Ornans*), Jean-François Millet (*The Sower, The Angelus*), and Honoré Daumier (*The Third-Class Carriage*).

Impressionism began with Edouard Manet in France in the 1860s. French artists continually blurred the boundaries of realism and abstraction. They used light and color to capture the impression of images as opposed to the "real image." The landscapes and everyday-life paintings of impressionist artists like Claude Monet, Camille Pissarro, Pierre-Auguste Renoir, Alfred Sisley, and Edgar Degas gave way to the more experimental arrangements of form and color of the great postimpressionists: Paul Gauguin, Vincent van Gogh, Georges Seurat, and Henri de Toulouse-Lautrec. Auguste Rodin produced powerful sculptures with the freedom of impressionist style.

Twentieth-century art provided new avenues for artistic expressions:

Surrealism is one of the new trends in painting that emerged in the 20th century. Inspired by the psychoanalytic writings of Sigmund Freud and Carl Jung, artists made the subconscious and the metaphysical important in their work. The influence of psychology is especially evident in the work of the surrealist Salvador Dali. Dali created surrealistic paintings as revealed in dreams, free of such conscious controls as reason and conventions.

Cubism and the abstract paintings of Pablo Picasso also emerged during the 20th century. This art represents the most direct call for the reduction and fragmentation of realistic depiction. Artists challenged common realistic conventions to create new representations of reality or imagination. Cubism is the most important and influential movement of European paintings and sculptures in the early 20th century.

Muralists and social realists between World War I and World War II created art that was physically interesting and with subjects accessible to the average person. John French Sloan, George Bellows, Edward Hopper, Thomas Hart Benton, Grant Wood, and John Steuart Curry were among those who celebrated the American scene in paintings, frequently in murals for public buildings and through widely available fine prints. The great Mexican muralists, who usually concentrated on political themes, include Diego Rivera, José Clemente Orozco, and David Siqueiros. They brought their work to the public in both Mexico and the United States.

Photorealism also emerged as a new art form in which paintings resemble lifelike photos. They are often portraits, *still lifes* (paintings of inanimate subjects), and landscapes.

Graffiti is a new and controversial art form that emerged in inner cities in America. Part of the controversy with this art is how the expression is conducted. Traditionally, through the use of spray-painting and brushes, the artists create the work on the surface of private and public buildings and often without the approval of the owners. For some, graffiti is a nuisance or worse. For others, it represents a liberating response to authority as well as the pressure of modern life.

Non-Western and Native American Artistic Traditions

Just as in European artistic traditions, **African art** illustrates the region's diversity and the many forms of artistic expression that developed across the African continent. Some of the world's most important **prehistoric art** can be found under rock outcroppings from sites in the Sahara to locations in southern African, especially in modern-day South Africa and Botswana. These rock etchings and paintings included mythical figures, portrayals of hunting and herding, and representations of daily life.

In areas where Africans developed settled agriculture, artists and craftsmen grew in importance and developed distinctive styles and artistic techniques. In sub-Saharan Africa, one of the earliest forms of lasting artistic expression was terracotta sculptures produced by the Nok culture that developed in western Africa, in what is now Nigeria. Other West African cultures also produced important fired clay sculptures in addition to carved wooden masks and statues, as well as bronzes and iron sculptures.

African artists both shaped and were influenced by artistic currents from nearby world regions. For example, the ancient kingdoms of Nubia, Meroe, and Axum, situated along the Nile River, produced temples, pyramids, statues, and bronzes that reflected their interaction with Pharaonic Egypt as well as the artistic traditions of Mesopotamia and the Mediterranean. Similarly, the later empires of West Africa, after their conversion to Islam, built mosques from unbaked clay, in distinctly African styles. And, in what is now the modern nation of Ethiopia, the production of Christian icons and architecture predominated from the fourth century to the present. In one of the most remarkable examples of Christian architecture, in **Lalibela, Ethiopia**, 11 churches were hewn from rock from nearby mountains sometime in the 12th or 13th centuries. These churches are among the many World Heritage sites located in Africa.

Frequently, African art was intended to serve ritual or ceremonial purposes. For example, throughout much of sub-Saharan Africa, elaborately carved masks and richly embroidered garments were used in religious ceremonies. African sculptures and masks had a profound impact on early 20th century artists like Pablo Picasso and Henri Matisse, who found inspiration in the angular and abstract forms used by African artists.

The progression of **Chinese art** is divided into periods according to the ruling dynasty and the development of technology. The earliest Chinese art products were made from pottery, jade, and eventually bronze. Porcelain art forms were introduced in early imperial China and were so refined that in English the word *china* came to mean high-quality porcelain. Buddhism arrived in China in the first century BCE and strongly influenced artists throughout the country. Calligraphy and painting were popular art forms, with artists working primarily on silk until paper was invented. Although classical sculpture was the dominant art form of the Tang dynasty, landscape painting, almost impressionistic in its portrayal of distance, dominated the Song dynasty. Color painting and printing were emphasized during the Ming dynasty and reached their peaks during the Qing dynasty when painters known as **Individualists** began to use free brushwork to express their ideas more openly. Beginning in the 19th century, Chinese artists were increasingly influenced by Western ideas and techniques. In the early 20th century, **social realism** was the dominant theme of Chinese artists. During the Cultural Revolution of the mid-20th century, art schools were closed and exhibitions were prohibited. Following the Cultural Revolution, however, art exchanges were established with other countries, and artists experimented with themes and methods. Wang Yani, a child prodigy whose work since 1975 has exemplified *xieyi hua*, a freehand style, has received much attention (Cultural China, n.d.).

Native American art, reflecting the traditions, cultures, and beliefs of the Indigenous peoples of the Americas, encompasses mixed media and techniques that include pottery, woodcarving, weaving, stitchery, painting, beadwork, and jewelry-making. Art forms and symbols vary across Native American tribes, who inhabited the Americas before the arrival of European colonists. Tribal artisans relied on available natural resources to determine the media in which they worked, and their art often beautified common items, creating objects of spiritual significance.

Integration of the Arts in the Content Areas

The arts can be easily integrated with other academic content areas. In reading, children can draw to present the main idea of a story. When they learn to write, they then can add words to their drawings. Art appreciation activities also provide an appropriate context for children to notice and discuss details in a painting. Through observation and description, children practice new vocabulary and use descriptive language. Scientific principles like light, color, and texture can be easily introduced through artwork. Likewise, art concepts of space, proportion, and balance can be introduced through mathematics. A history lesson can be enriched with a discussion of the key art movements and artists in each historical period. For example, Goya's paintings can enhance a discussion of the Napoleonic Era in Spain. Artworks in all media can provide meaningful visual contexts to frame discussions of culture and history.

Evaluating Works of Art

To judge the quality of a work of visual art, students should be given basic criteria for evaluation. These criteria can be derived through questions such as these: What is the artist's purpose? Does the work achieve that purpose? Does the artist have a unique voice, regardless of style, or could the artwork just as easily be someone else's? Does the artist's style serve the purpose of the work? (And if so, how?) Is the work memorable and distinctive? Was the work created to meet social or cultural needs? Has the artist used the elements and principles of art effectively?

COMPETENCY 002: MUSIC

The teacher understands the concepts, processes and skills involved in the creation, appreciation and evaluation of music and uses that knowledge to plan and implement effective and engaging music instruction.

The goal of music education is to develop independent musicians through the use of conceptual teaching of musical skills. It is expected that music teachers be literate in music in much the way English teachers are literate in language. Teachers of music should be able to teach children how to sing in tune, keep a steady beat, listen to different styles of music appropriately, and perform music expressively. Teachers should also learn and use music terminology and the elements of music. Additionally, they should learn the appropriate methodology to integrate music in the content areas, and apply knowledge for evaluating and critiquing musical performances

Elements of Music

Essential to the understanding of music are the key elements upon which all music is based—rhythm, melody, harmony, form, and expression. **Rhythm** is the varied lengths of sounds and silences in relation to the underlying beat. Usually children (K–3) confuse beat and rhythm and try to make them the same thing. Beat is the pulse that is felt in the music and rhythm is typically called the melodic rhythm or word rhythm found in the song. Audiate[7] the song "Happy Birthday"; the beat is the underlying pulse and the melodic rhythm is the words to the song. Now audiate "The Star-

---

[7] Audiation is the cognitive process of hearing music inside one's head.

SUBJECT TEST V: FINE ARTS, HEALTH & PHYSICAL EDUCATION (905)

Spangled Banner"; the beat may or may not be faster or slower (the speed of the underlying pulse of music is called **tempo**, see Table 7-2). The beginning of "The Star-Spangled Banner" has the same melodic rhythm as the beginning of "Happy Birthday." "Happy Birthday" begins with "Happy birthday to you" and has the same melodic rhythm as "Oh say can you see." After this beginning, the two songs do not have the same melodic rhythm. Melodic rhythm is identified using musical notation (the writing of music), which includes various types of notes and rests (see Figure 7-2).

Table 7-2. Tempo Markings

Tempo Marking	Speed
Grave	Extremely Slow
Largo	Very Slow
Adagio	Slow—leisure pace
Andante	Walking pace
Moderato	Moderate
Allegretto	Moderately quick
Allegro	Fast
Vivace	Lively
Presto	Quick

Figure 7-2. Musical Notes and Rests

Quarter Note · Quarter Rest · Two Eighth Notes · Eighth Note · Eighth Rest
Half Note · Half Rest · Whole Note · Whole Rest

Meter refers to how musicians group the steady beats. When the beat is grouped in 2s, it is in duple meter, which can be felt as marching or walking. When the beat is grouped in 3s, it is in triple meter, which can be felt as swaying to the music or a waltz.

Melody is the succession of sounds (or pitches) and silences that may move upward, downward, or stay the same. The "tune" or the singable part of the song is the melody. A **musical staff** (see Figure 7-3), consisting of five parallel lines and four spaces, is needed to read a musical tune. The **pitches** are represented by symbols called **notes** placed on the staff. There are seven letters found in the musical alphabet (A, B, C, D, E, F, and G). The **clef signs** at the beginning of the song determine the pitch level, either higher or lower. Typically, the **treble clef** is the singing range of women and the right hand on the piano; and the **bass clef** is the singing range of men and the left hand on the piano (see Figure 7-4). A grand staff combines both treble and bass clefs and can be seen in piano music and some hymns written for singers.

Figure 7-3. Musical Staff

Five Lines—a line going through the note head

Four Spaces—a note head between two lines

Figure 7-4. Musical Staff or Grand Staff with Clefs and Notes

Treble Clef

C D E F G A B C D E F G

C B A G F E D C B A G F

Bass Clef

Most music teachers use mnemonics when teaching the names of the lines and spaces in both clefs. The way to remember the names of the lines in the treble clef is the mnemonic "Every **G**ood **B**oy **D**oes **F**ine." The spaces of the treble clef spell **FACE**. The mnemonic for the lines in the bass clef is "**G**ood **B**oys **D**o **F**ine **A**lways" and the spaces are "**A**ll **C**ows **E**at **G**rass."

Interval is the distance between two pitches. For example, "Twinkle, Twinkle Little Star" has an interval of a 5th between the first and second *Twinkle*. That means that the first pitch (C) and the second pitch (G) are five steps apart. All intervals are identified by a number (e.g., 3rd) except for unison and octave. Unison is two sounds of an identical pitch and an octave is the distance between one pitch and the next pitch with the same name eight steps apart. When someone is singing or playing in tune (with correct pitch accuracy), they have good intonation; however, intonation can refer to one being flat (below the pitch) or sharp (higher than the pitch).

Harmony is usually the accompaniment or supportive sounds to a melody. These accompaniments are typically played by a pitched instrument, such as a piano, guitar, or autoharp. You can teach harmony to children at a young age by singing the melody and playing the simple accompaniment on the ukulele. Harmony can also be taught by having students sing in at least two parts. For example, ostinato, which is a pattern that repeats itself, is a great way to teach harmony to first- and second-grade students. You can sing the melody and have the students sing the ostinato (see Figure 7-5) or vice versa. Another way to produce harmony is through the use of singing rounds, such as "Row, Row, Row Your Boat." A round is where everyone sings the melody and subsequent voices enter at specific intervals after the leader. Partner songs are another example of harmony where two different songs can be sung at the same time.

Figure 7-5. Melody with Ostinato

Let Us Chase the Squirrel

Form is the structure or design of the music. A phrase, which is a musical line that contains groups of pitches, is similar to a sentence in language. Several musical phrases make up a song just like several sentences make up a paragraph. These phrases can define a song. Musical forms are analogous to mathematical patterns. Common forms in elementary music are binary (AB), ternary (ABA), theme and variation (A A1 A2 A3 A4 etc.), and rondo (ABACA). The different musical sections determine the form. For example, if there is a song that has a verse/refrain(chorus)/verse structure, it is labeled as ABA form. If the song has one section that keeps repeating the melody, then it is called rondo form where the A section (or melody) keeps returning. These forms are easy to identify through listening to orchestral literature.

Expression consists of dynamics and timbre. **Dynamics** is a term used by musicians to represent the louds and softs in music. Typically younger children (K–2) confuse dynamics with pitch level or melodic direction. The word "up" in music is usually associated with pitch level (the music moves up or goes higher) whereas, in the home, if children are asked to turn up the music or television, the word "up" is associated with a dynamic level (louder). Dynamics are expressed using the Italian language (see Table 7-3).

Table 7-3. Dynamics

Italian Term	Dynamic Level
Piano	Soft
Mezzo piano	Medium soft
Mezzo forte	Medium loud
Forte	Loud

Timbre is defined as tone color in music. This tone color refers to the quality of sound that distinguishes one voice or instrument from another. Kindergarten children distinguish between the four human voices—speaking, whispering, calling, and singing; whereas, older students are identifying the timbre of classroom instruments (woods, metals, and skins); singing voices (soprano, alto, tenor, baritone, bass); and orchestral instruments (strings, woodwinds, brass, percussion, and keyboard).

Curriculum Requirements

Texas has developed the Texas Essential Knowledge and Skills (TEKS) for music into four basic strands—music literacy, creative expression, historical and cultural relevance, and critical evaluation and response (see Table 7-4). The TEKS for music were revised and adopted in 2019. The TEKS are designed so students will be able to read, write, and create music; perform music from diverse cultures expressively; make musical connections to history, culture and the world; listen critically to music; and be able to evaluate, describe and respond to a wide variety of musical styles. Teachers of music are expected to have their students develop and master each strand within the prescribed state curricula.

**Table 7-4. Music Education Strands for K–5
TEA (2019, mod.)**

Grade Level	Music Literacy	Creative Expression	Historical/ Cultural Relevance	Critical Evaluation and Response
K	Identify the difference between the voices, timbre of voices, and instruments. Identify same/different in beat/rhythm, higher/lower, louder/softer, faster/slower, and simple patterns in musical performances. Identify beat, rhythm, and simple two-tone or three-tone melodies using iconic representation.	Sing or play classroom instruments independently or in groups from diverse cultures and styles. Move alone or with others to a varied repertoire of music using gross and fine locomotor and non-locomotor movement. Perform simple part work, including beat versus rhythm, and louder/softer and faster/slower.	Sing songs and play musical games, including rhymes, folk music, and seasons music. Identify simple interdisciplinary concepts related to music.	Identify and demonstrate audience behavior during live or recorded performances. Identify steady beat in music performances, and compare same/different in beat/rhythm, higher/lower, louder/softer, faster/slower, and simple patterns in musical performances.

(continued)

Grade Level	Music Literacy	Creative Expression	Historical/ Cultural Relevance	Critical Evaluation and Response
1	Identify the singing voices of adults and children. Identify visually and aurally the instrument families. Use basic music terminology in describing changes in tempo, including Allegro/Largo, and dynamics, including forte/piano. Identify and label representation and contrast in simple songs, such as AB, AABA, or ABAC patterns.	Sing tunefully or play classroom instruments, including rhythmic and melodic patterns from diverse cultures and styles, independently or in groups. Move alone or with others to a varied repertoire of music using gross and fine locomotor and non-locomotor movement. Perform simple part work, including beat versus rhythm, rhythmic ostinato, and vocal exploration. Perform music using tempo, including Allegro/Largo, and dynamics, including forte/piano.	Create short, rhythmic patterns using known rhythms, and melodic patterns using known pitches. Explore new musical ideas using singing voice and classroom instruments. Sing songs and play musical games, including rhymes, patriotic events, folk music, and seasonal music. Identify steady beat in short musical excerpts from various periods or times in history and diverse cultures. Identify simple interdisciplinary concepts relating to music.	Identify and demonstrate appropriate audience behavior during live or recorded performances. Recognize rhythmic and melodic elements in simple aural examples using terminology, and distinguish same/different between beat/rhythm, higher/lower, louder/softer, faster/slower, and simple patterns in musical performances. Respond verbally or through movement to short musical examples.
2	Identify choral voices, including unison versus ensemble, and instruments visually and aurally. Use music terminology to explain musical examples of tempo, including Presto, Moderato, and Andante, and dynamics, including fortissimo and pianissimo. Identify and label simple small forms such as AABA and ABAC. Read, write, and reproduce rhythmic patterns using standard notation in 2/4 meter, including half note/half rest; pentatonic melodic patterns using standard staff notation; and basic music terminology, including Allegro/Largo and forte/piano.	Sing tunefully or play classroom instruments, including rhythmic and melodic patterns from diverse cultures and styles, independently or in groups. Move alone or with others to a varied repertoire of music using gross and fine locomotor and non-locomotor movement. Perform simple part work, including rhythmic ostinato, and vocal exploration such as singing, speaking, and chanting. Perform music using tempo, including Presto, Moderato, and Andante, and dynamics including fortissimo and pianissimo. Create rhythmic phrases using rhythm, and melodic phrases using pitches. Explore new musical ideas in phrases using singing voice and classroom instruments.	Sing songs and play musical games, including patriotic, folk, and seasonal music. Examine short musical excerpts from various periods or times in history and diverse and local cultures. Identify simple interdisciplinary concepts relating to music.	Begin to practice appropriate audience behavior during live or recorded performances. Recognize known rhythmic and melodic elements in simple aural examples using terminology. Distinguish between rhythms, higher/lower pitches, louder/softer dynamics, faster/slower tempos, and simple patterns in musical performance, and respond verbally or through movement to short musical examples.

(continued)

Grade Level	Music Literacy	Creative Expression	Historical/ Cultural Relevance	Critical Evaluation and Response
3	Categorize and explain a variety of musical sounds, including voices, woodwind, brass, string, percussion, and instruments from various cultures. Use music symbols and terminology referring to rhythm, melody, timbre, form, tempo, and dynamics. Identify and label small and large musical forms such as ABAC, AB, and ABA. Read and write and reproduce rhythmic patterns using standard musical notation and pentatonic melodic patterns using standard staff notation.	Sing or play classroom instruments, with accurate intonation and rhythm, a varied repertoire of music such as American folk songs and folk songs representative of local cultures independently or in groups. Move alone or with others a varied repertoire of music using gross motor, fine motor, locomotor, and non-locomotor skills and integrated movement such as hands and feet moving together. Perform simple part work, including rhythmic and melodic ostinato, and interpret through performance music symbols and terms referring to tempo and dynamics. Create rhythmic phrases, melodic phrases, and simple accompaniment through improvisation and composition.	Perform a varied repertoire of songs, movement, and musical games representative of American and local cultures. Identify music from diverse genres, styles, periods, and cultures. Identify the relationships between music and interdisciplinary concepts.	Exhibit audience etiquette during live and recorded performances. Recognize rhythmic and melodic elements in aural examples using appropriate vocabulary. Identify specific musical events in aural examples, such as changes in timbre, form, tempo, or dynamics using appropriate vocabulary. Respond verbally and through movement to short musical examples. Describe a variety of compositions and formal or informal musical performances using specific music vocabulary.
4	Categorize and explain a variety of musical sounds including voices, woodwind, brass, string, percussion, keyboard, electronic instruments, and instruments of various cultures. Use music symbols and terminology referring to rhythm, melody, timbre, form, tempo, dynamics, and articulation to explain musical sounds. Identify and label small and large musical forms such as ABAC, AB, ABA, and rondo. Read, write, and reproduce rhythmic patterns using standard notation in 2/4, 4/4, and 3/4 meters; and extend pentatonic melodic patterns using standard staff notation. Identify music symbols and terms referring to tempo, dynamics, and articulation.	Sing and play classroom instruments, with accurate intonation and rhythm, a varied repertoire of music, such as American and Texan folk songs and folk songs representative of local cultures, independently or in groups. Move alone and with others to a varied repertoire of music using gross motor, fine motor, locomotor, and non-locomotor skills and integrated movement such as hands and feet moving together. Perform various folk dances and play parties. Perform simple part work, including rhythmic and melodic ostinato, derived from repertoire. Interpret through performance music symbols and terms referring to tempo, dynamics, and articulation. Create rhythm phrases, melodic phrases, and simple accompaniments through improvisation or composition.	Perform a varied repertoire of songs, movement, and musical games representative of diverse cultures such as historical folk songs of Texas and Hispanic and American Indian cultures in Texas, including "Texas, Our Texas." Identify and describe music from diverse genres, styles, periods, and cultures; and examine the relationships between music and interdisciplinary concepts.	Exhibit audience etiquette during live and recorded performances. Recognize rhythmic and melodic elements in aural examples using appropriate vocabulary. Describe specific musical events in aural examples, such as changes in timbre, form, tempo, dynamics, or articulation using appropriate vocabulary. Respond verbally and through movement to short musical examples. Describe a variety of compositions and formal or informal musical performances using specific music vocabulary. Justify personal preferences for specific music works and styles using music vocabulary.

(continued)

Grade Level	Music Literacy	Creative Expression	Historical/ Cultural Relevance	Critical Evaluation and Response
5	Distinguish among a variety of musical timbres, including voices, woodwind, brass, string, percussion, keyboard, electronic instruments, and instruments of various cultures. Use music symbols and terminology, referring to rhythm, melody, timbre, form, tempo, articulation, and meter to explain musical sounds presented aurally. Identify and label small and large musical forms such as ABAC, AB, ABA, rondo, and theme and variations. Read, write, and reproduce rhythmic patterns using standard notation in 2/4, 3/4, or 4/4 meters; and extend pentatonic and diatonic melodic patterns using standard staff notation. Identify and interpret music symbols and terms referring to tempo, dynamics, articulation, and meter.	Sing and play classroom instruments, with accurate intonation and rhythm, a varied repertoire of music such as American folk songs, patriotic music, and folk songs representative of local and world cultures independently or in groups. Move alone and with others a varied repertoire of music using gross motor, fine motor, locomotor, and non-locomotor skills and integrated movement such as hands and feet moving together. Perform various folk dances and play parties. Perform simple two-part music, including rhythmic and melodic ostinato, rounds, partner songs, and counter melodies. Interpret through performance music symbols and terms referring to tempo, dynamics, articulation, and meter. Create rhythm phrases, melodic phrases, and simple accompaniments through improvisation or composition.	Perform a varied repertoire of songs, movement, and musical games representative of diverse cultures such as historical folk songs of Texas and America and European and African cultures in America. Perform music representative of Texas and America, including "The Star Spangled Banner." Identify and describe music from diverse genres, styles, periods, and cultures. Examine relationships between music and interdisciplinary concepts.	Exhibit audience etiquette during live and recorded performances. Identify rhythmic and melodic elements in aural examples using appropriate vocabulary. Describe specific musical events such as changes in timbre, form, tempo, dynamics, or articulation in aural examples using appropriate vocabulary. Respond verbally and through movement to short musical examples. Evaluate a variety of compositions and form or informal musical performances using specific criteria. Justify personal preferences for specific music works and styles using music vocabulary.

Music in the Classroom

Elementary music teachers in Texas typically use two approaches to teach students music: The Kodály Method and Orff Schulwerk.

The Kodály Method

The Kodály Method is rooted in Zoltán Kodály's principles and step-by-step process for Hungarian teachers. This teaching technique is rooted in Hungarian culture, but can be adapted to other cultures and is used by some Texas music teachers. The main goals of the Kodály Method are to instill the love of music into all children; to have children achieve music literacy; start music education in early childhood; teach music sequentially; use quality folk songs; and cultivate the singing voice. The 3 P's (preparation, presentation, and practice) are vital to the teaching process in Kodály. These 3 P's are similar to the whole-part-whole approach where the teacher prepares a concept, teaches the concept, and then, through repetition and review, masters that concept. The tools used in Kodály are solfege (*do, re, mi, fa, sol, la, ti, do*), hand signs (to present a visualization in space of the high-low relationships of the pitches being sung), and rhythm syllables (quarter note = ta, eighth notes = ti, etc.). Other tools include musical flashcards, stick notation (the music notation without the note head) and musical ladders that show the melodic direction of the music.

One primary goal of Kodály is to teach music literacy, and singing is the vehicle to achieve this goal. In this method, students start with simple *sol mi* songs and then expand their musical vocabulary to include all pitches in the pentatonic scale (*do re mi sol la*). Singing is the major mode of communication and is as important to the current Kodály teacher as it was to Zoltán Kodály himself. Kodály believed that music was "meant to develop one's entire being personality, intellect, and emotions" (Organization of American Kodály Educators, 2015) and used folk songs as his basis of teaching music.

Orff Schulwerk

Orff Schulwerk[8] is a "learning by doing" approach to teaching music. It is based on what is most natural to children: singing, moving, chanting, creating, improvising, and playing instruments. In an Orff classroom, every child participates and experiences all aspects of music in a noncompetitive atmosphere. Orff Schulwerk begins with speech because Carl Orff, the creator of Orff Schulwerk, believed that speech is tied to rhythm and rhythm is the strongest musical element. These speech rhythms are transferred to the body in the form of body percussion (snap, clap, patchen,[9] and stamping). Special Orff instruments are used to accompany the songs or rhymes. These instruments (unpitched and barred) allow students to be creative, which leads to improvisation and later composition.

Unpitched rhythm instruments or classroom percussion (e.g., wood block, triangle, claves, drums, finger cymbals, etc.) and melodic instruments or barred instruments (xylophones, metallophones, and glockenspiels) make up the Orff ensemble. Usually the unpitched instruments play rhythmic figures and add a nice contrast to the Orff ensemble.

The barred (or melody) instruments are unique to Orff Schulwerk and can be found in classrooms all over the world. "The xylophone and metallophone are similar to traditional xylophones and vibes, but are small and have removable bars" (Lange, p. 9, 2005). The easy removal of bars enables children to set up the instruments into a pentatonic scale (see Figure 7-6). Notice that the F's and B's (half steps) are removed from the instrument. Because the pentatonic scale removes the half steps from the instrument, it allows students to have greater success during the instrumental experience because they can play anything on the instruments as a group and there is no dissonance. The pentatonic scale also allows the students to play simple melodies with greater success because with bars missing, they can visually see the melody. "There are three sizes of xylophones and metallophones: bass, alto, and soprano. The bars on the xylophone are made of wood; the bars on the metallophone are made of metal and have a ringing timbre that is important in the

---

[8] Schulwerk means "schoolwork" in German.
[9] Patchen means "patting legs" in German.

ensemble because of the contrast in sound with xylophones" (Lange, p. 9, 2005). The glockenspiels are smaller (alto and soprano only) and have removable metal bars, similar to the xylophone and metallophone.

Figure 7-6. Pentatonic Scale on Barred Instruments

These Orff instruments are what is typically found and played in elementary music classes. They can be used to play simple songs and can accompany singing and other rhythmic and melodic instruments. Traditional band and orchestral instruments are not taught by the classroom music teacher. Usually study of these instruments begins in middle school or junior high with a specialized band or orchestra teacher. The sounds of the band and orchestral instruments are taught to the students during listening lessons by the elementary music teacher. Learning the names and aural identification of these instruments may aid in the selection of playing one of these instruments later in their musical career.

Singing

For young children to learn to sing well, they must sing songs that will not strain the undeveloped vocal chords by singing too high or too low. Typically the classroom teacher sings too low for children and as a result, children strain their voices or do not sing along with the teacher. The best singing range for students in K–2 is from D–A (see Figure 7-7). Students in Grades 3–6 can sing a little higher, usually from D–D (see Figure 7-8). Children, in K–6, have a breathy tone quality and should not be asked to sing louder or project their voice. If a louder sound is necessary, add more children. If an adult asks children to sing louder, children will typically yell instead of sing and therefore damage their voice.

Figure 7-7. Singing Range of Students in K–2

Figure 7-8. Singing Range of Students in 3–6

When selecting music for students in K–6, make sure that most of the pitches fall within the desired range listed above. Avoid songs that are too low, which will cause strain and harm to the voice. There are several music collections from around the world that are appropriate for children. When choosing this music, try to choose recordings that are as authentic to the culture as possible.

Repertoire

Historically, folk songs were taught through oral transmission. Nowadays, folk songs are typically learned through written music, except in the elementary music classroom. In this environment, folk songs are taught to students by rote by echo-singing each phrase until the songs are learned. There are different types of folk songs, such as work songs, cowboy songs, and sailor songs. There are also folk songs from different cultures, such as *Sakura* from Japan and *De Colores* from Mexico. Some of the most popular American folk songs are seasonal and patriotic songs.

Singing patriotic songs is an important component in the Texas music curriculum. There are national patriotic songs, such as "The Star-Spangled Banner," "America the Beautiful," and "God Bless America." Explaining the historical significance behind each song is one of the TEKS for music. For example, the text to "The Star-Spangled Banner" was written during the War of 1812 by Francis Scott Key. He was detained on a British ship, in the harbor, while the British bombed Fort McHenry in Baltimore, Maryland. Key wrote the poem on an envelope early the next morning when he saw the American flag still flying over the fort (Star-Spangled Banner n.d.). The poem was later set to a tune written by John Stafford Smith and approved by Congress as the National Anthem on March 3, 1931.

Music has the power to heal wounds, and patriotic songs, because of their unifying nationalistic motifs, typically help in national healing. Since the terror attacks on the United States on September 11, 2001, the singing of "God Bless America," which can be heard regularly at Major League Baseball games, has played an important part in American culture. For younger students (K–2), "America (My Country 'Tis of Thee)" is an appropriate patriotic song that allows for discussion of American history. Another patriotic song appropriate for middle- to upper-elementary students (Grades 3–6) to teach history and culture is "America the Beautiful." The text of this song was written by an American educator, Katharine Lee Bates, and describes the landscape of the country.

Texas has an amazing history that can be taught in music class through song. For example, "The Old Chisholm Trail" is a traditional folk song that teaches students about the Chisholm Trail that Texas ranchers used to drive cattle to Kansas. Also, students need to know "Texas, Our Texas," which was adopted in 1929 by the Texas Legislature as the Texas state song. It was modified once in 1959 when Alaska became a state and therefore the wording in the song needed to be changed from "largest" state to "boldest" state in the third line of the song (Texas State Libraries and Archives, 2015). Other Texas songs that should be taught in elementary school are: "Deep in the Heart of Texas," "The Yellow Rose of Texas," "San Antonio Rose" and several others that discuss the history and culture of Texas.

Music from diverse cultures is not only one of the TEKS for music, but is popular in Texas schools. For example, Tejano and Mariachi are prevalent in several districts throughout the state. Tejano music dates back to 1690 when Spain settled the area that is now known as Texas. The music developed over the centuries with new settlers from different parts of the world, thus combining several ethnic backgrounds—Mexican, Cuban, German, and Czech. The featured instrument is the accordion and the Tejano orchestra has been influenced by Mexican, Cuban, German, and Czech brass bands. In addition to the instrumentation, the roots of Tejano include various dance styles, which adds to its diversity and cultural heritage (The Roots of Tejano and Conjunto Music, 2015).

Mariachi is a traditional form of Mexican folk music that has become popular in Texas schools. The instrumentation consists of violins, trumpets, a Spanish guitar, and a guitarrón (a large deep-bodied six-stringed acoustic bass from Mexico). Typically several of the band members will sing along while playing an instrument. Usually the group all dress in the same attire with silver studded charro outfits with wide brimmed hats. The size of the group varies from three to fifteen.

Listening/Concert Etiquette

Teaching elementary-aged students how to listen to music and what to listen for in music is important for musical understanding. If students are not taught what to listen for in a piece of music, they will typically begin talking and the music therefore becomes background noise. Preparation of a listening lesson should consist of historical background of the music (e.g. time period and composer biography) followed by information of the music itself (e.g. main theme, instrumentation, musical form, dynamics, etc.). This preparation prior to listening to music, recorded music or a live performance, allows for the students to be actively engaged while listening and should ensure greater concert etiquette. Students in Grades K–6 are expected to demonstrate appropriate concert etiquette. Whispering, talking, and turning around in a seat are unacceptable in most classical concert settings. The National Association for Music Education has developed "The Ten Rules for Students" (National Association of Music Educators, 2015). These rules are reproducible for distribution so inappropriate behavior at concerts does not occur. Other inappropriate behaviors, in addition to the three listed above, are dangling jewelry, watch alarms, cellphones ringing, and chewing gum loudly (National Association of Music Educators, 2015). Teaching students the expectations at a concert will benefit everyone involved—performers and audience members alike.

Evaluation

Evaluation is subjective and evaluating musical performances is no different. The way to add objectivity to evaluating music is to use **performance evaluations** (rubrics). A well-written rubric gives students positive feedback to improve their performance, and allows the teacher to measure many students performing at the same time. Rubrics identify critical components to be assessed, and communicate acceptable levels of student performance or expected behavior. Any rubric should be simple enough to allow the students opportunities for self-assessment.

The RubiStar provides opportunities for teachers to create their own rubric. This interactive site lets you choose from a list of music assessment components. Included are rubrics for judging classical concert etiquette, a general rubric for elementary standards and benchmarks, and a rubric for judging instrumental musical performance and music composition. Teachers select the area to be measured and the system provides a description of the levels of performances or the expected behavior. The system also allows the option to customize the rubric. See an example of a customized version to assess classical concert etiquette for elementary education students (see Table 7-5).

Table 7-5. Sample Rubric for Elementary Education Students

CATEGORY	4	3	2	1
Entering the Hall or Auditorium	Stands quietly outside the door, then follows usher quietly to assigned seat.	Talks in a soft voice outside the door, and then follows the usher quietly to assigned seat.	Talks in a soft voice while waiting and while being seated.	Talks in a loud voice while waiting or being seated.
Showing Appreciation	Claps at an appropriate volume at the end of all musical selections. Has pleasant expression and looks toward the performers while clapping.	Claps at an appropriate volume at the end of all musical selections. Does not look at performers when clapping.	Does not clap for all selections or claps at the wrong time.	Claps too loudly, drawing audience attention, or whistles and screams while clapping.
Attention	Listens politely to the music. Has an interested expression almost all the time.	Listens politely to the music. Looks interested some of the time. Does not distract others when not listening.	Does not appear to be listening or interested, but keeps quiet and does not distract others.	Distracts others by talking, moving, rattling things, playing with toys, etc. during the actual performance.

(continued)

CATEGORY	4	3	2	1
Stays seated	Student keeps all body parts within own seating area during entire performance, politely sharing armrest with at least one neighbor.	Student keeps all body parts within own seating area during most of the performance, politely sharing armrest with at least one neighbor. Movements do not distract or irritate others.	Student leans toward another student to talk quietly, but stays in seat and keeps hands and feet to himself/herself.	Student gets out of seat or lets arms, hands, legs stray into the space of another.

Integration

Music can easily be integrated into other subject areas. For example, music can easily be integrated into English Language Arts and Reading through the use of singing books. There are several songbooks, such as *Down by the Bay*, *Señor Don Gato*, and *The Star Spangled Banner*, for various grade levels. Music also reinforces poetry when students respond to rhythm, rhyme, and repetition of simple songs and chants. Since music uses text, teachers can teach alliteration, onomatopoeia, and rhyme scheme. When integrating music and math, students use rhythm and meter to count and skip numbers when moving, playing, or singing music. Music also integrates history and culture, as explained earlier in this chapter. Music can be used to teach almost any concept and can be a useful vehicle to help students respond and retain important facts.

COMPETENCY 003: HEALTH

The teacher uses knowledge of the concepts and purposes of health education to plan and implement effective and engaging health instruction.

Enhancing Wellness

The leading causes of illness, disease, and death are not infectious by nature, but rather lifestyle related. Some common diseases such as heart disease, obesity, and cancer are influenced by people's chosen behaviors. The key to achieving good health is taking responsibility for daily actions and creating a proactive lifestyle. Many benefits result from a consistent program of diet and exercise. Improvements in cardiac output, maximum oxygen intake, and mood stabilization, as well as enhancing the blood's ability to carry oxygen, are just a few of them. Health education also includes the awareness and avoidance of risks present in everyday life. Some of the risks include smoking, using drugs, and having unprotected sex. Education is the key to minimizing such risks.

Body Systems

The body has a system of interrelated subsystems working together to keep it functioning properly. Cells are the building blocks of the body, and tissues are groups of similar cells working together to perform a specific job. An organ consists of many kinds of tissues working together for a larger purpose, and a group of organs working together is called an organ system. Several organ systems work in the human body.

Circulatory System. The heart pumps blood in the circulatory system. The blood passes through the right chambers of the heart and through the lungs, where it acquires oxygen. It then passes back into the left chambers of the heart where it is pumped into the aorta, which branches into increasingly smaller arteries, veins, and capillaries throughout the body. Beyond that, blood passes through tiny, thin-walled structures called capillaries. In the capillaries, the blood gives up oxygen and nutrients to tissues and absorbs metabolic waste products containing carbon dioxide. Finally, blood completes the circuit by passing through small veins, joining to form increasingly larger vessels until it reaches the largest veins, which return it back to the right side of the heart.

Respiratory System. Respiration results from the expansion and contraction of the lungs for gas exchange in the body. In the lungs, oxygen enters tiny capillaries, where it combines with hemoglobin in the red blood cells and is carried to the body's tissues. At the same time, carbon dioxide passes through capillaries into the air contained within the lungs. Inhaling draws air that is higher in oxygen and lower in carbon dioxide into the lungs. Exhaling forces the air that is high in carbon dioxide and low in oxygen from the lungs.

Digestive System. Food provides the energy required for sustenance of the body. After the fragmenting of food by chewing and mixing with saliva, digestion begins. Chewed food passes down the esophagus into the stomach, where gastric and intestinal juices continue the digestion process. Thereafter, the mixture of food and secretions makes its way down the alimentary canal using peristalsis (the rhythmic contraction of the smooth muscle of the gastrointestinal tract). The smallest units of food are ultimately absorbed into the bloodstream and transported throughout the body for use.

Immune System. The body defends itself against foreign proteins and infectious microorganisms by means of a complex immune system. The immune system is composed of a dual system that depends on recognizing a portion of the surface pattern of the invader and the generation of lymphocytes and antibody molecules to destroy invading molecules.

Skeletal System. The human skeletal system consists of more than 200 bones held together by connective tissues called ligaments. The bones are attached to the skeletal muscles, and contractions of these skeletal muscles affect movements.

Nervous System. The nervous system controls muscular contractions. The nervous system has two divisions: the somatic, which allows voluntary control over skeletal muscle; and the autonomic (or involuntary), which controls cardiac and glandular functions. Nerve impulses carried by cranial or spinal cord nerves that connect the brain to skeletal muscles cause voluntary movement. Involuntary, or reflex, movement occurs in direct response to outside stimulus. Nerve terminals called receptors constantly send impulses to the central nervous system. Each type of receptor directs nerve impulses to specialized areas of the brain for processing.

Diet and Exercise

Statistics show that Americans get more obese every year (Centers for Disease Control and Prevention, 2018). Although countless books and magazine articles are available on weight control, students often get reliable information about diet and exercise only in the classroom. People who are overweight on average do not live as long as those who maintain optimal weight. Being overweight has been isolated as a major risk factor in certain types of cancer, in heart and kidney disease, and in gall bladder problems. Chronic diseases such as diabetes and high blood pressure are also aggravated by, or caused by, being overweight. Maintaining a good weight and body-fat ratio can definitely affect people's quality of life.

Conversely, being underweight also presents health risks. Society often places too much emphasis on losing weight and being thin. Women are especially prone to measuring their self-worth by the bathroom scale. Young girls are particularly susceptible to these messages, and eating disorders can result (National Institute of Mental Health, 2014). Ideal weight and a good body fat ratio should be the goals when trying to lose weight. A correlation also exists between body fat and high cholesterol. Diet and exercise are the keys to maintaining a good body fat ratio. Exercise helps keep the ratio low, improves healthy cholesterol levels, and prevents heart disease.

Metabolism is a set of chemical processes that occur in the body to keep it functioning and growing as well as responding to the environment and maintaining life balance. The Basal Metabolic Rate (BMR) is the pace at which the body burns the vast majority of calories efficiently at rest. Adjustments in the BMR are slow, occur over time, and are dependent upon the demands put upon the body physically (i.e., exercise) as well as on the consumption of calories. If calorie intake is too restricted, the body goes into starvation mode and operates by burning fewer calories to conserve energy. Just a 250-calorie drop a day combined with a 250-calorie burn will result in a loss of one pound a week. Crash diets, which bring about rapid weight loss, are unhealthy and ineffective. Slower weight loss lasts longer. Aerobic exercise is a major component of successful weight loss. Exercise speeds metabolism and causes the body to burn calories efficiently. The timing of exercise may also enhance the benefits. Exercise before meals speeds metabolism and helps suppress appetite. Education should help people realize that maintaining a healthy weight is crucial to a healthy and higher quality life.

Combined with exercise, a healthy diet is vital to good health, learning, academic achievement, and longevity. The elements of good nutrition, the role of vitamins, elimination of risk factors, and strategies to control weight are all part of a healthy lifestyle. In June 2011, the USDA changed its symbol for healthy eating from a Food Pyramid to a Healthy Plate. Instead of having Americans consider their daily intake, the USDA is encouraging consumers to think about building a healthy diet one plate at a time. The colorful, four-part plate is divided into four sections (Figure 7-9). Fruit and vegetables take half of the plate while one quarter each is reserved for protein and grains. A side container represents dairy.

Figure 7-9. Choose My Plate

Source: U.S. Department of Agriculture, *MyPlate*,
www.teamnutrition.usda.gov/myplate.htm.

Recommendations include:

1. One-half of the plate should be whole grains (e.g., bread, cereal, rice, and pasta) and proteins, which should vary between animal proteins and legumes.

2. Vegetables and fruit should comprise the other half.

3. Milk products should be low-fat (1%) or fat-free.

4. Compare sodium contents in soups and frozen foods and choose lower sodium products.

5. Drink water instead of sugary drinks.

Nutrients are divided into two main groups: macro-nutrients (carbohydrates, proteins, and fats) and micro-nutrients (vitamins and minerals). Most foods contain a combination of the two groups. Complex carbohydrates (e.g., vegetables, fruits, whole grain breads, and cereals) are the preferred energy source and should comprise up to one-half of the diet. These foods provide fiber, which helps digestion, reduces constipation, and reduces the risk of colon cancer. Proteins (e.g., milk, eggs, meat, fish, and beans) are one of the most essential nutrients because the body uses them to build and repair itself in more ways than any other food. Fats (e.g., olive and canola oils) are important to the body for regulating blood pressure, forming cell structures, transporting vitamins, and triggering immune system responses. Vitamins are essential because they perform highly specific metabolic processes in the cells and aid with many other functions, such as the growth and maintenance of the body. Minerals (e.g., calcium, iron, potassium, and zinc) help build strong bones and teeth, aid in muscle function, and help the nervous system transmit messages. Keeping a consistent balance of nutrients combined with hydration will keep systems functioning properly and thus minimize overall health risk. Much nutrition information is available to teachers at the Dietary Guidelines for Americans, published by the U.S. Department of Health and Human Services (2015).

Stress Management

Stress is the product of change, either negative or positive. Multiple components and situations can cause stress. Some of these are:

- Environmental factors such as noise, air pollution, and crowding

- Physiological factors such as sickness and physical injuries

- Psychological factors such as self-deprecating thoughts and negative self-image

Besides the normal stressors that everyone experiences, some students may live in dysfunctional families. Some also may be dealing with substance abuse and addictions, and some may be experiencing sexual abuse.

People have many sources of stress, and students and teachers should learn acceptable ways to cope with stress. The first step is to recognize the role that stress plays in daily life. A teacher might lead a class through a brainstorming activity to help the students become aware of the sources of stress that affects them. Next, the teacher could identify positive ways of coping with stress, including positive self-talk, physical exercise, proper nutrition, adequate sleep, outdoor play activities, time-management techniques, good study habits, and relaxation exercises.

Students facing stress often experience a range of emotions. They may be sad, frustrated, or afraid. Effective teachers realize that students' emotions play a significant role in students' classroom performance and achievement. Thus, they should seek to create a classroom environment supportive of students' emotional needs. They should have appropriate empathy and compassion for the emotional conflicts facing students. Teachers also should have a realistic awareness that students need to attain crucial academic and social skills that will help them control their environment as they become increasingly independent individuals and, eventually, productive citizens.

The state curriculum for health (Texas Essential Knowledge and Skills) has incorporated objectives and standards to prepare school-age children to face the multiple physical, environmental, and emotional challenges that children face in the United States. Health education teachers and teachers in general are required to teach these health objectives in formal health classes through the integration of health components in the general curricula. All Texas teachers should know the state health curriculum. An analysis of the health curriculum mandates in Texas follows.

Curriculum Requirements for Health

The Texas Essential Knowledge and Skills (TEKS) prescribes state curriculum for health education teachers (Texas Education Agency, n.d.). In conjunction with the national initiative, the TEKS curriculum provides strategies for teaching developmentally appropriate content in health education to children in Grades K–12. Some key components of the TEKS require children to develop an understanding of their body as well as of proper nutrition practices and safety procedures. It also requires that children be able to use reliable information to make personal health decisions. Topics introduced in Grades K–6 include:

1. Making healthy food choices.

2. Strategies to avoid health and safety risks.

3. Strategies for protection against sexual predators.

4. How media influence health decisions.

5. Assertive behaviors and strategies to deal with risky situations.

6. Gang-prevention programs.

7. Drug- and alcohol-prevention programs.

8. Knowledge of the human body.

9. Safety procedures in school and the community.

Key skills and activities required in the Texas K–6 curriculum are listed as follows.

Kindergarten

Children in Kindergarten should be able to:

1. Identify types of foods that help the body grow.

2. Identify the purpose of such protective equipment as a seat belt and a bicycle helmet.

3. Identify how to get help from a parent and/or trusted adult when made to feel uncomfortable or unsafe by another person/adult.

4. Demonstrate procedures for responding to emergencies, including calling 911.

5. Demonstrate how to seek the help of parents/guardians and other trusted adults in making decisions and solving problems.

First Grade

Children in first grade should be able to:

1. Name safe play environments.

2. Describe the harmful effects of alcohol, tobacco, and other drugs as well as explain how to avoid them.

3. Identify and practice safety rules during play.

4. Identify common illnesses and diseases as well as their symptoms.

5. Name members of his/her family who help him/her to promote and practice healthy habits.

Second Grade

Children in second grade should be able to:

1. Describe and demonstrate such personal health habits as brushing and flossing teeth and exercising.

2. Identify the major organs of the body and describe their primary functions.

3. Apply practices to control spread of germs, including hand washing and skin care.

4. Demonstrate refusal skills.

5. Identify media that provide health information.

Third Grade

Children in third grade should be able to:

1. Describe ways to improve personal fitness.

2. Identify types of nutrients.

3. Explain the body's defense systems and how they fight disease.

4. Relate how protecting the environment promotes individual and community health.

5. Describe how the media can influence healthy behaviors.

Fourth Grade

Children in fourth grade should be able to:

1. Identify information on menus and food labels.

2. Explain how to develop a home-safety and emergency response plan such as fire safety.

3. Explain how sleep affects academic performance.

4. Identify the importance of taking responsibility for developing and maintaining a personal health plan for such subjects as fitness, nutrition, stress management, and personal safety.

5. Identify ways to avoid drugs and list alternatives for the use of drugs and other substances.

Fifth Grade

Children in fifth grade should be able to:

1. Apply information from the food guide plate to make healthy food choices.

2. Calculate the relationship between caloric intake and energy expenditure.

3. Explain strategies for avoiding violence, gangs, weapons, and drugs.

4. Explain the impact of neglect and abuse.

5. Assess the role of assertiveness, refusal skills, and peer pressure on decision-making and problem-solving.

Sixth Grade

Children in sixth grade should be able to:

1. Analyze healthy and unhealthy dietary practices.

2. Explain the consequences of sexual activity and the benefits of abstinence.

3. Seek the input of parents and other trusted adults in problem-solving and goal-setting.

4. Make such healthy choices as leaving a smoke-filled room or selecting healthy snacks from vending machines.

5. Describe chemical dependency and addiction to tobacco, alcohol, and other drugs and substances. (Texas Education Agency, n.d.)

Human Growth and Development

A teacher does not have to be an expert in anatomy and physiology to see the physical changes that accompany students' growth and maturity. The preschool child has trouble grasping pencils and crayons to facilitate handwriting. However, even most two-year-olds can grasp crayons well enough to make marks on papers and thus enjoy the creative excitement of art. Physiological changes play a significant role in children's development as they increase their control of bodily movements and refine their motor skills. Their ability to engage in simple to complex classroom and playground activities increases as they develop. Teachers must adjust and adapt classroom and playground activities to be developmentally appropriate for students' skill levels.

Girls typically reach maturational milestones before boys. Physical changes may embarrass girls and boys when they draw unwelcome attention. These changes usually create discomfort as adolescents find their body to be quite different, sometimes seemingly overnight. Teachers should make children aware that these changes are part of their natural development.

To build social and emotional health, teachers should understand principles of human development as well as its multiple dimensions (e.g., physical, mental, emotional, and social). Teachers also must appreciate a dynamic and interactive view of human development. This approach to understanding human development recognizes that people do not develop in a vacuum. They instead develop in an environment that, friendly or unfriendly, supportive or non-supportive, evokes and provokes reactions from individuals. Human development also is not a one-way street with the environment doing all the driving. People also act to shape and form their environment.

People constantly interact with their environments. Teachers must know and be sensitive to the personal characteristics of students (internal factors) and the characteristics of the environment. Beyond the characteristics humans share as they grow and mature, internal factors also include students' personalities as well as their self-concept and self-esteem, their self-discipline and self-control, their ability to cope with stress, and their outlook on life (attitude).

Empowerment has many components, including self-concept. A good definition of self-concept is what we believe to be true about ourselves, not what we think about others and not what they think about us. Self-efficacy is related to self-concept and refers to the confidence a person has in his/her ability to cope with challenges. Self-efficacy is the sense of control over life or over the responses to life. Ideas about self-efficacy get established by age four. Because of this early establishment of either a sense of control or a sense of having no control, classroom teachers may find that even primary grade students believe they lack control over their lives and that it makes no difference what they do or how they act. Therefore, teachers must help students gain coping skills and develop a sense of self-efficacy.

Substance Use and Abuse

Drug and alcohol problems can affect anyone, regardless of age, sex, race, marital status, place of residence, income level, or lifestyle. However, certain risk factors are identifiable for substance abuse and have individual, familial, social, and cultural characteristics.

The personal characteristics linked to substance abuse include aggressiveness, emotional problems and low self-esteem as well as the inability to cope with stress. Feelings of failure and a fragile ego can also contribute to substance abuse. Physical disabilities, physical or mental health problems, and learning disabilities can add to a student's vulnerability to substance abuse. Students at risk for academic problems are also susceptible to substance-abuse problems.

Several family characteristics are associated with substance abuse. First, the alcohol or other drug dependency of a parent or both parents may be most important. This characteristic might relate to another significant factor: parental abuse and neglect of children. Antisocial and/or mentally ill parents also put children at risk for drug and/or alcohol abuse. Family unemployment or underemployment is another characteristic. Parents with little education or who are socially isolated are also risk factors. Single parents without family or other support, as well as family instability, and a high level of marital and family conflict or violence are other risk factors. Parental absence—because of separation, divorce, or death—can also increase children's vulnerability to substance abuse. Finally, other considerations include a lack of family rituals as well as inadequate parenting, little child-to-parent interaction, and frequent family moves. These factors describe children without affiliation or a sense of identity with their families or the community. Any of these family factors could lead to a substance abuse.

Living in an economically depressed area with high unemployment, inadequate housing, a high crime rate, and a prevalence of illegal drug use are social characteristics that can put some-one at risk for substance abuse. Cultural risk factors include racial discrimination, differing gen-erational levels of assimilation, low levels of education, and low achievement expectations from society. All the recognized risk factors are indicators of potential substance abuse. They do not necessarily predict a proclivity to drug or alcohol abuse. Some children who are exposed to very adverse conditions grow up to be healthy, productive, and well-functioning adults. Yet, knowing the risk factors, teachers are better able to identify children vulnerable to substance abuse and develop prevention-education strategies. If teachers recognize the risk factors in some of their stu-dents, teachers can take action designed to increase the chances that the child will resist the lures of illegal and dangerous alcohol and drug abuse.

It can be hard to tell whether someone is using illegal drugs or alcohol. People (including young people) who abuse drugs or alcohol go to great lengths to keep their behavior a secret. They deny and/or try to hide the problem. However, certain warning signs indicate that someone is using drugs or drinking too much alcohol: (1) Lying to teachers and family members, (2) Avoiding people who are longtime friends or associates, (3) Having slurred speech, (4) Complaining of headaches, nausea, or dizziness, (5) Having difficulty staying awake in class, and (6) Bloodshot, glazed over, and/or squinting eyes. These signs alone will not confirm a substance abuse problem, but in com-bination and when displayed consistently over time, they are strong indicators. Teachers should record their observations and keep written reports of behavioral changes they witness. Moreover, they should report their suspicions to the appropriate school authorities.

Violence and Abuse

Child abuse is a common problem in the United States. According to the American Academy of Pediatrics, more than 2.5 million cases of child abuse and neglect are reported annually (Shelov & Remer, 2009). Half the cases involve neglect, and the other half involves physical and sexual abuse.

Abused children typically show signs of overstimulation—being "wired," unruly, and/or bel-ligerent. By contrast, the behaviors of neglected children point to understimulation—all they want is to be left alone and typically they are unsociable, sedate, and/or withdrawn. The child learns this behavior at home during periods of neglect. The neglect may change the child's behaviors from almost flat (registering no emotion) to anger. Although poor attention, tears, violence, and apathetic behavior may indicate either abuse or neglect, neglected children usually have feelings of hopeless-ness and cannot adequately control their thoughts and emotions. Students either become obsessed with the neglect or refuse to acknowledge that the neglect is really happening.

Despite the media attention given to child abuse and neglect, many teachers still believe that it cannot happen to one of their students. They may think, "This is a nice neighborhood," or "Most of these students have both a mother and a father living at home." But teachers should instead keep in mind that it can happen to *their* students.

One of the most obvious visible signs of child abuse is red swelling or bruising caused by being hit. The appearance of marks on a child may prove child abuse, and the teacher must report the evidence immediately. Visible signs are also one way teachers can separate real abuse cases from unfounded ones. While marks from the hand, fist, or belt are usually recognizable, other marks in geometric shapes (i.e., eating utensils, paddles, coat hangers, or extension cords) can signify child abuse as well.

Besides showing the physical marks, victims of child abuse and neglect can also exhibit non-traditional behaviors. The most common documented characteristics include: (1) frequent illness; (2) hyperactivity disorders; (3) depression; (4) bowel or bladder control problems; (5) impulsivity, aggressiveness, or defiance; and (6) academic difficulties. Neglect is more common than abuse but gets less attention because it fails to show easily observable manifestations.

Teachers hope they will never have to manage a disclosure of any kind of maltreatment of a child, but such revelations are the responsibility of these trusted adults and student advocates. When a child discloses abuse, teachers should respond calmly and thank/support the child for bringing this matter to their attention. Teachers should not question the child about the details but should gather the information and follow-up with administrators, counselors, and/or nurses. The best course of action is to make an immediate referral or report of these suspicions.

Teachers in Texas are required by law to report any suspicion of child abuse or neglect to Texas Health and Human Services. Thus, they must be vigilant for possible symptoms or indications of child abuse. Failure to file a report of suspicion of child abuse or neglect has consequences and can result in legal action against the teacher. After reporting the abuse, the teacher should realize that the child may feel that his or her teacher has exposed the child's private life. While accepting the child's feeling of betrayal, the teacher should explain that the report was necessary and assure the child of protection against reprisals for telling about the abuse. Sometimes the child benefits from just knowing that others care about his or her well-being.

Safety and Accident Prevention

Peer counseling, peer mediation, and peer leadership programs have shown little effectiveness in reducing violence, encouraging safety in schools, and preventing accidents. Restricting promotion to succeeding grades for violent students has shown negative effects on achievement and attendance as well as behavior toward school. Research shows that the most successful programs are multifaceted and linked to a variety of services. Characteristics of such programs include: (1) early start and long-term commitment; (2) strong collaborative leadership that enforces explicit disciplinary policies; (3) ongoing staff development; (4) parental involvement and parental education (e.g., home visits); and (5) role-modeling activities designed to be culturally relevant.

School Violence

Violence of one form or another is prevalent in American schools. Findings by the U.S. Centers for Disease Control and Prevention help delineate the scope of the problem. In 2019, CDC's nationwide Youth Risk Behavior Survey asked high school students across the United States to report instances of violence. According to YRBS results from 13,677 students:

- About 1 in 5 high school students said they'd been bullied on school property in the past year.

- 8% of high school students reported being in a physical fight on school property at least once during the 12 months before the survey.

- More than 7% of high school students said they had been threatened or injured with a weapon (e.g., a gun, knife, or club) on school property at least once during the 12 months before the survey.

- Nearly 9% of high school students had skipped school at least 1 day during the 30 days before the survey, believing they would be unsafe at school or going to or from school

The CDC says, "School is the location where the violence occurs, not a type of violence."

Some elements that contribute to school violence are: (1) overcrowding, (2) poor design and use of school space, (3) lack of disciplinary procedures, (4) student alienation, (5) multicultural insensitivity, (6) rejection of at-risk students by teachers and peers, and (7) anger or resentment at school routines.

Factors that contribute to school safety include (1) a positive school climate and atmosphere, (2) clear and high performance expectations for all students, (3) practices and values that promote inclusion, (4) bonding of the students to the school, (5) high levels of student participation and parental involvement in school activities, and (6) opportunities to acquire academic skills and develop socially.

Teachers must be alert to the signs of potentially violent behavior, while acknowledging that signs can be misinterpreted and misunderstood. Warning signs should be used to get help for children, not to exclude, punish, or isolate them. Some of the imminent warning signs of school violence are: (1) serious physical violence with peers or family members; (2) serious destruction of property; (3) rage for seemingly minor reasons; (4) detailed threats of lethal violence; (5) possession and/or use of firearms and weapons; and (6) self-injurious behaviors or threats of suicide. Teachers should recognize these signs of violence and notify the appropriate authorities. Violence prevention strategies range from adding social skills training to the curriculum to installing metal detectors at the entrances to buildings. Schools should teach all students procedures in conflict resolution and anger management and should explain the school's rules, expectations, and disciplinary policies.

Mental and Emotional Health

Mental and emotional disorders present emotional and physical signs. Depression can manifest itself in an overall lack of interest in activities as well as constant crying or talk of suicide. Anxiety or obsessive thoughts also indicate a possible mental or emotional disorder. Physical signs include a disruption in eating or sleeping patterns as well as headaches, nausea and stomach pain, or diarrhea. The teacher should consider these signs as a cause for serious concerns and treatment.

Psychotic disorders, such as schizophrenia, are serious emotional disorders. These disorders are rare in young children and difficult to diagnose, although one of the warning signs for psychotic disorders is that the student experiences a complete break from the reality of his or her surroundings. Schizophrenics may have difficulty expressing themselves, resulting in unusual speech patterns or even muteness. Schizophrenics are more likely to be boys than girls and may also exhibit facial expressions that are either absent of emotion or overly active.

Infantile Autism

Infantile autism is another serious emotional disorder that appears in early childhood. Characteristics include withdrawn behavior and delayed or absent language and communication skills. Symptoms of autism can appear in children between four and eighteen months of age. Autistic children will usually distance themselves from others and may be unable to experience empathy. In addition, they often cannot distinguish or appreciate humor. Autistic children may have a preoccupation with particular objects or may perform particular activities repeatedly. While autistic children can range in intelligence, some children may have particular skills in focused areas, such as music or math. Diagnosis might inaccurately determine mental retardation, hearing/auditory impairment, or brain damage. Treatment for autistic children may involve therapy, drugs, or residential living. However, only 5% of autistic children become socially well-adjusted adults. Many of these high-functioning autistics are placed in the regular classroom, some with personal aides to facilitate their success.

Eating Disorders

Eating disorders are a real, treatable medical illness in which certain maladaptive patterns of eating take on a life of their own (National Institute of Mental Health, 2014). The main types of eating disorders are anorexia nervosa (lack of desire or interest in food, which results in starvation of the body) and bulimia nervosa (episodes of secretive excessive eating followed by inappropriate methods of weight control such as self-induced vomiting). A third problem that exhibits a total lack of control for eating is compulsive overeating or binge-eating disorder. Many professionals have suggested this condition as a formal disorder although it has not yet been approved as a formal psychiatric diagnosis. Eating disorders frequently develop during adolescence or early adulthood, but some reports indicate their onset can occur during childhood or later in adulthood. Treatments for eating disorders are complex and most often require professional help (e.g., psychotherapy, support groups, and/or hospitalization).

Healthy Interpersonal Relationships

The social domain of health is manifested in our ability to practice good social skills and maintain comfortable relationships with others. Socially, healthy people communicate respect for others, show tolerance and patience, and accept differences without compromising relationships. Successful teachers listen and recognize the needs of others. Ultimately, effective educators recognize ways they enrich and are enriched by their relationships and use these skills to role-model appropriate behaviors.

To become effective communicators, students need learning opportunities to practice interpersonal skills in situations they are likely to encounter (e.g., communicating empathy, resisting peer-pressure, managing conflicts, and asking for help). By practicing such methods, students establish a natural link to express their healthy intentions when the correct situation/environment arises. Educators should look for such ways to practice assertive communication as stating a position, offering a reason that makes sense or is healthy, and acknowledging others' feelings.

Health Care Information

The *Surgeon General's Report on Health Promotion and Disease Prevention* was first released in 1979, creating a public health revolution that emphasized disease prevention and taking personal responsibility for one's health. In 1990, the United States Department of Health and Human Services published *Promoting Health/Preventing Disease: Objectives for the Nation*, which outlined specific objectives for meeting those goals identified in the earlier *Surgeon General's Report*.

These objectives led to the development of *Healthy People 2000*, a document that aimed to reduce preventable death and disability and enhance the quality of life for American society. Today, *Healthy People 2030* is setting the current decade's data-driven health and well-being agenda for the United States, using science, technology, and education. Administrators, teachers, and health professionals must become familiar with the policy of the federal government and incorporate its principles in schools.

Health Care Professionals

School health services typically include policies and programs that assess and protect the health of students. Specifically, the school nurse leads this collaborative effort to direct patient care, screen and diagnose symptoms, promote health counseling services, participate in health promotion and disease prevention, and maintain relationships with allied health professionals and community health service providers. School administrators have the legal responsibility for the safety of all students and for the supervision of the health services program offered in school. Regrettably, many school districts have assigned these tasks to untrained teachers and/or staff, which leads to dangerous practices for the students, teachers, and school district.

Like other states, Texas has a legislative mandate requiring all children to be immunized against certain communicable diseases (e.g., polio, diphtheria, measles, mumps, rubella, chicken pox, and hepatitis) before enrolling in public school. All policies governing communicable diseases should be available to teachers and school employees to promote collaboration and risk reduction. Teachers should always be proactive in obtaining information when a child who suffers from a communicable disease can safely return to school. Besides any formal instruction in health, other teachers should integrate the content areas (e.g., social studies, science, art, and music) to health-related issues. Examples of topics that can be integrated easily into other content areas are:

1. the effects of pollution on health and occupational-related disease (e.g., "black lung" disease)

2. the health care options available to people in different parts of the world and in different economic circumstances

3. differentiation between communicable and non-communicable diseases

4. the importance of washing hands frequently

Older children should be able to explain the transmission and prevention of communicable diseases, and all children should learn which diseases cannot be transmitted through casual contact.

Students as young as kindergartners and first graders can learn how to recognize advertisements that might lead them to make unhealthy choices (e.g., for candy or sugar-laden cereal). By third or fourth grade, children should be able to show they can make health-related decisions regarding advertisements in media. Teachers can encourage students to: (1) avoid alcohol, tobacco, stimulants, and narcotics; (2) get plenty of sleep and exercise; (3) eat a well-balanced diet; (4) receive the proper immunizations; and (5) avoid sharing toothbrushes, combs, hats, beverages, and food with others.

External Influences

The school is a community agency that cannot function properly in isolation. The range of problems associated with students, results from not only school but also parents/family, neighborhoods, and the larger community (e.g., consumerism, media, and environment). Those who advocate for students must realize that the complexity of health and social problems require all community stakeholders to take responsibility and work with the schools to improve the health of students. An important step to confront these challenges is the need for local districts to establish a school health advisory council that includes members from all segments of the community (e.g., school personnel, medical professionals, nonprofit organizations, and the business sector). Such committees work to increase visibility of initiatives, increase the quantity and quality of health-promotion efforts, and reduce duplication of services.

First Aid

First aid is the immediate, temporary care of an injured or ill person. Occasionally, during physical education classes or during school hours, injuries and illnesses occur. Therefore, knowledge of first aid is important for physical education teachers and other instructors. However, a teacher should not attempt first aid if the procedures are unclear. A course in first aid is important for the classroom teacher, and they are readily available from your local chapter of the American Red Cross.

The following are some common injuries and a brief description of their emergency treatments:

1. **Bone Fracture:** A fracture is a break in a bone. Fractures can be simple, multiple (many breaks in the bone), or compound (a break in the bone and the skin).

   Treatment: Immobilize, use ice to control swelling, and seek medical aid. In the case of a compound fracture, it is important to stop the bleeding.

2. **Traumatic Shock:** Traumatic shock is the severe compression of circulation caused by injury or illness. Symptoms include cool sweaty skin and a rapid weak pulse.

   Treatment: Minimize heat loss and elevate the legs without disturbing the rest of the body. Seek medical help.

3. **Sprain Injury:** A sprain is an injury to a joint caused by the joint being moved too far or away from its range of motion. Both ligaments and tendons can be injured in a sprain. Ligaments join bone to bone, and tendons join muscle to bone.

   Treatment: Guide the victim to rest, apply ice to the injury, and compression. The use of the acronym RICE—Rest, Ice, Compression, and Elevation—provides an easy way to remember the appropriate treatment for sprains.

4. **Strain Muscle:** A strain is a muscle injury caused by overuse.

   Treatment: Use ice to lessen the swelling and rest. Applying some heat after icing can be beneficial although opinion on the value of heat varies.

5. **Dislocation of a Joint:** In this injury, the bone becomes out of place at the joint. As a result, ligaments can be severely stretched and/or torn.

   Treatment: Immobilize and seek medical help. Some people advocate "popping" the dislocation back into place, but this can be risky for both the injured person and for the person giving the first aid (liability). Therefore, let the medical professionals put the joint back in place.

6. **Heat Exhaustion:** The symptoms of heat exhaustion include cold and sweaty skin, nausea, dizziness, and paleness. Heat exhaustion is not as severe as heat stroke.

   Treatment: Increase water intake, replace salt, and get out of the heat.

7. **Heat Stroke:** The symptoms of heat stroke include high fever, dry skin, and possible unconsciousness.

   Treatment: Try to cool off the body gradually, get into the shade, and seek medical attention immediately.

8. **Heart Attack:** The symptoms of heart attack include shortness of breath, pain in the left arm, pain in the chest, nausea, and sweating.

   Treatment: Elevate the head and chest, give cardiopulmonary resuscitation if indicated, and seek medical assistance. If the heart stops, apply resuscitation techniques. Resuscitation is a first-aid technique that provides artificial circulation and respiration. Remember the ABCs: *A* is for "airway," *B* is for "breathing," and *C* is for "circulation." Check the airway to make sure it is open and check breathing and circulation.

9. **Seizures:** The cause of seizures is often epilepsy.

   Treatment: Clear the area around the victim to avoid injury during the seizure. Do not place anything in the victim's mouth. Seek medical help after the seizure, if necessary.

COMPETENCY 004: PHYSICAL EDUCATION

The teacher uses knowledge of the concepts, principles, skills, and practices of physical education to plan and implement effective and engaging physical education instruction.

Principles of Physical Education and Physical Activity

The Society of Health and Physical Educators (SHAPE) has defined what a student should know and be able to do as a result of a quality physical education program. A quality physical education program provides learning opportunities, appropriate instruction, meaningful and challenging content, as well as regular student and program assessment. SHAPE recommends that schools provide 150 minutes of instructional physical education for elementary school children, and 225 minutes for middle and high school student per week (Society of Health and Physical Educators, 2015).

With this definition in mind, SHAPE has developed the National Standards for Physical Education:

Standard 1: The physically literate individual demonstrates competency in a variety of motor skills and movement patterns.

Standard 2: The physically literate individual applies knowledge of concepts, principles, strategies, and tactics related to movement and performance.

Standard 3: The physically literate individual demonstrates the knowledge and skills to achieve and maintain a health-enhancing level of physical activity and fitness.

Standard 4: The physically literate individual exhibits responsible personal and social behavior that respects self and others.

Standard 5: The physically literate individual recognizes the value of physical activity for health, enjoyment, challenge, self-expression, and/or social interaction.

To help students achieve these standards, physical education teachers must understand the human body and how physical activity can affect it. Knowledge of anatomy and physiology can guide teachers in the selection and implementation of games and physical activities appropriate for development. Anatomy describes the structure, position, and size of body parts and organs. Because our bones adapt to fill a specific need, exercise benefits the skeletal system. Bones that anchor strong muscles thicken to withstand the stress put on them. Weight-bearing bones can develop heavy mineral deposits while supporting the body. Because joints help provide flexibility and ease of movement, it is important to know how each joint moves. Types of joints are ball and socket (e.g., shoulder and hip), hinge (e.g., elbow and knee), pivot (e.g., head of the spine), gliding (e.g., carpal [wrist] and tarsal [ankle] bones), angular (e.g., wrist and ankle joints), partially movable (e.g., vertebrae), and immovable (e.g., bones of the adult cranium).

Muscles are the active movers in the body. To teach physical education activity, the functions and physiology of the muscles must be understood. Because muscles move by shortening or contracting, proper form should be taught so that the student gets the most out of an activity. Knowing the location of each muscle is important to help in teaching proper form while participating in physical education activities. Understanding the concept of antagonistic muscles, with the related information concerning flexors and extensors, is also vital to the physical educator. Imagine trying to teach the proper form of throwing a ball if the instructor does not understand the mechanics. Knowledge of anatomy and physiology is also necessary to teach proper techniques for calisthenics as well as all physical activities. Without applying this knowledge, exercise can harm the body.

Exploration of movement through fun activities constitutes the main focus of physical education in the early grades. However, the curriculum also can provide more organized activities like yoga or low impact aerobic exercise. Aerobic exercise involves muscle contractions and body movement. Because aerobic exercise requires large amounts of oxygen, it will condition the cardiovascular system when done regularly. Some aerobic exercises are suited to developing aerobic training benefits, with a minimum of skill and time. Good aerobic activities include walking, running, swimming, and bicycling. These activities develop fitness and can be done alone with a minimum of equipment. True aerobic conditioning means an activity must require the body to use a lot of oxygen. It also must be continuous and rhythmic, exercise major muscle groups and burn fat as an energy source. Finally, it must last for at least 20 minutes in a person's target heart rate range. Children can participate in low-impact aerobics training, but parents and teachers must monitor their performance. Children will probably try to keep up with adults, and they may not have the strength, flexibility, and/or skill to keep pace. This could lead to undue fatigue, needless muscle soreness, and/or injury.

Benefits of an Active Lifestyle

The axiom "use it or lose it" holds for the human body. Our bodies thrive on physical activity, which is any bodily movement produced by skeletal muscles and resulting in energy expenditure. Fitness enables a person to meet the physical demands of work and leisure comfortably. A physically fit person can enjoy a better quality of life and minimize the development of life-threatening diseases. Unfortunately, Americans tend to be inactive.

Lack of activity can cause many problems, including weak muscles, poor circulation, shortness of breath, obesity, coronary artery disease, hypertension, type II diabetes, osteoporosis, and certain types of cancer. Overall, mortality rates from all causes are lower in physically active people than in sedentary people. Physical activity also can help people manage mild-to-moderate depression, control anxiety, and prevent weakening of the skeletal system. By increasing physical activity, a person may improve heart function and circulation, respiratory function, and overall strength and endurance. These benefits lead to improved vigor and vitality. Exercise also lowers the risk of heart disease by strengthening the heart muscle, lowering pulse and blood pressure, and lowering the concentration of fat in both the body and the blood. It can also improve appearance, increase range of motion, and lessen the risk of back problems associated with weak muscles, weak bones, and osteoporosis. Every person should engage in regular physical activity and reduce sedentary activities to promote health, psychological well-being, and a healthy body weight. Children should engage in at least 60 minutes of physical activity every day.

Proper hydration is also important during physical activity. To help prevent dehydration during prolonged physical activity or when it is hot, people should consume water before, during, and after the activity.

Evaluating and Monitoring Fitness Levels

Two chief reasons for teaching physical education are to instill a willingness to exercise and to encourage students to make good decisions about their health. The evaluation of student performance and progress thus is an essential responsibility of the physical education teacher. In 2007, the Texas Legislature passed a law that requires all students in Grades 3–12 to be measured annually on the Fitnessgram. The Fitnessgram is not a test of athletic ability but is rather a health-related fitness assessment that uses criterion-referenced standards to measure physical health (i.e., muscular fitness, aerobic fitness, and flexibility). With regular physical activity, all students should achieve a score on the Fitnessgram that will place them within or above the Healthy Fitness Zone on all test items. The idea is that all students should learn to assess their own level of fitness, interpret assessment results, plan personal programs, and motivate themselves to remain active throughout their lives.

The assessment plan for an elementary physical education program determines the degree to which students reach the identified goals. These critical objectives or "performance indicators" ensure that the teacher focuses activities on skill development and improved performance during movement games and activities. To obtain good body management skills is to acquire, expand, and integrate elements of motor control. This is done through movement experiences based on a creative and exploratory approach. Children not only manage their body with an ease of movement but also realize that good posture and body mechanics are important to their movement process and patterns. A child with good motor control is a child who is confident and graceful. This is important not only for playing games and sports but also for safety. Children without these skills are more prone to accidents and injury. The physical educator should identify and halt incorrect movement patterns, demonstrate proper forms of movement, and help learners to perform the desired movement pattern.

Development of Motor Skills

Physical changes play a significant role in children's development as they gain control of their body's movements and functions. As they develop physically, children refine their motor skills, enabling them to engage in increasingly complex movement lessons and/or activities. To identify patterns of physical development, teachers must first assess the level at which students can control specific movement patterns and then create activities that are developmentally appropriate for their students' physical abilities.

Children between three and four years have mastered standing and walking. At this stage, children are developing gross motor skills, including the ability to hop on one foot and balance, climb stairs without support, kick a ball, throw overhand, catch a ball that has bounced, move forward and backward, and ride a tricycle. Children between three and four are also developing fine motor skills, such as using scissors, drawing single shapes, and copying shapes like capital letters. By age four or five, when most children enter school, they are developing the gross motor ability to do somersaults, use a swing, climb, and skip. These skills require many movement patterns with increasing coordination. Children at this age can dress themselves using zippers and buttons, and they can possibly tie their shoes. They can also eat independently using utensils. Children at this age are increasingly capable of copying shapes, including letters and numbers. They can cut and paste and draw a person with a head, body, arms, and legs. These fine motor skills develop quickly in children at this age. By age six, children can bounce a ball, skate, ride a bike, skip with both feet, and dress themselves independently. As the student develops yearly, the physical skills (both fine and gross motor) become increasingly complex and involve more muscles and coordination. By age nine, children can complete a model kit, learn to sew, and cook simple recipes. By age ten, children can catch a fly ball and participate in all elements of a softball game.

Recognizing the TEKS milestones that most children will achieve by a certain age will help teachers make decisions about academic lessons and tasks. Teachers also may identify children who are not reaching their developmental milestones with the rest of the class. The physical ability of students to engage in simple to complex activities in school gradually increases as they develop.

Physical Educators must adjust and adapt classroom and playground activities to be developmentally appropriate for the specific skill levels of students.

During play, a child engages in meaningful movement patterns that use large muscle groups. Movement education helps a child to develop competency in those general movement patterns. Movement education has been defined as learning to move and moving to learn. Movement competency requires the student to manage his or her body through space, time, and direction with the ability to accomplish basic and specialized physical tasks and traverse obstacles. Basic movement skills are necessary for a child's daily living, whereas specialized skills are required to perform sports and other complex activities with clear techniques. Basic skills must be mastered before the child can develop specialized ones.

Perceptual motor competency is another consideration in teaching body management. Perceptual motor concepts relevant to physical education include those that give attention to balance, coordination, lateral movement, directional movement, awareness of space, and knowledge of one's body. Basic skills can be divided into three categories, locomotor, non-locomotor, and manipulative skills. A more complex movement pattern might include skills from each category. **Locomotor skills** describe the movement children must master to travel or move within a given space. These include walking, running, leaping, jumping, hopping, galloping, sliding, and skipping. **Non-locomotor skills** are used to control the body in relation to gravity. These are typically done while in a stationary position (i.e., kneeling or standing). Some of these activities include pushing, pulling, bending, stretching, twisting, turning, swinging, shaking, bouncing, rising, and falling. **Manipulative skills** are used when a child handles, moves, or plays with an object. Most manipulative skills involve using the hands and feet, but other parts of the body may be used as well. Hand-eye and foot-eye coordination are improved when manipulating objects. Throwing, batting, kicking, and catching are important skills to be developed using balls and beanbags. Starting a child at a less challenging level and progressing to a more difficult activity is an effective method for teaching manipulative activities. Most activities begin with individual practice and evolve into partner activities. When teaching throwing and catching, for example, the teacher should emphasize skill performance, principles of opposition, weight transfer, eye focus, and follow through. Some attention should be given to targets when throwing because students need to be able to catch and throw to different areas and levels. For detailed information on physical education activities for K–6 children, visit the PE Central website at *www.pecentral.org*.

Promoting Physical Fitness

Children in early childhood are not concerned with physical fitness. They are interested in having fun. Based on this premise, a physical education program for this age group should reflect this interest. The child who participates in fun physical activities will get the same benefits as children in a highly structured physical fitness program. It is thus important for K–6 physical educators to understand that programming activities that focus on the students' enjoyment of moving their bodies is much more important than grooming them for success at an event or sport.

Movement education enables children to choose the activity and the method they wish to use. Teachers can structure learning situations so that the child can be challenged to develop his or her own means of movement. The child becomes the center of learning and is encouraged to be creative in carrying out the movement. In this method of teaching, the child is encouraged to progress according to his or her abilities. The teacher is not the center of learning but offers suggestions and stimulates the learning environment through guided discovery. Student-centered learning works well when there is a disparity of motor abilities. If the teacher sets standards too high, the less talented students may become discouraged and lose motivation. Conversely, if the teacher sets standards too low, the more talented students will become bored and also lose interest. Providing options for learners is the best way to facilitate movement games and activities. Learners can identify which option or challenges are most appropriate and perform up to their developmental level with little help and/or cues from the teacher. Movement education tries to develop children's awareness not only of what they are doing but how they are doing it. Each child is encouraged to succeed in his or her own way according to his or her own capacity. If children succeed at developing basic skills in elementary school, they will have a much better chance at acquiring the specialized skills required for sports, events, and specific activities later in secondary school.

To teach a basic or specialized movement to a variety of learners, the instructor must present and use explanation, demonstration, and drill. Students can do demonstrations if the teacher monitors the demonstration and gives cues for proper form. Drills are excellent to teach specific skills but can become tedious unless they are done creatively. Using simulated games to practice skills can also work to maintain interest during a practice. Teachers should use observation and feedback when teaching a skill or activity. Positive feedback is more conducive to skill acquisition than negative feedback. The "old school" intimidation tactics of physical education coaches will not work for children at this age. Appropriate feedback means correcting with suggestions to improve. A student who continually misses the ball or kicks the ball out of play during kickball is aware that something is not right. The teacher should indicate what the problem is and show the student how to succeed when kicking the ball (and, of course, practice, practice, practice . . . time on task).

Many physical education professionals advocate the Teaching Games for Understanding model as a sound philosophy for teaching movement games. It is a socio-constructivist teaching and learning approach to physical education that emphasizes the learners' engagement in the construction of knowledge, skills, and experience. This student-centered model builds upon critical thinking, problem-solving, observation, and debriefing the experience for specific learning outcomes (i.e., teamwork, sportsmanship, and skill performance). Strategies of this model can be used across the physical education curriculum and include adventure education, cooperative learning, fitness education, tactical games, and sports education.

Curriculum Requirements for Physical Education

The TEKS comprises all the curriculum components in physical education. Physical education teachers are expected to use the prescribed state curriculum (Texas Education Agency, n.d.). In conjunction with the national initiative, TEKS requires children to show knowledge and skills for movement that provide the foundation for enjoyment, continued social development through physical activity, and access to a physically active lifestyle. All children are expected to develop muscular strength and endurance of the arms, shoulders, abdomen, back, and legs. They are also expected to become aware of how the muscles, bones, heart, and lungs work in physical activity. The activities and skills for children in K–6 are designed to keep children active, to develop the fitness necessary for appropriate physical development, and to maintain a healthy body and mind. Some of the key skills and activities required in the state K–6 curriculum are listed below (Texas Education Agency, n.d.).

Kindergarten

Children in Kindergarten should be able to:

1. Play with other children within boundaries during games and activities.

2. Develop muscular strength and endurance of the arms, shoulders, abdomen, back, and legs in such activities as hanging, hopping, and jumping.

3. Demonstrate such relationships as under, over, behind, next to, through right, left, up, down, forward, backward, and in front of.

4. Roll sideways (right or left) without hesitating.

5. Toss a ball and catch it before it bounces twice.

First Grade

Children in first grade should be able to:

1. Show proper foot patterns in hopping, jumping, skipping, leaping, galloping, and sliding.

2. Demonstrate the ability to work with a partner in such activities as leading and following.

3. Clap in time to a simple rhythmic beat; create and imitate movement in response to selected rhythms; jump a long rope; and demonstrate on cue key elements in overhand throw, underhand throw, and catch.

4. Describe how muscles and bones work together to produce movement.

5. Demonstrate control in balancing and traveling activities.

Second Grade

Children in second grade should be able to:

1. Demonstrate skills of chasing, fleeing, and dodging to avoid or catch others.

2. Show mature forms of walking, hopping, and skipping.

3. Display good sportsmanship and treat others with respect during game play.

4. Demonstrate simple stunts that exhibit personal agility, such as jumping with one- and two-foot takeoffs and landing with good control.

5. Demonstrate on cue key elements of hand dribble, foot dribble, kick and strike, such as striking a balloon or ball with a hand.

Third Grade

Children should be able to:

1. Show mature forms in jogging, running, and leaping.

2. Demonstrate control and appropriate form, such as curled position and protection of neck in rolling activities.

3. Transfer their bodies on and off equipment with good body control with such items as boxes, benches, stacked mats, horizontal bar, and balance beam.

4. Clap echoes in one measure rhythmical patterns.

5. Demonstrate key elements in such manipulative skills as underhand throw, overhand throw, catch and kick.

Fourth Grade

Children in fourth grade should be able to:

1. Change speed during straight, curved, and zigzag pathways.

2. Catch a football pass on the run.

3. Jump and land for height and distance absorbing force such as bending knees and swinging arms.

4. Perform basic folk dance steps such as schottische (German folk dance), and step-together-step.

5. Demonstrate key elements in such manipulative skills as volleying, hand dribble, foot dribble, and punt, also, striking with a body part, racquet, or bat.

Fifth Grade

Children in fifth grade should be able to:

1. Show smooth combinations of such fundamental locomotor skills as running and dodging and hop–step–jump.

2. Demonstrate the ability to contrast a partner's movement.

3. Identify common phases such as preparation, movement, follow through, or recovery in such movement skills as a tennis serve, handstand, and free throw.

4. Self-monitor the heart rate during exercise.

5. Identify potentially dangerous exercises and their adverse effects on the body.

Sixth Grade

Children in sixth grade should be able to:

1. Use relationships, levels, speed, direction, and pathways in such complex group and individual physical activities as crouching low for volleyball digs, stretching high during lay-ups, positioning for a soccer pass, or passing ahead of a receiver.

2. Move in time to such complex rhythmical patterns as ¾ time or ⁶⁄₈ time.

3. Hand and foot dribble while preventing an opponent from stealing the ball.

4. Practice in ways appropriate for such learning skills as whole/part/whole; shorter practice distributed over time is better than one long session; or practicing is best in game-like conditions.

5. Select and use proper attire that promotes participation and prevents injury.

Managing Instruction

Managing a large class of children in a loud gymnasium or outdoor learning environment is no easy task. Therefore, a major goal of the physical education teacher is to have all students listen to directions before activity. The instructions should be short, to the point, and as clear as possible. A teacher who talks longer than 20 seconds during any single instructional period will soon find the class losing interest. This leads to an environment difficult to manage. Teachers thus should alternate short instructional episodes including one or two points of focus with longer periods of activity. Minimizing instructional content will reduce student frustration and difficult situations. Most students and teachers enjoy an organized and efficient learning environment that devotes maximum class time to physical activity and learning skills.

Especially early on, the instructor must regularly enforce management behavior routines. Otherwise, the environment will be chaotic and difficult to manage. Effective physical educators identify a consistent keyword to use with learners to start a new activity (i.e., "Begin" or "Ready, Go"). This implies encouraging youngsters to listen to the entire set of instructions before preparing for the next exercise. Since the keyword is not given until all directions have been issued, students cannot begin until they hear the keyword. Similarly, a consistent signal should be established for stopping an activity (i.e., "Freeze" or "Clap once . . . Clap twice . . . Clap three times . . ."). The signal must be practiced daily so that the signal becomes second nature to the learners. Using an audio signal (i.e., whistle blast) with a visual signal (i.e., raising the hand overhead) may also be effective, since some youngsters may not hear the audio signal if they are engrossed in loud activity. A loud audio signal may be used to stop a class, but a voice command should always be used to start the class. If children do not respond to these signals, the procedure must be practiced. If a teacher settles for less than full attention, students will fulfill expectations of being chaotic and unmanageable.

Physical education teachers should also know how to divide students into teachable groups quickly. Simple games can accomplish this, such as "Back to Back" or "Foot to Foot," in which individuals get back to back (or foot to foot, etc.) with a partner as fast as possible. Students without a partner are instructed to go to the center of the teaching area (marked by a cone or spot) to find someone else without a partner. If students are staying near a friend, teachers can tell the class to move throughout space using a locomotor skill and then find a different partner each time the body part is called. If arranging students in groups larger than two people, Whistle Mixers work well. When the whistle is blown a certain number of times, students form groups corresponding to the number of whistle blows and sit to signify that they have the correct number of people in their group.

Physical education teachers need to use a consistent approach for dealing with undesirable behavior, and "Time-Out" is generally used. The time out approach moves youngsters out of the class setting and places them into a designated area when they misbehave. Placement in the time-out area does not imply that the student is a "bad person." It just means he or she has forgotten to follow the rules. When placing students in time-out, teachers should communicate that the children are loved but their misbehavior is unacceptable. Hence, they are placed in time-out.

To minimize undesirable behavior, teachers should develop a set of expectations and rules for the class. The expectations should be no more than five items, posted in the teaching area for easy reference. The rules should be discussed regularly so that children understand the expected behaviors and consequences. A set of consequences might be as follows: First misbehavior—the student is warned quietly to avoid embarrassment. Students sometimes are unaware they are bothering others, and a gentle reminder is all that is needed to refocus the behavior. Second misbehavior—the student is told to go to a designated time-out spot. The student must stay there until ready to reenter the activity and show the desired behavior. The student might to go to the area for a short period and return almost immediately to the activity. The assumption is that the student has agreed to stop misbehaving. Third misbehavior—the student goes to time-out for a longer period or the remainder of the period. Besides negative consequences, teachers also should identify positive consequences. The reward system is used to acknowledge students who follow the rules and comply with instructions and to motivate others to exhibit appropriate behavior.

Adaptive Physical Education

The Americans with Disabilities Act (n.d.) requires the placement of students in the least restrictive environment. For most "handicapped children," the least restrictive environment is the regular classroom, which includes participation in physical education activities. The challenge in teaching physical education to handicapped children is tailoring activities to fit each child. For example, blind or partially sighted students can participate in dance and some gymnastic and tumbling activities. These students can also participate in other activities with modifications. A beeper ball together with verbal cues can be used for T-ball or even for softball. If a beeper is unavailable, the teacher can put the student in position and assist in aiming and cueing when to hit the ball. Students using assistive devices like walkers or crutches can be allowed to hit the ball from a seated position and use the crutch to bat. If the child is unable to run, allow a substitute runner. Many games and activities can be modified for the handicapped child. Sometimes all it takes is a little ingenuity to change activities so handicapped students can enjoy participating.

COMPETENCY 005: THEATRE

The teacher understands the concepts, processes and skills involved in the creation, appreciation and evaluation of theatre, and uses that knowledge to plan and implement effective and engaging theatre instruction.

Introduction

The term **theatre** describes a dramatic theatrical live performance in front of an audience. The origin of this kind of performance has been highly debated; however, wall paintings, hieroglyphics, and artifacts suggest that the creation of theatre was heavily influenced by religious ceremonies and public celebrations as well as by the art of storytelling (Robinson, n.d.). The available evidence suggests that theatre/drama originated in Ancient Greece (and indeed the word *theatre* is rooted in the Greek *theaomai*, "to see") around the sixth century BCE, as part of the celebration of Dionysus, the god of fertility and wine (Gascoigne, n.d.). Thespis, a priest of Dionysus, is said to have introduced the first form of theatre in Greece. In this initial play, Thespis engaged in a dialogue with the chorus. With this performance, he became the first person to take the stage as an actor. It is the dialogue that marks the birth of theatre.

Most plays of the time were performed by a single actor and staged in improvised outdoor scenarios with little or no technical support. For many years, theatre was a one-actor show. Later, additional actors were added to the performance.

From its humble beginnings, theatre is now a well-established industry with multiple actors and large crews. Modern performances require large financial investments, with multimillion-dollar revenues. Most major U.S. cities and universities have some form of theatre activity. The most successful locations for theatre in the United States are New York and Las Vegas.

When students are introduced to theatre and its inherent creative and critical aspects, a gateway to a new world of perception and experience opens to them. These perceptual experiences include the physical, emotional, intellectual, aesthetic, social, moral, and spiritual aspects of what it is to be human.

When they act in plays, students shift their perceptions from self to others through voice and physical action as well as through interaction with other performers. Perceptions of reality expand as youngsters interpret the characters in the play.

Genres of Theatre

Traditionally, theatre productions were classified in two main areas—comedy and tragedy. The symbol of theatre, the laughing and weeping masks, represents this historical association. The literature also talks about *drama* as a theatre classification. In its narrow sense, drama refers to a play that deals with a serious topic but cannot be classified as tragedy or comedy. However, modern theatre has developed beyond these classifications. An analysis of some of the key categories of drama follows:

- **Tragedy** is one of the original forms of theatre, developed in Ancient Greece around the sixth century BCE. A tragedy is a dramatic composition of serious and often somber themes. It generally portrays the life and misfortunes of the main characters, leading to their downfall and destruction. Two of the best-known tragedies are *Oedipus the King* by Sophocles and *Hamlet* by Shakespeare. In each case, the play has a tragic ending. In *Oedipus the King* the protagonist—Oedipus—killed his father, married his mother, and finally blinds himself as punishment. In *Hamlet*, the protagonist deals with disloyalty, murder and finally, he is killed.

- **Comedy** is another form of theatre developed in Ancient Greece. This type of play uses humor to represent simple topics of daily life. It always ends happily. One of the first comedies produced in Greece is *Wasps* by the Greek playwright Aristophanes, considered to be the father of comedy. This play satirizes an Athenian government official and his demagogic practices.

- **Melodrama** represents the struggle between good and evil. It uses such theatrical elements as music, dialogue, pantomime, and acting to lead to a moral conclusion. One of the first melodramas was *Pygmalion* from the French philosopher Jean-Jacques Rousseau. In this story, a sculptor falls in love with one of his sculptures, and Venus, the goddess of love, feeling his pain, brings the sculpture to life. Modern melodramas adapted or created for television are characterized by extravagant theatricality and oversimplifies and often one-dimensional characterization. Both Spanish and U.S. soap operas fall within this tradition.

- **Satire** uses irony and exaggeration to ridicule such targets as unquestionably held beliefs, extreme religious positions, and human vices to teach a moral. A modern example of a satirical play is *The American Dream* by the playwright Edward Albee, who uses the play to critique the American family.

- **Farce** is a comedy in which the plot is developed around a situation instead of the characters. In lay terms, it has been called situational comedy, or sitcom and has been among the most durable and popular forms of teleplay. Popular television sitcoms that have also earned critical acclaim have included *I Love Lucy, All in the Family, M*A*S*H,* and, more recently, *Seinfeld, Frasier, The Big Bang Theory*, and *black-ish*.

Elements and Conventions of Theatre/Drama

To appreciate theatre, teachers should understand the components of a play as well as the elements and conventions of drama and theatre. The playwright, with the support of the stage manager and the actors, uses all the elements of theatre to create a play. Besides the elements of theatre, the playwright uses the conventions of theatre to communicate with the audience. An analysis of these components follows.

Basic Elements of Theatre

Theatre has four main elements: script/scenario, the process, the product, and the audience (Adair-Lynch, n.d.).

1. **Script/scenario** is the foundation of a theatrical performance. The playwright writes the script and conceptualizes the scenario for it. The script and details about the scenario are used to produce the actual performance.

2. In the **process,** the director becomes the artistic visionary who brings to life the ideas of the playwright. The *director,* in consultation with such specialists as the casting director, movement coach, custom designer, vocal coach, and choreographer, designs the structure and the process to lead the play to completion.

3. The **product** is the result of all the efforts and the collaboration of the production crew (producer, director, production manager, stage manager, designers, sound engineers, stage crew, the actors, etc.). It includes every aspect of the performance, including casting, sound and light effects, and the creation of the scenario for the play.

4. The **audience** is the most important component of the theatrical experience. They decide the fate of the play. To engage the audience, modern productions often allow opportunities for actors to interact directly with the audience. Involving the audience in the actual play provides a different experience for both the actors and the audience. This strategy has been used extensively in such modern theatrical presentations as the *teatro campesino*, a theatrical production developed by artistic director Luis Valdez. This type of theatre for the masses emerged as a cultural tool of Cesar Chavez's United Farmworkers strikes of the 1960s (El teatro campesino, n.d.). Eventually, it became a national form of theatre and a tool for the development of Mexican-Americans' consciousness of their social, political, and economic position in society (Library USB, n.d.).

Elements of Drama

The elements of drama or a play are the stagecraft, plot, conflict, mood, music, and theme as well as characters and the form of communication.

- **Stagecraft/Spectacle**

  The stagecraft, or spectacle, describes the creation and preparation needed to stage a play. It includes the special effects, lighting, set, and props as well as the make up, hairstyle, and costumes for the performers.

  The stage manager, together with the costume and scenic designers, creates the stagecraft for the performance.

- **Plot**

  The plot is the storyline. Traditionally, the play has an introduction that sets up a complication that comprises the main action and entwines the characters. The rising action leads to a climax, and the falling action then leads to a resolution.

- **Conflict**

  A struggle between opposing forces. The struggle may be internal (within a character) or external (between characters or between a character and an idea or entity).

- **Mood**

  The feeling or atmosphere of both the physical space and the dramatic action stemming from the characters' performance as well as special effects.

- **Music**

  The music encompasses not only the musical composition for the play but also the rhythm of the dialogues and speeches. It can also include sound effects and the actors' voices as well as songs and instruments.

- **Theme**

  The theme is the central idea of the play. The theme should be thoroughly and consistently integrated into the plot and the dialogue.

- **Characters**

  The characters are the central figures of a play. Through them, the playwright introduces the plot, the theme, and the mood of the play.

- **Communication/Language**

  Communication encompasses all the information presented verbally and nonverbally to stage the play. It includes the design of the stagecraft, the interaction among the characters, and the interaction of the characters with the audience. For oral communication, the playwright can use dialogues, monologues, and soliloquy—in which a character talks alone to convey thoughts to the audience—to communicate the information and create the dramatic mood of the play.

Conventions of Theatre

The conventions of theatre refer to the rules established by the playwright, the director, and the actors to replicate reality and communicate with the audience. Some of these conventions are:

1. Use of a narrator or a chorus to provide information about the scene

2. Using the stage curtain to signal the end of scene, to make changes to the stage, or to allow actors to change costumes

3. Use of realistic or expressionistic costumes

4. Use of strategies for sequencing time—change of lights, change of scenery, change of characters, or the use of make up

5. Use of flashbacks and flash-forwards to clarify and present information

6. Use of music and songs to set up scenes and provide information to the audience

7. Use of pantomime and exaggerated movement to provide details of a scene

8. Control of the tempo (speed) of the scenes

9. Use of split scenes/conversations—two separate scenes presented concurrently

10. Use of light or sounds to replicate the time of day

11. Use of costumes, sounds, or artifacts to represent a symbol (e.g., using the howling of the wind to create a sense of mystery or foreboding).

How to Teach Elements and Conventions of Theatre

Dramatic play is a natural process that children use to cope with problems and to help them understand the world. It represents one of the earliest manifestations of symbolic thought, which is one of the foundations for the development of language and creative thinking. Dramatic play helps children make sense of the world and practice the language skills needed for further development.

One of the key components of the Texas K–6 state curriculum (TEKS) is to begin developing *self-awareness*, especially in early childhood. Dramatic play gives children opportunities to develop self-awareness in the controlled and protected classroom environment. Through these activities, children also develop problem-solving and socialization skills and improve their understanding of human behavior and conflicts. Dramatic play also lets children practice expressive movement, voice, and characterization. To accomplish these goals, teachers provide opportunities for children to initiate dramatic play in a non-restrictive environment. For students in early childhood, these activities should be spontaneous, as opposed to having the students memorize a script or mimic a structured behavior. Dramatic play offers an effective way to teach these components.

What are the key features of dramatic play?

The Center for Best Practices in Early Childhood (September 2002) identified the following key features of dramatic play:

1. It is a form of pretending that includes role-playing, the use of puppetry, and fantasy play.

2. It can be part of solitary play, which gives children the option of using toys or artifacts to play on their own.

3. It can also become social play, including interaction with the teacher and other students.

4. It can include reading stories to children or showing video presentations to them. In these cases, children can interpret and recreate the story.

5. It can also include props and costumes to provide a framework for the activity, or it can be spontaneous improvisation and child-generated.

Moreover, dramatic play lets children create their own voices to represent different characters of a story. For example, in the Norwegian fairy tale *The Three Billy Goats Gruff*, children can practice their theatrical voices by imitating a timorous voice to represent the fear of the first two goats and a more assertive voice for the third goat. They can also recreate a strong and menacing voice to represent the troll. In the same story, children can practice *expressive movement* by walking nervously over the bridge and *characterization* by using facial expressions to show the fear of the first two goats and the challenging behavior of the third goat. Moreover, they can practice *sound effects* with music and the sound of the goat walking over the bridge. All these components of theatre can be practiced in the relaxed and controlled environment of the elementary school classroom.

Older students can be exposed to theatre in a more in-depth fashion through mature and structured play. They can be exposed to play that requires holding auditions, memorizing a script, organizing a crew, setting up the stage, and presenting the play to an audience. Some of the key steps in presenting a theatrical production are:

- **Running a production.** Teachers coordinate scheduling and organize resources. It helps to list the resources available to the production. The teacher may need to check with school administrators and other teachers about the budget and equipment as well as the availability of school facilities. The teacher can then set priorities about the choice of play, auditions, rehearsals, and performance.

- **Selecting a play.** The play should be age-appropriate for the students and approved by school administrators. The stage also should have the necessary technical capabilities for the production.

- **Holding auditions.** Teachers should encourage students to try out for the roles in the play. Teachers often will steer leading roles to older students capable of performing the parts, but this is optional. Students not selected for the play can be encouraged to become part of the production, such as working on the stage crew. The key goal is to involve all students who want to participate.

- **Organizing a stage crew.** The production will require crew members capable of handling sound, lighting, props, costumes, and other technical details. Students who act in one production may take stage crew positions in another.

- **Rehearsing.** The teacher should oversee all the details of preparing the production, from holding rehearsals with the actors to arranging for the stage crew to practice their duties. The teacher must also monitor the students who are acquiring props, building sets, and creating costumes. For a musical play, the teacher should also insist that the musicians join several rehearsals.

Brief History of Theatre

As long as humans have been capable of communication, they have probably employed some form of drama and performance. Cave paintings supply evidence for the early use of costumes and masks to bolster mimetic performances. As either magic or prayer, these performances hoped to encourage nature's productivity. A historical analysis of theatre follows (Adapted from Life 123, n.d.; Educational Portal, n.d.).

Ancient History

Greek plays began around 700 BCE with seasonal ritualistic performances celebrating their multiple deities (Robinson, n.d.). During the festivities different groups competed against each other to win the challenge. Later, Thespis, known as the founder of classical **tragedy,** brought these early performances to the level of drama. He is credited with inventing a new breed of performer, the actor, who would engage the audience by impersonating one or more characters between the dances of a chorus. From the connection of the founder of classical tragedy, the word *thespian* was coined to refer to actors in theatre.

Some of the greatest accomplishments in theatre during this period were (Educational Portal, n.d.):

1. The production of plays by Aeschylus (*Agamemnon*), Sophocles (*Antigone* and *Oedipus the King*), and Euripides (*Medea*).

2. The introduction of dance as part of plays. Euripides is considered the first choreographer in the history of theatre.

3. During the Hellenistic (350–250 BCE) period, *comedy* replaced *tragedy* as the preferred form of theatre. The themes for drama move from politics and philosophy to portrayals of the follies and daily life of people.

Middle Ages

With the fall of the Roman Empire in 476 CE, popular theatre practically disappeared from public view. A new form of play emerged in its place: the **morality** play. Morality and religious plays became the main representation of drama during the dark ages. Medieval theatre in Europe began as a springtime religious observance. This communal and public event drew large audiences to celebrate the teachings of the Old and New Testaments of the Bible. Religious theatre was restricted by such elements as the liturgy, church calendar, and ecclesiastical dress. **Morality** plays were also performed then, and they show the conscience of the Middle Ages. After approximately 200 years, drama moved out of the church to the streets and theatre halls. Historians document that women never performed in medieval plays for two reasons. First, male-dominated, rigidly hierarchical groups like clergy, craftsmen, and merchants predominated. Second, it was believed that boys with trained voices could produce more volume than women.

Contributions of Chinese Theatre

One of the first theatrical performances in China was recorded during the Shang Dynasty (618–907 CE) (Miettinen, n.d.). These original plays used dance, masked performers, and music to develop the plot. They also used puppetry in street performances. The developments of stringed and shadow puppetry are two of the greatest contributions of China to European and world theatre. Early evidence of this type of art goes back to the Han Dynasty (206 BCE to 220 CE).

Renaissance

The European Renaissance began in Italy, where theatre experienced key changes in production and content. The use of music, songs, acrobatics and dance were incorporated as part of theatrical productions. One of the greatest contributions of Italy was the development of commedia dell'arte or Italian comedy around the mid-1500s. This was a popular form of entertainment akin to street theatre, designed to appeal to a mass audience. The home page of the Commedia dell'arte describes it as a colorful theatrical production that uses masks with exaggerated features. It also uses acrobatics to entertain the audience and support the comic plot (n.d.) This type of comedy is one of the greatest contributions of Italian playwrights to theatre.

In France similar changes were taking place. Molière was the chief French playwright among those who changed the world of comedy and drama. Costumes, hairstyles, and makeup on the French stage mirrored popular fashions on the streets and among the nobility. The comedy of Molière stands as one of the most remarkable contributions of France to world theatre. In Spain, dramatists Lope de Vega, Pedro Calderón de la Barca, and Miguel Cervantes helped create the Golden Age of Spanish literature. However, by 1700 Spain's world influence was declining, and its influence on European theatre declined as well.

England joined the movement during Queen Elizabeth I's reign, a period known as the *Elizabethan Era* (1558–1603). In England, theatre was used for the first time as a commercial enterprise.

The stage became lavish with detailed scenery and colorful costumes. The two basic types of costumes were contemporary and symbolic. Symbolic costumes were worn to distinguish the important characters from the ordinary people. This period produced world-renowned playwrights such as Christopher Marlowe and Ben Johnson as well as William Shakespeare, the author who best represents the era. Shakespeare created enduring characters and addressed timeless questions that resonate today. Through his plays, Shakespeare also provided an interesting historical overview of the monarchy because his plays often represented real historical characters and periods.

Romanticism

The Romantic period began in Germany around 1800 CE. During this period, the plot of the drama focused on a hero fighting for justice and against the forces of evil. Melodramas became the preferred form of this artistic movement. Special effects were used to provide the emotion that typifies this form of drama. During this period, women also began acting in plays. Some of the best known plays of the time are:

1. The German Wolfgang von Goethe's tragic play *Faust*, and

2. The French playwright Alexander Dumas' script for the novels *The Three Musketeers* and *The Count of Monte Cristo*.

Modern Era

Political and economic forces of the early 19th and early 20th centuries changed the view of theatre. Theatre became a source of communication with the masses and often a source of political voices. This period also saw the development of technological innovations to facilitate and improve theatre. Some of these were: revolving stage or elevator stage to change scenes, electric lights, and voice amplification technology to communicate with spectators.

The modern era also brought the use of radio, movies, and television. As new technologies took hold, the interests of the audience shifted to the new media. During the first part of the 20th century, radio theatre became the most popular form of theatre in the United States and in the world. Through radio, producers recreated the theatrical experience for larger audiences. Radio delivered live performances with actors, music, and special effects. Radio required listeners to use their imagination to "see" the story unfold before a national audience. Popular stories in drama, mystery, and comedy motivated families to regularly congregate around the radio.

Later, television sought to recreate the theatrical experience through different types of drama, comedy, and mystery shows. The television and movie industries now represent some of the most successful enterprises in the world. People around the world can choose from hundreds of specialized channels presenting their version of theatre. Due in part to the plethora of entertainment options available electronically and the cost for attending theatre performances, today theatrical performances are largely an entertainment for the upper classes.

Despite these changes, the theatre industry has prevailed and continues expanding. Musical dramas have become popular and, in fact, one of the key exponents of modern theatre. Musical productions have become very elaborate, with large casts and extensive ensembles, and the use of sophisticated choreography. In the United States, one of the most memorable musicals of the mid-20th century was Leonard Bernstein's *West Side Story*. In the latter part of the 20th century, musical productions became even more elaborate, with productions like *Cats* and *The Lion King*, and later *Frozen*, which all became huge box office successes on Broadway.

Realism in Theatre

As a result of the Realism movement of the 20th century, drama instruction moved from the exaggerated acting style of the past to a more realistic and natural performance. Improved acoustics in modern theatres and the use of voice amplification technology made this transition possible. In this movement, the characters are real, and the costumes are authentic. The stage in this type of theatre is simple, with three physical walls and a fourth imaginary wall facing the audience (Cash, 2014). The dialogues use everyday speech, including the use of the vernacular to provide a natural view and to identify with the audience. Modern drama is still strong in the United States and the world. However, the high price of admission associated with the costs of production has helped make theatre less accessible to a mass audience.

Modern Acting Theory

Russia's Konstantin Stanislavsky (1863–1938) is a major force in the development of modern acting theories. He developed a technique that became standard for acting classes. He maintained that actors should bring to the play their personal emotions and experiences to prepare for the role. If the character requires a show of anger, for example, the actors should search deep in their subconscious to find when they experienced the emotion. They then should use that experience and the emotion it creates to add realism and credibility to their character. Stanislavsky's theories of acting today provide the main way to teach acting in the United States and perhaps the world.

Texas Essential Knowledge and Skills (TEKS) for Theatre

Theatre, or drama, falls under the umbrella of the fine arts curriculum of the Texas Essential Knowledge and Skills (TEKS). The TEKS for theatre are organized around four main strands—observation and perception; creative expression/performance, historical and cultural relevance; and critical evaluation and response (TEA, 2013 mod.). These strands constitute the core components of the EC–6 state curriculum.

The key components of the EC–6 curriculum can be summarized as follows (TEA, 2013 mod.):

(1) Through perceptual studies, students increase their understanding of self and others and develop clear ideas about the world. Through theatrical experiences, students com-

municate in a dramatic form, make artistic choices, solve problems, build positive self-concepts, and relate interpersonally.

(2) Students increase their understanding of heritage and traditions and the diversity of world cultures through historical and cultural studies in theatre. The study of theatre can promote thinking and further discriminating judgment, developing students who are appreciative and evaluative consumers of live theatre, film, television, and other technologies.

The goal of theatre arts in the elementary grades is to guide learners to use their imagination, improvise dramatization, and use short stories or historical events to foster original thought and creativity (Center for Educator Development in Fine Arts, 2013). These key components of the TEKS are introduced in Kindergarten and continue to increase in complexity from the early grades to sixth grade and beyond. The expectations are that by the sixth grade, students develop a strong foundation in the elements and conventions of theatre and can analyze and evaluate theatrical performance.

Traditionally, a fine arts teacher in collaboration with EC–6 teachers delivers these curricular components. However, EC–6 teachers often lack the preparation to deliver and integrate quality theatre instruction in school.

Table 7-6 shows an example of how these strands can be integrated in the Kindergarten curriculum to promote original thought among students (Adapted from Center for Educator Development in Fine Arts, 2013).

Table 7-6. Theatre Arts Kindergarten Strand Content

Theatre Arts Strands	Content/skills	Activities
Perception	listening and observation skills	• Guide children to arrange illustrations from a story in the correct sequence. • Allow students to use movement to imitate objects and actions from their environment. • Ask children to imitate such sounds as wolves howling, dogs barking, birds singing, or, say, a dripping faucet or the sound of the wind.
Creative Expression/ Performance	Add sounds and movement to a story	• Children stage a simple play after reading the story of the Three Little Pigs. They imitate the walk of the characters and the sounds they make. • They can also practice facial expressions to express surprise, fear, and other emotions.

(continued)

Theatre Arts Strands	Content/skills	Activities
Historical/ Cultural Relevance	Recreating tales from other cultures to better understand people's point of view.	• After listening to the story: "The Legend of the Blue-bonnet" (Tomie DePaola)—students recreate the story to explore the concept of sacrifice. • After reading about the Columbus voyage and contacts with the natives of America, students can stage a play to represent this initial contact.
Evaluation/ Response	Analyzing and evaluating a performance	• Students view a live or video presentation of a play. While watching the presentation, they model the appropriate behavior of an audience.

For further details on the Theatre TEKS, go to *https://tea.texas.gov/about-tea/laws-and-rules/ texas-administrative-code/texas-administrative-code-title-19-part-2.*

Integration of Theatre in the Content Areas

Theatre can be easily integrated with multiple content areas. Integration of content with the arts has been linked to increased student achievement (De Moss & Morris, 2002). In social studies, teachers can guide students to improvise conversations between and among historical characters. For example, students might improvise conversations among the defenders of the Alamo and leaders of the Mexican Army. In science class, teachers can guide students to represent the life and accomplishments of key scientists. Teachers can also use actors to represent and perform how these scientists use the scientific process.

In language arts, one of the most widely used activities to integrate theatre education is **Readers' Theater**. In this activity, a story is modified so that characters read portions of the text. Students rehearse their reading part and then create a theatre format to present the reading. Although Readers' Theater does not require setting up a stage, students can still practice stagecraft, develop costumes, and set up lights and the stage to improve the quality of the performance. On stage, students can also use drawings to represent the background of the story. Children enjoy this approach, and it improves reading. This activity can be especially appropriate for English learners (ELs) at different stages of development because the script can be changed to address individual differences. Teachers can modify the script to include non-English speakers through the use of onomatopoeia—sounds of a rooster, a cat, an explosion—that require minimum linguistic development. Table 7-7 presents examples of additional activities to integrate theatre with the content areas.

Table 7-7. Integration of Theatre Arts and the Content Areas

Social Studies	• Guide students to improvise conversations among historical characters. • Develop mock elections in class and guide students to represent political figures. • Guide students to analyze ways in which social and cultural values are expressed throughout history (MLDE, 2006). • Identify the types of jobs available in theatre—actors, producers, stage crew . . .
Arts and Music Education	• Guide students to develop a stage for a performance, using drawing and artifacts. • Select the music for a performance.
Science	• Role-play the life of important scientists and their contribution to society. • Link the scientific principles and manipulation of light, sound, and space in theatrical productions (MLDE, 2006).
Mathematics	• Apply mathematical concepts in the set design and stage directions in theatrical enactment (MLDE, 2006).
Language Arts	• Interpret literary texts. • Identify characters and use of terms like protagonist, villain, etc. • Identify the elements of theatre.

For more information about Readers' Theater and free scripts, visit Aaron Shepard's Readers' Theater website at *www.aaronshep.com/rt/RTE.html*.

Benefits of Theatre

Good dramatic experience develops reading in all curriculum areas. Reading with expression and with performance gestures, stage presence and concentration can carry over for the rest of a student's life. The arts involve the use of multiple skills and abilities and can lead students to explore issues in an integrated fashion in authentic situations (Champions of change, n.d.). Moreover, learning expands when students can represent concepts from the content areas through the arts (Seidel, n.d.).

The American Alliance for Theatre and Education (AATE) provides an overview of research on the benefits of participation in theatre arts programs (n.d.). Among the most relevant findings are:

1. Drama promotes student engagement in school and improves reading comprehension.

2. Participation in drama has also been linked to improved attendance.

3. Participation in drama also improves social interaction and communication skills. This interaction improves self-esteem among participants in drama programs.

Drama also can give students opportunities to take risks with language, to connect with their emotions, and to enhance their cognitive abilities. Drama also provides students with opportunities for social interaction, and lets them practice academic content in non-threatening situations. The commitment required from participation in drama and the skills practiced by the participants supports the linguistic and academic performance of all students. It especially can support the performance of diverse student populations.

Visual Arts Sources

American Orff Schulwerk Association (AOSA). Retrieved from *https://aosa.org* (accessed July 6, 2009).

Cultural China (n.d.) The main artistic features in the development of Chinese paintings, from *https://arthistoryteachingresources.org/lessons/chinese-art-before-1300.*

National Gallery of Art (n.d.). Washington, D.C. Retrieved from *https://www.nga.gov.*

Organization of American Kodály Educators (OAKE). Retrieved from *https://www.oake.org/default.aspx.*

Public Domain Information Project. Retrieved from *http://www.pdinfo.com/index.php.*

Ray, B.C. 1997. *African art: Aesthetics and meaning.* Retrieved from *https://static.lib.virginia.edu/artsandmedia/artmuseum/africanart.*

Ryan, V. (2002–2009). Primary, secondary and complementary colours. Retrieved from *https://technologystudent.com/designpro/pricol1.htm.*

Shirrmacher, R., and Fox, J.E. (2009). *Art and creative development for young children.* 6th ed. Upper Saddle River, NJ: Cengage Learning.

TEA (2013 mod.) Texas Essential Knowledge and Skills by Chapter. Retrieved from *https://tea.texas.gov/about-tea/laws-and-rules/texas-administrative-code/texas-administrative-code-title-19-part-2.*

Witcombe, C.L. (1995). Art history resources. Retrieved from *http://arthistoryresources.net.*

Music Sources

Lange, D.M. (2005). *Together in harmony: Combining Orff Schulwerk and music learning theory.* Chicago: GIA Publications.

Mariachi. (n.d.) Retrieved from *http://www.mariachi.org/history.html*.

National Association of Music Educators. (n.d.). Retrieved from *http://musiced.nafme.org/resources/concert-etiquette-home/*.

Organization of American Kodály Educators (n.d.) Retrieved from *http://www.oake.org/about-us/who-was-kodaly/*.

The Roots of Tejano and Conjunto Music. (n.d.). Retrieved from *https://www.lib.utexas.edu*.

RubiStar: Create rubrics for your project-based learning activities (n.d.). Retrieved from *http://rubistar.4teachers.org/index.php?screen=ShowRubric&rubric_id=1837253&*.

Star-Spangled Banner. (n.d.). Retrieved from *https://amhistory.si.edu/starspangledbanner*.

Texas State Libraries and Archives. (n.d.). Retrieved from *https://www.tsl.texas.gov*.

Health and Physical Education Sources

Americans with Disabilities Act. *Search ADA (n.d.)*. US Department of Justice, Retrieved from *https://www.ada.gov*.

Centers for Disease Control and Prevention (2014). *Overweight and Obesity*. Retrieved from *https://www.cdc.gov/obesity/data/index.html*.

Fitnessgram (n.d.). *Activity and fitness assessment*. The Cooper Institute, Retrieved from *https://fitnessgram.net*.

Healthy People 2020 (n.d.). *Search Healthy People.gov Homepage*. Office of Disease Prevention and Health Promotion. Retrieved from *https://health.gov/healthypeople*.

National Institute of Mental Health (2014). *Eating Disorders*. US Department of Health and Human Service. Retrieved from *http://www.nimh.nih.gov/health/topics/eating-disorders/index.shtml*.

PE Central. *The Premier Website for Health and Physical Education* (n.d.). Retrieved from *https://www.pecentral.org*.

Shelov, S., & Remer. T. (2009). *Caring for baby and young child: Birth to age 5*. American Academy of Pediatrics. New York City, Bantam Books.

Society of Health and Physical Educators (2015) *National Standards*. SHAPE America. Retrieved from *http://www.shapeamerica.org/standards/*.

Texas Education Agency (n.d.). *Texas Essential Knowledge and Skills*. Retrieved from *https://tea.texas.gov*.

U.S. Department of Agriculture (n.d.). *Search ChooseMyPlate.gov*. USDA Center for Nutrition Policy & Promotion. Retrieved from *https://www.myplate.gov*.

U.S. Department of Health and Human Services (2015). *Dietary Guidelines*. Office of Disease Prevention and Health Promotion. Retrieved from *www.health.gov/DietaryGuidelines/*.

Theatre Sources

AATE (n.d.). The effects of theatre education. Retrieved from *https://www.aate.com/?page=effects*.

Adair-Lynch, T. (n.d.). Elements of theatre and drama. Retrieved from *https://www.smc.edu*.

Cash, J. (2014). Realism and naturalism theatre conventions. The Drama Teacher. Retrieved from *http://www.thedramateacher.com/realism-and-naturalism-theatre-conventions/*.

Center for Best Practices in Early Childhood (2002). Dramatic play in early childhood. Retrieved from *http://dramaticplay.wordpress.com/*.

Center for Educator Development in Fine Arts (CEDFA) (2013). Theatre curriculum framework. Retrieved from *https://www.cedfa.org*.

Champions of change (n.d.). The impact of the arts on learning (Edward B. Fiske, ed.). Retrieved from *http://artsedge.kennedy-center.org/champions/pdfs/champsreport.pdf*.

DeMoss, K. & Morris, T. (2002). How arts integration supports student learning: Students shed light on the connections. Chicago, IL: Chicago Arts Partnerships in Education (CAPE).

Educational Portal (n.d.) *History of Drama: Dramatic Movements and Time Periods*. Retrieved from *http://education-portal.com/academy/lesson/history-of-drama-dramatic-movements-and-time-periods.html*.

El Teatro Campesino (n.d.) Retrieved from *https://elteatrocampesino.com*.

Home page of *commedia dell'arte* (n.d.) A brief history of *commedia dell'arte*. Retrieved from *https://www.shane-arts.com*.

Library USB. El teatro campesino. Online: *http://www.library.ucsb.edu/special-collections/cema/etc*.

Life 123 (n.d.). A brief history of drama. Retrieved from *https://www.life123.com*.

Miettinen, J.O. (n.d.). Early history of Chinese theatre (n.d.). Retrieved from *https://disco.teak.fi/asia*.

MLDE (2006). Benefits of integrating fine arts across the curriculum. Maryland Department of Education. Retrieved from *https://www.msdefinearts.org*.

Robinson, S.R. (n.d.) Theatre and Drama in Ancient Greece. CWU Department of Theatre Arts. Retrieved from *http://www.cwu.edu*.

Seidel, S. (n.d.). Stand and unfold yourself: A monogram on the Shakespeare & Company—Harvard Program Zero. Retrieved from *https://www.kennedy-center.org*.

TEA (2013 mod.) *Texas Essential Knowledge and Skills by Chapter*, Retrieved from *https://tea.texas.gov*.

TExES Core Subjects EC–6 (391) Practice Test Battery

TExES Core Subjects EC–6 Practice Test 1: English Language Arts and Reading

This practice test and an additional test are available at the online REA Study Center (*www.rea.com/studycenter*).

The TExES Core Subjects EC–6 ELA and Reading (901) test is computer-based, so we strongly recommend that you take our online practice tests to simulate test-day conditions and to receive these added benefits:

- **Timed testing conditions**—Gauge how much time you can spend on each question.

- **Automatic scoring**—Find out how you did on the test, instantly.

- **On-screen detailed explanations of answers**—Learn not just the correct answer, but also why the other answers are incorrect.

- **Diagnostic score reports**—Pinpoint where you're strongest and where you need to focus your study.

ELA and Reading Practice Test Answer Sheet

1. Ⓐ Ⓑ Ⓒ Ⓓ   16. Ⓐ Ⓑ Ⓒ Ⓓ   31. Ⓐ Ⓑ Ⓒ Ⓓ
2. Ⓐ Ⓑ Ⓒ Ⓓ   17. Ⓐ Ⓑ Ⓒ Ⓓ   32. Ⓐ Ⓑ Ⓒ Ⓓ
3. Ⓐ Ⓑ Ⓒ Ⓓ   18. Ⓐ Ⓑ Ⓒ Ⓓ   33. Ⓐ Ⓑ Ⓒ Ⓓ
4. Ⓐ Ⓑ Ⓒ Ⓓ   19. Ⓐ Ⓑ Ⓒ Ⓓ   34. Ⓐ Ⓑ Ⓒ Ⓓ
5. Ⓐ Ⓑ Ⓒ Ⓓ   20. Ⓐ Ⓑ Ⓒ Ⓓ   35. Ⓐ Ⓑ Ⓒ Ⓓ
6. Ⓐ Ⓑ Ⓒ Ⓓ   21. Ⓐ Ⓑ Ⓒ Ⓓ   36. Ⓐ Ⓑ Ⓒ Ⓓ
7. Ⓐ Ⓑ Ⓒ Ⓓ   22. Ⓐ Ⓑ Ⓒ Ⓓ   37. Ⓐ Ⓑ Ⓒ Ⓓ
8. Ⓐ Ⓑ Ⓒ Ⓓ   23. Ⓐ Ⓑ Ⓒ Ⓓ   38. Ⓐ Ⓑ Ⓒ Ⓓ
9. Ⓐ Ⓑ Ⓒ Ⓓ   24. Ⓐ Ⓑ Ⓒ Ⓓ   39. Ⓐ Ⓑ Ⓒ Ⓓ
10. Ⓐ Ⓑ Ⓒ Ⓓ   25. Ⓐ Ⓑ Ⓒ Ⓓ   40. Ⓐ Ⓑ Ⓒ Ⓓ
11. Ⓐ Ⓑ Ⓒ Ⓓ   26. Ⓐ Ⓑ Ⓒ Ⓓ   41. Ⓐ Ⓑ Ⓒ Ⓓ
12. Ⓐ Ⓑ Ⓒ Ⓓ   27. Ⓐ Ⓑ Ⓒ Ⓓ   42. Ⓐ Ⓑ Ⓒ Ⓓ
13. Ⓐ Ⓑ Ⓒ Ⓓ   28. Ⓐ Ⓑ Ⓒ Ⓓ   43. Ⓐ Ⓑ Ⓒ Ⓓ
14. Ⓐ Ⓑ Ⓒ Ⓓ   29. Ⓐ Ⓑ Ⓒ Ⓓ   44. Ⓐ Ⓑ Ⓒ Ⓓ
15. Ⓐ Ⓑ Ⓒ Ⓓ   30. Ⓐ Ⓑ Ⓒ Ⓓ   45. Ⓐ Ⓑ Ⓒ Ⓓ

Practice Test 1: ELA and Reading

TIME: 1 hour and 10 minutes
45 selected-response questions

Directions: Read each item and select the correct response or responses. Most items on this test require you to provide the one best answer. However, some questions require you to select all the options that apply.

---

1. Which of the following statements best explains the semantics of language?

   A. The study of meaning in a language

   B. How words can be combined in language

   C. Letter-sound relationships

   D. Sounds of a language and how they combine

2. Which of the following approaches ***does not*** provide conditions for learning that would support English learners' acquisition of language and content?

   A. Explaining a new concept by building upon the background knowledge of the students

   B. Using actions and gestures to explain the definitions of words

   C. Letting students talk to a classmate about what they learned after reading a small chunk of information in a chapter before asking students to share with the whole group

   D. Asking students to look up definitions of unfamiliar words in a dictionary

3. Which of the following pertains to phonemes of language?

   A. The study of meaning in a language

   B. How words can be combined in language

   C. Letter-sound relationships

   D. Sounds of a language and how they combine

4. A teacher presents the word *destruction*. The teacher points out to the students that *struc*t, a Latin root, means "to build." The teacher adds that *de-* is a common prefix that means "opposite." The teacher also points out how *construct* and *restructure* are related. Which of the following best explains why this instruction would help students?

   A. The teacher is helping the students gain in applying phonics for word identification.

   B. The teacher is helping students gain in phonemic awareness.

   C. Morphemic analysis can help students learn about word structure and meaning.

   D. Using knowledge of syntax can help students identify words.

5. Which of the following words is irregular in spelling?

   A. Stay

   B. Have

   C. Wait

   D. Name

6. Which of the following words contains an open syllable?

   A. Begin

   B. Running

   C. Wishing

   D. Finish

7. A teacher presented the following pair of sentences and read each to his students:

   The **object** of the game is to score more points than your opponent.

   The people did not **object** to the change in the delivery date.

   Which of the following indicates what the teacher is showing students with regard to the words in bold in the sentences above?

   A. How to use a word in more than one sentence to provide more than one example

   B. How derivatives can be used to find meaning

   C. That some words can be spelled the same but pronounced differently, depending on whether they are used as nouns or verbs

   D. That reading a word twice makes students more apt to remember how to recognize it

8. Which of the following best describes affixes?

   A. Another name for suffixes

   B. Another name for prefixes

   C. Root or base words

   D. Prefixes and suffixes

9. Which of the following statements best describes the cloze procedure?

   A. Encourages students to recognize the purpose of headings

   B. Helps students examine the structure of expository texts

   C. Helps students examine the structure of a story through a graphic organizer

   D. Has students fill in deleted words by using context clues

10. When listening to a student read individually during instruction, the teacher observes that the student stops reading when seeing the word *father*. Which of the following can the teacher do to provide effective support?

    A. The teacher should ask the student to read to the end of the sentence to determine what the word is, based upon the way the initial sound of the word is spoken.

    B. The teacher should ask the student to "sound it out" to determine the word.

    C. The teacher should ask the student to "look for the little word" in the word.

    D. The teacher should tell the student the word.

11. A teacher observes that a student can identify words when reading, but the student does not read smoothly and does not change intonation when a sentence has a question mark. Which of the following types of instruction does the student need?

    A. Structural analysis

    B. Fluency

    C. Visualization

    D. Phonics

12. Which of the following statements best describes how to foster fluency?

    A. Encourage students to recognize the purpose of headings.

    B. Provide students reading materials that have challenging words to foster growth.

    C. Make sure students can recognize text structure.

    D. Provide opportunities for students to read texts a second time to foster word identification and allow for the monitoring of students' reading.

13. Which of the following statements *does not* describe the significance of text organization as students read to learn or study?

    A. Students can use the text structure to help them remember how individual ideas are connected to each other and to major ideas.

    B. Text features include headings, captions, illustrations, index, and table of contents.

    C. Students need to figure out text structure when reading expository texts.

    D. Helping students read smaller chunks of information and take notes makes it easier for them to retain new academic vocabulary and related concepts in textbooks.

14. Fiction includes all but which of the following?

    A. Fantasy

    B. Mystery

    C. Folktales

    D. Biography

15. Which of the following best describes the omniscient point of view?

    A. The events that take place in the story

    B. What each character feels, thinks, says, and does

    C. When the story is told by a narrator from one character's viewpoint

    D. When a character tells the story

16. Which of the following strategies describes anticipating what the text will be about before reading and what will happen next during reading?

    A. Summarizing

    B. Recalling

    C. Predicting

    D. Making inferences

17. Which of the following statements best explains why even advanced readers can find reading the expository text of textbooks challenging?

    A. Students are unfamiliar with some types of poetry.

    B. Students need to use strategies, such as reading manageable chunks and figuring out the text organization, to help them remember new information.

    C. Students may not understand that the theme is inferred.

    D. Students need to use story structure to understand what they read.

18. A teacher is focusing on the following words in working with students: *for example*, *for instance*. Which of the following statements describes how such instruction could contribute to literacy development?

   A. The teacher is showing common affixes used in words.

   B. The teacher is teaching antonyms.

   C. The teacher is showing how a cohesive tie can be used by writers.

   D. The teacher is showing how to use visualization when reading.

19. Which of the following represents a way a teacher could use a visual organizer to help students think about new concepts and see the relationships among concepts?

   A. Directed Reading Thinking Activity

   B. Concept Maps

   C. Reciprocal Teaching

   D. Question-Answer Relationships

20. Which of the following is *not* accurate in describing what is needed for vocabulary development?

   A. Students should be given time to read daily and read various types of texts.

   B. Teachers need to be intentional in selecting words for instruction that meets students' needs.

   C. Teachers can help students by modeling their own strategies for determining the meanings of words.

   D. Teachers need to give and monitor the results of vocabulary tests on a regular basis.

Use the information below to answer questions 21 to 26.

Part 1. The teacher meets with students in small groups for reading. In preparing English learners to read a story, the teacher presents the word *exit*. The teacher tells the students that one of the words they will read in the story is *exit*. The students look at the word and say it. The teacher then shows the sentence that appears in the story where the word is used, and the teacher explains what the word means.

Part 2. The teacher shows students a photo of an exit sign above a door in a building, and she explains that the sign indicates where to leave the building.

Part 3. The teacher then tells students that she is going to exit the classroom and briefly walks out the door and comes back in.

Part 4. After students have read the story silently, they retell the story and share their responses. The teacher brings up the point that the people had difficulty when they tried to exit the building because of the location of the fire.

Part 5. On the next day, the teacher says, "Now we are going to exit our classroom to go to the cafeteria."

Part 6. In a subsequent lesson, the teacher reminds students that they learned the meaning of *exit*. The teacher then shows students the following words: *export*, *expel*. The teacher and students discuss the meaning of the prefix *ex-* and how this helps lay the basis for understanding a word's meaning.

21. In Part 1, the teacher provides pre-reading instruction for English learners: The students look at the word *exit* and then say it. The teacher then shows the sentence that appears in the story where the word is used, and explains what the word means.

   Which of the following is a rationale for the teacher's instruction?

   A. The teacher wants students to preview text features.

   B. The teacher wants to provide direct instruction on a word in the story that English learners may not understand by using only context clues.

   C. The teacher wants to teach phonics so students can make gains in word identification.

   D. The teacher wants to equip students to make predictions.

22. In Part 2, the teacher shows students a photo of an exit sign above a door in a building, and she explains that the sign indicates where to leave the building. Which of the following is a rationale for the teacher's instruction?

   A. The teacher is using a visual to help provide a variety of ways to help students understand unfamiliar vocabulary vital to understanding the story.

   B. The teacher is helping students preview text features.

   C. The teacher is teaching phonics so the students can make gains in word identification.

   D   The teacher is helping students learn to spell the word by seeing it again.

23. In Part 3, the teacher then tells students that she is going to exit the classroom and briefly walks out the door and comes back in. Which of the following is a rationale for the teacher's instruction?

   A. The teacher is helping students develop a concept map.

   B. The teacher is helping students preview text features.

   C. The teacher wants students to be able to use pantomime.

   D. The teacher is teaching vocabulary briefly, but the instruction is in-depth by using multiple ways of showing meaning.

24. In Part 4, students have read the story silently. Next, they retell the story and share their responses. The teacher brings up the point that the people had difficulty when they tried to exit the building because of the location of the fire. How does the teacher contribute to English learners' literacy development?

   A. In the course of sharing their responses, the students are able to use language to communicate the information with the whole class in talking before a whole class.

   B. The teacher can provide feedback by grading the students' contributions to the discussion.

   C. The teacher can ask comprehension questions to make sure the English learners understand the story.

   D. Through talking about what took place and sharing personal responses, the students are able to expand on their own experiences with the story.

25. On the next day, in Part 5, the teacher says, "Now we are going to exit our classroom to go to the cafeteria." Which of the following is a rationale for the teacher's decision to focus again on the word *exit*?

   A. The students will be able to write the word in their personal dictionary.

   B. Teaching a set of vocabulary words over several days helps English learners master unknown words.

   C. The teacher can use the talking experiences as a basis of students' writing.

   D. By talking about what took place and sharing personal responses, the students are able to expand their experiences with the story.

26. In a subsequent lesson, described in Part 6, the teacher reminds students that they learned the meaning of *exit*. The teacher then shows students the following words: *export, expel*. The teacher and students discuss the meaning of the prefix *ex-* and how this helps lay the basis for understanding a word's meaning.

Which of the following highlights why the teacher's instruction is beneficial?

A. The teacher is helping students apply phonics generalizations.

B. The teacher is helping students be prepared for a vocabulary quiz.

C. The teacher is preparing students to write sentences using the new words.

D. The teacher is helping students determine the meaning of words on their own by using morphology.

Use the information below to answer questions 27 and 28.

Students in fifth grade started the school year by writing personal narratives and informal reports drawing upon their experiences. Now, the students are going to learn how to write a report. The teacher knows that even when students are competent writers, they can find it challenging to orchestrate the skills needed to locate information and write a report.

27. Which of the following is an effective way to support students' initial learning of how to write a report?

A. The teacher needs to make sure each student knows how to develop an outline.

B. The teacher should provide differentiated instruction for English learners so they create an oral version on their own.

C. The teacher and students could collaborate on writing a shorter report first to ensure students know strategies to use.

D. The teacher needs to tell students to make sure they do not copy from a text as they take notes.

28. Which of the following tells how teachers can help ensure that students use quality sources that meet their needs as they begin to learn how to write a report?

A. The teacher can locate material and websites that students will find helpful.

B. The teacher can provide a checklist on how to evaluate a website.

C. The teacher can show students how to search for a website.

D. The teacher can let students work in pairs to support each other.

29. The teacher reads aloud over a period of days from an informational book that provides an overview of wolves as a research topic. The teacher and students work together to decide on questions or aspects of the topic they want to address. The teacher writes questions each at the top of a sheet for note-taking. The teacher then tells the students that they can add other aspects if they develop other questions as they read to gain information.

Which of the following statements indicates how this demonstration can help students gain in inquiry skills?

A. The teacher is providing background knowledge students need for reading.

B. The students are learning how to read purposefully and organize their note-taking as they gather information from sources.

C. The students are using fiction and nonfiction to learn.

D. The students are learning how to use cohesive ties.

30. The teacher reads aloud an excerpt from an informational book that addresses the topic and that focuses upon one of the categories of the topic, baby wolves, or pups. The teacher then closes the book and makes a list of what she remembers about pups on the page for note-taking that is devoted to the category of baby wolves.

How can this demonstration help students gain in inquiry skills?

A. The teacher is ensuring students have the background knowledge they need.

B. The teacher shows how to preview a text.

C. The teacher can now ask students to copy the notes to use when they write that part of the report.

D. The teacher shows how to take notes without copying the text.

Use the information below to answer questions 31 to 34.

The teacher is helping students learn about state government, and he also is teaching students how to read, organize ideas, and learn when using informational texts. In addition, the teacher knows that these learning experiences will help students when they learn to gather information to write reports. Parts of the unit of study are presented below.

Part 1. Before students begin to read the chapter about the branches of state government, the teacher directs their attention to the title of the chapter and guides them to notice the chapter headings: *Executive*, *Legislative*, and *Judicial*.

Part 2. The teacher and students read the introduction. Thinking aloud, the teacher says, "The introduction tells us that the chapter will describe what each branch of government consists of and who heads it, the role of each branch, and the terms of office. We can develop questions we will try to answer as we read." The teacher adds questions to a table that will be completed by the students and the teacher as the students read the chapter.

Branch of Government	Executive	Legislative	Judicial
What does the branch include? Who heads it?			
What is the role of the branch?			
How long is the term of office?			

31. Which of the following is a major rationale for Part 1?

A. The teacher is providing shared reading to help students acquire new information.

B. The teacher is helping students understand academic vocabulary presented in the chapter.

C. The teacher is helping students develop comprehension monitoring.

D. The teacher is helping students preview the chapter to gain an understanding of how the overall topic is organized.

32. In Part 2, the teacher shares his thinking about the overview of the chapter and guides students in developing questions. Which of the following explanations best conveys why this approach is effective?

A. The teacher provides modeling to help students understand what to do in reading to learn from expository text.

B. The teacher is building background knowledge.

C. The teacher is helping students be able to complete the table.

D. The teacher is activating students' prior knowledge.

33. In Part 2, the teacher displays a chart the students complete with the teacher's guidance as they learn about each branch of their state government. After reading about the executive branch, the teacher asks students to tell what they have learned, and the teacher adds the information to the chart. In the next lesson, the students continue in this way after encountering additional information. Which of the following represents how this approach can help students remember new information?

A. The categories of the table help students organize individual facts in memory.

B. Building background knowledge helps students relate the new to the known.

C. Students can copy the chart and complete it.

D. Previewing headings can help students before reading a text.

34. In Part 2, the teacher does not require students to complete the reading and chart on their own. Which of the following is the best rationale for the teacher's approach?

A. The teacher is providing shared reading to help students who read below grade level.

B. The teacher knows that the students have difficulty with academic vocabulary.

C. The teacher is providing ample modeling, which is necessary for students to succeed in learning strategies for navigating expository text.

D. The teacher is helping students for the first lesson, but they will work on their own after that.

35. A teacher presents four pairs of words for spelling instruction: *bridal—bridle, coarse—course, hair—hare, fair—fare*. Which of the following best describes the purpose of this instruction?

A. To help students master irregular plurals

B. To help students learn multisyllabic words

C. To help students learn synonyms

D. To help students learn to learn to spell commonly confused words

36. Which of the following is *not* a coordinating conjunction?

A. Because

B. And

C. So

D. But

37. As part of her read-aloud program, a teacher includes quality nonfiction books the students enjoy. As part of teaching students how to write a report, the teacher rereads the lead-ins of several books. Which of the following is a rationale for the teacher's instruction?

A. The teacher can ask students to write a lead-in like one in the books.

B. The teacher can show students how to preview a book.

C. Books that students have heard or read can serve as mentor texts, helping students become familiar with strategies and techniques writers use.

D. Students can find it difficult to comprehend nonfiction versus fiction, so the teacher is reading a part again.

38. Given that the writing process can be recursive, which of the following indicates where in the process the writer devotes attention to establishing content as a rough draft?

   A. Prewriting

   B. Drafting

   C. Revising

   D. Editing

39. Which of the following best illustrates how viewing a video can be incorporated effectively as part of a unit of study?

   A. Test students afterward to make sure they gained from the video.

   B. Have students find a video online to learn about using digital resources.

   C. Ask students to discuss what they learned and add information to notes based upon other sources used during the unit of study.

   D. Provide differentiated instruction by having English learners use the video instead of reading the text.

40. In evaluating whether to use a website, which of the following is a factor that suggests that a site should *not* be used for instruction?

   A. Most pages present large amounts of information.

   B. The site has accurate, understandable content that relates to the objectives of instruction.

   C. The site has multimedia and visual materials that contribute important information.

   D. The site is easy to navigate.

41. Examine the student's writing sample below. Which of the following is an accurate assessment of the student's abilities in using writing conventions?

   My best friend lives next to my house, we have fun. Last Friday we had a sleep over at her house, we stayed up until midnite.

   A. The student does not use correct subject-verb agreement.

   B. The student knows how to use a period and a comma correctly.

   C. The student needs to learn how to avoid a comma splice.

   D. The student needs to learn about capitalization.

42. A student wrote the following:

   I had to go to the emergency room last summer. Because I broke my arm.

   Which of the following statements accurately describes the child's mastery of writing conventions based on the writing sample?

   A. The student has difficulty with using verb tenses.

   B. The student does not know that a clause that begins with a subordinating conjunction is not an independent clause.

   C. The student does not know about capitalization of seasons.

   D. The student has difficulty spelling high-frequency words.

43. Which of the following is an effective rationale for asking students in a group to retell what they have read as part of a grand conversation?

   A. The teacher can determine whether the student can make inferences.

   B. The teacher can determine whether the student can evaluate information.

   C. The teacher can determine whether the student is making text-to-self connections.

   D. The teacher can determine whether the student understands at a literal level what was read.

44. When teachers require students to read texts independently, the teacher needs to make sure the students can comprehend what they read. What percentage of the words should students be able to identify so that they can devote attention to constructing meaning?

   A. 95%–100%

   B. 90%–94%

   C. 85%–89%

   D. 80%–84%

45. If a school district wants to monitor each student's abilities in learning to understand and spell commonly confusing words, which of the following types of assessment should be used?

   A. Criterion-referenced

   B. Norm-referenced

   C. Running records

   D. Anecdotal accounts

ELA and Reading Practice Test Answer Key

1. A.
2. D.
3. D.
4. C.
5. B.
6. A.
7. C.
8. D.
9. D.
10. A.
11. B.
12. D.
13. B.
14. D.
15. B.

16. C.
17. B.
18. C.
19. B.
20. D.
21. B.
22. A.
23. D.
24. D.
25. B.
26. D.
27. C.
28. A.
29. B.
30. D.

31. D.
32. A.
33. A.
34. C.
35. D.
36. A.
37. C.
38. B.
39. C.
40. A.
41. C.
42. B.
43. D.
44. A.
45. A.

ELA and Reading Practice Test 1
Detailed Answers

1.   A.

Option (A) is correct because semantics pertains to the study of meaning. Option (B) is incorrect because syntax pertains to how words can be combined in a language. Option (C) is incorrect because letter-sound relationships pertain to phonics. Option (D) is incorrect because phonemes pertain to sounds of a language and how they combine. **(901-001—Oral Language)**

2.   D.

Option (D) is correct. Students do need to learn to use the dictionary, but English learners and other students are not apt to understand the meanings of unfamiliar words by looking up definitions. Options (A), (B), and (C) are incorrect because they are ways to develop students' language in effective ways while also making it possible for English learners to participate in subject-matter learning. **(901-001—Oral Language)**

3.   D.

Option (D) is correct because the phonemes refer to the sounds of a given language and how these are combined to communicate orally. Option (A) is incorrect because semantics pertains to the study of meaning. Option (B) is incorrect because syntax pertains to how words can be combined in a language to create phrases and sentences. Option (C) is incorrect because letter-sound relationships pertain to phonics. **(901-001—Oral Language)**

4.   C.

Option (C) is correct because the teacher is showing how a Latin root word is featured in words and how this relates to meaning, which can help students also understand other words they encounter. Option (A) is

incorrect because phonics is learning about sound-symbol correspondences to identify words. Option (B) is incorrect because phonemic awareness is accounting for sounds in words. Option (D) is incorrect because readers use syntax when they use their knowledge of how words can be combined in a language. **(901-002—Word Analysis and Identification Skills)**

5.   B.

Option (B) is correct; *have* is irregular in spelling because it does not adhere to the phonics generalization for a long vowel sound where a vowel "says" its name (vowel-consonant-silent *e* pattern). Students must learn to read/spell high-frequency words and cannot sound out these words. Options (A) and (C) are incorrect because they are words that do adhere to phonics generalizations (or how a vowel team forms long *a* by *ay, ai*), thereby being regular spellings. Option (D) is incorrect, as it shows a word that features a phonics generalization, or a way to create a long *a* (by the vowel-consonant-silent *e* pattern). **(901-002—Word Analysis and Identification Skills)**

6.   A.

Option (A) is correct. A syllable is open when a vowel is at the end of the syllable, which leads to a long sound, such as in the first syllable of *bē-gin*, where the *a* is long, or says its own name. The syllable is not closed by a consonant. Options (B), (C), and (D) are incorrect. These options represent words that have closed syllables, where the syllable ends in a consonant, resulting in a short vowel sound. **(901-002—Word Analysis and Identification Skills)**

7. C.

Option (C) is correct. Words with the same spelling can be a noun or verb, depending upon the placement of the main stress in the word. Option (A) is incorrect because the intent of the sentences is not to provide additional examples of word usage. Option (B) is incorrect because the sentences do not illustrate words that are derivatives, but rather show differences in the pronunciation of a word, depending upon whether it is used as a noun or verb. Option (D) is incorrect because the word featured in each sentence is not pronounced the same way, students do not practice reading each word twice. **(901-002—Word Analysis and Identification Skills)**

8. D.

Option (D) is correct. Affixes are prefixes and suffixes which can be added to a base word or root word to from a new word. Options (A) and (B) are incorrect because affixes include both prefixes and suffixes. Option (C) is incorrect because affixes are combined with root, or base, words. **(901-002—Word Analysis and Identification Skills)**

9. D.

Option (D) is correct. The cloze procedure can be used to determine whether students understand vocabulary or a text as a whole. To this end, students use context clues or syntax and semantics to identify and understand words. Option (A) is incorrect because helping students to recognize the purpose of headings pertains to the organization of the information in a text. Option (B) is incorrect because the cloze procedure focuses on understanding words well enough while reading to supply a missing word from a sentence; it does not relate to the way the information is organized. Option (C) is incorrect because story maps are graphic organizers that can help visualizing information, but they do not address the purpose of cloze procedure. **(901-002—Word Analysis and Identification Skills)**

10. A.

Option (A) is correct because the teacher is showing how to use context and initial letter sounds to identify an unknown word, which is an effective strategy the student also can apply in other situations. Option (B) is incorrect because the word represents an irregular spelling, as do many words in English, so the strategy of "sounding out" will not work for students in many situations. Option (C) is incorrect because using structural analysis or word parts does not work for this word because *fat* is not a root word nor part of a compound word in *father*. Option (D) is incorrect because the first response should be to show students how to identify unknown words so that students can be self-reliant in reading. **(901-002—Word Analysis and Identification Skills)**

11. B.

Option (B) is correct. Fluency entails being able to read smoothly so what is read can be remembered, and prosody is needed because readers understand better when they read with expression and make changes in intonation in response to indicators in the text. Options (A) and (D) are incorrect because the student does not need word identification instruction. Option (C) is incorrect because the assessment has not focused upon comprehension, and visualization is used to help students create images in their minds to read actively and comprehend. Though comprehension can be affected when students do not read fluently, comprehension assessment is not described in this situation. **(901-003—Reading Fluency)**

12. D.

Option (D) is correct. Reading fluency is developed when students read materials again to be able to read more smoothly and accurately and use the appropriate intonation to better comprehend what is being read. Teachers can monitor students' reading to ensure students read fluently and model, as needed. Option (A) is incorrect because recognizing the purpose of headings pertains to noting the text structure of expository text. Option (B) is incorrect. Students do need to gain in sight vocabulary words to read fluently, but fluency is developed when students can read the words of the text easily and can devote attention to reading smoothly with expression. Option (C) is incorrect because noting text structure is useful for understanding the way information is presented in expository text, which can foster comprehension and learning. **(901-003—Reading Fluency)**

13. B.

Option (B) is correct because this statement pertains to text features, not text organization. Helping students understand how to use text features and text organization are both important, and the instruction works together to help students navigate expository text, but text organization pertains to the body of the text. Options (A), (C), and (D) are incorrect, as they *do* apply specifically to text organization. **(901-004—Reading Comprehension and Applications)**

14. D.

Option (D) is correct. Though biography, memoirs and other types of nonfiction can certainly engage readers, the information in them is not fictional and thus unresponsive to the question. Options (A), (B), and (C) are incorrect because they are types of fiction. **(901-004—Reading Comprehension and Applications)**

15. B.

Option (B) is correct because the term *omniscient* implies that the author is aware and able to communicate internal emotions of the characters. Option (A) is incorrect because it pertains to the plot of the story. Option (C) is incorrect because it pertains to limited third-person point of view. Option (D) is incorrect because it pertains to first-person narrative point of view. **(901-004—Reading Comprehension and Applications)**

16. C.

Option (C) is correct. Proficient readers use their prior knowledge along with information they see in the text, such as the title, to predict before reading, and they continue to predict and revise predictions based on what the text presents. Option (A) is incorrect. Summarizing is a strategy that helps readers be aware of what is important in a text and bring together ideas, explaining text in their own words. Option (B) is incorrect. Recalling is when students tell what they remember about what they have read, which depends upon their prior knowledge of the topic and the reading level of the text not being too difficult for students to read. Option (D) is incorrect. Readers make inferences when they use their past experiences to understand ideas that are implied, but not stated explicitly, in the text. **(901-004—Reading Comprehension and Applications)**

17. B.

Option (B) is correct because expository texts make different demands on readers. Students need to be shown they cannot rely on the approach they have used in reading fiction because expository texts can require understanding how unfamiliar, abstract concepts relate to one another and the broader topic at hand. Options (A), (C), and (D) are incorrect because they pertain to reading fiction or poetry, not expository texts. **(901-004—Reading Comprehension and Applications)**

18. C.

Option (C) is correct. The words represent cohesive ties writers can use to connect ideas; knowing this helps students to comprehend and compose text. Option (A) is incorrect because affixes are prefixes and suffixes. Option (B) is incorrect because the words are not opposite in meaning. Option (D) is incorrect because visualization is a comprehension strategy in which students are encouraged to think about what they are reading. **(901-004—Reading Comprehension and Applications)**

19. B.

Option (B) is correct. Concept Maps are visual organizers that can help students understand main ideas and how ideas relate to each other as they learn in content areas. Option (A) is incorrect. The Directed Reading Thinking Activity (DRTA) is a comprehension strategy that guides students to ask questions, make predictions, and then read to confirm or refute their predictions. Option (C) is incorrect. In reciprocal teaching, the teacher models, and then students take on the role of teachers by using four strategies to have a dialogue about what they have learned: summarizing, question generating, clarifying, and predicting. Option (D) is incorrect. Question-Answer Relationships is a strategy that helps students think about what can be required to answer questions about material they have read: (1) Look in one place in the text; (2) Search in more than one place in the text; (3) Use what is read in combination with what the reader has experienced; and (4) Use prior knowledge of the reader. **(901-004—Reading Comprehension and Applications)**

20. D.

Option (D) is correct because research does not show that tests foster vocabulary development; in fact, students often forget the meanings of words and only gain a superficial understanding when memorizing definitions. Option (A), (B), and (C) are incorrect because they describe instruction that is effective in helping students gain in vocabulary development. **(901-005— Vocabulary Development)**

21. B.

Option (B) is correct. If students apply context clues to identify a word, but they are not successful, the teacher should present direct instruction to clarify the meaning of an unfamiliar word if students cannot understand the meaning by using context clues. Option (A) is incorrect. The teacher is not focusing on examining the title, headings, or illustrations of text to be able to improve comprehension. Option (C) is incorrect

because the focus of instruction is on the meaning of a word. Option (D) is incorrect because the focus of this situation is on vocabulary development, not predicting what will take place in the story. **(901-005—Vocabulary Development)**

22. A.

Option (A) is correct. The teacher is strategically using a photo that will help students understand what they will be reading and how they may see the word in other settings. Option (B) is incorrect. The teacher is not focusing on examining the title, headings, or illustrations of text to be able to comprehend. Option (C) is incorrect because the focus of instruction is on the meaning of a word, not on using letter-sound relationships to identify the word. Option (D) is incorrect because the focus of this scenario is on vocabulary development, not on spelling. **(901-005—Vocabulary Development)**

23. D.

Option (D) is correct. The teacher is using actions to add to the other activities used to foster vocabulary development. Option (A) is incorrect. Concept maps can help students understood words and how concepts are related, but this is not what the teacher is addressing in this situation. Option (B) is incorrect. The teacher is not focusing examining the title, headings, or illustrations of text to be able to comprehend. Option (C) is incorrect because the focus of instruction is on the meaning of a word, not on informal drama. **(901-005—Vocabulary Development)**

24. D.

Option (D) is correct because students gain in oral and written language when given the opportunity to talk about what why have read in authentic ways. The teacher has shared, which also contributes to the students' understanding of the story. Option (B) is incorrect. Teachers should make observations about students' participation to inform their teaching, but grading students is not a way to motivate students. Option (C) is incorrect because the teacher is not asking questions but rather is using retelling and discussion to enhance comprehension. Option (A) is incorrect because the students are talking in a small-group, not a whole-class situation. **(901-001—Oral Language)**

25. B.

Option (B) is correct because students profit from multiple learning experiences across several days when learning vocabulary. Option (A) is incorrect because the teacher is not helping students write in personal dictionaries in this situation. Option (C) is incorrect. Talking is effective for helping students establish content when they write, but the students are not writing in this situation. Option (D) is incorrect because in this situation, the teacher is focusing upon helping students have in-depth experiences with new vocabulary, not on talking about what takes place in the story. **(901-005—Vocabulary Development)**

26. D.

Option (D) is correct. Teachers should help students relate new concepts to what they know, as well as understanding the meanings of prefixes, suffixes, and word roots—which is effective in enabling students to learn new vocabulary independently. Option (A) is incorrect. The focus of instruction is on morphology, or word parts, not phonics. Option (B) is incorrect. Research does not show that giving a vocabulary quiz helps students make gains. Option (C) is incorrect because the teacher is not focusing upon writing sentences in this situation. **(901-005—Vocabulary Development)**

27. C.

Option (C) is correct because students need support as they engage in strategies associated with writing a research report. When the teacher demonstrates and works with students, students are more apt to be able to write independently. Option (A) is incorrect because even though students are often told to develop an outline, they need to read first to get an overview of a topic as well as

any sub-topics that may need to be addressed. Writers often change outlines as they do research on a topic and when they start writing. Option (B) is incorrect. Making it possible for students to talk about what they want to write about is helpful for all students because it provides scaffolding. In the case of English learners, participating in writing through sheltered instruction helps them grow as writers. Option (D) is incorrect because students need to be shown what to do, not just told. If students are told not to copy what the text says, they often just change a few words in a sentence. **(901-006—Reading, Inquiry, and Research)**

28. A.

Option (A) is correct. Students eventually do need to learn how to locate and evaluate websites, but, as novices, they can easily be overwhelmed or end up using poor quality web sources. In the course of being directed to, and using, high-quality sites, students will gain expertise in understanding what a good site is. When a teacher narrows the web search, it allows students to focus on other skills, such as note-taking, noting sources, and writing a draft. Option (B) is incorrect because criteria on a checklist will not be understood if students are not familiar with the criteria. Option (C) is incorrect. Even if students know how to search for a site, they may not find one of quality. Option (D) is incorrect because students who are novices will not be able to support each other's learning in this situation even though working in pairs is effective for many other types of learning situations. **(901-006—Reading, Inquiry, and Research)**

29. B.

Option (B) is correct. The designated questions or subject areas provide structure and purpose for students as they read and record information. Option (A) is incorrect. The teacher is not providing information students need to be able to understand a text. Option (C) is incorrect because the teacher has used only nonfiction in this situation. Option (D) is incorrect because cohesive ties pertain to words that connect ideas, such as *further-*

more, a word that signals addition. **(901-006—Reading, Inquiry, and Research)**

30. D.

Option (D) is correct. Note-taking can be difficult for students to learn, which is why the teacher shows how to read short segments and then write notes without looking at the text so that students see a way to accurately put ideas into their own words. Option (A) is incorrect because the teacher has not focused upon building background knowledge in this learning experience. Option (B) is incorrect. Previewing a text entails looking at titles, headings, illustrations, photographs, and captions to prepare for reading. Option (C) is incorrect because when students copy the notes, they are directing their attention to copying, not observing what process the teacher is modeling. Instead, the teacher should continue to model or work together with students to provide gradual release of responsibility. **(901-006—Reading, Inquiry, and Research)**

31. D.

Option (D) is correct because students often overlook text features, such as headings, and are better able to organize and memorize individual facts when they understand the text structure and how the topic is organized. Option (A) is incorrect because the teacher does not provide shared reading, which involves the teacher and students reading a text together to help students who cannot deal with this on their own. Option (B) is incorrect because, at this point in the lesson, the teacher is not focusing on unfamiliar concepts or terms. Option (C) is incorrect because the teacher is directing students' attention to the title and heading, not helping them engage in metacognition, which would have them check their understanding as they read. **(901-006—Reading, Inquiry, and Research)**

32. A.

Option (A) is correct because teachers can support students' learning by thinking aloud and demonstrating

before asking students to engage in a strategy for reading expository text. Option (B) is incorrect because the teacher is not building background needed to understand the text. Option (C) is incorrect because the objective of the instructions is to help students learn how to preview a text and use the introduction as a guide, not merely to complete a table. Option (D) is incorrect because the teacher is not activating prior knowledge so students can relate the new information to what they know at this point. **(901-006—Reading, Inquiry, and Research)**

33. A.

Option (A) is correct because students need to understand and remember important details and how individual details relate to retain information they read. Option (B) is incorrect because the teacher is not building background as the students complete the chart, but rather is helping students record information. Option (C) is incorrect because the teacher is writing what the students dictate, and it is best that the students focus on the process and not on copying information. Option (D) is incorrect because previewing headings takes place before reading to help students understand how a topic is organized. **(901-009—Viewing and Representing)**

34. C.

Option (C) is correct because gradual release of responsibility helps students incrementally grasp and use strategies. Students receive the support they need by first watching the teacher, and then working with the teacher, and next working with other students under the teacher's guidance. Option (A) is incorrect because the teacher does not provide shared reading, where the teacher and students read a text together that they cannot read on their own. Option (B) is incorrect because the teacher is not focusing on unfamiliar concepts or terms at this point in the lesson. Option (D) is incorrect because the teacher should work with students until the they can work on their own, which can require more than one lesson for complex tasks; students learn even as they work with the teacher. **(901-006—Reading, Inquiry, and Research)**

35. D.

(D) is correct because homophones are words that are pronounced the same but have different meanings and spellings, so they can be confusing. Option (A) is incorrect because plural forms of words are not featured. Option (B) is incorrect because some of the words have one syllable. Option (C) is incorrect because pairs of words are not alike in meaning. **(901-007—Writing Conventions)**

36. A.

Option (A) is correct since the word *because* is a subordinating conjunction, which creates a dependent clause. A dependent clause must be used with an independent clause to create complete sentences not be a fragment. If the dependent clause is first, a comma is used prior to the independent clause. Options (B), (C), and (D) are incorrect because they are coordinating conjunctions, which can be used to combine two independent clauses and require a comma. **(901-007—Writing Conventions)**

37. C.

Option (C) is correct. Students can learn about how to write effectively through their read-aloud and reading experiences. Teachers can help students notice strategies and techniques writers use by looking back at works, which serve as mentor texts. Option (A) is incorrect. Mentor texts show students options, but they are not used as a model that students must follow. Option (B) is incorrect because the teacher is not focusing on preparation for reading in this situation. Option (D) is incorrect. Students can find it more challenging to read and remember expository text, but the teacher is focusing on showing students how to write an effective lead-in in this situation. **(901-008—Written Communication)**

38. B.

Option (B) is correct because drafting is where writing a rough draft is created to establish rather than polish content or place emphasis on writing conventions (mechanics). Option (A) is incorrect because prewriting is where writers brainstorm and think about what to write before actually writing. Option (C) is incorrect because revising is where changes are made in establishing content. Option (D) is incorrect because editing is where proofreading takes place, entailing a focus on writing conventions, or mechanics, of writing, including spelling punctuation, capitalization, and usage. **(901-008—Written Communication)**

39. C.

Option (C) is correct because this activity helps students learn techniques for selecting, organizing, and evaluating information from an electronic environment. Option (A) is incorrect because students need guidance in learning from the video and ample time for learning new information before taking a test. Option (B) is incorrect because the teacher needs to ensure that the students view a quality video, and students need guidance in locating quality electronic sources. Option (D) is incorrect because all students need to participate in reading the textbook to gain in proficiency, and teachers can provide scaffolding to support English learners so they participate in reading a text. **(901-009—Viewing and Representing)**

40. A.

Option (A) is correct because large amounts of information on a page can be overwhelming. Options (B), (C), and (D) are incorrect because they present criteria that help ensure students can gain from a website. **(901-009—Viewing and Representing)**

41. C.

Option (C) is correct. The student has joined two independent clauses together with a comma, which is incorrect and is a comma splice. Option (A) is incorrect because the student did use correct subject-verb agreement. Option (B) is incorrect because the student has not used a comma correctly. Option (D) is incorrect because the student has used correct capitalization in the sample. **(901-010—Assessment of Developing Literacy)**

42. B.

Option (B) is correct. All clauses have a subject and a verb, but a subordinating conjunction such as *because* and *although* creates a dependent clause, which must be joined to an independent clause to avoid being a fragment. Option (A) is incorrect because this writing sample does not show difficulties with using the correct verb tense. Option (C) is incorrect because seasons are not capitalized. Option (D) is incorrect because the writing sample contains no spelling errors of any kind. **(901-010— Assessment of Developing Literacy)**

43. D.

Option (D) is correct. When students retell, they tell what happened in the story, which requires literal-level comprehension as well as an accurate understanding of what took place. Options (A), (B), and (C) are incorrect because retelling does not primarily encourage or reveal that the student is able to think at higher levels, including the ability to make inferences, or to evaluate or relate what they have read based on their own experiences. **(901-010—Assessment of Developing Literacy)**

44. A.

Option (A) is correct because students typically need to be able to read 95%–100% of the words to be able to comprehend a story. Being able to read words does not ensure comprehension, so students could need additional support, but do need to be able to read texts easily to focus on meaning. Option (B) is incorrect. A text is considered to be at a student's instructional level when he or she can read at least 90%–94% of words, as the student needs instructional support to comprehend what's being read. Options (C) and (D) are incorrect because when a student reads below 90% of words, the text is considered to be too hard, or at the frustration level. **(901-010—Assessment of Developing Literacy)**

45. A.

Option (A) is correct because criterion-referenced tests can provide information about what students know in regard to a specific set of predetermined outcomes. Option (B) is incorrect because the scores of a norm-referenced test provide information about a student's ranking in comparison to other students, not specific information of what a student knows and can do. Option (C) is incorrect because running records provide information about a student's oral reading, but not a specific assessment of a set of confusing words. Option (D) is incorrect because anecdotal accounts may not include observing students using confusing words in their reading and writing even though anecdotal accounts can be beneficial in other ways. **(901-010—Assessment of Developing Literacy)**

TExES Core Subjects EC–6 Practice Test 1: Mathematics

This practice test and an additional test are available at the online REA Study Center (*www.rea.com/studycenter*).

The TExES Core Mathematics (902) test is computer-based, so we strongly recommend that you take our online practice tests to simulate test-day conditions and to receive these added benefits:

- **Timed testing conditions**—Gauge how much time you can spend on each question.

- **Automatic scoring**—Find out how you did on the test, instantly.

- **On-screen detailed explanations of answers**—Learn not just the correct answer, but also why the other answers are incorrect.

- **Diagnostic score reports**—Pinpoint where you're strongest and where you need to focus your study.

Mathematics Practice Test Answer Sheet

1. Ⓐ Ⓑ Ⓒ Ⓓ   15. Ⓐ Ⓑ Ⓒ Ⓓ   29. Ⓐ Ⓑ Ⓒ Ⓓ

2. Ⓐ Ⓑ Ⓒ Ⓓ   16. Ⓐ Ⓑ Ⓒ Ⓓ   30. Ⓐ Ⓑ Ⓒ Ⓓ

3. Ⓐ Ⓑ Ⓒ Ⓓ   17. Ⓐ Ⓑ Ⓒ Ⓓ   31. Ⓐ Ⓑ Ⓒ Ⓓ

4. Ⓐ Ⓑ Ⓒ Ⓓ   18. Ⓐ Ⓑ Ⓒ Ⓓ   32. Ⓐ Ⓑ Ⓒ Ⓓ

5. Ⓐ Ⓑ Ⓒ Ⓓ   19. Ⓐ Ⓑ Ⓒ Ⓓ   33. Ⓐ Ⓑ Ⓒ Ⓓ

6. Ⓐ Ⓑ Ⓒ Ⓓ   20. Ⓐ Ⓑ Ⓒ Ⓓ Ⓔ   34. Ⓐ Ⓑ Ⓒ Ⓓ

7. Ⓐ Ⓑ Ⓒ Ⓓ   21. Ⓐ Ⓑ Ⓒ Ⓓ   35. Ⓐ Ⓑ Ⓒ Ⓓ

8. Ⓐ Ⓑ Ⓒ Ⓓ   22. Ⓐ Ⓑ Ⓒ Ⓓ   36. Ⓐ Ⓑ Ⓒ Ⓓ

9. Ⓐ Ⓑ Ⓒ Ⓓ   23. Ⓐ Ⓑ Ⓒ Ⓓ   37. Ⓐ Ⓑ Ⓒ Ⓓ

10. Ⓐ Ⓑ Ⓒ Ⓓ   24. Ⓐ Ⓑ Ⓒ Ⓓ   38. Ⓐ Ⓑ Ⓒ Ⓓ

11. Ⓐ Ⓑ Ⓒ Ⓓ   25. Ⓐ Ⓑ Ⓒ Ⓓ   39. Ⓐ Ⓑ Ⓒ Ⓓ

12. Ⓐ Ⓑ Ⓒ Ⓓ   26. Ⓐ Ⓑ Ⓒ Ⓓ   40. Ⓐ Ⓑ Ⓒ Ⓓ

13. Ⓐ Ⓑ Ⓒ Ⓓ   27. Ⓐ Ⓑ Ⓒ Ⓓ

14. Ⓐ Ⓑ Ⓒ Ⓓ   28. Ⓐ Ⓑ Ⓒ Ⓓ

Practice Test 1: Mathematics

TIME: 1 hour and 10 minutes
40 selected-response

> **Directions:** Read each item and select the correct response or responses. Most items on this test require you to provide the one best answer. However, some questions require you to select all the options that apply.

1. The concept of the zero evolved in India but was also developed, independently, by the

   A. Babylonians.

   B. Mayans.

   C. Arabs.

   D. Romans.

2. While students in a sixth-grade class work in small groups on an ungraded discovery activity involving linear functions, the teacher circulates through the class asking individual students questions such as, "Why did you choose to assign the height variable to the vertical axis?" and "What happens to the graph if you use different-sized cups for the experiment?"

   Based on the scenario, which of the following is a primary purpose of these questions?

   A. To provide a formal assessment that can be used to encourage students to work harder.

   B. To gauge student progress in developing conceptual understanding in a way that will not penalize the student.

   C. To show the students that the teacher cares about the work they are doing.

   D. To provide an informal summative assessment that can be used to determine each student's grade for the assignment.

3. Carlos wants to bring cookies for each student in his entire elementary school. He knows there are 800 students in the school. His teacher asks him to make sure he buys enough bags to carry all of the cookies, assuming each bag can hold 38 cookies. Carlos goes to the store and buys 20 bags, then brings the cookies to school the next day. He finds out that he doesn't have enough cookies for all the students at the school. Which of the following is Carlos most likely to have done to obtain the incorrect number of bags?

   A. Rounded 38 to 40

   B. Neglected to count 2 classrooms of students

   C. Baked at 375 degrees for too long

   D. Used plastic bags

   > Word problem: Tripti has 10 apples and 20 oranges. Tripti's mother doubles the total number of apples and oranges she has. Meanwhile, Gahn's mother gives Gahn twice as many apples and twice as many oranges as Tripti started with.

4. A teacher creates the word problem shown above for a math lesson. Based on the word problem, the lesson will most likely cover which of the following mathematical properties?

   A. Associative property

   B. Distributive property

   C. Commutative property

   D. Dissociative property

5. Simplify: $6 \cdot 2 + 3 \div 3$.

   A. 18

   B. 5

   C. 10

   D. 13

6. Which of the following is an expression that represents the following statement: three times one-half of a number less eighty percent?

   A. $3 \times \dfrac{4}{2} - 0.8$

   B. $3 \times \dfrac{x}{2} - \dfrac{8}{100}$

   C. $3 \times \dfrac{x}{2} - 0.8$

   D. $3 \times \dfrac{x}{2} - 80$

7. Divide 6.2 by 0.05.

   A. 124

   B. 1.24

   C. 12.4

   D. 0.124

8. Multiply $\dfrac{3}{4}$ by $\dfrac{2}{3}$. Show your answer in simplified form.

   A. $\dfrac{5}{7}$

   B. $\dfrac{5}{12}$

   C. $\dfrac{1}{2}$

   D. $\dfrac{6}{12}$

9. What is the mode of the following data set? 4, 12, 3, 15, 8, 3, 9, 9, 8, 10, 12, 14, 3, 2.

   A. 3

   B. 9

   C. 8

   D. 14

10. A card is drawn from a standard deck of cards, what is the probability that the card is a queen or a black four?

   A. $\dfrac{6}{52}$

   B. $\dfrac{8}{25}$

   C. $\dfrac{25}{52}$

   D. $\dfrac{12}{52}$

11. A pair of 6-sided dice is rolled. What is the probability the sum of the dice is less than 13?

   A. $\dfrac{1}{12}$

   B. $\dfrac{35}{36}$

   C. 1

   D. $\dfrac{1}{18}$

12. What is the formula for the relationship between the number of faces, vertices, and edges of a cube?

   A. $F + E = V + 2$

   B. $E + V = F + 2$

   C. $F + V = E - 2$

   D. $F + V = E + 2$

13. What is another way to write $4 \times 4 \times 4$?

   A. 4^3

   B. 3^4

   C. 4×3

   D. 12

14. An isosceles triangle is a polygon with two equal sides. What else does this imply?

   A. It is equilateral.

   B. Its angles sum to greater than 180°.

   C. It is also scalene.

   D. It has two equal angles.

15. Two fair two-sided coins are tossed at the same time. What is the probability that only one head is obtained in each of the tosses?

   A. 0.25

   B. 0.75

   C. 0.5

   D. 0.1

16. The main advantage of using hands-on activities in mathematics is to

   A. enhance students' ability to think abstractly.

   B. make the lesson more enjoyable.

   C. lead the students to active learning and guide them to construct their own knowledge.

   D. promote equity, equality, and freedom for the diverse ethnic groups in the nation.

Use the figure below to answer the question that follows.

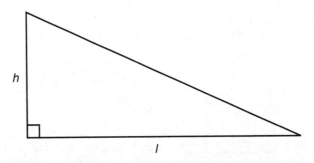

17. Which formula can be used to find the area of the triangle?

   A. $A = \dfrac{(l \times h)}{2}$

   B. $A = \dfrac{(l + h)}{2}$

   C. $A = 2(l + h)$

   D. $A = 2(l \times h)$

18. If a can weighs 14 oz., how many cans would you need to have a ton? (Round your answer to the nearest ones place and pick the best answer.)

   A. 2285

   B. 2286

   C. 2287

   D. 2300

19. How many faces does a cube have?

   A. 7

   B. 6

   C. 5

   D. 4

Use the figures below to answer the question that follows.

20. In each of the figures shown above, made up of circles, rectangles, triangles, and parallelograms, the shaded area represents a region in which flowers will be planted costing $2.50 per square foot. Which of them costs under $300 to plant the flowers?

    Select *all* that apply.

    A. Figure A

    B. Figure B

    C. Figure C

    D. Figure D

    E. Figure E

21. Students in Ms. Lopez's class are solving this problem by the discovery method:

    A sheet of paper 16 by 30 inches has squares of side x cut out from the corners as shown in the diagram below. The paper is folded on the dotted line to create a rectangular solid. The volume of the solid is $V = x(30 - 2x)(16 - 2x)$.

    Which of the following activities is most effective in helping students understand how length, width, and height contribute to the volume of a rectangular solid?

    A. Have students cut out squares of various sizes and determine the area of the resulting piece of paper.

    B. Have students cut out squares of various sizes, bend up the sides, and determine the volume of the resulting shape.

    C. Have students plug in various values of x into the given formula.

    D. Have students watch a YouTube video of the problem.

22. For what value of x is the expression $\dfrac{5}{x}$ undefined?

    A. 9

    B. 1,000,000,000.1123

    C. 0

    D. 1E – 14

23. Which of the following sets of numbers is not an integer followed by its square?

    A. −8, 64

    B. 8, 64

    C. 6, 32

    D. −9, 81

24. Which of the following statements best represents the value of manipulatives as part of an instructional strategy?

    A. Manipulatives are more appropriate for students at the preoperational stage of cognitive development.

    B. The use of manipulatives should be restricted to children in Kindergarten to fourth grade.

    C. The use of manipulatives is more appropriate for teaching computation skills and geometry.

    D. Manipulatives can be used to teach mathematics in grades Pre-K to high school.

25. Which of these numbers or number representations are irrational numbers? Select *all* that apply.

    A. π

    B. $\sqrt{2}$

    C. $e \approx 2.71828182845\ldots$

    D. $\dfrac{5}{8}$

26. Which of the following would be the best set of units to use when measuring a football field?

    A. Centimeters

    B. Inches

    C. Meters

    D. Miles

27. Which of the following were the first mathematicians to impact the development of modern-day mathematics?

    A. Greeks and the Aztecs

    B. Egyptians and Babylonians

    C. Hindus and Aztecs

    D. Arabs and the Mayans

28. Perform the indicated operation: $(-36) - 11$.

    A. 47

    B. 25

    C. −47

    D. −25

29. In the problem, $5 + 6 \times \dfrac{3}{2}$, what is the first operation which should be performed according to the order of operations?

    A. Exponent

    B. Multiply

    C. Subtract

    D. Add

30. A local Brownie troop uses the model $y = 2x - 25$ to calculate the money earned in a bake sale, where x is the number of cookies sold. If the troop sold 75 cookies, how much money did the troop earn?

    A. $75

    B. $150

    C. $175

    D. $125

31. In Ms. Leal's class, there are 18 blondes, 17 brunettes, and 5 redheads. Rodrigo is asked to determine the probability of Ms. Leal randomly selecting a redhead from her class to answer a question. His answer is 8. Which of the following best describes how Rodrigo went wrong in finding the solution?

    A. He divided 40 by 5.

    B. He divided 5 by 40.

    C. He added 7 and 1.

    D. He subtracted 1 from 9.

32. Two paper bags are each filled with four blue marbles and four red marbles. What is the probability of selecting a blue marble from the first bag and a blue marble from the second bag?

    A. $\dfrac{1}{4}$

    B. $\dfrac{2}{16}$

    C. $\dfrac{1}{2}$

    D. $\dfrac{4}{8}$

33. An example of a prime number is

    A. 9

    B. 682

    C. 49

    D. 67

34. Which of the following numbers cannot be used to express probability?

    A. −0.004

    B. 0.2

    C. 0

    D. 0.99

35. Solve the following problem. Express the answer as a mixed number. $1.6 - \dfrac{3}{8} =$

    A. $\dfrac{49}{40}$

    B. 1.225

    C. 1.23

    D. $1\dfrac{9}{40}$

36. There are 16 more apples than oranges in a basket of 62 apples and oranges. How many oranges are in the basket?

    A. 23

    B. 39

    C. 32

    D. 30

37. Valerie has a bathtub that she needs to fill with water. To fill the tub, she first needs to fill a bucket with water and then dump this into the bathtub. If the bucket is a cylinder with a radius of 6 in. and a height of 12 in., how many buckets will it take to fill the 5 ft. × 3 ft. × 3 ft. tub?

    A. 50 buckets

    B. 48 buckets

    C. 57 buckets

    D. 62 buckets

38. Dan and Stacy live on a farm where they are no longer allowed to let their cattle roam free. They need to add a fence around their land, which has a rectangular shape like the figure below. How many feet of fence do they need to buy in order to fence in all of their land?

223 ft

467 ft

   A.   103,341 ft.

   B.   104,141 ft.

   C.   1,380 ft.

   D.   690 ft.

39. Simplify to a single term in scientific notation: $(2 \cdot 10)^3 \cdot (6 \cdot 10^4)$.

   A. $0.12 \cdot 10^7$

   B. $12 \cdot 10^7$

   C. $4^8 \cdot 10^8$

   D. $4.8 \cdot 10^8$

Use the figure below to answer the question that follows.

40. Given that the radius of the circle shown is 6 units and that the circle is inscribed in the square, which of the following is the approximate area of the shaded region?

   A.   106 square units

   B.   31 square units

   C.   77 square units

   D.   125 square units

Mathematics Practice Test Answer Key

1. B	15. C	29. B
2. B	16. C	30. D
3. A	17. A	31. A
4. B	18. B	32. A
5. D	19. B	33. D
6. C	20. A, D, E	34. A
7. A	21. B	35. D
8. C	22. C	36. A
9. A	23. C	37. C
10. A	24. D	38. C
11. C	25. A, B, C	39. D
12. D	26. C	40. B
13. A	27. B	
14. D	28. C	

Mathematics Practice Test 1
Detailed Answers

1. **B.**

The correct answer is (B). The Mayans developed the concept of the zero around 700 CE. However, there is no evidence to suggest that its discovery has any connection with the development of the same concept in India. Choice (A) is incorrect because there is no evidence to suggest that the Babylonians developed the concept of the zero as part of their numeric system based on 60. Choice (C) is incorrect because most historians agree that the Arabs used information from the Hindus to develop our modern numeric system, which includes the zero. Choice (D) is incorrect because there is no evidence to suggest that the Romans developed the concept of the zero as part of their numeric system. **(902-003 Patterns and Algebra)**

2. **B.**

The correct answer is (B). Because no grades are being assigned, the students will not be penalized if they cannot answer the question. The questions themselves are focused on key concepts in linear functions such as the meaning of the y-intercept (question No. 1) and the linear function as a model of the physical world (question No. 2). Choice (A) can be ruled out because the fact that the teacher is asking the questions in a conversational tone without mention of grades being assigned makes this an informal assessment. Choice (D) can be ruled out because the teacher is assessing the students as they work on the content. This means the teacher is using a formative, not summative, assessment. Though choice (C) may initially seem appealing, it is not correct because a teacher who maintains a neutral relationship with his or her students can still perform these tasks effectively; thus, the notion of caring in itself is not integral to this test item. **(902-001 Mathematics Instruction)**

3. **A.**

The correct response is (A). It is most likely that Carlos rounded 38 to 40 in order to make his division process easier. This would then explain how he came to purchase 20 bags because 800 students divided by 40 yields 20. **(902-006 Mathematical Processes)**

4. **B.**

The correct response is (B). The distributive property best describes the statement. Tripti initially had (10 + 20) apples and oranges and then the amount is doubled: $2 \times (10 + 20)$. Gahn was given twice as many apples and oranges from the beginning: $(2 \times 10 + 2 \times 20)$. Choice (A) is a play on the associative property and therefore is incorrect. Answers (C) and (D) do not apply. Therefore, the best answer is choice (B). **(902-006 Mathematical Processes)**

5. **D.**

The correct answer is (D). The order of operations must be obeyed here. Remembering the saying "Please Excuse My Dear Aunt Sally (PEMDAS)" allows us to remember the order in which mathematical operations must be carried out: Parentheses Exponent Multiply Divide Add Subtract. Following this, multiply 6 by 2 to obtain 12. Then, divide 3 by 3 obtaining 1. Finally, add the two results together to obtain $12 + 1 = 13$. **(902-001 Mathematics Instruction)**

6. **C.**

The correct answer is (C). The statement "three times one-half of a number less eighty percent" implies that we do not know the actual number. Therefore, it must be represented by a variable. This fact eliminates choice (A). Knowing that 80% is equivalent to $\dfrac{80}{100}$ or

0.8 eliminates choices (B) and (D). Therefore, the only choice that is left happens to be choice (C). **(902-006 Mathematical Processes)**

7. A.

The correct answer is (A). The traditional whole number division algorithm (method) is helpful when dividing decimals longhand. The work can be set up like this:

$$0.05\overline{)6.2}$$

Dividing (while temporarily ignoring the zeros and decimal points) gives

$$
\begin{array}{r}
124 \\
0.05\overline{)6.2} \\
\underline{5} \\
1\,2 \\
\underline{1\,0} \\
20 \\
\underline{20} \\
0
\end{array}
$$

Next, you count the number of digits to the right of the decimal point in the divisor (two). Two, then, is the number of places that you shift the "inside" decimal point to the right, and then "up" into the answer:

$$0.05\overline{)6.2} \longrightarrow 0.05\overline{)6.2}$$

Because the answer is a whole number, the decimal point does not have to be shown. **(902-002 Number Concepts and Operations)**

8. C.

The correct answer is (C). The useful, traditional approach to multiplying simple fractions (those between 0 and 1) is to first multiply the numerators together and then to multiply the denominators together to find the product. In this case, $\frac{3}{4} \times \frac{2}{3} = \frac{6}{12}$. That fraction is then shown in simplest form, $\frac{1}{2}$. Based on the explanation, choices A, B, and D are incorrect. **(902-002 Number Concepts and Operations)**

9. A.

Choice (A) is the correct answer. The mode is the number that occurs most often. From looking at the data we see that the number 3 occurs 3 times, the most of all the numbers. **(902-005 Probability and Statistics)**

10. A.

The correct answer is (A): $\frac{6}{52}$. In a standard deck of cards there are 52 total cards. Of the 52 cards, there are four suits and 13 cards per suit. Therefore, there are four queens in the deck. Additionally, of the four suits, two are black and two are red. So, there are two black fours giving a grand total of six cards of 52 that meet the criteria. **(902-005 Probability and Statistics)**

11. C.

The correct answer is (C): $\frac{36}{36} = 1$. On a single die there are six numbers, 1–6. On a pair of dice, the values of the sums range from 2–12. All values are clearly less than 12. Therefore, all rolls will be less than 13. Additionally, with a pair of dice, there are 36 possible outcomes (6 each) and, therefore, the answer is (C). **(902-005 Probability and Statistics)**

12. D.

The correct answer is (D): $F + V = E + 2$. Recall that the Face (F) of a cube is a plain region of a geometric body, the Edge (E) is a line segment where two faces of a three-dimensional figure meet, and a Vertex (V) is the union of two segments or the point of intersection of two sides of a polygon. Knowing this we can see that for a cube there are 6 faces, 8 vertices, and 12 edges. Substituting these numbers into the appropriate spot in each formula allows us to determine option (D) as the only correct answer. **(902-004 Geometry and Measurement)**

13. A.

Recalling that exponential notation is used when numbers are multiplied by themselves numerous times, try to simplify the expression. Option (B) is not correct because this implies 3 is multiplied by itself 4 times. Options (C) and (D) are the same answer in different representations, but both are incorrect. Since 4 is multiplied by itself 3 times in this problem, we know the answer should be option (A). **(902-002 Number Concepts and Operations)**

14. D.

In any triangle, the sum of the angles must equal 180°. If a triangle has two equal sides, the third side cannot be unique and must be a set length. The lines associated with the equal sides will intersect the third side at the same angle. Therefore, the only answer that can be determined to be true from the information is option (D). **(902-004 Geometry and Measurement)**

15. C.

Since tossing two separate coins does not affect the outcome of the other coin, we know that the probability of getting heads on either coin is $\frac{1}{2}$. The probability of the outcome is thus $\frac{2}{4}$ or 0.5. Alternatively, the possibilities are HH, HT, TH, and TT. Since there are 4 possibilities and 2 of them have only one H, the probability is $\frac{2}{4} = \frac{1}{2} = 0.5$. **(902-005 Probability and Statistics)**

16. C.

The correct answer is (C). Hands-on activities can make the curriculum more relevant and guide children to construct their own knowledge. Hands-on activities can probably lead children to think abstractly (A), but the activity is not designed exclusively to accomplish this goal. Hands-on activities can make the class more interesting and enjoyable (B), but they are not the reasons for the activities. (D) is incorrect because there is no evidence to suggest that hands-on activities can promote equity, equality, or freedom among students. **(902-001 Mathematics Instruction)**

17. A.

The area of any rectangle is equal to the measure of its length times the measure of its width (or to say it differently, the measure of its base times the measure of its height). A right triangle can be seen as half of a rectangle (sliced diagonally). Choice (A) represents, in effect, a rectangle's area cut in half (i.e., divided by 2). Based on this explanation, choices (B), (C), and (D) are incorrect. **(902-004 Geometry and Measurement)**

18. B.

The correct answer is (B), 2286. An easy way to solve this problem is to use basic algebra. Knowing that there are 16 oz. in a pound and that there are 2,000 lbs. in a ton helps ease the difficulty of the problem. We want to find out the number of cans x it will take to obtain a ton. Therefore, we have $\frac{14}{16}x = 2000$. If both sides of the equation are multiplied by 16 and then we divide both sides by 14, we will obtain the approximate number of cans it will take to obtain one ton. $x = \frac{16 \times 2000}{14} = \frac{32000}{14} \approx 2285.7$. We see that many of the answers are close to this value. When we round this number, we will obtain 2,286. **(902-003 Patterns and Algebra)**

19. B.

The correct answer is (B): 6. Remembering that a face is a plane region of a geometric body, one can determine that since there are six sides to a cube, there are also six faces. **(902-004 Geometry and Measurement)**

20. A., D., E.

The correct answers are (A), (D), and (E). This problem tests the area of regular polygons.

A. Area = $\pi(6^2) = 36\pi$. Cost = $36\pi(2.5) = 90\pi$ dollars = \$282.74, which is less than \$300
B. Area = $\pi(64) - \pi(9) = 55\pi$. Cost = $55\pi (2.5) = 137.5\pi$ dollars = \$431.97, which is not less than \$300
C. Area = $13(10) = 130$. Cost = $130(2.5) = \$325$, which is not less than \$300

D. Area = $\frac{1}{2}$ (20)(4) = 40. Cost = 40(2.5) = $100, which is less than $300

E. Area = 18(7) − 9 = 117. Cost = 117(2.5) = $292.50, which is less than $300

(902-004 Geometry and Measurement)

21. B.

The correct answer is option (B) because having students cut out the squares gets them to see that the larger the square, the smaller the length and width. Being able to have a physical model of these solids allows students to see readily which ones are obviously larger in volume than others. Option (A) is incorrect as cutting squares out and examining the area tells students nothing about the volume. Option (C) is incorrect because although plugging different values of x will give different volumes of V, students do not see how the size of x affects the length and the width. Option (D) is incorrect because unless this video shows someone performing option (B), it cannot be as effective a learning tool. **(902-001 Mathematics Instruction)**

22. C.

Until more advanced mathematics are incurred, the standard definition of division states that an expression is undefined if it contains division by 0. Option (D) is a number very close to zero. Although option (D) will make the expression a huge number, it is still not undefined. Therefore, the response that best corresponds to the question is choice (C). **(902-003 Patterns and Algebra)**

23. C.

An integer number is a whole number that is either positive or negative. Remembering that a negative times a negative gives a positive means that any of the answers could be possible and we cannot rule any out by process of elimination. Knowing that 8 times 8 gives 64 and −8 times −8 gives 64 means both choices (A) and (B) are true. Similarly, −9 times −9 results in 81 (D), meaning 81 is true. However, 6 times 6 gives 36, not 32. This means

that choice (C) is not a true statement and is the solution to the problem. **(902-003 Patterns and Algebra)**

24. D.

The correct answer is (D). Manipulatives can be used to simplify the teaching of mathematics in all grade levels—Pre-K to high school. Choices (A) and (B) are incorrect because the use of manipulatives does not have to be restricted to early childhood (Pre-kindergarten through fourth grade). Choice (C) is incorrect because manipulatives can be used to teach concepts including computation skills and geometry but its use is not limited to these two components. **(902-001 Mathematics Instruction)**

25. A., B., and C.

The correct answers are (A), (B), and (C). An irrational number is a number that cannot be expressed as a fraction. π is one of the most well-known irrational numbers. Additionally, the square root of 2 and Euler's number (e) are well-known numbers that are irrational (at no known point does a pattern appear in the decimals of these numbers). Choice (D) is not correct because any number that can be written as a fraction is a rational number. **(902-006 Mathematical Processes)**

26. C.

While all of these units will accurately express the length of the football field, centimeters and inches would not be a convenient scale to use, as the resolution of the measurement would be too great resulting in an extremely large number (or a long time to measure). Miles are another inconvenient method to measure a football field, as a mile is much larger than a single football field. **(902-002 Number Concepts and Operations)**

27. B.

While other groups made significant contributions to mathematics, choice (B), the Egyptians and Babylonians (third millennium BCE) were the first groups to make an impact on the development of modern-day mathematics. **(902-006 Mathematical Processes)**

28. C.

When subtraction involves any negative numbers, a good rule to use is, "Don't subtract the second number. Instead, add its opposite." Using that rule, the original expression, $(-36) - 11$, becomes $(-36) + -11$. To be "in debt" by 36, then to be further "in debt" by 11, puts one "in debt" by 47, shown as -47. **(902-002 Number Concepts and Operations)**

29. B.

Using the acronym PEMDAS as a mnemonic device to remember the order of operations, it allows us to see that the first operation required in the problems is multiplication. That is, the acronym calls for the following order: parenthesis, exponents, multiplication, division, addition, and subtraction. However, since the problem does not contain parenthesis or exponents, the first operation required in the problem is multiplication. **(902-006 Mathematical Processes)**

30. D.

(D) is the correct answer. The Brownie troop sold \$125 worth of cookies. The amount of money, y, is found by substituting the number of cookies sold, 75, for x in the given equation: $y = 2x - 25 = 2(75) - 25 = 150 - 25 = 125$. **(902-006 Mathematical Processes)**

31. A.

The correct answer is (A). Choices (C) and (D), while matching Rodrigo's answer, would seemingly come from nowhere which is highly unlikely. Choice (B) would produce a number less than 1, the correct answer for the problem asked of Rodrigo, and therefore would not match Rodrigo's answer. It is most likely that Rodrigo divided 40, the number of students in the class, by 5, the number of redheads, to obtain his answer of 8. **(902-005 Probability and Statistics)**

32. A.

There are equal numbers of blue and red marbles in each bag. For a single bag on a single draw, the probability of pulling a red or a blue marble is equal to $\frac{4}{8}$, or $\frac{1}{2}$. Selecting a marble from one bag does not affect the probability of selecting a specific marble from the other bag, therefore these events are said to be independent. When dealing with the probability of independent events, one may multiply the probabilities together to obtain the overall probability. In this case, we know the probability of selecting a blue marble is $\frac{1}{2}$ for the first bag and it is also $\frac{1}{2}$ for the second bag. Therefore, the overall probability of the independent events is $\frac{1}{4}$. **(902-005 Probability and Statistics)**

33. D.

A prime number is a number whose only factors are one and itself. Even numbers greater than 2 can always be factored by 2, eliminating (B). (A) can be factored as 3 times 3 and (C) can be factored as 7 times 7. Therefore, (D) must be the right answer as it only has factors of 1 and 67. **(902-002 Number Concepts and Operations)**

34. A.

A probability can be expressed as a number from 0 to 1, or with percentage or decimal numbers. A percent is a representation of a decimal number relative to 100. Therefore, the only number shown which does not fit is the negative number. **(902-005 Probability and Statistics)**

35. D.

This problem can be solved by converting the decimal to a fraction, or the fraction to a decimal and then subtracting. If the decimal is converted to a fraction, 1.6 becomes $1.6 - \frac{3}{8}$ becomes $\frac{16}{10} - \frac{3}{8}$. In order to subtract, we should now get a common denominator. The lowest common denominator between 8 and 10 is 40. Therefore, the answer becomes $\frac{64}{40} - \frac{15}{40} = \frac{49}{40}$. Since the problem asks for a mixed number, the answer is $1\frac{9}{40}$. **(902-002 Number Concepts and Operations)**

36. A.

This problem is easily solved by using some basic algebraic reasoning. Since we are interested in determining the number of oranges that are in the basket, we will set this as a variable called r. The number of apples, a, and the number of oranges, r, sum to a total of 62. We also know that there are 16 more apples than oranges ($a = r + 16$). This gives $r + (r + 16) = 2r + 16 = 62$. Solving for r yields 23 oranges in the basket. **(902-003 Patterns and Algebra)**

37. C.

This problem requires critical thinking and some basic knowledge of math. Solving for the volume of the bathtub, one obtains 45 ft^3 and the volume of the bucket is $\pi \cdot 0.5^2 \times 1 \approx 0.7854$ ft^3. To find how many buckets of water it will take to fill the tub, we must divide 45 by 0.7854. This gives approximately 57 buckets (C). **(902-003 Patterns and Algebra)**

38. C.

This problem deals with finding the perimeter of the rectangle. Since the two short legs of fence have the same length and the two long legs have the same length, we know $P = 2l + 2w$. This gives us a value of $2 \cdot 223 + 2 \cdot 467 = 1380$ ft. So you should have chosen option (C). **(902-004 Geometry and Measurement)**

39. D.

First simplify the expression $(2 \cdot 10)^3 \cdot (6 \cdot 10^4)$; rewrite as $(2^3 \cdot 10^3) \cdot (6 \cdot 10^4) = 8 \cdot 10^3 \cdot 6 \cdot 10^4$. Rearrange the terms so they appear as $(8 \cdot 6) \cdot (10^3 \cdot 10^4)$ to assist in multiplying the "like" numbers. The first group results in 48. To calculate $(10^3 \cdot 10^4)$ we use a specific rule for exponents. To multiply quantities with the same base (in this case 10), add the exponents: $10^3 \cdot 10^4 = 10^{(3+4)} = 10^7$, which produces a value of $48 \cdot 10^7$. To place this into scientific notation, the first number's absolute value should be between 0 and 1. For the leading number, move the decimal point one place to the left and add 1 to the exponent of the 10. Our final answer would then be $4.8 \cdot 10^8$. **(902-002 Number Concepts and Operations)**

40. B.

First, it is helpful to view the shaded area as the area of the square minus the area of the circle. With that in mind, you simply need to find the area of each simple figure, and then subtract one from the other. You know that the radius of the circle is 6 units in length. That tells you that the diameter of the circle is 12 units. Because the circle is inscribed in the square (meaning that the circle fits inside of the square touching in as many places as possible), you see that the sides of the square are each 12 units in length. Knowing that, you compute that the area of the square is 144 square units (12×12). Using the formula for finding the area of a circle (πr^2), and using 3.14 for π, you get approximately 113 square units. ($3.14 \times 6 \times 6$). Then, you subtract 113 (the area of the circle) from 144 (the area of the square) for the answer of 31. Based on the explanation given, choices (A), (C), and (D) are incorrect. **(902-004 Geometry and Measurement)**

TExES Core Subjects EC–6 Practice Test 1: Social Studies

This practice test and an additional test are also available at the online REA Study Center (*www.rea.com/studycenter*).

The TExES Core EC–6 Subjects Social Studies (903) test is computer-based, so we strongly recommend that you take our online practice tests to simulate test-day conditions and to receive these added benefits:

- **Timed testing conditions**—Gauge how much time you can spend on each question.

- **Automatic scoring**—Find out how you did on the test, instantly.

- **On-screen detailed explanations of answers**—Learn not just the correct answer, but also why the other answers are incorrect.

- **Diagnostic score reports**—Pinpoint where you're strongest and where you need to focus your study.

Social Studies Practice Test Answer Sheet

1. Ⓐ Ⓑ Ⓒ Ⓓ
2. Ⓐ Ⓑ Ⓒ Ⓓ
3. Ⓐ Ⓑ Ⓒ Ⓓ
4. Ⓐ Ⓑ Ⓒ Ⓓ
5. Ⓐ Ⓑ Ⓒ Ⓓ
6. Ⓐ Ⓑ Ⓒ Ⓓ
7. Ⓐ Ⓑ Ⓒ Ⓓ
8. Ⓐ Ⓑ Ⓒ Ⓓ
9. Ⓐ Ⓑ Ⓒ Ⓓ
10. Ⓐ Ⓑ Ⓒ Ⓓ
11. Ⓐ Ⓑ Ⓒ Ⓓ
12. Ⓐ Ⓑ Ⓒ Ⓓ
13. Ⓐ Ⓑ Ⓒ Ⓓ
14. Ⓐ Ⓑ Ⓒ Ⓓ

15. Ⓐ Ⓑ Ⓒ Ⓓ
16. Ⓐ Ⓑ Ⓒ Ⓓ
17. Ⓐ Ⓑ Ⓒ Ⓓ
18. Ⓐ Ⓑ Ⓒ Ⓓ
19. Ⓐ Ⓑ Ⓒ Ⓓ
20. Ⓐ Ⓑ Ⓒ Ⓓ
21. Ⓐ Ⓑ Ⓒ Ⓓ
22. Ⓐ Ⓑ Ⓒ Ⓓ
23. Ⓐ Ⓑ Ⓒ Ⓓ
24. Ⓐ Ⓑ Ⓒ Ⓓ
25. Ⓐ Ⓑ Ⓒ Ⓓ
26. Ⓐ Ⓑ Ⓒ Ⓓ
27. Ⓐ Ⓑ Ⓒ Ⓓ
28. Ⓐ Ⓑ Ⓒ Ⓓ

29. Ⓐ Ⓑ Ⓒ Ⓓ
30. Ⓐ Ⓑ Ⓒ Ⓓ
31. Ⓐ Ⓑ Ⓒ Ⓓ Ⓔ
32. Ⓐ Ⓑ Ⓒ Ⓓ
33. Ⓐ Ⓑ Ⓒ Ⓓ
34. Ⓐ Ⓑ Ⓒ Ⓓ
35. Ⓐ Ⓑ Ⓒ Ⓓ
36. Ⓐ Ⓑ Ⓒ Ⓓ
37. Ⓐ Ⓑ Ⓒ Ⓓ
38. Ⓐ Ⓑ Ⓒ Ⓓ
39. Ⓐ Ⓑ Ⓒ Ⓓ
40. Ⓐ Ⓑ Ⓒ Ⓓ

Practice Test 1: Social Studies

TIME: 50 minutes
40 selected-response questions

> **Directions:** Read each item and select the correct response or responses. Most items on this test require you to provide the one best answer. However, some questions require you to select all the options that apply.

1. Which of the following best describes how elementary teachers should prepare students for their roles as citizens of the United States?

   A. They lay the foundation of American core values, citizenship, democracy, and patriotism.

   B. They have students in upper elementary grades prepare reports on the values and beliefs of America's forefathers.

   C. They ask students in lower elementary grades to role-play key historical figures in school plays and other events.

   D. They provide basic information when they can, so students can fit social studies content into their daily schedules.

2. Which of the following best describes the women's suffrage movement in Texas?

   A. Women activists in Texas became involved when the suffrage movement was popular in the United States.

   B. Many women in Texas embraced change and sought an equal status in all parts of society.

   C. Texas women believed that the suffrage movement was a natural extension of the work they did at home.

   D. The suffrage movement was a long fight, lasting nearly 60 years, to convince the male-dominated political establishment and other women of the merit of enfranchising women.

3. The Virginia House of Burgesses was established in Jamestown to

   A. function as the official body of the U.S. government.

   B. regulate trading among colonies.

   C. function as a form of representative government.

   D. regulate the establishment of religions.

4. Identify the order of the products that have supported the Texas economy through its history.

   A. Petroleum, cotton, oranges, and cattle

   B. Cattle, corn, petroleum, and education

   C. Cotton, cattle, petroleum, and computers and electronics

   D. Cattle, petroleum, beef, venison, and poultry

5. The Imperial Forces of Japan attacked Pearl Harbor on Sunday, December 7, 1941. Once the attack began, the officer in charge called President Roosevelt and notified him of the attack. During the communication, the president was able to hear the noise of the bombs exploding and the struggle of the battle. Recently, a reporter from the *Dallas Morning News* was researching the details of the attack and found a transcription of the official diary of Emperor Hirohito, in which he indicated the following: "The Imperial forces of Japan destroyed the American fleet in Hawaii Monday, December 8, 1941." If the attack occurred on December 7, why did the official document from the Japanese government indicate that the attack happened on December 8? Select the statement that best explains this discrepancy.

   A. The Americans knew that the attack was going to happen and assumed that it had happened the day before.

   B. The U.S. government had spies in Japan who knew when the attack was going to take place.

   C. There is a one-day difference between the two regions.

   D. Emperor Hirohito learned about the attack the day after, and he assumed that it happened on the same day he was apprised of it.

6. The U.S. Constitution was designed so that no single branch of the government—executive, judicial, or legislative—could exert full control over the other two. This unique feature of the Constitution is known as

   A. judicial review.

   B. the pocket veto.

   C. checks and balances.

   D. habeas corpus.

7. Advanced organizers and graphic representations are commonly used in social studies. What is the advantage of using these strategies to teach content?

   A. They make content accessible to all children.

   B. They make learning more interesting.

   C. They can be used to teach other content areas.

   D. They can be used to teach higher-order thinking skills.

8. The Mayflower Compact was one of the earliest agreements to

   A. establish a political body and to give that political body the power to act for the good of the colony.

   B. establish rules for farming and trading.

   C. establish a plan to implement plantation systems.

   D. establish a policy for settlement.

9. What is the function of the lines of latitude and longitude on a map?

   A. They form a grid system that emphasizes a cylindrical projection.

   B. Together, they provide the coordinates for the absolute location of a place.

   C. They form a grid system that measures distance in meters.

   D. Together, they are used to explain the relative location of a place.

10. A globe is a scale model of the Earth shaped like a sphere. A globe shows sizes and shapes more accurately than

   A. a compass rose.

   B. a Mercator projection map.

   C. a map scale.

   D. a thematic map.

11. The Sumerians, Akkadians, Babylonians, and Assyrians were some of the civilizations that flourished in Mesopotamia—the land between the rivers. What rivers are being alluded to in this statement?

    A. Nile and Amazon

    B. Tigris and Euphrates

    C. Nile and Indus

    D. Volga and Danube

12. A compass rose is a design printed on a chart to

    A. show the orientation of a map of Earth.

    B. show the distance between two places in the world.

    C. represent features such as elevations and divisions.

    D. show the distance between two corresponding points.

13. The tallest mountains in the world are part of the

    A. Andes Range.

    B. Himalayas Range.

    C. Karakoram Range.

    D. Kunlun Range.

14. The Battle of Gettysburg was the most disastrous episode of which of the following?

    A. American Civil War

    B. American Revolution

    C. Second World War

    D. Texas Revolution

15. The economic theory that states that prices vary based on the balance between the availability of a product or service at a certain price and the desire of potential purchasers to pay that price is known as

    A. free enterprise.

    B. the law of supply and demand.

    C. the interplay of inflation and deflation.

    D. economic interdependence.

16. What is the main purpose of the Federal Reserve System?

    A. To promote fiscal stability and provide stimulus money to balance the economy

    B. To promote economic growth

    C. To create inflation and deflation

    D. To keep the banking industry strong enough to ensure a supply of currency

17. The Texas state curriculum officially introduces children to U.S. history in

    A. second grade.

    B. third grade.

    C. fourth grade.

    D. fifth grade.

18. There are two categories of maps: reference maps and thematic maps. An atlas is an example of

    A. a reference map.

    B. a thematic map.

    C. a physical map.

    D. a population map.

19. The New England colonies consisted of

    A. Maryland, Virginia, North Carolina, South Carolina, and Georgia.

    B. Massachusetts, Connecticut, Rhode Island, and New Hampshire.

    C. New York, New Jersey, Delaware, and Pennsylvania.

    D. North Carolina, Rhode Island, Delaware, and Maryland.

20. To apply the concept of time zones, students need to have a clear understanding of

    A. the international date line.

    B. the Earth's yearly revolution.

    C. the concept of the meridians of longitude.

    D. the concept of the parallels of latitude.

Use the photograph below to answer the question that follows.

21. Which of the following court cases saw the U.S. Supreme Court rule that the conditions of segregation illustrated in the photograph above violated the Fourteenth Amendment?

   A. *Plessy v. Ferguson*

   B. *Marbury v. Madison*

   C. *Brown v. Board of Education of Topeka*

   D. *Dred Scott v. Sandford*

22. The earliest European colonization efforts in North America began with the founding of which of the following?

   A. Virginia and Massachusetts

   B. Texas and New Mexico

   C. Saint Augustine and Roanoke

   D. New York and New Jersey

Use the information below to answer the question that follows.

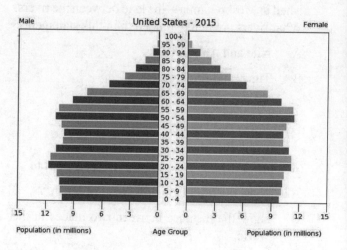

Source: United States Census Bureau

23. A population pyramid as seen above is a complex example of what type of chart, diagram, or graph listed below?

   A. Bar graph

   B. Pie graph

   C. Pedigree chart

   D. Dot plot

24. The first 10 amendments to the U.S. Constitution are known as the

   A. doctrine of the separation of church and state.

   B. Bill of Rights.

   C. Right to Privacy.

   D. Right to Due Process.

25. Students are expected to have received how many years of daily social studies instruction before entering middle school?

   A. As much as possible

   B. Two years

   C. Four years

   D. Seven years

26. Why are Indian tribes from the Central and Great Plains of Texas better known than their counterparts from the Coastal Plains?

   A. They had a more advanced civilization.

   B. They were sedentary and built better ceremonial sites and permanent structures.

   C. They domesticated the horse, which made them better hunters and warriors.

   D. They had an abundance of food sources and were stronger.

27. The United States has 50 states and at least four territories. Based on these figures, what is the maximum number of senators who can serve in the U.S. Senate?

   A. 50

   B. 100

   C. 54

   D. 435

Revere, Paul, engraver. "The BLOODY MASSACRE perpetrated in King Street BOSTON on March 5th 1770 by a party of the 29th REGT." 1770. Courtesy of Prints and Photographs Division, Library of Congress.

28. The Paul Revere engraving of the Boston Massacre (1770), pictured above, is taught at what grade level?

   A. 6th grade

   B. 5th grade

   C. 4th grade

   D. 3rd grade

29. Cinco de Mayo is a holiday commemorating the victory of the Mexican army over the French forces of Napoleon III on May 5, 1862. This event is important to Mexican Americans because

   A. the Mexicans defeated a ragtag army.

   B. it led to Mexican Independence Day.

   C. the general who led the Mexican forces was born in present-day Texas.

   D. President Benito Juarez joined forces with the United States to defeat France.

30. The Fifteenth Amendment to the U.S. Constitution was ratified in 1870 to grant

   A. Black women and men the right to vote.

   B. citizenship for Blacks.

   C. freedom of slaves.

   D. Black men the right to vote.

31. Determining which globes to use for a first grade classroom should be based on which of the following characteristics? Select *all* that apply.

   A. Three or fewer colors to represent land.

   B. At least seven colors to represent land.

   C. Two or fewer colors to represent water.

   D. Three or more colors to represent water.

   E. A 12-inch globe.

32. Probably as a response to the war in Iraq and Afghanistan, the Organization of Petroleum Exporting Countries (OPEC) cut the production of oil. As a result of this action, the cost of gasoline increased to almost $3.00 per gallon in 2005. What is the economic principle or statement that best represents this scenario?

   A. During war, the prices of fossil fuels increase.

   B. The American economy is dependent on foreign oil.

   C. The law of supply and demand determines the prices of goods and services.

   D. OPEC was boycotting the United States.

33. Identify the statement that best describes the country of Iraq.

   A. It is a linguistically and ethnically homogeneous Muslim nation.

   B. It is a Muslim nation with multiple ethnic groups within its borders.

   C. It is located in Southeast Asia.

   D. It is a province of Pakistan.

Use the information below to answer the question that follows.

Texas GDP Ranking among Nations
Gross Domestic Product, 2014
(in billions of U.S. dollars)

Rank	Nation	Billion $
1	United States*	$17,418
2	China	$10,380
3	Japan	$4,616
4	Germany	$3,859
5	United Kingdom	$2,945
6	France	$2,846
7	Brazil	$2,353
8	Italy	$2,147
9	India	$2,049
10	Russia	$1,871
11	Canada	$1,788
12	**TEXAS****	**$1,648**
13	Australia	$1,444
14	Korea	$1,416
15	Spain	$1,406
16	Mexico	$1,282
17	Indonesia	$888
18	The Netherlands	$866
19	Turkey	$806
20	Saudi Arabia	$752

*Includes Texas
**If Texas were a nation

Sources: International Monetary Fund and the U.S. Bureau of Economic Analysis. Based on data provided by the Texas Comptroller of Public Accounts staff. Published June 2015.

34. Based on the table above, if Texas were an independent nation, its annual economic output would be which of the following? Select *all* that apply.

   A. Ahead of Canada by approximately US$140 billion

   B. More than double the GDP of Saudi Arabia

   C. More than half the GDP of the United Kingdom

   D. One notch above Australia

35. The Spaniards Francisco Pizarro and Hernán Cortés conquered, respectively, which of the following two civilizations?

   A. Mayan and Aztec

   B. Inca and Aztec

   C. Toltec and Olmec

   D. Taino and Quechua

36. Identify the statement that best describes the relationship between the eight social studies strands and the TEKS in the implementation of the Texas curriculum.

   A. There is no connection between the TEKS and the social studies strands.

   B. The social studies strands have been used as a foundation for the development of the state curriculum.

   C. The strands apply to programs at the university level and the TEKS applies to K–12 curricula.

   D. The strands apply to programs at the high school level, while the TEKS applies to all grade levels.

37. Why might children in prekindergarten and Kindergarten have problems understanding how the Earth is represented in globes and flat representations?

   A. They might not be developmentally ready to understand symbolic representations.

   B. They might pay more attention to the colors and features of globes and maps than the concepts being taught.

   C. They might not be interested in maps and globes.

   D. They might have problems recognizing the Earth's features presented on a 12-inch globe representation.

38. Which of the following has a government that is an example of a theocracy?

   A. Jordan

   B. China

   C. Iran

   D. India

39. A census of the population of the United States is conducted every 10 years. Based on census results, which of the following can be affected by population changes?

   A. U.S. House of Representatives

   B. U.S. Senate

   C. Justices of the Supreme Court

   D. The Executive Branch

40. In Texas, the course that focuses on human or cultural geography is introduced in which of the following grades?

   A. Third

   B. Fourth

   C. Fifth

   D. Sixth

Social Studies Practice Test Answer Key

1.	A	15.	B	29.	C	
2.	D	16.	D	30.	D	
3.	C	17.	D	31.	A, C, and E
4.	C	18.	A	32.	C	
5.	C	19.	B	33.	B	
6.	C	20.	C	34.	B, C, and D
7.	A	21.	C	35.	B	
8.	A	22.	C	36.	B	
9.	B	23.	A	37.	A	
10.	B	24.	B	38.	C	
11.	B	25.	D	39.	A	
12.	A	26.	C	40.	D	
13.	B	27.	B			
14.	A	28.	B			

Social Studies Practice Test 1
Detailed Answers

1.   A.

The correct answer is (A). All elementary teachers play an important role in students' civic education. They introduce and instill the core values and ideals of what it means to be an American. Additionally, they provide foundational understanding of concepts upon which subsequent grade levels build. Social studies education also teaches students to consider events and situations from different points of view and to connect information learned in other disciplines, such as science or English language arts. Option (B) may occur; however, writing such reports is not central to preparing students for their role as citizens. Option (C) is correct in that students in lower elementary do learn about key historical figures. Some teachers may ask them to role-play. However, the answer does not specifically describe the elementary teacher's responsibility to prepare students for their role as citizens of the United States. Option (D) is incorrect. It is expected in the state of Texas that students will receive daily instruction in social studies. **(903-001 Social Science Instruction)**

2.   D.

The correct answer is (D). After being left out of the Fifteenth Amendment (right to vote), women across the United States, and in Texas and other states, began to fight for equal rights. Option (A) is incorrect because women in Texas were involved in the suffrage movement from the mid-1800s to the early 1900s. As it turns out, many women had to be persuaded that equal rights would not detract from their role and responsibility as wife and mother (C). The suffrage movement was a long struggle in Texas that required the dedication of great numbers of women and men to see it through to fruition. In 1919, Texas became the ninth state in the Union to ratify the Nineteenth Amendment, which guaranteed all American women the right to vote. **(903-002 History)**

3.   C.

The correct answer is (C). Established in 1619, the Virginia House of Burgesses was the first democratically elected legislative body in the British American colonies. Option (A) is incorrect because the U.S. government did not exist during this time (1619). Option (B) is incorrect because England regulated trading with the colonies. Option (D) is incorrect because there was no official entity in the colony to regulate the establishment of religions. **(903-005 Government and Citizenship)**

4.   C.

The correct answer is (C). Cotton and eventually cattle were the main products produced in Texas during the 19th and early 20th centuries. Later, with the discovery of petroleum in the 20th century, it became one of the most important exports for Texas. In the latter part of the 20th century, computers and electronics replaced oil as the main products of the state. Based on this explanation, options (A), (B), and (D) are eliminated. **(903-004 Economics)**

5.   C.

The correct answer is (C). There is a difference of one day from Honolulu to Tokyo. Honolulu is located east of the International Date Line (IDL), while Japan is west of the line. That is, if we travel from Honolulu toward the west on December 7, crossing the IDL to get to Tokyo, we would get there on December 8. The attack was recorded on December 7, 1941, in Honolulu, but the equivalent date for Japan was December 8, 1941. Options (A), (B), and (D) are incorrect because they do not explain the real reason for the date confusion. Additionally, the scenario does not provide information to support the position that Emperor Hirohito was confused about the dates. **(903-003 Geography and Culture)**

6.   C.

The correct answer is (C). The U.S. Constitution set up a system so that each branch of the government has the power to control or regulate the power of the other two. Option (A) is incorrect because judicial review addresses only the power of the judicial branch. Judicial review is the power to review legislation enacted by Congress and signed by the president. If the legislation is unconstitutional, it can be invalidated. Option (B) is incorrect because it addresses the power of the president to veto or refuse to sign legislation approved by Congress. Option (D) is incorrect because habeas corpus is one of the civil rights that guarantees people the right to a quick trial by jury. **(903-005 Government and Citizenship)**

7.   A.

The correct answer is (A). Information in social studies can be presented in graphic form through the use of graphs and charts. This makes the content accessible to all children, including ELs. Options (B), (C), and (D) describe possible ways to use advanced organizers and graphic representations, but individually these options do not fully explain their value. **(903-001 Social Science Instruction)**

8.   A.

The correct answer is (A). The Mayflower Compact was drawn up and signed by the Pilgrims aboard the *Mayflower*. They pledged to consult one another to make decisions and to act by the will of the majority. It is one of the earliest agreements to establish a political body and to give that political body the power to act for the good of the colony. Options (B), (C), and (D) are incorrect because these were aspects of colonial life but not the purpose of the Mayflower Compact. **(903-005 Government and Citizenship)**

9.   B.

The correct answer is (B). The coordinates provide the precise, or absolute, location of any place, thing, or person on Earth. The coordinates provided from the latitude/

longitude grid system support all map projections, not just cylindrical projections (A). The lines of latitude and longitude support all units of measure for distance, not only meters (C). The combination of latitude and longitude provide the exact or absolute location of something on Earth. Relative location is the description of the general location of a place in relation to another geographic point. **(903-003 Geography and Culture)**

10.   B.

The correct answer is (B). A globe is a scale model of the Earth shaped like a sphere. Because a globe is the same shape as the Earth, it shows sizes and shapes more accurately than a Mercator projection map (a flat representation of the Earth). Option (A) is incorrect because a compass rose is a design used to show the relative position of the cardinal points (north, south, west, and east) and not a representation of the Earth. Option (C) is incorrect because a map scale is used to show the distance between two places in the world. Option (D) is incorrect because thematic maps are not used to show the size and shape of the Earth. **(903-003 Geography and Culture)**

11.   B.

The correct answer is (B). The convergence of the Tigris and the Euphrates created a fertile region where some of the greatest civilizations of the world emerged. This part of the world has been called the Fertile Crescent, and it is part of the area called the Cradle of Civilization. Option (A) is incorrect because the Nile gave birth to the Egyptian civilization, and the Amazon River is located in South America, far away from Mesopotamia. Option (C) is incorrect because the Indus River is located in modern-day India. Option (D) is incorrect because the Volga and Danube rivers are located in Europe. **(903-002 History)**

12.   A.

The correct answer is (A). A compass rose is a design printed on a chart or map for reference. It shows the orientation of a map on Earth and shows the four cardinal directions (north, south, east, and west). A compass rose may also show in-between directions such as northeast or northwest. Option (B) is incorrect because a map scale shows the distance between two places in the world. Option (C) is incorrect because features such as elevations and divisions are represented by different colors. Option (D) is incorrect because the ratio of the distance between two points on the Earth and the distance between the two corresponding points on the map is represented by a scale and not by a compass rose. **(903-003 Geography and Culture)**

13. B.

The correct answer is (B). With the exception of peak K2, the top 10 mountain peaks are all part of the Himalayas Range. Choice (A) is incorrect, because, despite the fact that the Andes Range contains several high mountains, none of them ranks within the top 50 in the world. Choice (C) is incorrect because only three of the top 20 mountains in the world are part of the Karakoram Range. Choice (D) is incorrect because only one mountain from the Kunlun Range ranks within the first 25. **(903-003 Geography and Culture)**

14. A.

The correct answer is (A). The Union and the Confederate armies fought from July 1 through July 3, 1863, southwest of Harrisburg, Pennsylvania, in the Battle of Gettysburg. More than 50,000 soldiers were casualties—killed, wounded, captured or missing in what the Gettysburg Foundation terms "the largest battle ever fought in North America." In November 1863, President Lincoln dedicated the National Cemetery at the site of the battle by delivering his Gettysburg Address. In 1895 the battlefield became a national military park. **(903-002 History)**

15. B.

The correct answer is (B). The economic theory that states that prices vary based on a balance between the availability of a product or service at a certain price and the desire of potential purchasers to pay that price is known as the law of supply and demand. Free enterprise (A) is a generic term to describe capitalism and entrepreneurship. Inflation and deflation (C) are, respectively, the prevailing rate at which prices for goods and services are rising or declining. Economic interdependence (D) characterizes the relationship between people, regions, nations or other entities that has each dependent on the other. **(903-004 Economics)**

16. D.

The correct answer is (D). The main purpose of the Federal Reserve System is to keep the banking industry strong enough to ensure a supply of currency. When the banking industry is strong and there is an adequate supply of currency, fiscal stability and economic growth are more likely to occur. However, the direct role of the Fed is not to provide stimulus money to balance the economy (A), promote economic growth (B), or create inflation and deflation (C) in the country. Policies adopted by the Fed can lead to a healthy economy—or a weak economy resulting in inflation or deflation. **(903-004 Economics)**

17. D.

The correct answer is (D). The TEKS introduces the history of the United States in fifth grade. Option (A) is incorrect because in second grade the social studies curriculum covers local communities. Option (B) is incorrect because in third grade the curriculum centers on how individuals change their communities and the world. Option (C) is incorrect because in fourth grade students are familiarized with the history of Texas. **(903-001 Social Science Instruction)**

18. A.

The correct answer is (A). Reference maps show the locations of places, and boundaries of countries, states, counties, and towns. Atlases or road maps are examples of reference maps. Option (B) is incorrect because thematic maps show a particular topic such as population density, distribution of world religions, or physical, social, economic, political, agricultural, or economic features. Option (C) is incorrect because a physical map is a thematic map that shows the topography of the land including land features and elevations. Option (D) is incorrect because population maps are thematic maps that are used to show where people live in a particular region. **(903-003 Geography and Culture)**

19. B.

The correct answer is (B). The New England Colonies consisted of Massachusetts, Connecticut, Rhode Island, and New Hampshire. Option (A) is incorrect because Maryland, Virginia, North Carolina, South Carolina, and Georgia formed the Southern Colonies. Option (C) is incorrect because New York, New Jersey, Delaware, and Pennsylvania formed the Middle Colonies. Option (D) is incorrect because this answer represents a combination of some of the Southern Colonies and some of the Middle Colonies. **(903-002 History)**

20. C.

The correct answer is (C). The Earth is divided into 24 zones based on the meridians of longitude, which are determined using the rotation of the Earth and its exposure to sunlight. This rotation creates day and night, and consequently the concept of time. Option (A) is incorrect because the international date line is only one of 24 meridians of the Earth. Option (B) is incorrect because the term *revolution* describes the movement of the Earth around the Sun, which affects the seasons but not necessarily the time zones. Option (D) is incorrect because the parallels of latitude do not affect the time zones. **(903-003 Geography and Culture)**

21. C.

The correct answer is (C). The conditions represented in the photograph, which shows separate drinking fountains for whites and for African Americans, were ruled unconstitutional by the U.S. Supreme Court in *Brown v. Board of Education of Topeka* in May 1954. The case struck down *Plessy v. Ferguson* (A), the 1896 case in which the High Court had established the "sepa-

rate but equal" doctrine for determining the constitutionality of racial segregation laws. The High Court's ruling in *Marbury v. Madison* (B) in 1803 established the doctrine of judicial review, but did not touch on issues of racial segregation. In contrast, race was central to the thesis put forth in the Supreme Court's *Dred Scott* decision (D) in 1857: that African Americans, regardless of whether they had been slaves or been granted their freedom, were not protected by the U.S. Constitution and could never become U.S. citizens. **(903-002 History)**

22. C.

The correct answer is (C). The Spaniards established Saint Augustine, the first permanent European colony in North America, in 1565 near what is today Jacksonville, Florida. Subsequent to this, the English made an attempt to establish a colony off the coast of North Carolina—Roanoke. Choice (A) is incorrect because Virginia, Massachusetts, and all the other American colonies were established in the 17th century. Choice (B) is incorrect because New Mexico was established a few years later, in 1598, to become the first European colony west of the Mississippi. The first mission in Texas was established more than one hundred years later, in 1682. Choice (D) is incorrect because the Dutch did not begin bringing families to the area of New York and New Jersey until 1624. **(903-002 History)**

23. A.

Option (A) is correct. A population pyramid uses a series of bar graphs to represent the population of males and females at different ages. A population pyramid is a critical resource in social studies education. Elementary teachers should use them often to help students stay in practice with reading and interpreting the data on these graphs as they apply to different cultures and/or time periods in history. Option (B) refers to a circle divided into parts to represent data. Option (C) is a diagram that looks like a flow chart and is used to show lineage, or a family tree. Option (D) is a type of graph that is often seen in mathematics. It is like a bar graph except that it uses a dot to identify data. For example, if the bar graph extends a bar, or thick line, to the number 9, the dot plot uses a dot at the number 9 to represent the same information. Elementary teachers should use this commonality to help students transfer skills for reading and analyzing data in multiple forms. **(903-001 Social Science Instruction)**

24. B.

The correct answer is (B). Civil rights are the legal and political rights of the people who live in a particular country. In the United States, the Constitution and the Bill of Rights guarantee civil rights to American citizens and residents. The first 10 amendments to the U.S. Constitution are known as the Bill of Rights. Choices (A), (C), and (D) are incorrect because these name certain rights included in the Bill of Rights, but fail to address the question. **(903-005 Government and Citizenship)**

25. D.

The correct answer is (D). In Texas, teachers are required to teach social studies in every grade level. Therefore, by Grade 7 students are expected to have seven years of social studies (Kindergarten through 6th grade). Because the answer hinges on the amount of instruction to be received by middle school, response options (A), (B), and (C) can be ruled out. **(903-001 Social Science Instruction)**

26. C.

The correct answer is (C). The Apache and the Comanche domesticated the horse and became skillful hunters and warriors. These skills allowed them to fight the whites for many years for control of the Central and Great Plains of Texas. Choice (A) is incorrect because the tribes from the plains were nomads and did not develop an advanced civilization. Choice (B) is incorrect because both the Comanche and the Apache were nomads and did not leave permanent constructions. Choice (D) is incorrect because the tribes from the area had to hunt for survival and they had to move continuously to find adequate food supplies. **(903-002 History)**

27. B.

The correct answer is (B). The U.S. Constitution provides for two senators to represent each of the 50 states, for a total of 100. Territories are not represented in the U.S. Senate. Choice (D) is incorrect because it represents the current number of members of the U.S. House of Representatives. **(903-005 Government and Citizenship)**

28. B.

Option (B) is the correct answer. Students are taught U.S. History in Grade 5. The Boston Massacre was an important part of the Revolutionary War. Option (A) refers to World Cultures. Option (C) refers to Texas History. Option (D) refers to the social studies topic, "How Individuals Change their Communities and their World." **(903-001 Social Science Instruction)**

29. C.

The correct answer is (C). General Ignacio de Zaragoza was one of the leaders of the Mexican Army. He was born south of the city of Goliad, when this region was part of Mexico. Because the region is now part of Texas, Mexican Americans celebrate the accomplishment of this "Mexican American" hero. In the Battle of Puebla, the Mexican forces faced anything but a ragtag army (A); Napoleon III's French troops represented one of the world's best fighting forces, so the victory took on symbolic significance. Cinco de Mayo has nothing to do with Mexican Independence Day (B), which was established in 1810, a full half-century before the Battle of Puebla. Option (D) is incorrect because the United States did not participate in this war. The U.S. was fighting its own war—the American Civil War (1860-1865). **(903-002 History)**

30. D.

The correct answer is (D). The Fifteenth Amendment granted Black males the right to vote. Option (A) is incorrect because the voting right was given to Black males only, not women. Option (B) is incorrect because the Fourteenth Amendment granted citizenship to former slaves. Option (C) is incorrect because the Thirteenth Amendment granted freedom to slaves. **(903-005 Government and Citizenship)**

31. A., C., and E.

Options (A), (C), and (E) are correct because lower elementary grades (Pre-K–3) should use a smaller, simpler globe than upper elementary grades (4–6). Options (B) and (D) are characteristics of a globe for older elementary students. **(903-001 Social Science Instruction)**

32. C.

The correct answer is (C). Reducing the production of oil while keeping the same demand for the product creates an imbalance between supply and demand. This imbalance results in a price increase. Options (A) and (B), while potentially and flatly true, respectively, do not articulate an economic principle, as the question requires. Option (D) presents an opinion that fails to address the true question. **(903-004 Economics)**

33. B.

The correct answer is (B). Iraq is a Muslim nation with multiple ethnic groups within its borders. The largest groups are the Arabs, consisting of Shiite and Sunni Muslims. The Kurds are the largest minority group. (A) is incorrect. The multiple groups living in Iraq speak Arabic, Kurdish, Turkish, Assyrian, and other languages. (C) is incorrect because Iraq is located in the Middle Eastern part of Asia. (D) is incorrect because Pakistan is a Muslim country from the region, but there is no political association between the two nations. **(903-003 Geography and Culture)**

34. B., C., and D.

Options (B), (C), and (D) are correct. Option (B) is correct because Texas's US$1.65 trillion GDP in 2014 was more than double Saudi Arabia's US$752 billion. Option (C) is correct because the United Kingdom chalked up approximately US$2.95 trillion in GDP in

2014, half of which would be US$1.48 trillion. Option (D) is correct because Texas ranks 12th while Australia ranks 13th, according to the table. Option (A) is incorrect because the statement is actually the inverse of the reality: the figures show Canada in 11th place in terms of GDP, a notch above Texas. **(903-003 Economics)**

35. B

The correct answer is (B). Francisco Pizarro conquered the Incas of Peru, and Hernán Cortés conquered the Aztecs of Mexico. Choice (A) is incorrect because the Maya had virtually disappeared before the arrival of the Spaniards in America. Choice (C) is incorrect because these Mesoamerican groups, the Toltec and Olmec, disappeared before the Spanish colonization. Choice (D) is incorrect because the Tainos were from the Caribbean, an area that was under Spanish control before the intervention of Cortés and Pizarro. Additionally, the word *Quechua* refers to the language spoken by the Incas and other groups in the Andes Mountains. **(903-002 History)**

36. B.

The correct answer is (B). The social studies strands are systematically integrated throughout the social studies state curriculum in Grades K–12. Option (A) is incorrect based on the previous explanation. Options (C) and (D) are incorrect because the social studies strands are used in public education as well as in higher education. **(903-001 Social Science Instruction)**

37. A.

The correct answer is (A). Maps use symbolic representation, and children at that age (Pre-K and Kindergarten) rely mostly on concrete experiences for learning. The abstraction typical of maps' legends and other symbolic representations might not be developmentally appropriate for this age group. Choice (B) is a plausible statement but not the best answer. Children initially will be inclined to use the globe as toys and pay attention to colors, but eventually they will understand its function through classroom instruction. Choice (C) is incorrect

SOCIAL STUDIES PRACTICE TEST 1: DETAILED ANSWERS

because it presents an opinion not supported in the scenario. Choice (D) is probably a true statement: Children will have problems conceptualizing how the Earth can be represented in a small 12-inch globe, but this choice is not the best answer because it addresses only one component of the question—globe representation. **(903-001 Social Science Instruction)**

38.   C.

The correct answer is (C). Iran is a theocratic Islamic republic ruled by a supreme religious leader, a president, and a parliament. Jordan (A) is a constitutional monarchy. China (B) is ruled by a strictly hierarchical, highly centralized government led by the Chinese Communist Party. India (D) is a constitutional democracy led by a president, a prime minister, and a parliament. **(903-005 Government and Citizenship)**

39.   A.

The correct answer is (A). The number of members of the House of Representative is adjusted to reflect a proportion of the total U.S. population; thus, every time there is a census, the number can change. Choices (B), (C), and (D) are incorrect because population changes do not affect the composition of the Senate, the Supreme Court, or the Executive Branch. **(903-005 Government and Citizenship)**

40.   D.

The correct answer is (D). The course designed to introduce students to cultural or human geography is introduced in sixth grade. Unfortunately, some teachers teach this from a world history perspective, not from a geographic perspective. A geographic perspective includes history as well as other information such as culture, geopolitics, demographic, and human-environment interaction. Geographic concepts and skills are taught at each grade level. However, the World Cultures course is designed to teach basic understanding of cultural geography in preparation for World Geography at the high school level. **(903-001 Social Science Instruction)**

TExES Core Subjects EC–6 Practice Test 1: Science

This practice test and an additional test are available at the online REA Study Center (*www.rea.com/studycenter*).

The TExES Core Subjects EC–6 Science (904) test is computer-based, so we strongly recommend that you take our online practice tests to simulate test-day conditions and to receive these added benefits:

- **Timed testing conditions**—Gauge how much time you can spend on each question.

- **Automatic scoring**—Find out how you did on the test, instantly.

- **On-screen detailed explanations of answers**—Learn not just the correct answer, but also why the other answers are incorrect.

- **Diagnostic score reports**—Pinpoint where you're strongest and where you need to focus your study.

Science Practice Test Answer Sheet

1. Ⓐ Ⓑ Ⓒ Ⓓ   16. Ⓐ Ⓑ Ⓒ Ⓓ   31. Ⓐ Ⓑ Ⓒ Ⓓ

2. Ⓐ Ⓑ Ⓒ Ⓓ   17. Ⓐ Ⓑ Ⓒ Ⓓ   32. Ⓐ Ⓑ Ⓒ Ⓓ

3. Ⓐ Ⓑ Ⓒ Ⓓ   18. Ⓐ Ⓑ Ⓒ Ⓓ   33. Ⓐ Ⓑ Ⓒ Ⓓ

4. Ⓐ Ⓑ Ⓒ Ⓓ   19. Ⓐ Ⓑ Ⓒ Ⓓ   34. Ⓐ Ⓑ Ⓒ Ⓓ

5. Ⓐ Ⓑ Ⓒ Ⓓ   20. Ⓐ Ⓑ Ⓒ Ⓓ   35. Ⓐ Ⓑ Ⓒ Ⓓ

6. Ⓐ Ⓑ Ⓒ Ⓓ   21. Ⓐ Ⓑ Ⓒ Ⓓ   36. Ⓐ Ⓑ Ⓒ Ⓓ

7. Ⓐ Ⓑ Ⓒ Ⓓ   22. Ⓐ Ⓑ Ⓒ Ⓓ   37. Ⓐ Ⓑ Ⓒ Ⓓ

8. Ⓐ Ⓑ Ⓒ Ⓓ   23. Ⓐ Ⓑ Ⓒ Ⓓ   38. Ⓐ Ⓑ Ⓒ Ⓓ

9. Ⓐ Ⓑ Ⓒ Ⓓ   24. Ⓐ Ⓑ Ⓒ Ⓓ   39. Ⓐ Ⓑ Ⓒ Ⓓ

10. Ⓐ Ⓑ Ⓒ Ⓓ   25. Ⓐ Ⓑ Ⓒ Ⓓ   40. Ⓐ Ⓑ Ⓒ Ⓓ

11. Ⓐ Ⓑ Ⓒ Ⓓ   26. Ⓐ Ⓑ Ⓒ Ⓓ   41. Ⓐ Ⓑ Ⓒ Ⓓ

12. Ⓐ Ⓑ Ⓒ Ⓓ   27. Ⓐ Ⓑ Ⓒ Ⓓ   42. Ⓐ Ⓑ Ⓒ Ⓓ

13. Ⓐ Ⓑ Ⓒ Ⓓ   28. Ⓐ Ⓑ Ⓒ Ⓓ   43. Ⓐ Ⓑ Ⓒ Ⓓ

14. Ⓐ Ⓑ Ⓒ Ⓓ   29. Ⓐ Ⓑ Ⓒ Ⓓ   44. Ⓐ Ⓑ Ⓒ Ⓓ

15. Ⓐ Ⓑ Ⓒ Ⓓ   30. Ⓐ Ⓑ Ⓒ Ⓓ   45. Ⓐ Ⓑ Ⓒ Ⓓ

Practice Test 1: Science

TIME: 55 minutes
       45 selected-response questions

> **Directions:** Read each item and select the correct response or responses. Most items on this test require you to provide the one best answer. However, some questions require you to select all the options that apply.

1. Which of the following instruments should be used to most accurately measure a liquid in milliliters in a laboratory investigation?

   A. Flask

   B. Beaker

   C. Graduated cylinder

   D. Test tube

2. Which of the following scientists first proposed the theory of plate tectonics, which maintains that the Earth's continents were formed long ago as part of a single landmass?

   A. Robert Hooke

   B. Sir Isaac Newton

   C. Charles Darwin

   D. Alfred Wegener

3. Which of the following is a non-renewable source of energy?

   A. Wind

   B. Solar

   C. Natural gas

   D. Hydroelectric

4. In which of the following ways does deforestation (cutting down) of the rainforests in South America impact residents of the United States?

   A. Deforestation does not impact the U.S. population.

   B. Deforestation results in a decrease in the amount of carbon dioxide in the atmosphere, which decreases the threat of global warming.

   C. Deforestation results in contaminated food crops that may be consumed by U.S. residents.

   D. Deforestation results in an increase in the amount of carbon dioxide in the atmosphere, which contributes to the threat of global warming.

5. Which of the following gases comprises the majority of the air in Earth's atmosphere?

   A. Oxygen

   B. Carbon Dioxide

   C. Nitrogen

   D. Water vapor

6. Which of the following is the most effective, concrete way to teach elementary students the concept of diffusion for the first time?

   A. Present a lecture giving the definition of diffusion for students to write in their notebooks.

   B. Make a drawing of diffusion on the board showing how diffusion happens while at the same time providing the definition.

   C. Give students a clear, plastic cup of water and ask them to place one drop of food coloring in the water without stirring and observe; then follow up with discussion on their observations.

   D. Assign students a textbook reading on diffusion, with review questions to complete when finished reading.

7. Mr. Garcia spends three weeks teaching students about ecosystems. At the end of the unit, he gives students a 45-minute unit exam consisting of a variety of question formats, such as short-answer, multiple-choice, and essay. After grading the exam, he is surprised and disappointed that his students did not perform well on the exam, with most students failing. What is the most important thing Mr. Garcia should have done to prevent this disaster?

   A. He should have used different assessments throughout the unit instead of waiting until the end to measure his students' learning.

   B. He should have spent another week lecturing students on ecosystems.

   C. He should have made his assessment all multiple-choice items.

   D. He should have made the test longer than 45 minutes by adding more test items.

8. What is the usefulness of informing students of their results on a test or project?

   A. It creates a competitive environment in your classroom for students when they take tests or work on projects.

   B. It provides both the student and teacher with information on the extent to which the students have learned the material.

   C. It creates anxiety among students that negatively impacts future performance on tests and projects.

   D. It allows administrators to report scores to the state education agency.

9. The students in Ms. Johnson's class are rolling a toy convertible car down a slanted ramp with a brick at the end of it. They place a small stuffed animal in the convertible, unrestrained, and then let the car roll down the ramp. The car hits the brick and stops. What happens to the stuffed animal as soon as the car hits and is stopped by the brick? Why?

   A. The stuffed animal stays in the car because an object at rest stays at rest unless acted upon by a force.

   B. The stuffed animal flies out of the car backwards because for every action there is an equal and opposite reaction.

   C. The stuffed animal flies out of the car forward because an object in motion will continue to stay in motion unless acted upon by a force.

   D. None of the above is correct.

10. A rocket burns fuel in bursts out of a nozzle, allowing it to maneuver and turn in the vacuum of space. Which of Newton's Laws of Motion explains how this maneuvering is able to occur?

    A. An object in motion stays in motion unless an outside force acts on it.

    B. For every action there is an equal and opposite reaction.

    C. Fast-moving air has low pressure.

    D. An object at rest stays at rest unless an outside force acts on it.

11. What does using two pulleys in a single system (movable pulley) to lift an object do to the force required compared to lifting the object without the movable pulley?

    Select from the following.

    A. The use of the movable pulley reduces the amount of force required by one-half.

    B. The use of the movable pulley increases the amount of force required by one-half.

    C. The use of the movable pulley changes the amount of force required to 5 Newtons.

    D. The use of the movable pulley changes the amount of force required.

12. Which of the following is a chemical change in matter?

    A. Ice melting

    B. Paper tearing

    C. Paper burning

    D. Crushing chalk

13. The chemical formula for water is H_2O, making water which of the following?

    A. Element

    B. Compound

    C. Atom

    D. Ion

14. When does cellular respiration occur in plants?

    A. Cellular respiration does not occur in plants, only photosynthesis.

    B. Cellular respiration occurs only at night, because photosynthesis occurs during the day.

    C. Cellular respiration occurs only during the day, because photosynthesis occurs at night.

    D. Cellular respiration occurs all day and night, the same as in animals.

15. What is the proper sequence of energy transformations that occurs in ringing a doorbell?

    A. Mechanical, electrical, sound

    B. Electrical, mechanical, sound

    C. Sound, electrical, mechanical

    D. Electrical, sound, mechanical

16. In Ms. Sullivan's class, the students measured the starting temperature of two thermometers. They used one thermometer to measure the temperature at the surface of a pond. The second was attached onto a sinker on an eight-meter rope and was dropped to near the bottom of the pond. They repeated the experiment several times, recording their findings. The students' results revealed that the temperature at the surface was on average four degrees higher than the temperature near the bottom of the pond. Which of the following forms of energy transfer best explains their findings?

    A. Conduction

    B. Radiation

    C. Convection

    D. Evaporation

17. Jorge and Rita were working on a laboratory activity where they connected one end of an electric wire to the positive node of a new 6-volt battery, then wound the wire around an iron nail with 20 twists, then attached the other end of the wire to the negative node of the battery. The students then plunged the point of the nail into a pile of small paper clips and made observations. They repeated this experiment three more times. The two students then changed the number of times the wire was wound around the nail to 10 twists, and plunged the point of the nail in the paper clips again. The students made observations and again repeated this experiment three more times. What did the students observe happen in the first trial with 20 twists of the wire around the nail compared to the second trial with 10 twists of the wire around the nail, and why?

A. The first trial with 20 twists attracted and "picked up" fewer paper clips than the second trial with 10 twists because the electric field was weaker with 20 twists compared to 10 twists of the wire.

B. The first trial with 20 twists attracted and "picked up" more paper clips than the second trial with 10 twists because the electric field was stronger with 20 twists compared to 10 twists of the wire.

C. The first trial with 20 twists attracted and "picked up" and equal number of paper clips as the second trial with 10 twists because the electric field was equally strong with 20 twists and 10 twists of the wire.

D. Neither trial produced an electric field and could not attract and "pick up" the paper clips.

18. What do green plant leaves do with green wavelengths of visible light in the electromagnetic spectrum, and what is the evidence?

A. Green plants absorb green wavelengths, and the evidence is that the leaves are green in color.

B. Green plants refract green wavelengths, and the evidence is that the leaves may be green or yellow in color.

C. Green plants absorb green wavelengths, and the evidence is that the leaves turn red and yellow in the fall.

D. Green plants reflect green wavelengths, and the evidence is that the leaves are green in color.

19. What is the energy source for each of the following nonrenewable and renewable energy types used to generate electricity for human use, listed in the same order as the energy type?

Nonrenewable and Renewable Energy Types:

Hydroelectric – Nuclear – Fossil Fuel – Geothermal – Solar

A. Heat from beneath Earth's surface – Coal – Moving Water – Soil – Sun

B. Soil – Uranium – Wind – Volcanoes – Heat from beneath Earth's surface

C. Moving Water – Uranium – Coal – Heat from beneath Earth's surface – Sun

D. Moving Water – Sun – Heat from beneath Earth's surface – Sun – Uranium

20. Mr. Littlejohn hands his students a seed, and then hands them a log from a tree. He discusses with students that somehow this tiny seed becomes a great tree, part of which the students are holding in their hands as a log. He asks the students, "Where does all the mass come from that allowed this tiny seed to grow into a tree?" What is the correct response to this question?

   A. The mass that made the tree came from nutrients in the soil.

   B. The mass that made the tree came from the soil itself.

   C. The mass that made the tree came from nitrogen in the soil.

   D. The mass that made the tree came from carbon dioxide in the air.

21. The students in Mrs. Leone's class are studying mealworms. They fill the bottom of a petri dish with oatmeal for food and tiny slices of apple for moisture, and then place three mealworms in the dish and replace the cover (which allows air in). The students observe the mealworms over several days, drawing their observations. After several days the students notice their mealworms are shorter, curled up, and no longer moving. The students are concerned but continue to draw and write observations of their three mealworms. After several more days, the students observe that there are three black beetles in their petri dishes and no curled up mealworms. What is the best explanation for what happened?

   Select from the following:

   A. The mealworms became ill and the beetles got inside the petri dishes and ate them.

   B. The mealworms underwent metamorphosis, changing from larva to pupa to adult.

   C. The mealworms underwent metamorphosis, changing from egg to pupa to larva.

   D. The mealworms underwent metamorphosis, changing from adult to larva to pupa.

22. The forest and pond area inhabited by wildlife including raccoons was demolished to build a large restaurant. It so happens the restaurant disposes of uneaten meals in an open dumpster in the far end of the parking lot behind the building. Which of the following basic needs specifically among the raccoons likely changed the *least* due to the construction of this building?

   A. Shelter

   B. Water

   C. Food

   D. Air

23. In sexual reproduction, what is the process that occurs in specialized cells to produce the gametes before fertilization, and the process that then occurs in the fertilized egg or zygote to begin development of the embryo?

   A. Mitosis occurs to produce the gametes, and then meiosis occurs in the zygote.

   B. Binary fission occurs to produce the gametes, and then meiosis occurs in the zygote.

   C. Asexual reproduction occurs to produce the gametes, and then sexual reproduction occurs in the zygote.

   D. Meiosis occurs to produce the gametes, and then mitosis occurs in the zygote.

24. Black fur (B) in guinea pigs is dominant over white fur (b). If a homozygous black-furred female guinea pig mates with a heterozygous black-furred male guinea pig, what percentage of their offspring will have white fur?

   A. 25% white

   B. 50% white

   C. 75% white

   D. 0% white

25. Which of the following options explains why some species of animals may be unable to adapt and no longer survive in its environment? Select *all* that apply.

    A. The environment changed from forest to industrialized city.

    B. The amount of water in lakes and marshlands in the environment significantly decreased.

    C. The predator population in the environment significantly increased in number.

    D. The population moved to urban areas and became dependent on humans.

26. Giraffes with long necks have survived over time because they can reach treetop leaves, which they eat for nourishment. What is one reason giraffes developed long necks over time?

    A. Giraffes in the past constantly stretched their necks to reach leaves on tall trees and thus developed long, strong muscles in their necks.

    B. Trees grew taller over time, so giraffes grew longer necks to accommodate this tree growth and reach their food.

    C. Genetic mutations occurred over time, resulting in some giraffes developing longer necks than others; these giraffes were more likely to survive than those with shorter necks.

    D. The types of leaves giraffes fed on consisted of rich sources of calcium that strengthened and lengthened their vertebrae over time.

27. Working in groups, the students in Ms. Rosa's class plant three seeds in a pot of soil, then water them, and place the pot in a tall, narrow cardboard box with a half-dollar-sized circular hole cut out on one side near the top of the box where light can enter. The students only briefly open the box each day to measure their plant's growth and add water, then close it again. They keep their boxes on the window sill with the hole-side facing the outside light. After several weeks, what will students most likely observe happening to the plant, and why?

    A. Students will observe the plant stem bending toward the hole in the side of the box due to the stimulus produced by light, called phototropism.

    B. Students will observe the plant stem bending away from the hole in the side of the box due to the stimulus produced by the dark, called anti-phototropism.

    C. Students will observe the plant stem bending toward the bottom of the box due to the stimulus produced by the water, called hydrotropism.

    D. Students will observe the plant stem bending toward the bottom of the box due to the stimulus caused by gravity, called geotropism or gravitropism.

28. Which of the following organisms in a food chain or food web absorbs and holds the most energy?

    A. Producers

    B. Secondary consumers or carnivores (2nd level)

    C. Primary consumers or herbivores (1st level)

    D. Decomposers

29. Which of the following represents the order of the layers of the Earth if one were to travel from the surface to its center?

    A. Crust, outer core, mantle, inner core

    B. Mantle, crust, inner core, outer core

    C. Outer core, inner core, crust, mantle

    D. Crust, mantle, outer core, inner core

30. Which of the following is a rocky planet?

   A. Jupiter

   B. Neptune

   C. Mars

   D. Uranus

31. Which of the following *best* describes the transpiration in the water cycle?

   A. The evaporation of water from the surface of lakes

   B. The condensation of water on the leaves of green plants

   C. The evaporation of water from the leaves of green plants

   D. The precipitation of water on the leaves of green plants

32. Which of the following is a property of water?

   A. When water freezes to ice it expands

   B. When water freezes to ice it contracts

   C. Water is a nonpolar molecule

   D. Most water on Earth is freshwater

33. What is relative humidity and what instrument is used to measure it?

   A. Relative humidity is a measure of the wind speed in a specific region and time, and is measured by an anemometer

   B. Relative humidity is a measure of the amount of moisture in the air in a specific region and time, and is measured by an anemometer

   C. Relative humidity is a measure of the moisture in the air in a specific region and time, and is measured by a psychrometer

   D. Relative humidity is a measure of the air pressure in a specific region and time, and is measured by a barometer

34. Which of the following is the symbol for a stationary front on a weather map?

   A.

   B.

   C.

   D.

35. What time of day or night would the New Moon phase be as close to directly overhead as possible for your location?

   A. The Moon would be directly overhead at midnight

   B. The Moon would be directly overhead at dawn

   C. The Moon would be directly overhead at noon

   D. The Moon would be directly overhead at dusk

36. The students in Mr. Lawson's class are going to engage in an inquiry-based laboratory investigation in which they will be placing a glass thermometer in a beaker of ice and heating it on a hot plate so they can graph the heating curve of water. What is the first and most important thing Mr. Lawson should do before students begin this investigation?

    A. Provide students with the materials needed to conduct the investigation and let them begin

    B. Give students a review sheet that explains and shows a completed graph of the heating curve of water before they begin the investigation

    C. Read aloud and discuss all safety precautions of the investigation, including wearing safety goggles and the use of glassware and heating surfaces

    D. Instruct students on the clean-up procedures to follow after the investigation, including where to store the glassware

37. Which of the following indicates the type of questioning used to gain the most participation from students?

    A. Calling the name of the student to respond first, then asking the question

    B. Asking students to raise their hands

    C. Asking the question first, then calling on students at random to respond

    D. Asking students to "call out" the response

38. Which of the following types of rock is formed from other types of rock listed below after it has been subjected to extreme pressure and temperature over time?

    A. Igneous

    B. Metamorphic

    C. Sedimentary

    D. Conglomerate

39. The students in Mr. Gonzales's class are reading about a research scientist who believes she has found the cure for lung cancer tumors with a new medication that needs to undergo further research. Her research involves 200 lung cancer patients. Half are given the new medication and half are given a "placebo" pill, which is simply a sugar pill. None of the patients know whether they are receiving the actual medication or the placebo. After three months of recording data measuring the size of cancer tumors in the lungs of all patients, the scientist finds that the size of the cancer tumor has not grown in about 3% of the patients receiving the new medication. However, all patients receiving the new medication are exhibiting severe and unusual mental side-effect reactions, including fits of rage and physical violence toward others and themselves. Which of the following is the ethical course of action for this scientist to take in testing this cancer medication?

    A. Stop the experiments immediately and return to the laboratory for more testing, without using humans, on the mental side effects it has caused.

    B. Continue the experiments with humans because it is helping some of the cancer patients, and wait to see if the mental issues resolve themselves.

    C. Provide the placebo group with the new medication because it is helping a few of the patients in the group who are receiving the medication.

    D. Recruit another sample of 200 patients and repeat the same experiment with new groups receiving either the medication or the placebo.

40. In using the 5E (learning cycle) inquiry model in teaching, which of the following is the best way to introduce new science-concept vocabulary to students and English learners in particular?

    A. List, define, and review the science vocabulary words and definitions before students begin the exploration.

    B. Have students read the textbook definitions of new science vocabulary the day before class and quiz them before beginning the exploration.

    C. Introduce science vocabulary that labels the science concept after students have conducted an exploration, but before the students state the concept.

    D. Introduce science vocabulary that labels the science concept after students have conducted an exploration and have stated the concept.

41. Which is longer, three yards or 25 decimeters?

    A. 3 yards

    B. 25 decimeters

    C. Both distances are the same

    D. The answer cannot be determined

42. What is true about using models in teaching to represent the natural world in science?

    A. Models are exact in their representation of the actual phenomena.

    B. Models only work as a representation of actual phenomena if computer generated.

    C. Models will always differ from the actual phenomena they represent.

    D. Models of natural phenomena will always lead students to form misconceptions.

43. In an exploration activity, the students measure 50 ml of water and pour it into one cup, and 50 ml of isopropyl alcohol and pour it into a second cup. They then drop one ice cube in the cup of water and one ice cube in the alcohol. The students observe that the ice cube floats in the water but sinks in the isopropyl alcohol. Why?

    Select from the following.

    A. The ice cube is less dense than the water and denser than the alcohol.

    B. The ice cube is denser than the water and less dense than the alcohol.

    C. The ice cube has a density equal to that of the water and is denser than the alcohol.

    D. The ice cube has a density equal to that of both the water and the alcohol.

44. What is the proper instrument to use in measuring the mass of an object?

    A. Meter stick

    B. Graduated cylinder

    C. Triple beam balance

    D. Sling psychrometer

45. Which of the following is the best way to evaluate whether students are able to determine the density of an irregular object?

    A. Give them a multiple-choice test item to demonstrate their knowledge.

    B. Provide them with a true-false test to demonstrate their knowledge.

    C. Give them a fill-in-the-blank test to demonstrate their knowledge.

    D. Have students conduct a hands-on lab practical test to demonstrate their knowledge.

Science Practice Test Answer Key

1. C	16. C	31. C
2. D	17. B	32. A
3. C	18. D	33. C
4. D	19. C	34. C
5. C	20. D	35. C
6. C	21. B	36. C
7. A	22. D	37. C
8. B	23. D	38. B
9. C	24. D	39. A
10. B	25. A, B, C, and D	40. D
11. A	26. C	41. A
12. C	27. A	42. C
13. B	28. A	43. A
14. D	29. D	44. C
15. A	30. C	45. D

Science Practice Test 1
Detailed Answers

1. C.

Option (C) is correct because a graduated cylinder precisely measures liquid amounts in milliliters. Options (A), (B), and (D) are not used to measure precise amounts of liquid, but actually are vessels mainly used to carry out various experiments, such as mixing liquids to produce a chemical reaction. Flasks and beakers can measure liquids in larger units of volume, whereas graduated cylinders are used to measure liquids in smaller standard units with greater precision. **(904-001 Lab Processes, Equipment, and Safety)**

2. D.

Option (D) is correct. Alfred Wegener first described the theory of plate tectonics in the early 1900s. Options (A), (B), and (C) are incorrect. Robert Hooke (A) first described cell theory: that all living things are composed of cells. Sir Isaac Newton (B) is known for discovering the Laws of Motion and Gravity. Charles Darwin (C) described natural selection, which led to the theory of evolution. **(904-002 History and Nature of Science)**

3. C.

Option (C) is correct. Natural gas is a non-renewable source of energy because it is a fossil fuel. Natural gas, which is a gas mixture of methane and other hydrocarbon compounds, comes from deep in the Earth, as does oil and coal. Natural gas is formed when ancient buried plants and the gases they produce are exposed to intense heat and pressure over many thousands of years. Once the natural gas is used to produce energy (e.g., electricity), it cannot be replaced. Options (A), (B), and (D) are all renewable sources of energy. These sources are not depleted upon use. The wind produces

energy (generates electricity) whenever it blows, solar power results from the capture of energy from the sun, and hydroelectric energy uses the forces of moving water—as in a waterfall—to produce electricity. **(904-003 Impact on Science)**

4. D.

Option (D) is correct because the high quantity of trees and massive foliage in South America carry on photosynthesis, which utilizes carbon dioxide gas to produce glucose, thus decreasing the amount of carbon dioxide in the atmosphere. Carbon dioxide gas in excess has been shown to absorb heat and increase warming of the atmosphere. If the foliage is removed, there will be fewer plants to take carbon dioxide out of the atmosphere, and it will accumulate in ever-increasing amounts. Global warming impacts the growth of food plants elsewhere across the globe, including the U.S., and these food plants have optimal growth within particular temperature and climatic ranges, which could be detrimental to their growth if conditions change. Option (A) is incorrect because there are interactions and interrelationships between what happens in one part of the globe and another. Option (B) is incorrect because the carbon dioxide in the atmosphere will increase rather than decrease. Option (C) is incorrect in that deforestation is not related to crop contamination. **(904-003 Impact on Science)**

5. C.

Option (C) is the correct response. Nitrogen comprises most of the Earth's atmosphere. The percentages are: Nitrogen at 78 percent, Oxygen at 21 percent, Argon at 0.93 percent, and Carbon dioxide at 0.038 percent. Even smaller percentages of water vapor and other gases are also in the atmosphere. Therefore, options (A), (B), and (D) are incorrect. **(904-015 Structure and Function of Earth Systems)**

6.   C.

Option (C) is correct because elementary school children are in the concrete stage of intellectual development, meaning they need hands-on, direct experiences with objects and phenomena. Options (A) and (D) will be mundane, negatively affect student motivation, cause confusion, and likely lead to significant misconceptions of the concept. This is because lecturing and reading are abstract, which is beyond what these students are ready for the first time they are learning a new concept. Drawing by the teacher (B) should be done after the students experience and observe a form of diffusion as described in option (C). An even better teaching strategy is for students to draw and develop a definition themselves. **(904-005 Students as Learners and Science Instruction)**

7.   A.

Option (A) is correct because it is important to monitor and measure student learning throughout the unit using various assessment techniques. In doing so, the teacher can adjust teaching to match what students are and are not learning during the unit. Assessments throughout the unit reveal difficulties and misconceptions students may be forming. Such knowledge of student learning throughout the unit will allow the teacher to better help all students achieve success. Option (B), teaching the unit for a longer period of time, would not help the students because even more time would have passed in the unit without monitoring student learning. Option (C) is incorrect because using only one testing format does not fully reveal what students have learned. Many students have difficulty, and even anxiety, with multiple-choice questions but do well with short answer and essay. Using only short-answer and essay formats may cause such stresses for other students. Therefore, using a variety of testing formats gives all students an opportunity to express their knowledge. Option (D) is incorrect because more test items would have produced the same result. **(904-006 Science Assessment)**

8.   B.

Option (B) is correct because it allows the teacher to adjust instruction according to the needs of the students, and for the students to gauge their levels of learning of the concepts. Options (A) and (C) indicate that not informing the students may lead to a negative learning environment in the classroom. Reporting scores (D) is typically done within school districts on standardized tests *after* learning has taken place; the scores achieved do not provide information on students' understandings and potential difficulties as learning progresses throughout the school year. **(904-006 Science Assessment)**

9.   C.

Option (C) is correct because the stuffed animal and car become one object. The stuffed animal is in motion with the car as it rolls down the ramp. The stuffed animal is unrestrained, however, so when the car stops, the stuffed animal remains in motion, flying forward out of the car until gravity acts upon it and it lands on the floor. Option (A) is incorrect because the object is or was in motion and so the stuffed animal will not remain in the car when it hits the brick unless it is attached to the car (as with seatbelts in actual cars). Option (B) is incorrect because the stuffed animal will continue its forward motion when it suddenly stops by hitting the brick and cannot reverse its motion and fly backwards. Option (D) is incorrect because there is indeed a correct answer in option (C). **(904-007 Forces and Motion)**

10. B.

Option (B) is the correct answer because burning the fuel causes the gases released to be expelled at a very high speed out of a nozzle, which is computer controlled in the desired direction to push the rocket in the opposite direction. This is Newton's third law—that for every action there is an equal and opposite reaction. Options (A) and (D) are incorrect because the force is not from outside of the rocket in this case. Option (C) is incorrect as it is a simplified version of Bernoulli's principle of lift. **(904-007 Forces and Motion)**

11. A.

Option (A) is correct. A single pulley and movable pulleys are classified as simple machines. The amount of force required to lift an object with two pulleys in a single system reduces the force required to lift the object by one-half. Option (B) is incorrect because the movable pulley will not increase but rather decrease the amount of force required. Option (C) is incorrect because the force will not be changed to a definite value of force; the reduction of force to be applied depends on the weight of the object to be lifted and the number of pulleys in the system. Option (D) is incorrect because the use of a movable pulley does reduce the amount of force required to lift the object. **(904-007 Forces and Motion)**

12. C.

Option (C) is correct because burning is when oxygen in the air chemically combines with the hydrocarbon molecules in the paper, which are long connected chains of glucose ($C_6H_{12}0_6$) molecules. Burning the hydrocarbons results in new substances, including carbon dioxide (CO_2), carbon monoxide (CO), and water (H_2O). The new substances are no longer hydrocarbon molecules, but new products; thus the reaction is not reversible. The reaction also showed classic signs of chemical reactions, including a change in color, heat produced, and gas released. The changes listed in Options (A), (B), and (D) indicate physical changes because the substances do not change their chemical compositions; the liquid water is still H_2O after it melts; the paper is still made up of the hydrocarbons and possible other molecules in the torn pieces; and the chalk is still made up of the same molecules of chalk (typically calcium carbonate, $CaCO_3$) only now it is in tiny pieces. **(904-008 Physical and Chemical Properties)**

13. B.

Option (B) is correct because water is made up of two or more different kinds of atoms: hydrogen (H) and oxygen (O), which is a compound. Option (A) is incorrect because elements are made up of only one kind of

atom. Option (C) is incorrect because water is made up of more than a single atom. Option (D) is incorrect because ions are positively or negatively charged atoms or molecules and water is a stable molecule. **(904-008 Physical and Chemical Properties)**

14. D.

Option (D) is correct because cellular respiration is a life function that uses oxygen to burn glucose to produce energy as an end product. Just as in animals, cellular respiration must occur during the day and night, for the entire 24-hour cycle. If cellular respiration were to stop, the plant would die. Option (A) is incorrect because respiration does occur in plants, very much the same as in animals. Options (B) and (C) are incorrect because cellular respiration occurs all day and night. **(904-008 Physical and Chemical Properties)**

15. A.

Option (A) is correct because mechanical energy pushed the doorbell and closed the circuit. The closed circuit allowed for the transfer of energy from mechanical to electrical energy. The electrical energy was transferred into sound energy. Options (B), (C), and (D) indicate an incorrect sequence in the transformation of energy. **(904-009 Energy and Interactions)**

16. C.

Option (C) is the correct answer because convection is the transfer of heat energy through liquids and gases. In convection, warmer air or liquid expands and rises, and cooler air or liquid contracts and sinks. Convection explains why the water at the surface was slightly warmer than the water near the bottom of the pond. Convection also explains why a home's attic is warmer and its basement is cooler than the rest of the house; it also explains ocean currents and lake turnover in the spring in cold climates. Option (A) is incorrect because conduction is the transfer of heat energy through solids, such as through a metal spoon placed in a hot liquid—the heat from the liquid travels through the spoon to the handle, and the handle soon becomes hot. Option (B) is incorrect because radiation is the transfer of heat energy through space, as with the sun's radiation. Option (D) is incorrect because evaporation is the phase change in which a liquid changes to a gaseous state of matter. **(904-009 Energy and Interactions)**

17. B.

Option (B) is correct because the laboratory activity described is transforming the nail into a temporary magnet or electromagnet. The more twists of the wire around the nail, the greater the electric field produced, and the stronger the electromagnet. Thus, the trials with 20 twists of the wire around the nail would pick up more paper clips than the trials with 10 twists of the wire around the nail. Option (A) is incorrect because the trials with 20 twists of wire around the nail would have a stronger rather than weaker electric field and would thus pick up more paper clips compared to the trials with 10 twists. Option (C) is incorrect because the different number of twists produces stronger and weaker electric fields and the strengths of these fields would not be equal. Option (D) is incorrect because a 6-volt battery or any battery would create an electric field and therefore attract some number of paper clips in the example given. **(904-009 Energy and Interactions)**

18. D.

Option (D) is correct because the colors we see around us are the wavelengths of light reflected by that object or substance. Green plants, therefore, do not absorb green light waves, but this color of visible light of the electromagnetic spectrum reflects off the plant's surface and our eyes see the color green. Option (A) is incorrect because if the plant absorbed green wavelengths, the color green would not be seen by our eyes because it would be absorbed into the substance of the leaves. Option (B) is incorrect because refraction is the bending of light rather than reflection, so the color would be bent rather than reflected to our eyes. Option (C) is incorrect because green plants in the growing season

reflect and do not absorb green wavelengths of light, so the color we see is green. However, in the fall, deciduous trees, which are plants in which the leaves change color and fall off in the winter, stop producing chlorophyll (the green pigment in plants), and instead produce other pigments, including red and yellow, as they become dormant. The red and yellow colors taken on by these leaves indicate a shift in the wavelengths of light reflected. If our eyes see the color red, then the leaves are reflecting light in the red wavelength region of the electromagnetic spectrum. **(904-009 Energy and Interactions)**

19. C.

Option (C) is correct in that hydroelectric energy produces electricity through fast-moving water as in Niagara Falls. Nuclear energy utilizes the radioactivity of uranium. Fossil fuel energy produces electricity through the burning of coal, oil, and/or natural gas. Geothermal energy produces electricity by harnessing the energy beneath the Earth's surface to produce electricity. Solar energy captures the energy of the sun to produce electricity. Options (A), (B), and (D) are listed in the incorrect order and/or are incorrect sources of energy. **(904-010 Energy Transformations and Conservation)**

20. D.

The correct answer is (D). Photosynthesis is the process by which plants take carbon dioxide (CO_2) from the air and combine it with water (H_2O) to make glucose with the formula $C_6H_{12}O_6$. Glucose is a simple sugar that joins together with other glucose molecules to form starch or carbohydrates—long chains of sugar molecules. These carbohydrates become the substance of plants—the roots, stems, leaves, and in angiosperms (flowering plants), also the flowers and fruits. Carbohydrates, for example, form the cellulose in the stems of plants. Plants, therefore, are basically made from "air"—namely, the carbon dioxide gas in the air. Option (A) is incorrect. The nutrients in the soil or fertilizers we apply only provide vitamins for the plants; they do not form the structure or substance of the plant. Option

(B) is incorrect as plants do not absorb the soil itself. This can be demonstrated by measuring the mass of the soil in a pot before planting seeds in that soil, and again after the seeds grow into plants (ensuring approximately equal moisture is in the soil at both measurement times). The measures will reveal that the soil has the same mass before and after plant growth. Option (C) is incorrect because although nitrogen is an element plants utilize, it accounts for only a small percentage of the mass of a plant. **(904-010 Energy Transformations and Conservation)**

21. B.

The correct answer is (B). The mealworm is not actually a worm, but instead the larva stage in the life cycle of a darkling beetle. The larva feeds on the oatmeal, uses the moisture from the apple, and grows. After gaining the necessary nutrition, the mealworm will undergo metamorphosis and change into a pupa. In this stage the mealworm shortens, curls up, and does not move, yet many changes are taking place. The pupa undergoes metamorphosis and changes into the adult, which is the darkling beetle. The only stage not observed in this life cycle is the egg stage; however, if the adults are left to remain together long enough in the petri dish, there likely will be eggs, and the four-stage life cycle will begin again with new offspring (egg, larva, pupa, adult). Option (A) is incorrect, and though students may believe this to be what happened, the beetles did not come into the petri dish from outside, but were the mealworms after undergoing complete metamorphosis into the adult stage. Options (C) and (D) are incorrect because the correct sequence in the life cycle of a mealworm that undergoes complete metamorphosis is egg to larva (mealworm) to pupa to adult, then back to new eggs as the offspring. **(904-011 Structure and Function of Living Things)**

22. D.

The correct answer is option (D). The air likely changed the least as the concentration of oxygen in the atmosphere remains relatively constant and will be sufficient for the survival of the raccoons. All three remaining options would have been likely to undergo a greater change. In the case of option (A), the shelter likely changed because the raccoons, a nocturnal animal, no longer have the trees and shrubs to inhabit. In the case of option (B), the water likely changed because the pond was taken out or filled in to construct the restaurant. In the case of option (C), the food likely changed because the raccoons now had the uneaten food to forage upon rather than seeking insects, frogs, and other food typical of its diet in a forest environment. **(904-011 Structure and Function of Living Things)**

23. D.

The correct answer is (D). Meiosis forms the gametes or the egg and sperm cells. In this process the beginning primary sex cells, called oocytes in the female and spermatocytes in males, undergo various stages of division in which chromosomes are replicated followed by two cell divisions. The result of meiosis is half the number of chromosomes (haploid) in each of the four resulting sperm and egg cells, although only one of the four cells in females is the true egg capable of being fertilized. Fertilization is the union of the single viable egg cell produced in meiosis and a single sperm cell. Fertilization of the haploid egg and sperm cells restores the chromosome number (genetic material) to the proper number for that organism, which is double (diploid), and where each chromosome has a pair from the opposite cell that codes for the same types of traits. After fertilization of the egg cell has occurred, the resulting zygote now divides by mitosis to make exact copies of the chromosomes it contains and maintain the full diploid number of chromosomes necessary for the organism's growth, development, and by and large, its survival. Mitosis also goes through a series of distinct stages where the first step is the duplication of chromosomes, followed by one cell division that produces two new cells from the original cell—each an exact copy. Option (A) reverses the process that occurs to produce the gametes and to form the embryo after fertilization. Options (B) and (C) are incorrect to explain the process that occurs to produce the gametes and the embryo after fertilization. **(904-012 Reproduction and the Mechanisms of Heredity)**

24.   D.

Option (D) is correct: None of the offspring will have white fur. If the female is homozygous black, then her gene combination is BB, and if the male is heterozygous black, he has a gene combination of Bb. That is, for the female, both chromosomes that code for fur color code for the dominant trait, black fur (BB). For the male, only one of the chromosomes out of the pair codes for black fur, and the second inherited chromosome codes for white fur color (Bb). In using a Punnett square diagram to determine the offspring, the result will show 100% of the offspring have black fur, and 0% have white fur. However 50% of the offspring carry the hidden trait for white fur color, so white color is still carried on in future generations. The Punnett square for this genetic cross is shown below. Options (A), (B), and (C) are incorrect because none of the offspring will have white fur. **(904-012 Reproduction and the Mechanisms of Heredity)**

	Father (sperm cell) B	Father (sperm cell) b
Mother (egg cell) B	BB	Bb
Mother (egg cell) B	BB	Bb

25.   A., B., C., and D.

The correct answer requires that you select all four options because options (A), (B), (C), and (D) are all experienced by animals as stresses that may displace them, cause a significant decline in population, or lead to extinction. Adaption requires time and generations of chance genetic mutations in animals, with some of those mutations proving beneficial to the animal and the offspring in the new environment. Those animals with the mutation would survive and produce more offspring, whereas those animals without the mutation would perish. Moving to urban areas sometimes results in the decline or even extermination of animal populations. **(904-013 Adaptations and Evolution)**

26.   C.

Option (C) is correct because genetic mutations randomly occur over time. If the genetic mutation happens to be beneficial to the organism in the environment, such as a giraffe having a longer neck than others within the species, then the organism with that mutation is more likely to survive, thrive, and produce offspring with the inherited mutation compared to those organisms without the mutation. Over time, the offspring that have the mutation and generations that follow are likely to continue to prosper and reproduce in this environment; and those organisms without the mutation are more likely to die off. Options (A) and (D) are both incorrect because stretching the neck in the past or eating calcium would not produce the result described, nor would offspring inherit this same trait as their parents. Option (B) is incorrect because organisms cannot choose to change in ways to match the environment. **(904-013 Adaptations and Evolution)**

27. A.

The correct answer is (A). The plant stem and leaves will grow toward the light. The plant responds to the stimulus of light as its means for initiating photosynthesis, which produces the plant's food or glucose. Hormones within the plant called Auxins respond to stimuli and produce this result. Option (B) is incorrect because plants will grow toward light rather than away from light. Options (C) and (D) are incorrect because the plant would not respond in these ways to water or gravity. **(904-014 Organisms and the Environment)**

28. A.

Option (A) is correct because producers are plants that receive the energy directly from the sun to produce food in the form of glucose. Option (C) is incorrect because primary consumers obtain their food from producers; however, some of the energy it receives has already been lost because it was used by the plant to maintain its own life functions. Option (B) is incorrect because secondary consumers are carnivores that obtain food from primary consumers; however, even more of the energy has been lost due to it being utilized to maintain life functions of the producers and the primary consumers. Decomposers are the final stage; however, much of the energy has already been lost through the various consumers in the food chain or web, so decomposers receive the least amount of energy. **(904-014 Organisms and the Environment)**

29. D.

Option (D) shows the correct order of the layers of the Earth from surface to center: crust, mantle, outer core, inner core. Options (A), (B), and (C) show an incorrect sequence of the layers of the Earth. **(904-015 Structure and Function of Earth Systems)**

30. C.

Option (C) is correct. Mars, Earth, Venus, and Mercury are rocky planets, whereas Jupiter, Saturn, Uranus and Neptune are gaseous planets. Therefore, options (A), (B), and (D) are incorrect. **(904-018 Solar System and the Universe)**

31. C.

Answer (C) is correct. Transpiration is the evaporation of water from the stomata located on the underside of leaves on plants. Liquid water is absorbed through the roots, is carried through the plant in small vessels called the xylem, and water that is not needed or excreted evaporates, meaning it changes from liquid to gas (water vapor) as it leaves the stomata. This moisture in the air from transpiration contributes to humidity and to cloud formation along with water evaporated from lakes, rivers, and oceans, which is eventually precipitated to Earth again in the water cycle. Option (A) is incorrect because evaporation from lakes and other bodies of water is simply evaporation—molecules of liquid water on the surface leave the surface in the form of water vapor. Option (B) is incorrect because condensation is water changing from water vapor (gas) to liquid water. Option (D) is incorrect because precipitation is water falling to Earth from clouds in the form of rain, snow, sleet, or hail. **(904-016 Cycles in Earth Systems)**

32. A.

The correct answer is (A). When water freezes, its molecules arrange in crystalline form because it is a polar molecule (has a positive and negative end). The arrangement of molecules in ice takes up more space than it does in liquid form. This property explains why potholes in roads are caused by freezing and thawing (melting) of water in the cracks of roads in winter, and why the ice cubes in an ice cube tray in a freezer are larger than the liquid water that was originally poured into the tray. Option (B) is incorrect because water expands when it freezes. Option (C) is incorrect because water is a polar molecule. Option (D) is incorrect because most water on Earth is saltwater, with only 2.5 percent freshwater. **(904-016 Cycles in Earth Systems)**

33. C.

Option (C) is correct because relative humidity is the percentage of water in the air and is measured by a psychrometer. Options (A) and (B) are incorrect because an anemometer measures wind speed. Option (D) is incorrect because humidity is not a measure of air pressure. **(904-017 Energy in Weather and Climate)**

34. C.

Option (C) is the correct symbol for a stationary front. Stationary fronts occur when a cold front or warm front stops moving. Stationary fronts result from warm and cold air masses that are in the same region pushing against each other, but they are of equal power. Option (A) is incorrect because it is the symbol for a cold air front. The spikes are facing the direction the cold air mass is moving. Option (B) is incorrect because it is the symbol for an occluded front. An occluded front is when a cold air mass is trailing right behind a warm air mass, and there is already a cold air mass ahead of the warm front that the warm front is pushing into. The cold front that is following the warm air mass overtakes the warm front and connects with the cold front that is ahead of the warm front. The warm air mass rises and there is usually precipitation when this happens. Option (D) is the symbol for a warm front. As with the cold front, the warm air mass is behind the curved line and the half-circles represent the leading edge of the front. **(904-017 Energy in Weather and Climate)**

35. C.

The correct answer is (C). The New Moon phase is when the Moon is not visible because it will be daytime, likely near or at 12 noon. The spatial position of the New Moon phase is between the Sun and Earth, so it will not

be visible because the light from the Sun conceals it from view. Options (A), (B), and (D) are incorrect because the New Moon is only out and "visible" (although not typically seen with the naked eye) during the daytime. **(904-018 Solar System and the Universe)**

36. C.

Option (C) is correct because presenting the safety precautions is the first step in any laboratory investigation. The safety procedures should be in printed form on the students' laboratory sheets, posted on the walls of the classroom, and read aloud to students before beginning any investigation. Option (A) is incorrect because giving students the materials should not be done prior to a thorough explanation and discussion of both the safety precautions and the laboratory procedures. Failure to do so before allowing students to begin could have disastrous results and cause harm to students. Option (B) is incorrect because providing the "answers" and giving away the concepts to students should not be done before an inquiry investigation—students are to discover the concepts based on their own experiences and data. Option (D) is incorrect because although clean-up instructions are important, these instructions should not precede a discussion on safety. Safety precautions must be implemented throughout the investigation, including during clean-up activities. **(904-002 History and Nature of Science)**

37. C.

This question addresses the beginning teacher's knowledge of "how to guide students in making systematic observations and measurements and posing questions to guide investigations," as stated under TExES Core Subjects EC–6 Science Competency 002. Option (C) is correct because by asking the question first and then randomly calling the name of a student to respond, the students do not know who will be called on to respond. Therefore, more of the students will be attentive and prepared to respond compared to other styles of questioning. Option (A), in which the name of student is called before the question, may promote a situation where other students do not feel they need to listen to the question or answer; only the student called upon needs to respond. Options (B) and (D) are incorrect because students who do not want to participate can simply choose to not raise their hand or refrain from calling out a response. **(904-002 History and Nature of Science)**

38. B.

Option (B), metamorphic rock, is correct because this type of rock is formed from igneous or sedimentary rock that is deep in the Earth and has been subjected to extreme pressure and temperature. Metamorphic rock may also exhibit signs of the Earth's folding due to plates colliding, which may also bend and twist the rock. Igneous rock (A) is the rock produced from hot lava or magma prior to exposure to pressure and/or folding. Sedimentary rock (C) is rock formed from eroded rock carried in bodies of water as sediments such as clays and sand. The sediments settle out of the water and form rock such as sandstone and shale. Conglomerate rock (D) is coarse grained sedimentary rock. In conglomerates, rocks of different shapes and sizes are cemented together. **(904-016 Cycles in Earth Systems)**

39. A.

Option (A) is the correct response because the new medication is causing harm to the patients receiving it and to others. Options (B), (C), and (D) are incorrect because it is unethical to continue and/or expand upon experiments with patients knowing it is also causing them harm. The benefits of the new medication are not significant enough to place all patients in danger. **(904-003 Impact on Science)**

40. D.

Option (D) is correct because all students, including ELs, will best understand new terminology/vocabulary after they have experienced the concept in a concrete, hands-on manner. The new terms that label the new con-

cept they have defined through their explorations will have meaning to them because they experienced it. Options (A), (B), and (C) are incorrect because they force students to learn new vocabulary words and definitions before they have experienced their meanings through their own explorations. The students will tend to simply memorize the terms, which will have little to no meaning to them, and will likely form misconceptions about those terms, or they will not retain their meanings. **(904-005 Students as Learners and Science Instruction)**

41. A.

The correct answer is (A). First, calculate how many meters are in a yard. To do this, you have to know the following: 1 yard = 0.9144 meters and 0.9144 meters = 9.144 decimeters. The measurement known as the yard is an imperial, U.S. length unit. It equals 3 feet, or 36 inches. The meter is a length unit of the metric system with a base-10 structure. The measurement of 0.9144 meters = 9.144 decimeters. First convert decimeters to meters. In this problem, 25 decimeters = 2.5 meters. Since 1 yard = .9144 meters, then 3 yards is calculated as .9144 x 3 = 2.7 meters. So 3 yards is a slightly longer distance. Option (B) is incorrect because it is a shorter distance than 3 yards as previously shown. Option (C) is incorrect because the lengths are not equal. Option (D) is incorrect because the answer can be found by knowing the conversion of non-standard units to standard units. **(904-001 Lab Processes, Equipment, and Safety)**

42. C.

Option (C) is correct because it is not possible to create a model that is exactly the same as the actual scientific phenomena or object being represented. For example, a ball-and-stick model of molecules is only a representation of an atom; the ionic or covalent bonding is due to the charges in the atoms, particularly electrons, which cannot be adequately represented by a stick. Option (A) is incorrect because no model is exact in its representation; it is impossible to represent every detail of a phenomenon with a model—it would simply have to end up being the real phenomenon instead. For example, you can make a marsh ecosystem in the classroom in an aquarium to represent an actual marsh, but it could not possibly have all of the elements of the actual marsh ecosystem in nature. Option (B) is incorrect because although computer-generated models are often useful, many physical models are equally or more useful than computer-generated ones. Making and flying an actual paper airplane to represent real airplane flight gives learners a different experience than making virtual paper airplanes on the computer. Option (D) is incorrect because, although sometimes students may develop misconceptions through the use of models, if models are implemented correctly, they will actually help students build more sound understandings of natural phenomena. In using models, teachers should ask the students to point out differences between the actual phenomena and the model. Students should understand that the model is simply a tool to help us visualize the natural phenomena, and that models have inherent limitations in their applicability. **(904-004 Concepts and Processes)**

43. A.

Option (A) is correct because for something to float, it must be less dense than the liquid it is in, and for an object to sink it must be denser than the liquid it is in. Density is a measure of how tightly packed the matter is (mass) within a given amount of space (volume), or D = M/V. Water is unique with respect to its density because it is the only substance on Earth that is less dense in solid form (ice) than in liquid form (water); therefore, the solid form floats in its own liquid. Alcohol is less dense (molecules are less tightly packed) than water, so the ice cube sinks. Option (B) is incorrect because if the ice cube was denser than liquid water it would sink in the water, and if less dense than the alcohol it would float in this liquid. Option (C) is incorrect because if a substance has equal density as the liquid it is in, it would be suspended in the middle of the liquid. This statement is incorrect even though the second part of it—which states that the ice is denser than the alcohol—is correct. Option (D) is incor-

rect because again, equal density means the ice cube would be suspended (i.e., neither sink nor float) in both the water and in the alcohol. **(904-008 Physical and Chemical Properties)**

44. C.

Option (C) is correct because in science the triple beam balance is the instrument or piece of equipment used to measure mass. Option (A), the meter stick, measures length. Option (B), the graduated cylinder, measures liquid amount or volume. Option (D), the sling psychrometer, measures relative humidity. **(904-001 Lab Processes, Equipment, and Safety)**

45. D.

Option (D) is correct because the best way to evaluate a laboratory skill such as determining density is to ask students to perform the skill. This evaluation measures learning and skill as authentic, alternative assessment—in this case, the laboratory practical. Demonstrating skill is superior to any other method of evaluation in this particular example because the teacher can observe students performing the technique and students can earn a grade for successful performance. Choices (A), (B), and (C) are not the best evaluation methods because although students may be able to learn the correct answers on how to measure density, knowing the correct answers does not mean the students know how to perform the laboratory technique. **(904-006 Science Assessment)**

TExES Core Subjects EC–6 Practice Test 1: Fine Arts, Health, and Physical Education

This practice test and an additional test are available at the online REA Study Center (www.rea.com/studycenter).

The TExES Core Subjects EC–6 Fine Arts, Health, and Physical Education (905) test is computer-based, so we strongly recommend that you take our online practice tests to simulate test-day conditions and to receive these added benefits:

- **Timed testing conditions**—Gauge how much time you can spend on each question.

- **Automatic scoring**—Find out how you did on the test, instantly.

- **On-screen detailed explanations of answers**—Learn not just the correct answer, but also why the other answers are incorrect.

- **Diagnostic score reports**—Pinpoint where you're strongest and where you need to focus your study.

Fine Arts, Health, and Physical Education Practice Test Answer Sheet

1. (A) (B) (C) (D)
2. (A) (B) (C) (D)
3. (A) (B) (C) (D)
4. (A) (B) (C) (D)
5. (A) (B) (C) (D)
6. (A) (B) (C) (D)
7. (A) (B) (C) (D)
8. (A) (B) (C) (D)
9. (A) (B) (C) (D)
10. (A) (B) (C) (D)
11. (A) (B) (C) (D)
12. (A) (B) (C) (D)
13. (A) (B) (C) (D)
14. (A) (B) (C) (D)

15. (A) (B) (C) (D)
16. (A) (B) (C) (D)
17. (A) (B) (C) (D)
18. (A) (B) (C) (D)
19. (A) (B) (C) (D)
20. (A) (B) (C) (D)
21. (A) (B) (C) (D)
22. (A) (B) (C) (D)
23. (A) (B) (C) (D)
24. (A) (B) (C) (D)
25. (A) (B) (C) (D)
26. (A) (B) (C) (D)
27. (A) (B) (C) (D)
28. (A) (B) (C) (D)

29. (A) (B) (C) (D)
30. (A) (B) (C) (D)
31. (A) (B) (C) (D)
32. (A) (B) (C) (D)
33. (A) (B) (C) (D)
34. (A) (B) (C) (D)
35. (A) (B) (C) (D)
36. (A) (B) (C) (D)
37. (A) (B) (C) (D)
38. (A) (B) (C) (D)
39. (A) (B) (C) (D)
40. (A) (B) (C) (D)

Practice Test 1:
Fine Arts, Health, and Physical Education

TIME: 35 minutes
40 selected-response questions

> **Directions:** Read each item and select the correct response or responses. Most items on this test require you to provide the one best answer. However, some questions require you to select all the options that apply.

1. Identify an activity that can guide children to see the tangible value of the visual arts in our lives.

   A. Present a picture and guide children to notice the concept of perspective.

   B. Present examples of sculpture and guide children to determine the materials used to create it.

   C. Prepare a list of occupations and guide students to link them with skills taught in visual arts.

   D. Post students' drawings in the school hallways, so people can appreciate their accomplishments.

2. What is the glycemic index?

   A. A list of foods that illustrate carbohydrate impact on blood sugar

   B. The usable energy part of the Krebs Cycle

   C. The amount of sugar grams on a food label

   D. The rate at which a person's metabolism burns glycogen

3. Which of the following developed a teaching method that emphasizes rote learning?

   A. Gordon

   B. Orff

   C. Suzuki

   D. Jaques-Dalcroze

4. Ceramics is an art form that is accessible to elementary-level students. However, it is also a form that is highly specialized because it requires

   A. an understanding of the concepts of perspective and color.

   B. the use of an oven and a specialized type of paint.

   C. an awareness of tridimensional figures and details of human form.

   D. the application of highly flammable paint to create a shiny look.

5. Fifth grade students are singing a song accompanied by the piano. The piano is playing which part?

   A. Rhythm

   B. Melody

   C. Form

   D. Harmony

6. A high male voice is classified as which of the following?

   A. Soprano

   B. Tenor

   C. Bass

   D. Baritone

7. Count Basie, a jazz pianist and band leader, employed which style of playing in his accompaniment?

   A. Comping

   B. Scat singing

   C. Riffs

   D. Figured bass

8. Horseshoe making and jewelry making are examples of which of the following?

   A. Art forms developed in the United States

   B. Metalworking

   C. Functional art

   D. Forms developed in China

9. What is Basal Metabolic Rate (BMR)?

   A. How efficient the body is at burning calories at rest

   B. How the body regulates hormone production

   C. The level at which metabolism burns calories best

   D. How diet impacts metabolic functions

10. After the game has started, which of the following would be the least advisable method for modifying a physical activity or game?

    A. Switching out equipment to increase/decrease the difficulty level

    B. Changing the rules to accommodate large groups

    C. Altering the size of the playing environment

    D. Applying rules of elimination from game play

11. Flashbacks and flash-forwards are used to do which of the following?

    A. Clarify and present important information

    B. Establish differences among the characters

    C. Lead the audience to the climax of the play

    D. Add realism to the drama

12. Dramatic play includes a variety of activities, but it rejects

    A. interaction with the teacher and students.

    B. the option of having children-initiated activities.

    C. the use of solitary play.

    D. memorization of lengthy dialogues.

13. Dramatic play is commonly used to introduce students to theatre arts. This strategy is most appropriate for which of the following?

    A. Children in upper elementary grades

    B. Children with prior experience in theatre

    C. Children in early childhood education

    D. Children learning English as a second language

14. Inactivity can increase the risk factor of contracting which of the following diseases or conditions?

    A. Heart disease

    B. Anemia

    C. Sleep apnea

    D. Psoriasis

15. Which of the following characteristics of a quality physical education (PE) program would the Society of Health and Physical Education (SHAPE) advocate most to policy makers regarding elementary PE?

A. Curriculum stressing lessons that keep students happy and busy

B. Student involvement in moderate-to-vigorous physical activity for at least 90% of class time

C. The number of students in physical education class should be the same as the number of students in a regular classroom

D. Students participating in physical education and physical activity every school day

16. Which of the following identify key arts movements of the 19th century?

A. Romanticism and Impressionism

B. Impressionism and Idealism

C. Cubism, Realism, and Surrealism

D. Rococo and Baroque

17. Which of the following statements describes the key characteristic of a farce in theatre?

A. It is shorter than a traditional drama.

B. The plot is developed around a situation.

C. The plot is developed around the main characters.

D. The characters sing their lines instead of saying them.

18. Which of the following sets of symptoms best describes heat stroke?

A. Cool, moist, pale skin

B. Red, hot, dry skin, unconsciousness

C. Nausea and dizziness

D. Headache and excessive sweating

19. Fourth grade students are singing a song where they all sing the melody and come in at specific intervals after group No. 1. What type of song are they singing?

A. Round

B. Partner Song

C. Call and Response

D. The speed of the underlying pulse in music

20. A physical education teacher is planning a skipping and galloping lesson based on the TEKS requirements. These requirements suggest this type of lesson is most appropriate for which of the following age groups?

A. Children 5–6 years of age

B. Children 8–9 years of age

C. Children 11–12 years of age

D. Children 14–15 years of age

21. During Ancient History and again during the Renaissance, artists sought to perfect representation of the human body. To accomplish this goal in sculpture, artists studied

A. pictures or drawings representing the human body.

B. the skin texture of models.

C. the human anatomy.

D. the type of bones and composition of human tissue.

22. In music, the words "up" and "down" are usually associated with which of the following?

A. Fast and slow

B. Loud and soft

C. High and low

D. Strong and gentle

23. Which of the following statements about human metabolism is inaccurate?

    A. More total calories are expended during rest (Basal Metabolic Rate) than exercise

    B. "Fasting" (not eating for long periods of time) speeds up metabolism

    C. Exercise stimulates metabolism

    D. Adjustments in metabolism are slow and take place over long periods of time

24. Based on the Individuals with Disabilities Education Act (IDEA), children with crutches or any other types of assistive devices should

    A. not be allowed to participate in physical education activities.

    B. be allowed to participate like any other student.

    C. be provided with appropriate modification for participation in physical education activities.

    D. be provided with a special physical education class designed for them.

25. When teaching students the structure of music, to which of the following could a musical phrase be likened in terms of the structure of language?

    A. A letter

    B. A word

    C. A sentence

    D. A paragraph

26. Gothic architecture, which spawned magnificent churches with pointing arches and towers reaching to the sky, flourished in Europe during which of the following?

    A. The Roman Empire

    B. The Greek Empire

    C. The Middle Ages

    D. Ancient Civilization

27. Which of the following enable the playwright, the director, and the actors to establish the guidelines and limitations to deliver a realistic and convincing play?

    A. Elements of theatre

    B. Stagecraft and the plot

    C. Conventions of theatre

    D. Theme and communication

28. In the Pre-kindergarten and Kindergarten reading classroom, children use drawings to

    A. represent the main idea of a story.

    B. communicate their emotions.

    C. practice muscular coordination.

    D. practice with primary and secondary colors.

29. Nine-year-old Jesse is having difficulty hitting a ball with a bat. Which of the following activities is likely to be most effective for helping him learn how to hit a ball successfully?

    A. Working cooperatively with another learner who has similar difficulties hitting the ball

    B. Striking whiffle balls on the ground with a short-handed hockey stick

    C. Participating in games that require fast reflexes and advanced eye–hand coordination skills

    D. Hitting a larger ball placed on a batting tee

30. Select the letter that contains the correct sequence of Kodály rhythm syllables for this song line, "Twinkle, Twinkle Little Star."

    A. Ta Ta Ta Ta Ti ti Ta

    B. Ta ti Ti ti Ta Ta Ti

    C. Ti ti Ti ti Ti ti Ta

    D. FACE

31. Which of the following systems is most affected by aerobic activity?

   A. Muscular system

   B. Digestive system

   C. Cardiovascular system

   D. Skeletal system

32. One of the most famous scenes in Hamlet is when the main character speaks to himself and shares with the audience his internal thoughts and indecisions: "To be or not to be, that is the question." What element of drama was William Shakespeare using in this performance?

   A. A farce

   B. A satire

   C. A dialogue

   D. A soliloquy

33. In traditional theatre, actors use which of the following to communicate directly with the audience?

   A. Artifacts and non-verbal communication

   B. A monologue

   C. Questions and answers before the play

   D. A soliloquy

34. From a learner's perspective, what sequence (from start to finish) best represents the progression for learning a motor skill?

   A. Student Demonstration > Transfer of Knowledge & Information > Assessing that Knowledge & Information > Summary

   B. Stating Objectives > Providing Examples > Teaching Rules of the Game > Playing the Game > Closure & Summary

   C. Clear Idea of the Task > Motivational Disposition to the Skill > Practice > Feedback > More Practice > Skill Utilization

   D. Introduction Using Visual Aids > Demonstration of All Related Modifications > Assessment & Evaluation of Skill

35. A build-up of paint on canvass can be used to create a sense of which of the following?

   A. Energy

   B. Texture

   C. Intensity

   D. Empty space

36. What are the letter names of the spaces on the musical staff?

   A. FACE

   B. ABCD

   C. ACEG

   D. FGAB

37. A teacher asked a health class to complete a written homework assignment involving an analysis of the physiological effects of participating regularly in physical activity as well as the risk factors associated with inactivity. For which of the following is physical inactivity a risk factor?

   A. Heart disease

   B. Anemia

   C. Sleep apnea

   D. Psoriasis

38. A teacher notices multiple bruising marks on a child. The teacher should then do which of the following?

   A. Ask the child about their home life for more information

   B. Do nothing, it is not a teacher's responsibility

   C. Talk with the parents about child abuse

   D. Report the evidence immediately

39. Flying buttresses, pointed arches, and stained glass windows are characteristic of which historic style of architecture?

    A. Romanesque

    B. Renaissance

    C. Byzantine

    D. Gothic

40. Artists Edouard Manet, Camille Pissarro, Auguste Renoir, and Edgar Degas were the leading painters of which of the following movements?

    A. Impressionism

    B. Romanticism

    C. Realism

    D. Surrealism

Fine Arts, Health, and Physical Education Practice Test Answer Key

1.	C	15.	D	29.	D
2.	A	16.	A	30.	C
3.	C	17.	B	31.	C
4.	B	18.	B	32.	D
5.	D	19.	A	33.	B
6.	B	20.	A	34.	C
7.	A	21.	C	35.	B
8.	B	22.	C	36.	A
9.	A	23.	B	37.	A
10.	D	24.	C	38.	D
11.	A	25.	C	39.	D
12.	D	26.	C	40.	A
13.	C	27.	C		
14.	A	28.	A		

Fine Arts, Health, and Physical Education Practice Test 1 Detailed Answers

1. C.

The correct answer is (C). Linking visual arts with actual occupations (e.g., architecture or advertising) can guide students to appreciate its practical value. It can also spark interest in the arts. Bringing notice to the concept of perspective (A) and posting students' art on the wall (D) will not significantly establish a connection between the arts and its impact in our lives. Knowing about the materials (B) used in different types of sculpture may be interesting to children, but it falls short in tangibly connecting the visual arts with our daily lives. **(905-001 Visual Arts)**

2. A.

The glycemic index is a system that ranks a variety of foods on a scale from 1 to 100 based on their effect on blood sugar levels. Thus, option (A) is the correct answer. The glycemic index has nothing to do with the Krebs Cycle (B) or glycogen utilization in the body (D). Although the amount of sugar intake can directly affect blood sugar levels (C), the glycemic index has nothing to do with the amount of sugar, only the body's response to a particular food with sugar in it. **(905-003 Health)**

3. C.

The correct answer is (C). Dr. Shinichi Suzuki developed a teaching philosophy called "Talent Education," which used the so-called mother-tongue method. This means that music is taught in a similar fashion to the way children learn their native language: by rote. The use of imitation, repetition, and observation are stressed. Edwin Gordon emphasized audiation, the use of inner hearing, making option (A) incorrect. Carl Orff's approach employed the use of rhythm, ruling out choice (B). Émile Jaques-Dalcroze is primarily recog-

nized for his use of eurythmics and improvisation. **(905-002 Music)**

4. B.

The correct answer is (B). Ceramics requires the use of an oven and specialized paints to create the final glossy shine of the work. Traditionally, the pieces are bought raw and students are guided to paint them. The firing of the pieces is generally done in a specialized shop. Understanding colors (A) is not required to begin creating ceramic work. The paint used in ceramics changes drastically once the piece is fired in the kiln. Because ceramics is traditionally part of the elementary school art program, knowledge of tridimensional figures and human forms is not required to create this type of art (C). The materials and the paint used in ceramics are generally not flammable (D). Glaze is typically used to create the shiny appearance. **(905-001 Visual Arts)**

5. D.

The correct answer is (D). Harmony is the accompaniment or supportive sounds to a melody. Choice (A) is incorrect because rhythm is varied lengths of sounds and silences. Choice (B) is incorrect because melody is the singable part of a song. Choice (C) is incorrect because form is the structure of the music analogous to mathematical patterns. **(905-002 Music)**

6. B.

A tenor (B) is a high male voice. The range of voices is classified from high to low; that is, soprano, alto, tenor, baritone, bass. A soprano (A) is a high female voice. A bass (C) is the lowest male voice. A baritone (D) has a range between the tenor and the bass. **(905-002 Music)**

7.   A.

The correct answer is (A). Comping, short for accompaniment, is the style of playing that Count Basie mastered. Often used in jazz, comping has a bounce, syncopation, and flexibility that allows soloists the freedom to improvise. Scat singing (B) is also used in jazz; it is a vocal technique, popularized by Louis Armstrong, that does not use words. Riffs are short phrases often used as accompaniment. Figured bass is a notation below the bass line that tells the performer which chords to follow. **(905-002 Music)**

8.   B.

The correct answer is (B). Both horseshoe making and jewelry making are forms of metalworking. The first is an instrumental and highly functional form of art, while the second is focused on the creation of adornments (C). There is no conclusive historical evidence to identify a country where horseshoe making was developed (A) and (D). Though horseshoe making was used extensively in the United States during the 18th and 19th centuries, both it and jewelry making long predated the founding of the U.S. **(905-001 Visual Arts)**

9.   A.

The correct answer is (A). BMR is the basic rate at which the body burns calories at rest (A). It may have peripheral effects on certain kinds of hormone function (B), but is not defined by this. Diet may also affect the BMR slightly (D), but is not defined by this either. Option (C) is a distractor answer: It sounds good, but there is no "best" way for the body to burn calories; there is just the rate at which it does so. **(905-003 Health)**

10.   D.

The correct answer is (D). You never want to design, modify and/or play games in which students are eliminated from participation during a lesson, game or physical activity (e.g., dodgeball). Inevitably the highest-skilled kids will receive all the activity/opportunity provided and the lowest-skilled kids will become

spectators. Options (A), (B), and (C) are all appropriate modifications a teacher could use to bring out the best in students, activity levels, and game play. **(905-004 Physical Education)**

11.   A.

The correct answer is (A). The use of flashbacks and flash-forwards is a strategy to present information and clarification of the plot. Whereas this two-pronged strategy can theoretically be used to establish distinctions among the characters (B), to lead the audience to a climax (C), or to add realism (D) to the drama, it was not designed for that purpose. **(905-005 Theatre)**

12.   D.

The correct answer is (D). Dramatic play can include interactions with teachers and students (A), or it can be a form of solitary play (C), or it can be teacher- or student-initiated (B). However, since this activity is designed mostly for younger children, the use of memorization of dialogues is not recommended. **(905-005 Theatre)**

13.   C.

The correct answer is (C). Dramatic play is a spontaneous activity in which students are allowed to recreate scenes based on their interpretation of the world. It is not scripted, and it does not require memorization because the target group is students in early childhood. Dramatic play can be used for upper elementary (A) and for English learners (D), but it was not expressly designed for these groups. Option (B) should be cast aside because no prior experience in theatre is required to participate in dramatic play. **(905-005 Theatre)**

14.   A.

Sedentary lifestyle behavior is a primary risk factor for heart disease as well as other preventable diseases. (B), (C), and (D) are not directly caused by inactivity. **(905-003 Health)**

15. D.

Option (D) is the best answer for physical education in EC–6 school settings. The No. 1 issue physical education professionals face (and advocate for) at the elementary school level is that students receive structured physical activity and exercise every school day. This is how lifestyle patterns are shaped and formed; thus, the goal of PE is to create lifelong movers. Currently, the vast majority of elementary children receive physical education only once or twice per week. Option (A) is vague and does not ensure any kind of structured physical activity that is beneficial to the student for health purposes. Option (B) is unrealistic, even the best physical education classes struggle to keep students motivated to exercise at a moderate-to-vigorous level for more than half of the class time. Option (C) applies more to PE at the secondary level, where multiple regular-sized classes are combined into one large class, making it more difficult for a teacher to manage and teach. **(905-004 Physical Education)**

16. A.

The correct answer is (A). Romanticism and Impressionism were key art movements of the 19th century. Cubism and Surrealism (C) were two movements of the 20th century. Baroque and Rococo (D) were two European movements of the 17th and 18th centuries. Baroque paintings and sculptures were characterized as extravagant, beautiful, and complex. This movement is best represented in the sculptures of Bernini, and the paintings of Caravaggio, Rubens, and van Dyck. In painting, the Rococo (later Baroque) portraits representing pastoral life—relaxing, playful scenes. One of the best representations of the Rococo paintings is *The Swing* by French painter Jean-Honoré Fragonard. **(905-001 Visual Arts)**

17. B.

The correct answer is (B). A farce can be identified as "situational comedy," where the plot develops around a situation, not necessarily around the characters (C).

There are not strict guidelines to determine the length of a farce versus other forms of theatre (A). Option (D) describes opera instead of farce. **(905-005 Theatre)**

18. B.

The correct answer is (B). Heat stroke is best recognized and described by red, hot, dry skin due to lack of hydration, leaving the body unable to cool itself efficiently. Unconsciousness is another sign of heat stroke in extreme situations. Option (A) does not include the typical signs of heat stroke rather heat exhaustion which is not as severe. Options (C) and (D) may accompany heat stroke but are not by themselves primary indicators of the problem. **(905-003 Health)**

19. A.

The correct answer is (A). A round is a musical form that creates harmony, which consists of simultaneous combination of tones. Typically when thinking of harmony, one thinks of melody and accompaniment. However, when singing a round, everyone sings the melody and then the students break into groups and enter at different intervals creating musical harmony. A famous round is "Row, Row, Row Your Boat." Option (B) is incorrect because a Partner Song consists of two songs that have the same harmonies that can be sung together. Option (C) is incorrect because a Call & Response is having one leader sing in solo and the rest of the class sings a response. Option (D) is incorrect because a Play Party Song is a song that is sung at social events and contains movements, similar to folk dancing. **(905-002 Music)**

20. A.

Skipping and galloping are basic locomotor skills that can first be introduced at the Kindergarten level and then practiced throughout the elementary grade levels and beyond. Most children are ready to learn skipping and galloping skills at age 5, which makes option (A) the correct answer. **(905-004 Physical Education)**

21. C.

The correct answer is (C). During the Renaissance, painters and sculptors studied the human body, even using cadavers to see muscle formation. While it's true that some studied the drawings of others (A), and the texture of the skin (B), and the structure of bones (D) to do their work, the study of cadavers was instrumental in developing the drawings and information to recreate human-like paintings and sculptures. **(905-001 Visual Arts)**

22. C.

The correct answer is (C). Pitch describes how high and low sounds, or up and down, are produced. Option (A) is incorrect because it describes characteristics of rhythm. Option (B) is incorrect because it describes characteristics of dynamics. Option (D) is incorrect because it describes characteristics of weight. **(905-002 Music)**

23. B.

The only inaccurate answer about metabolism is choice (B). Fasting does not speed up metabolism but rather shuts metabolism down in order to conserve energy due to little or no calories fueling the body. Choice (A) is true because your basal metabolism (basal metabolic rate) is constantly burning calories and converting energy. Choice (C) is correct because physical activity always stimulates metabolic function. Choice (D) is correct in that metabolism slowly adjusts to the demands placed on the body over long periods of time. **(905-003 Health)**

24. C.

The correct answer is (C). The ADA required school districts to place special education children in the least restrictive educational environment; thus, an orthopedic-handicapped student would be placed in mainstream classrooms. Students are required to receive physical education using appropriate accommodations to allow their successful participation. Choice (A) is incorrect because only in extreme cases are special education children excluded from participating in the school curriculum. Choice (B) is only partially correct, as it fails to mention the need to make accommodations for successful participation in physical education activities. Choice (D) is incorrect because it adopts an extreme position not applicable to limited mobility. **(905-004 Physical Education)**

25. C.

The correct answer is (C). The form or structure of music is analogous to the structure or design in language. A letter in language is equivalent to a pitch in music. A word in language is equivalent to a musical pattern. A phrase is a group of musical patterns, which is similar to a sentence in language. Several musical phrases are similar to a paragraph in language. **(905-002 Music)**

26. C.

The correct answer is (C). Gothic architecture spanned a period from the mid-12th century to the 16th century. The Middle Ages gave birth to an architectural style with religious themes brought to life with the help of the rib vault, flying buttress, and pointed, or Gothic, arch – all of which made it possible to create vast expanses while allowing for natural light. The church spires symbolically reached for God. The Greek (B) and Roman (A) empires as well as the Ancient Period (D) all preceded the Middle Ages. **(905-001 Visual Arts)**

27. C.

The correct answer is (C). The conventions of theatre describe all the details needed to deliver a realistic performance. Some of the conventions of theatre are: the use of a narrator, costumes, sequencing time, lights and makeup, and flashbacks. The stage and the plot (B) and theme and communication (D) are four of the six elements of theatre (A). **(905-005 Theatre)**

28. A.

The correct answer is (A). Since children in Kindergarten and below may have problems answering comprehension questions in written form, the teacher guides them to draw to represent their understanding of a story. It is difficult to determine if in the reading class, students will use drawing just to represent their emotions (B) or to practice muscular coordination (C). Practicing with primary and secondary colors (D), might be more appropriate in art class rather than in reading class. **(905-001 Visual Arts)**

29. D.

In order to create opportunities for success with a physical task, educators need to find creative ways of making the task easier for student of varying skill levels. By placing a larger ball on a fixed tee, the task becomes much easier and doable for a less skilled student like Jesse. Therefore, option (D) is the best answer. Option (A) is incorrect because two low-skilled students are not going to be able to help each other progress with the skill. Options (B) and (C) may be indirectly helpful in the process but will not directly train the muscles needed to accomplish the task at hand. **(905-004 Physical Education)**

30. C.

The correct answer is (C). The question addresses the basic understanding of the Kodály rhythm syllables. The two syllables included in this example are ta, which would be notated as a quarter note on the staff; and ti, which would be notated as an eighth note on the staff. If a person were to keep the beat and sing the song "Twinkle, Twinkle Little Star," it should be apparent that the answer is (C). Options (A) and (B) begin with the wrong note (ta), and option (D) ends with the wrong note (ti). **(905-002 Music)**

31. C.

The correct answer is (C). Although options (A) and (D) are largely necessary for participating in aerobic kinds of activity, it is the cardiovascular system that works the hardest to support and sustain the energy and oxygen utilization necessary for continuous activity (via blood circulation). Option (B) is not directly relevant to aerobic activity. **(905-003 Health)**

32. D.

The correct answer is (D). A soliloquy is a form of a monologue in which the character engages in introspection, expressing intimate thoughts and emotions. The term *soliloquy* comes from the Latin—*solus* (alone) and *loqui* (to speak). Soliloquy is similar to a monologue, but in a monologue the actor presents a speech directly to the audience. This indirect communication with the audience provides information about his/her state of mind and indecisions. A farce (A) is comedy, and a satire (B) has features of comedy. In a dialogue (C) two characters share information through a conversation. **(905-005 Theatre)**

33. B.

The correct answer is (B). In a monologue, a single actor presents a speech directly to the audience. Artifacts and non-verbal communication (A) are used to present information in an indirect fashion to the public. Traditionally, actors do not engage the audience prior to the play (C). In a soliloquy (D), the actor engages in a conversation with himself/herself in which the actor provides insights into emotions the character is experiencing internally. **(905-005 Theatre)**

34. C.

The correct answer is (C). In order to learn a motor skill, learners need to have a clear idea of what the task is before they can begin to practice and improve that task or activity. In order to account for diverse learning styles, good teaching includes visual, auditory, and kinesthetic exemplars to the task at hand. In addition, a focus on practice with feedback is fundamental to mastering a motor skill. Thus, option (C) is the progression that clearly makes the most sense for learning psycho-motor skills. **(905-004 Physical Education)**

35. B.

The correct answer is (B). Building up paint with thick brushes is generally used to create texture, even if the surface appears flat. A build-up of paint generally is not used exclusively to create a sense of energy (A) or intensity (C). An empty space (D) is generally not created through a build-up of paint, either. **(905-001 Visual Arts)**

36. A.

The correct answer is (A). The spaces in the treble clef spell FACE. It is easy to remember because space and face rhyme. **(905-002 Music)**

37. A.

The correct answer is (A). Sedentary lifestyle behavior is a primary risk factor for heart disease as well as other preventable diseases. Options (B), (C), and (D) are not directly caused by inactivity. **(905-003 Health)**

38. D.

The correct answer is (D). If a teacher notices abuse or neglect with a child, he or she should calmly and immediately report it to the proper authorities at the school (i.e., principal or assistant principal). Although options (A) and (C) may appear to be natural choices for humanistic educators, it is not a good course of action for a variety of reasons. First, the teacher is not trained in the field(s) of counseling or psychology. Second, the teacher will not be as familiar or knowledgeable with the leadership policies and procedures regarding abuse as an administrator should be. Third, the teacher no longer

remains anonymous and/or protected by the school district in case of legal issues that may result. Option (B) is not an option as the teacher has a responsibility to advocate for (act on behalf) of the child. **(905-003 Health)**

39. D.

The correct answer is (D). The flying buttress was a device invented specifically to support the high vaults of Gothic churches. Flying buttresses, pointed arches, and stained glass windows appear together only on Gothic style buildings, most of which were built between 1150 and 1500. Choice (A) is incorrect because buildings of the Romanesque period (c. 1050–1150) usually employ wall buttresses and rounded arches, with only a few having pointed arches. Choices (B) and (C) are also incorrect because Byzantine and Renaissance buildings are often characterized by domes and rounded arches. **(905-001 Visual Arts)**

40. A.

The correct answer is (A). Impressionism was a movement of the 19th century which shifted away from the realistic and detailed paintings of the Realism movement (A) of the late 1800s to a new way to represent an impression of reality. Impressionism used bright and vibrant colors to capture the impression of the images. Surrealism (C) is a movement of the 20th century. Romanticism (B) was a movement of the 18th century that tried to depict an escape from the pressures of the industrial period and the scientific rationalization of life. Its adherents communicated strong emotions and liberalism in their paintings. **(905-001 Visual Arts)**

Index

English Language Arts and Reading Practice Test 1

Practice-test questions are sorted here by competency. To get an idea of your level of mastery, check the box under the question numbers that you answered correctly.

901-001 Oral Language

1	2	3	24

901-002 Word Analysis and Identification Skills

4	5	6	7	8	9	10

901-003 Reading Fluency

11	12

901-004 Reading Comprehension and Applications

13	14	15	16	17	18	19

909-005 Vocabulary Development

20	21	22	23	25	26

901-006 Reading, Inquiry, and Research

27	28	29	30	31	32	34

901-007 Writing Conventions

35	36

901-008 Written Communication

37	38

901-009 Viewing and Representing

33	39	40

901-010 Assessment of Developing Literacy

41	42	43	44	45

Total: _____/45

Mathematics Practice Test 1

Practice-test questions are sorted here by competency. To get an idea of your level of mastery, check the box under the question numbers that you answered correctly.

902-001 Mathematics Instruction

2	5	16	21	24

902-002 Number Concepts and Operations

7	8	13	26	28	33	35	39

902-003 Patterns and Algebra

1	18	22	23	36	37

902-004 Geometry and Measurement

12	14	17	19	20	38	40

902-005 Probability and Statistics

9	10	11	15	31	32	34

902-006 Mathematical Processes

3	4	6	25	27	30	31	32	33

Total: _____/40

Social Studies Practice Test 1

Practice-test questions are sorted here by competency. To get an idea of your level of mastery, check the box under the question numbers that you answered correctly.

903-001 Social Science Instruction

1	7	17	23	25	28	31	36	37

40

903-002 History

2	11	14	19	21	22	26	29	35

903-003 Geography and Culture

5	9	10	12	13	18	20	33

903-004 Economics

4	15	16	32	34

903-005 Government and Citizenship

3	6	8	24	27	30	38	39

Total: _____/40

Science Practice Test 1

Practice-test questions are sorted here by competency. To get an idea of your level of mastery, check the box under the question numbers that you answered correctly.

904-001 Lab Processes, Equipment, and Safety

1	41	45

904-002 History and Nature of Science

2	36	37

904-003 Impact on Science

3	4	39

904-004 Concepts and Processes

42

904-005 Students as Learners and Science Instruction

6	40

904-006 Science Assessment

7	8	45

904-007 Forces and Motion

9	10	11

904-008 Physical and Chemical Properties

12	13	14	43

904-009 Energy and Interactions

15	16	17	18	19

904-010 Energy Transformations and Conservation

20

904-011 Structure and Function of Living Things

21	22

904-012 Reproduction and the Mechanisms of Heredity

23	25

904-013 Adaptations and Evolution

25	26

904-014 Organisms and the Environment

27	28

904-015 Structure and Function of Earth Systems

5	29

904-016 Cycles in Earth Systems

31	32	38

904-017 Energy in Weather and Climate

34

904-018 Solar System and the Universe

30	35

Total: _____/45

Fine Arts, Health, and Physical Education Practice Test 1

Practice-test questions are sorted here by competency. To get an idea of your level of mastery, check the box under the question numbers that you answered correctly.

905-001 Visual Arts

1	4	8	16	21	26	28	35	39

40

905-002 Music

3	5	6	7	19	22	25	30	36

905-003 Health

2	9	14	18	23	31	37	38

905-004 Physical Education

10	15	20	24	29	34

905-005 Theatre

11	12	13	17	27	32	33

Total: _____/40